SONS OF ARTHUR, CHILDREN OF LINCOLN

Sons of Arthur, Children of Lincoln

Welsh Writing from the American Civil War

JERRY HUNTER

UNIVERSITY OF WALES PRESS
CARDIFF
2007

British Library Cataloguing-in-Publication Data
A catalogue record for this book is available from the British Library

ISBN 978-07083-2019-8 Paperback
ISBN 978-0-7083-2020-4 Hardback

Printed in Great Britain by Antony Rowe Ltd, Wiltshire

For my mother and my father

Contents

Prologue

Fredericksburg, 13 December 1862

The Union army suffered nearly 13,000 casualties that day, most of them in a series of futile assaults upon well-defended Confederate positions.[1] Thousands of wounded men were left stranded between the two opposing armies, and soldiers on both sides later described the horrible chorus of cries which came from the field of Fredericksburg. One Union survivor, Thomas Griffiths, wrote about the experience in his native language:

> Wrth ddringo i fyny y bryn, lle yr oedd ein gelynion yn gwylied ein holl symudiadau, ac wedi ymbaratoi i'n derbyn, a agorasant arnom o'u gwrthgloddiau, gan ysgubo ein dynion wrth y canoedd i fyd arall. O! y llefain, yr wylo, yr ysgrechiadau a'r gwaeddi! y Sais, yr Allman, y Gwyddel, a'r Cymro, a floeddiasant yn nghyd! O! y gruddfan a'r ochain mawr oedd gan y rhai a orweddent yn eu gwaed.[2]

> 'While climbing up the hill, where our enemies were watching all of our movements, and where they had prepared to meet us, they opened on us from their entrenchments, sweeping our men by the hundreds to another world. Oh! the lamenting, the weeping, the screams and the yelling! The English-speaker,[3] the German, the Irishman and the Welshman crying together! Oh! the wailing and the great sighing which came from those who lay in their blood.'

Like several thousand other Union soldiers, and tens of thousands of Northern civilians, Thomas Griffiths was a Welsh-speaking American. This passage reminds us that the Union army was linguistically diverse; Griffiths's description of the mournful Babel which he heard at Fredericksburg provides a horrible version of the American melting pot, a version which also draws our attention to language. Speakers of English, German, Irish and Welsh cry out together in the wake of the very act of sacrifice which affirms their place in the nation which they die serving.[4]

For in spite of these cultural differences, or perhaps *because* of them, Thomas Griffiths saw service in the Union army as a unifying experience. Whatever language they spoke, he and his fellow soldiers were all children of the same symbolic father, Abraham Lincoln:

> . . . nis gallant feddalhau dim ar yspryd gwrol a phenderfynol milwyr yr Undeb, a phlant eu hen dad, Abraham Lincoln, y rhai sydd wedi llyncu ei ysbryd rhydd a dyngarol, a phenderfyniad i golli y diferyn olaf o waed dros ryddid dynoliaeth, a darostyngiad caethiwed, trais a gormes – un wlad yw eu *motto*[.][5]

> '[The Southerners] can not weaken the heroic and determined spirit of the Union's soldiers, children of their old father, Abraham Lincoln, who have imbibed his free and humane spirit, as well as his determination to lose the last drop of blood for the freedom of humanity, and the overthrow of slavery, violence and oppression – one country is their *motto*.'

Other writers expressed similar sentiments in English, but the simple fact that Thomas Griffiths wrote this in Welsh in extremely significant. The Welsh language was an essential component in a constellation of factors which made soldiers like Griffiths part of a distinct sub-culture within the Union army, just as it differentiated Welsh-speaking civilians in New York, Pennsylvania, Ohio, Wisconsin and other Northern states from their non-Welsh neighbours.

While much of what the minority of Welsh-speaking soldiers and civilians wrote about the American Civil War reflects the kinds of things which the English-speaking majority was expressing in newspapers, journals, letters and diaries, the language difference often meant more than just a different way of saying the same thing. Language is a social phenomenon and each language is part of a complex web of social practices. As is the case today, in the mid-nineteenth century the Welsh language brought with it unique modes of cultural expression and reference, ranging from the medieval intricacies of bardic poetry to the religious culture of the Non-conformist chapel. Welsh-American writers employed these cultural resources as they attempted to analyse and interpret the Civil War, and the war in turn forced them to treat subjects and themes foreign to previous generations of Welsh authors.

The United States is now, and has always been, a multilingual nation, and the wartime writings of Welsh-speaking Americans constitute a compelling part of the country's multilingual history.[6] By the same token, this large body of writing constitutes a forgotten chapter in the history of Welsh literature. The linguistic difference which was so essential to Welsh-American identity at the time of the war has also meant that Anglophone American scholars have subsequently ignored the thousands of pages of primary sources written by Welsh-speaking Americans during the Civil War.[7] Research to date has uncovered around 10,000 pages written in the Welsh language which stem directly from the American Civil War. Many of these are print sources, for Welsh-speaking Americans had their own weekly newspaper as well several monthly journals in the 1860s. A considerable amount of manuscript material has also survived, including letters and diaries written by soldiers from camp, battle field, and hospital. The book you are about to read is an introduction to this vast body of Welsh-language Civil War writing.

NOTES

[1] David J. Eicher, *The Longest Night* [:] *A Military History of the Civil War* (New York, 2001), pp. 399–405.

[2] *Y Drych*, 31 January 1863.

[3] The word *Sais*, commonly used by Welsh-speakers today to mean 'Englishman', was often employed in the nineteenth century to mean 'English-speaker'. See *Geiriadur Prifysgol Cymru* (Cardiff, 1950–2002), p. 3169. In the Middle Ages, the epithet *Sais* was sometimes applied to a Welshman to signify that, unlike most people of Wales, he could speak English. Though less common today, some Welsh speakers still use the word to denote somebody who speaks English or who can not speak Welsh.

[4] The term 'melting pot' itself was not to be coined for nearly half a century: Israel Zangwill, *The Melting Pot: Drama in Four Acts* (New York, 1909).

[5] *Y Drych*, 31 January 1863.

[6] The last few years have witnessed a drive to draw attention to American literatures in languages other than English. See Werner Sollors (ed.), *Multilingual America* [:] *Transnationalism, Ethnicity, and the Languages of American Literature* (New York and London, 1998); Marc Shell (ed.), *American Babel* [:] *Literatures of the United States from Abnaki to Zuni* (Cambridge MA, 2002); Marc Shell and Werner Sollors (eds), *The Multilingual Anthology of American Literature* (New York and London, 2000).

[7] One short introductory pioneering article was published nearly fifty years ago: Alan Conway, 'Welshmen in the Union Armies', *Civil War History*, 4 (1958), 143–74. Otherwise, very little work has been published in this field. The only book-length study to date is my own Welsh-language volume: Jerry Hunter, *Llwch Cenhedloedd* [:] *Y Cymry a Rhyfel Cartref America* (Llanrwst, 2003).

Acknowledgements

This project has a twenty-year history, and the best way to acknowledge the many debts I've accumulated along the way is to recount some of that history. It begins in 1986 when my step-sister Joyce Whitney discovered a copy of William Davies Evans's *Dros Gyfanfor a Chyfandir* in a second-hand bookstore in Columbus, Ohio.

This was the first time that I came across a Welsh-language text written by somebody who had taken part in the American Civil War. Thanks to Joyce and her discovery, I started keeping an eye out for similar kinds of sources. While studying in Aberystwyth in the 1980s I had a chance to collect relevant material in the National Library of Wales; I am extremely grateful to the Library's staff for the help rendered at that time and at many other junctures since then.

I got to know Eirig Davies shortly after moving to Cambridge, Massachusetts, in 1990. Eirig has spent a lot of time searching for Welsh-American publications in a number of libraries and archives, and – like many people interested in this field – I have been inspired by his enthusiasm and enlightened by his many discoveries. While a graduate student at Harvard University, and during several research trips in subsequent years, I was greatly aided by the staff of Widener and Houghton libraries.

When I joined Cardiff University's Welsh Department in 1996 I found myself part of a group of scholars interested in the Welsh Diaspora. I am grateful to Sioned Davies, Robert Owen Jones and Colin Williams for their support and help in founding the Cardiff Centre for Welsh-American Studies, and special thanks are due to Wyn James and Bill Jones for their continuing help over the years. In addition, I am indebted to Bill for reading and commenting upon early drafts of this book's first two chapters. This community of scholars also included Huw Griffiths, who has provided valuable insights regarding several illusive primary sources. Thanks, also, to Dylan Foster Evans and Angharad Price for their support and encouragement.

Since joining the Welsh Department at the University of Wales, Bangor, I have been aided and encouraged in numerous ways by Jason Walford Davies, Branwen Jarvis, Gwyneth Lewis, William Lewis , Peredur Lynch, John Rowlands, and Gwyn Thomas. I have benefited especially from Gerwyn

Wiliams's own work on Welsh-language war literature, and our many conversations over the years have enriched my own understanding of the subject. It is also a pleasure to thank Bangor's library and archive staff for many kinds of help provided over the years. The wider community at Bangor includes a number of other scholars interested in the Welsh Diaspora; I am grateful to Margaret Deuchar, Densil Morgan and Duncan Tanner for working with me in forming an AHRC-funded Research Network ('Language, Religion and Print Culture in the Welsh Diaspora'), and to the AHRC for their support. I am also indebted to Densil for reading and commenting on drafts of several chapters.

Similarly, I am grateful to Daniel Williams for reading early drafts of the first two chapters and for many inspiring conversations. Thanks also to Edgar Slotkin, Mark Nevins, Elio Brancaforte, Richard Wyn Jones, Rhys Jones, Rhys ap Rhisiart, Tim Correll, Anna Surany, and Jay Williams for encouragement at various crucial junctures.

The experience of working on the documentary *Cymry Rhyfel Cartref America* deepened my appreciation of many aspects of the field. Thanks to all those individuals at S4C and Cwmni Da who were involved in the project, and especially to Dafydd Baines, Gareth Owen, Rolant Jones, Steve Martin and Ifor ap Glyn. Indeed, because Ifor immersed himself in the subject to such a great extent, I have subsequently benefited on numerous occasions from his informed comments and suggestions. During our work on the documentary I came into contact with some of Welsh America's most enthusiastic local historians, and it is a pleasure to acknowledge the aid of Bet and Evan Davis, John and Joan Jones, Bob Jones and Leonard Wynne. I am especially indebted to Leonard for introducing me to Michael and Anne Everett; the Everetts have contributed greatly to my research by making available their amazing archive of family papers. Special thanks to Dave, Libby and their families for many kinds of support rendered during several extended research trips.

Parts of this book were written during the Spring of 2004 while I was a visiting professor in Harvard University's Department of Celtic Languages and Literatures. It is a pleasure to acknowledge the support of old friends who became temporary colleagues at that time: Patrick K. Ford, Barbara Hillers, Tomás Ó Cathasaigh, and Margo Granfors.

A host of individuals have enabled me to gather a wealth of primary sources over the years, generously sharing their personal collections (including a great deal of unpublished manuscript material). While I have not been able to cite all of these texts directly in this book, they have all contributed by enabling me to form a background data base; this is the field against which I examine individual texts in this study. I have surely lost some names over the years, and I apologize sincerely to individuals who have slipped through my large and less-than-perfectly organized record of correspondence. It is a pleasure to thank the following for their help: Ronald

Crewe, Alun Davies, Gareth Davies, Leslie Davies, D. Merrill Davis, John Ellis, Albert Gregorovich, Gareth Griffith, Amos Hawkins, Joan Huff, Iwan Hughes, J. O. Hughes, T. Meirion Hughes, Richard Humphreys, William Humphries, Ann Humphries, Evan James, Ifan James, J. Greville James, Susan James, Arfon Jones, Bryan Jones, David Jones, Eric Jones, Evan Jones, Gwawr Jones, John Jones, Martin Jones, Mary Jones, Rhys Jones, Sylvia Jones, Tom H. Jones, Gary Knepp, David Knight, Anne Knowles, Bryn Lloyd-Jones, Rhoswen Llywelyn, John Wyn Lewis, Gethin Matthews, Edward Miller, Carol Mills, David Morgan, Evan Morgan, Alan Owen, Trefor Owen, Marcia Richards, Thomas Richards, David Roberts, Emyr Roberts, G. Roberts, David R. Smith, Georgia Snoke, A. Thomas, J. D. R. Thomas, M. E. Thomas, Nadine Thomas, Richard A. Thomas, T. Islwyn Walters, David White, Alan Williams, David Williams, Evan Williams, Gwyn Williams, Ifan Williams, Rhian Williams, Richard Williams, Robert Williams and T. Alun Williams. Thanks also to Kate Olson and Aled Llion Jones for help offered along the way.

In addition, I would like to acknowledge help rendered by the staff of a number of other libraries, archives and museums: The Camp Dennison Museum; The National Archives; The National Library of Congress; The Madog Center, Rio Grande University; the Vermont Historical Society's Library; The Cincinnati Library; The Ironton, Ohio, Library; The Emory University Library; The Old Slave Mart Museum (Charleston, S.C.).

I gratefully acknowledge the AHRC for a research leave award which enabled me to complete this book, and I would like to thank everybody at the University of Wales Press for their hard work.

I am extremely grateful to Kevin Van Anglen for reading the entire typescript and providing valuable comments. In addition, I am indebted to Kevin for a great deal of advice generously offered over many years.

As always, thanks to Mom, Dad, Tove and Keith for their continuing support in this and all endeavours. Ac yn olaf, diolch o galon i Judith, Megan a Luned am eu cariad a'u cefnogaeth.

The scope of this study

This book focuses on Welsh writing stemming directly from the American Civil War. The first two chapters are an exception in that they examine the history of Welsh-American literature and culture during the period from roughly 1838 to the start of the war. It is impossible to understand the reactions of Welsh-language writers to the conflict without first knowing something about the cultural composition and ideological disposition of Welsh America during the antebellum period.

The rest of this book is concerned with Welsh-language texts written and/or published in the United States during the war years (1861–5). This means that a large amount of writing published in Wales during the war has been ignored for the most part. Similarly, while a substantial body of retrospective war literature was produced by Welsh-American writers after 1865 (including a massive 631-page history), these texts constitute a field which lies beyond the scope of the present study.[1]

NOTE

1 J. W. Jones and T. B. Morris, *Hanes y Gwrthrfyel Mawr yn y Talaethau Unedig; Yn Nghyd A Byr Grybwyllion Am y Prif Ddigwyddiadau O Ddarganfyddiad America Hyd Adferiad Heddwch, Yn 1865* (Utica, 1866). The title translates as 'History of the Great Rebellion in the United States; In Addition to Short Discussions of the Main Events from the Discovery of America up to the Restoration of Peace, In 1865'. See Jerry Hunter, *Llwch Cenhedloedd* [:] *Y Cymry a Rhyfel Cartref America* (Llanrwst, 2003), 254–6.

Part One

Welsh America on the Eve of Civil War

1

The Bards and the Bowie Knife

On the first day of 1862 the bards gathered in Utica, New York. Perhaps the most lively and prestigious festival of its kind in the United States, Utica's annual *eisteddfod* was held every New Year's Day. The gathering on the first day of 1862, however, was different, for the shadow of Civil War darkened the celebration of Welsh culture and identity. John Edwards, one of the poets who attended the event, captured the sombre spirit in verse:

Llonyddodd ein llenyddiaeth – a rhyfel
    Arafodd Farddoniaeth,
  Diwrnod Eisteddfod os daeth,
  Mae hwn i mi'n amheuaeth.[1]

'Our literature has grown still – and war
    Has slowed the pace of poetry,
  If the *Eisteddfod* day has come,
  This is for me an uncertainty.'

Edwards was known to Welsh-speaking Americans as Eos Glan Twrch, 'The Nightingale of the Twrch River'. While his bardic name harked back to the valley in North Wales where he had been born, for years he had been composing and publishing a great deal of Welsh-language literature focusing on life in his adopted country. Before the war, Edwards had been one of many Welsh-American writers who harnessed their literary talents to promote the anti-slavery cause. After the outbreak of hostilities in 1861, he turned his verse to the pressing events of the times, publishing poetry which praised the deeds of Welsh Americans on the battlefield and voiced the war-time fears of Welsh-speaking civilians.

Eos Glan Twrch was but one of many Welsh bards who put their poetry at the service of the Union war effort, and the circumstances of many of them would change dramatically during the war years. Indeed, despite his public support for abolition and the Union cause, before the end of the war Eos Glan Twrch would be accused – perhaps falsely – of being a Copperhead (a member of the Democratic Party's anti-war faction). John E. Roberts, known to fellow-poets as Cymro Brith ('Motley Welshman'), would serve as wagon master with the 5th Pennsylvania Cavalry. David Cadwgan, called simply Cadwgan Fardd ('Cadwgan the Bard'), lived in a Welsh settlement in eastern Tennessee; like several of his pro-Union neighbours, he would become a fugitive in the mountains, hiding from Confederate raiders. The Reverend Lewis Meredith, who used the bardic name Lewys Glyn Dyfi ('Lewis of the Dovey Valley'), would travel back to Wales during the war while seeking foreign support for the Union war effort.

'MAINTAINING HAPPILY OUR CUSTOMS': AMERICAN *EISTEDDFODAU*

Before the Civil War, all of these poets had been engaged in the process of creating a Welsh-language American literature, thus contributing to the larger project of constructing and maintaining a distinct Welsh-American identity. *Eisteddfod* festivals like the one held in Utica offered a potent way of publicly articulating that identity. By the end of the Middle Ages the word *eisteddfod* was being used to refer to a special kind of Welsh cultural practice, 'a kind of congress of bards held to formulate rules in connexion with their craft and to organize themselves into a guild of craftsmen or graduates'. The medieval tradition was reinvented and re-imagined during the eighteenth and nineteenth centuries, and *eisteddfod* came to mean 'an event or festival at which competitions are held in music, elocution, literature, arts and crafts, &c'.[2] Other kinds of competitions – especially singing – became increasingly prominent parts of the nineteenth-century *eisteddfod* (plural *eisteddfodau*), yet poetry competitions remained a definitive component of the institution.[3]

As early as 1838 one Welsh immigrant published a treatise suggesting how various 'means' (*moddion*) and 'institutions' (*sefydliadau*) could be used for preserving the Welsh language in the United States. After first stressing the important roles played by Sunday schools and the printing press in nurturing Welsh-language culture, this anonymous author drew attention to the literary festivals of Wales: 'Hefyd, nis gallaf fyned heibio heb wneud sylw ar yr *Eisteddfodau, Cymdeithasau Cymreigyddol, Gwleddoedd a gwyliau* Cymreig, sydd wedi bod yn dra chyffredin gan ein cenedl' ('Also, I can not pass by without making mention of the *Eisteddfodau, Welsh Societies, Feasts and* Welsh *festivals,* which have been popular amongst our nation').[4] These cultural festivals soon became a prominent part of Welsh-American life as well; the ten years before the start of the Civil War witnessed a surge of *eisteddfodic* activity in the northern United States. Taking Pennsylvania as an example, annual festivals were being established all across the state by the middle of the 1850s, with some of the better-publicized *eisteddfodau* being held in Danville, Minersville and Carbondale.[5] By 1860, Pittston had its own *eisteddfod* as well. And Pennsylvania had no monopoly; Welsh communities in New York, Ohio and

Wisconsin were successful in staging similar events.[6] Detailed records of many of these early American *eisteddfodau* are rare, and it is often difficult to tell exactly when these local festivals were first held. Some, however, are better documented. For example, the *eisteddfod* held in Carbondale, Pennsylvania on Christmas Day 1854 was described in print as the third annual festival, allowing us to date the first Carbondale *eisteddfod* to Christmas 1852.[7]

The Carbondale event was sponsored by a local organization, 'The Literary Society of the Welsh' (*Cymdeithas Lenyddol y Cymry*), and the *eisteddfod* which it held on Christmas Day 1854 appears to have been a particularly successful one. The essays were judged by the Revd R. R. Williams of Minersville while the poetry judge, Dewi Emlyn, came from Ohio. One participant saw the *eisteddfod* as heralding Carbondale's ascension to the status of Welsh-American cultural capital. He wrote that 'Carbondale intends to claim that she is the Welsh "Athens" of America' ('Y mae Carbondale am hawlio mai hi yw "Athen" Gymreig America'). In order to underscore his point, this writer signed his letter 'Athenydd Bach' – 'A Little Athenian'.[8]

Despite this aspiring Athenian's enthusiasm, it appears that the rest of Welsh America did not support the claims of Carbondale and its festival to such national status. On the contrary, the early 1850s witnessed a campaign to establish a National Eisteddfod in New York City. Although the Old Country was not short of *eisteddfodau* during the first half of the nineteenth century, it was only in the 1850s that a serious campaign was started to found a truly National Eisteddfod in Wales.[9] The American campaign was thus very much a direct reflection of the current mood in Wales, with the important exception that the national cultural institution was being discussed in relation to a very different nation. In 1851–2 a Welsh minister named R. D. Thomas travelled to the United States. Known as Iorthryn Gwynedd in bardic circles, he was an enthusiastic champion of Welsh literary culture. The Revd Thomas was impressed by the growing Welsh-language literary culture which he found in the United States, and in order to help support it he published an open letter addressed to 'The Welsh in general in the United States' ('At y Cymry yn gyffredinol yn yr Unol Daleithiau'):

> Y mae yn America, yn ddiau, lawer o *feirdd rhagorol*, ac o *lenorion medrus*, a gallent gyrhaedd mawredd mwy a defnyddioldeb eangach pe caent fwy o gefnogaeth deilwng. Darllenasom rai darnau campus, yn cynnwys gwir farddoniaeth, a rhai traethodau penigamp, yn cynnwys gwir chwaeth, athrylith, a goreuddawn, yn y *Cyhoeddiadau Cymreig Americanaidd*. Cawsom y fraint o weled, ac o gyfeillachu â'r awduron. Pwy oeddynt? *Cymry pur, diledíaith, dyngarol, awenyddol, aiddgar*, – GOREUON ein gwlad – pobl wedi gwenud, ac yn barod eto i wneud llawer o aberthau pwysig, er mwyn coethi a chefnogi eu hiaith, a llesoli eu cenedl. Am ysbaid blynyddau lawer llafuriasant yn galed a ffyddlon er eich mwyn chwi, collasant lawer o'u hamser gwerthfawr, a threuliasant lawer o'u harian a'u heiddo er mwyn codi, sefydlu, a pheri i lenoriaeth Gymreig fod yn anrhydeddus,

> dylanwadol a llesiol. Onid yw golygyddion, gohebwyr, a beirdd medrus eich Cyhoeddiadau, ynghyd ag awdwyr y *llyfrau Cymreig yn America*, wedi gwneud y pethau hyn?[10]
>
> 'There are in America, without doubt, many *exceptional bards*, and many *capable writers*, and they might achieve a greater greatness and a wider usefulness if they were to receive further fitting support. I read some excellent pieces, including true poetry, and some masterful essays, displaying true taste, genius and finest art, in the *Welsh-American Publications*. We had the privilege of seeing, and of socializing with the authors. Who were they? *Pure, untarnished, humanitarian, poetic, ardent Welsh people* – THE BEST of our country – people who have done, and are ready to do again, much for your sake[;] they have lost much of their precious time, and they have spent a lot of their own money in order to start, establish, and cause Welsh literature to be honourable, effective and beneficial. Have not the editors, correspondents, and capable poets of your Publications, in addition to the authors of the *Welsh books in America*, done these things?'

Like many nineteenth-century Welsh literary critics, R. D. Thomas describes the role of the Welsh-language writer as one of community service. He argues that the Welsh poets, authors and editors of the United States have done all that can be expected of a community's *literati*; they have spent their own valuable time and money in order to serve their fellow Welsh-speaking Americans. The tone of his open letter is one of advocacy, and the piece finds its rhetorical centre with a sentence carrying the air of prophecy: 'Their labour will not be in vain, and they will never lose their reward' ('Ni bydd eu llafur yn ofer, ac ni chollant eu gwobr byth').

The proper reward for those engaged in creating America's Welsh literature, Thomas suggests, would be to establish an American National Eisteddfod:

> Edrychwch i'r Eisteddfodau a'r cymdeithasau llenorol lluosog ac anrhydeddus sydd yn yr Hen Wlad! . . . Efallai nad allech chwi, ar unwaith, eu hefelychu a'u dilyn ym mhobpeth – byddai yn anhawdd, efallai, cael a chynnal *Eisteddfod Urddasol* yn unman yn *America y flwyddyn nesaf* – y mae yn rhy fuan eto i wneud hyny – nid ydych yn ddigon aeddfed eto, – ac efallai na roddid cefnogaeth unol a theilwng i hyny yn awr. Diau fod genych ddynion digon teilwng i fod yn Feirdd *Cadeiriol*, ac yn *Feirniaid* medrus a diduedd ar y cyfansoddiadau mwyaf rhagorol ac etholedig[.][11]
>
> 'Look to the numerous and estimable Eisteddfodau and the literary societies which are in the Old Country. . . . It's possible that you can not, immediately, imitate and follow them in every aspect – it would be difficult, perhaps, to set and hold a *Dignified Eisteddfod* anywhere in *America next year* – it is yet too early to do that – you are not mature enough yet, – and perhaps united and proper support for that would not be given at this time. Yet it is likely that you have men suitable enough to be *Chaired* Bards, and capable and unbiased *Judges* of the most excellent and choicest compositions[.]'

The editor who published this letter applauded the idea, adding that 'the supporters of Welsh literature in America' – '[c]efnogwyr llenyddiaeth Gymreig yn America' – would definitely take note of the idea put forth by R. D. Thomas. Continuing in this vein, he suggested that this kind of *eisteddfod* was exactly what Welsh America needed and that New York City was exactly the venue for such an event: 'Diau mai dyma y peth sydd arnom eisiau er cefnogi gwir deilyngdod yn mhlith ein cenedl, ac nis gwyddom am un lle cymhwysach i gynnal yr Eisteddfod gyntaf na dinas Caerefrog-Newydd' ('It's certain that this is the thing which we need in order to support true merit amongst our nation, and we do not know of any more fitting place to hold the first Eisteddfod than the city of New York').[12] A movement was set in motion. While the campaign to establish a Welsh-American National Eisteddfod surely involved canvassing potential supporters and other activities which went unrecorded, some written traces of that work have survived on the pages of the Welsh-American press. Eight months later, the same editor who had published R. D. Thomas's open letter summed up the state of the campaign: 'Mae cryn son, a pheth ysgrifenu, yn bresennol yn mhlith Cymry America am gael Eisteddfod Genedlaethol, a rhai cynlluniau wedi eu gwneud i gario yr amcan allan yn llwyddiannus' ('There is a great deal of talk, and some writing, at present amongst the Welsh of America about getting a National Eisteddfod, and some plans have been made in order to carry out the goal successfully').[13] Two months later, in May 1854, a Mr W. Jones of New York published yet another open letter addressed to 'The Welsh throughout the United States' ('At y Cymry trwy y Talaethau Unedig'); its purpose was to continue the discussion on *Yr Eisteddfod Genedlaethol* – 'The National Eisteddfod'.[14] This writer's argument in favour of establishing such a festival took the form of a potted – and slanted – history of Western culture. His 'history' is written in such a way as to imply that holding an *eisteddfod* in New York City would be a development in accordance with the natural progress of 'Western Civilization'. If the Welsh of Carbondale, Pennsylvania, saw their town as the Welsh Athens of America, this writer argued that the ancient cultural glory of the real Athens had yielded in time to great cultures in the West – meaning, specifically, Wales. This cultural force was now moving westwards once more, he suggested, crossing the Atlantic and taking root in New York.

This Mr Jones thus generated a Welsh version of the 'westward-ho' slogan which was becoming such an entrenched part of American public life. It was less than a decade since the editor of *The Democratic Review*, John L. O'Sullivan, had coined the phrase 'manifest destiny', creating a specific rhetorical label for the political and economic impetus which would ensure the colonization of the entire continent and the conquest of the remaining free Native Americans.[15] Unlike that other influential newspaperman, Horace Greeley, who issued American colonists of 'the West' with their trademark battle-cry, 'Go West, young man', this Welsh writer was not arguing specifically for expansion across all of North America. He was, rather, using a well-established trope as a rhetorical frame for his own agenda, that is, legitimising the establishment of a Welsh cultural institution in New York City. Since the eighteenth century American writers had been developing the 'translation of empire' trope which the British Bishop George Berkeley had articulated memorably in his 1726 poem 'On the Prospect of Planting Arts and Learning in America.'[16] Berkeley's line, 'Westward the course of empire takes its way', had long since been incorporated into the language of American expansionism, and the influence of that language upon this Welsh-American writer is revealed by the English phrase opening the following quotation:

> *But the progress of civilization is westward;* ac felly cawn fod graddau o wybodaeth wedi dyfod i Gymru yn bur foreu; îe, mae y llanerch fechan hono . . . wedi bod yn tywynu fel haul o ran gwybodaeth yn flaenorol i'r un man arall yn Ewrop, ac yno, mae'n debyg, y cynnaliwyd yr Eisteddfodau Llenyddol cyntaf [.][17]

> '*But the progress of civilization is westward;* and thus we find that degrees of knowledge came to Wales fairly early on; yes, that small glade . . . has been shining like a sun of knowledge prior to any other region in Europe, and there, it's likely, the first literary Eisteddfodau were held.'

The force of this stilted historiography suggests that Welsh culture, having thus inherited the mantle of classical Greece, was now yielding that honour to a new society growing in the west. 'The progress of civilization is westward,' and the cultural glories of Wales were being transferred, by means of this supposedly natural law, to Welsh America. The rest of the letter presents practical details – mundane after the historiographical contortions contained in the first part – regarding the preparations for the New York festival, which was to be held on Christmas Day 1855.

An *eisteddfod* was indeed held in New York City. However, judging by the surviving print record, it did not achieve the status of an American National Eisteddfod any more than did Carbondale's annual gathering.[18] Despite the aspirations of their local Welsh communities, neither Carbondale nor New York City could realistically claim to be the Welsh Athens of the United States. That honour belonged to Utica, in Oneida County, New York.

When Oliver Wendell Holmes declared Boston to be 'the thinking centre of the continent', a Utica resident could easily have answered by describing his own town as the 'hub' of Welsh America's cultural life.[19] Oneida County boasted dozens of Welsh-speaking chapels by the middle of the nineteenth century.[20] It also housed the lion's share of the Welsh-American press, located for the most part in the town of Utica itself. Not surprisingly, many of the more prominent religious, cultural and political leaders of Welsh America made their home in the area. A joke still told in Utica today describes Welshmen emigrating to the United States, bound ultimately for Utica. They land first in

New York City, and, as they wander through the busy streets, marvelling at the mass of humanity and the numerous cultural and economic activities taking place there, one turns to the other and says: 'if this is New York, what must Utica be like?'[21] While this punch-line would puzzle most Americans today, it makes perfect sense to anybody familiar with the nature of nineteenth-century Welsh America; new Welsh immigrants would have looked to Utica as their new cultural capital. All told, it is no surprise that Utica's annual *eisteddfod* was so successful. Held for the first time in 1856, the festival achieved something of the status of an unofficial National Eisteddfod, as the Utica-based press made sure that compositions produced for the event and reports of the proceedings were disseminated widely throughout Welsh-speaking America.[22]

The published poetry of John Edwards – or Eos Glan Twrch – serves as a chronicle of the yearly life of the festival. If the lines which he published in 1862 reflect the sombre atmosphere of the first *eisteddfod* held in war-time Utica, a longer poem which the Eos published back in 1856 praised the first ever Utica *eisteddfod* as a model for Welsh-American cultural practice. Both of these poems use the *englyn* form (plural *englynion*), one of the traditional strict metres codified by Welsh bards in the Middle Ages and kept in use throughout the modern period right up to the twenty-first century.[23] The opening lines of the 1856 poem utilize a culinary metaphor, stating that Oneida County has set out 'on its good table' (*ar ei bwrdd da*) 'provisions for feasting' ([*d*]*efnyddiau gwledda*). We are then told that 'crowds of people with the same intention' (*niferi oll o'r un fwriad*) answered the invitation, gathering together in Utica in order to enjoy 'the delicacies of their country' ([*d*]*anteithion eu gwlad*).[24]

The 'country' described here by Eos Glan Twrch is unspecified, perhaps an intentional introduction of a meaningful ambiguity. The cultural feast does in fact bring two countries together; the 'delicacies' – or at least the recipes with which they are produced – come ultimately from Wales, yet they are consumed on the American 'table' provided in Utica. While we might take the word *gwlad*, 'country', to mean alternately both Wales and the United States, it also suggests the Welsh America which these *eisteddfod*-goers were in the process of creating.[25]

If the poem begins with unchecked praise for those taking part in the metaphorical feast, it soon turns in the opposite direction in order to heap scorn on those who shun the *eisteddfod*. Eos Glan Twrch sets the festival's supporters against the [*b*]*alch goegddyn* – the 'vain false man' – who 'turns his posed nose up on his mother' (*gwneyd trwyn syn – ar ei fam*), and:

Gwadu'i iaith, ac wedi hyn,
Gwadu pob rhinwedd gwed'yn.

'Denies his language, and after this,
Denies every virtue afterwards.'

In marked contrast, the Welsh-Americans who gather in Utica on New Year's Day are made to represent 'the honest man' (*y gwr gonest*) who 'loves his nation every day' (*Gâr ei genedl beunydd*). The poet links this love of nation to a love of language, adding that, for Welsh speakers, this also means loving poetry:

A charu ei iaith berffaith bydd,
Wed'yn fe gara Brydydd.

'And he will love his perfect language,
And then he will love [the] Poet.'

For Eos Glan Twrch, the *eisteddfod* is a civilizing force, a vehicle for 'getting music [and] getting morals in Welsh' (*cael miwsig, / Cael moesau yn Gymraeg*). It is a way of preserving culture and all the benefits provided by culture:

Cadw'n llon ein defion, a'n dysg,
Awenyddol, iawn addysg.

'Maintaining happily our customs, and our
Poetic learning, a proper education.'

The adjective translated here as 'poetic', *awenyddol*, comes from *awenydd*, one of several Welsh words meaning 'poet' or 'bard'. This noun in turn stems from the word *awen*, a term which has been used since the earliest history of the Welsh language to describe poetic inspiration.[26] In addition to being 'poetic', the 'learning' and 'proper education' which the *eisteddfod* provided for Welsh-Americans was, quite literally, 'inspiring'. It inspired Welsh immigrants and their children to create and maintain Welsh-language culture in the United States.

Eos Glan Twrch wanted all of Welsh-speaking America to take note of the Utica *eisteddfod*. To that end, he accompanied his poem with a prose piece praising the festival:

Cefais yr hyfrydwch . . . o fod yn Eisteddfod Utica y Calan, ac yn wir yr oedd yno le difyrus ac adeiladol; cefais fy moddhau yn fawr ar lawer golygiad, megys yn lluosogrwydd y dyrfa, yn nghyda'r dull gweddus y dygwyd y cyfarfod yn mlaen. Yr oedd cynyrchion Barddonol lled dda. . . .[27]

'I had the pleasure . . . of being in the Utica Eisteddfod on New Year's Day, and truly there was a pleasant and constructive time to be had there; I was greatly satisfied on many accounts, such as the great size of the crowd, as well as the proper manner in which the gathering was conducted. There were fairly good Poetic compositions. . . .'

One of the main reasons why he was holding up the Utica *eisteddfod* as a model for Welsh-American cultural practice was that the proceedings were conducted entirely in Welsh:

> Treuliwyd y cyfarfodydd yn Gymraeg yn ddieithriad, ac, yn fy meddwl i, i hyny y mae eu dyddordeb idd ei briodoli. Chwi a wyddoch mai troi cyfarfodydd ac Eisteddfodau o'r Gymraeg i'r Saesonaeg sydd wedi bod yn niwed a gwarth i'r cyfryw yn yr Hen Wlad a'r wlad hon[.][28]

> 'The meetings were conducted in Welsh without exception, and, to my mind, that is the reason for their appeal. You know that it is changing meetings and Eisteddfodau from Welsh to English which has been a damage and a disgrace to such proceedings in the Old Country and this country[.]'

Despite the general feeling that promoting Welsh-language culture was at the very heart of the *eisteddfod* tradition, many of the festivals of Victorian Wales were giving increasing prominence to the Queen's English. This was part of what Hywel Teifi Edwards has described as 'the psychology of "post-1847" Wales.'[29]

The year 1847 saw the publication of the infamous 'Blue Books', a governmental report on the condition of education in Wales. The investigation had been conducted on behalf of the government by three English barristers; they could neither read nor speak Welsh, despite the fact that they were sent to assess the state of education in Wales, where at least 70 per cent of the population – and a much higher percentage of the children – could speak only Welsh.[30] The cultural gap was widened by the fact that they were Churchmen with little sympathy for the Nonconformist chapels which dominated the educational institutions of Wales. Despite the fact that literacy rates among Welsh speakers were probably higher on average than among their English-speaking counterparts over the border, the Queen's investigators took the lack of English in Welsh schools as an indicator of poor educational standards.[31] They linked the perceived educational failings to perceived moral failings, and the result was a lengthy report which roundly condemned the language, culture and morals of the Welsh. The appearance of the report in 1847 was a devastating blow to Welsh national pride: over 1,000 pages, contained in three volumes, bound in blue leather and bearing the mark of Queen Victoria's government, officially condemned Welsh culture as inferior. Heaping condescension on Wales and Welsh-language culture was nothing new; what the 'Blue Books' provided was a codified, official version of a kind of discourse which had characterized the relationship between Wales and the British Empire for a long time.

The Welsh reacted in various and often schizophrenic ways. One post-1847 literary impulse, usually seen as the 'healthy' response by modern advocates of Welsh-language culture, was crystallized by R. J. Derfel in his 1854 play, *Brad y Llyfrau Gleision*. The title, which translates as 'The Treachery of the Blue

Books', was a conscious reworking of 'The Treachery of the Long Knives' (*Brad y Cyllyll Hirion*), an episode in the colourful pseudo-history of medieval Wales which, in various versions, was extremely popular in the nineteenth century. Other prominent Welshmen went the way suggested by the Blue Books themselves, striving to present a version of Wales which would be acceptable to the Victorian English status quo. One of the era's more popular slogans, 'progress', was levelled against Welsh culture, and this had a very direct effect upon the Welsh *eisteddfod*, as certain influential figures sought to make the institution a reflection of Anglocentric Victorian values. In Hywel Teifi Edwards's memorable analysis, 'Esgorodd y Llyfrau Gleision ar haid o ymarferolwyr a fynnai weld y Cymry yn ymsythu ac ymwroli yng ngoleuni a gwres haul "Cynnydd" Oes Victoria' ('The Blue Books gave birth to a flock of pragmatists who wanted to see the Welsh straightening up and taking heart in the light and warmth of the Victorian Age's sun of "Progress"').[32] This meant that traditional Welsh cultural practices should take second place to the 'useful' sciences, and it meant that English was increasingly given pride of place over Welsh. Indeed, by the early 1860s, the newly organized National Eisteddfod of Wales had become so Anglicised that supporters of the Welsh language held their own alternative festival in protest.[33]

This Victorian Anglophilia was carried by some Welsh immigrants to the United States, and it must have been compounded by the desire of a certain portion of Welsh-Americans to assimilate and replace Welsh with American English. On the other hand, it appears that the vast majority of Welsh immigrants saw maintaining a lively Welsh-language culture as being thoroughly compatible with their new lives as American citizens. Thus in praising the Utica *eisteddfod* Eos Glan Twrch stressed that the event was extremely popular because of the fact that all proceedings were conducted exclusively in Welsh: 'The meetings were conducted in Welsh without exception, and, to my mind, that is the reason for their appeal.'

'AT THE SERVICE OF THE WELSH NATION IN THE UNITED STATES': PRINT CULTURE, LANGUAGE AND IDENTITY

The poetry and prose by Eos Glan Twrch discussed so far appeared in *Y Drych* ('The Mirror'), a weekly newspaper which was published in New York City during the 1850s. While earlier attempts at establishing Welsh-language newspapers in the United States had failed, *Y Drych*, which first appeared in January 1851, succeeded.[34] After its owners obtained a year-old rival, *Y Gwyliedydd* ('The Sentinel'), the paper was renamed *Y Drych a'r Gwyliedydd;* it was this composite title which the paper carried when the Eos published his praise of the Utica *eisteddfod* in 1856. In 1858 the *Gwyliedydd* part of the name was discarded, and *Y Drych* would remain a corner-stone of Welsh-American culture throughout the period of the Civil War – and, indeed, well into the twentieth century.[35] Less than a year before the outbreak of the Civil War, the paper was moved to Utica, logically taking its place at the hub of Welsh America's cultural life.

Y Drych's mast-head boasted that the paper was a 'National Newspaper at the Service of the Nation of the Welsh in the United States' – *Newyddiadur Cenedlaethol at Wasanaeth Cenedl y Cymry yn y Talaethau Unedig*. The exact wording of the paper's claim is extremely significant, as the word *cenedl*, 'nation', appears twice, once on its own, referring to 'the *Nation* of the Welsh', and once as the root of the adjective *cenedlaethol*, 'national', referring to the United States. This encapsulates a version of Welsh-American identity which pervades the Welsh-language literature published in the United States at the time; *Y Drych* catered for people who saw themselves as being both Welsh and American, and the paper itself was a means of fostering that Welsh-American national identity.

Y Drych allowed Welsh-speaking Americans to maintain a national discussion in their native language, a discussion which included subjects ranging from current United States politics to the poetry competitions of various *eisteddfodau*. Benedict Anderson has suggested that the ideational network provided by the printing press helped to generate modern nationalism: 'These fellow-readers, to whom they were connected through print, formed . . . the embryo of the nationally imagined community.'[36] The Welsh-language press of the United States certainly allowed the country's Welsh citizens to form their own meaningful community on the national level, the community which we can call 'Welsh America'. *Y Drych* lived up to its boast; it was 'at the service of the nation of the Welsh in the United States', helping to construct and maintain a distinct Welsh-American identity. One Welshman from Cattaraugus County, New York, described this process in a letter published by the paper in March 1858:

> Yn mhlith yr amrywiol a'r lluosog bethau sydd yn gwneyd eich cyhoeddiad mor dderbyniol gan bob Cymry o chwaeth, nid y lleiaf ydyw, fod y Cymry, er mor wasgaredig ydynt ar hyd a lled y Cyfandir mawr hwn, yn cael cydgyfarfod i ysgwyd llaw â'u gilydd ar faes y Drych[.][37]
>
> 'Among the various and numerous things which make your publication so acceptable to all Welsh people of taste, not the least is that the Welsh, however dispersed they may be all across this great Continent, get to meet and shake hands with each other on the field of *Y Drych*.'

In addition to keeping far-flung communities in contact with one other, thus fostering this sense of Welsh-American identity on the national level of the United States, the press was an essential part of the context which made Welsh-language American literature possible. The Welsh-American press provided the essentials necessary for maintaining literary culture: readers, a way of reaching those readers, and a critical forum. However, before exploring further the literary culture of Welsh America, we need to look more closely at the way in which we are defining Welsh-American identity.

Defining national identity can be an extremely complex endeavour. Welsh identity in the twenty-first century is constructed and defined in a number of often very different ways, some of which depend to varying degrees on the Welsh language and some of which emphasize other factors. In the middle of the nineteenth century, the vast majority of the people in Wales were Welsh speakers, and the majority of that majority spoke no English; language was for them the main way of defining their Welshness.[38] Virtually all of those people who emigrated to the United States from Wales before and during the Civil War would have spoken Welsh as their native language, and it is likely that around 70 per cent of these immigrants did not speak English upon arrival in their new country.[39] As William D. Jones has concluded, this held true for Welsh immigrants for well after the Civil War:

> Mewn gwirionedd, y mae amrywiaeth eang o ffynonellau ansoddol a thystiolaeth oddrychol ar gael sy'n awgrymu'n bendant fod y rhan fwyaf o ddigon o'r Cymry a ymfudodd i'r Unol Daleithiau, am y rhan helaethaf o'r ganrif, yn siaradwyr Cymraeg.[40]
>
> 'In truth, a wide range of quantitative sources and subjective evidence is available which suggests clearly that the vast majority of the Welsh people who immigrated to the United States, for the greatest part of the century, were Welsh speakers.'

This conclusion stems from a detailed study of the Welsh community of Scranton, Pennsylvania, yet the analysis is easily applied to communities across the United States. Indeed, if the Welsh of urban, industrial communities like Scranton were able to maintain the Welsh language while living and working in close proximity to other ethnic and linguistic groups, it was even easier for more isolated rural communities to do so. Not only did these immigrants continue to speak Welsh in their new American homes; the language 'penetrated every aspect of the immigrant's life' ('wedi treiddio i bob agwedd ar fywyd yr ymfudwyr').[41] After surveying ways in which these immigrants' (non-Welsh-speaking) neighbours described them, Jones adds that 'the Welsh language had an important role in giving a special and separate identity to immigrants from Wales, along with a great deal of unity as a group' ('bod i'r Gymraeg swyddogaeth bwysig o ran rhoi hunaniaeth arbennig a neilltuedig i ymfudwyr o Gymru, ynghyd â chryn fesur o undod fel grŵp').[42]

How large was the Welsh-speaking population of the United States? In 1850 the US Census recorded 29,868 Welsh natives living in the US, and by 1860 the number had reached 45,763.[43] For the most part they emigrated for economic reasons. Although citing 'social ideals' ('[d]elfrydau cymdeithasol') as a significant factor, Glanmor Williams concludes in his study that 'economic incentives' ('cymhellion economaidd') were more powerful forces.[44] This is supported by the detailed analysis conducted by Anne Knowles, who shows that 'Welsh emigration did indeed follow national economic trends' with '[t]he peaks of departure' corresponding to 'economic depressions and recoveries'.[45] However, the economic reasons driving emigrants from Wales during the first half of the nineteenth century were to a great extent bound up with politics and public moral debate. Wealthy landlords often persuaded Parliament to pass acts of enclosure which helped them appropriate what had been common land, thus undermining aspects of traditional life in rural Wales and placing increasing economic pressure on village and farming communities.[46] Most Welsh people emigrated for economic reasons, but these reasons were also often perceived as stemming from social injustices. In 1856 the editor of one Welsh-American journal contrasted the freedom which his countrymen were enjoying under American democracy with the unfair system which they had left behind in the Old Country, described specifically in terms of the 'high rents and heavy taxes' ('y rhenti uchel, trethoedd trymion') which oppressed poor farmers in Britain and the way in which Welsh Nonconformists were 'forced to pay to maintain a religion which [they] did not love' ('orfod talu i gynnal crefydd nad ydym yn ei charu').[47] The Church of England could still claim a tithe in this period, forcing Nonconformist Welsh farmers to pay 10 per cent of their produce to support a church which they did not attend. The resentment engendered by this unfair system would eventually lead to *Rhyfel y Degwm*, 'The Tithe War' of the late 1880s. Really a series of (often violent) protests and riots, the 'Tithe War' which swept through rural Wales twenty years after the American Civil War was foreshadowed by verbal protests like the ones lodged by immigrants to America during the 1850s. The reasons for emigrating to the United States may be analysed in terms of economic hardship, but it is also clear that many immigrants viewed this hardship as the direct result of injustice.

Since at least the late eighteenth century, radicals had suggested that Welsh people should turn their backs on the circumstances which oppressed them in Britain in order to build a new and better society across the sea.[48] This utopian discourse often included an express desire to preserve Welsh-language culture without the interference and condescension of the British state. Whether or not the majority of Welsh immigrants accepted this premise, they did nonetheless take part in constructing new Welsh-speaking communities in the United States; since virtually all Welsh immigrants were Welsh speakers, when the 1860 Census tells us that 45,763 people born in Wales were living in the United States, we can take this to mean that well over 45,000 Welsh speakers were living in America. Indeed, the actual number of Welsh-speaking Americans was much larger than this as the children, and sometimes grandchildren, of immigrants were raised speaking Welsh as a first language in many American communities.[49] The linguistic infrastructure of these communities was maintained first and foremost by numerous Welsh chapels. The Welsh-language culture of nineteenth-century America was defined to a great extent by radical Protestant Nonconformity; none of the nineteenth-century Welsh writers discussed in this study were Anglicans, and all who professed religion in their writings (and most did) were either Calvinistic Methodists, Baptists, Congregationalists or Wesleyans (with an occasional Unitarian as well). As in Wales, the Welsh-American Chapel played a role in supporting various other social and cultural institutions; Sunday School, for adults as well as children, was an important vehicle for maintaining literacy in Welsh (in addition to the more obvious religious functions), and chapels were often the sponsors of other kinds of societies such as Welsh-speaking branches of various temperance and anti-slavery movements. These religious institutions also supported literary culture; the considerable social infrastructure provided by the Welsh chapel helped the *eisteddfod* institution to take root in the United States.

The Welsh-language American press served as hand-maiden to these other institutions, fostering that sense of Welsh-American national identity described above. By mid-century Welsh America had, in addition to its weekly newspaper, three substantial monthly journals. While numerous other books, pamphlets and short-lived papers and journals were produced by the Welsh presses in Utica and other communities, it is *Y Drych* and these three monthlies which formed the back-bone of Welsh-American print culture in the middle of the nineteenth century.[50] A poet using the pen-name Aderyn Du o'r Dyffryn, 'The Black Bird of the Valley', composed a short poem in 1847 praising the three journals. This simple rhymed exhortation was published under the title 'Lines to the Descendants of Gomer in America' ('Llinellau at Hil Gomer yn America'); it presents the three monthly publications as organs essential to the life of Welsh America. The first couplet states in no uncertain terms that it is the duty of Welsh-Americans to support the journals:

> Cydunwn Hil Gomer, yn seinber ein sain,
> I ddangos fod mawredd a rhinwedd yn rhain[.][51]

> 'Let us join together, Descendants of Gomer, melodious our sound,
> To show that there is greatness and virtue in these[.]'

Nineteenth-century writers often described the Welsh as *Hil Gomer*; like many phrases enjoying cultural currency at the time, it drew blithely upon medieval Welsh pseudo-history. As early as the ninth century, Welsh authors were writing that the first son of Japheth was named Gomer, and that the Ancient Britons or Welsh were descended from him.[52] As Japheth was himself the son of Noah, this genealogical invention fashioned a lineage for the Welsh which took them back to the time of the biblical flood. While some medieval Welsh writers had gone a large step farther and traced their people's history all the way back to Adam and Eve, Gomer was the favourite ultimate ancestor of nineteenth-century Welsh-American writers. The name was helped to pride of place in Welsh literary consciousness by the fact that Joseph Harris, who established the first weekly Welsh-language newspaper in Wales in 1814, used the pen-name Gomer. His paper, the direct ancestor of Welsh-American publications like *Y Drych*, was called *Seren Gomer* ('Gomer's Star').

Thus in 1847, the same year in which the Blue Books were published back in Britain, this Welsh-American poet could call on the loyal 'Descendants of Gomer' in America to join together in praise of their three monthly journals. He then states that these publications were a means of keeping the immigrants and their descendants from living as strangers' – 'byw fel dieithriaid' – in their new country; they would not be 'strangers' in the United States because these journals helped make their America into a Welsh America. Following this, the poet commands Welsh-Americans to 'nurture bardic inspiration' – 'Meithrinwch yr awen' – in order to support the 'cheerful, beneficial and fluid' Welsh language in America ('iaith siriol, ireiddiol a rhwydd'). The poem closes by invoking the three journals by name:

> Cewch ryddid dan haulwen, a'r SEREN i'r swydd,
> Cyfryngau gwybodaeth ryw doraeth a dardd.
> CENHADWR, cain odiaith, mwyn helaeth mae'n hardd,
> A CHYFAILL iach hefyd er bywyd i'r bardd.

> 'You will have freedom under the sun, with the STAR at work,
> Media for a considerable multitude's knowledge springs forth.
> A MISSIONARY, most fair, [with] great wealth, is handsome,
> And a sturdy FRIEND as well to give life to the bard.'

These journals are said to support the 'freedom' of Welsh America. While the exact nature of that liberty is not specified, it is connected to the dissemination of knowledge and the health of Welsh letters in America; the very 'life' of the bard depends upon the success of these publications.

The last journal named in this poem, *Y Cyfaill o'r Hen Wlad*, was the oldest of the three, having started publication in 1838. The title translates as 'The Friend from the Old Country', and the significance of this phrase was explained on the first page of the journal's very first number. The piece is a fanciful dialogue which, due to the fact that it appeared early in January 1838, begins as a New Year's greeting:

> *Y Cyfaill*. Blwyddyn newydd dda i chwi, a llawer o honynt.
> *Cymro*. Diolch yn fawr i chwi, am eich cyfarchiad caredig. Dymunwn yr un peth i chwithau. Ond y mae yn beth go ryfedd genyf glywed iaith fy mam gan wr dieithr

> yn y wlad yma. Pwy ddywedaf fi ydych chwi?
> *Y Cyf.* Cyfaill yw 'mhenw. Nid wyf yn meddwl ei wadu. Gall dyn gonest ddweud ei enw yn mhob gwlad, heb ofn. Yr wyf yn hoff iawn o'm henw hefyd; a gobeithiwyf gael dod i brofi i chwi, nad ydwyf yn hollol annghymmwys i'r enw osodwyd arnaf.[53]

> '*The Friend.* A happy new year to you, and many of them.
> *Welshman.* Thank you very much, for your kind greeting. I would wish the same thing for you. But it is a very strange thing for me to hear the language of my mother from a stranger in this country. Who will I say you are?
> *The Friend.* Friend is my name. I do not intend to deny it. An honest man can speak his name in every country, without fear. I am very fond of my name as well; and I hope to come to prove to you, that I am not completely unlike the name which has been given to me.'

The Welshman, thrilled with the name, invites the personified journal into his house, asking his new 'Friend' to put his bag down and rest. The Welshman asks the *Cyfaill* what is in his bundle (*sypyn*), and is told that it contains 'valuable treasures . . . to share amongst the Welsh in America' ('Trysorau gwerthfawr . . . i'w gyfranu yn mhlith y Cymry yn America'). The curious Welshman enquires about the exact nature of these riches, and his Friend tells him simply that they 'are from the old country' ('o'r hen wlad'). The Welshman finds this to be ironic, confessing that he has emigrated to the United States in search of 'treasures' because he had given up hope of ever growing wealthy in Wales. The Friend corrects him, detailing the exact nature of the treasures contained between its covers: 'It is not treasures of gold and silver that I have – but treasures of knowledge, which, despite that, are better than the best kinds of creation's ore' ('Nid trysorau aur ac arian sydd genyf – ond trysorau gwybodaeth, y rhai er hyny, ydynt yn rhagori ar fwnau goreu'r grëadigaeth'). This explanation of the journal's name, the opening gambit in the publication's long life, proved to be no idle boast: the 'Friend from the Old Country' did indeed earn its place on the bookshelves of Welsh America, and it would remain a friend to Welsh-speaking Americans up to its end in 1933.

The second of these three journals, *Y Cenhadwr Americanaidd*, started publication in 1840 in Utica (and was moved shortly thereafter to the nearby village of Remsen).[54] Translating as 'The American Missionary' (or 'Messenger'), the journal's title revealed the ambitious moral agenda pursued by its editor, the Revd Robert Everett. The *Cenhadwr*'s first title-page, however, described the monthly's remit as including a variety of subjects:

> Bywgraffiadau, Duwinyddiaeth, Hanesyddiaeth, Amaethyddiaeth,
> Ynghyd a
> **Newyddion Americanaidd a Thramor:**
> Hefyd, Cyfansoddiadau Mewn
> **Barddoniaeth a Pheroriaeth.**

'Biographies, Theology, Historiography, Agriculture,
Along with
American and Foreign News:
Also, Compositions in
Poetry and Music.'

While the *Cenhadwr* was wide-ranging, the bold-faced print drew the attention of prospective readers to two aspects of its contents. As will be seen in Chapter Two, Robert Everett's 'Missionary' was indeed a potent vehicle for reform, championing abolition as well as temperance and women's rights; the lasting importance of this journal would ultimately lie in the political and moral arguments which it disseminated throughout Welsh America. However, in presenting the new publication to Welsh-American readers, it was not this moral agenda which the editor emphasized but rather two other things: the journal contained 'news', both 'American' and 'Foreign', and it also contained 'Poetry and Music', lending credence to the poet's claim that these journals gave 'life to the bard'.

The third journal appeared first in 1844. *Y Seren Orllewinol*, 'The Western Star', was published originally in Utica before being moved to New York and then to its final home in Pottsville, Pennsylvania.[55] While all three of these journals aimed at serving Welsh America in general, they also had their denominational affiliations: the *Cyfaill* was the publication of the Welsh Calvinistic Methodists in the United States, the *Cenhadwr* provided a forum for the Welsh Congregationalists of America, and the *Seren* served the country's Welsh Baptists. (While there were a substantial number of Welsh-speaking Wesleyans living in America as well, they did not have their own journal; they either contributed to one of the other publications or published in the denomination's monthly back in Wales, *Yr Eurgrawn Wesleyaidd*.) The denominational arguments which so characterized the Nonconformist chapel culture of Wales did at times temper the contents of these journals. For example, when the Methodists and Baptists of Cattaraugus, New York, fell out over the organization of a new Sunday School, they traded blows from the denominational platforms offered by the *Cyfaill* and the *Seren*.[56] However, as all three publications presented the news of the day as well as discussions of events like *eisteddfodau* which were of interest to Welsh America in general, they at least tried to transcend their sectarian associations. And, like *Y Drych* newspaper, all three monthlies presented passionate arguments in favour of maintaining Welsh-language culture in the United States.

As early as February 1838, the second issue of the *Cyfaill* carried a treatise on 'Preserving Welsh' ('Cadw y Gymraeg'), penned by a writer from Ohio calling himself Gomeriad ('One of Gomer's people').[57] He welcomed the new journal enthusiastically, playing upon the way in which the first issue's opening dialogue had described the personified publication as a new 'Friend' visiting the Welsh immigrant's home:

Y CYFAILL CYWIR – Er pan ddeallwyd eich bod yn golygu cynnysgaeddu y Cymry yn America, a math o Gylchgrawn Cymreig misol, mawr yr hyfrydwch a barodd hyny yn y fro dywyll y preswyliwyf; ac nid llai y trydar a'r cynnwrf yn mysg fy nghymydogion yn nghylch y 'Cyfaill o'r Hen Wlad,' er ys amrai fisoedd bellach; a minau yn lled ddistaw yn eu mysg, ond nid llai fy awyddfryd am ddyfodiad dechreu y flwyddyn 1838, pryd yr hyderwn gael prawf o fedusrwydd y Cyfaill hwnw i ddisychedu trigolion yr ardal hon. Ond pa fodd bynag, yr amser nodedig a ddaeth, y Cyfaill a ymwelodd a'n bro, ac a ymbresenolodd yn ein tai cyffion.[58]

'TRUE FRIEND:- Since it was first learned that you intended to endow the Welsh in America with a kind of monthly Welsh Journal, great is the joy which that [news] has caused in the dark region where I reside; and no less is the murmur and excitement amongst my neighbours concerning the 'Cyfaill o'r Hen Wlad', for some months now; while I have been fairly quiet in their midst, no less was my desire for the coming of the year 1838, when I knew I would get to experience the ability of that Friend to quench the thirst of this region's inhabitants. At any rate, the appointed time came, the Cyfaill visited our regions, presenting itself [or 'himself'] in our log cabins.'

The last sentence describes the *Cyfaill*'s visit to the Welsh of this unspecified Ohio community in an extremely interesting manner. First of all, the journal's arrival is described using the verb *ymbresenoli*, a word which combines the verb *presenoli*, 'to present oneself', with the reflexive affix *ym-*, intensifying the emphasis on the person who is making an appearance. The new Friend, having reached the distant community in a 'dark' part of Ohio, presents himself in order to be counted; he has presented himself in order that he be reckoned as a part of this Welsh-American community's cultural life. Secondly, the houses of these Welsh Ohioans are described as *tai cyffion*, 'log cabins', emphasizing the Welsh publication's ability to reach what is presented as a new frontier community.

The journal's visit to Ohio's log cabins is then praised by Gomeriad as a means of 'freeing the Welsh from the English[-language] enslavement of this country' ('i ryddhau y Gymraeg o gaethiwed Seisnigaidd y wlad hon'). The writer continues by wishing the *Cyfaill* and all similar publishing ventures success, noting that they are especially crucial for those Welsh-Americans who do not speak English.[59] The essential logic of maintaining Welsh-language culture in America is emphasized repeatedly by Gomeriad:

Gwallgof y cyfrifwyf y dyn, yn enwedig y Cymro, a ddywed mai afreidiol a diles cadw a choleddu yr iaith Gymraeg yn y wlad hon; y mae ei thrysorau yr un mor llawn o eiriau cynnwysfawr yn America ac yn Nghymru. Ond gwir fod ein helyntion ni yn wahanol i'n cydgenedl yno, gan ein bod yn ymddibynu ar ein cyfeillion Americanaidd am gyfryngau gwybodaeth mewn iaith estronol; ond eto credwyf a llawenychwyf fod Cymraeg i gael ei siarad gan genedl y Cymry yn y rhan hyn o'r ddaear, tra huan a lloer yn rhoi eu llewyrch.

> 'I consider to be insane any man, especially a Welshman, who says that preserving and embracing the Welsh language in this country is unnecessary and unbeneficial; its treasures are just as full of comprehensive words in America as [they are] in Wales. Yet it is true that our experiences are different to [those of] our nation there, since we depend upon our American friends for the means of knowledge in a foreign language; but yet I believe and I take joy [in the fact] that Welsh will be spoken by the nation of the Welsh in this part of the earth, as long as sun and moon give their light.'

The 'enslavement' to the English language which this writer describes is clearly not seen as the fault of his 'American neighbours', for they are only trying to help the emigrants by providing 'knowledge' in English.

This favourable description of the writer's English-speaking neighbours was more than unsolicited politeness. Indeed, rather than seeking actively to discourage the immigrant's native tongue, state governments at times made special concessions for the Welsh. One writer, also from Ohio, published a piece in *Y Cyfaill o'r Hen Wlad* in 1839 praising his state's linguistic sensitivity.[60] The Ohio state government, he said, 'had ordered the printing of one thousand papers containing the recent Address of the State Governor in the Welsh language' ('wedi gorchymyn argraffu mil o bapyrau yn cynnwys Cenadwri ddiweddar y Llywydd Taleithol yn yr iaith Gymraeg').[61] The author then describes the state government's actions as a 'sign of respect for those of our nation as citizens in the West' ('Mae hyn yn arwydd o barch i'n cyd-genedl fel dinasyddion da yn y Gorllewin'). This piece was given a simple subtitle which describes its contents in plain terms: 'Yr Iaith Gymraeg yn Ohio', 'The Welsh Language in Ohio'.

The main title, however, is taken from an old Welsh prophecy: 'Eu Hiaith a Gadwant' – 'they will keep their language.'[62] Welsh tradition attributed these words to Taliesin, an early medieval poet who by the later middle ages had generated a legendary persona. A great deal of poetry and prose contained in medieval and early modern manuscripts depicts Taliesin as a supernatural shape-shifting poet, at times described as the very incarnation of *awen*, or bardic inspiration. The supernatural powers attributed to Taliesin by legend also made him a prophet, and a range of vaticinatory material is attributed to him in several centuries' worth of manuscripts and books.[63] What is interesting concerning the nature of Welsh culture in the United States is that an article discussing the relationship between the Ohio State Government and the Welsh language is presented to readers using the best-known line from Taliesin's poetic prophecy. As is seen in so many Welsh-American writings from the period, this piece seeks to inspire (Welsh-)American patriotism by using a loaded concept drawn from a much earlier phase of Welsh cultural history. Like that supporter of the New York City *eisteddfod* who saw the progress of civilization as leading naturally to the Welsh-American cultural festival, so this writer had no trouble in melding a prophecy about the fate of the Welsh language in Wales with a jubilant report of the welcome extended to Welsh immigrants by the government of Ohio. Welsh-Americans were led to read the prophetic line in the context of recent state politics; the quotation suggested that the spirit of Taliesin, age-old culture hero of the Welsh, was guiding events in the Ohio State House.

To return to Gomeriad's description of the *Cyfaill*'s arrival in Ohio's log cabins, it was not his 'American neighbours' who challenged the relevance of Welsh, but rather the 'insane' immigrant who viewed maintaining Welsh-language culture in the United States as 'unnecessary and unbeneficial.' As suggested already by the brief discussion of the Blue Books and their effect upon the Victorian *eisteddfodau* of Wales, there were plenty of Welsh people in the nineteenth century who embraced the process of Anglicization, eschewing their native language and its associated culture in the face of the English language's hegemonic force. This process had been started by the Welsh gentry of the sixteenth century who left Wales for London, either literally or metaphorically, Anglicizing themselves while pursuing the favours of the nascent British Empire. By the early nineteenth century, the London-based satirist Jac Glan-y-gors had invented the name 'Dic Siôn Dafydd', and it soon came to be used as a pejorative label for a Welshman who pretended to forget his native language. Jac Glan-y-gors's long satirical poem bearing that title became extremely popular in nineteenth-century Wales (and America), and the theme was taken up by other writers and poets. 'Dic Siôn Dafydd' became a part of Welsh folk consciousness, surviving through the twentieth century as the linguistic 'Uncle Tom' of Welsh-language popular culture.

Eos Glan Twrch's 1856 poem praising the supporters of Utica's *eisteddfod* contrasted them with the 'vain false man' who had no interest in such cultural pursuits; while avoiding the stock character's name, this was his way of describing Dic Siôn Dafydd's American cousin. Similarly, in 1847 a writer calling himself 'Ab Gomer' ('Son of Gomer') published a letter in *Y Seren Orllewinol* which, like the poem by Aderyn Du discussed above, praised the services rendered by America's three Welsh-language monthly journals. While expressing joy over the fact that there were 'enough of Gomer's descendants on this side of the Atlantic to support three Welsh publications in an honourable fashion' ('Y mae digon o hil Gomer yr ochor hyn i'r Mor-werydd i gynnal tri o gyhoeddiadau Cymreig mewn modd anrhydeddus'), this Son of Gomer also bemoaned the fact that the children of Dic Siôn Dafydd had followed more honourable emigrants across the sea:

> ond fel y mae gwaethaf y modd, y mae rhai o'r Cymry, ar ol iddynt ddyfod yr ochor hyn i'r môr, yn gwadu eu hiaith a'u cenedl, fel ag y gwnaeth eu hen dad Dic o'u blaen, ac yn resu eu hunain gyda y Saeson . . . Mae y rhai hyn yn ddigon i wneuthur dyn rhesymol i chwydu ei berfedd allan wrth eu clywed yn siarad mor ffroen-uchel, a chyda y fath lediaith Saesnigaidd am eu cenedl, eu hiaith, a'u cyhoeddiadau, fel pethau rhy isel a gwael iddynt *hwy* i wneuthur sylw o honynt[.][64]

'however, more's the pity, some of the Welsh, after coming to this side of the sea, deny their language and their nation, as their old father Dic did before them, enlisting with the English . . . These people are enough to make a reasonable man vomit his insides out at hearing them speak so snobbishly, and with such an Englishy patois, about their nation, their language, and their publications, as things too low and base for *them* to notice.'

Fortunately, according to Ab Gomer, the American children of Dic Siôn Dafydd were few and had little impact on the developing character of Welsh America:

er eich cysur nid yw y pleidiau a nodwyd genyf ddiweddaf yn lluosog iawn, trwy drugaredd; ac nid yw eu dylanwad ond bychan yn mhlith ein cenedl: ac heblaw hyn, y mae genyf i ddywedyd fod gyda ni amryw o gewri cryfion ar y maes; ac y mae genym bleidwyr selog a ffyddlon, ac ysgrifenwyr medrus a galluog, y rhai a allant eich cynnorthwyo[.][65]

'in order to comfort you [I can say that] the parties which I noted above are not very numerous, mercifully; and their influence is but small among our nation; and besides this, I can say that we have several strong giants on the field; and we have zealous and faithful advocates, and capable, skilful writers, who can help you.'

These champions are described explicitly as authors; it is 'skilful writers' ('ysgrifenwyr medrus') who come as giants to the field of cultural combat in the face of the threat posed by Dic Siôn Dafydd's American offspring. Welsh-language writers were singled out for praise because of the part they played in constructing and maintaining a Welsh-American identity.

Ab Gomer was referring to people like E. D. Thomas, a writer who published a short article in *Y Seren Orllewinol* in 1850. The ostensible purpose of the piece was to praise a recent series of lectures on Welsh history delivered by Iorwerth Owen in Cincinnati's Independence Hall. However, Thomas used his glowing review of the lectures as a platform from which to berate Dic Siôn Dafydd's American children, mixing his discourse on the edifying virtues of historiography with bare-knuckle satire:

Llawer Dic Shon Dafydd a welir yma a thraw yn y wlad. Mor gynted ag y gallant siarad ychydig mewn iaith estronol clywir hwynt yn brygawthwn, *"Me can no' 'stan' Wels," "Me was be Englis,"* &c. Ffei arnynt! A dyweded pob Cymro, *"Oes y byd i'r Iaith Gymraeg."*[66]

'Many a Dic Shon Dafydd is seen here and there in the country. As soon as they can speak a little in a foreign language they are heard to blather, *"Me can no' 'stan' Wels," "Me was be Englis,"* &c. Fie upon them! And let every Welshman say, *"Long live the Welsh language.'*

E. D. Thomas's complaint that 'many a Dic Shon Dafydd' was to be found in the United States goes against Ab Gomer's assurance that such characters were 'not very numerous, mercifully'. Whatever the real number of Dic's American children, Ab Gomer's conclusion that 'their influence is but small among our nation' is supported by other kinds of evidence.[67]

At least one American Dic Siôn Dafydd wielded enough influence to worry Welsh America's *literati.* A writer using the pen-name Wil Milltiroedd ('Wil of the Miles', or, perhaps, 'Well-travelled Wil'), used the publication *The Old Countryman* to attack the supporters of Welsh-language culture, writing that 'We are of the opinion that the preservation of the Welsh language has retarded the Welsh in intellectual pursuits, and crippled the literature of Wales.'[68] *The Old Countryman* was a short-lived English-language journal for British immigrants which at times printed Welsh material. Judging by surviving publications from the period, it had little effect on Welsh-American culture and was virtually ignored by Welsh-speaking Americans; however, the fact that such an attack was mounted from its pages did not go unnoticed. In the October 1846 number of *Y Seren Orllewinol,* a writer calling himself Taliesin ab Gwilym ('Taliesin son of Gwilym' or 'William'), provided a spirited response. He called Wil Milltiroedd 'the modern Dic Shon Dafydd', further describing him as being 'remarkably unpopular because of his lack of patriotism, his hypocrisy, his selfish whim, and his jealousy of whoever happens to be popular' ('nodedig o anmhoblog o herwydd ei anwladgarwch, ei ragrith, ei fympwy hunanol, a'i eiddigedd wrth y sawl a fyddo yn boblog').[69]

It is perhaps no coincidence that this American champion of Welsh-language culture used the name Taliesin. After all, Taliesin was the archetypical bard of medieval Welsh tradition, personifying the power of poetry and the poet's ability to speak truth. In the sixteenth-century 'Tale of Taliesin', the protagonist triumphs over a group of self-important court poets, thus making Taliesin, among other things, a name to be invoked during bardic debates. Appropriately enough, this American Taliesin finished his attack on the 'modern Dic Siôn Dafydd' with a satirical poem. Beginning with verses in the *englyn* metre, this poem is in fact an *awdl,* a combination of several of the medieval strict-metres seen traditionally as the Welsh bard's formal *tour de force.*[70] Indeed, as bardic satire was an important feature of the medieval Welsh literary tradition, there are many aspects of this poem which recall Welsh poetry's golden age.[71] A poet calling himself Taliesin was composing bardic satire using a combination of the medieval strict metres; this tells us something about the way in which new Welsh-American writing was being placed in productive association with (an imagined version) of the classical Welsh past:[72]

Gelyn mwyaf digywilydd – yw hwn
    O hil Dic Shon Dafydd,
  Ei swn cyfeiliornus sydd
  Aruthr wawd, oer athrodydd.[73]

'The most shameless enemy – is this man
From the lineage of Dic Siôn Dafydd,
His misleading noise is
A great shame, heartless slanderer.'

In this *englyn*, the poem's opening stanza, Taliesin ab Gwilym draws upon old linguistic registers in creating a pointedly contemporary satire. The penultimate line, describing the despised figure's 'misleading noise', refers directly to the way in which this American version of Dic Siôn Dafydd tried to undermine the contemporary discussion of the nature of Welsh-American culture. Despite its contemporary subject-matter, the two phrases which make up the last line – *aruthr wawd* and *oer athrodydd* – would not have been out of place in a fourteenth-century bardic debate.

While Taliesin ab Gwilym attacked the Welsh-American advocate of Anglicization by means of traditional bardic satire, a satirist using the name 'Welsh Yankee' used humorous fiction for the same purpose:

> Mr. Editor, – Fi dim gwybod a fyddwch chi boddlon i mi rito i'r Seren, but fi wedi meddwl rito iddi lawer tro. Fi wedi colli yr Welsh, am bod tad a mam fi wedi dysgu fi i speco English. . . .[74]

It is hard to render this quotation in English. While the English words and forms are readily discernible – 'Welsh' and 'English' (instead of *Cymraeg* and *Saesneg*), 'rito' ('to write') instead of *ysgrifennu* and 'speco' ('to speak') instead of *siarad* – the piece is impossible to translate. The reader of Welsh will appreciate the satire immediately, as torturously bad grammar is used to mimic the speech of a Welsh-American raised by parents who shunned their native language. The following translation is an attempt at doing approximately the same thing with English grammar:

> 'Mr. Editor, – Me no know if you will be willing for me to write to the Seren, but I have thought to write to it many times. Me have lost the Welsh, since my father and mother taught me to speak English.'

The writings of the 'Welsh Yankee' in fact constituted a kind of column in *Y Seren Orllewinol*, appearing sporadically during the 1840s and 1850s.[75] Ab Gomer assured the *Seren*'s readers that Dic Siôn Dafydd's American children were 'not very numerous', while Taliesin ab Gwilym declared with confidence on the pages of the same journal that the advocate for linguistic assimilation was 'remarkably unpopular' among Welsh-Americans. However, the very fact that these authors felt a need to take their arguments to press, coupled with the fact that the Welsh Yankee's column appeared intermittently throughout this period, suggests strongly that such forces were an ever-present threat to those concerned with maintaining a Welsh-language American culture.

Other than the two-dimensional caricatures of satirical fiction, most of the real immigrants inclined towards the views of Dic Siôn Dafydd are absent from the literary record; their willing linguistic assimilation took them out of the ambit of Welsh-speaking America and its publications. However, studies to date suggest that the vast majority of nineteenth-century Welsh immigrants continued to use their native language in fashioning the 'special and separate identity' of Welsh America described by William D. Jones. The present study is concerned with Welsh-language writing stemming from the American Civil War, and for present purposes 'Welsh' will be defined in terms of the Welsh language. This methodological guideline is in keeping with the way in which identity was defined by Welsh people, both in Wales and in the United States, in the mid-nineteenth century. While other ways of articulating Welsh identity have played a prominent role in the history of twentieth- and twenty-first century Wales, the main way of assessing Welsh identity in Wales and America at the middle of the nineteenth century was the language. For the purposes of the present study, Welshness is defined in terms of language and culture, not in terms of 'blood' and 'race'. This book thus ignores the English-speaking descendants of Welsh immigrants, a fact which greatly effects the way in which Welsh-American involvement in the Civil War is assessed. There were plenty of people in the Southern United States with Welsh surnames; many of them, including Jefferson Davis himself, were the descendants of Welsh immigrants. However, English-speaking Southerners of distant Welsh descent differed greatly – in terms of language, culture and, as will be seen in the next chapter, ideology – from the Welsh-speaking Americans living in the North.

Nineteenth-century Welsh America was located overwhelmingly in the Northern states. Around 90 per cent of the Welsh immigrants recorded in the 1850 and 1860 censuses were living in four states – New York, Pennsylvania, Ohio and Wisconsin – and most of the remaining 10 per cent were residing in other Northern states.[76] A number of Welsh people had emigrated to Virginia and the Carolinas during the eighteenth century, but their descendants had long since lost the Welsh language. There were small Welsh-speaking communities in Tennessee and Maryland when the Civil War broke out, yet these isolated groups of people can only be described as exceptions to the rule that Welsh America was located almost exclusively in the free states of the North. Indeed, judging by the evidence provided by the Welsh-American press, an emphasis on the political and moral distinction between free state and slave state played an increasingly important role in defining Welsh-American identity during the decade before the Civil War. In their history of the newspaper, Aled Jones and Bill Jones note that *Y Drych* started life in 1851 by ignoring politics, focusing instead on cultural concerns. This soon changed.

> By February 1855 editorials on slavery and politics were appearing whilst the 1856 presidential campaign, and the political loyalties of the Welsh, were discussed in detail. In November 1856 *Y Drych* asserted that never before had the Welsh in America shown so much interest in politics. Particular emphasis was put on the Republican opposition to slavery.[77]

As will be seen in detail in the next chapter, a study of other print sources supports this analysis of *Y Drych*'s development. One might even conclude that this process of politicization above all else characterizes the history of Welsh America during the decade leading up to the Civil War.

Of course, the term 'process of politicization' is shorthand for a number of complicated historical developments which are now lost to us. The complex 'reality' of Welsh-language American culture of the period is gone, and we have to depend almost entirely upon surviving written sources. This book presents history woven primarily from various kinds of texts written by Welsh-speaking Americans. It can be seen as literary history in two senses of the term: I am attempting to assess literature stemming from a particular historical experience and, at the same time, I am also writing a narrative history by using literature as my primary source. This book, then, is in essence a study of the relationship between literature and history; it takes as a starting point the assumption that literary texts and historical context are 'mutually self-constituting.'[78] In keeping with the way in which nineteenth-century Welsh and Welsh-American writers used the word *llenyddiaeth*, I am defining 'literature' broadly.[79] This includes the range of texts produced by the Welsh-American press – newspaper articles, sermons, and essays in addition to fiction and poetry – as well as unpublished letters and diaries.

THE BARDIC MEASURING STICK: DEFINING WELSH-AMERICAN LITERATURE

Since literature, broadly defined, is at the centre of this study, and since the articulation of Welsh-American identity by means of writing and publishing is the main subject explored in this chapter, it is worth asking a series of related questions which follow from these starting points. First of all, if we can describe Welsh-American identity, can we can also talk of a Welsh-American literary identity? Did Welsh-Americans writing on the eve of the Civil War produce what we might call a Welsh-American literature? Academic departments at universities all over the world promulgate the concept of (an English-language) 'American Literature' as distinct from the 'English Literature' of England; to what extent can we treat Welsh texts written in the United States as part of a Welsh-American Literature, closely related to – and yet also distinct from – the Literature of Wales? What did Welsh-American writers and readers think? Do we have any way of knowing what they actually thought?

We can start answering these questions by returning to the texts themselves. In fact, we can return to the same issue of *Y Drych* which carried Eos Glan Twrch's elaborate praise for the Utica *eisteddfod*, namely the one published on 15 March 1856. That same issue carried a letter by Ellis Owain Ellis, an artist who was part of Liverpool's large Welsh community. He was working on a book of engravings which he planned to publish under the title *Oriel Beirdd a Llenorion Cymru*, 'A Gallery of the Bards and Writers of Wales'. In his open letter, Ellis asked the Welsh of America to help him by sending 'pictures of Williams, New York, and other Welsh authors who had moved to America' ('lluniau Williams, New York, ac eraill o awduron Cymreig a symudasant i'r America'). The paper's editor added his own comments to the engraver's letter, drawing his readers' attention to the importance of the venture: 'It's true that there are various bards here famous enough to have a Place in the *Gallery*' (*'Mae yn wir fod yma amryw feirdd digon enwog i gael lle yn yr* Oriel'). This was a chance for the Welsh of America to prove to themselves and to people back in the Old Country that they had a literary culture of note. The editor thus urged 'the friends of the bards in this country' (*'gyfeillion y beirdd yn y wlad hon'*) to form committees in order to pursue the project in an orderly fashion. They were to obtain daguerreotypes of the poets and send them without delay to the artist in Liverpool. He helped the future committee-members by providing a list of America's Welsh poets, using their bardic names:

> Nid ydym ni yn gwybod yn bresenol ond am y beirdd canlynol, ac os dygwydd i ni beidio enwi rhai a ystyrir yn feirdd, na fydded i neb gymeryd hyny yn dramgwydd, canys nid yn fwriadol y bu. Enwn y rhai isod. Eos Glan Twrch, Floyd, E. N. Ionoron Glandwyryd, Fairhaven, Vt. Dewi Emlyn, Parisville O., Iolo Mynwy, Hyde Park, Pa. Llinos Glan Ohio, Minersville, Pa. Iorthryn Gwynedd, Rome, E. N.
>
> 'We do not know at present of any except for the following poets, and if it happens that we do not name same who are considered to be poets, let no one take it as offence, for it was not intentional. We name those below. Eos Glan Twrch, Floyd, N. Y. Ionoron Glan Dwyryd, Fairhaven, Vt. Dewi Emlyn, Parisville, O[hio], Iolo Mynwy, Hyde Park, Pa., Llinos Glan Ohio, Minersville, Pa., Iorthryn Gwynedd, Rome, N. Y.'

Since the artist had asked for 'Williams, New York' by name, the editor singled out this poet for special attention: 'Bydd i gyfeillion "Williams, New York", sef Wm. J. Williams (Gwilym ab Ioan,) ofalu cael ei arlun mewn pryd i'w anfon i'r Oriel'; 'Let the friends of "Williams, New York", that is W[illiam] J. Williams (Gwilym ab Ioan), take care to get his picture in time to send to the Gallery.'[80]

Thus, in 1856 the editor of *Y Drych* was composing a list of Welsh-American poets in order that they receive their proper 'place' in the literary gallery being assembled back in Britain. However, the editor's list was produced in response to the artist's request; it was quite literally an after-thought, a short paragraph appended to another text. While this was a move towards canonizing and promoting the Welsh-language literature of the United States, it was an extremely tentative step. And it was taken in the context of canonizing and promoting the Welsh-language literature of Wales, not as an independent project designed to present Welsh-American literature as a field in its own right.

Exactly three years and three months later, on 15 June 1859, *Y Drych* was presenting a very different kind of literary exercise to Welsh America. In fact, that edition of the newspaper carried three pieces about poetry, providing a journalistic echo of Eos Glan Twrch's versified boast that the good Welsh-American who loved his language also by definition loved poetry. First of all, the newspaper published Caledfryn's official adjudication of the bardic compositions produced for that year's Utica *eisteddfod*.[81] Caledfryn (or William Williams) was a mainstay of bardic culture back in Wales. In 1832 he won the Chair at an Anglesey *eisteddfod* with an *awdl* that soon became one of the most popular strict-metre poems of its time.[82] He published several books on Welsh grammar and bardic craft, and by the time he was invited to judge the Utica contest Caledfryn was one of the most popular – and rigorous – *eisteddfod* adjudicators in Wales. The literary criticism which Caledfryn delivered from the stages of numerous *eisteddfodau* has been credited with raising the standards of poetry in early Victorian Wales; the organizers of the Utica festival had chosen just the person to help ensure that Welsh-American poets were being tested carefully. And by publishing Caledfryn's criticism, *Y Drych* was ensuring that the whole of Welsh America benefited from the Utica *eisteddfod*'s literary enterprise.

Secondly, the edition of *Y Drych* published on 15 June 1859 carried an instalment of 'Dydd Lyfr Guto', 'Guto's Day-book', a humorous column which appeared in the newspaper intermittently throughout the period. The 'Day-book' is satirical fiction written in the first-person by Guto, a fictional poet. This 1859 entry lampoons those poets who frequented the American *eisteddfodau*, thus emphasizing with the tribute of satire the importance of these cultural festivals to Welsh-American life. Guto places his trust in nepotism rather than his own talent, hoping that his friendship with the judge will ensure him a victory in the bardic competition. Whoever the author of this piece was, he took aim unflinchingly at that idealized version of Welsh America which many of its publications were promoting, linking his satire of the *eisteddfod* culture to a corner-stone of Welsh America's public morality, the temperance movement:

> Tachwedd 12. – Yr wyf wedi teneuo llawer wrth fyfyrio mor galed erbyn Eisteddfod Utica. Credaf y byddwyf yn sicr o'r gwobrwyon. Yr wyf yn hen gyfaill

> i Caledfryn. Ysgrifenais ato heddyw gan awgrymu y caiff weled fy ngwaith cyn hir. Dysgwyliaf wneyd tri-ugain dolar yn glir yn yr eisteddfod hon. Nid wyf yn Deedotal mwy na'r hen Galedfryn.[83]
>
> 'November 12. – I have grown thin [with worry] while preparing so thoroughly for the Utica Eisteddfod. I believe that the prizes are certainly mine. I am an old friend of Caledfryn's. I wrote to him today suggesting that he will get to see my work before long. I expect to make 60 dollars easily in this eisteddfod. I am no more of a Teetotaller than is old Caledfryn.'[84]

The fictitious diary then jumps to 1 January, the day of the *eisteddfod*. Guto is denied the prize money he had expected to win so easily, and he has to 'borrow ten dollars from E. G. T., the poet, to pay for lodgings' ('Benthyg deg dolar gan E. G. T., y bardd, i dalu am *lodgings*').[85]

Guto's benefactor is Eos Glan Twrch. As seen in the reference to Caledfryn, the fiction is woven with strands of reality, making the satire all the more powerful. John Edwards (or Eos Glan Twrch) was indeed one of the most successful poets then competing in the American *eisteddfodau*, and thus Guto's decision to ask the Eos for a ten-dollar loan would have made sense to *Y Drych*'s readers. The 'Day-Book' is a short, compact piece, presented – between the columns of other, longer articles – for the enjoyment of the newspaper's readers. However, it carries all the hallmarks of much more lengthy and elaborate works of Welsh satire. It could even be viewed as a precursor to *Wil Brydydd y Coed* ('Wil, the Poet of the Forest'), the memorable satire by David Owen which was serialized in a Welsh journal between 1863 and 1865. Like Guto, Wil is a bumbling protagonist who has completely unrealistic pretentions to bardic greatness. And, like the poet of Guto's 1859 'Day-Book' entry, Wil supports himself by means of sponging and deceit, thus making up for his lack of honest talent.[86] Though a fraction of the length of even one of *Wil Brydydd y Coed*'s chapters, this instalment of 'Guto's Day-book' contains all the constituent elements of that elaborate satire: the protagonist's self-importance, his delusions of bardic grandeur, and his precarious survival enabled by his parasitic behaviour. In addition to this kind of prose satire, there was a well-established Welsh tradition of writing poetry which lampooned the pretensions of aspiring bards. Guto's satirical piece is easily situated within the literary culture of nineteenth-century Wales.

The 'Day-book', however, is also made to be explicitly American. It is located in and around the most prestigious annual *eisteddfod* of the United States, the one held in Utica, New York. Furthermore, a number of well-known Welsh-American poets are made to interact with the fictional protagonist. In addition to Eos Glan Twrch, Gwyneddfardd appears at the Utica event. This poet, otherwise known as T. B. Morris, was one of *Y Drych*'s co-editors; like the hapless Guto, he is said to have grown thin with anxiety while awaiting the bardic competition's results.[87]

In addition to Caledfryn's adjudication and 'Guto's Day-Book', the 15 June 1859 edition of *Y Drych* contains a piece entitled 'Y Beirdd Wrth Lathen', 'The Bards put to the Yard Stick'. Its author used the pen-name 'John Bunnau'; like the author of 'Dydd-Lyfr Guto', his real name remains a mystery. As the piece presents often scathing literary criticism, it is possible that the real 'John Bunnau' intended to remain anonymous. While he did give Utica as his place of residence, it is hard to know whether this is a genuine hint as to the author's identity or a handy way of misleading readers (as the best known Welsh community in the United States at the time, Utica was readily believable as an address).

The body of the piece is a chart which compares twenty Welsh poets in various categories; this is the 'yard stick' (*llathen*) of the title. John Bunnau's critical measuring stick is a simple list of names and numbers. The long paragraph which introduces the chart is, however, an extremely interesting piece of prose:

> Hynaws Olygydd. – Ar noswaith hafaidd hyfryd a mi yn eistedd wrthyf fy hun ar lan afon sydd yn rhedeg heb fod yn mhell o ddrws fy nhy, daeth i fy meddwl dafoli Beirdd Cymreig America; ac os gwelwch yn dda gyhoeddi y tafoliad yn y DRYCH, wele ef i chwi. Nid wyf yn dysgwyl y bydd pawb o'r frawdoliaeth nac allan o honi o'r un farn a mi yn nghylch y Beirdd, ond yr wyf yn cyfansoddi hon, gan gredu fy mod yn gwneuthur cyfiawnder a'r oll yn ol eu hanfodol deilyngdod. Felly os bydd rhai o honynt yn tramgwyddo na buasai eu rhifnodau yn uwch eu gradd rhaid iddynt gofio mai nid bai y casglydd yw hyny. Buasai yn dda genyf fod yn alluog i roddi rhif 20 wrth yr holl enwau a than y gwahanol ddosranau; ond rhaid oedd gwneuthur fel hyn ol cydwybod.[88]
>
> 'DEAR EDITOR. – Upon a lovely summery evening, and me sitting by myself on the bank of a river which runs not far from the door of my house, it came to my mind to assess the Welsh Bards of America; and if you see fit to publish the assessment in the DRYCH, here it is for you. I do not expect that everybody within and outside of the brotherhood will be of the same opinion as myself concerning the Bards, but I am composing this believing that I am doing justice to all according to their essential worthiness. Thus if some of them are offended that their scores are not of a higher degree then they must remember that it is not the fault of the one carrying out the assessment. I would have liked to have been able to place the number 20 by all of the names and under the various categories; yet one must act according to conscience.'

This paragraph provides a narrative context for the literary criticism which is the piece's *raison d'être*. Its opening sentence contrasts pointedly with what follows; this blithe introduction lulls readers into a false sense of security and calmness before John Bunnau launches into his aggressive criticism, pummelling a series of poets mercilessly with his 'yard stick'. The first sentence, which dramatizes the genesis of the piece, has the fictionalized author placed in an idealized rural setting. The 'lovely summery evening' and the peaceful house near the river's bank might seem to derive from the romantic pastoral aesthetics driving so many works of nineteenth-century Welsh literature.[89] However, as the piece is signed 'John Bunnau, Utica', this particular pastoral scene is romanticizing the terrain of Oneida County, New York; while the author may be using tropes derived from his exposure to Welsh literature, he is using them to draw a markedly American landscape.

The whimsical opening soon gives way to serious criticism. If the first sentence softens the bardic assessment by describing the dreamy setting in which it was composed, John Bunnau's next sentence refers directly to the unforgiving nature of his criticism; he does not expect 'that everybody within and outside of the brotherhood' will share his opinion. The 'brotherhood' of course refers to the community of poets (although women were publishing poetry in Welsh-language journals on both sides of the Atlantic at the time, the public face of bardic culture remained overwhelmingly masculine). The Welsh bardic fraternity was – and perhaps still is – notoriously quarrelsome, with disputes over *eisteddfod* adjudications often reaching epic proportions; the nit-picking exactitude of John Bunnau's assessment, mixing vicious humour with serious criticism, is in many ways an accurate reflection of *eisteddfod* culture. There is no doubt that his 'yard stick' was intended as a serious piece of literary criticism; the bards given the highest marks by John Bunnau were, in fact, poets who did well in the American *eisteddfodau* and who were published and praised widely in the Welsh-American press. Yet it is also in part a work of humour or, to be more exact, it is like 'Guto's Day-Book' in that it uses satire to underline the importance of poetry to Welsh-Americans.

Perhaps the most significant thing about John Bunnau's preface to the 'yard stick' is the way in which he describes the 'brotherhood' in question. The twenty poets assessed in the chart are described specifically as *Beirdd Cymreig America*, 'the Welsh Bards of America'. Back in 1856 the editor of *Y Drych* appended as an afterthought a list of Welsh bards who deserved a place in the British artist's gallery of *literati*. John Bunnau's 1859 piece is fundamentally different; it was presented to readers of *Y Drych* from start to finish as an assessment of America's Welsh poets. Every one of the twenty poets named was living in the United States and composing poetry in the Welsh language. Moreover, the fact that he names all but two of them using their bardic names suggests that he was writing about an established literary culture; Welsh-American readers knew who he was talking about, for he was assessing *their* poets. Whoever John Bunnau really was, he was a Welsh-American literary critic. He used his own literary artifice to locate himself in an idealized version of rural Oneida County, New York, and he was concerned solely with assessing the work of American bards. The publication of 'Y Beirdd Wrth Lathen' in June 1859 heralded – or at least confirmed – the birth of a Welsh-American literature. John Bunnau was a Welsh-American critic concerned with assessing specifically Welsh-American poets on the pages of a Welsh-language newspaper published in the United States for a primarily American readership. Unlike the tentative nature of the editor's note in 1856, this represents a confident assertion of a distinctly Welsh-American literary identity; this short piece of critical writing takes as its starting point the assumption that there is such a thing as Welsh-language American poetry. It tells us that at least some Welsh-speaking Americans thought that they had their own distinct literary culture.

The critical yardstick itself is a simple chart; it lists the twenty poets in a vertical row and gives them marks in four categories listed horizontally at the top. The first category is *awen*, or 'bardic inspiration', followed by 'knowledge' (*gwybodaeth*). In Hywel Teifi Edwards's assessment of the effect of the 'Blue Books' and British hegemony upon the *eisteddfodau* of Wales, he notes the desire to make Welsh culture 'useful' to that powerful god of Victorian society, 'Progress': 'Eu dyletswydd, bellach, oedd ymgymhwyso ar gyfer y dyfodol cyffrous a'u hwynebai a chasglu ffeithiau materol-fuddiol trwy bob dull a modd' ('Their duty, now, was to adapt themselves in preparation for an exciting future which faced them and collect useful material facts by all sorts of means').[90] It might have been an American god of science who influenced John Bunnau here, and it would be worth exploring his emphasis on 'knowledge' in terms of the intersection between philosophy, science and literature which occurred in certain American intellectual circles in the nineteenth century. However, it might have been an importation from Wales, perhaps rejuvenated by cultural influences in the United States. Whatever the impetus, it is surely significant that, immediately after measuring a poet's *awen* – one of the oldest, most traditional and culturally-laden terms available to a Welsh literary critic – John Bunnau assesses him according to his *gwybodaeth*, his empirical 'knowledge'.

The third column in the chart gives marks for *cynghanedd*, the complex system of internal line ornamentation which is a mandatory part of the traditional strict metres.[91] This detailed series of metrical rules, formalized in the bardic grammars of the later middle ages, were still a very real part of Welsh literary culture in the nineteenth century (as indeed they still are in the twenty-first). John Bunnau's final category, *barn*, 'opinion', seems to refer to the correctness of the opinions expressed by the poet. No more details are provided, but given the themes common to Welsh-American poetry of the 1850s, we can conjecture that he is referring to the poets' opinions on questions of a religious and/or political nature.[92]

In theory, twenty was the highest score possible in each of the four categories. John Bunnau, however, was a harsh critic, and not one of the twenty poets earned a score of twenty in any of the four categories. On the other hand, he did frequently employ the lower range of the scale, thus providing that element of satiric humour referred to above. For example, a poet who used the name Mwyniant Maldwyn – 'Montgomeryshire's Joy' – had no joy at the hands of John Bunnau: he was given zero in each of the four columns. Coch Bach ('The Little Red[-haired ?] One') was judged to be literally a fraction better, receiving zero in three of the four categories, and a mere 1/100 – one per cent of one point – for his knowledge! These two losers were barely beaten by Meirionwyson ('One from Merioneth'), who earned only 1/4 point – one quarter of one point – for his knowledge. Cymro Brith, the 'Motley Welshman', received a motley score, earning one point for his *cynghanedd*, one half of one point for his *awen*, and zero in the other two categories.

Cymro Brith's real name was John E. Roberts; this is the man who, less than three years later, would find himself serving as wagon master for the 5th Pennsylvania Cavalry. Despite having his poetry slated in this fashion on the newspaper's pages, he would continue to support *Y Drych*, sending the editor letters chronicling his regiment's campaigns in Virginia. In fact, several of the poets whom we have already met in this chapter were included in John Bunnau's list of twenty Welsh-American bards. The highest marks on the 'yard stick' were given to Gwilym ab Ioan, the 'Williams of New York' mentioned in the letter published in 1856. The second highest score went to none other than Eos Glan Twrch, that giant of the nascent Welsh-American literary scene who chronicled the fortunes of the Utica *eisteddfod* in prose and verse and earned a place in Guto's satirical fiction. Eos Glan Twrch and Gwilym ab Ioan both figured prominently on the pages of the Welsh-American press during the 1850s; despite the fun which John Bunnau had in splitting hairs and splitting marks, the fact that he gives these two the highest scores strongly suggests that this exercise was also grounded in the reality of Welsh America's literary culture.

Several of the other bards measured by the 'yard stick' will also be mentioned in later chapters. Cadwgan Fardd – who in several years' time would find himself hiding from Confederate raiders in the mountains of eastern Tennessee – scored in the top half of John Bunnau's ranking. He was beaten slightly by Lewys Glyn Dyfi, the Reverend Lewis Meredith, who in 1863 would replace poetry with diplomacy, travelling back to the land of his birth while seeking foreign support for the Union cause. Other bards measured on the pages of *Y Drych* in June 1859 would use the newspaper as well as Welsh America's journals to publish poetry dealing with the war. For example, the former editor *Y Seren Orllewinol*, the Revd J. P. Harris – referred to by John Bunnau under his bardic name, Ieuan Ddu – would publish poetry treating the grief which the conflict visited upon Pennsylvania's Welsh communities. Ionoron Glan Dwyryd, Dewi Emlyn, Ap Cinmerchyn, Gwentydd Bychan, Iorthryn Gwynedd and R. L. Herbert would also publish poetry interpreting the war's effect upon – and meaning for – their communities. This last poet was one of two whom John Bunnau listed using their real names; Herbert was extremely well-known to Welsh-American readers as he had been active for some time publishing material against slavery and in favour of the new Republican party, which opposed the spread of that Southern institution.

The other poet not referred to by a bardic pseudonym was Llewelyn Ioan Evans; while he would play an important role in the intellectual and religious life of Welsh America for decades to come, Evans had given up writing poetry by the start of the war.[93] Indeed, by the time John Bunnau's criticism was published in 1859, Llewelyn Ioan Evans had already bade a bitter farewell to bardic pursuits, an event precipitated by a quarrel with another of John Bunnau's poets, Iorthryn Gwynedd. This was the Revd R. D. Thomas, the same poet who, after visiting the United States in 1851–2, had published an exhortation urging Welsh-Americans to support their writers and poets by establishing a National Eisteddfod. Thomas had since emigrated with his wife to the United States, and the writings he published as Iorthryn Gwynedd had become a regular feature of several Welsh-American publications. Iorthryn weighed in on John Bunnau's chart with mediocre marks (9, 11, 8 and 6). As he was roundly beaten by Llewelyn Ioan Evans (who scored 16, 17, 10 and 16), the Revd Thomas must have been irked; the two poets had been engaged in a vitriolic dispute – made very public by means of the Welsh-American press – for some time.

Like many other bardic quarrels, the trouble began with an *eisteddfod* competition. Evans won the main prize in Wisconsin's State *eisteddfod* ('Eisteddfod Daleithiol Wisconsin'), beating, among others, the experienced and over-confident Thomas. The minister did not show much magnanimity in defeat, and he criticized the winning poem on the pages of *Y Cymro-Americaidd* ('The American Welshman'), a newspaper which was started in order to compete with *Y Drych*.[94] In addition to trashing his opponent's poem, R. D. Thomas attacked the victorious poet directly, accusing him, among other things, of plagiarism. It appears that Llewelyn Ioan Evans threatened to bring a law suit against Thomas for these slanderous statements, and the contentious minister had to change his tactics. Rather than publishing under his own name, and rather than publishing under his well-known bardic name, Iorthryn Gwynedd, he published a 'review' of Evans's poem under another pen-name, Hoffwr Barddoniaeth ('Poetry Lover').

While this bardic war raged in the pages of the Welsh-American press, the press itself was engaged in its own publication war. This ended with *Y Drych* defeating its upstart rival, *Y Cymro-Americaidd*, and that short-lived paper came to an end. The 'review' by Hoffwr Barddoniaeth was thus published in *Y Cenhadwr Americanaidd*, the monthly journal of the Welsh-American Congregationalists. Llewelyn Ioan Evans answered on the pages of the same publication, and the war of words raged on for another year. In the November 1858 number of the journal, R. D. Thomas – aka Iorthryn Gwynedd, aka Hoffwr Barddoniaeth – pronounced with swagger that he had won the argument and that Welsh America was on his side:

> Deallwn fod ein hadolygiad ar bryddest Ll. I. Evans wedi enill cymeradwyaeth prif ddynion ein cenedl ar y cyfandir hwn; ond adolygiad gwael iawn ydyw yn ngolwg Ll. I. E. ei hun; ac mae'n debyg nad oedd y wlad yn dysgwyl iddo ddweyd dim yn amgen[.][95]

> 'I understand that our review of Ll. I. Evans's poem has won the commendation of the chief men of our nation on this continent; yet it is a very poor review in the eyes of Ll. I. E. himself; and it's likely that the country did not expect him to say anything else[.]'[96]

These two poets were contending for the commendation of a specific community of readers and critics, defined here as 'the chief men of our nation on this continent'. The judge of the Wisconsin *eisteddfod*'s poetry competition was Gwilym Hiraethog, one of the more famous poets and writers of Wales; like the Utica *eisteddfod*'s decision to employ Caledfryn as an adjudicator, the Wisconsin festival enlisted Gwilym Hiraethog in order to lend his prestige and experience to the American competition. R. D. Thomas did fight on the Welsh front as well, sending personal letters to Gwilym Hiraethog in Wales during the course of the protracted dispute. Yet the main front of this bardic war was located in the United States; the two opponents faced off on the pages of several different Welsh-language American publications, and, according to their own words, they were fighting for the approval of Welsh-speaking Americans.

To use Stanley Fish's term, the collective group of Welsh-American readers, poets and literary critics made up the specific 'interpretive community' for whom these two poets were writing.[97] In addition to the obvious facts that the original poems were composed for an *eisteddfod* in Wisconsin and that the debate over the poetry was carried out on the pages of the Welsh-American press, the argument was punctuated with cultural and historical references which locate the writings in a self-consciously American *milieu*. For example, Llewelyn Ioan Evans claimed that Hoffwr Barddoniaeth should reveal his real name (knowing full well that he was Iorthyn Gwynedd, aka R. D. Thomas). Thomas refused – or rather, his *alter alter ego* refused – stating that revealing his true name would endanger his life:

> wrth ofyn am enw priodol H[offwr] B[arddoniaeth] mae . . . yn peri i ddrychiolaeth Junius a'i *bowie knife*; Brooks a'i ffon; a *rifle* yn y llwyn hofran yn union o flaen ein llygaid.[98]

> in asking for Poetry Lover's proper name, he is . . . causing the apparition of Junius and his bowie knife; Brooks and his cane; and the rifle in the bushes to hover directly before our eyes.

This sentence contains a density of specifically American references. Junius was the pen-name used by another Welshman who had recently threatened his literary opponents on the pages of the Welsh-American press. Full of insincere melodrama, R. D. Thomas states here that he fears for his life, suggesting that Llewelyn Ioan Evans might murder him with that characteristically American weapon, the Bowie Knife. His bardic opponent's words are also said to conjure up the threatening spectre of Preston 'Bully' Brooks, who had recently beaten the anti-slavery orator Charles Sumner to a bloody pulp with his cane on the Senate floor in Washington. It is unclear whether or not the 'rifle in the bushes' was meant to refer to a specific event; however, given that this piece was published in 1858, it is quite possibly an attempt to index the bloody guerrilla war which had been taking place in Kansas. Whatever the source of this final image, all three references are used to suggest an imminent threat, and the first two – the cane of Bully Brooks and the Bowie Knife – are violent images with a distinctly American flavour.

This was not the first time that a Welsh-American writer used the Bowie Knife as a trope. R. D. Thomas associates the image with 'Junius'; little is known about this shadowy figure and no known copies of his writings have survived.[99] Whoever Junius was and whatever he wrote, he was not the first writer to wave the bardic Bowie Knife on the pages of the Welsh-American press. In fact, that very image appeared in the dialogue which presented the new *Cyfaill o'r Hen Wlad* to its readers back in 1838. During the course of that fictional discussion, the *Cymro* ('Welshman'), given a surprise visit by his new *Cyfaill* ('Friend'), asks the personified journal what religious denomination (*enwad*) it supports. It was no secret that this publication was produced for the Welsh-speaking Calvinistic Methodists of the United States, yet, given the fact that Welsh-American print culture was still in its infancy in the 1830s, the *Cyfaill* strove to serve all of Welsh America and thus its editor claimed repeatedly to be unbiased.[100] The 'Welshman' refers to the sectarian divisions which riddled Welsh society, warning his new 'Friend' that the field of Welsh-American writing could easily run red with figurative blood:

> Dychymygaf y gwelaf y gwahanol enwa[da]u yn ymfyddino yn erbyn eu gilydd, wedi eu cyflawn arfogi a gwaywffyn ac a chleddyfau – *bwlets* papyr yn chwyrnu heibio fy nghlustiau, a'u dudalenau yn gochion gan waed y gwahanol bleidi[a]u.[101]
>
> 'I imagine that I see the various denominations mustering against each other, armed thoroughly with spears and swords – paper bullets whining past my ears, and their pages red with the blood of the various parties.'

The Friend answers, easing the jumpy Welshman's fears:

> Peidiwch a dychrynu, Gymro bach. Garw yr ydych yn agor eich llygaid. Nid felly chwaith. Mae eisiau deall y cwbl yn peri i'ch dychymyg gyfeiliorni yn ei ddarluniau. Mae genyf borth bychan, yn mha le, y mae pob ymgeisydd yn cael ei chwilio cyn ei ollwng i mewn, ac os bydd ganddo arfau tân, *dirks, bowie knives*, neu ryw beth cyffelyb, y mae yn rhaid iddo eu gadael y tu allan i'r drws. Ni oddefir ar faes y Cyfaill, unrhyw arfau ond rhesymau, a rhaid trin yr arfau hyny yn foneddigaidd, heb gnoi na thraflyncu. Eithr nid ydym yn erbyn dadl, ond ei chadw o fewn terfynau rheolaidd a buddiol.[102]

> 'Don't be afraid, dear Welshman. It is to an uncouth sight that you turn your eyes. Yet it is not thus. Your desire to understand all of this causes your imagination to go astray in the images which it conjures. I have a narrow gate, in which each contestant much be searched before being let inside, and if he happens to have fire arms, *dirks, bowie knives*, or something similar, then he must leave them outside of the door. On the field of the Cyfaill no arms will be tolerated other than reasons, and those weapons must be handled politely, without biting or gorging. However, we are not against an argument, but rather for keeping it within regular and constructive boundaries.'

Continuing the martial metaphor which the Welshman uses to describe literary debate, the Friend describes his field of combat as the interior of a castle; there is an open arena, yet it is surrounded by walls and protected by a carefully-watched gate. While welcoming those who would enter into civilized contest, the *Cyfaill* assures its reader that potentially dangerous literary combatants will be disarmed at the gate ahead of time, thus keeping the journal's pages free of blood. Proper literary debate is described in terms of a gentlemen's duel, controlled and bound by rules. This rule-bound contest is set against the vindictive feuding of the frontier ruffian with his guns and bowie knives. The extended metaphor is shaded with a characteristically American colour, prefiguring the way in which R. D. Thomas would answer his opponent's challenge twenty years later. The *Cyfaill*'s opening dialogue, like the writings which constituted the dispute between R. D. Thomas and Llewelyn Ioan Evans, was addressed to a specific interpretive community, a community which we can define as the writers, readers and critics of Welsh America.

Llewelyn Ioan Evans was not about to surrender that community's approval without a fight. Rather than dragging the dispute on through the pages of *Y Cenhadwr Americanaidd* and other monthly and weekly publications, he devised a massive, final counter-attack in order to end the war of words. In 1859 Evans published an entire pamphlet, sixty-four pages in length, using a Welsh press in New York City. He entitled his tour-de-force *Crach-feirniadaeth; neu Amddiffyniad yn Ngwyneb Ysgrifau Hoffwr Barddoniaeth.*[103] The second part of the title translates easily as 'or a Defence in the Face of the Writings of Poetry Lover'. The main part of the title, *Crach-feirniadaeth*, combines the term for (literary) criticism, *beirniadaeth*, with *crach*, a word possessing a wealth of pejorative meanings, ranging from 'scabby' or 'vile' to 'contemptible'. It sometimes has the force of the prefix 'pseudo-', a meaning which fits the context perfectly; labelling R. D. Thomas's literary arguments once and for all as 'pseudo-criticism' was indeed the main purpose of the pamphlet.

The pamphlet begins with a *Rhaglith* or 'Foreword,' and this introductory essay is given a sub-title which tells us exactly who the target audience was: 'At Gymry yr Unol Daleithia'; 'To the Welsh of the United States'.[104] Like the audience specified by Thomas in his 'review' ('the chief men of our nation on this continent'), the way in which Evans begins his protracted 'defence' tells us in simple and unmistakable terms that he was defining the readers for whom he was writing as Welsh-speaking Americans. The first sentence of the first chapter restates this point: 'Yn mlaenaf oll, yr wyf yn dymuno galw yr holl genedl Gymreig yn yr Unol Dalaethau yn dyst mai mewn hunan-amddiffyniad yr wyf yn ymddangos o'u blaen y waith hyn'; 'First and foremost, I desire to call all of the Welsh nation in the United States as a witness that it is in self-defence that I appear before them this time.'[105] Following this introduction, Evans engages his opponent's pretentious rhetoric head-on, picking at Thomas's claim that he had won 'the commendation of the chief men of our nation on this continent'.

> Nid at y Cyhoedd Mawr, [sef] dau neu dri o 'brif ddynion ein cenedl ar y cyfandir hwn' [yr wyf yn apelio]. Yr wyf yn apelio . . . at y *Cyhoedd Bach* hwnw, ag sydd yn gynwysedig o ychydig filoedd o genedl y Cymry yn y wlad hon.[106]

> 'It is not to the Great Mass, [namely] two or three 'of the chief men of our nation on this continent' [to whom I am appealing]. I am appealing . . . to that *Small Mass*, which includes a few thousand of the nation of the Welsh in this country.'

Evans then says that he is ready to take the war of words from the printed page to the public stage of each of Welsh-America's individual communities; he boasts that he is 'ready to meet' Thomas 'publicly in every Welsh settlement from New York to South Bend' ('yn barod i gyfarfod . . . yn gyhoeddus yn mhob sefydliad Cymreig o Efrog Newydd i South Bend').[107]

Like the metaphorical Bowie Knife invoked by R. D. Thomas, the very language used by Ioan Llewelyn Evans was in part anchored in the recent political and cultural history of the United States. In questioning the winning poem Thomas had also questioned the rules adopted by the organizers of the Wisconsin *eisteddfod*. Evans struck back, supporting the right of Wisconsin's Welsh community to run their own affair by referring to 'the spirit of the great principle of these days, *Popular Sovereignty*' ('ysbryd egwyddor fawr y dyddiau hyn, *Popular Sovereignty*').[108] The pamphlet was published a year after the Douglas–Lincoln debates of 1858, and Evans drew upon Stephen Douglas's definition of 'popular sovereignty' in driving his point home:

> Gwasanaetha hynyna gystal a rhagor er dangos fod Wisconsin, yn ysbryd egwyddor fawr y dyddiau hyn, *Popular Sovereignty*, sef yn ol esboniad Douglas, hawl pob Talaeth a Thiriogaeth i defnu ei sefydliadau ei hun, yn dewis trefnu ei Heisteddfodau yn ol ei chwaeth ei hun, ac nid yn ol *dictum* un Buchanan crachfarddol[.][109]

> 'That will serve as well as anything to show that Wisconsin, in the spirit of the great principle of these days, *Popular Sovereignty*, which according to Douglas's explanation, [is] the right of each State and Territory to organize its own

> institutions, chooses to organize its Eisteddfodau according to its own taste, and not according to the *dictum* of one pseudo-bardic Buchanan.'

In other words, the rights and freedoms which the political system of the United States confers on its citizens extend to Welsh-American literary culture. Evans also calls Iorthryn Gwynedd a 'pseudo-bardic [James] Buchanan'; the president's failure to deal with the pressing questions which were rending the United States becomes a metaphor for Iorthryn's ineffectual critical pronouncements. The phrase 'Buchanan crachfarddol' in itself provides a concise reminder of the fact that this writer's cultural horizons were drawn along lines which were both Welsh and American. As the pejorative prefix *crach-* appears in medieval Welsh bardic debates (called *ymrysonau barddol*), the coupling of the compound adjective *crachfarddol* with the name of the U. S. president provides a striking example of how traditional Welsh literary culture was reworked in an American context.[110]

Crachfeirniadaeth, the closing blow in a bardic dispute which had raged on the pages of the Welsh-American press for several years, appeared in the same year as John Bunnau's critical 'yardstick' (*llathen*). When readers scanned the list of twenty Welsh-American poets 'measured' by John Bunnau, they would surely have paused over the names of Iorthryn Gwynedd and Llewelyn Ioan Evans, for the venomous debate between the two had become a prominent feature of Welsh-American print culture during the late 1850s. Indeed, reading the 'yardstick' in the context of the protracted debate reveals one extremely important point. During the course of the dispute, both poets repeatedly defined a specifically Welsh-American community of critics, writers and readers, and the existence of this community is the underlying assumption of John Bunnau's attempt to assess what he calls 'the Welsh Bards of America'. We thus find between 1856 and 1859 a series of writings which tell us that Welsh-speaking Americans were thinking of their own literature, perhaps for the first time, as constituting a distinct sphere of cultural activity. Welsh-Americans, or at least the ones who wrote for the Welsh-language press of the United States, thought that such a thing as 'Welsh-American literature' did, in fact, exist. By the eve of the Civil War, Welsh America had its own nascent literary tradition.

This was not a result of sheer geographical necessity, for the Welsh-language writers of the United States were not irrevocably separated from those of the Old Country. People travelled back and forth across the ocean, and this was especially true for the intelligentsia who were actively engaged in the process of creating and maintaining Welsh America's literary culture.[111] In his study of Welsh emigration, Glanmor Williams suggests that 'on average, more Welsh people crossed and re-crossed the Atlantic than the subjects of any other country' ('mwy o Gymry ar gyfartaledd wedi croesi ac adgroesi Môr Iwerydd na deiliaid yr un wlad arall').[112] The momentous journey from Wales to North America surely engendered a certain psychological distance, yet this distance was not insurmountable. In addition to numerous personal letters, print culture kept the Welsh-language communities on both sides of the Atlantic in contact with each other; ships carrying newspapers, journals and books from British ports would pass ships travelling in the other direction which carried *Y Drych*, *Y Cyfaill o'r Hen Wlad* and other Welsh-American publications to Wales. The same year which saw the publication of Llewelyn Ioan Evans's pamphlet witnessed laying what Welsh-American publications called *y pellebyr tanforawl*, the trans-Atlantic telegraph cables connecting Britain and the United States. And, as we have seen, leading literary figures from Wales such as Caledfryn and Gwilym Hiraethog were employed as judges in American *eisteddfodau*.

Rather than being cut off from the Old Country, Welsh America's literary life was on the contrary in direct contact with the literary culture of Wales. This nascent Welsh-American tradition did not have a declaration of literary independence akin to Ralph Waldo Emerson's cry that (Anglophone) Americans had 'listened too long to the courtly muses of Europe'.[113] Surviving writings from the period suggest that, while Welsh-American *literati* did think in terms of something we can call Welsh-American literature, they did not define that new entity in rebellious opposition to the Welsh-language tradition(s) of Wales. The guiding muse – or *awen* – of the mother literature would continue to shape Welsh-American writing throughout the period of the Civil War and beyond, and American poets and writers would continue to draw upon the forms, images and themes generated by more than a thousand years of Welsh cultural history. At the same time, the very fact that Welsh America remained so connected with Wales highlights the emergence of this new Welsh-American literary identity. The Welsh-language poets, writers, critics and editors of the United States could have conceivably described their work as only a sub-set of the literature of Wales. But they did not. Instead, they chose to create a literature which, if markedly *Welsh*-American, was also specifically Welsh-*American*.

In describing the Civil War's effect on the Utica *eisteddfod*, Eos Glan Twrch wrote that 'our literature has grown still – and war has slowed the pace of poetry' ('llonyddodd ein llenyddiaeth – a rhyfel / Arafodd Farddoniaeth'). There is no question that those people who gathered in Utica on the first day of 1862 would have taken the words *ein llenyddiaeth* – 'our literature' – to mean Welsh-American literature. And, while the war's shadow certainly made for a more sombre *eisteddfod* that year, in many ways the Civil War actually 'quickened' Welsh-American literature, forcing writers and poets to treat a range of new themes, and challenging them to interpret the ways in which the bloody events of 1861–5 were transforming their communities and the very nature of their Welsh-American identity. That war-time transformation of Welsh-American literature is the central topic of this book.[114]

NOTES

1 *Y Cenhadwr Americanaidd*, February 1862.

2 *Geiriadur Prifysgol Cymru* (Cardiff, 1950–2002), p. 1201: '(modern sense) event or festival at which competitions are held in music, elocution, literature, arts and crafts, &c.' and '(formerly) a kind of congress of bards held to formulate rules in connection with their craft and to organize themselves into a guild of craftsmen or graduates.'

3 While it is true that poetry remained a definite part of the *eisteddfod* concept, the British-English hegemony of the Victorian heyday seduced many of Wales's festival organizers and led them to promote 'useful' pursuits over the traditional emphasis on poetry and literature. This is eloquently described by Hywel Teifi Edwards, *Gŵyl Gwalia* [:] *Yr Eisteddfod yn Oes Aur Victoria 1858/1868* (Llandysul, 1980), Chapter 3.

4 *Y Cyfaill o'r Hen Wlad*, February 1838. The italics are in the original.

5 *Y Seren Orllewinol*, October 1854; November 1854; *Y Drych*, 15 March 1856.

6 *Y Drych*, 12 May 1860.

7 *Y Seren Orllewinol*, February 1855.

8 Ibid.

9 Hywel Teifi Edwards, *Gŵyl Gwalia*, pp. 1–18.

10 *Y Seren Orllewinol*, May 1852.

11 Ibid.

12 Ibid.

13 *Y Seren Orllewinol*, February 1853.

14 *Y Seren Orllewinol*, May 1854.

15 Frederick Merk, *Manifest Destiny and Mission in American History* [:] *A Reinterpretation* (New York, 1963), pp. 25–52.

16 See, for example, Richard Ruland and Malcolm Bradbury, *From Puritanism to Postmodernism* [:] *A History of American Literature* (New York, 1991), pp. 47–8.

17 *Y Seren Orllewinol*, May 1854.

18 It seems that the first truly National Eisteddfod of the United States was held in Hyde Park, Scranton, Pennsylvania on 15–16 September 1875; *Y Drych*, 23 September 1875. See also, Hywel Teifi Edwards, *Eisteddfod Ffair y Byd* (Llandysul, 1990), p. xvii.

19 Oliver Wendell Holmes, *The Professor at the Breakfast-Table* (1860), in *The Works of Oliver Wendell Holmes* (Boston, 1892), vol. 2, p. 83. Holmes also named Boston the 'hub' by stating famously that the 'Boston State-House is the hub of the solar system'; Oliver Wendell Holmes, *The Autocrat of the Breakfast-Table* (1858), in *The Works of Oliver Wendell Holmes* (Boston, 1892), vol. 1, p. 125.

20 R. D. Thomas, *Hanes Cymry America* (Utica, 1872), pp. 82–101.

21 Recited by Mr Robert A. Jones, originally of Utica and now of New Hartford, Oneida County, New York, and recorded by the writer in 2002. For a general discussion of Utica's Welsh culture, see Emrys Jones, 'Some Aspects of Cultural Change in an American Welsh Community', *Transactions of the Honourable Society of Cymmrodorion* (1952), 15–41.

22 David M. Ellis, 'The Welsh in Utica', *Transactions of the Honourable Society of Cymmrodorion* (1981), 131.

23 The poems published by John Edwards in 1856 and 1862 use the *englyn union unodl* form, one of the traditional strict metres. It consists of four lines, the first

two of which constitute a *toddaid byr* (one ten-syllable line the caesura of which rhymes with the end of a following six-syllable line). The final two lines are made up by a *cywydd* couplet (two seven-syllable lines, one ending in an accented rhyme, the other in an unaccented rhyme). The same end-rhyme links all four lines, and *cynghanedd* (the system of internal line ornamentation) is mandatory. See note 91 below.

24 *Y Drych*, 15 March 1856.

25 Welsh-American writers occasionally use the word *gwlad* to mean 'state' (more normally rendered *talaith* or *talaeth* when referring to a state within the United States).

26 Welsh *awen*, cognate with Irish *ái*, has come down to Modern Welsh from the earliest period of Celtic culture. See Patrick K. Ford, *The Celtic Poets* (Belmont [Mass.], 1999), p. xxvii.

27 *Y Drych*, 15 March 1856. John Edwards first sent this description as a part of a letter to his friend Robert Richards in New York City. It is possible that Richards, and not Edwards, was responsible for sending the letter on to the press.

28 Ibid.

29 The original phrase is 'seicoleg Cymru "post-1847"; Hywel Teifi Edwards, *Codi'r Hen Wlad yn ei Hôl* [:] *1850–194* (Llandysul, 1989), p. 40.

30 See Gareth Elwyn Jones, 'The Welsh Language in the Blue Books of 1847,' in Geraint H. Jenkins (ed.), *The Welsh Language and its Social Domains 1801–1911* (Cardiff, 2000), p. 433: 'The pedigrees of the commissioners predetermined their views on the Welsh language.'

31 The bases for widespread literacy in Wales were laid back in the eighteenth century. The historian Geraint Jenkins concludes that '[m]any factors contributed to the dramatic upsurge of literacy in Wales after 1730', citing, among other influences, 'the role of Methodism and revivified Dissent' as well as 'the growth of flourishing printing-presses', while stressing that 'none of these played such a decisive role in the dissemination of reading habits as the circulating schools. For the first time . . . most rural inhabitants had access to elementary schooling in the vernacular'. As Jenkins notes, the network of schools established by Welsh reformers such as Griffith Jones were so successful 'that, in 1764, Catherine II of Russia instructed a commissioner to investigate . . . and to prepare a detailed report.' Geraint H. Jenkins, *The Foundations of Modern Wales* (Oxford and New York, 1993), p. 379.

32 *Hywel Teifi Edwards, Gŵyl Gwalia*, p. 61.

33 Ibid., p. 19.

34 Two Welsh-language American newspapers are known to have been started in the United States before *Y Drych*. The first, *Y Cymro America* ('The Welsh-American'), appeared in 1832, and the second, *Haul Gomer* ('Gomer's Sun'), appeared in 1848; neither lasted more than a year. The first issue of *Y Drych* was dated 2 January 1851, and was apparently printed in November 1850. See Aled Jones and Bill Jones, *Welsh Reflections [:] Y Drych & America 1851–2001* (Llandysul, 2001), p. 1; see also Chapter 4 in the MA thesis which Paul D. Evans presented to Cornell University in 1914, 'The Welsh in Oneida County, New York.' The thesis has been published online by Siloam Road Enterprises (2001): *http://members.aol.com.siloamroad/oneidawelsh*.

35 For a concise survey of the paper's entire history, see Aled Jones and Bill Jones, *Welsh Reflections*.

36 Benedict Anderson, *Imagined Communities[:] Reflections on the Origin and Spread of Nationalism* (London, 1983), p. 44.

37 *Y Drych*, 15 March 1858.

38 Describing the situation at the start of the nineteenth century, Geraint Jenkins states that 'yr iaith Gymraeg oedd yr arwydd amlycaf o hunaniaeth Gymreig' ('the Welsh language was the most obvious sign of Welsh identity'); Geraint H. Jenkins, 'Rhagymadrodd' ('Introduction'), in Geraint H. Jenkins (ed.), *Iaith Carreg Fy Aelwyd* (Cardiff, 1998), pp. 1–2.

39 Present research has not uncovered any Welsh immigrants in this period who could not speak Welsh. The percentage is my own estimate, based on the linguistic situation in the later part of the nineteenth century, which has been better documented; there was no census in Wales until 1851 and no question asked about the Welsh language before the census of 1891. See Geraint H. Jenkins, *Iaith Carreg Fy Aelwyd*, p. xiii.

40 William D. Jones, 'Y Gymraeg a Hunaniaeth Gymreig mewn Cymuned yn Mhennsylvania', in Geraint H. Jenkins (ed.), *Iaith Carreg Fy Aelwyd* (Cardiff, 1998), p. 256.

41 Ibid., p. 260.

42 Ibid., p. 264.

43 U. S. Bureau of the Census, *The Seventh Census of the United States: 1850* and *The Eighth Census of the United States: 1860.*

44 Glanmor Williams, *Y Baradwys Bell?* (Cardiff, 1976), p. 9.

45 Anne Kelley Knowles, *Calvinists Incorporated* [:] *Welsh Immigrants on Ohio's Industrial Frontier* (Chicago and London, 1997), p. 23.

46 Ibid., pp. 17–19 and 93–101.

47 *Y Cenhadwr Americanaidd*, August 1856. The piece was by Robert Everett, the journal's editor.

48 The efforts of Morgan John Rhys and John Evans during the 1790s are chronicled by Gwyn A. Williams, *The Search for Beulah Land* (London, 1980). The best-known example from Welsh history is Michael D. Jones's drive to establish a Welsh colony overseas, a campaign which eventually led to the Welsh settling of Patagonia. See, for example, Glyn Williams, *The Welsh in Patagonia [:] The State and the Ethnic Community* (Cardiff, 1991), pp. 23–31

49 As late as the 1890s, the young people in southern Minnesota's Welsh community were still learning Welsh as a first language; see T. E. Hughes, David Edwards, Hugh Roberts and Thomas Hughes (eds.), *Hanes Cymry Minnesota [:] History of the Welsh in Minnesota* (Mankato, 1895), p. 158. My own fieldwork – conducted between 1999 and 2002 in Welsh communities in Ohio and New York – has suggested that Welsh survived as the language of the home in some American families for as long as four generations. There are still some people living in the United States today who, though native-born Americans, were raised speaking Welsh. See also Anne Kelly Knowles, *Calvinists Incorporated*, pp. 221–4.

50 See Henry Blackwell, *A Bibliography of Welsh Americana* (Aberystwyth, 1977 [2nd edition]) and D. Eirug Davies, 'Llyfrau a Phamffledi Cymraeg a gyhoeddwyd yn yr Unol Daleithiau', *Llên Cymru*, 26 (2003), 106–33.

51 *Y Seren Orllewinol*, March 1847.

52 See, for example, the ninth-century Latin text, *Historia Brittonum*; John Morris (ed. and trans.), *Nennius*[:] *British History and The Welsh Annals* (London and Chichester, 1980), pp. 22 and 63.

53 *Y Cyfaill o'r Hen Wlad*, January 1838.

54 *Y Cenhadwr Americanaidd* was officially published in Remsen, as that was the nearest post-office designation; the journal was actually printed in the Everetts' house in Steuben, a small hamlet up the road from Remsen.

55 *Y Seren Orllewinol* began publication in July 1844 in Utica. It was relocated to New York in May 1845 because the editor, W. F. Phillips, had changed jobs and moved from Utica to New York. When J. P. Harris of Minersville, Pennsylvania, became the editor in December of that year, the *Seren* was moved to his town.

56 See *Y Cyfaill o'r Hen Wlad*, September 1842, and, especially, a piece published by 'Pererin yn Cattaraugus' in *Y Seren Orllewinol*, January 1845.

57 While no more details about this writer are known, it is quite possible that he lived in the community of Gomer, in Allen County, Ohio, established in the early 1830s.

58 *Y Cyfaill o'r Hen Wlad*, February 1838.

59 He describes Welsh publications as 'ymborth prydlon a rheolaidd i'r Cymry uniaith' ('regular and punctual sustenance for the monolingual Welsh'). *Y Cyfaill o'r Hen Wlad*, February 1838.

60 *Y Cyfaill o'r Hen Wlad*, February 1839.

61 Interestingly, in 1848, William Bebb (1802–1873), the son of Welsh immigrants, would be elected Governor of Ohio. However, in the late 1830s Bebb was still practising as a lawyer, and I am not aware of any direct evidence connecting him with these Welsh-language measures.

62 *Y Cyfaill o'r Hen Wlad*, February 1839.

63 The exact date of the original prophecy and the exact identity of Taliesin are complicated matters. Taliesin is generally taken to have been an historical poet who composed heroic praise poetry in the 6th or 7th centuries AD. During the later Middle Ages, Taliesin developed into a legendary figure, supposedly capable of shape-shifting, prophecy, and other supernatural feats. While there are poems attributed to the persona of the 'legendary Taliesin' in manuscripts from the early fourteenth century onwards, most of this prophetic material is actually contained in manuscripts from the sixteenth and seventeenth centuries. See Marged Haycock, 'Llyfr Taliesin: Astudiaethau ar Rai Agweddau' (unpublished PhD thesis, University of Wales, Aberystwyth, 1983); Patrick Ford, 'Introduction,' *Ystoria Taliesin* (Cardiff, 1992); Gruffydd Fôn Gruffydd, 'Cerddi Taliesin Ben Beirdd y Gorllewin [:] detholiad o gerddi a briodolir i Daliesin wedi eu golygu' (unpublished PhD thesis, University of Wales, Bangor, 1997); Jerry Hunter, *Soffestri'r Saeson*[:] *Hanesyddiaeth a Hunaniaeth yn Oes y Tuduriaid* (Cardiff, 2000).

64 *Y Seren Orllewinol*, January 1847.

65 Ibid.

66 *Y Seren Orllewinol*, January, May 1850.

67 See the conclusions of William D. Jones cited in notes 40–2 above.

68 *Y Seren Orllewinol*, October 1846.

69 Ibid.

70 Ibid.

71 An influential literary critic, Saunders Lewis, dubbed the years 1435–1535 as '*Y Ganrif Fawr*' ('The Great Century'), because so much high-quality strict-metre poetry was composed by the Welsh 'poets of the gentry' during that period. However, Lewis also stressed that this late-medieval bardic golden age was prefigured by the work of the 'poets of the princes,' a period ending in 1282 with

the death of the last native prince of Wales. Saunders Lewis, *Braslun o Hanes Llenyddiaeth Gymraeg* (Cardiff, 1932), pp. 30 and 115–33.

72 The term 'classical', when used in the context of Welsh-language poetry, refers to the great body of medieval strict-metre poetry.

73 *Y Seren Orllewinol*, October 1846.

74 *Y Seren Orllewinol*, March 1851, 'Y Welsh Yankee' and April 1851.

75 A writer using the name 'Voty Hall' published a similar kind of satire in the short-lived paper *Cymro America*, 1 February and 15 February 1832.

76 See Anne Kelly Knowles, *Calvinists Incorporated*, p. 4.

77 Aled Jones and Bill Jones, *Welsh Reflections*, p. 17.

78 I have borrowed and reworded Richard Helgerson's phrase, '[t]he discursive forms of nationhood and the nation's political forms were mutually self-constituting.' Richard Helgerson, *Forms of Nationhood* [:] *The Elizabethan Writing of England* (Chicago and London, 1992), p. 11.

79 See, for example, the way in which Aled Jones describes the nineteenth-century Welsh conception of *llenyddiaeth*, 'literature': 'Distinctions between literature and reportage, between the book and the newspaper, in effect between "high" and "low" forms of literary culture, came to be made in literary criticism only towards the end of the nineteenth century'; Aled Jones, 'The Welsh Newspaper Press', in Hywel Teifi Edwards (ed.), *A guide to Welsh literature c.1800–1900* (Cardiff, 2000), p. 1.

80 At the end of his list of Welsh-American poets, the editor adds the names of famous Welsh bards who had died in America: 'Y mae yr enwogion canlynol wedi meirw yn y wlad hon ['The following famous ones have died in this country'], Goronwy Owain, Gwenffrwd, Abraham Williams, o'r Cwm Glas, J. A. Williams, A Don Glan Towy.'

81 *Y Drych*, 15 June 1859. The adjudication was printed under the headline 'Beirniadaeth Caledfryn ar Gyfansoddiadau Barddonol Eisteddfod Utica' ('Caledfryn's Criticism of the Utica Eisteddfod's Bardic Compositions').

82 William Williams, or Caledfryn, won in the Beaumaris Eisteddfod of 1832 with his *awdl* on 'Drylliad y Rothesay Castle' ('The [Ship-]Wreck of the Rothesay Castle'). His works on grammar and bardic craft include *Drych Barddonol neu Draethawd ar Farddoniaeth* ('A Bardic Mirror or an Essay on Poetry'), published in 1839 and *Grammadeg Cymreig* ('A Welsh Grammar'), which appeared in 1851. His autobiography was published posthumously: William Williams, *Cofiant Caledfryn* (Y Bala, 1877).

83 *Y Drych*, 15 June 1859.

84 This humorous reference to Caledfryn's (supposed) fondness for drink could be taken in several ways. Caledfryn did condemn the drunken behaviour which some poets exhibited in Welsh *eisteddfodau*; see Hywel Teifi Edwards, *Gŵyl Gwalia*, p. 123. However, while speaking out against drunkenness he also at times took a stand seen by some as in opposition to the temperance movement's campaigning, for he suggested that 'moderation' instead of complete abstinence should be the rule.

85 *Y Drych*, 15 June 1859.

86 While David Owen, or 'Brutus', is best known for *Wil Brydydd y Coed*, which did not begin to appear until 1863 (and thus well after the publication of this instalment of *Dydd-Lyfr Guto*), he had published other works of satirical prose as early as the late 1830s. Thus my suggestion that this short piece of Welsh-American satire most closely resembles one of Owen's later works does not rule

out the possibility that *Y Drych*'s satirist was influenced by some of Owen's earlier prose. See Thomas Jones's introduction ('Rhagymadrodd') in David Owen, *Wil Brydydd y Coed*, ed. Thomas Jones (Cardiff, 1949), pp. xx–xxxii. It should be noted that one main difference between the American 'John Bunnau' and David Owen is that the latter was a Churchman who used the character of Wil to satirize what he saw as the fake intelligentsia of Welsh chapel culture.

87 'Yr wyf wedi teneuo llawer wrth fyfyrio mor galed' ('I have grown very thin from studying so hard'); *Y Drych*, 15 June 1859. Gwyneddfardd's real name was Thomas B. Morris; see R. D. Thomas, *Cyflawn Olygfa ar Gymry America* (Utica, 1872), p. 42.

88 *Y Drych*, 15 June 1859.

89 Of course, this kind of romantic pastoral imagery was by no means confined to Welsh literature in the nineteenth century. However, this strain of writing gained an increasing hold upon Welsh literary tastes during the first half of the nineteenth century (particularly in the context of lyric poetry). See, for example, Huw M. Edwards, 'The Lyric Poets', in Hywel Teifi Edwards (ed.), *A Guide to Welsh Literature c.1800–1900*, p. 104. John Bunnau's opening sentence might be also read in relation to a much earlier work of Welsh literature; it in part echoes the opening sentence of Ellis Wynne's prose masterpiece, *Gweledigaetheu y Bardd Cwsc* (1703).

90 *Hywel Teifi Edwards, Gŵyl Gwalia*, p. 61.

91 The word *cynghanedd*, which can be translated literally as 'harmony', describes the system of internal line ornamentation which is mandatory in the traditional strict metres. There are four main types of *cynghanedd*, each requiring either a specific kind of internal rhyme (*cynghanedd lusg*), alliteration (*cynghanedd groes* and *cynghanedd draws*), or, in the case of *cynghanedd sain*, both rhyme and alliteration. Each of these four types is further subdivided into more categories based on the relationship between the line's main accents and the patterns of alliteration and/or internal rhyme.

92 The four categories are represented in this way: *Awen. Gwybth. Cyngdd. Barn.* As *gwybth.* and *cyngdd.* are abbreviations for *gwybodaeth* and *cynghanedd*, it is possible that *barn.* is also an abbreviation, although this is not likely.

93 D. Densil Morgan, 'Cymru a Diwinyddiaeth Princeton 1: Gyrfa Gynnar R. S. Thomas, Abercynon (1844–1923)', *Cylchgrawn Hanes Cymdeithas Hanes y Methodistiaid Calfinaidd*, 25 (2001), pp. 59–68.

94 Aled Jones and Bill Jones, *Welsh Reflections*, pp. 16–17.

95 *Y Cenhadwr Americanaidd*, November 1858.

96 The word translated here as 'poem' is *pryddest*, which normally means a long free-metre poem (as opposed to an *awdl*, which is a long poem in a combination of the strict metres).

97 Stanley Fish, *Is There a Text in This Class? The Authority of Interpretive Communities* (Cambridge, Massachusetts and London, 1980).

98 *Y Cenhadwr Americanaidd*, November 1858.

99 Ibid. Junius seems to have published in editions of *Y Drych* which are not extant. There were, of course, other writers working in other languages who had used this name prior to the 1850s; it is clear, however, that the writer referred to in *Y Cenhadwr Americanaidd* had recently published in Welsh in America.

100 This was stressed in the very first issue of the journal, and repeatedly throughout the 1830s and early 1840s. See, for example, *Y Cyfaill o'r Hen Wlad*, January 1838.

101 *Y Cyfaill o'r Hen Wlad*, January 1838.

102 Ibid.

103 Ioan Llewelyn Evans, *Crach-feirniadaeth; neu Amddiffyniad yn ngwyneb ysgrifau 'Hoffwr Barddoniaeth', yn cynnwys ymchwiliad i egwyddorion beirniadaeth. . . .* (New York, 1859).

104 Ibid., p. iii.

105 Ibid., p. 5.

106 Ibid., p. 8.

107 Ibid., p. 10.

108 Ibid., p. 54.

109 Ibid.

110 For the abusive language used in medieval Welsh bardic debates, see Jerry Hunter, 'Professional Poets and Personal Insults: Ad Hominem attacks in Late Medieval Welsh Ymrysonau', *Proceedings of the Harvard Celtic Colloquium*, 13 (1993), 54–65, and 'Cyd-destunoli Ymrysonau'r Cywyddwyr: Cipolwg ar "Yr Ysbaddiad Barddol"', *Dwned* 3 (1997), 33–52.

111 For example, two prominent Welsh-American ministers, Robert Everett and Ben Chidlaw, travelled back to Wales and conducted well-publicized preaching tours there. Chidlaw was also actively engaged in promoting emigration from Wales, and to this end he published his pamphlet *Yr American* (Llanrwst, 1840).

112 Glanmor Williams, *Y Baradwys Bell?* (Cardiff, 1976), p. 11.

113 Ralph Waldo Emerson, 'The American Scholar', in Nina Baym *et al* (eds), *The Norton Anthology of American Literature* (New York and London, 1998), p. 1113.

114 Alice Fahs's pioneering study has influenced my use of the phrase 'war-time transformation of literature'; Alice Fahs, *The Imagined Civil War [:] Popular Literature of the North and South 1861–1865* (Chapel Hill and London, 2001).

2

Frederick Douglass's 'Welsh Friend'

The Reverend R. D. Thomas claimed that, in addition to the ruffian's Bowie knife, his bardic opponent's threats conjured up the bloody stick of Preston 'Bully' Brooks. Thomas's loaded reference served several rhetorical ends at once. As was suggested in the last chapter, this is one of several details which helped to locate the bardic debate between Thomas and Ioan Llewelyn Evans within specifically American parameters. While asking readers to view Evans's writings as the literary equivalent to Brooks's bloody cane, this rhetorical strategy simultaneously invited Welsh-Americans to view Thomas as being similar to Charles Sumner, the moral champion whom Brooks had assaulted so viciously – and publicly – on the floor of the Senate. Thomas's jibe was well aimed, for Sumner's anti-slavery orations had made him a hero in the eyes of Welsh America.

The speech which precipitated the infamous beating was given considerable attention by the Welsh-American press. In October 1856 *Y Cyfaill o'r Hen Wlad* published a short piece under the title *'Y Trosedd yn erbyn Kansas – Araeth Sumner'* ('The Crime against Kansas – Sumner's Speech'):

> Cawsom trwy garedigrwydd rhywun, gopi trwy'r *Post* o'r araeth gynhyrfiol a gwerthfawr uchod, wedi ei chyfieithu i'r Gymraeg; ac erbyn myned i Scranton, gwelsom gan ein cyfaill Lewis . . . sypyn o honynt yn cael eu gwasgaru gyda haelfrydedd arferol y gwr da hwnw. Byddai yn hoff genym glywed iddynt gael lledaeniad helaeth trwy yr holl sefydliadau Cymreig, a hyny ar frys.[1]
>
> 'We received through the mail, by means of somebody's kindness, a copy of the stirring and valuable speech noted above, translated into Welsh; and after going to Scranton, we saw that our friend Lewis had . . . a bundle of them being distributed with the usual generosity of that good man. It would please us to hear that they have been distributed widely throughout all of the Welsh communities, and that in a hurry.'

William Rowlands, the editor of the *Y Cyfaill o'r Hen Wlad*, is here describing a Welsh translation of Sumner's oration, published as a pamphlet on a press in Scranton, Pennsylvania, and distributed widely throughout Welsh America. A translation of the entire speech was also published in the September 1856 number of *Y Seren Orllewinol*. The *Cyfaill* was the monthly journal of America's Welsh Methodists and the *Seren* served the country's Welsh-speaking Baptists, yet both publications were supporting the anti-slavery cause by 1856, as was the Congregationalists' journal *Y Cenhadwr Americanaidd*. Abolition had been gaining support in the Welsh-speaking communities of the United States, and by the middle of the 1850s anti-slavery declarations were a central part of Welsh America's communal ideology. Abolition was preached from the pulpits of America's Welsh-language chapels. Anti-slavery slogans were shouted from the stages of Welsh America's political rallies. Prose and poetry describing slavery as 'a sin against God and humanity' were published on the pages of the Welsh-American press.

The Welsh of America had not always felt this way. On the contrary, a number of early Welsh immigrants who settled in America prior to the nineteenth century were slave-owners. One of them, Goronwy Owen, is considered by many literary historians to be the most important Welsh poet of the eighteenth century. Earning his living as an Anglican clergyman and teacher, Owen emigrated to Virginia in 1758 in pursuit of the wealth which had escaped him back in Britain. Having failed in other lines of work, he bought a small tobacco plantation and at the time of his death in 1769 he owned four slaves.[2] Rather than being part of a distinct Welsh community, Goronwy Owen was an isolated settler. There was, however, at least one Welsh colony which accepted the institution of slavery. Recent research by D. Hugh Matthews details the history of sixteen Baptists who left Wales in 1701. They settled a place which became known as Welsh Tract (now in Delaware), and in 1736 as many as forty-eight members of the growing community moved to Welsh Neck, South Carolina. Tax records prove that six of these forty-eight Welsh immigrants owned a total of seventeen slaves at the time of the move to South Carolina; Matthews suggests that other members of the community may have sold their slaves before moving to avoid paying South Carolina's import tax.[3] Welsh Neck's Church remained Welsh-speaking up until the mid-1760s, and at least one member of the community could still speak the language as late as 1786.[4] While the history of other eighteenth-century settlements has not been so thoroughly documented, we can assume that Welsh Neck was not the only community of slave-owning Welsh immigrants in eighteenth-century America.

Another Welsh Baptist, very different from the residents of Welsh Neck, emigrated to America in 1789. Morgan John Rhys championed radical causes on both sides of the ocean, and he published anti-slavery material while in America.[5] Other thinkers back in Wales including the visionary Iolo Morganwg and William Williams of Pantycelyn – author of many of the Welsh language's most popular hymns – were speaking out against slavery by the end of the eighteenth century.[6] However, Welsh America would not raise anything like a collective voice against slavery until the middle of the nineteenth century. It is tempting to see the development of Welsh-American ideology in terms of the radical voice of Morgan John Rhys slowly gaining ground, gradually winning the hearts and minds of the majority of Welsh-Americans. The history of Welsh America between 1701 and 1860, however, is not a story of fluid development and transformation; it is, rather, one of disruptions, with the ends of old communities being separated temporarily and geographically from the beginnings of new ones. Southern slave-owning communities like Welsh Neck had ceased being Welsh by the end of the eighteenth century; as far as the development of Welsh America, they proved to be dead ends (as did the Utopian community which Morgan John Rhys himself tried to found in western Pennsylvania). On the other hand, new Welsh communities were being founded in northern states during the early years of the nineteenth century, communities which would form the back-bone of Welsh America by the time of the Civil War.

Some nineteenth-century immigrants brought new, radical ideals with them from Wales, and others found such ideas in their new American home. Some came with views on issues like women's rights, temperance, and the evils of slavery which were fed and amplified by the intellectual and religious stimuli they found in the United States. The evolution of the ideology or ideologies which came to characterize Welsh America is a complex subject; such processes are difficult to pin down, and the details of this history are still waiting for the illumination which future research will surely provide. For the purposes of our present study, we can start by noting this: surviving records and writings suggest that by about 1840 Welsh-speaking Americans tended to think that slavery was wrong. They did not on the whole do much about it, condemning slavery with their words but not with their actions. In this respect they resembled a great many of their non-Welsh neighbours in the northern United States. The situation which existed in 1840 changed dramatically over the next two decades; this is the process of politicization discussed in the last chapter, a process which Aled Jones and Bill Jones see as characterizing the early history of Welsh America's weekly paper, *Y Drych*.[7]

The ideological transformation of Welsh America was described by Paul D. Evans in a Master's thesis presented to Cornell University back in 1914. In addition to studying the literature produced by the country's Welsh press, Evans was also able to draw upon the oral history of Welsh-Americans who still remembered many of the details of their communities' mid-nineteenth-century history. He was drawing on sources now lost to us, and his analysis is thus all the more valuable:

> In [1840] was begun the abolition movement among [the Welsh in America], which was destined to excite more political feeling than anything before or after. Up to that time little attention was paid by the Welsh to the subject of slavery. They were opposed to the institution on principle but it did not immediately concern them and they were content to leave it alone. They had no more love for the abolitionist

> than the ordinary Northerner at that time. The few abolitionists among the Welsh . . . who had agitated the subject during 1839 had received very little sympathy. They were thought a group of dreaming radicals and ignored. The Welsh were soon, however, to find this small group growing, and the principles of abolition were soon to become a live issue among them.[8]

Perhaps the main event which made 1840 a significant year was the start of Robert Everett's journal, *Y Cenhadwr Americanaidd* ('The American Missionary').[9] For over thirty years he would edit and publish the monthly on a press in his own home near Remsen, New York.[10] In addition to using the *Cenhadwr* to attack slavery, Everett published another journal, *Y Dyngarwr* ('The Humanitarian') in 1843, a publication solely devoted to two issues, temperance and abolition. He tried to post a free copy of *Y Dyngarwr* to every Welsh-speaking minister in America, and it is no surprise that the venture proved too costly to continue. However, Robert Everett's *Cenhadwr* would continue to publish potent anti-slavery material up to the end of the Civil War.

Robert Everett worked in a number of overlapping areas; he was, at one and the same time, writer, editor, publisher, minister and political activist, and he used all of these spheres of activity to intensify Welsh-American opposition to slavery. Everett's activities also helped keep the growing circle of Welsh-speaking abolitionists in contact with their Anglophone colleagues. After all, while the abolitionism of Everett and his supporters was Welsh in articulation, it was also part of the broader culture of American abolitionism. It is thus extremely significant that Everett, a Congregational minister who emigrated from Flintshire in 1823, made his home in Oneida County, New York. In addition to living near Utica, the cultural capital of Welsh America, he was also living in an area of special significance in terms of American religious culture. Oneida County formed part of the 'burned-over district', so called because the fires of revival had burned so often in the area, leaving in their wake numerous vibrant strains of radical evangelical Protestantism.[11]

The burned-over district spawned, or attracted, its share of abolitionists. Milton Sernett has recently named the region 'North Star Country', taking as his starting point Frederick Douglass's decision to relocate to up-state New York and start publishing his own paper, the *North Star*, in Rochester in 1847; 'the decision to relocate to Upstate New York proved to be a wise one for, by the 1840s, the region rivalled New England in importance to the continuing battle against slavery.'[12] This move helped signal Douglass's ascendancy as one of the country's leading abolitionists.[13] Since escaping from slavery in 1838, he had been steadily acquiring a reputation as a powerful speaker on abolitionism, and his fame was enhanced substantially by the publication of his autobiography in 1845, the *Narrative of the Life of Frederick Douglass, An American Slave*.[14] Before relocating to up-state New York, Douglass had been part of William Lloyd Garrison's circle of New England abolitionists. He had also worked on Garrison's paper, *The Liberator*, and, in the words of John Stauffer, 'his move to Rochester to establish the *North Star* was itself an assertion of independence from his former employer.'[15]

In 1851 Douglass changed the name of the *North Star* to *Frederick Douglass' Paper*. And the 3 November 1854 edition of the paper drew attention to *Y Cenhadwr Americanaidd*, translated as 'The American Messenger':

> Y CENHADWR AMERICANAIDD. Remsen, N.Y.: J. R. Everett. We have made more than one resolution . . . not to increase our list of Exchanges; but we cannot deny ourselves the gratification of sending our Paper (as requested) to the Editor of The American Messenger, and, at the same time, of expressing our satisfaction at learning that there is, at least, one 'purely Anti-Slavery Paper,' published by the Welsh people of this country. This is as it should be. It is consistent that a people who have loved Freedom so much, for themselves, should lend their efforts towards obtaining it for others.[16]

Frederick Douglass continued to receive the *Cenhadwr*, duly referring to it time and again in his paper as 'our Welsh friend', sometimes voicing 'regret that we cannot speak with him,' and noting once that 'it needs an interpreter before we can converse with him'.[17] However, Douglass – and/or Julia Griffiths, who helped Douglass with the paper – thumbed the journal's pages on occasion, searching for the names of Welsh abolitionists and religious leaders who were known to them.[18] Shortly after the first appearance of *Uncle Tom's Cabin*, two different Welsh-language translations were published in Oneida County, New York, one by Robert Everett.[19] *Frederick Douglass' Paper* duly informed its readers of these developments, noting that 'Uncle Tom's Cabin has been translated into Welsh, and bears the title of "Caban F'Ewthyr T[w]m" '.[20]

In addition to giving regular notice to the literary endeavours of Welsh-American abolitionists, *Frederick Douglass' Paper* also reported their practical support. In September, 1854, it published an account of a series of anti-slavery meetings held in Oneida County, noting that 'one of the best meetings of the series' was held at Waterville, New York. The report adds that 'there are in Waterville, a considerable number of Welsh, who are to a man, go-ahead Abolitionists'.[21] This evidence supports the records which the Welsh of Oneida County have left regarding their own activities (with one exception: Douglass – or his editorial assistant – should have amended the piece to read that the Welsh were 'go-ahead abolitionists to a man and to a woman'; like the Anglophone abolitionist press, the Welsh-American press was publishing a number of anti-slavery poems by women at the time).

While journals such as *Y Cenhadwr Americanaidd* and *Y Dyngarwr* provide the greatest body of evidence concerning the work of Welsh-American abolitionists, there is also some surviving manuscript evidence which helps us reconstruct the methods which they used. One of these documents records an anti-slavery meeting held in Capel Uchaf, Oneida County on 'Friday evening, Jan[uar]y 6, 1843.'[22] It was 'organized by the appointment of Austin Ward, chairman,' and Robert Everett played the part of 'secretary'. The document, written in English by Everett himself, describes some of the evening's proceedings: 'George French, a fugitive slave, from Tennessee gave a short sketch of his life, family, & escape from slavery.'[23]

The short record of the evening's meeting ends with a list of names, entitled 'Pledges of time to circulate petitions, & disseminate anti-slavery truth.' The list contains the names of twenty-three individuals, most of whom pledged between two and six days of their time to this particular campaign. Robert Everett's name is the very first on the list; the *Cenhadwr*'s editor pledged ten days, an amount of time matched by only one other, the Reverend John Howe. Everett's wife, Elizabeth, was also present; she promised to spend two days distributing material from door to door. Several of the activists were women, both unmarried (Miss Gwen Prichard and Miss Elizabeth Williams) and married (Mrs Eleanor Pugh, Mrs Howe and Mrs Everett). All of the twenty-three were Welsh-speaking Americans.

The campaign strategies adopted by Oneida County's Welsh abolitionists were surely based at least in part upon the methods used by the American Anti-slavery Society and the New England Anti-Slavery Society.[24] It is also likely that the involvement of Everett and other Welsh-American ministers in the temperance movement provided them with organizational models. A wider context for the meeting held on 6 January 1843 is suggested by the fact that Robert Everett recorded the proceedings in English, presumably because he was sending the details on to the national organizers of the American Anti-Slavery Society. He also published a record of the meeting in Welsh, holding it up as an example for all of Welsh America to follow.[25] While Everett used his press to ensure that the wider community of Welsh-speaking Americans took note of the Oneida County abolitionists' activities, the surviving manuscript record shows the localized nature of their grass-roots campaigning; the territory assigned these bearers of 'anti-slavery truth' reads like a map of the local Welsh community. While one concentrated on the 'Village of Remsen and district by the turnpike gate' (the Everett family's own immediate neighbourhood), another worked the 'Fairchild and Enlli districts' (Enlli being a Welsh-language chapel in the area named after the island off the Llŷn Peninsula from which some of Oneida County's immigrants had come). Another was sent to the area around Penymynydd chapel, while others knocked on doors in 'Tŷ coch district' and 'Felyn y dwyrain'.[26]

With both parents pounding the snowy roads of up-state New York in winter distributing anti-slavery material, it is no surprise that the many Everett children grew up to be active abolitionists. In addition to helping their father and mother publish and distribute *Y Cenhadwr Americanaidd* for decades, the children would take their own active roles in the fight against slavery. Two of

Everett's sons were educated at Beriah Greene's Oneida Institute, that radical school described by Milton Sernett as the home of 'Abolition's axe'.[27] In the 1850s, one of them would move to Kansas as a free-soil settler. The daughters were equally active; one of them became one of the first women doctors in the United States, and another would travel to the South immediately after the Civil War in order to work in a school for former slaves. In September 1849 the Everetts' daughter Elizabeth attended the Free Baptist Quarterly Conference held in Clinton, New York. Though a Congregationalist like her parents, Elizabeth was reporting on the New York Baptists' stance on abolition. She dutifully sent a letter back to her parents, describing with evident pleasure the 'anti-slavery resolutions' which the Baptists had adopted.[28]

The notices published by Frederick Douglass show that Robert Everett corresponded with him. Everett also wrote to Harriet Beecher Stowe, seeking permission to publish his Welsh translation of *Uncle Tom's Cabin*.[29] Stowe's reply was short but supportive:

> Dear Sir,
> You have my full permition to translate Uncle Tom into Welch and do any thing with it in that language that shall seem to you most fit and desireable. I shall be happy if it does any good.
> Yours very truly
> H B Stowe[30]

Like many of Robert Everett's other activities, publishing a Welsh version of the popular anti-slavery novel obviously did – to rephrase Stowe's letter – do some good. The majority of Welsh-speaking Americans, though thinking slavery evil, did not at first take kindly to Everett's mixing of politics with religion. Like many other abolitionists, Robert Everett was abused by mobs early in his political career; in the late 1830s and early 1840s he was even pelted with eggs and hymn books from the gallery of chapels where he preached![31] However, by 1856 Welsh-Americans were flocking to the newly-formed Republican Party. In the words of Paul Evans, '[t]he Welsh were now united in one party and . . . organized on the principle of opposition to slavery. It was what Everett and his supporters had worked for and the work, once done, was permanent.'[32]

A wealth of surviving manuscript sources attests to the hard work carried out by the Everett family and their colleagues.[33] These people literally took the cause of abolition from door to door, slowly radicalizing their Welsh-American communities house by house, street by street and village by village. Of extreme significance is the fact that ministers like Robert Everett used the pulpit to preach against the evils of slavery, thus radicalizing the chapels which lay at the heart of Welsh-American society. And, as editor of *Y Cenhadwr Americanaidd* and owner of his own printing press, Everett worked to dissemi-nate anti-slavery sentiments by means of the written – and printed – Welsh word. In praising Everett's publication, his 'Welsh Friend', Frederick Douglass stated that there was 'at least one "purely Anti-Slavery Paper" published by the Welsh people of this country.'[34] While Everett's *Cenhadwr* was solidly anti-slavery from the beginning, it was by no means the only publication presenting Welsh-speaking Americans with anti-slavery material. A study of the views on slavery published in the other two main Welsh-American journals – *Y Seren Orllewinol* and *Y Cyfaill o'r Hen Wlad* – as well as the weekly newspaper, *Y Drych*, reveals much about the way in which Welsh-American thinking on the subject was brought into sharper focus during the twenty years before the Civil War. Indeed, before the end of the 1850s Frederick Douglass could have referred to the Welsh-American press in general as his 'Welsh friend'.

Y Cyfaill o'r Hen Wlad, the oldest of the three main monthly journals, began publication in 1838. As was seen in the last chapter, its editor, William Rowlands, insisted that he abstained from revealing his personal opinion, and that the publication was an unbiased forum open to all viewpoints. Despite this professed neutrality, the journal presented an anti-slavery perspective from the beginning; otherwise generic news summaries described southern slave owners as *gwrthwynebwyr rhyddid*, 'the opponents of freedom'. In September 1838 a letter was published by a reader calling himself Jonathan, who stated that he was against slavery. He was writing to the journal because he was worried by some of his neighbours, for they quoted the Old Testament in defence of the immoral institution, and he was looking for professional help in countering these Christian supporters of slavery.[35] Jonathan was answered during the following months by a series of Calvinistic Methodist ministers who gave him a string of Biblical arguments against slavery.[36]

Throughout the first year and a half of the journal's existence, the *Cyfaill*'s pages presented an untroubled consensus of opinion concerning the evils of slavery. However, this consensus was shattered in the summer of 1839, after a writer using the name 'Hebog Du' ('Black Hawk') wrote in to applaud all of the journal's anti-slavery essays and letters and to ask a simple question. Hebog Du knew that there were two groups opposed to slavery, the Abolitionists and the Colonization Society, and he was not sure which one he should support.[37] This letter was answered in November 1839 by a writer using the name 'Chwarae teg i Bob Ochr' ('Fair Play for Both Sides') supporting the colonizationists' view that freed slaves should be sent to Africa.[38] A different answer also reached the journal's pages, as William Thomas of Utica wrote in to champion pure and immediate abolition over African colonization. This debate raged on the pages of the *Cyfaill* throughout 1840 and 1841, until the Welsh colonizationist was beaten (or at least decided to withdraw from the debate).

Nothing more is known about the individual who used the name 'Chwarae teg i Bob Ochr', and it is difficult to find other Welsh writers who voiced direct support for African colonization. However, future investigation into this subject might benefit from considering the fact that Pennsylvania had one of the largest Welsh-speaking populations in the country in connection with that state's importance to the colonization movement. According to Richard Newman, Pennsylvania was by the early 1830s 'a hotbed of colonization as auxiliary societies spread rapidly throughout the state. By 1831 Pennsylvanians had formed over eighty local groups, more than a third of all national auxiliaries.'[39] Wherever this Welsh colonizationist lived, and however many supporters he had within the larger community of Welsh America, his debate with the abolitionist William Thomas was in many ways simply a Welsh version of the national struggle between the two anti-slavery movements. William Lloyd Garrison's 'conversion from colonization to immediate abolition' ten years before had been a seminal moment in the evolution of American abolitionism, and the increasingly vocal supporters of the radical stance which came to be called 'Garrisonism' had been attacking colonization throughout the 1830s.[40] In the words of Robert Fanuzzi, the 'ascent of Garrison and the Massachusetts Anti-Slavery Society opened up a contentious . . . sphere of debate . . . as the discussion of abolition antagonized the lay and clerical supporters of African colonization.'[41]

As far as the Welsh articulation of abolitionism is concerned, the series of letters published in *Y Cyfaill o'r Hen Wlad* served to bring the real issues at stake into sharper focus. In addition to condemning slavery, abolitionists like William Thomas and Robert Everett advocated complete equality of the races. Thus, rather than accepting the colonizationist as a brother in the fight against slavery, William Thomas condemned him for being racist.[42]

> Egwyddorion y Gymdeithas Drefediaethawl yw, dysgu fod lliw y croen yn anaddasu dynion i gydfwynhau breintiau crefyddol, gwladol, teuluaidd, a pherthynasol. . . . Ond egwyddorion y Gymdeithas Wrthgaethiwawl yw dysgu nad yw lliw y croen, yn fwy na hyd a lled yn y corph, yn gwneyd dyn yn rhinweddol; ond fod pob dyn, gwyn a du, yn ddeiliaid llywodraeth foesol[.][43]

> 'The principles of the Colonization Society teach that skin colour makes men incapable of enjoying together the privileges of religion, politics, family and relations. . . . However the principles of the Abolition Society teach that skin colour does not, any more than does the shape and size of one's body, make a man virtuous; but that every man, white and black, possesses moral judgement.'

William Thomas won the argument with a moral check-mate. Although thinking slavery wrong, colonizationists wanted to send former slaves 'back' to Africa; they believed that people with black skin and those with white skin could not be neighbours. This, Thomas quips, is as ridiculous and as bigoted as assuming that people of different sizes are unsuited to live together. Like the Revd Thomas Roberts of Freedom, New York, who believed that 'all of the earth's races are equal in every way' ('fod holl genedloedd y ddaear yn gydraddol yn mhob ystyr'), this writer believed that all people were equally subject to the same moral forces.[44]

While the Calvinistic Methodists who read *Y Cyfaill o'r Hen Wlad* followed this debate over the relative merits of different kinds of anti-slavery movements, the Welsh Baptists of the United States were conducting a different kind of debate on the pages of their monthly journal. In June 1845, a long exhortation was published in *Y Seren Orllewinol*, expressing joy over the fact that no Welsh people were profiting from slavery, calling for immediate abolition, and urging Welsh-Americans to use their votes to oust pro-slavery politicians from office. The editor supported this step into the realm of political action by publishing in the same issue a Welsh translation of a decree issued by the Baptist elders of Geneva, New York, condemning slavery.[45] As Robert Everett's daughter Elizabeth had remarked in a letter to her parents, the Baptist Union of the United States was taking an official stance on the evils of slavery.

The following month, July 1845, the *Seren* published a letter by Mr L. James of Utica, reacting to the anti-slavery exhortation. He stated that he was greatly pleased with the first half of the essay, agreeing that slavery was indeed a great evil. However, this writer did not think that the pages of a religious journal should be used to urge specific political action. Like those Welsh-Americans who had attacked Robert Everett for preaching politics from the pulpit five years earlier, Mr James complained that the *Seren*'s editor had been tricked into turning the Baptists' publication into a political forum: 'rhaid imi gyfaddef i ryw arswyd anghyffredinol afaelyd ynof, rhag iddynt fod yn llwyddiannus i droi y SEREN ORLLEWINOL yn *bolitical arena* – anharddu gwynebpryd y SEREN fwyn, gu!' ('I must confess that a strange terror seized hold of me [when I realized] that they might succeed in turning the SEREN ORLLEWINOL into a *political arena* – disfigure the countenance of the dear, tender SEREN!').[46] Despite decrying the journal's political turn, Mr James stressed that his complaint involved only the mixing of politics and religion, and that he did, in fact, oppose slavery. To that end, he concluded his letter with some conciliatory remarks: 'Hyderaf, syr, y parhewch i amddiffyn rhyddid – rhyddid gwirioneddol – rhyddid cyffredinol – rhyddid i bob lliw, iaith a chenedl, dan y nefoedd' ('I am sure, sir, that you will continue to defend freedom – true freedom – general freedom – freedom for every colour, language and nation, under heaven').

This letter sparked a heated debate on the pages of the *Seren*, resulting in what can be interpreted as a triumph for those abolitionists who did believe in mixing politics and religion.[47] By the end of the 1840s the journal was publishing sermons demonstrating that Christian teaching required Welsh-Americans to take direct political action in order to end slavery.[48] Despite the protestations of Mr James and his supporters, the Welsh Baptists' journal did indeed become a 'political arena', and abolition was the main cause championed in that arena. Looking at all three of the Welsh-American denominational publications reveals a gradual focusing of attention on the evils of slavery. While the *Cenhadwr* was solidly abolitionist from the start, the readers of the

Cyfaill had to work through a debate over the relative merits of colonization and abolition, and the *Seren*, against the wishes of some its readers, worked towards transforming its religious forum by including within in it a place for the politics of abolition.[49] By the start of the Civil War, all three journals were solid supporters of abolition.

If these three publications constituted the flesh and blood of Welsh-American print culture on the eve of the war, *Y Drych* was the backbone. The newspaper first appeared in January 1851, and the very first edition of the weekly contained an article on the Fugitive Slave Law. While condemning the law and questioning the right of Congress to pass any law which supported slavery, the paper walked a middle path. It likened 'the poor Negro who is fleeing for his freedom' ('y Negro tlawd sydd yn diangc am ei ryddid') to the fugitives of ancient Israel. The paper stated clearly that Congress had no authority to pass legislation 'incommensurate with reason and humanity' ('anghyson â rheswm a dynoliaeth'), but it also condemned the 'hot-headed Abolitionists of the North' – 'Gwrthgaethyddion penboethlyd Gogleddol' – who would break laws in order to free the slaves in the south.[50]

By 1857, the paper's editor was singing a very different tune. When one Welsh Democrat wrote in to complain that the newspaper was an organ for Republican propaganda, the editor replied with a protracted anti-slavery essay, supporting the actions of radical Free-soil settlers in Kansas. Sounding more and more like the abolitionists who had been publishing in the three monthly journals for years, *Y Drych* attacked those who would 'condemn human beings' to abuse merely 'because of their colour' ('tynghedu bodau dynol . . . oherwydd eu lliw').[51] The paper's editor also followed the debate which *Y Seren Orllewinol* fielded over mixing politics and religion. When George Cheever published his book *God against Slavery* in 1857, *Y Drych* presented Welsh readers with a glowing review, urging members of all Welsh denominations in America to view the fight against slavery as a Christian duty.[52]

While a study of these four publications allows us to follow the main contours of Welsh America's political geography during the quarter century before the Civil War, they do not tell the whole story. Several short-lived journals had a significant effect, none more than Robert Everett's second journal, *Y Dyngarwr*. It lasted only one year, from January to December 1843. The individual issues were not long – about eight pages each on average – and the total twelve issues constitute one slim volume, ninety-six pages in length. The journal's impact, however, should not be underestimated. Everett tried to send *Y Dyngarwr* to all the ministers of all the Welsh denominations in the United States, and the publication was thus widely read by those individuals who were directly involved in shaping Welsh America's public morality.[53] For example, the journal's contributors included the Revd J. P. Harris, who later in the 1840s would inject his own journal, *Y Seren Orllewinol*, with the kind of anti-slavery writings which he first published in *Y Dyngarwr*.[54] Harris was a Baptist and Everett was a Congregationalist; the journal served – perhaps more than any other Welsh-American monthly published before the Civil War – to bridge the sectarian divide. Given Everett's desire to distribute so many copies free of charge, it is perhaps no surprise that publishing *Y Dyngarwr* in addition to *Y Cenhadwr Americanaidd* proved too costly a venture. However, the ninety-six pages which he produced in 1843 carried a wealth of weighty moral arguments, providing Welsh America with material which they could draw upon during the next two decades.

Each issue was divided into two parts, *Dirwest* ('Temperance') and *Rhyddid* ('Freedom'). This attempt at giving equal attention to the two favourite causes of radical Welsh Nonconformists was undermined by Everett's devotion to abolition. While the first issue was closely balanced – with about three and a half pages devoted to temperance and four and a half devoted to abolition – by November 1843 the evils of alcohol took a definite second seat to the sin of slavery, occupying only one half of one page. Moreover, while the 'Temperance' section was placed first originally, the two parts were reversed in the June issue, and for the rest of its short life 'Freedom' would greet readers upon turning to *Y Dyngarwr*'s first page. Robert Everett was truly concerned with the temperance movement, as indeed he was with other causes such as women's rights, yet, in the words of one of his admirers, despite his work on many moral fronts, 'Dr. Everett's name, as a reformer, will be remembered, most especially, in connection with the anti-slavery cause' ('bydd enw Dr. Everett, fel diwygiwr, mewn coffadwriaeth, yn fwyaf neillduol, yn ei gysylltiad â'r achos gwrthgaethiwol').[55]

The first piece published under the first 'Freedom' section in January 1843 was penned by Robert Everett himself. Bearing the simple title 'Beth yw Rhyddid?' – 'What is Freedom?' – the essay presents total racial equality as the moral benchmark for Welsh America:

> Mae dyn yn mwynhau rhyddid pan y mae yn cael cwbl dawelwch gan ei gyd greaduriaid yn nghyflawniad ei orchwylion a'r dyledswyddau gorphwysedig arno, fel bod rhesymol, taug at Dduw, tuag ato ei hun, ei deulu, ei gymydogion, a dynolryw yn gyffredinol. Yr hawlfraint i'r pethau hyn sydd yn eiddo i bob dyn, o bob lliw, iaith a chenedl, trwy ddwyfol roddiad, a'i ymddifadu o un o honynt sydd yn gysegr yspail ar eiddo yr Arglwydd, ac yn ymgais at ymddifadu dyn o'i ddynol a'i hanfodol iawnderau.[56]
>
> 'Man enjoys freedom when he is given complete peace by his fellow-creatures to fulfil his tasks and the obligations placed upon him, as a reasoning being, towards God, towards himself, his neighbours, and human kind in general. The right to these things is the possession of every man, of every colour, language and race, by divine gift, and depriving him of one of them is an unholy theft of the Lord's property, and an attempt to deprive man of his human and essential rights.'

Citing 'language' along with 'colour' and 'race' was a way of including the rights of the Welsh in this general definition of freedom and equality; the language, after all, was the main yardstick used in delineating Welsh identity during the first half of the nineteenth century. Everett's next sentence connects these fundamental rights to the crime against humanity being committed in the southern United States: 'Mae y caethwas wedi ei ymddifadu trwy y gorthrwm mwyaf o'r hawliau hyn' ('the slave has been denied these rights by means of the greatest oppression'). This was *Y Dyngarwr*'s manifesto, a plain declaration of war on the slave system.

The journal linked abstract (and theological) reasoning with practical action, often drawing attention to the resources available to abolitionists. For example, it carried a piece by the Revd John Howe – one of Everett's abolitionist colleagues in Oneida County, and one of the twenty-three activists present at the 1843 meeting described above – on the effectiveness of anti-slavery narratives. The essay, entitled 'Chwedl Effeithiol' ('An Effective Tale'), describes a recent sermon preached by yet another Welsh minister, the Revd William Rowlands, to the Calvinistic Methodist congregation in Remsen.[57] The preacher's subject was 'secret prayer' ('gweddi ddirgel'), and, though he took as his starting point Matthew 6:6, the rhetorical centre of Rowlands's sermon came in the form of a story about a religious slave. After providing a synopsis of the didactic tale, Howe concludes his treatise with some general observations regarding the usefulness of such narratives:

> Credwyf pe byddai i bawb wnaed cystal tegwch a'r hanesion sydd yn dyfod o'r Deheubarth ag a wnaeth Mr. Rowlands, mai buan iawn y byddai cant i un o bleidleiswyr dros ryddhad y caethwas, yn lle 'un i gant' fel yr hysbysir yn y 'Cyfaill' diweddaf.[58]
>
> 'I believe that, if everybody did justice to the stories which are coming from the South equal to that which Mr. Rowlands has done, the supporters of the slave's freedom would soon be one hundred to one, in stead of "one in a hundred" as is noted in the most recent *Cyfaill*.'

John Howe was describing the role which carefully crafted language could play in the campaign against slavery; he was offering advice to public speakers and authors as to how they might employ their talents in the service of the cause. The aim was to take the 'stories' which were 'coming from the South' and present them artfully, thus 'doing fairness' to them. The role of the morally-minded orator and writer, then, was to search out the relevant raw materials and craft narratives which would release the stories' latent ability to motivate the public. However simple and short, this sentence presents the essence of what we might call a poetics of the anti-slavery narrative.

Robert Everett also highlighted the role which Welsh writers could play in the great moral struggle. He asked the question 'Beth A All Y Cymry Wneud?'

– 'What Can the Welsh Do?' – in order to free the slaves, before answering with ten specific suggestions. These solutions ranged from the religious (praying for freedom) to the political (sending letters and petitions to the government), but they also included the artistic:

> Cyfansodder emynau ar ryddid fel y gwneir ar ddirwest, a chaner hwynt yn fynych yn nghynulleidfa yr Arglwydd. Peth yn effeithio yn fawr ar y meddwl dynol yw canu; canu emynau dirwestol a fu yn un moddion neillduol i ddeffroi teimladau priodol yn yr achos hwnw. Gwneler hyny yn yr achos hwn hefyd; dysger ein hieuenctid a'n plant bychain o'u mebyd i ganu emynau gwrthgaethiwol, ac i folianu yr Arglwydd am fendithion rhyddid.[59]
>
> 'Let hymns to freedom be composed as they are [on the subject of] temperance, and let them be sung often in the Lord's congregation. Song is something which affects the human mind greatly; singing temperance hymns was one of the particular means used to awaken appropriate feelings for that cause. Let that be done for this cause as well; let our youth and our little children be taught to sing anti-slavery hymns from their childhood, and to praise the Lord for freedom's blessings.'

Leading Welsh-American abolitionists thus encouraged different kinds of literary activity. While John Howe asked writers to publish anti-slavery narratives, Robert Everett urged poets to compose hymns which would move the emotions of singers and listeners. Everett's idea was not new; the Welsh-American press had already been producing such hymns. For example, in June 1839 *Y Cyfaill o'r Hen Wlad* published 'Cwyn y Caeth', 'The Slave's Complaint', by a Cincinnati poet who used the name 'Ab Ioan'. It begins as an address to the Welsh of America: 'At Gymry mwynion Unol Wlad, / Er cofio'r Caethion heb nacad . . .' ('To the gentle Welsh of a United County, / That the Slaves be remembered without refusal . . .'). Having first worked through a concise description of the evils of slavery, the poem ends with a prayer, suggesting that it was in fact meant to be sung as a hymn in public meetings or religious services: 'Doed, doed y dydd i ben / Na byddo caethion mwy. Amen' ('May it come, may the day come / When there will no longer be any slaves. Amen').[60]

Some of the better anti-slavery hymns which the Welsh-American press published were composed by female poets; it is perhaps no coincidence that Everett followed his exhortation to the country's Welsh bards with a plea directed at Welsh America's women: 'Bydded i'n mamau a'n chwiorydd . . . roddi eu llais a'u gwerthfawr ddylanwad o blaid rhyddhad y caethwas' ('Let our mothers and sisters . . . lend their voices and their valuable influence in favour of the slave's freedom').[61] Like Frederick Douglass, Robert Everett linked the fight for women's rights directly to the fight for the rights of slaves: 'Llawer chwaer ddu, ïe llawer chwaer wen (yn mron yn hollawl felly) sydd yn dyoddef y cam mwyaf'; 'Many a black sister, yea, many a white sister (almost completely thus) is suffering the greatest injustice.'[62]

One of the more interesting writers who answered the literary call to arms issued by Howe and Everett was the future editor of *Y Seren Orllewinol*, J. P. Harris. Known in bardic circles as Ieuan Ddu, Harris published a great deal of Welsh poetry in a number of journals. A moral fable which he published in *Y Dyngarwr* demonstrates that Harris was also a gifted prose stylist.[63] The piece is entitled, simply, 'Gweledigaeth', 'A Vision', and it is a fiction. The fiction, however, is presented within a frame which offers the reader a way of suspending disbelief. Using the guise of mundane discourse, it begins as a letter to the journal's editor, Robert Everett. Like that piece which 'John Bunnau' would publish in *Y Drych* over a decade later, this 'letter' begins by describing an idealized pastoral setting before quickly shifting frames of reference as the otherworldly dream vision takes hold.

> Mr. Golygydd, – Ni ddileuir argraffiadau dwys y weledigaeth a ddarganfyddais yn ddiweddar o'm meddwl, tra côf yn dal ei heisteddle. Un diwrnod wrth synfyfyrio ar geulanau anial yr Afon Ddu – yn yfed yr awelon adfywiol a chwareuant ar ei hwyneb llon – ac yn mynych wrando y tônau peroriaethol, mor fedrus a chwareuai i loni plant y goedwig, – diosgwyd fi o'm gwisgoedd is-loerawl, gorlanwyd fy meddwl â phethau uwch sêr y nef, sef pleserau gwynfa; yn fy myfyrdod ehedwn ar edyn Cerub drwy frôydd Paradwys, a theimlwn fy hun mor ddedwydd a neb o'r côr nefolaidd a gylchynent yr orsedd.[64]

> 'Mr. Editor, – the deep impressions of a vision which I happened upon recently can not be deleted from my mind as long as memory retains its seat. One day while meditating upon the uninhabited hollowed banks of the Black River – drinking the revivifying breezes which play across its happy surface – and persistently listening to the musical tunes, so skilfully playing to cheer the children of the woods, – I was removed of my earthly garments, my mind was filled with things above heaven's stars, namely the pleasures of paradise ; in my meditation I flew on the wings of a Cherub through the regions of Paradise, and I felt myself as content as any member of the heavenly choir which encircled the throne.'

This romanticized rural landscape, like the summery Utica evening described by John Bunnau, is specifically American; it is the 'refreshing breezes' of the Black River, and 'the sweet songs' of local birds – 'children of the woods' – which lull Ieuan Ddu's fictitious persona into sleep, thus preparing him for the ensuing dream.

Despite being grounded in an idealized version of familiar American geography, this opening paragraph draws heavily upon the Welsh literary tradition. Ieuan Ddu is constructing a literary vision which, while arguably traceable back to medieval dream literature, is reminiscent of Ellis Wynne's 1703 book, *Gweledigaetheu y Bardd Cwsc*, 'Visions of the Sleeping Bard', a popular and influential part of the Welsh literary canon (reprinted several times, in

Wales and the United States, during the nineteenth century).[65] The way in which the Welsh-American writer structured his prose, grounding the central vision in (an imagined and highly stylized) 'reality', is reminiscent of Wynne's masterpiece. The 1703 book contains three 'visions'; all of them are placed within a similar introductory frame, and two of them open with this kind of idealized pastoral setting. The introduction to the first of Wynne's vision has the 'sleeping bard' climbing the mountains of Wales 'on a fair afternoon during a long, sunny, warm summer' ('Ar ryw brydnhawngwaith têg o hâ hir felyn tesog'). The scene introducing his third and final vision is set on 'one of gentle April's fair mornings' ('Ar ryw foreu têg o Ebrill rywiog'), and has the bard 'strolling . . . along the banks of the Severn, amidst the sweet songs of the little musicians of the Woods' ('rhodio . . . ynglann Hafren, ynghanol melys-byncieu cerddorion bâch y Goedwig').[66]

The bird-song of the Severn's banks prefigures the musical 'children of the woods' who sing near the American river, and the persona constructed by J. P. Harris, who walks 'meditating along the hollowed banks of the Black River', is imitating the way in which Ellis Wynne's bard strolls along the banks of the Severn. The transition from rural bliss to disturbing vision in the Welsh-American piece also echoes the *Bardd Cwsc*. In the first of Wynne's visions, the Sleeping Bard is carried by an Angel to view supernatural realms. Harris claims to have 'flown on the wings of a Cherub through the regions of Paradise', before meeting a supernatural 'gentleman riding as upon a cloud' ('[b]onheddwr yn marchogaeth fel ar y cwmwl').[67] This character gives his name as Y Dyngarwr; he is the new journal personified, and he berates the dreaming Welsh-American: '"O ddyn marwol! beth a wnei DI yma? Heddyw yw'th amser i weithio. Mae dy frawd yn gruddfan mewn caethiwed. Tyred a chanlyn fi." ('"O mortal man! what do YOU do here? Today is your time to work. Your brother is suffering in slavery. Come and follow me."')[68]

The personified journal then takes the dreaming mortal 'towards the south' ('tua'r deheu'), where they encounter a very different kind of supernatural figure:

> canfyddais Bendefiges rodresgar mewn gwisg ysgarlad; ei llygaid ydoedd gochion; ei chroen lliwus gwedi gwywo gan belydr yr haul; ei hedrychiad yn sarug a dychrynadwy; yn ei llaw aswy yr oedd fflangell '*Massa*', ynghyd a haiarn nodi; ac yn ei llaw ddeheu gwpan aur yn orlawn o win; yn ei chylchynu yr oedd gosgorddlû, y rhai a waeddant yn awr ac yn y man, 'Mawr yw Arglwyddes y deheu!'[69]

> 'I perceived a pompous Aristocratic woman in scarlet clothes; her eyes were red; her tanned skin withered by the sun's rays; her gaze was surly and fear-inspiring; in her left hand was the whip of "Massa," along with a branding iron; and in her left hand there was a golden cup overflowing with wine; there was a retinue surrounding her, yelling now and again, "Great is the Lady of the south!" '

This monstrous Lady is based directly upon the description of 'the whore of Babylon' found in the Book of Revelation 17.4: 'The woman was clothed in . . . scarlet . . . In her hand she held a gold cup.'[70] Harris transforms the Revelation's 'scarlet woman' into a grotesque version of the stereotypical Southern Belle, and – also following the typological template of the Book of Revelation – he inscribes each part of this allegorical picture was a specific meaning. The personified journal, like the guide which Wynne gave his sleeping bard (and the Angel who interprets the vision in Revelation), explains the apparition in detail. Also echoing Wynne's description of the deceiver Belial as an enchanter ('hudol'), this guide tells the dreaming mortal that the 'Lady of the south' is a 'deceitful enchantress' ('Hudoles dwyllodrus').[71] In describing her further, he gives her real name:

> ei henw priodol yw CAETHWASANAETH; ei 'gwisg ysgarlad' a ddynoda ei syched am waed; ei 'llygaid cochion' a arddangosant ei meddwdod; 'lliw ei chroen' a brofa boethder yr hinsawdd lle y preswylia; ei hedrychiad 'sarug a dychrynadwy' a dystia ei hamddifadrwydd o deimlad dynol; y 'fflangell a haiarn nodi yn ei llaw aswy' a arwyddant greulondeb ei llywodraeth; y 'gwin yn y cwpan aur yn ei llaw ddeheu' oedd waed yr *Ethiopiad* tlawd.

> 'her proper name is SLAVERY; her "scarlet clothes" represent her thirst for blood; her "red eyes" show her inebriation; "the colour of her skin" testifies to the heat of the climate where she dwells; her "surly and fear-inspiring" gaze proves that she is bereft of human feeling; the "whip and branding iron in her left" hand symbolize the cruelty of her rule; the "wine in the golden cup in her right hand" was the blood of the poor *Ethiopian*.'

This last phrase is an explicit reference to Revelation 17.6: 'The woman, I saw, was drunk with the blood of God's people and with the blood of those who had borne their testimony to Jesus.'[72] The oppressed slaves are defined as God's people, just as personified Slavery is made to partake of the Antichrist. While carefully crafted to elicit the desired emotional – and political – response, this typological morality tale was not meant to be subtle.

After returning from the allegorical dream vision to the real world of 1843, J. P. Harris ends his piece by calling on readers to make sure that none of 'Meibion Gwalia', 'the Sons of Wales', support the evil 'Enchantress' of the south. His appeal for action is presented as an appeal to history, for he asks Welsh-Americans to remember that their ancestors were made slaves and sent 'for sale in the markets of Rome' ('ar werth yn marchnadoedd Rhufain'). He would not be the last Welsh-American writer to link the historical experience of the Welsh to the current experiences of slaves in the American south, although most did not follow Harris in venturing as far back as the Roman period. This kind of discourse would be used during the Civil War to link southern slave owners directly to the British aristocrats who had oppressed the Welsh through history, and it was crystallized on the pages of *Y Dyngarwr* back in 1843. One writer from Pittsburgh calling himself 'Iorwerth' published an essay in the April issue of the journal, entitled 'Caethiwed Cymru,' 'The Slavery of Wales.'[73] In describing the 'slavery which prospers in the dear land of our brothers and fathers, namely Wales' ('[y] caethiwed a ffyna yn hoff wlad ein brodyr â'n tadau, sef Cymru'), Iorwerth laid out what he saw as its historical basis, the medieval conquest of Wales's native rulers and the destruction of their society by the Anglo-Norman invaders:

> Bu ein cenedl yn gref a chyfoethog gynt, yn meddu gwledydd, Brenhinoedd Cymreig, a chyfreithiau o'u cyfansoddiad eu hunain, ac yn eu hiaith eu hunain, ac wrth feddwl am yr hyn a fuont a'r hyn yw eu sefyllfa yr awr hon y mae yn ddigon i dori y galon galetaf ac i achosi ffynonau o ddeigrau o'n llygaid.[74]
>
> 'Our nation was once strong and wealthy, having lands, Welsh Kings, and laws of their own composition, and in their own language, and thinking about that which they were and that which is their situation now is enough to break the hardest heart and to bring fountains of tears from our eyes.'

Iorwerth's highly politicised historiography traces the current situation of Wales ultimately to the conquest of 1282, seen by him as the historical milestone marking a 'free' and 'independent' Wales from the 'enslaved' nation it became. The Welsh in the 1840s, he states, still have to suffer the rule of men 'who are not of their own choosing' ('nid o'u dewisiad hwy'). He contrasts the tyranny of the English monarchy's hold on Wales with American democracy, exclaiming that, unlike Welsh-American voters, 'the poor Welsh people [of Wales] have no hope of changing their crowned Head except by death' ('nid oes obaith i'r Cymry druain i gael newid eu Pen coronog ond trwy angau'). He ends by praying for the immediate end of all kinds of slavery 'all over the world' ('trwy'r byd'), while also reiterating his central point: 'O! am i ein cenedl . . . gael eu gwaredu . . . o dan draed eu creulon orthrymwyr' ('O! that our nation . . . be delivered . . . from under the feet of their cruel oppressors').[75]

While seeking the support of readers by referring to the oppression visited upon the Welsh in the Old County, *Y Dyngarwr* remained focused on American slavery. Like its sister publication, *Y Cenhadwr Americanaidd*, it published the proceedings of various anti-slavery societies, helping Welsh-speaking campaigners across the United States to establish a national network and thus benefit from each other's efforts. In November 1843, Robert Everett published a record of Utica's Welsh-language anti-slavery society. In a meeting held in Utica's Congregational Chapel on October 30, the society passed five resolutions:

> 1af – Ar fod y Gymdeithas hon i gydweithredu â Chymdeithas Steuben mewn dosbarthu traethodau Cymreig i'n cyd genedl yn y ddinas hon a'i hymgylchoedd.

2. Fod y gymdeithas hon yn cymeradwyo y penderfyniad hyny a basiwyd gan Gynadledd Steuben, sef, fod Cynadledd Wrthgaethiwol i gael ei chynal yn Utica yn yr iaith Gymraeg mor gynted ag y bydd cyfleusdra yn rhoddi i'w chynnal.

3. Ein bod yn teimlo yn ddiolchgar i'r Gweinidogion hyny o wahanol enwadau crefyddol, am y parodrwydd a ddangosasant a'r cefnogiad calon a roddasant yno i gael Cynhadledd yn y ddinas hon; ac hefyd am eu haddewid a roddasant y bydd iddynt ddyfod yma i'w chynal.

4. Nad ydyw y pethau ag y mae y ddwy blaid, sef y Whigiaid a'r Democratiaid yn gwahaniaethu yn eu cylch ond megys dim yn eu pwysfawrogrwydd a'u canlyniadau wrth eu cydmaru a'r CAM a wneir a'r rhai a ddelir mewn caethiwed.

5. Nad yw yn ddigon i ni basio Penderfyniadau fod caethiwed yn ddrwg mawr, heb ein bod yn ymdrechu trwy bob moddion cyfreithlon yn ein cyraedd fel Dinasyddion er hollol ddileu y pechod gwarthus hwn o'r byd.

'1st – That this Society is to work together with the Steuben Society in distributing Welsh essays to those of our nation in this city and its environs.

2. That this society applauds that decision passed by the Steuben Conference, namely, that an Anti-slavery Conference be held in Utica in the Welsh language as soon as convenience allows it to be held.

3. That we feel thankful to those Ministers from different religious denominations for the readiness which they have shown and the hearty support which they have provided there for having a Conference in this city; and also for the promise which they gave that they will come here to hold it.

4. That the things which the two parties, namely the Whigs and the Democrats, are arguing over are but nothing in their significance and their consequences in comparison with the WRONG which is done to those who are held in slavery.

5. That it is not enough for us to pass Resolutions that slavery is a great evil, without us striving through every legal means within our reach as Citizens in order to completely remove this shameful sin from the world.'

The censure directed at 'the two parties' is in many ways characteristic of this period of Welsh-American abolition. Like Louis Menand's description of New England's abolitionists, whose 'renunciation of politics was the secret of their politics', the Welsh abolitionists of Oneida County were refusing to cooperate with the two main political parties, the Whigs and the Democrats.[76] However, rather than rejecting party politics completely, the records of meetings like the one held in Utica reveal that Welsh voices were calling for a new kind of political party, one which would seek to free the slave.

Robert Everett did campaign on behalf of the Liberty Party during the early 1840s, intensifying this activity when James Birney was nominated as the party's presidential candidate in 1844. The Whigs, who had claimed the majority of Welsh America's votes prior to this time, fought back by producing their own Welsh-language publication prior to the election. This came in the form of *Seren Oneida* ('The Oneida Star'), which appeared on 22 October 1844. While presented as a paper, it was really a one-off propaganda stunt, and it appears that only this one pre-election edition was published.[77] The *Seren Oneida* was briefly resurrected in 1845, but it had disappeared for good by the middle of 1846. This Whig-funded publishing venture proved a resounding failure and seems to have had very little impact upon the public face of Welsh America. However, as it attacked Robert Everett, portraying him as a divisive figure, it does show that America's leading Welsh abolitionist met resistance within his own community during the first half of the 1840s. Like the eggs and hymn books thrown at Everett in those early days, this Welsh publication, however unsuccessful, nonetheless constituted an attack aimed at him by other Welsh-Americans (if ultimately inspired and funded by the Whig party organizers).[78]

Everett and his fellow abolitionists persevered, radicalizing Welsh America by means of the pulpit, the printing press and the political party. As will be seen below, the fruits of their labours were readily apparent by 1856, when the Welsh threw their support *en masse* behind the newly formed Republican Party, a support predicated on that party's opposition to slavery. As the resolutions passed by the 1843 Utica meeting demonstrate, the development which ended with unified Welsh backing of the Republican Party began with a rejection of the two old parties, the Whigs and the Democrats. This political move carried Welsh radicals through the experiments of the short-lived anti-slavery parties of the 1840s before eventually landing them solidly in the Republican camp in 1856. The political trajectory of these Welsh abolitionists was extremely similar to the one followed by many of their English-speaking colleagues, although Everett and his supporters often provided a distinctly Welsh articulation of (what were becoming) familiar abolitionist principles. The five resolutions passed in Utica in 1843 refer directly to the Welsh language twice; in addition to 'distributing Welsh essays' to their *cydgenedl* (those of 'the same nation'), the Utica abolitionists specified that their anti-slavery conference is to be conducted 'in the Welsh language'.

The published record of the Utica meeting helps us to detail the way in which abolition spread throughout that large part of Welsh America contained in Oneida County, New York. Counter to what twenty-first-century readers with an urban bias might think, the movement did not start in the 'city' (*dinas*) of Utica, but rather in the small outlying hamlet of Steuben. While the nearby village of Remsen was cited on the title page of Robert Everett's publications, his press was actually located in his Steuben home, the seat of his ministry and the base for his anti-slavery campaigning. Though no individuals are named in the Utica society's proceedings, the thanks given to Steuben's 'Ministers' would have been understood by readers as a reference to the Revd Everett and his Steuben colleagues. Oneida County was not the only place where Welsh America was being politicized in this manner, and some of the other more radical communities were, in fact, located in cities like Cincinnati and Pittsburgh. As early as June 1840 a Welsh-speaking Pittsburgh branch of the American Anti-slavery Society was publishing its own resolutions.[79] However, the cultural capital of Welsh America, Utica, received much of its moral conscience from the nearby Steuben area, thanks largely to the efforts of Robert Everett, his family, and the members of his congregations.

Manuscript evidence like Robert Everett's list of volunteers pledging 'to circulate petitions, & disseminate anti-slavery truth' tell some of the story of how he worked to radicalize his own community.[80] Records like the published resolutions of the Utica meeting suggest some of the ways in which Everett's followers carried their campaign into more densely-populated areas near by. And the literature published on Robert Everett's press shows how he used the printed word to solicit the aid of the whole of Welsh-speaking America. This is acutely evident in the twelve issues of *Y Dyngarwr* which Everett produced in 1843. The essence of *Y Dyngarwr*'s message was not new to Everett's press; the very first issue of his flagship publication, *Y Cenhadwr Americanaidd*, published in January 1840, carried an essay by Cadwalader Jones of Cincinnati bemoaning 'the pitiful situation' ('sefyllfa druenus') of the slaves and asking the Welsh to support the Anti-Slavery Society ('Y Gymdeithas Wrthgaethiwol').[81] *Y Dyngarwr* helped solidify Everett's moral agenda, bolstering the foothold which the *Cenhadwr* had gained in the conscience of Welsh America. Appearing as it did in 1843, it was a part of that crucial early period of activity, the time when the Welsh of America were being pushed from their passive opposition to slavery to a state where 'the principles of abolition were . . . a live issue among them.'[82]

Everett's press, which included *Y Cenhadwr Americanaidd*, the monthly journal serving America's Welsh Congregationalists, was used to support abolition from its start in 1840. If anything, the appearance of *Y Dyngarwr* in 1843, like the publication of Everett's Welsh version of *Uncle Tom's Cabin* ten years later, increased the anti-slavery credentials of his press. As has been seen already in this chapter, the monthly journals of the Welsh-American Methodists and Baptists, as well as the weekly newspaper *Y Drych*, were also solidly anti-slavery by 1856. The contents of a short-lived publication, *Yr Arweinydd* ('The Leader'), show the extent to which the Welsh-American press was committed to the cause. This fortnightly paper, published in Rome, Oneida County, first appeared on 10 January 1858. It lasted for slightly more than three years, ending six months after the start of the Civil War. Edited by Revd William Hughes, a Calvinistic Methodist minister, the contents of *Yr Arweinydd* were almost exclusively religious. It lacked the zeal and fire of *Y Dyngarwr* and *Y Cenhadwr Americanaidd*, and readers apparently found it bland in comparison to *Y Cyfaill o'r Hen Wlad* and *Y Seren Orllewinol*. However, *Yr Arweinydd* did present its readers with anti-slavery material, and the fact that a publication which otherwise eschewed politics in favour of theology did this testifies to the hold which abolition had on Welsh America's public life by 1858.

John Edwards, whose enthusiastic support for the Utica *eisteddfod* was discussed in the last chapter, was *Yr Arweinydd*'s poetry editor. Also known to his readers as Eos Glan Twrch, Edwards was chiefly responsible for the anti-slavery sentiments published on the pages of *Yr Arweinydd*. Back in 1843 Robert Everett and John Howe had used the pages of *Y Dyngarwr* to suggest ways in which Welsh-American writers could use their talents in the struggle against slavery. In 1858 Eos Glan Twrch published a didactic essay in *Yr Arweinydd* which linked the literary talents of Welsh-Americans to their Christian commitment to the anti-slavery cause:

> bydded eu crefydd yn eu dysgu i bleidleisio o du rhyddid a chyfiawnder, ac yn erbyn trais a gormes caethiwed yn ei holl orthrwm a'i ysgelerder. Yn eu cyfarfodydd addysgiadol, a'u Heisteddfodau, bydded llygad eu llawforwyn, *Llenyddiaeth*, bob amser ar law ei meistress, *Crefydd*.[83]

> 'let their religion teach them to vote in favour of freedom and justice, and against slavery's violence and tyranny with all of its oppression and villainy. In their educational meetings and their Eisteddfodau, let the eye of their handmaiden, *Literature*, be always at the service of their mistress, *Religion*.'

Perhaps lacking appropriate contributions at times, the paper's poetry editor often published his own verse in *Yr Arweinydd*. One such poem by the Eos, possibly meant to be sung as a hymn, was on 'Y Beibl' ('The Bible'). In addition to describing the Holy Book as 'freedom . . . for the slave' ('[rh]yddhad i'r . . . caeth'), the verse welcomed people of all colours to the Bible's sanctuary:

> Y newydd taened Seion wiw,
> Nes cyraedd conglau pella'r llawr,
> A dyfod dynion o bob lliw,
> I feddiant o'u gwaddoliaeth fawr.

> 'Let the news be spread through comely Zion,
> Until it reach the farthest corners of the earth,
> And men of every colour come,
> To partake of their great inheritance.'

Though perhaps lacking the acumen of Robert Everett's writings, and though not approaching the elaborately drawn allegory of J. P. Harris's dream vision, the prose and poetry published by Eos Glan Twrch three years before the start of the Civil War shows the degree to which anti-slavery sentiments had penetrated Welsh America's communal ideology. The main purpose of the essay quoted above was to show 'The Best Means . . . for Ensuring the Usefulness of America's Welsh Youth' ('Y Moddion Goreu . . . Er Sicrhau Defnyddioldeb Ieuenctyd Cymry America'); it was not an abolitionist tract, yet it nonetheless included an attack on 'slavery's violence and tyranny'. Eos Glan Twrch suggests that America's Welsh youth were expected to embrace this anti-slavery ideology, echoing Robert Everett's declaration that children be 'taught to sing anti-slavery hymns from their childhood'.

Anti-slavery sentiments had penetrated virtually every corner of Welsh-American print culture by the middle of the 1850s. There was one small exception, *Y Gwron Democrataidd* ('The Democratic Hero'), which appeared briefly in 1856 and then disappeared. This paper, which was apparently published only twice, was really no more than an ephemeral pamphlet pretending to be a newspaper. It was very much like the Whig-funded propaganda published in Welsh during the mid-1840s. The appearance – and immediate disappearance – of the *Gwron* can only be interpreted as a failed attempt on the part of the Democratic party to counter all the pro-Republican material being published by the Welsh-American press.[84] This Democratic publication was brought out during the run-up to the 1856 election in an attempt to deter Welsh-Americans who were flocking to the new Republican Party. As Paul Evans noted in 1914, the simple fact that a publication supported the Democratic Party 'was reason enough for its failure among the Welsh'.[85] The Democrats' venture into the world of Welsh-language publishing failed as soon as it was begun, and the *Gwron* sank without a trace.[86]

In fact, the greatest trace which *Y Gwron Democrataidd* has left is the hostile reaction of the mainstream Welsh-American press. In November 1856, one month after the *Gwron*'s appearance, the Welsh Baptist journal, *Y Seren Orllewinol*, ran a scathing 'review' (*adolygiad*), presumably penned by its editor. The title, which simply reads 'Y Gwron Democrataidd,' is followed by a sentence which attaches a string of pejorative adjectives to the Democrats' publication:

> Mae y papyr disynwyr, anghysson, a chelwyddog hwn yn gabledd ar synwyr cyffredin ei ddarllenwyr. Rhaid fod y golygydd yn meddwl fod y Cymry yn 'ffolach na'r dyn a osododd ei fam yn y ffald' os methant ganfod ei dwyll a'i waeledd.[87]

> 'This senseless, inconsistent, lying paper is an affront to its readers' common sense. The editor must think the Welsh "more stupid than the man who put his mother in the sheep-pen" if they fail to perceive its deceit and lowness.'

The *Seren*'s editor said in no uncertain terms that the *Gwron* supported slavery:

> Amddiffyna gaethwasanaeth yn y modd mwyaf digywilydd; a gwae i bwy bynag a ddywedo air yn erbyn helaethiad y gyfundraeth felltigedig. Mae y rhan fwyaf o'i

> gynnwysiad y fath nad yw hyd y nod pleidwyr y weinyddiaeth halogedig bresennol yn cynnyg son am danynt ond yn unig wrth y dosbarth mwyaf anwybodus a rhwydd eu twyllo.
>
> 'It defends slavery in the most shameless manner; and woe to the person who happens to utter a word against the extension of the accursed institution. Most of its contents are of the sort that not even the supporters of the present sullied government dare mention but only when addressing the most unlearned and easily deceived category [of individual].'

There is only one surviving copy of the *Gwron*, and if it is representative of the publication's short life then we must conclude that the portrait painted by the *Seren* is not entirely accurate. Rather than supporting slavery directly, the *Gwron* described it as a distraction used to divert the attention of Welsh immigrants from their own best interests: 'Yn yr ymdrech presennol am allu politicaidd, ceisiwyd denu eich sylw oddiwrth gadwraeth a pharhad eich hawliau politicaidd, i'r ochr gynhyrfiol o'r frwydr diriogaethol, yn nghylch caethiwed y Negro' ('in the present struggle for political power, an attempt has been made to draw your attention away from the maintenance and continuation of your political rights to the agitating side of the territorial battle relating to the enslavement of the Negro').[88] According to *Y Seren Gorllewinol*'s editor, the Democratic paper attacked most of the other Welsh-American publications, not surprisingly given their open and fiery support for John C. Frémont and the Republican Party. The *Gwron* referred to Robert Everett's *Cenhadwr* as 'one of the "Black Republicans" ' ('un o'r "Gweriniaid Duon" '), and it accused *Y Seren Orllewinol* of 'selling out' ('ymwerthu') to the Republicans.

While the *Seren*'s editor apparently exaggerated the 'crimes' of the Democratic publication in places, these last accusations are more believable. Not wanting to stand alone in a field dominated by Republican publications, the *Gwron*'s editor apparently misrepresented the politics of *Y Cyfaill o'r Hen Wlad*, claiming that the Calvinistic Methodists' journal 'opposed the Republicans, and supported Pierce [and] Buchanan' ('wrthwynebu y Republicaniaid, a phleidio Pierce, Buchanan'). In fact, while the *Cyfaill*'s editor had since the journal's start in 1838 professed political neutrality, he had come out solidly against slavery. In September 1856, one month before the *Gwron*'s abortive appearance, the *Cyfaill* had published a piece praising the resolution of a Wisconsin Methodist Congregation to condemn slavery. The editor, William Rowlands, used some carefully crafted rhetoric in attempting to walk a middle path between his old principle that religious figures should not lend direct support to political parties and his desire to see slavery ended.

> Mae yn hyfrydwch genym weled cynnrychiolwyr eglwysi y Trefnyddion Calfinaidd yn Wisconsin mor Fethodistaidd a pheidio 'anog neb i bleidio unrhyw blaid wladyddol fel y cyfryw,' ac eto yn medru dwyn eu tystiolaeth yn eofn, yn syml, ac yn benderfynol yn erbyn drygau caethwasiaeth.[89]

'It pleases us to see that the representatives of the Calvinistic Conveners in Wisconsin are so Methodist as to refuse "to urge anybody to support any political party as such," while still being able to bear their witness fearlessly, simply, and determinedly against the evils of slavery.'

Rowlands then reiterated the neutral editorial policy which he had professed for nearly twenty years, adding: 'Eto gwyddom fod corff y genedl, yn gystal a rhan luosocaf ein derbynwyr, o blaid rhyddid mewn cyssylltiad â Freemont' ('Yet we know that the body of the nation, along with the most numerous portion of our subscribers, are in favour of freedom in alliance with Frémont'). He thus went through the motions of rejecting politics while at the same time stating that the majority of his readers, and the majority of Welsh-Americans, supported 'Frémont and freedom'. Before ending, the *Cyfaill*'s editor did say that he did not support the methods – 'llwybrau,' literally 'paths' – used by some abolitionists, but this caveat was only presented as an aside while welcoming the new Republican Party: 'y mae yn llawenydd calon genym ni, wedi dysgwyl am flynyddau[,] gael plaid wladol y gallwn rhoddi ein pleidlais gyda hi yn gydwybodol o du rhyddid ac yn erbyn caethwasiaeth' ('it is our heart's own pleasure, after waiting for years, to have a political party to which we can give our vote conscientiously in favour of freedom and against slavery').

William Rowlands, the most 'neutral' of Welsh America's editors, thus stated in no uncertain terms that he was giving his own vote to the new Republican Party. Moreover, the *Cyfaill*'s editor could count among his anti-slavery credentials the fact that he had used his journal to publish one of the two Welsh translations of *Uncle Tom's Cabin* which appeared in America during the early 1850s. *Y Gwron Democrataidd* had indeed misrepresented the *Cyfaill*'s stance, and the *Seren*'s Baptist editor came to the defence of his Calvinistic Methodist colleague:

Nid ydym yn prisio llawer am gableddau dynion drwg, yn ein beio am bleidio egwyddorion daionus rhinwedd a chyfiawnder, ond am dderbyn eu canmoliaeth am gydsynio â hwy i wneud drwg a chefnogi trais a chreulondeb, mae hyny yn ormod i ni ei oddef. Da genym nad yw y 'Cyfaill' yn euog o bleidio y pethau anfad y dywed y Gwron ei fod, ac yn hyn eto y mae haerllugrwydd Gol. y Gwron yn ymddangos. Diau mai ei amcan oedd dangos fod ganddo rhyw Gyhoeddiad Cymreig yn debyg iddo ei hun.

'We do not place much value in the blasphemies of evil men, blaming us for supporting the good principles of virtue and justice, but as for accepting their praise for agreeing with them to do evil and support violence and oppression, that is too much for us to bear. It pleases us [to say] that the *Cyfaill* is not guilty of supporting the bad things which the *Gwron* says it supports, and in this again the impudence of the *Gwron*'s editor is made evident. It is certain that his intention was to show that he had some other Welsh Publication similar to his own.'

The *Seren*'s editor finished his reply to the *Gwron* by dancing on the grave of his dead enemy, noting with pleasure that the Democratic publication had already ceased to exist: 'Gwelsom . . . fod y "Gwron" wedi diflanu gyda yr ail rifyn. Yr oedd yn llawn bryd iddo' ('We saw . . . that the *Gwron* has disappeared with the second number. It was high time for it to do so').[90]

It is impossible to find support for the ill-fated *Gwron* on the pages of the other surviving publications, and, as it was such a complete divergence from the political norm of Welsh-American print culture, it seems that most of Welsh America's intelligentsia paid it the ultimate insult by completely ignoring it. At the same time, it is no surprise that *Y Seren Orllewinol* produced such a caustic response in November 1856; while Robert Everett and his *Cenhadwr* had been consistently drawing the attention of Welsh-Americans to the anti-slavery virtues of the Republican Party, the *Seren* became wholeheartedly absorbed with party politics during the 1856 election season.

In October 1856 the *Seren* was presented under a special title, 'Yr Etholiad Llywyddol' ('The Presidential Election'); the entire issue was devoted to what constitutes, in effect, a Welsh-language Republican manifesto. It is an intentionally eclectic document, beginning with articles gleaned from other Welsh-American publications in what must be interpreted as a way of demonstrating Welsh America's united political front. In doing so, the *Seren*'s editor was following the lead of a new Welsh paper, *Y Cymro Americaidd* ('The American Welshman'), founded in New York City in May 1855 in order to compete with *Y Drych*.[91] Thus the first page of the *Seren*'s special election issue reprinted an editorial published in *Y Cymro Americaidd* that September (the original of which has apparently not survived). The *Cymro*'s editor, J. Henry Puleston, himself a Republican Party organizer, begins by urging all Welsh-Americans to join him in the fight for freedom:

> *Anwyl Gydwladwyr*, – Wedi penderfynu i neillduo ychydig wythnosau yn gwbl at achos Rhyddid yn eich plith, er ymdrechu eich cynorthwyo yn yr ymdrechfa bwysig ddyfodol, a dymuno arnoch wneud eich rhan er hwylusu Ymadrodd rhydd, Kansas rydd, Llafur rhydd, a'r Undeb, yr wyf yn awyddus i wasgaru yn eich plith y fath wybodaeth ag a'ch galluoga i weithio yn gyfiawn yn yr achos.[92]
>
> '*Dear Fellow Countrymen*, – Having decided to devote several weeks completely to the cause of Freedom amongst us, in order to strive to help you in the future important struggle, and desiring you to do your part in order to aid free Speech, a free Kansas, free Labour, and the Union, I am eager to disseminate amongst you such information as will enable you to labour righteously in the cause.'

Puleston then proceeds to summarize and praise the various pro-Republican and anti-slavery articles gathered together for the election issues of the *Cymro* and the *Seren*. He urges readers to analyse this collection of material carefully and to be wary of the 'deceitful traps' ('maglau dichellgar') which the Democrats are preparing for them. Using that ancient emotive term, he urges 'hil Gomer' – 'the descendants of Gomer' – to recall that they have 'always stood in favour of freedom and justice' ('bob amser wedi sefyll o blaid rhyddid a chyfiawnder').[93] He describes Frémont as a candidate who should appeal to the Welsh voter for several reasons: 'Y mae Fremont yn gyfaill nid yn unig i'r caeth, ond hefyd i'r ymfudydd; mewn gair cyfaill dynoliaeth, casawr gorthrwm, a Phrotestant gwirioneddol ydyw' ('Frémont is a friend not only of the slave, but also of the immigrant; in a word, he is a friend of humanity, a hater of oppression, and a true Protestant'). In concluding this introductory editorial, Puleston appeals again to his readers' pride, calling upon all Welsh people in America 'to ease the way of Freedom in this important era, and by this we will maintain our national honour without tarnishing it' ('hwyluso ymdaith Rhyddid yn y cyfnod pwysig presennol, trwy hyn y cadwn i fynu ein hanrhydedd cenedlaethol heb ei difwyno').[94]

Of all the articles gathered from other publications and presented in the *Seren*'s special election issue, the least enthusiastic endorsement for Frémont and the Republicans came in the editorial quoted above which William Rowlands first published in the *Cyfaill*. However, despite pretending to eschew the worldly stain of politics, the Calvinistic Methodist journal's editor described the Republicans as 'a political party to which we can give our vote conscientiously in favour of freedom and against slavery.' Though appearing lukewarm when compared to some of the fiery pieces with which it was reprinted in the *Seren*, Rowlands's editorial does nonetheless come down solidly in favour of 'Freedom and Frémont'.

Not surprisingly, one of the most memorable endorsements was reprinted from Robert Everett's *Y Cenhadwr Americanaidd*.[95] This is a compelling piece of persuasive prose, working on several levels ranging from the theological to the politically savvy to the emotional. It also appeals to Welsh pride, claiming to have heard an American say that: 'y Cymry ydyw y genedl fwyaf dros ryddid o neb o'r ymfudwyr yma, a'u bod yn llawer mwy felly na lioedd o hiliogaeth yr hen Buritaniaid' ('the Welsh are the nation most in favour of freedom of all of the immigrants here, and that they are much more so than hosts of the race of the old Puritans'). Taking a chapter out of the Anglophone Americans' popular history, the editorial states that the Welsh in the United States outshine the descendants of those Puritan settlers so lauded in mainstream nationalistic discourse as the founders of American freedom. It also contrasted the freedom which his countrymen were enjoying under American democracy with the unfair political system which they left behind in the Old Country, the 'high rents and heavy taxes' ('y rhenti uchel, trethoedd trymion') which oppress poor farmers in Britain and the way in which Welsh Nonconformists were 'forced to pay to maintain an [Anglican] religion which [they] did not love' ('orfod talu i gynnal crefydd nad ydym yn ei charu').[96]

Having reminded Welsh-Americans of the freedom they had found in their adopted country, the *Cenhadwr*'s essay then twists the rhetorical knife by stating that, despite all this, they are subject 'to a government of slave-masters' ('o dan llywodraeth caethfeistri').[97] It returns to what is described as the Welshman's innate love of freedom, supporting the point by echoing the editors of the *Seren* and the *Cymro* and noting that 'just about all of the Welsh[-American] Publications have come out as one man in favour of the cause' ('y Cyhoeddiadau Cymreig o'r bron yn dyfod allan fel un gwr dros yr achos'). Practical advice is offered as well, urging Welshmen to get their citizenship papers in order and claim the right to vote. The piece describes the mobilization of Welsh Republican voters as 'preparing for the day of the great battle' ('ymbaratoi erbyn dydd y frwydr fawr'). The Republican Party is called 'Byddin Rhyddid,' 'Freedom's Army', and Frémont is made into an American version of 'Moses, gwaredwr Israel' ('Moses, saviour of Israel').[98]

The *Cenhadwr*'s editorial, reprinted for the benefit of the *Seren*'s readers, paints a nasty picture of the Democrats. They are connected with the violence that was rending the nation from Bleeding Kansas to the Senate's floor, recently stained with blood by Preston Brooks 'who tried to kill the renowned Charles Sumner . . . only because he spoke his mind in a speech against slavery' ('a geisiodd ladd yr enwog Charles Sumner . . . yn unig am draethu ei feddwl mewn araeth yn erbyn caethiwed').[99] According to the *Cenhadwr*, the only 'laws' upheld by the Democratic Party were those of force and oppression: 'Eu cyfraith hwy ydyw y rhychdryll, y pastwn, a'r gyllell, a'r "Trecha treisied, a'r gwanna' gwaedded" ' ('Their law is the rifle, the cudgel, and knife', and "Let the strongest despoil, and let the weakest scream" ').[100] Like the imagery which R. D. Thomas would use two years later in attacking his bardic enemy, this rhetoric is grounded in a description of a characteristically American kind of violence, that being perpetrated by pro-slavery ruffians in Kansas. However, this analysis of United States politics is clinched with a traditional Welsh proverb – *trecha treisied, a'r gwanna gwaedded* – used for centuries by Welsh people to describe those who rule by force instead of law.

In addition to these editorials gleaned from the *Cymro*, the *Cyfaill* and the *Cenhadwr, Y Seren Orllewinol*'s editor contributed his own treatise to this special election issue. Opening with the question 'Paham y Mae y Cymry yn Werinwyr?' – 'Why are the Welsh Republicans?' – he then proceeds to present a dizzying number of answers, fielding a range of theological, moral and political reasons. This editorial also appeals to the emotional gut-level: 'Mae gormes fel tân ar groen y Cymro' ('Oppression is like fire on the skin of a Welshman'). The *Seren*'s special election issue augmented these four editorials with a potent assemblage of various pro-Republican and anti-slavery pieces. There was an article by the poet-preacher R. L. Herbert saying, in effect, that Welsh-Americans had no choice in the coming election: they had to vote for Frémont because the contest would decide 'whether *Freedom* or *Oppression* would rule' the United States ('pa un ai *Rhyddid* ai *Gorthrwm* a lywodraetha').[101] This was followed by a poem by Ohio's poet-preacher, Dewi Emlyn, entitled

'Achwyniadau y Caethion' ('The Slaves' Complaints'), which in turn was followed by a piece praising Frémont. Then came a short treatise called, simply 'Buchanan is Two-Faced' ('Buchanan yn Ddau-Wynebog'), followed by a Welsh translation of the Republican Party's official platform.[102]

While evidence provided by other Welsh publications supports the same conclusion, the October 1856 issue of *Y Seren Orllewinol* substantiates beyond any doubt the claim that Welsh-Americans were flocking *en masse* to the Republican Party. Paul Evans – combining a study of the Welsh press, the English-language Oneida County Press, and oral history – reached this same conclusion more than ninety years ago:

> In Oneida County there was the same general union of Welshmen in the new party as elsewhere. They held a meeting in Holland Patent, October 11, 1856, at which were present delegates from all of the Welsh settlements in the county. Reports from these delegates showed that in many of the towns nearly every Welsh voter was openly for Freedom and Frémont while in several others the 'black list' was hopelessly small.[103]

The vast majority were voting 'for Freedom and Frémont', yet it was the first of the pair, 'Freedom', which brought them into the new party. It would appear that Welsh-Americans on the whole were one-issue voters at this time; they were becoming Republicans because that party opposed the slave-owning powers.

The Welsh-language publications of the United States were used to galvanize the actions of abolitionists, and in doing so they drew upon the combined literary and theological talents of America's Welsh intelligentsia. Analysing the way in which this literature translated into tangible political support for the Republican Party is a study in the relationship between words and actions, between theory and praxis. Stanley Cavell has focused attention on Ralph Waldo Emerson's views on the topic: 'Philosophy cannot abolish slavery, and it can only call for abolition to the extent, or in the way, that it can call for thinking.'[104] Writers and publishers like Robert Everett helped transform the thinking of Welsh America, and they did so using all the literary, cultural and religious resources available to them. In the second issue of *Y Cenhadwr Americanaidd* Everett had urged his readers to 'Pray for Slaves' ('Gweddio Dros y Caethion'), focusing on the mental act of remembering. He presented five aspects to this remembering:

> 1. Dylem eu cofio mewn gweddi, oblegid mawredd y gorthrymder y maent dano.
> 2. Dylem eu cofio, o herwydd eu bod mor ddiymddiffynol.
> 3. Dylem eu cofio, oblegid fod cymmaint yn eu hangofio.
> 4. Dylem eu cofio, oblegid eu cymmeriad personol a moesol.
> 5. Byddai eu cofio yn fynych ger bron ein Tad nefol . . . dan ddylanwadau ac arweiniad ei Ysbryd, yn debyg o'n dwyn i deimlo yn addas tuag atynt yn eu

hadfynd, ac i weithredu yn effro a diflino yn ofn yr Arglwydd er eu rhyddhad a'u hiechydwriaeth.

'1. We should remember them [i.e., the slaves], because of the greatness of the oppression they are suffering.
2. We should remember them, because they are so defenceless.
3. We should remember them, because so many others forget them.
4. We should remember them, because of their personal and moral character.
5. Remembering them frequently before our heavenly Father . . . under the influence and guidance of his Spirit is likely to bring us to feel appropriately towards them in their affliction, and to take action in a wide-awake and untiring fashion in fear of the Lord in order to free them and bring about their salvation.'

If Ralph Waldo Emerson thought that philosophy 'could only call for abolition to the extent . . . that it can call for thinking', Robert Everett presented a different view of the relationship between thought and action. Focusing thought through prayer led to morally appropriate feelings – 'i deimlo yn addas', 'to feel appropriately', are his words – and these feelings in turn are said to engender action. Everett describes a chain reaction, providing Welsh-Americans with a template allowing them to connect their own personal religious beliefs with the process of moral meditation which leads to direct political action. Moreover, he asked his readers to follow this practice 'daily before the Lord' ('yn feunyddiol ger bron yr Arglwydd'), thus motivating action with what was for him the ultimate leverage, each Christian's individual relationship with his or her God.

As was discussed earlier in this chapter, Robert Everett, John Howe and Eos Glan Twrch all provided views on the relationship between literature and the campaign against slavery. They urged the Welsh-language poets and writers of the United States to compose verse and narrative which would help the process by which thought and prayer engendered action. The historiographical efforts of the Welsh-American press also promoted this alliance between literature and abolition, presenting figures from the Welsh past as heroes for the present. One of these was Iolo Morganwg (or Edward Williams), a poet and thinker who was at the centre of a group of radical eighteenth-century Welsh *literati*. Calling himself 'the Bard of Liberty', Iolo had been an outspoken opponent of slavery; in addition to attacking slavery in his writings, he took actions of other kinds which made him an example to future abolitionists. Iolo Morganwg died in 1826, and fifteen years after the bard's death *Y Cyfaill o'r Hen Wlad* presented his biography to its American readers, holding Iolo up as a model of moral behaviour:

I Edward Williams (Iolo Morganwg) yr oedd amrai frodyr, y rhai, yn moreuddydd eu hoes, a ymfudasant i'r India Orllewinol, lle y cynnyrchasant eiddo mawr. Buont feirw yn olynol, a disgynodd yr holl eiddo i Iolo, yr hwn oedd ganddo

> deulu mawr, ac mor dlawd ag y dichon maen-saer a bardd fod. Ei gyfeillion a'i llon-gyfarchasant ar ei dynged dda; ond, er eu syndod, na dderbyniai byth geiniog o honynt, oblegid mai gwerth rhyddid, esgyrn, gwaed ac eneidiau ei gyd-greaduriaid oeddynt. "Y mae yn felldigedig," ebai, "a dygai felldith Duw ar fy mhlant – nis mynaf ddim o hono." Glynodd wrth y penderfyniad hwn.[105]
>
> 'Edward Williams (Iolo Morganwg) had several brothers, who, early in life, emigrated to the West Indies, where they accumulated substantial possessions. They died in succession, and all of the property came down to Iolo, who had a large family, and was as poor as it is possible for a stone-mason and bard to be. His friends congratulated him on his good fate; but, to their surprise, he never received a penny of [the monies left him], because they carried the price of the freedom, bones, blood and souls of his fellow-creatures. "It is accursed," he said, "and it would bring the curse of God upon my children – I do not want any of it." He stuck to this decision.'

Like that Welsh-American poet R. L. Herbert who wrote in 1856 that voters had no choice but to vote for freedom, the story of Iolo Morganwg's life is turned into a narrative which rules out the possibility of moral equivocation.

By the time of the 1856 election, the vast majority of Welsh America's cultural resources – its chapels, its presses, the talents of its poets and writers – were being used to support the Republican Party. The Welsh knew that they constituted a tiny fraction of the US population, but Robert Everett reminded them that their vote could still make a difference:

> Yr ydym ni y Cymry yn un o'r llawer cenedlaethau sydd yn gwneud i fynu ddinasyddion America: ac er nad ydym ond cenedl fechan mewn cydmariaeth, eto yr ydym yn 'Benjamin fychan,' yn mysg y llwythau, ac mae yr un un rhwymedigaethau pwysig yn gorphwys arnom ni . . . Gallai y cyfan . . . droi ar fwyafrif bychan, a gallwn ni fod yn gwneud i fynu y mwyafrif hwnw.[106]
>
> 'We the Welsh are one of the many peoples which constitute America's citizens: and although we are but a small nation by comparison, still we are a "little Benjamin" amongst the tribes, and the same important obligations rest upon us . . . The whole thing might . . . turn upon a small majority, and we can make up that majority.'

While helping make up the vote which handed states like New York, Wisconsin and Ohio to Frémont, the Welsh-American 'little Benjamin' was not nearly enough of a 'small majority' to tip the balance in the end. Although Buchanan gained only a minority of the popular vote (45 per cent), his 174 electoral votes put him well ahead of Frémont who, having won eleven northern states, had a total of 114.[107]

Buchanan's 1856 victory was seen as a disaster for freedom, and widely described as such by the Welsh-American press. In a June 1858 editorial, Robert

Everett saw the divisive administration's actions as sowing the seeds of disunion:

> Tra mae dwy gyfundrefn mor wrthwynebol i'w gilydd (sef caethiwed a rhyddid,) yn cydfodoli dan yr un Cyfansoddiad gwladwriaethol, a'r un Gydgynghorfa, a'r un Llywydd, dan rwymau llw swyddogol, i ymgeleddu ac amddiffyn y ddau drefniant, pa fodd y gallwn ddysgwyl i'r ddwyblaid gael eu boddloni.[108]
>
> 'As long as two systems so opposed to each other (namely slavery and freedom) co-exist under the same national Constitution, and the same Congress, and the same President, under the obligations of official oaths to protect and defend the two organizations, how can we expect the two sides to be satisfied?'

It was also in June 1858 that Abraham Lincoln delivered his 'House Divided' speech. Placing the key sentences from that oration side by side with Everett's editorial shows a striking degree of similarity:

> 'A house divided against itself cannot stand.' I believe this government cannot endure, permanently half *slave* and half *free*. I do not expect the Union to be *dissolved* – I do not expect the house to *fall* – but I do expect it will cease to be divided. It will become *all* one thing, or *all* the other.[109]

Like the more famous members of the Republican Party, Welsh Republicans were describing the failings of the current Democratic president in terms of an expanding crisis which was increasingly difficult to address. In addition to suffering through the years of Buchanan's 'pro-slavery' government, another experience gave the writings of Welsh-American abolitionists a sharper edge during the second half of the 1850s – the violent events in 'bleeding Kansas'.

Several of Welsh America's religious leaders had preached pacifism during the early 1850s, and the Welsh-American press had published material arguing in favour of the peace movement. In 1850 *Y Seren Orllewinol* printed 'Anerchiad Cymdeithas Heddwch', 'The Peace Society's Address', which stated in plain terms that 'all sorts of wars were inconsistent with the spirit of Christianity and the well-being of humanity' ('fod pob math o ryfeloedd yn anghysson ag ysbryd Cristionogaeth a daioni dynolryw').[110] Eight months later *Y Cenhadwr Americanaidd* published an essay by William R. Jones of Neenah, Wisconsin, entitled 'Rhagorfraint Heddwch' ('The Privilege of Peace'). The journal's editor, Robert Everett, prefaced the treatise with his own supportive comments:

> Yr ydym yn ddiolchgar i ysgrifenydd y llinellau canlynol . . . am ei sylwadau ar yr egwyddor werthfawr a bleidir yma ganddo. Credym nad oes eisiau dim i roi terfyn effeithiol ar ryfeloedd a thywallt gwaed, ond i'r werin yn gyffredinol gael ei dwyn i ddeall, i goleddu ac i fabwysiadu egwyddorion heddwch ac i sefyll yn gadarn mewn gwrthwynebrwydd i ryfel.[111]

> 'We are grateful to the author of the following lines . . . for his observations on the valuable principle which he supports here. We believe that nothing more is needed to put an effective end to wars and the spilling of blood than to bring the people in general to understand, to embrace and to adopt the principles of peace and to stand firmly in opposition to war.'

Connections between Welsh America and the Old Country helped channel this pacifism into the Welsh pulpits and publications of the United States, for Nonconformist Welsh ministers were playing a key role in Britain's peace movement at this time.[112] In 1849 the Welshman Henry Richard became secretary of the British Peace Society. Richard wrote for the Society's journal, *The Herald of Peace*, and several years later he also became its editor.[113] Another Welsh stalwart of the British peace movement was Samuel Roberts, a well-known minister, author and radical thinker whose commitment to pacifism would draw heavy criticism from the Welsh-American press during the Civil War.

At the start of the 1850s Robert Everett had urged his fellow Welsh-Americans to 'embrace and to adopt the principles of peace and to stand firmly in opposition to war'. And, while it is impossible to gauge the feelings of those people who have left no written record of their beliefs, it appears that the moral and religious leaders of Welsh America were indeed embracing the principle of pacifism at mid century. However, by the start of the Civil War they were for the most part prepared to jettison this commitment to peace. Several factors contributed to the decline of pacifism in Welsh America, not the least of which was the bloody guerrilla war which raged in Kansas during the 1850s. By 1856 Robert Everett was using the *Cenhadwr* to support the armed free-soil settlers in Kansas; this was not at all surprising, for his son John was one of them. *Y Drych* presented the news from 'bleeding Kansas' in a way which favoured the actions of the anti-slavery faction: the 'settlers from the Free States had to take up arms in self defence' ('[yr] ymfudwyr o'r Talaethau Rhyddion wedi eu gorfodi i gymeryd arfau i fyny mewn hunanamddiffyniad'), for 'the supporters of Slavery . . . had committed a multitude of outrages' ('Mae pleidwyr Caethwasiaeth . . . wedi cyflawni lluaws o ysgelerderau').[114]

The political resolve of Welsh-speaking Americans had been consolidated in the camp of the Republican Party during the 1856 election; if anything, the events of the following four years served to strengthen this resolve even more. When the 1860 election came, the resources of Welsh America were again thrown behind the Republicans. As early as July of that year *Y Seren Orllewinol* was engaged in heavy campaigning, publishing a Welsh translation of the Republican Party's platform as well as a translation of a letter by William Seward intended to display party unity. The same issue of the journal carried an article about the up-coming Republican convention, telling readers that 'cyfeillion rhyddid a chyfiawnder', 'the friends of freedom and justice', will be happy to know that Lincoln was tipped as the party's nominee.[115] The

Republicans' hold on the Welsh-American vote was implicitly acknowledged by the Democratic Party; there was no attempt to field another version of the aborted *Gwron Democrataidd*.

Not surprisingly, Lincoln's election victory was roundly applauded by the Welsh-American press. The weekly newspaper, *Y Drych*, declared that 'the battle was hot, and the victory is glorious' ('Yr oedd y frwydr yn boeth, ac mae y fuddugoliaeth yn ogoneddus').[116] All three of the denominational journals responded with similar joy. The editor of *Y Seren Orllewinol* declared with confidence that the country was now in safe hands: 'Mae genym bob ymddyried yn noethineb Mr. Lincoln' ('We have every confidence in Mr. Lincoln's wisdom').[117] Having backed the winning party in 1860, having so tightly yoked the resources of their press and pulpit to Lincoln's campaign, Welsh-speaking Americans gained a new enfranchisement, a more deeply-vested interest in the political life of the United States.

If the groundswell of support for Lincoln tightened the hold of the Republican Party upon Welsh America's political consciousness, the events surrounding John Brown's failed insurrection had already sharpened the edge of Welsh-America's moral conscience. Following Brown's execution, even *Y Cyfaill o'r Hen Wlad*, the most cautious and 'politically neutral' of the Welsh-American publications, added its voice to the chorus proclaiming Brown to be freedom's martyr. In February 1860 it published a translation of Victor Hugo's well-publicized letter.

> Y Caethion hyn, y Negröaid hyn, mynai dyn gwyn, dyn rhydd, un John Brown, eu gwaredu. Yn sicr, os ydyw gwrthryfel (*insurection*) yn ddyledswydd grefyddol mewn unrhyw amgylchiad – y mae yn erbyn caethwasiaeth. Dymuniad John Brown oedd dechreu y gwaith da trwy waredigaeth y caethion yn Virginia.[118]

> 'A white man, a free man, one John Brown, strove to deliver these Slaves, these Negroes. Indeed, if insurrection be considered a religious duty in any situation – it is [a religious duty] against slavery. John Brown's desire was to begin the good work by achieving the deliverance of the slaves in Virginia.'

The editor of the *Cyfaill* printed Hugo's translated words in order to endorse them. The Welsh Methodist journal was presenting its readers with a radical interpretation of Brown's actions; it was suggesting that Christians could – and perhaps even should – view armed insurrection against slave owners as 'a religious duty'.

Brown's execution remained a favourite topic of discussion for some time, and it was thus no surprise that, when the next Utica *Eisteddfod* was announced, 'John Brown' was set as the subject for a composition in the strict *englyn* metre. The winning poem was composed by that stalwart supporter of the Utica festival, Eos Glan Twrch, and it was later published. The poem's six short stanzas provide a narrative summary of Brown's armed struggle against slavery.

The first verse (or *englyn*) describes his efforts in Kansas as a struggle against 'gorthrymwyr [y] caethwas', 'the slave's oppressors'. The poem's final two *englynion* describe Brown's ill-fated attack on Harpers Ferry, Virginia, ending with an interpretation of the resulting execution's significance:

Virginia, drigfa drygfoes – a thywell
    Fam caethiwed eisoes;
  I'r ddalfa mewn traha'i troes,
  A mwy'n iawn, mynu'i einioes!

Rhoi'n Brown ar hyn o bryd – wna'i i oddef
    Dienyddol ddedryd;
  A'i enw'n sarn, ond mewn barn byd,
  Merthyr oedd yn mhorth rhyddyd![119]

'Virginia, dwelling-place of evil – and the dark
    Mother of slavery already;
  He [Brown] was interned in the prison with arrogance,
  And more than that, his life was demanded!

Our Brown given now – to suffer
    A judgement of execution;
  His name trampled upon, but in the opinion of the world
  He was a Martyr in freedom's gate!'

As always, the Utica *Eisteddfod* in 1861 was held on New Year's Day. It was a charged time; Lincoln had won the presidential election less than two months previously, triggering flowery praise and self-congratulations on the pages of the Welsh-American press. The new president, however, was not to be inaugurated until the first week of March, and Buchanan's ignominious stint as a 'lame duck' president witnessed the beginning of the Union's dissolution. On December 20 – twelve days before the Welsh bards gathered in Utica – the state of South Carolina passed its secession ordinance. The event had been foreseen by *Y Drych*'s editor; in the 1 December 1860 edition of the paper he noted that Lincoln's election by the free states was being used as 'an excuse' by Southern secessionists:

> mae y ffaith fod y Rhydd Dalaethau wedi mynu clywed eu llais am unwaith, wedi taflu rhai o'r Talaethau Caethwasaidd i deimladau anfoddog a hyd yn oed gythruddedig. Mae yn fwy na thebyg nad ydyw etholiad Lincoln ond math o rithesgus dros y cam y mae rhai o'r Talaethau Deheuol yn fygwth gymeryd[.][120]

> 'the fact that the Free States have demanded that their voice be heard for a change has thrown some of the Slave States into discontented and even ferocious feelings.

> It is more than likely that Lincoln's election is but a flimsy excuse for the step that some of the Southern States are threatening to take.'

People were already talking of forcing the discontented states to remain in the Union, but the paper's editor felt that 'there is a kind of nasty sound to our ears in the word *force*' ('mae rhyw swn cas i'n clustiau ni yn y gair *gorfodi*').[121] In the event of disunion, he continued, the free states should be happy enough to be rid of 'the filth and pollution of Slavery's accursed plague' ('ffieidd-dra a halogrwydd pla melldithfawr Caethwasiaeth').[122]

Y Drych's editor set out another important point before his readers; 'forcing' the slave states to remain in the Union would mean civil war: 'In order to force, one would have to send an army of soldiers there, civil war would surely begin to fertilize the south's sunny glades with human blood' ('Wrth orfodi, rhaid anfon yno fyddin o filwyr, bydd rhyfel cartrefol yn sicr o ddechreu gwrteithio llenyrch heulog y deheu â gwaed dynol').[123] The exact language used by the newspaper bears close scrutiny for it combines a shrinking from the spectre of war with an element of belligerent boasting. The North does not want war, the editor suggests, but if war should come it will be Southern soil which is stained with blood. Moreover, the kinds of expressions one might expect here – for example, *cochi â gwaed*, 'to redden with blood', or *staenio â gwaed*, 'to stain with blood' – are passed by in favour of another phrase; he writes that the 'South's sunny glades' will be 'fertilized' with blood. His choice of the verb *gwrteithio*, 'to fertilize', is significant. The suggestion is that, however horrible and undesirable such a conflict might be, if war does come it will cultivate the land, perhaps in order to plant a new and better society there.

Whatever the reasons for choosing these exact words, the newspaper was once again accurate in its prediction. The Rebels fired on Fort Sumter in April, starting a civil war which would eventually stain the ground with far more blood than any of *Y Drych*'s readers could have ever imagined. According to *Y Seren Orllewinol* the coming of war was 'the worst blow that our adopted country has ever suffered' ('yr ergyd gwaethaf a ddyoddefodd ein gwlad fabwysiedig erioed').[124] When the news reached Wales, the editor of one monthly journal, *Y Cronicl*, claimed to have written his own headline as if in a dream, not believing the words which he himself was putting on paper: 'WAR IN AMERICA. – We are dreaming as we write these words. We cannot believe that we are seeing them, though they have come to hand, and we're looking at them' ('RHYFEL YN AMERICA. – Yr ydym yn breuddwydio wrth ysgrifenu y geiriau hyn. Nis medrwn gredu ein bod yn eu gweled, er eu dod i lawr, ac edrych arnynt').[125] While other people in Wales reacted in a similar fashion, the feelings of *Y Cronicl*'s editor must have been amplified by personal concerns; his brother, the Revd Samuel Roberts – a staunch supporter of pacifism, abolition and other radical causes – had in 1857 led a small number of immigrants to found a Welsh settlement in Tennessee. By the time his brother was composing this headline back in Wales, Samuel Roberts and his fellow-settlers were in a difficult situation; they were anti-slavery and pro-Union residents of a slave state moving to secede from the Union.

Benjamin T. Jones was another Welshman living in the South when the Civil War started. An ardent abolitionist, he was working as a missionary in Marion, Arkansas. On the morning of the first Sunday in May 1861, Jones was on his way to preach. It was a volatile time, less than a month after the fall of Fort Sumter and the very week that Arkansas's state legislature was voting to secede from the Union. Before reaching his destination, the young missionary was accosted by secessionist ruffians.

> [F]el yr oeddwn yn myned i'r capel i bregethu, daeth deuddeg o ddynion drygionus ar geffylau i gyfarfod â mi, yn gorchymyn trwy fygythion fy mod i ymadael oddiyno yn ddi-oed. Felly cymerasant fi ymaith yn uniongyrchol, a bu raid i mi ymadael heb ond y nesaf i ddim o'm dillad, llyfrau, arian, &c – a da oedd cael y bywyd, o herwydd wedi i'r dorf derfysglyd dd'od yn nghyd . . . yr oeddynt am fyned â fy mywyd, o herwydd fy mod, meddant, yn *Abolitionist*, hyny yw, am *ddiddymu caethiwed*. Ond o ddaioni yr Arglwydd cefais fyw[.][126]

> 'As I was going to chapel to preach, twelve wicked men on horseback came to meet me, ordering me by way of threats to leave there without delay. They thus took me away quickly, and I had to leave with next to none of my clothes, books, money, &c. – and I was lucky to get away with my life, because after the riotous mob came together . . . they wanted to take my life, because I was, they said, an *Abolitionist*, that is, in favour of *ending slavery*. But by the Lord's goodness my life was spared.'

Benjamin Jones managed to escape from Arkansas, apparently helped through Tennessee by Samuel Roberts. He eventually reached a Welsh settlement in Allen County, Ohio. The place was called Gomer, named after that legendary ancestor of the Welsh: though not returning to Wales, Jones had returned to what was – at least culturally, if not geographically – familiar ground. He was immediately offered work as a schoolteacher and, having settled into a new, safer existence, he sat down to write a letter to his mother. She lived in Llanidloes back in Wales, and Jones sent his long epistle to her via Robert Everett, giving the editor permission to publish it in *Y Cenhadwr Americanaidd*.

The story of the abolitionist's narrow escape was presented on the journal's pages with all of the personal letter's trappings, beginning 'Fy anwyl, anwyl Fam' ('My dear, dear Mother') and ending 'Oddiwrth eich anwyl a'ch unig fab, Benjamin' ('From your dear and your only son, Benjamin'). Yet despite this intimate frame, the printed letter was a public document; by publishing the personal letter Robert Everett turned it into a piece of literature for his readers' consumption. It was made into a didactic narrative, a moral treatise packaged as an exciting tale of narrow escape and near death. The piece presented a damning picture of violent, slave-owning secessionists, and it thus suited

Everett's war-time agenda perfectly. The editor who, ten years before, had urged Welsh-Americans 'to stand firmly in opposition to war', was now using his journal to temper the metal of Welsh America, preparing it for what he saw as a holy war against slavery. The same process which turned Benjamin Jones's personal narrative into a public text would generate a considerable body of literature by the end of the Civil War, as the Welsh-American press took the war-time experiences of its readers and converted them into literature which was, in turn, used to reconfirm that same anti-slavery and pro-Union ideology which Welsh America carried into war.

If Welsh-Americans carried this ideology with them into war, that ideology also carried *them* into war. Despite the fact that the vast majority of Welsh-Americans had no military experience before April 1861, and despite the fact that many of their religious leaders had preached pacifism not long before, Welsh America did to a great extent accept, and in a sense even welcome, the advent of war. This, at least, is the impression given by the considerable body of Welsh-language writing published during the Civil War. A few months before the start of hostilities *Y Drych* had recoiled at the thought of using war to 'force' the Southern states to remain in the union. As soon as it became obvious that 'the south's sunny glades' would indeed be 'fertilized' with blood, the Welsh-American press transformed itself into a pro-war press. Immediately after the fall of Fort Sumter it became clear that the Welsh press of the United States would unite behind the Union's war effort, just as it would unite in portraying the conflict as a struggle against slavery. Frederick Douglass's Welsh friend would go to war.

NOTES

1 *Y Cyfaill o'r Hen Wlad*, October 1856.

2 Alan Llwyd, *Gronwy Ddiafael, Gronwy Ddu* [:] *Cofiant Goronwy Owen 1723–1769* (Llandybïe, 1997), p. 316.

3 D. Hugh Matthews, 'Bedyddwyr Cymraeg a Chaethwasiaeth,' *Y Traethodydd* (April, 2004), 87.

4 Ibid., 86–7.

5 Gwyn A. Williams, *The Search for Beulah Land* (London, 1980), pp. 81–7.

6 E. Wyn James, 'Caethwasanaeth a'r Beirdd, 1790–1840', *Taliesin* 119 (Summer, 2004), 37–60.

7 See Aled Jones and Bill Jones, *Welsh Reflections* [:] *Y Drych & America 1851–2001* (Llandysul, 2001), p. 69.

8 Paul D. Evans, 'The Welsh in Oneida County, New York' (MA thesis, Cornell University, 1914). The thesis has been published online by Siloam Road Enterprises (2001): *http://members.aol.com.siloamroad/oneidawelsh*.

9 This analysis differs from that of Maldwyn Jones, who states that '[b]y 1845, then, after a decade of steadily increasing anti-slavery activity, Everett had made little impression on his fellow-country-men'; Maldwyn A. Jones, 'Welsh-Americans

and the Anti-Slavery Movement,' *Transactions of the Honourable Society of Cymmrodorion* 1985, 117. While it is true that the real fruits of Everett's labour would not be evident until the 1856 election, the Welsh-American press in general (beyond Everett's own publications) was coming around to the anti-slavery point of view in the 1840s, as discussed in this chapter. Maldwyn Jones underestimates the extent to which Welsh America was being radicalised in this period; for example, he states that another prominent Welsh-American minister, Benjamin Chidlaw, 'stopped short of advocating abolition' (119); this is contrary to the considerable body of material published by and about Chidlaw in the period before the Civil War.

10 Remsen was given on the title page of Robert Everett's publications. However, the press was really located in Everett's house in Steuben, a small hamlet down the road from Remsen. I am grateful to Leonard Wynne for clarifying this and other details concerning Oneida County geography.

11 The considerable body of scholarship on this topic includes: Whitney R. Cross, *The Burned-over District: The Social and Intellectual History of Enthusiastic Religion in Western New York, 1800–1850* (Ithaca [New York], 1950); Michael Barkun, *Crucible of the Millennium: The Burned-Over District of New York in the 1840s* (Syracuse [New York], 1986); Judith Wellman, *Grass Roots Reform in the Burned-Over District of Upstate New York* (New York and London, 2000).

12 Milton C. Sernett, *North Star Country[:]Upstate New York and the Crusade for African American Freedom* (Syracuse [New York], 2002), p. xiv.

13 For a description of the process by which Douglass broke away from the orbit of the New England abolitionists, see William S. McFeely, *Frederick Douglass* (New York, 1991), pp. 146–82.

14 Ibid., 115–17.

15 John Stauffer, *The Black Hearts of Men* [:] *Radical Abolitionists and the Transformation of Race* (Cambridge, MA, 2002), p. 158.

16 'Literary notices'; *Frederick Douglass' Paper*, 3 November 1854.

17 For example, *Frederick Douglass' Paper*, 12 October 1855.

18 For example, *Frederick Douglass' Paper*, 16 February 1855: 'Y CENHADWR AMERICANAIDD. We are glad to see our Welsh friend. We wish we could comprehend his language, so that we might have a little chat together. We desire this the more just now, since the only word we can make out is that of a name once famous in Welsh annals. . . .' While her name suggests that Julia Griffiths might have had some Welsh ancestry, I have to date found no references to this effect. For her work on *Frederick Douglass' Paper*, see McFeely, *Frederick Douglass*, pp. 162–8.

19 In addition to the Welsh translations published in the United States (by Robert Everett in book form and as a serial on the pages of *Y Cyfaill o'r Hen Wlad*), several different versions were published in Wales, for example *Crynodeb o Gaban 'Newyrth Tom, neu, Fywyd Negroaidd yn America* (Swansea, 1853) and *Caban F'ewyrth Twm* (Wrexham, 1853). Gwilym Hiraethog's version was a free reworking of Harriet Beecher Stowe's novel, placing the narrative within a Welsh framework in addition to translating it into the Welsh language; William Rees, *Aelwyd F'ewythr Robert* (Denbigh, 1853). The Welsh appetite for versions of the novel in their own language would continue through the period of the Civil War, as evidenced by another edition, *Caban F'ewythr Tomos, neu, Hanes Caethwas Cristnogol* (Caernarfon, 1862). The Welsh Methodists had frowned upon fiction, considering it to be a frivolous form of literature. As Stowe's novel had an overt moral purpose, all of these Welsh versions helped convince the

Welsh reading public that it was possible to write and read fiction without compromising one's religious convictions. In a very real sense, Harriet Beecher Stowe's book thus helped pave the way for the development of the Welsh-language novel. See E. G. Millward, *Cenedl o Bobl Ddewrion* [:] *Agweddau ar lenyddiaeth Oes Victoria* (Llandysul, 1991), pp. 120–26; Melinda Gray, 'Uncle Tom's Welsh Dress: Ethnicity, Authority and Translation' in Alyce von Rothkirch and Daniel Williams (eds), *Beyond the Difference* [:] *Welsh Literature in Comparative Contexts* (Cardiff, 2004).

20 *Frederick Douglass' Paper*, 31 December, 1852.

21 *Frederick Douglass' Paper*, 3 September 1854.

22 Manuscript in the collection of Michael Everett.

23 Ibid.

24 For the methods developed by the New England Anti-Slavery Society and the American Anti-Slavery Society – especially the use of travelling 'agents' – see Richard S. Newman, *The Transformation of American Abolitionism* [:] *Fighting Slavery in the Early Republic* (Chapel Hill, 2002), pp. 131–2, 146, and 154–5.

25 *Y Dyngarwr*, January 1843.

26 Manuscript in the collection of Michael Everett.

27 See Milton C. Sernett, *Abolition's Axe: Beriah Green, Oneida Institute, and the Black Freedom Struggle* (Syracuse, NY, 1986).

28 Letter from Elizabeth Everett to her parents, sent from Clinton, New York, dated September 8, 184[9]. The final number in the year is unclear. Manuscript in the collection of Michael Everett.

29 *Caban F'Ewythr Twm; neu fywyd yn Mhlith yr Iselradd* (Remsen, 1854). While Everett took as the basis of this work a translation by Hugh Williams, he revised it substantially.

30 Letter from Harriet Beecher Stowe to Robert Everett, dated November 22, 1852, Andover. Collection of Michael Everett.

31 Dewi Emlyn (ed.), *Bywyd a Gwaith Dr Everett* (Utica, 1879), p. 185. These abuses are also mentioned in several manuscripts in the collection of Michael Everett, and in Paul D. Evans, 'The Welsh in Oneida County, New York'.

32 Paul D. Evans, 'The Welsh in Oneida County, New York'.

33 I am basing this analysis on a range of manuscripts in the collection of Michael Everett.

34 See notes 16–18 above; it is not always clear whether these references were written by Frederick Douglass himself or by one of his assistants (such as Julia Griffiths). I am taking *Frederick Douglass' Paper* to stand as a representative of Douglass's public voice, just as I am following the lead of Douglass's paper by personifying *Y Cenhadwr Americanaidd* as his 'Welsh friend'.

35 *Y Cyfaill o'r Hen Wlad*, September 1838.

36 In answering Jonathan's question, anti-slavery theology was provided by, for example, Owen Jones of Philadelphia (*Y Cyfaill o'r Hen Wlad*, January 1839) and W. H. Thomas of Utica (*Y Cyfaill o'r Hen Wlad*, January 1839 and February 1839).

37 *Y Cyfaill o'r Hen Wlad*, June 1839.

38 *Y Cyfaill o'r Hen Wlad*, November 1839.

39 Richard S. Newman, *The Transformation of American Abolitionism*, p. 117.

40 Robert Fanuzzi, *Abolition's Public Sphere* (Minneapolis, 2003), p. 107. Fanuzzi points out that it was 'William Watkins, an African American minister from Baltimore, who convinced [Garrison] to use *The Liberator* as an anticolonizationist organ in the tradition of the colored newspaper.'

41 Ibid., p. 140.

42 He did not use the term *hiliol*, 'racist' – indeed this Welsh word is not attested until 1850, a decade after this letter was published. However, the words used by William Thomas did accuse the Colonization Society of a stance which would be called *hiliol* or 'racist' today.

43 *Y Cyfaill o'r Hen Wlad*, January 1840.

44 *Y Seren Orllewinol*, April 1858.

45 See, for example, *Y Seren Orllewinol*, June 1845.

46 *Y Seren Orllewinol*, July 1845.

47 The resolutions passed by the congregations of individual chapels show that America's Welsh Methodists were also working through this same debate during the 1840s. For example, a Welsh Methodist chapel in Remsen passed the following in March 1844: 'Ein bod yn gwrthod rhoddi ein capeli i'r gwrthgaethiwyr politicaidd' ('We refuse to give our chapels over to the political abolitionists'), adding that they were 'as opposed to slavery as anybody, but that they did not think it appropriate to place the chapels at the service of political agitators' ('mor wrthwynebol i gaethiwed a neb, ond nad oeddynt yn ystyried yn briodol i roddi y capelau at wasanaeth cynyrfwyr politicaidd'). Hugh Davies, *Hanes Cymanfa Dwyreinbarth Pennsylvania* (Scranton, 1898), p. 36.

48 See, for example, *Y Seren Orllewinol*, May and June 1847, October 1848, and January 1850.

49 Note that another argument erupted on the pages of the *Cyfaill* in the 1850s, with an old-fashioned Calvinist who, though thinking it evil, said slavery could be seen in terms of pre-ordination being attacked by Eos Glan Twrch, who forwarded passionate and uncompromising anti-slavery arguments. See *Y Cyfaill o'r Hen Wlad*, Novemember 1855, and January, April and July 1856.

50 *Y Drych*, 2 January 1851.

51 *Y Drych*, 3 October 1857.

52 George B. Cheever, *God against Slavery; and the Freedom and duty of the Pulpit to Rebuke it as a sin against God* (1857). 'Adolygiad y Wasg' ('Review of the Press'), *Y Drych*, 6 June 1857.

53 *Y Dyngarwr*, January 1843: 'Gwneir anrheg o'r "Dyngarwr" am y fl[wyddyn] hon i bob gweinidog yn mhlith y Cymry, o bob enwad crefyddol ag a ddewiso ei dderbyn, cyn belled ag y maent yn adnabyddus i ni' ('A gift of the "Dyngarwr" for this year is made to every minister amongst the Welsh, of every religious denomination, who decides to accept it, as long as they are known to us').

54 *Y Dyngarwr*, February 1843.

55 A piece contributed by Revd E. Davies of Waterville, New York, to Dewi Emlyn (ed.), *Bywyd a Gwaith Dr Everett* (Utica, 1879), p. 121.

56 *Y Dyngarwr*, January 1843.

57 While the piece does not provide any more biographical details, it is very likely that this was the same Revd William Rowlands who edited *Y Cyfaill o'r Hen Wlad*.

58 *Y Dyngarwr*, January 1843.

59 Ibid.

60 *Y Cyfaill o'r Hen Wlad*, June 1839.

61 *Y Dyngarwr*, January 1843.

62 Ibid.

63 *Y Dyngarwr*, February 1843.

64 Ibid.

65 Ellis Wynne, *Gweledigaetheu y Bardd Cwsc* (London, 1703). Tracing the lineage of Welsh literature of this type is a complicated endeavour. In addition to medieval narratives such as 'Breuddwyd Rhonabwy' and 'Breuddwyd Macsen Wledig' ('The Dream of Rhonabwy' and 'The Dream of Macsen Wledig'), a wealth of visionary material made its way into the Welsh tradition by means of translation; for example, a Welsh version of Bunyan's *Pilgrim's Progress* (which first appeared in print in 1688) was extremely popular throughout the nineteenth century. Biblical themes and images, especially those drawn from the Book of Revelation, also had a profound influence upon Welsh vision literature. The most detailed discussion of Ellis Wynne and his influences is found in Gwyn Thomas, *Y Bardd Cwsg a'i Gefndir* (Cardiff, 1971).

66 Ellis Wynne, *Gweledigaetheu y Bardd Cwsc*, pp. 5 and 83.

67 *Y Dyngarwr*, February 1843.

68 Ibid.

69 Ibid.

70 *The New English Bible* (New York and Oxford, 1972); New Testament, p. 327.

71 *Y Dyngarwr*, February 1843.

72 *The New English Bible*; New Testament, p. 327.

73 *Y Dyngarwr*, April 1843.

74 Ibid.

75 Ibid.

76 Louis Menand, *The Metaphysical Club* [:] *A Story of Ideas in America* (New York, 2002), p. 13.

77 Paul D. Evans, 'The Welsh in Oneida County, New York', p. 36. Little is known about the history of *Seren Oneida*, and Paul Evans himself had to rely upon oral history in order to flesh out the details.

78 I am extremely grateful to Huw Griffiths for the illumination on this subject which he provided during several conversations between 2000 and 2003.

79 *Y Cenhdawr Americanaidd*, June 1840: 'Cymdeithas Wrthgaethiwol Gymreig Pittsburg' ('The Welsh Anti-slavery Society of Pittsburg').

80 Manuscript in the collection of Michael Everett.

81 *Y Cenhadwr Americanaidd*, January 1840.

82 For example, Robert Everett also published another short-lived journal, *Y Detholydd* ('The Eclectic'), between 1850 and 1852. More concerned with literature and less political than the other two, its primary purpose was to present American readers with a selection of prose and poetry drawn from the publications of Wales.

83 *Yr Arweinydd*, 25 February 1858.

84 I am grateful to Huw Griffiths for this observation, made during an informal conversation in 2001.

85 Paul D. Evans, 'The Welsh in Oneida County, New York', p. 20.

86 The only extant copy of *Y Gwron Democrataidd* of which I am aware is dated 'Hydref 29' ('October 29'); the fact that the year, 1856, was not included is indicative of the fact that it was an ephemeral publication only produced for the 1856 election.

87 *Y Seren Orllewinol*, November 1856.

88 *Y Gwron Democrataidd*, 29 October [1856].

89 *Y Cyfaill o'r Hen Wlad*, September 1856.

90 *Y Seren Orllewinol*, November 1856.

91 While *Y Drych* was publishing anti-slavery material by this time, and while it did not support the Democratic party, its owner did allow *Y Gwron Democrataidd* to be

printed in its offices. This apparently alienated Welsh-American readers, thus lending temporary support to the soundly Republican *Y Cymro Americaidd*, established as it was to rival *Y Drych*.

92 *Y Seren Orllewinol*, October 1856.
93 Ibid.
94 Ibid.
95 *Y Cenhadwr Americanaidd*, August 1856.
96 Ibid.
97 Ibid.
98 *Y Seren Orllewinol*, Hydref 1856.
99 *Y Cenhadwr Americanaidd*, August 1856 and *Y Seren Orllewinol*, Hydref 1856.
100 Ibid.
101 *Y Seren Orllewinol*, Hydref 1856.
102 Ibid.
103 Paul Evans, 'The Welsh in Oneida County, New York', p. 47.
104 Stanley Cavell, *Philosophical Passages: Wittgenstein, Emerson, Austin, Derrida* (Oxford, 1995), p. 29.
105 *Y Cyfaill o'r Hen Wlad*, February 184.
106 *Y Cenhadwr Americanaidd*, August 1856. This is part of the editorial which was also reprinted by *Y Cymro Americaidd* and *Y Seren Orllewinol* during the 1856 election.
107 Eric Foner, *Free Soil, Free Labor, Free Men* (Oxford and New York, 1995), pp. 107–8; James M. McPherson, *Battle Cry of Freedom* (London, 1988), p. 162.
108 *Y Cenhadwr Americanaidd*, June 1858.
109 Abraham Lincoln, 'Speech Delivered at Springfield, Illinois, at the Close of the Republican State Convention, June 16, 1858', in John Grafton (ed.), *Abraham Lincoln* [:] *Great Speeches* (New York, 1991), p. 25.
110 *Y Seren Orllewinol*, June 1850.
111 *Y Cenhadwr Americanaidd*, February 1851.
112 On the history of the Welsh peace movement and its connections with the wider British movement, see Goronwy J. Jones, *Wales and the Quest for Peace* (Cardiff, 1969); Iorwerth C. Peate, 'Y Traddodiad Heddwch yng Nghymru 1800–1899', *Transactions of the Honourable Society of Cymmrodorion* (1957); Geraint H. Jenkins, *Cadw Tŷ Mewn Cwmwl Tystion* (Llandysul, 1990), pp. 29–50.
113 Lewis Appleton, *Henry Richard* [:] *The Apostle of Peace* (London, 1889); D. Ben Rees (ed.), *Oriel o Heddychwyr Mawr y Byd* (Llandysul, 1983).
114 *Y Drych*, December 1860.
115 *Y Seren Orllewinol*, July 1860.
116 *Y Drych*, 1 December 1860.
117 *Y Seren Orllewinol*, December 1860.
118 *Y Cyfaill o'r Hen Wlad*, February 1860.
119 Published in *Y Cenhadwr Americanaidd*, June 1862. The poem also appeared in *Y Drych*.
120 *Y Drych*, 1 December 1860.
121 Ibid.
122 Ibid.
123 Ibid.
124 *Y Seren Orllewinol*, May 1861.
125 *Y Cronicl*, June 1861.
126 *Y Cenhadwr Americanaidd*, June 1862.

Part Two

Welsh America and the Union War Effort: An Overview

3

Sons of Columbia, Sons of Arthur: The Militarization of Welsh America and the Literature of Enlistment

One Sunday during the first October of the Civil War, the Reverend Benjamin Chidlaw preached a sermon in Paddy's Run, Ohio. He discussed *yr amseroedd*, 'the times' which the war had brought to the Welsh-speaking Christians who listened to him that day, adding that it was [*e*]*u delydswydd*, 'their duty', to support the government. The Revd Chidlaw was using his position as minister to urge young Welsh-Americans to join the Union army, and he apparently succeeded. In his published account of the event, Chidlaw noted with satisfaction 'that twenty-five of the comely young men had already enlisted, with others to follow them' ('fod 25 o ddynion ieuainc glandeg wedi enlistio yn barod, ac ereill i'w canlyn').[1] Another of Ohio's Welsh ministers, Dewi Emlyn, had also been preaching the Union cause from the pulpit during the first months of the war. This prompted Gwilym Glyn Ebbw to publish a simple 'Question' (*Gofyniad*) in *Y Cenhadwr Americanaidd*, asking: 'Is it in keeping with Christianity for a minister of the Gospel to recruit on the Sabbath? [The question is] directed at Dewi Emlyn' ('A yw un unol â Christionogaeth i weinidog yr Efengyl i recrutio ar y Sabboth? Yn gyfeiriedig at Dewi Emlyn').[2] Benjamin Chidlaw and Dewi Emlyn were the two most famous and influential Welsh ministers in the state of Ohio at the time, and it is clear that at least part of the robust network of chapels serving Welsh America was being turned into an unofficial mechanism for recruiting Union soldiers.[3] Both these ministers were writers, and they published regularly in *Y Cenhadwr Americanaidd*; while it is impossible to know exactly what was taking place in all of America's Welsh chapels, there is no mistaking the fact that the country's Welsh-language religious press supported the Union's war effort from the very start.[4]

One of the ways in which the religious journals of Welsh America went to war was to portray the bloodshed as the result of the nation's sins. In July 1861 *Y Cenhadwr Americanaidd* published an essay by Iorthryn Gwynedd, the same poet who had conjured up the image of the bardic Bowie knife in his debate with Ioan Llewelyn Evans during the late 1850s.[5] Like the *Cenhadwr*'s editor, Robert Everett, Iorthryn – otherwise known as the Revd R. D. Thomas – was a Congregational minister, and he imbued this piece with the hottest fire and brimstone which the rhetoric of the Welsh pulpit had to offer.

Gall fod yn *fflangell* drom i'r *Gogledd* am eu bydolrwydd, a'u ffurfioldeb crefyddol; ond bydd yn *ddinystr* i fasnach, uchelgais, a balchder, a llwyddiant, y *Deheubarth*, am eu rhagrith a'u caledwch, eu twyll a'u creulonderau yn hir orthrymiad y Negro Du.[6]

'It might be a heavy *scourge* to the *North* for their worldliness, and their religious formality; but it will be the *destruction* of the economy, ambition, pride and success of the *South*, for their hypocrisy and their hardness, their deceit and their cruelties in the long oppression of the Black Negro.'

Iorthryn's explanation of the relationship between God's will and the suffering which the war had brought to the North is presented conditionally; rather than being an unqualified statement, it is a suggestion, a possible interpretation (*gall fod* are his exact words: 'it can be' or 'it might be'). On the other hand, he had no doubt whatsoever as to the meaning of the war in terms of the South's sins; the conflict *was* divine retribution for their 'long oppression' of the slave.

Before John Brown went to the gallows he penned what was to become one of the central prophecies of American history: 'I, John Brown, am now quite certain that the crimes of this guilty land will never be purged away, but with Blood'.[7] Welsh America – by means of its main literary event, the Utica *Eisteddfod*, and by means of its press – was transforming Brown into a 'martyr at freedom's gate.'[8] Like Iorthryn Gwynedd, and like many of the North's radical Protestants in general, other Welsh-American writers interpreted the Civil War as God's way of opening freedom's gate, welcoming the sacrificial blood spilled by the 'scourge' of war as a means of purging the crimes of their adopted country.[9] One of the best examples of this kind of discourse was published later in the war by Erasmus W. Jones, Chaplain of the 21st US Colored Regiment.

Mae yr Unol Daleithau yn awr, y Gogledd fel y De, o dan wialen geryddol Jehofa. Mae gwaedd wylofus pedair miliwn o eneidiau 'dros ba rai y bu Crist farw' wedi cyrhaedd clustiau Arglwydd y lluoedd ac wedi llwyddo yn y llys fry. Lled gyndyn ydym wedi bod, mae'n wir, i gydnabod llais Jehofa uwch ein penau yn gwaeddi 'torrwch bob iau a gollwngwch y gorthrymedig yn rhydd!' Bu gorfod i Dduw lindagu y llywodraeth cyn iddi addaw gwneud cyfiawnder â'r negro. Diolch iddo, hyd yn oed am *geryddon*! Credaf fod ein 'hymwared yn agoshau'. Caiff ein gwlad ei 'hadgenedlu drachefn i obaith bywiol.' O'r bedydd gwaed, cawn 'gyfodi i newydd-deb buchedd.' Ar ol y gwyntyllio ofnadwy ceir ni yn wenith mwy pur, a deuwn allan o'r 'ffwrn danllyd boeth' fel aur wedi ei buro trwy dân.

'The United States now, the North and South alike, are under Jehovah's chastising rod. The doleful cry of four million souls "for whom Christ died" has reached the ears of the Lord of Hosts and has been heard in the court on high. We have been fairly reluctant, it's true, to recognize Jehovah's voice above us crying "sever every yoke and set the oppressed free!" God had to strangle the government before it would promise to do justice to the negro. Thank Him, even for *chastisements*! I believe that our "deliverance is growing near". Our land will be "reborn again to

> living hope." From this baptism of blood we will be able "to awaken to the newness of life". After this horrible winnowing we will be found to be purer wheat, and we will come out of the "hot fiery furnace" like gold purified by fire.'

Like Iorthryn Gwynedd and Robert Everett, Erasmus Jones had been a Congregational minister in Oneida County before the war, and like them he took his theological interpretation of the conflict from the pulpit to the printing press. In doing so, these ministers were asking all of Welsh America to view the war as God's bloody vengeance visited upon the entire nation for its sins, chief of which was the oppression of the slave. The Welsh-language press of the United States had established a national community of readers, and this provided minister-authors like Jones with a kind of national church, a congregation which extended far beyond the walls of their individual chapels. From the literary pulpit provided by *Y Cenhadwr Americanaidd* Iorthryn Gwynedd, Erasmus Jones and Robert Everett were asking this national communion of Welsh-speaking Christians to view the war as a 'hot fiery furnace' from which a new nation would emerge, cleansed of the sin of slavery.[10]

While this kind of theological discourse provided one way of interpreting the advent of war, the Welsh-American press also discussed the conflict in other ways. When war broke out the Revd John Jay Butler and his wife Elizabeth were staying with her parents in Oneida County, New York. Like his father-in-law, Robert Everett, Butler was a minister and an abolitionist, and also like his father-in-law, he had a talent for writing fiery rhetorical essays. Butler quickly penned a short piece on the war for a Connecticut paper, *The Morning Star*.[11] However, before sending it to that English-language publication, he showed his treatise to Everett, who immediately translated his son-in-law's essay into Welsh. The piece appeared in the May 1861 issue of *Y Cenhadwr Americanaidd*, and it describes the events of April in memorable terms: 'Mae y newydd am gwymp amddiffynfa Sumter wedi effeithio fel disgyniad taranfollt ar yr holl wlad'; 'The news of Fort Sumter's fall has affected the whole country like the strike of a lightning bolt.'[12] If the lightning's strike was a traumatic experience for the nation, it was also an electrifying agent which prompted action: 'Mae Cyhoeddeb y Llywydd, am 75,000 o wyr arfog i'r maes, yn derbyn atebiad calonog o bob parth o'r talaethau rhyddion'; 'The President's Call for 75,000 armed men on the field has received a hearty response from each part of the free states.'[13]

The same adjective, *calon[n]og* – 'hearty' – was used by the editor of *Y Seren Orllewinol* to describe the response of the nation's Welsh communities to Lincoln's call:

> O bob cenedl yn y wlad, nid oes neb wedi dyfod allan yn fwy calonog ar alwad yr Arlywydd, i amddiffyn y llywodraeth nâ'r Cymry. Y maent wedi ymddwyn yn deilwng o'u cymeriad fel gwladgarwyr, a gwyddom y byddant gyda y mwyaf gwrol ar faes y gwaed pan fydd galwad am hynny. Aeth 2,000 o filwyr allan o

> Swydd Schuylkill – rai cannoedd o honynt yn Gymry, tua 50 o Minersville yn unig . . . yn debyg yr un fath yr oeddynt yn myned o ardaloedd Scranton, Danville, Pittsburg, &c. Sicrhawyd ni gan gyfaill a ymwelodd â 'Camp Curtin', yn Harrisburg, ddechreu y mis diweddaf, y gallesid clywed y Gymraeg yn cael ei siarad yno braidd yn mhob rhan o'r gwersyll. Yn Efrog Newydd, Ohio, a thalaethau eraill, mae amryw Gymry wedi ymres[tr]u; er fod yn anhawdd roddi cyfrif o'u nifer.[14]
>
> 'Of all the nations in the country, nobody has come out more heartily at the President's call to defend the government than the Welsh. They have behaved in a manner fitting their character as patriots, and we know that they will be amongst the most heroic on the field of blood when there is call for that. 2,000 soldiers left Schuylkill County – some hundreds of them Welsh, about 50 from Minersville alone . . . similarly they were departing from the regions of Scranton, Danville, Pittsburgh, &c. We were assured by a friend who visited "Camp Curtin" in Harrisburg at the start of last month that one could hear Welsh being spoken in just about every part of the camp. In New York, Ohio, and other states, a number of Welsh have enlisted; although it is difficult to provide a tally of their number.'

This editorial was published at the start of June 1861, and it thus testifies to the fact that comparatively large numbers of Welsh-speaking citizens were enlisting during the early months of the war. The new Welsh soldiers are described by reference to two aspects of their character: they are 'patriots' (*gwladgarwyr*) who have volunteered 'to defend the government', and they are Welsh speakers whose native language 'can be heard in just about every part of the camp'.

The *Seren* was published in Pottsville, Pennsylvania, and the editor had information from the state's individual Welsh communities concerning the number of volunteers leaving home as well as the first-hand account provided by a friend who had visited the army camp at Harrisburg; he could report with some authority as to the number of Welsh-speaking soldiers in Pennsylvania's new volunteer army. However, while knowing that Welsh communities in other northern states had also contributed 'a number' of volunteers, the editor notes with regret that 'it is difficult to provide a tally of their number.' If the editorial begins by praising the Welsh volunteers, it then turns to lamenting the fact that they can not be counted accurately.

> Y mae yn ddrwg genym hyn. Y mae cannoedd o Gymry yn cael eu colli yn mhlith cenedloedd eraill, fel nad yw eu cenedl eu hunain yn cael yr anrhydedd oddi wrthynt. Nid oes nemawr o honynt ychwaith yn swyddogion; dim ond milwyr cyffredin. Pe ffurfiesent gwmnïau eu hunain, gallasent ddewis swyddogion o'u plith eu hunain, a buasent fel y cyfryw yn cael eu hystyried a'u cydnabod yn Gymry, a diau y buasai eu cydwladwyr yn llawenhau o'u herwydd; ond gan mai yn wahanol y maent, nid oes genym ond dymuno eu llwyddiant.[15]
>
> 'We consider this to be a pity. Hundreds of Welshmen are being lost amongst other nations, so that their own nation does not receive the honour from them.

> Furthermore, hardly any of them are officers; only common soldiers. If they had formed their own companies, they could have chosen officers from amongst themselves, and as such they would be considered and recognized as Welsh, and it is likely that their countrymen would take joy because of them; but since it is otherwise, we can only wish them success.'

The war was giving these Welsh-speaking Americans a chance to prove themselves to be 'patriots', yet 'their own nation' – what we are calling *Welsh* America – was losing the chance to earn the large-scale 'honour' which this wave of volunteering merited. The new soldiers were 'being lost amongst other nations' in the army, and, unlike the soldiers of specifically Irish and German regiments, they would not be 'recognized as Welsh' by non-Welsh-Americans.

While plenty of Welsh-Americans were turning out for service, they were for the most part not being recruited in an organized fashion during the first weeks of the war. Although communities like those in the relatively populous industrial areas of Pennsylvania did provide hundreds of Welsh volunteers early on, the enlistment trend in some sparsely populated rural communities would take time to gain momentum. This was the case in southern Minnesota; while claiming the honour of being the first Welshman in the United States to volunteer in answer to the president's call, William D. Howells was also the only Welsh soldier from his community who joined the 1st Minnesota Infantry, the first new regiment presented for service to Abraham Lincoln. Another solitary Welshman, Isaac Morgan, joined the 2nd Minnesota Infantry. By the time the 9th Minnesota Infantry was formed in August 1862, the enlisting trend had spread among the area's small Welsh population: that new regiment had twenty-one Welsh-speaking soldiers. As some of Minnesota's Welsh writers would boast in print decades after the war, even though these soldiers came from a thinly populated rural community, by the end of the war the area's Welsh families had sent sixty-six of their men to join the Union army.[16]

One of the 9th Minnesota's twenty-one Welshmen, John R. Roberts, was appointed Lieutenant.[17] Early in the war the soldiers elected officers from among their own ranks; in the words of Bell Irvin Wiley, 'Election of captains and lieutenants' – that is, the company officers – 'by the men and of colonels and majors by company officers was common practice, with governors issuing commissions to those so elected'.[18] The social, political and ethnic ties which had bound groups of soldiers together in civilian life before enlisting greatly influenced the election process, and most Welsh volunteers did not have enough numbers to ensure the appointment of their own officers in the manner suggested by *Y Seren Orllewinol* in June 1861. It was often men who took upon themselves the task of recruiting a company who were elected as captain of the new unit, and colonels were frequently those individuals who had recruited the entire regiment. As Wiley notes, 'frequently, if not usually, the voting was a mere formality, it being a foregone conclusion that persons responsible for recruiting the units, or previously approved by the governor, would become the officers.'[19] As the standard number of a company at time of enlistment was 100 men (with an infantry regiment of ten companies containing 1,000 soldiers), the demography of Welsh America mitigated against this kind of recruiting effort; while there were notable exceptions such as the Utica community and the large mining towns of Pennsylvania, a great percentage of the country's Welsh-speaking population was spread out in rural villages, hamlets and farms. This absence of organized, large-scale recruiting early in the war was reflected by the lack of Welsh officers. The *Seren*'s editor thus highlights this lack as one obvious aspect of the process by which Welsh volunteers were being 'lost amongst other nations' in the Union army.

While Welsh officers were extremely rare at the start of the war, there were a few Welshmen who had influence within the army's ranks. After being made chaplain of several new Pennsylvania regiments, John M. Thomas published a letter urging other Welsh-Americans to join him: 'it would be no small joy for me to see hundreds of the sturdy youth of our nation turning out with us' ('byddai yn llawenydd nid bychan genyf weled cannoedd o gedyrn ieuaingc ein cenedl yn troi allan gyda ni').[20] He tempted potential recruits by noting that he could offer them services in the Welsh language, and he also informed them that, as a Welshman enjoying the commanding officer's confidence, he could intercede on their behalf in times of trouble:

> Caiff y milwyr gymmaint o fanteision . . . ag a gânt gyda neb, beth bynag; a chânt y manteision canlynol: – Pregethwr a all gymdeithasu â hwynt yn Gymraeg – y bydd y pregethwr hwnw, yn rhinwedd ei swydd yn dal cyfrinach â'r prif swyddogion, ac y bydd yn gofalu am danynt pan yn glaf ac yn glwyfedig; ac, fe allai, yn gweinyddu iddynt yn iaith eu rhiaint.[21]

> 'The soldiers will receive as many advantages [with us] as they will with anybody, at any rate; and they will get the following advantages: – A preacher who can socialize with them in Welsh – [and] that preacher, by virtue of his job, enjoys the confidence of the chief officers, and he will take care of them when they are sick and injured; and, perhaps, he will provide religious service for them in the language of their parents.'

Thomas's letter, published in September 1861, also expresses the general concern of *Y Seren Orllewinol*'s editor. Although many Welshmen were enlisting, Revd Thomas complained that these soldiers were not being organized in Welsh companies and regiments:

> Y mae cannoedd o Gymry, yn ddiau, yn bwriadu myned allan i'r rhyfel mewn ychydig wythnosau o wahanol fanau yn y dalaeth hon, fel taleithiau ereill; a difyr iawn fyddai cael llu o honynt gyda'u gilydd. Nid oes dim yn fy nghymmhell i

roddi y gwahoddiad hwn ond teimlad o barch i'r Cymry. Trueni na buasai y Cymry wedi deffro yn brydlawn, ac wedi ymrestru dan swyddogion o'r eiddynt eu hunain, ac wedi cynnyg eu gwasanaeth fel catrodau Cymreig. . . . Er fy mod yn awyddus i weled y Cymry yn troi allan gyda mi, etto byddai yn well genyf eu gweled yn ffurfio catrawd hollol Gymreig.[22]

'Hundreds of Welshmen, without doubt, intend to go off to the war within a few weeks from various parts of this state, like other states; and it would be very pleasing to have a host of them together. Nothing compels me to place this invitation other than a feeling of respect for the Welsh. It's a pity that the Welsh did not awaken in time and enlist under officers of their own and offer their service as Welsh regiments. . . . Although I am eager to see the Welsh turning out with me, I would yet prefer to see them forming a completely Welsh regiment.'

This letter is a call to arms which includes a specific invitation to join Thomas in the new Pennsylvania regiments which he was serving. However, he relegates his personal recruitment drive to a place of secondary importance; the chaplain states that he would be willing to slow the flow of volunteers into the ranks of his own units in order to realize the dream of 'forming a completely Welsh regiment'. What he saw as the national needs of Welsh America were placed above local and personal needs.

More than two years after publishing his complaint about the lack of Welsh officers and companies, the *Seren*'s editor was still voicing regret that his 'countrymen' were being 'swallowed' by the army and thus losing an opportunity to be seen by all of the Union as *Welsh-American*s.

Er nad yw y Cymry yn cael llawer o anrhydedd cyhoeddus oddiwrth genedloedd eraill am eu gwroldeb a'u gwladgarwch yn y rhyfel presennol, eto, da genym hysbysu nad ydynt yn ol i gyflawni eu dyledswydd, a chredwn fod cymmaint o honynt wedi myned allan â neb eraill yn gyfatebol i'n rhifedi: Ond wedi y cwbl llyngcir ni o'r golwg gan y mwyafrif.[23]

'Although the Welsh are not receiving much public honour from other nations for their heroism and their patriotism in the present war, still, we are pleased to inform that they are not behind in performing their duty, and we believe that as many of them have turned out as any other [nation] comparable to our numbers: But after all we are swallowed from sight by the majority.'

However, by the time this editorial was published in August 1863, he had to admit that things had improved somewhat. The editor noted that the Welsh Captain, William H. Hopkins, had a number of Welsh soldiers in his company, and that 'Mr. John E. Davies, Minersville, had set out to raise a Welsh company, and had succeeded to get men' ('Mr John E. Davies, Minersville, [wedi gwneud c]ynnig i godi cwmni Cymreig, ac wedi llwyddo i gael dynion').[24]

There were, in fact, several Welsh, or mostly Welsh, companies by the start of 1863. It appears that the regiment with the largest number of Welsh-speaking soldiers was the 56th Ohio Volunteer Infantry, organized during the fall and winter of 1861. One of them, William S. Jones, provided the following assessment of the regiment's Welsh component to the readers of *Y Drych*:

> Yr oedd yn gwneyd i fyny y gatrawd hon ar y cyntaf, y rhan fwyaf o ddau gwmni o Gymry, sef cwmnioedd C ac E. Yr oedd Capteiniaid y ddau gwmni hyn yn Gymry, ac un Is-gapten. Yr oedd hefyd amryw Gymry yn wasgaredig mewn cwmnioedd eraill yn gyffredin, yng nghyd a'r *Adjutant* a'r Capelydd. Yr oll yn gwneyd i fyny 150, ond fod rhai o honynt o deulu Dic Sion Dafydd, yn gwadu iaith eu mamau.[25]
>
> 'There were making up this regiment at its start the better part of two companies of Welsh, namely companies C and E. The Captains of these two companies were Welsh, and one Lieutenant. There were also other Welshmen dispersed in other companies in general, along with the Adjutant and the Chaplain. All making up 150, except that some of them belong to Dic Siôn Dafydd's family, denying the language of their mothers.'

Even within the 56th Ohio, surely the most Welsh of the Union's regiments, the level of Welsh organization and identity varied considerably. Upon the regiment's formation, the Welsh could boast of three field officers – two captains and one lieutenant – as well as one line officer, the adjutant, and the regimental chaplain. Welsh-speaking enlisted men also made up 'the better part' of the two companies commanded by the Welsh captains. On the other hand, there were also 'other Welshmen dispersed in other companies', a phrase echoing the *Seren*'s complaint that Welsh soldiers were 'being lost amongst other nations' in the army. In other words, some of the regiment's Welsh soldiers were recruited and organized together in distinct groups and commanded by Welsh officers, while others blended into the melting pot of other companies in the same regiment. While this may reflect the varying degrees of success enjoyed by different Welsh communities in the area when it came to recruitment drives, it also shows that some Welsh-Americans were assimilates who were just as happy to turn their backs on 'the language of their mothers'. The published letters by William S. Jones and other Welsh-speaking soldiers of the 56th Ohio testify to the fact that two of the regiment's companies were characterized by a lively Welsh-language culture, while other volunteers in the same regiment were what contemporary writers like Jones described as the American children of Dic Siôn Dafydd.[26] In the case of this Ohio regiment, the differing degrees to which individual Welsh-Americans embraced their Welsh identity before the war were recreated within the new society of the army camp; most of them ('the better part') congregated in distinct groups where they could use their own language and maintain a Welsh sub-culture within the regiment's ranks, while others were apparently content to exist in a 'dispersed' state within the culturally diverse yet predominantly Anglophone population which constituted most of the regiment.

An entire company of the 118th Ohio, mustered in Cincinnati in September 1862, was made up of Welsh volunteers. One of them, D. M. Hughes, wrote to *Y Cyfaill O'r Hen Wlad* in order to ensure that Welsh America at large was aware of the unit's Welsh company:

> Yr ydwyf wedi meddwl rhoddi ychydig o hanes y 118fed Gatrawd Ohio, yn yr hon y mae 110 o fechgyn gwrol Cymry Putnam, Gomer, a Vanwert, y rhai a ymunasant â hi yn mis Awst diweddaf, ac a aethant i Wersyllfa Lima i ddysgu y gelfyddyd o ryfela.[27]

> 'I have thought of giving a little of the history of the 118th Ohio Regiment, in which there are 110 of the heroic boys of the Welsh of Putnam, Gomer and Vanwert, who joined it last August, and went to Camp Lima to learn the art of warfare.'

Similarly, Daniel T. Jones, a sergeant with Company H, 126th Illinois Infantry, opened his letter to *Y Drych* by boasting of his unit's Welsh character: 'Mr. Editor: Here is for the *Drych*'s readers a little of our history as a company, the majority of which is composed of Welshmen' ('Mr Olygydd: Wele i ddarllenwyr y *Drych* ychydig o'n helynt fel cwmni, y mwyafrif o ba un sydd yn Gymry').[28] One soldier from Company F of the 22nd Wisconsin Infantry wrote to *Y Cenhadwr Americanaidd* noting simply that the 'majority' (*mwyafrif*) of the company's soldiers were Welsh.[29] Later in the war, another of the company's soldiers would express thanks for this Welsh companionship on the pages of *Y Cyfaill o'r Hen Wlad*: 'Bum yn ffodus iawn trwy ymrestru yn y cwmni yma mewn llawer ystyr. Y mae tua dwy ran o dair i'r cwmni yn Gymry, a'r swyddogion bron i gyd yn Gymry' ('I was very fortunte in enlisting in this company in many ways. Two parts of three of the company are Welsh, and the officers are almost all Welsh').[30] In order to emphasize its overwhelmingly Welsh character, Company F of the 22nd Wisconsin was given the name 'The Cambrian Guards'; the captain commanding the company, Owen Griffith, also spoke Welsh.

Owen Griffith in fact provides one example of a Welsh-American who was elected captain because of the crucial role he played in recruiting his company's soldiers. A description of the way in which this company was recruited was published years after the war in the *Racine County Militant*:

> On August 12 [1862], a large and inspiring war meeting of Welsh citizens was held for the purpose of securing recruits for Owen Griffith's company of the Twenty-second [Wisconsin]. Speeches were made by Rev. W. J. Hopkins, Owen Griffith, W. G. Roberts, Robert O. Jones, John Bowen and W. W. Vaughan. The following vigorous patriotic resolutions were adopted by the meeting. . . . Committees were appointed at this meeting to solicit funds and volunteers among the Welsh citizens at Skunk Grove and at Pike Grove.[31]

Following these activities in August, the company became part of the new regiment, which was officially mustered into service on 2 September 1862. We thus find Owen Griffith, the man who would become captain of the 'Cambrian Guards', as one of the dignitaries who spoke from the stage at the 'war meeting'. Important members of the local Welsh community were central to this process, including an influential minister, the Revd W. J. Hopkins. As the report of the 'war meeting' was published years later in English, it is not known to what degree the proceedings of 12 August 1862 were conducted in Welsh. At least some of the speeches would have been in the recruits' mother-tongue; surviving manuscript evidence proves that some of Wisconsin's Welsh soldiers had little knowledge of English upon enlisting, and all the speakers mentioned in the report were Welsh.[32]

Events such as the 'war meeting' held by Racine's Welsh community characterized the recruiting efforts of all kinds of communities across the United States. The company of soldiers was seen as an extension of the local community on the battlefield, and the close relationship between the new soldiers and their civilian base began at the very moment that soldiers were recruited for the new military unit. In the words of Reid Mitchell,

> . . . soldiers believed that they were fighting for their families and communities. The homefolk had sent them to war. Rallies, public meetings, exhortations from the press and pulpit had encouraged the teenagers and men of the North to enlist; their communities presented them with homemade American flags, promised always to remember their bravery, and marched them out of town to the accompaniment of brass bands.[33]

Civilians with no intention of enlisting, including women, who could not enlist, joined together with potential soldiers in a public ceremony which served to articulate the patriotism and war-time aspirations of the community. Thus the resolutions passed by the Welsh of Racine constitute public articulations of their American patriotism as well as an affirmation of their Welshness.

> Whereas, in our opinion, the present crisis in which this treasonable rebellion involves the fate of the republic, that no man or woman is worthy of the name or title of American citizen that will not with his influence, wealth and blood, come to the support of the government in its present peril, therefore be it
>
> Resolved, that we, the Welsh citizens of Racine, do hereby tender to the government our warmest sympathy, with the assurance that we will with our treasure and blood support it in its efforts to put down this rebellion.
>
> Resolved, that we denounce as forever unworthy of our country, any Welshman, or any other adopted citizen, come from what country he may, who shall become so base to every impulse of manhood and truth as to apply to a British consul, or any other consul, for protection, or the more cowardly base act of fleeing to

> Canada from the United States, which has given us a home and protection in time of peace. We deem it our duty to stand by this government in time of need and peril, and share the fortunes of the republic in victory or death.
>
> Resolved, that in the opinion of this meeting, the late act of Congress confiscating all rebel property, should be put in force with the greatest vigor, and that all slaves owned by rebel masters should be hereafter and forever declared free.[34]

With these words the community defines its own identity. The people present at the meeting describe themselves as 'the Welsh citizens of Racine', while declaring that 'no man or woman is worthy of the name or title of American citizen' who does not 'support the government in its present peril'. Perhaps foreseeing the draft which was soon to come, they passed a pre-emptive measure, condemning ahead of time 'any Welshman' who might in future consider absconding to Canada or Britain. The resolutions are soundly pro-government and pro-Union, yet the Welsh citizens of Racine did not hesitate to offer Lincoln's government and the Union army some antislavery advice, urging them to declare 'all slaves owned by rebel masters . . . hereafter and forever . . . free'.

The resolutions passed at this public meeting can be seen as an ideological agenda presented formally by the community to the new military unit it was generating. This agenda would in fact be pursued rigorously by the Welsh soldiers of the 22nd Wisconsin during the war; within a year they would be taking direct action in order to free slaves, even when those actions contradicted the orders of their own commanding general. Not surprisingly, the 22nd Wisconsin Infantry would earn the sobriquet 'the abolitionist regiment'.[35] The bond between civilians and soldiers was actively maintained after the volunteers left home; as Mitchell notes, the 'community never entirely relinquished its power to oversee its men at war'.[36] The surviving print and manuscript sources relating to the Welsh soldiers of the 22nd Wisconsin show the degree to which these soldiers kept in close contact with their civilian community; in addition to personal letters carried by the postal service, Welsh-speaking Methodists in Company F corresponded as a group with the congregation of their home chapel in Racine by means of *Y Cyfaill o'r Hen Wlad*, and Captain Owen Griffith published reports on the conduct of his Welsh soldiers for readers in Wisconsin on the pages of *Y Drych*. Formalized initially in the heightened public displays of the rallies and ceremonies with which the civilians honoured their new volunteers, these Welsh-language publications helped to preserve the bond between civilian and soldier during the war years.

August 1862 marked an increase in Welsh America's organized recruiting efforts. While Owen Griffith was hard at work in Racine, Wisconsin, a Welsh physician in Ebensburg, Pennsylvania, was busy recruiting what became Company F of the 133rd Pennsylvania Volunteer Infantry. The influence and popularity which Dr J. M. Jones enjoyed in his local community was cited by one Ebensburg poet as the reason why so many young Welshmen followed him into the army.

Enwog ydoedd ef fel meddyg
Hoffai pawb ei wyneb llon,
Credai llawer nad oedd debyg
Iddo ar y ddaear hon;
Gado wnaeth ei alwedigaeth
A'i gyfeillion hefyd am
Fod ei gariad ef yn wresog
At ei wlad, a'i sel fel fflam.

Aeth yn Gadben ar gwmpeini
Hardd o fechgyn – Cymry mad,
Ymrestrant Awst diweddaf
I wneyd rhan yn mrwydrau'r wlad[.][37]

'He was famous as a doctor;
Everybody liked his happy face,
Many believed that there was nobody like
Him on this earth;
He left his calling,
And his friends as well, because
His love was burning
For his country, and his zeal was like a flame.

'He became Captain of a beautiful company
Of boys – good Welshmen,
They enlisted last August
In order to do their part in the country's battles.'

The poet's description of the doctor-turned-captain provides a look at the way in which civilian bonds merged into military structure. Well liked and 'famous as a doctor' in the area, Dr Jones replaced his civilian 'calling' with a military one. However, while he traded the art of healing for the practice of killing, his relationship with the community who so respected him remained the same. One of the functions of a civilian doctor was, quite literally, to bring children into the world and help oversee their successful progress to adulthood; Dr Jones's role as company captain is described metaphorically in terms of caring for children or 'boys': 'He became Captain of a beautiful company / Of boys.'

This use of the word *bechgyn*, 'boys', is entirely characteristic of Civil War literature. As Reid Mitchell demonstrates, despite the fact that 'the median age of the northern soldier was . . . twenty-four', and despite 'how elderly Civil War armies were compared to the ones produced by mass conscription in the twentieth century,' there was an overwhelming tendency to describe the soldiers as 'boys'.[38] This rhetorical commonplace served several functions, one of which we might define as stressing the close emotional bond between the 'boy' solders and their 'parent' communities. Another is described by Mitchell in terms of the conceptual passage from civilian to soldier: 'as Americans tried to make sense of the war, they linked the transformation of the civilian into a soldier and the passage of a boy into adulthood.'[39] In the case of this particular Welsh poem, the common war-time trope is rendered more powerful by the fact that it is used to describe a doctor who led his peace-time patients into the ranks of the Union army.

This Welsh poet from Ebensburg was a woman; while otherwise anonymous, she used the pen-name 'Cymraes', 'A Welsh woman'. The single word *Cymraes* follows the published poem in *Y Cenhadwr Americanaidd*; the only aspect of the poet's identity which she chose to reveal was her sex, and this surely affected the way in which contemporary readers reacted to the poem. In stressing the 'need for femininity' in the masculine context of the army, Mitchell writes that 'Northern culture put domesticity at the centre of society and women at the centre of domesticity'.[40] In that sense, this poem provides a Welsh example of a national phenomenon: published texts or public ceremonies stressing the close ties between soldiers and civilian community often foregrounded feminine aspects of that community.

According to this Welsh woman poet, Dr Jones's success as a recruiter was grounded in his patriotic zeal as well as his popularity in the local community; his burning love of country is described as a beacon, a 'flame' which drew the Welsh 'boys' of Ebensburg into the new company. J. H. Evans, who recruited Welsh soldiers in Centreville, Ohio, apparently relied more heavily upon the talents and charisma of another young Welsh-American from the area; according to a text published in the December 1862 issue of *Y Cenhadwr Americanaidd*, Evans employed Tom Thomas as a kind of pied piper, 'play[ing] his whistle skilfully' in order to draw volunteers into the ranks of what would become the 56th Ohio Infantry. As suggested above, Welsh soldiers for the 56th Ohio were apparently recruited in various ways and with varying degrees of organization. This text, published by a writer using the pen-name 'Cymro Tawel' ('Quiet Welshman'), describes the process by which the soldiers of Company F – one of the two described by William S. Jones as being mostly Welsh – were recruited.

> Yn ddiweddar ymosododd ein cydwladwr caredig, Mr. J. H. Evans, Centreville, sef mab Mr. Thomas Evans, masnachwr cyfrifol yn y lle hwnw, ar y gorchwyl o godi cwmni o wirfoddiaid i fyned allan yn erbyn y creulawn, a da genym ddweyd fe lwyddodd hefyd. – Dechreuodd o dde, ac yna aeth rhag ei flaen yn llwyddiannus. Aeth at fab y Parch. D. C. Thomas, llwyddodd gyda y bachgen *llon*

> *heini* hwn sydd a'i sirioldeb yn enill pawb o'r bron. Aeth Tom serchog allan gyda Mr. Evans a chwareuodd ei chwibanogl gyda y fath fedusrwydd, y canlyniad fu i fechgyn dewrion Cymry ymrestru yn y cwmni nes ei wneud mewn ychydig amser braidd yn llawn. Yn awr maent yn Camp Morrow, ger Portsmouth, ac yn gwneud yn rhagorol.[41]

> 'Recently our kind fellow countryman, Mr J. H. Evans, Centreville, the son of Mr. Thomas Evans, a responsible merchant in this place, tackled the job of raising a company of volunteers to go out against the cruel, and we are pleased to say that he succeeded at that. – He started on the right foot, and progressed successfully. He went to the son of Revd D. C. Thomas, he succeeded with this *cheerful, sturdy* boy who with his pleasant demeanour wins just about everybody over. Personable Tom went out with Mr. Evans and played his whistle with such skill, the result was that the brave boys of the Welsh enlisted in the company until it was within a short time rather full. They are now in Camp Morrow, near Portsmouth, doing exceptionally well.'

This paragraph provides another example of that well-worn convention, describing Tom Thomas as a 'cheerful, sturdy boy' and referring to the entire group of volunteers as 'brave boys'. It also hints at the ways in which the bonds and networks of the peace-time community were transformed into a recruitment mechanism; J. H. Evans is described as the son of one of Centerville's 'responsible merchant[s]', and he starts by enlisting the aide of a local minister's son, who presumably took advantage of his social position in addition to his musical talents in order to attract potential soldiers. The social networks and hierarchies which had articulated the life of Centerville's Welsh community before the war were transformed by means of the way in which the company was recruited into the structure of the new military unit. J. H. Evans was mustered as a lieutenant of Company E and was later promoted to be its captain. Thomas D. Thomas, the minister's 'cheerful boy', remained a musician with the same company.

One Welshman who had considerable influence in his community before the war was William H. Powell. Living in Ironton, Ohio, Powell was manager in the Lawrence rolling mill, one of the area's many ironworks. When the war broke out, he recruited a company of cavalry and became its captain. Unlike Captain Evans of Centreville, Ohio, Powell did not attempt to recruit a specifically Welsh company. Several Welshmen from the area did follow him into service, however, and some of these soldiers sent letters to *Y Drych* informing the broader community of Welsh America as to Powell's progress up through the ranks. One of them was E. A. Rosser, who described the former mill manager as 'the right man in the right place':

> Mae genyf i'ch hysbysu am ddyrchafiad Cymro yn ein catrawd, sef y Capt. Powell, o Ironton, O., i fod yn *Major*, ac mewn llai na dau fis, cafodd eilwaith ei

> ddyrchafu i fod yn *Lieu. Col.* Llwyddiant iddo ac i bob Cymro arall sydd yn cyflawni ei ddyledswydd. Y siarad yma yw mai efe yw yr 'Iawn ddyn yn yr iawn le.'[42]
>
> 'I have to have inform you of the promotion of a Welshman in our regiment, namely Captain Powell, from Ironton, Ohio, to Major. And, in less than two months, he got promoted a second time to Lieutenant Colonel. Success to him and to every other Welshman who fulfils his duty. The talk here is that he is the "right man in the right place".'

When Powell was sent home to Ohio from Virginia in order to recover from illness, another of his Welsh soldiers, Howell G. Hopkins, reported dutifully to the paper:

> Y mae ein cydfilwr a'n cydwladwr, W. H. Powell, yn awr gartref yn glaf o'r Typhoid Fever, ond ein gobaith ni oll yw ei fod wedi ei adferyd erbyn hyn, am mai efe yw ein swyddog goreu, a chyn bo hir os adferir ei fywyd, bydd yn un o sywddogion goreu y wlad.[43]
>
> 'Our fellow soldier and our fellow countryman, W. H. Powell, is now home sick with the Typhoid Fever, but our hope is that he is better by now, because he is our best officer, and before long if his life is restored, he will be one of the best officers in the country.'

Powell did indeed survive the fever, and by May 1863 he was promoted to full Colonel and given command of the 2nd West Virginia Cavalry, the Union regiment containing the company of Ohio soldiers which he had recruited at the start of the war. William Powell was a successful officer, distinguishing himself in the fight against Mosby's Confederate raiders in Virginia, and he was eventually promoted to Brigadier General at the war's end.

Both these soldier-correspondents stress Powell's Welsh identity as well as his success as an officer; Hopkins does this by writing that his 'fellow countryman' (*cydwladwr*) is destined to become 'one of the best officers of the country' ('un o swyddogion goreu y wlad'). The fact that the word *gwlad* – 'country' – is used in two different ways in the same sentence might force twenty-first-century readers into a kind of interpretive double-take, as the *gwlad* of the word *cydwladwr* is Wales and the *gwlad* of the second phrase is the United States.[44] Pride in the Welshness of the successful officer is combined with an expression of patriotic pride in the United States and the Union army which these Welsh-American soldiers were serving. This duality of expression was entirely characteristic of Welsh-American writings of the time. Indeed, as these letters were published by *Y Drych*, it is worth recalling Chapter One's discussion of the newspaper's boast that it was a 'National Newspaper at the Service of the Nation of the Welsh in the United States' – *Newyddiadur Cenedlaethol at Wasanaeth Cenedl y Cymry yn y Talaethau Unedig*. Like the word *gwlad* in the soldier's letter, the word *cenedl*, 'nation', appears twice in this phrase, once referring to 'the *Nation* of the Welsh', and once as the root of the adjective *cenedlaethol*, 'national', a reference to the United States.[45] Rather than seeing such dualities of expression as indicative of a schizophrenic identity, it is best to take them for what they are: the normal ways by which writers expressed what was for them a very coherent Welsh-American identity. Howell Hopkins described William H. Powell as a fellow-Welshman and an American patriot; as far as the surviving print and manuscript sources allow for broad generalizations concerning the identity of Welsh-speaking Americans, it is safe to assume that most of *Y Drych*'s readers would have liked to have been described in this manner.

Powell was an exception; on the whole, Welshmen did not climb high in the Union army. There were a number of Welsh field officers (that is, lieutenants and captains), and at least one Welsh soldier, Joseph Griffiths, won a comission to West Point because of his valour during the siege of Vicksburg, but very few Welsh-speaking Americans climbed higher than the rank of captain.[46] As has already been discussed, the demography of Welsh America mitigated against the kind of large-scale recruiting which would have allowed more Welsh community leaders to start military life as officers. This is especially obvious when the size of the Welsh population is measured against the larger immigrant groups. In comparison with the 1,611,304 Irish immigrants and the 1,301,136 'U. S. residents born in one of the thirty-four German-speaking states of central Europe,' the 45,763 Welsh immigrants noted by the 1860 US census constituted an extremely small population.[47] The leaders of these larger ethnic communities had access to considerable political networks in peacetime which were easily converted into recruiting mechanisms after the advent of war. For example, Carl Schurz, whose influence with German-speaking voters had made him an important campaigner for the Republican Party in the 1850s, provided a direct link between German-American society and the higher eschelons of Lincoln's war-time government. In describing Schurz's recruiting activities, William L. Burton states that:

> He contacted President Lincoln, U. S. senators, and state officials in an effort to establish an ethnic presence in the army. He sought a general's commission for himself, urged Lincoln to create a German brigade, and even won Lincoln's early agreement to create such a brigade.[48]

In addition to a number of Irish and German regiments, these ethnic communities were visible at an even higher level of army organization, as German and Irish brigades were also formed. Even the most influential Welsh-Americans lacked the kind of political leverage commanded by Schurz; on the whole, they could not claim a large enough voting base in their communities to draw the attention of the state and federal politicians who conferred the higher military ranks.

Furthermore, the very idea of military service was foreign to most Welsh-speaking Americans before the Civil War, and in this too they were unlike many of their German and Irish neighbours.[49] Some German-speaking immigrants had gained military experience during the 1848 Revolution, and a considerable number of Irish immigrants had joined peace-time militia companies; as Burton notes, 'many . . . Irish-Americans . . . saw militia activities as a gateway to the higher levels of Irish society'.[50] When the war came, influential Irish recruiters such as Michael Corcoran and Thomas Francis Meagher urged potential volunteers to join the Union army in order to gain military experience which might be used against the British during the future war for Ireland's liberation.[51] While connections between Ireland and Irish Americans often involved garnering support for the Irish nationalists' armed struggle against Britain, cultural connections between Welsh-Americans and the Old Country had, among other things, provided a channel for the pacifism of Henry Richard and the British Peace Society. The proto-pacifism discussed in Chapter Two was certainly part of the constellation of moral and cultural factors which kept Welsh-Americans decidedly un-military before April 1861.[52] According to the surviving evidence, very few Welshmen volunteered to fight in the Mexican War of 1848–50, even though the 1850 census recorded that 29,868 Welsh natives were living in the United States. Unlike other sectors of the emerging American middle class, those Welsh immigrants who succeeded economically did not on the whole see sending their sons to West Point as a desirable career option.

There were perhaps two or three dozen Welsh lieutenants and captains, with William H. Powell and a rare few gaining a higher rank.[53] However, the complaint published by *Y Seren Orllewinol*'s editor during the first weeks of the conflict remained for the most part valid throughout the war; while Welsh-Americans enlisted in comparatively large numbers (given that they were, after all, a relatively small group compared to other immigrant populations), they were nonetheless too small and too poorly organized to form many distinctly Welsh units within the Union army. The dream of a Welsh regiment was kept alive on the pages of the Welsh-American press for some time, fuelled partly by an awareness of the fact that a considerable number of German and Irish regiments were being formed; *Y Cenhadwr Americanaidd*, for example, published an article in September 1861 entitled 'Ellmyn Enwog yn y Fyddin' – 'Famous Germans in the Army'.[54] However, the gulf between dream and reality was insurmountable; the Welsh simply did not have the population to support the kind of large-scale effort which led to the formation of the German and Irish Brigades. Some Welsh communities – like the ones in Racine, Wisconsin and Centerville, Ohio – succeeded in recruiting Welsh or mostly Welsh companies, yet there would never be a Welsh regiment. This, seen by many war-time writers as a 'lack' or 'failure', would in fact have long-term consequences for Welsh America; as military historians have tended to focus on larger units of army organization (regiment, brigade, army), the lack of a Welsh regiment is one reason why Welsh-speaking soldiers have been virtually ignored by generation after generation of historians writing about the Union army.[55]

No historian has determined exactly how many Welsh-speaking Americans enlisted in the Union army. Indeed, the exact number will most likely always remain elusive; as the editor of *Y Seren Orllewinol* noted at the start of the war, since there were no regiments made up entirely of Welsh soldiers it is 'difficult to give an account of their number'.[56] According to the Revd Benjamin Chidlaw, there were 'thousands' of Welsh soldiers in the Union army by the summer of 1862: 'Mae miloedd o Gymry o New York, Pennsylfania, Ohio a Wisconsin ar y maes. Yr Hollalluog fyddo yn eu diogelu ac yn eu bendithio' ('There are thousands of Welsh from New York, Pennsylvania, Ohio and Wisconsin on the field. May the Almighty protect and bless them').[57] The Revd Chidlaw knew what he was talking about, and we can take him at his word. In addition to being chaplain of the 39th Ohio Infantry, Chidlaw was an active Christian missionary, and in this capacity he spent time with the soldiers of many different regiments. It is difficult to be more specific than Chidlaw's reference to 'thousands'. Remembering that, for the purposes of this study, 'Welsh' is defined as Welsh-speaking, we can at present account for a little over 3,000 Welsh soldiers. This is an extremely conservative number, based only on the hardest kinds of evidence; it is derived solely from surviving documents written by Welsh-speaking soldiers and civilians during the Civil War. The real number was surely much higher, and it is safe to suggest that there were at least 6,000 – and perhaps as many as 10,000 – Welsh-speaking soldiers in the Union army. While future research may allow for a slightly more specific number, we must be satisfied for now with the Revd Chidlaw's statement that there were 'thousands of Welshmen on the field'.

As seen in the cases of Benjamin Chidlaw and John M. Thomas, not every Welshman enlisted to fight with weapons; several Welsh ministers became chaplains with the Union army.[58] Other Welsh-speaking Americans enlisted as musicians. Daniel B. Davies was known as *y baswr mawr* – 'the big bass' – to the Welsh of Wisconsin before the war; he joined the 24th Wisconsin Infantry, playing tuba in the regimental band. Hugh Pritchard was born on a farm known as Garth Dorwen, near the village of Penygroes in Caernarfonshire. His family emigrated to Racine County, Wisconsin, naming their new farm Garth Dorwen as well. When the war broke out, Hugh enlisted as a musician with the 8th Wisconsin Infantry. And these two were not the only Welsh musicians to volunteer for Wisconsin regiments; Elias J. Prichard, another immigrant from Caernarfonshire, joined the band of the 22nd Wisconsin Infantry.[59]

Even before the first Welsh soldier went into battle, the war was bringing radical changes to the everyday life and language of Welsh America. Benjamin Chidlaw, undergoing the transformation from civilian minister to military chaplain, described life in the army camp succinctly as *dull newydd o fyw* – 'a new way of living'.[60] As Sgt. Daniel T. Jones noted in his letter to the press, the new Welsh recruits under his command had to learn 'the military way of eating, sleeping and walking' – 'y dull milwraidd o fwyta, cysgu a rhodio'.

> Pan ddaeth yr alwad . . . gadawsom ein cartref yn Coal Valley . . . Illinois. Siglasom ddwylaw a chanasom yn iach i'n hanwyl a hoff berthynasau, a ffwrdd a ni gyda brwdfrydedd dwys a theimlad anesgrifiadwy dros weriniaeth, rhyddid, ac iawnderau dynoliaeth . . . Arosasom am ychydig wythnosau yn Camp Dixon, Ill., lle y cawsom *slight introduction* i'r dull milwraidd o fwyta, cysgu a rhodio, ac erbyn ein bod wedi ein cyrchu i Camp Douglas ger Chicago, credem ein bod yn medru cerdded yn ddigon da gyda chynorthwy Corporal yn gweiddi *'Left, left, left,'* i osod holl filwyr *Jeff* dan ein traed a gwneyd holl dir cysegredig *Dixie* yn ddiffeithwch; wedi aros yno am ychydig ddyddiau cawsom ynau, blychau lledr, a *belts*, wedi eu haddurno a phres, &c., ac yr oeddem o ran golwg o leiaf yn ddynion hollol wahanol i'r hyn oeddem ychydig wythnosau cyn hynny[.][61]

> 'When the call came . . . we left our home in Coal Valley . . . Illinois. We shook hands and said farewell to our dear and beloved relatives, and off we went with deep enthusiasm and an indescribable feeling for democracy, freedom, and the rights of humanity . . . We stayed for a few weeks in Camp Dixon, Illinois, where we had a *slight introduction* to the military manner of eating, sleeping and marching, and by the time we reached Camp Douglas near Chicago, we thought that we could walk well enough with the help of a Corporal yelling *"Left, left, left"* to put all of the soldiers of *Jeff*[*erson Davis*] beneath our feet and turn all of the sacred land of *Dixie* into a wasteland; after waiting for a few days, we received guns, leather boxes and *belts*, adorned with brass, &c., and we were at least in appearance completely different men from that which we had been a few weeks before that.'

Crossing the threshold that separated civilian existence from military life was surely a big step for all Americans, yet it entailed an even greater change for those people for whom the very idea of soldiering was foreign. As discussed above, very few Welsh-speaking Americans had any military background before the war and the principles of pacifism had been embraced by some of their religious leaders during the 1850s. However, the changes that came after April 1861 were profound, and the rapid militarization of society touched all corners of Welsh America. Like the volunteers themselves, friends and family members who stayed at home had to adjust to new circumstances and modes of thinking, and letters published by soldiers like Daniel T. Jones ensured that Welsh readers across the northern United States had a taste – or at least a description – of the transformation from civilian to soldier which men like Jones were experiencing.

In describing the newness of army life, both Chidlaw and Jones use the word *dull*, meaning 'way', 'manner' or 'mode'. This also applied to their manner of speaking; language itself was tranformed by military experience. In recounting the Illinois Welshmen's introduction to military life, Daniel Jones focuses on 'eating, sleeping and marching', yet it can also be said that the Civil War brought a new way of *talking* for soldier and civilian alike. The coming of war and the subsequent militarization of society transformed the very language which people used on a daily basis, and for Welsh-speaking Americans this linguistic transformation was twofold.

Many of the new soldiers had little or no command of English, and this was true of some American-born Welsh speakers as well as recent immigrants; there were communities in rural Wisconsin, Ohio and New York where Welsh was the language of every aspect of life – home, farm, and chapel (supplemented by the literary culture of the *eisteddfod* and supported by the Welsh-language press of the United States). And there were even more people who, though more or less fluent in English, nonetheless lived most of their daily lives through the medium of Welsh. As already noted, some soldiers learned English only after enlisting in the Union army. Welsh speakers serving together could converse in their native language, and those lucky enough to have a Welsh-speaking chaplain had access to prayer meetings and perhaps the occasional sermon in their mother tongue. The few Welsh companies with 'fellow countrymen' for officers might even have received some orders and instructions in Welsh. Unlike German-speaking soldiers who, in addition to serving in German regiments, were often in German brigades, even those soldiers in Welsh companies had to use English for any communication outside the company's ranks (with the possible exception of those in the 56th Ohio Infantry who had a Welsh-speaking regimental adjutant). They all must have learned a great deal of English fairly quickly; in a very literal sense, their lives depended on it.

Thus the first kind of linguistic transformation involved a new or heightened familiarization with English. This is emphasized by the English words italicized in the published text of Daniel Jones's letter.[62] The volunteers are inducted into army life through the medium of English, as non-commissioned officers scream *'left, left, left'* at them on the drill grounds. Indeed, instead of writing *cyflwyniad* ('introduction'), or using any number of appropriate phrases which would have been available to Jones in Welsh, he uses the English *'slight introduction'*; the macaronic sentence gave civilian readers at home a taste of the military English surrounding the Welsh-speaking soldiers. And these civilians now had more cause to read English; while the Welsh press provided them with news of the war on a monthly and weekly basis, the desire for up-to-date reports from the front surely led more Welsh-Americans to turn to the English-language daily papers.

The other kind of linguistic transformation involved the Welsh language itself. Despite the heightened used of English, Welsh remained the main language of many communities, and, even if turning at times to English papers for news, Welsh-speaking Americans would discuss the war amongst themselves using their mother tongue. They thus had to familiarize themselves with phrases and terms which had not been part of their everyday vocabulary in peacetime. Both *Y Cenhadwr Americanaidd* and *Y Cyfaill o'r Hen Wlad* published lists of military terms which presented Welsh readers with the new words in their own language while also providing them with a linguistic mechanism for following the gist of news stories in the English-language papers. For example, readers were told in Welsh that the English word '*Ordnance*' was 'a name used for all types of large projectiles, in order to distinguish them from the category "Small Arms"'; '*Ordnance* – sydd enw a ddefnyddir ar bob math o gyflegrau mawrion, er mwyn eu gwahaniaethu oddiwrth yr enwad "Arfau Bychain" (*Small Arms*)'.[63] The development in military technology which would account for most battlefield casualties during the war was also explained to readers:

> . . . yn ddiweddar mae geu-dyllau *Muskets* y Talaethau wedi eu rhychu yn droellawg. Nid ydynt yn awr yn defnyddio yr hen fwled crwn, ond pelen bigyrnol, yr hon a deflir yn mhellach, a chyda mwy o gywirdeb[.][64]

> '. . . recently the barrels of the States' *Muskets* have been rifled in a spiral fashion. They do not now use the old round bullet, but rather a conical projectile, which is shot a greater distance, and with greater accuracy.'

Religious journals like *Y Cenhadwr Americanaidd* described the war as a 'fiery furnace' purging the nation of sin, presenting a theological interpretation of the conflict which drew upon the pyrotechnical rhetoric of the Welsh pulpit. Yet these same journals also ensured that Welsh-speaking Americans possessed the mundane vocabulary of warfare, the terminology which helped them understand how the modern technology of killing was transforming the fiery furnace of their ministers' rhetoric into tragic reality on the battlefield.

While these vocabulary lists and other similarly prosaic pieces were published in order to help Welsh-Americans adapt their language to wartime circumstances, some of America's Welsh bards turned this martial language into the stuff of poetry. The most famous of several Welsh poets who worked in the slate quarries of western Vermont and eastern upstate New York, Rowland Walter – commonly known by his bardic name, Ionoron Glan Dwyryd – composed an *englyn* on 'the Cannon':

> Offeryn ing o ffwrn angau – â thân
>   A thwrf rhwng ei weflau;
> O'i mîn hyll, dinistr mae'n hau –
> Gwae! yw anadl ei genau.[65]

'An instrument of agony from death's furnace – with fire
And tumult between its lips;
From its ugly orifice it sows destruction –
Woe! is the breath from its mouth.'

Like the theological interpretations of the war discussed at the beginning of this chapter, and like the list of military vocabulary, this *englyn* was published on the pages of *Y Cenhadwr Americanaidd*. Between April 1861 and April 1865, the Welsh-American press published a great amount of war poetry. Many of these verses appeared with the titles of melodies, a clear indication that the printed page was not the only medium by which this new war poetry was being transmitted to Welsh-speaking Americans; a large portion of these poems were in fact hymns and songs intended for performance during patriotic rallies and ceremonies. While some were sung, other poems were recited to crowds from the stages of American *eisteddfodau*.

As will be seen in Part Three, some of the poetry and prose published by the Welsh-American press after the fall of Fort Sumter did follow the darker, more meditative strain of war writing represented by this *englyn* to the Cannon. However, a great amount of Welsh-language war literature glorifies and romanticizes aspects of the conflict, and in that respect it was similar to much of what was being written and published in English at the time. This was in response to what we might call a pragmatic drive, as writers and poets placed their talents at the service of the Union war effort, producing material intended to bolster the morale of soldiers and civilians while also keeping them focused on the 'cause' or 'causes' of the war. As the new recruits marched off to fight, the Welsh press of the United States indulged in protracted literary adulations of the volunteers. In addressing the readers of his journal at the start of 1862, Robert Everett described the formation of the new volunteer army as one of the most memorable events of 1861:

> Ffurfiad y Fyddin Wladwriaethol ardderchog a godwyd er *hunanamddiffyniad* fydd un o'r pethau rhyfeddaf i'w cofio am y flwyddyn 1861. . . . [P]an ganfyddwyd y gelynion yn ymgodi yn ein plith, yn gwisgo eu harfau ac yn tanio eu magnelau, wele Fyddin o *saith gan' mil o wyr* yn dyfod i'r maes mewn ychydig wythnosau, oll yn *wirfoddolion*, heb na galw enwau na *drafftio* neb![66]

> 'The formation of the splendid National Army which was mustered for *self defence* will be one of the most wondrous things to remember about the year 1861. . . . When the enemies arose amongst us, bearing their arms and firing their canons, behold an Army of *seven hundred thousand men* coming to the field in a few weeks, all *volunteers*, without calling names or *drafting* anybody!'

Praising the volunteers with his own pen in this manner, Everett also rewarded them with the fruits of his printing press, sending copies of *Y Cenhadwr*

Americanaidd free of charge to soldiers. The *Cenhadwr*'s editor similarly urged other civilians to send Welsh-language reading material to friends and relatives in the Union army; if the publications of Welsh America went to war figuratively by supporting the Union's war effort, they also went to war literally, as will be seen in detail in Chapter Five.[67]

A number of writers published letters and articles suggesting that a formal record of all Welsh-American volunteers be kept. Evan Griffiths of Iowa presented his idea to the readers of the *Cenhadwr*:

> Mr. Golygydd, – Tybiwyf y byddai yn fuddiol a chyfiawn i'n cenedl, i gael hysbysrwydd trwy gyfrwng y cyhoeddiadau Cymreig o nifer eu meibion sydd wedi ymrestru yn myddinoedd yr Undeb er dechreu y rhyfel . . . Mae llawer o'n gwroniaid, ein dysgedion, ein llaw gelfyddydwyr, a'n duwinyddion . . . wedi eu claddu byth yn malurion yr oesau, heb gymaint a choffa am danynt, o eisiau rhagfeddwl a dal ar adeg fel hon i'w cofnodi. Nis gallaf gredu eu bod yn fwy hwyrfrydig i ddwyn arfau yn erbyn y gwrthryfel yn ein gwlad, na chenedloedd eraill; o ganlyniad, tegwch fyddai eu cofnodi, fel rhai a roddasant gymhorth i'r llywodraeth i lethu y gwrthryfel presenol.[68]

> 'Mr. Editor, – I think that it would be profitable and just for our nation to be informed by means of the Welsh publications of the number of their sons who have enlisted in the armies of the Union since the start of the war . . . Many of our heroes, our scholars, our craftsmen, and our theologians . . . have been buried forever in the debris of the ages, without so much as a memorial to them, for lack of forethought and failure to grasp a moment like this one in order to record them. I cannot believe that they [i.e. Welsh volunteers] have been slower to take up arms against the rebellion in our country than other nations; by result, it would be fair to record them as ones who gave support to the government in putting down the present rebellion.'

Griffiths's first sentence brings together a heady mixture of concepts and beliefs. He writes that it would be [*b*]*uddiol a chyfiawn* – 'beneficial and just' – for the Welsh of America – described as [*ei*]*n cenedl*, 'our nation' – to be informed by means of the press as to the number of their 'sons' (*meibion*) in the Union armies. Like the editorial published by *Y Seren Orllewinol* during the first weeks of the war, this writer calls for an exact count of all the Welsh volunteers. And, like so much Welsh writing during the war, Griffiths locates the separate identity of Welsh-Americans (*ein cenedl*) comfortably within the Union which they were fighting to preserve.

Having set out the general principle, Evan Griffiths then proceeds to provide a concrete example by listing the Welsh volunteers from his area who had joined the 22nd Iowa Infantry (a group which included his own son):

> Yn y *company* A, Cadben Lee, 22ain Gatrawd Iowa, y mae 7 o Gymry, sef David J. Roberts, Corporal; David J. Davies yn 1st Isgadben sef mab i'r Parch. John Davies,

> gynt o Ninetysix, ger Remsen, E[frog] N[ewydd]; William Hughes yn ail Isgadben; Samuel C. Jones yn Sergeant cyntaf, sef mab i'r Parch M. M. Jones; Samuel D. Price yn ysgrifenydd yr Isgadben; Richard Thomas, a Joshua Hughes yn filwyr cyffredin.
>
> Yn *company* I, Cadben Robertson, y mae Joseph E. Griffith yn ail Sergeant; Thomas T. Davies yn 6ed Corporal; Edward Breeze; John R. Hughes; Griffith N. Griffiths; Thos. P. Jones, a Thos. Marsden yn filwyr cyffredin.[69]
>
> 'In company A, Captain Lee, 22nd Regiment Iowa, there are 7 Welshmen, namely David J. Roberts, Corporal; David J. Davies, 1st Lieutenant, namely the Revd John Davies's son, formerly from Ninetysix, near Remsen, New York; William Hughes, second Lieutenant; Samuel C. Jones, first Sergeant, namely son to the Revd M. M. Jones; Samuel D. Price, secretary to the Lieutenant; Richard Thomas and Joshua Hughes, common soldiers.
>
> In company I, Captain Robertson, Joseph E. Griffith is second Sergeant; Thomas T. Davies 6th Corporal; Edward Breeze; John R. Hughes; Griffith N. Griffiths; Thos. P. Jones, a Thos. Marsden common soldiers.'

Other writers were to echo these sentiments on the pages of *Y Cenhadwr Americanaidd*, *Y Cyfaill o'r Hen Wlad*, *Y Seren Orllewinol* and *Y Drych* throughout the war. However, no formal printed record of all Welsh volunteers was kept.[70] On the other hand, these Welsh-American publications – and, indeed, many of the publications back in Wales – did perform the service in an ad-hoc fashion, publishing the names of volunteers, praising them in prose and verse, and recording the biographies of those Welsh-speaking soldiers who died in uniform.

Essays and letters like the one published by Evan Griffiths reveal a desire to record for posterity the exact facts regarding the numbers and names of Welsh recruits, thus providing a kind of utilitarian tribute to the volunteers. Other very different kinds of prose tributes were published, including short works of sentimental fiction, some of them translated from English. Robert Everett published the following piece in the pages of the *Cenhadwr*:

> Deuwch gyda mi i'r ystafell fach brydferth draw, a dangosaf i chwi eneth siriol yn brysur gyda ei gwaith yn gwau. Y lodes fach dlawd hon sydd gloff o'i mebyd, eto gwelwch mor gyflym y mae yn *ceisio gwneud daioni*. Gofynais iddi a oedd yr hosanau yr oedd mor brysur ar waith arnynt yn cael eu bwriadu i dad anwyl neu frawd ymhlith y gwirfoddolion. Atebodd yn anwylaidd ei gwedd, 'Nid oes genyf na thad na brawd; ond y mae yn hoff genyf am yr holl wirfoddolion, ac mae'r hosanau hyn i unrhyw filwr tlawd y byddo arno eu heisiau.' Dymunwn innau fod fy holl gyfeillion ieuainc yn dilyn siampl yr eneth fach haelionus ac anwyl hon, ac yn gwneud rhywbeth dros y milwyr, y rhai a aethant allan mor benderfynol dros ein gwlad yn ei chyfyngder mawr.[71]

> 'Come with me to the small beautiful room over there, and I will show you a cheerful girl busy at work knitting. This poor little lass who is lame from childhood, yet see how swiftly she is *trying to do good*. I asked her if the socks she was so busy working on were intended for a dear father or brother amongst the volunteers. She answered with a tender look, "I have neither father nor brother; but I like all of the volunteers, and these socks are for any poor soldier who might need them." I myself wish that all my little friends would follow the example of this generous and dear little girl, and do something for the soldiers, who went out so determinedly to help our country in its great hardship.'

This short narrative was obviously designed to engender action; the voice of the un-named narrator urges the youth of Welsh America to support the volunteers. Employing a kind of melodrama so common to Victorian fiction in Wales, England and America, the reader is introduced to an orphaned child, lame from birth. She is a girl, a member of the sex removed by nineteenth-century social convention and military practice from the battlefield. The character at the centre of this one-paragraph story is portrayed as the weakest possible member of society, existing in a state of compounded helplessness; she is an orphaned (and thus undefended) child, presented explicitly as alone, physically disabled and confined, it seems, to her chair. Yet she *'is trying to do good'*, and succeeds in doing so. If aimed specifically at the writer's 'young friends', this short piece of patriotic fiction carried a message for all the journal's readers; it told them that every single member of northern society could and should contribute to the Union war effort. However innocent and simple on the surface, this work of propagandistic literature suggests that the processes of militarization reached all corners of Welsh America.

Much of the early war literature centring on the volunteers originated with the community's public celebration of its soldiers. As noted above, these meetings and ceremonies served to articulate the links between volunteers and their civilian home communities. In addition to recruiting new soldiers, such events were used to present new companies and regiments with their battle flags and to see them off to war. Prose and poetry stemming from these ceremonies, while providing a good idea as to Welsh America's adulation of its volunteers, are only the literary remains of complex social interactions. We may have the published versions of songs sung at patriotic gatherings or 'war meetings', yet these published texts are but the traces of live performances, and these performances in turn were only part of the wider social context of the public celebration or ceremony. Such events are by their very nature ephemeral; we can only attempt to reconstruct these ceremonies by using the surviving print and manuscript sources as guidelines. Any public event has as many possible interpretations as participants; however, the published poetry and prose descriptions stemming from these ceremonies present what we might call a 'formal' or 'authorative' interpretation of the event. The author sending the piece for publication was often an important figure in the local

Welsh community (a minister and/or prominent poet or essayist), and in publishing the text that author was working with the editor of the journal or newspaper, a figure with authority at the national level of Welsh-American society. Together, author and editor produced a public record of the occasion which interpreted the event in a particular way and carried the stamp of their authority.

One of the most important of such events was the departure of the volunteers. Like the processes by which soldiers were recruited in Ohio and Wisconsin discussed above, the community's farewell celebration was a public event which provided a formal interpretation of the emotional basis for the link between soldier and home community, a bond which the recruits would carry with them to camp and battlefield. Surviving texts, both printed and in manuscript, all stress the emotional nature of the event. Indeed, many of the published texts which describe these farewell ceremonies can be seen as an attempt to enshrine the emotional force of the 'memorable day' forever in prose or poetry. The same writer who recorded the methods by which Welsh soldiers were recruited for the 56th Ohio Infantry also described the volunteers leaving home:

> Penodwyd diwrnod i'r meibion heini i ymadael â Centreville. – Ar y diwrnod hwnw casglodd rhyw lawer iawn ynghyd i ffarwelio â hwynt ac i ddymuno iddynt bob llwyddiant. – O'r teimladau a'r dagrau dywalltwyd yno y diwrnod hwnw! Yn nghanol y cynhwrf . . . sylwais ar un peth a effeithiodd yn rhyfeddol, ie, yn rhyfeddol iawn ar fy nheimladau. – Wel, beth oedd hyny? Gwelais ddynes ieuanc lanwedd, siriol ei gwedd, ymddangosai fel angyles i mi a siaradai yr iaith arferai fy mam anwyl ei siarad â mi yn *Nghymru wen*. Gwelwn hi yn estyn ei llaw arianaidd at y milwr hwn ac at y milwr arall, fel pe buasai yn rhoddi rhyw beth iddynt. Neseais ymlaen gael gweled y symudiad – a beth feddyliech chwi oedd hi yn ei wneud? O! 'r Arglwydd a'i bendithio hi; dim ond anrhegu y gwirfoddiaid â Thestament glân ein Harglwydd Iesu – ïe, dim ond hyny. Beth allasai wneud yn fwy, er dangos ei chariad at gyrff ac eneidiau y bechgyn gwiw.[72]
>
> 'A day was set for the sturdy boys to depart from Centreville. – On that day a great many gathered together to say farewell to them and to wish them every success. – Oh, the feelings and the tears which were spilled there that day! In the middle of the excitement . . . I noticed one thing which affected my feelings wondrously, yes, most wondrously. – Well, what was that? I saw I young pretty woman, cheerful of appearance; she appeared as an angel to me and she spoke the language my dear mother used to speak with me in *fair Wales*. I saw her extending her silvery hand to this soldier and to that soldier, as if she were giving something to them. I drew closer in order to see the movement – and what do you think she was doing? Oh! May the Lord bless her; only giving as a present to the volunteers the holy Testament of our Lord Jesus – yes, only that. What more could she have done in order to show her love for the bodies and souls of the comely boys.'

The writer's pen-name was 'Cymro Tawel', 'Quiet Welshman', a pseudonym belied by the agitated emotional state which he claims to have experienced during the event he describes. Indeed, the Quiet Welshman felt moved to compose a poem in praise of 'fair Gweni', the young woman who 'showed her love' to the volunteers in such a Christian fashion:

Pwy yw, medd rhyw un oddi draw,
Oedd â'r fath anrheg yn ei llaw?
I'w hoddi'n rhwydd a hyny'n rhad
I'n meibion mwyn ein meibion mâd?

O gwiw yw dweyd mai Gweni dlos,
Merch Davies fwyn o Ty'n y Rhos,
A wnaeth fath weithred fawr ei bri,
Bydd cofio byth am dani hi.[73]

'Who is she, asks somebody over yonder,
With such a gift in her hand?
To give freely and for free
To our gentle sons, our good sons?

'Oh, it is fitting to say that it was fair Gweni,
Daughter of gentle Davies from Tŷ'n Rhos,
Who performed an act of such great distinction,
She will always be remembered.'

Like the short fictional piece describing the orphaned girl knitting socks for the volunteers, the Quiet Welshman's tribute centres upon the support which the women of the community extend to the soldiers.

While this prose-and-verse piece takes as its starting point the volunteers' departure for war, the Quiet Welshman describes a bond between soldier and civilian which is anchored in peaceful qualities. The soldiers, like Gweni Davies's father, are described using the adjective *mwyn*, meaning 'kind', 'tender', or 'gentle'. These soldiers, also described as *mâd*, 'good', are presented explictly as the 'sons' (*meibion*) of those civilians remaining at home. As noted above, in his analysis of the domestic imagery used to interpret the experiences of Union soldiers, Reid Mitchell states that 'Northern culture put domesticity at the center of society and women at the center of domesticity'; he adds that, because 'the army was an exclusively male preserve', this 'presented a problem for soldiers who wanted their service to be a sign of their good moral conduct'.[74] This might have been all the more so for Welsh-Americans who had little or no direct experience of war before 1861, and whose religious leaders had embraced a kind of pacifism not long before. Rather than focusing on the violent nature of the experiences to which these Welsh Ohioans march, this writer chooses to praise the 'good sons' for their gentle qualities, and the point of reference from which he describes those virtues is provided by a female member of their community.

In her study of the (English-language) popular literature published during the Civil War, Alice Fahs discusses a range of 'writings [which] stressed the central importance of women in supporting men's enlistment'.[75] Fahs's analysis of what she calls 'The Feminized War', like the emphasis which Reid Mitchell places upon the importance of domestic imagery, help us to situate Welsh texts like this one within the broader context of wartime American writing.[76] In many ways the country's Welsh-language press was presenting its readers with imagery and modes of interpreting the war's meaning(s) which echoed prose and poetry being published by the English-language press of the United States. The Quiet Welshman's text, however, can also be read productively in relation to recent Welsh history, for that history conveyed a heightened significance to the way in which Welsh women were portrayed in writing. Among other things, the 'Blue Books' published in 1847 had questioned the morality of Welsh women, and the flurry of literary responses to the British government's degrading report included a concerted attempt to portray the mothers, sisters and daughters of Wales in a particular way.[77] Literary constructions of Welsh women stressed their morality and Christian virtue as well as their Welshness. In the words of Jane Aaron, 'O burdan enllib y Sais ymrithiodd yr arwres newydd, yn bur, yn dduraidd, ac yn hunanymwybodol Gymreig'; 'from the purgatory of the Englishman's slander the new heroine emerged, pure, steel-like, and self-consciously Welsh.'[78] The women of post-1847 Wales had a special role to play:

> Yr oedd anrhydedd ei chrefydd . . . yn ogystal ag enw da ei chenedl, yn dibynnu ar lwyddiant y Gymraes i ddinoethi celwydd Brad y Llyfrau Gleision trwy brofi ei bod yn 'bur fel y dur'.[79]
>
> 'The honour of her religion . . . in addition to her nation's reputation, depended on the Welsh woman's success at exposing the lie of the Blue Books' Treachery by proving that she was "pure like steel." '

The Quiet Welshman draws attention to the fact that Gweni Davies speaks Welsh in addition to praising her for encouraging the Welsh soldiers to (continue to) embrace Christianity while in uniform. He describes the young woman as an 'angel' – a patently Christian messenger – in the same sentence which stresses her Welshness: 'she appeared as an angel to me, and she spoke the language which my dear mother used to speak with me in *fair Wales*' ('ymddangosai fel angyles i mi a siaradai yr iaith arferai fy mam anwyl ei siarad â mi yn *Nghymru wen*').[80]

While Gweni Davies may well have been born in Ohio, this writer, who refers directly to his childhood in Wales, was an immigrant. As discussed in

Chapter One, aspects of what we might call post-1847 culture were brought to the United States by Welsh immigrants. When war came, what had by 1861 become traditional ways of portraying Welsh women melded easily with ways in which American popular culture was constructing a 'feminized war'. The Quiet Welshman's description of the volunteers' departure tells us something of the role played by Welsh-American women in the constellation of public ceremony and literary conventions linking the soldiers to their home communities. It also shows that this bond between soldier and civilian was often tempered with religious belief; Gweni is said to have given each of the departing soldiers a 'Testament', and it is this detail above all else which so excites the otherwise 'quiet' Welsh writer. Gweni Davies's Bibles reflect Robert Everett's published announcement that he was going to present volunteers with free copies of *Y Cenhadwr Americanaidd*. In both cases there is an actual physical gift made to symbolize the link between soldier and home community, and the present in both examples is explicitly defined as religious reading material (remembering that the *Cenhadwr* was the journal of the Welsh Congregationalists in America).

Writings like the text published by Cymro Tawel romanticized the volunteers' departure, providing the wider community of Welsh America with a specific ideological – and, often, theological – interpretation of the local community's farewell ceremony. While many soldiers would in time contribute hundreds of pages of prose and poetry to the Welsh-American press, most published descriptions of these kinds of events are told from the point of view of the civilians staying behind; these texts can be seen as literary manifestations of the public support offered by the community to its volunteers. The soldiers themselves are by no means silent regarding this aspect of their wartime experiences. Sergeant Daniel T. Jones, for example, described his company's departure from Coal Valley, emphasizing the emotional and patriotic aspects of the occasion: 'We shook hands and said farewell to our dear and beloved relatives, and off we went with deep enthusiasm and an indescribable feeling for democracy, freedom, and the rights of humanity' ('Siglasom ddwylaw a chanasom yn iach i'n hanwyl a hoff berthynasau, a ffwrdd a ni gyda brwdfrydedd dwys a theimlad anesgrifiadwy dros weriniaeth, rhyddid, ac iawnderau dynoliaeth').[81] This, however, is only one isolated sentence in an extended description of the Welsh company's introduction to military life, and it is thus very different from those poems and prose pieces devoted solely to the volunteers' departure.

One such poem was published in the October 1861 issue of *Y Cenhadwr Americanaidd*. It was composed by 'Josiah' of Lexington, Illinois, and bears the title 'Ychydig Linellau a gyfansoddwyd wrth weled cyfeillion yn ymadael tua maes y rhyfel' – 'A Few Lines composed at seeing friends depart for the field of battle'.[82] The title's short description provides a dramatic frame for the poem, asking us to imagine the event on which it is predicated: the poet is part of a crowd of civilians, cheering the volunteers who march south to war.[83] As some of the new recruits are described explicitly as *cyfeillion*, 'friends', the close bond between civilians and soldiers is emphasized. While Josiah tells us that he is watching his friends' departure, and thus staying behind, the poem itself elides the distinction between civilian observer and marching soldier; the poet uses the first person plural of the verb throughout, saying in effect, '*we* march to war'.

> Yn mlaen, yn mlaen yn awr
> Ymneswn oll yn nhgyd,
> Er maint y cyffro mawr
> Sy'n siglo seiliau'r byd;
> Dan faner Rhyddid awn yn glau
> Yn ngwyneb nerth y gelyn gau.[84]

> 'Onwards, onwards now
> We all draw closer together,
> Despite the scale of the great tumult
> Which shakes the foundations of the world;
> Under Freedom's banner we go quickly
> To face the false enemy's might.'

These short lines suggest the way in which the ceremonial farewell inspired the gathered crowd to identify with the departing soldiers; they are 'all draw[ing] closer together', marching as one under 'Freedom's banner'. The observer is included emotionally in the soldiers' departure, a reading confirmed by the first line of the final verse: 'Yn mlaen am hyny awn' – 'Onwards, because of that, we go'. The repetition of the words *Yn mlaen*, 'onwards', echo the 'on to Richmond' war cry which studded Northern papers during the early months of the war; this phrase, rooted in the popular pro-war culture of the time, lends rhythm to what is in effect a civilian's literary version of the soldiers' marching song.

Although published descriptions of the farewell written by volunteers themselves are relatively scarce, there are a number of unpublished diaries and letters which help us understand how the new soldiers experienced the occasion. (More precisely, what these texts show is how soldiers presented and interpreted their experiences in writing.) John Rowlands of the 14th Vermont Infantry described the day of departure in his diary: 'Dyma ddiwrnod byth gofadwy, pan yn ffarwelio a chyfeillion ac a'm annwyl wraig a blentyn'; 'This is an ever-memorable day, saying farewell to friends to my dear wife and child'.[85] He attempts to crystallize the experience in writing by using the compound adjective 'byth-gof[i]adwy', 'immemorial' or 'ever-memorable'. This same word also punctuates published descriptions of similar occasions, allowing us to conclude that private accounts reflect the published public record to a degree. David Davies, who recorded his personal experience of the event in his diary, also used this adjective:

> Sul 5 Ionawr. Diwrnod teg bythgofiadwy gennyf, teimladau rhyfedd yn fy meddiannu heddiw wrth feddwl efallai mai dyma y Sabbath olaf am byth ymhlith fy ffrindiau a'm cydnabod. Yn y capel y bore a'r nos. Ffarwelio a'm cyfeillion yn hen ac ieuainc a heno cyn ymadael, Leila Hughes yn troi ataf yn y diwedd i ffarwelio, i'r hon y rhoddais 'Farewell Kiss'; cefais gernod yn ad-daliad!
>
> Llun 6 Ionawr. Diwrnod teg a diwrnod hynod. Torri i lawr wrth gadw dyletswydd bore heddiw, felly fy ewyrth Daniel. Cychwyn o gartref am tua 8 a.m. mewn teimladau da (ar ol cael sbel dda o wylo ar ol brecwast [. . .]), y teulu oll yn fy hebrwng i'r 'Flatts'. Cyfarfod Mam yno yr hon oedd yn wylo yn ddrwg. Cael digon o beth yfed yno am ddim. Teimlo yn dda iawn yn cychwyn tua 9.30[.][86]
>
> 'Sunday 5 January [1862]. A beautiful ever-memorable day for me, strange feelings possessing me today at thinking that this may be my last Sabbath among friends and acquaintances forever. In the chapel morning and night. Said farewell to my friends old and young tonight before departing, Leila Hughes turned to me to say farewell, to whom I gave a 'Farewell Kiss'; I got a slap for repayment!
>
> 'Monday 6 January. A beautiful day and a remarkable day. Broke down while conducting family prayers this morning, thus also my uncle Daniel. Started from home about 8 a.m. in good spirits (after having a spell of crying after breakfast [. . .]), the entire family accompanying me to the 'Flats' [the local lowland area where the train station was located]. Met Mother there; she was crying badly. Got plenty enough to drink there for free. Feeling very well when starting about 9.30.'

Details such as David Davies's use of the word *bythgofiadwy* and his description of the big day as *hynod*, 'remarkable', resemble the language of published texts describing the same kind of event. However, the personal diary of this New York volunteer includes other details which are for the most part absent from the pages of the religious (and pro-temperance) journals of Welsh America, for he confesses to making bold with a female acquaintance and to exploiting the emotions of his friends in order to get drunk for free.

Published tributes to the departing volunteers often present an idealized description of the soldier's interior state, imagined as one of religious devotion and patriotic determination. Josiah's poem, for example, emphasizes the resolve of the Illinois soldiers, singing together as they march 'onwards' to battle 'under Freedom's banner'. David Davies's diary presents a slightly different picture. While agreeing with published texts in emphasizing the emotional nature of the event, this volunteer does not describe his own interior state in terms of patriotic resolve; he writes rather of *teimladau rhyfedd*, the 'strange feelings' which marked his last Sunday at home, recording a sense of foreboding. However, by the time he left he was 'feeling very well' thanks to the alcohol consumed during the tearful farewell. The denominational journals, presenting temperance as part of a constellation of causes which they saw as defining the public morality of Welsh America, tended to portray drinking alcohol and Christian virtue as diametrical opposites. This soldier's unpublished, personal text presents what is perhaps a more realistic picture, drawn in mixed, overlapping shades rather than the clear black and white moral tones of the religious press. Other parts of his diary attest to the fact that David Davies was a committed Christian, reading his Bible regularly, attending religious services whenever possible, and meditating on spiritual topics. Indeed, the same diary entry which records his farewell drinking binge also notes that he was in chapel 'morning and night' on his last Sunday at home and that he himself led 'family prayers' a few hours before his departure.

David Davies was from Nelson, New York. As the written record of his departure from that community focuses to an excent on its women – Leila Hughes, whom he attempted to kiss, and his mother, who saw him off while 'crying badly' – it's worth reading his diary in the context of a poem published by 'Rebeca', a Welsh woman from Nelson.[87] The verse, published in *Y Cenhadwr Americanaidd* in October 1862, is simply entitled 'Ein Milwyr', 'Our Soldiers', and is similiar to many other poems written in both Welsh and English in praise of the Union volunteers. It stresses their patriotic resolve to preserve the Union, painting a portrait of determined recruits who march south while 'their love for the Union / grows stonger continually' ('Eu cariad at yr Undeb / O hyd sydd yn cryfhau').[88] In her description of the volunteers' farewell, Rebeca, like David Davies, mentions the 'mother's tears':

Gadawsant eu hanwyliaid
  A'r dedwydd gartref clyd.
Wna dagrau mam na phriod
  Mo'u rhwystro i ymgasglu ynghyd.[89]

'They left their dear ones
  And the happy, warm home.
The tears of neither mother nor wife
  will keep them from mustering together.'

While both were written by Welsh-speaking Americans from Nelson, New York, the formal aspects of these two texts, as well as the circumstances in which they were produced, differ considerably. One is a piece of personal, unpublished prose written by a male volunteer, the other is a public, published poem composed by a female civilian. And while they diverge considerably in the case of David Davies's record of drinking and (what many

Welsh-Americans would interpret as) moral laxity, both writers focus on the image of the mother's tears in describing the volunteer's departure.

The soldiers' farewell was not the only kind of event which inspired Welsh-American poets and writers. On the Fourth of July 1861, a gathering was held by the Welsh community of Floyd, New York. This was the first Independence Day commemorated during the Civil War, and the usual expressions of patriotism were channelled into specific meditations on the crisis threatening the United States. A poem – composed specifically for the occasion by a local bard known as 'Ab Morydd' – was sung as part of a flag-raising ceremony organized by the Welsh residents of Floyd. The verse was published in *Y Cenhadwr Americanaidd* a few months later, proceeded by a description of the event.

> Yr Achlysur o Ddyrchafiad y Lluman Undebol yn Floyd.
>
> Datganwyd rhan o'r ganig ganlynol, gan bedwar o bersonau, er boddhad cynulleidfa luosog, pan yn dyrchafu "Lluman Undebol" ar Fryn Floyd, Gorph. 4, 1861 – eu ton – *Milford*.[90]

> 'The Occasion of Raising the Union Flag in Floyd.
>
> Part of the following song was performed, by four people, to the satisfaction of a large crowd, when the "Union Flag" was raised on Floyd Hill, July 4, 1861 – their tune – *Milford*.'

The piece was sent to the journal by the Revd R. Evans.[91] By taking this step to publish the prose-and-verse record of the occasion Evans was helping to transform an ephemeral event in the life of his local community into a lasting literary record of Welsh-American patriotism. And in presenting his text by means of the press to a wider readership, the author was working with the journal's editor to inspire other Welsh communities across the northern United States to hold similar meetings and to use their literary (and musical) talents in order to bolster the Union cause.

The poem itself is an extended meditation on the flag, and as such it had plenty of English-language parallels. The public-performative context in which it originated was also in many ways typical of wartime American culture, north and south. According to Alice Fahs:

> At the start of the war, it was widely assumed that poetry and song had an important patriotic role to play in the war. Numerous writers – both obscure and well known – produced poetry that asserted the communicative power of poetry in wartime. They wrote verse intended to inspire their compatriots to enlist in the war. They composed 'national songs' intended to be new symbols of nationality. They wrote paeans to the national flag. . . . And they sent hundreds of verses to newspapers. In writing such verse, they treated poems as imaginative acts that not only reflected a new nationhood but actively called it into being.[92]

Americans, she states, 'assumed' that verse and song would play a part in the war. This was a natural extension of pre-war American culture; as Richard Marius notes in the introduction to his anthology of English-language Civil War poetry, '[n]ineteenth-century Americans expected poetry to be served up on every occasion and devoured it when it was set before them'.[93]

In addition to reading songs like this one within the broader American context described by Fahs and Marius, the fact that Welsh-speaking Americans such as the residents of Floyd 'assumed that poetry and song had an important patriotic role to play in the war' can be interpreted as a logical extension of a specifically Welsh emphasis on these arts. As discussed in detail in Chapter One, Welsh-language literary and cultural societies were being formed in the United States as early as the 1830s, and by the 1850s *eisteddfodau* were taking root in American soil. In addition to the public role played by poetry in Welsh society, immigrants brought to the United States what was becoming an increasingly popular musical culture in Wales during the mid-nineteenth century. Welsh people were coming to call their country *Gwlad y Gân*, 'the Land of Song', a process described by Hywel Teifi Edwards:

> Erbyn diwedd y 60au roedd Cymru'n arddel y teitl, 'Gwlad y Gân,' ac yn cynnig i'r byd . . . ei diléit mewn cymanfa a sol-ffa, oratorio a chôr, telyn a chainc, piano a solo yn brawf o'i rhagoriaeth. . . . Un o gynhwysion pwysicaf myth Gwerin Cymru yw 'Gwlad y Gân'. Gellid 'canu'r byd i'w le' – o ganu'n ddigon uchel.[94]

> 'By the end of the 1860s Wales was adopting the title "the Land of Song", and offering to the world . . . its love of the singing festival and of sol-fa, of oratorio and choir, harp and tune, piano and solo as proof of its excellence. . . . "The Land of Song" is one of the most important ingredients in the myth of the Folk of Wales. It was possible "to sing the world into place" – if one sang loud enough.'

Whatever pre-war cultural influences helped shaped the performance which took place in Floyd, New York on 4 July 1861, the people who took part were certainly trying 'to sing the world into place'. They were attempting to sing their own Welsh-American world into place, using poetry and song to articulate their identity as loyal citizens in a country torn by civil war. Like so many other poems composed early in the war, the words written by Ab Morydd for the Floyd ceremony use the national flag as a symbol for focusing attention on the concept of nationhood and the attendant act of maintaining – or preserving – that nationhood.

The public performance of this song on the first Fourth of July of the war can be seen as an attempt to yoke a verbal meditation on the concept of nationhood to an actual physical artefact (the very real 'Union Flag' raised on Floyd Hill) which represents that abstract concept. Whatever actually happened in the New York town on that day, the prose introduction to the poem which the Revd Evans published in *Y Cenhadwr Americanaidd* certainly makes the connection between physical artefact and literary creation clear; the written record draws attention to the flag itself, bringing the speech act – that is, the public declaration of allegiance – together with the physical emblem of that allegiance.[95] The flag is described not as the 'United States Flag' but as 'Lluman yr Undeb', 'The Union Flag', the banner of the Union war effort. It is the abstract and imagined *Union* of the United States which the Welsh community of Floyd was emphasizing on the Fourth of July, and the local minister's reportage suggests this emphasis in several ways: the 'satisfied' crowd is described as *lluosog*, 'large' or 'numerous', and the poem itself, rather than being performed by a soloist, was sung by four different – yet, presumably, harmonized or harmonizing – individuals. The emphasis throughout is on the community, a real union of individuals which represents the imagined Union of the United States.[96]

Ab Morydd's first verse describes the act of raising the flag as an affirmation of faith in the concept of Union and the ultimate success of the Union's war effort:

Mae'n ffydd wrth ddyrchu'n Baner fraith,
Daw llwydd i'n gwaith mewn gwir,
Hi brofa nad am amser maith
Bydd gorthrwm yn ein tir.

'Our faith as we raise the spangled Banner is that
Success will come to our endeavour in truth,
It will prove that oppression
Will not last for a long time in our land.'

While neither the poem nor its prose introduction state specifically that the Fourth of July celebration was used to recruit soldiers, the event took place less than three months after the fall of Fort Sumter, during the first great volunteer drive. Moreover, Ab Morydd's words strongly suggest that the gathering was used to encourage potential volunteers. As the second and third verses emphasize, this New York community was using the event to boast of its contribution to the war effort; it declared in song that it was 'sacrificing' its young men for the cause.

Aberthu'n meib a wnawn i'r gâd;
Er cynydd rhif ein sêr,
A dwyn gwir ryddid trwy'n holl wlad,
Wrth gynllun doeth ein Nêr.

Ni welodd haul y nef erioed,
Fath Undeb mewn un wlad;

Hen famau serchog ar fryn Floyd,
  Yn foddlawn uno'r gâd!

'We will sacrifice our sons to the fight;
  In order to increase the number of our stars,
And bring true freedom throughout our country,
  According to the wise plan of our Lord.

'The sun of heaven has never witnessed
  Such a Union in any country;
Dear old mothers on Floyd Hill,
  Willingly join the fight!'

The mothers described by this poet may have been 'dear', but they are not portrayed as overly sensitive. If Welsh writers of Nelson, New York, drew attention to the mother's tears, this Welsh poet from Floyd invokes a more stoical image of the volunteer's mother. As noted above, in her discussion of 'The Feminised War', Alice Fahs describes the emphasis which popular literature placed upon 'the central importance of women in supporting men's enlistment'.[97] Despite the importance accorded to wives, sisters and daughters in Welsh and English wartime writing, no figure was more central to the patriotic literature of enlistment than the soldier's mother, and Welsh-American poets had a wealth of different images on which to draw in producing literary constructions of the volunteer's mother. Aspects of the American cultural heritage so readily adopted by immigrants and their children included the figure of the 'Republican Mother', described by Linda Kerber as a specific ideological development which followed the Revolution.[98] And, as Reid Mitchell has suggested, the image of the good Republican Mother influenced the domestic imagery of the Civil War; the 'Republican Mother raised virtuous Republican Children', and by the summer of 1861 the Union's pro-war writers were interpreting that to mean sons who volunteered to fight against the secessionist Rebels.[99]

In addition to this American rhetorical tradition, writers and poets like Ab Morydd could draw upon what were becoming traditional Welsh images of femininity and motherhood. It has already been suggested that the Welsh writer from Ohio who praised Gweni Davies for her Welshness and for her support of Christian values was drawing upon the post-1847 stream of writing which, in the words of Jane Aaron, portrayed the Welsh woman as supporting 'the honour of her religion . . . in addition to the good name of her nation . . . by proving herself to be "as pure as steel" '.[100] If 'pure', steel is first and foremost a hard metal, and Aaron describes the process by which an image of *Y Gymraes dduraidd*, the 'steel-like Welsh woman', was set against literary constructions of the 'soft' English woman.[101] Nineteenth-century Welsh writers were busy constructing what scholars such as Hywel Teifi Edwards have called 'myth Gwerin Cymru', 'the myth of the Welsh Folk', and one of the stereotypical images of that constructed mythology was *Y Fam Gymreig*, 'the Welsh Mother'. Jane Aaron stresses the role which biblical imagery played in the genesis of this figure:

> Defnyddiwyd yr ymadrodd 'mam yn Israel' dro ar ôl tro yn ysgrifau cofiannol y bedwaredd ganrif ar bymtheg i ddisgrifio'r Gymraes ddelfrydol, ac y mae ysbryd ymosodol Debora yn rhan o ddelwedd y Fam Gymreig. Ei phrif nodweddion yw diwydrwydd egnïol a dygnwch milwriaethus yn wyneb caledi bywyd[.][102]
>
> 'The expression "mother in Israel" was used time and again in the biographical essays of the nineteenth century to describe the ideal Welsh woman, and Deborah's aggressive spirit was part of the image of the Welsh Mother. Her main characteristics are an energetic diligence and a militant assiduity in the face of life's hardship.'

The Welsh-American mothers addressed in Ab Morydd's Fourth of July song can be seen as part *Mam Gymreig* and part Republican Mother. Unlike the very real and believable tearful mother of David Davies's diary, and unlike the sentimentalized weeping mothers portrayed by many Civil War poets, the women depicted by this poet have that steel-like quality described by Jane Aaron; they 'willingly' sacrifice their sons in order to 'increase the number of stars' on the Star-Spangled Banner. Like Deborah, who sent the hosts of Israel to fight Sisera, the Welsh mothers of Floyd send their sons to war against the Southern armies.[103]

Ab Morydd's first stanza gives two reasons for 'sacrificing' these mothers' sons: its second line states that they march to war in order to return the fallen stars of the Confederate states to the firmament of the United States flag, and the third line declares that Union volunteers fight in order to 'bring true freedom' to the country. While the exact nature of this 'freedom' is unspecified in the opening stanza, the second half of the poem interprets it explicitly in terms of freeing the slaves:

> O'n brodyr tlodion, fechgyn Ham!
> Er dued yw eu crwyn,
> A'n myrdd chwiorydd sy'n cael cam,
> Gwell meirw er eu mwyn.
>
> 'Oh, our poor brothers, sons of Ham!
> However black their skin may be,
> And our myriad sisters who are abused,
> It's better to die for their sake.'

The last five stanzas of the poem expand upon this theme, describing the war as a struggle to free the slaves. In his short introduction to Ab Morydd's composition, Evans tells us that 'part' (*rhan*) of the poem was sung to the tune of 'Milford' during the ceremony, and it is impossible to know exactly which verses were included in the public performance. However, as six of the published poem's nine verses concentrate on the evils of slavery, it is extremely likely that the abolitionist sentiments expressed by the poet played some part in the Welsh community's Fourth of July ceremony. Readers of *Y Cenhadwr Americanaidd*, like the 'large crowd' gathered in Floyd, are asked to consider '[c]aeth sefyllfa'r Negro tlawd' – 'the enslaved state of the poor Negro' – who is forced to witness 'the selling of his wife' ('gwerthu'i wraig'). The war fought by the young volunteers, newly 'sacrificed' by their 'dear old mothers', is cast as 'A stormy cloud which is over / Our county, with its dark slavery' ('Trydanawl gwmwl sydd uwch ben / Ein gwlad, a'i chaethglud ddu'). The Union cause, described in the first verse as restoring the flag's fallen stars and bringing a 'true', yet unspecified, 'freedom', is by the poem's end imagined in terms of shattering the slaves' chains:

Y llyffetheiriau ant cyn hir
  Bob un yn chwilfriw mân,
Er perffaith ryddid trwy'n holl dir
  A'r gaethglud seinia'i chân.

'The fetters before long will be
  Small shattered fragments, every one,
Bringing perfect freedom throughout all our land
  And those enslaved will sound its song.'[104]

Like the 'paeans to the national flag' which Alice Fahs describes as 'new symbols of nationality', this Welsh ode to 'The Union Flag' can be seen as an imaginative act which 'reflected a new nationhood' just as it 'actively called' – or 'sung' – 'it into being'.[105] The literary record published on the pages of *Y Cenhadwr Americanaidd* was made to recall the public meeting held in Floyd, New York, linking what was presented as the united stand of that specific Welsh community to the more abstract Union which they were supporting. Like the nationhood imagined by the poet, and like the nationhood invoked by the people who gathered to sing and hear the poet's verses on Floyd Hill, the nationhood suggested to the Welsh-Americans who read the printed poem on the pages of the journal was constructed so as to present the freedom of the slaves as an essential component of their idealized Union.

Family imagery underpins the poem's ideational structure, bringing together a series of charged relationships. The literal family bond connecting mother to son is replicated metaphorically on a number of levels, affecting the way in which the local community is portrayed and helping to forge the symbolic link between that community and the greater 'family' of the Union. Several scholars have stressed the role which family imagery played in the processes of imagining and articulating the Union. In his analysis of the writings by Union soldiers, Reid Mitchell states that:

> When these men spoke of the Union as a family, it was less than an identity, but it was more than a metaphor. The centrality of home and the family to northern culture made them central to the northern soldier's understanding of the Civil War.[106]

This connection between family and Union is suggested by the structure of Ab Morydd's second verse; the first couplet praises the Union ('The sun of heaven has never witnessed / Such a Union in any country'), and the final two lines focus on the mothers of the local community ('Dear old mothers on Floyd Hill, / Willingly join the battle!'). The twofold ideological impact of the piece is driven by this family imagery, for it encompasses the cause of abolition in addition to the cause of Union; the mothers of Floyd willingly sacrifice their sons in order to free the slaves, described specifically as the 'brothers' (*brodyr*) and 'sisters' (*chwiorydd*) of those Welsh-American volunteers. According to the last line of the first verse, the sacrifice of Welsh-American volunteers in the fight to shatter the chains of their enslaved brothers and sisters is all part of the 'Lord's wise plan' – 'cynllun doeth ein Nêr'.

Four months later Ab Morydd composed a similar poem, also designed for public singing. And, like his earler ode to 'The Union Flag', this piece was also offered up to the wider community of Welsh America on the pages of *Y Cenhadwr Americanaidd*.[107] The published poem was given the title 'Trem ar Amgylchiadau yr Unol Dalaethau – Tachwedd 1861', 'A Look at the Circumstances of the United States – November 1861'. However, the fact that it is in part another ode to the national flag is made manifest immediately by the note which the poet or editor added after the title, stating that it was to be sung to the tune (*ton*) of 'The Star-Spangled Banner'. While this song would not become the official national anthem of the United States until 1931, it was one of the country's favourite patriotic songs during the Civil War. What Ab Morydd did in November 1861 was rewrite 'The Star-Spangled Banner' in order to make it into a wartime expression of Welsh-American patriotism. Just as Francis Scott Key's original lyrics begin by describing the bombardment of Baltimore during the War of 1812, so the opening lines of this Welsh poem describe the martial scenes unfolding throughout the United States during the first months of the Civil War.

> Aruthrol yw trwst tabyrddau trwy'n holl wlad,
> Y magnel a'r cledd, yn crochlefain, dialer!

A mynant i lawr holl lunwyr llid a brad
A brofent eu twyll yn nistryw Caerfa Sumter.

'Terrible is the tumult of drums throughout our country,
The cannon and the sword cry hoarsely, "take revenge!"
And they desire the overthrow of all of the architects of anger and treachery
Who gave proof of their deceit in the destruction of Fort Sumter.'

The poet's description of the Civil War battlefield brings together the favourite symbolic weapon of romantic war poetry, the sword, and the roaring cannon of modern warfare. Having begun by presenting the 'terrible tumult' of war and the 'treachery' which started the conflict, Ab Morydd finishes the opening verse by referring to the recruiting drive at hand; like his Fourth of July meditation on the Union Flag, this song also portrays parents who willingly offer their sons up to the Union army:

Eirch rhiaint eu meibion, 'I'r frwydr yr ewch,'
A brodyr ar frodyr a floeddiant, 'dewch, dewch,
Ein baner ddyrchafwn, a'n fwyfwy o sêr,
A chwifio'n hardd wna hon, am byth tan nawdd ein Ner.'

'Parents beseech their sons, "To the battle you shall go,"
And brothers call to brothers, "come, come,
Our banner we shall raise, it will gain ever more stars,
And it will wave beautifully, forever under the protection of our Lord." '

Also like the earlier poem, these lines depict the march of volunteers to battle as an act of determination which will restore (and/or increase) the number of stars on the United States flag. The tune to which these words were sung presents it from the start as a Welsh ode to the national flag – the 'Star-spangled Banner' of the popular English-language song – yet it is only in the lines quoted above that the image of the flag is introduced directly into the poem. While the earlier song by Ab Morydd focused on the national flag being hoisted at the centre of a patriotic meeting, this poem describes the flag being carried by Union soldiers as they march to war.

This poem by Ab Morydd echoes his Fourth of July ode in that the relationship between civilian community, volunteer army, and the cause for which both are sacrificing is described in terms of an extended family. Parents urge their sons to go to war, and these sons call on their metaphorical 'brothers' to join them in bearing the Stars and Stripes off to battle. The suggestion that this song was composed in order to promote enlistment among Welsh-Americans is borne out by the first lines of its second verse: 'Mae cedyrn ein gwlad, a'u golwg oll yn llym, / Wrth ruthro i'r gâd, ar alwad yr Arlywydd' ('The strong ones of our country, with their eyes all fixed steadily, / Rush to battle, upon the call of the President'). As it praises those who have rushed off to answer the president's call for volunteers, so the song urges others to follow suit.

However, while urging Welsh-Americans to answer Lincoln's call and fight to preserve the Union, this poem, like Ab Morydd's 'Lluman yr Undeb', imbues that call to arms with a markedly Welsh-American ideology. Unlike Lincoln's government during the first months of the war, the leaders of Welsh America were openly interpreting the struggle as a war against slavery, and the words which Ab Morydd composed for the 'Star-Spangled Banner' made this point in a dramatic and unmistakable way:

Ein baner fu cynt, gan filain blant y fall,
Yn warthrudd i'n gwlad ar ororau tir Affric,
Ond mwyach ni ddaw yn ei chysgod fath wall[.]

'Our flag was made, by the devil's churlish children,
A disgrace to our country on the borders of Africa's land,
But now no such blemish will be found in its shadow.'

Rather than being a superficial patriotic hymn praising the United States as a perfect nation, the poem's martial flag-waving is tempered with the abolitionist's critical reflection on American history.[108] The same flag which Union volunteers now follow to war had in the past been turned into a mark of 'disgrace', for it was flown over slave ships anchored off Africa's coast. Like the religious discourse which interpreted the Civil War as divine retribution for the sin of slavery, this recruiting song urged Welsh-Americans to go to war in order to wipe the stain of slavery from the United States flag.

Ab Morydd's final verse returns to the martial imagery of Key's original English lyrics, recalling the 'bombs bursting in air' and the 'rocket's red glare' with a description of the Civil War battlefield's man-made lightning storm:

Er dued yw'r nos, a themhestl ar bob llaw;
Mellt pylor yn creu rhyw daranau cynddeiriog.
A miloedd trwy'n gwlad yn llesmeirio gan fraw;
Wrth wel'd pelau tân yn chwyrnellu'n fawreddog.
Er garwed y tywydd, daw'r tranoeth i'n rhan,
A'i hinon tra hyfryd, er gwynfyd i'r gwan,
Pan rodia'r caeth yn rhydd, ein baner a fydd ben,
Yn llaw ein cadarn Iôr, uwch tir a môr, Amen.

'However black the night, with a storm on every side;
Gunpowder's lightning creating a vicious thunder,

And thousands throughout our country fainting from fright
At seeing the balls of fire spinning boldly through the air,
Yet however rough the weather, a new day will come for us
With its weather most fair, bringing bliss to the weak,
When the slave walks freely, our flag will rule,
In our strong Lord's hand, above land and sea, Amen.'

The battlefield's storm takes place during a metaphorical night, a darkness covering the United States. The poet's concluding words – meant to be sung to the roaring crescendo which marks the end of the 'Star-Spangled Banner' – reassure Welsh-Americans that, 'however black the night' and 'however rough the weather', a new, gentler day will dawn.[109] The final couplet describes that bright new day explicitly in terms of the end of slavery; dawn will come 'when the slave walks freely'.

Both of these pieces by Ab Morydd were composed for singing during public events; they were a means of re-affirming the local Welsh community's ideological commitmment to the causes of Union and Abolition, and they were also a means of urging potential volunteers to join the Union army. And by printing these poems on the pages of *Y Cenhadwr Americanaidd*, the journal's editor, Robert Everett, was working with the poet in order to ensure that the broader community of Welsh America was touched by these same sentiments. Everett, like several other Welsh-American ministers, had embraced pacificism before the war. However, perhaps already galvanized by the recent history of 'Bleeding Kansas', when struck by the 'lightning-bolt' news of Fort Sumter's fall, he was quick to use his journal in support of the Union's war effort. Already anti-slavery and pro-Union, *Y Cenhadwr Americanaidd* became a pro-war publication, as did the Welsh-American press in general.[110]

Ab Morydd was by no means the only Welsh-American poet writing these kinds of poems during the early months of the war. In December 1861 *Y Cyfaill o'r Hen Wlad* published a poem by Ionoron Glan Dwyryd (otherwise known as Rowland Walter, the same poet who composed the *englyn* on the cannon discussed above; Ionoron was one of those bards assessed by John Bunnau on the pages of *Y Drych* in 1859). While specific details of the event are omitted, the journal's editor notes that the poem was composed at the request of a local dignitary, 'the Honorable Henry Nicoll, N.Y.' ('a gyfansoddwyd ar gais yr Anrh. Henry Nicoll, E. N.'). The request, it seems, was for a poem which could be read (or sung) during some kind of public ceremony or gathering. Like Ab Morydd's 'Lluman yr Undeb' ('The Union Flag'), Ionoron's poem is entitled 'Baner yr Undeb' ('The Union Banner'). And just as the prose introduction to Ab Morydd's work seeks to link the poem to the actual flag raised by the Welsh residents of Floyd, New York, so the *Cyfaill*'s editor sought to make manifest the link between the poet's abstracted meditation and the literal flag which Union volunteers were carrying into combat: he placed Ionoron's poem beneath an illustration of a fluttering United States flag.[111]

While this poem employs the patriotic clichés which characterize so much wartime poetry, it also engages in a more subtle kind of discourse. The first verse moves from the ultimate metonymical symbol of the United States, the Stars and Stripes, to 'The Guardian Angel of the Union' who sits beneath the flag.

Ar aden yr awel, yn tyner ymdoni,
 Mae Baner ein Rhyddid yn amlwg uwch ben,
A golwg ysblenydd y Ser a'r Brithresi
 Mor siriol ag amlryw dlos lanerch o'r nen;
O dani'r eistedda hen Angel Gwarcheidiol
 Yr Undeb, a'i olwg yn ddwys ac yn syn –
Ei wisg yn rhwygiedig – ei drem yn fawreddol,
 A'i wefus yn sibrwd rhyw linell fel hyn:[112]

'On the wings of the breeze, gently fluttering,
 The Banner of our Freedom flies prominently above,
And the splendid appearance of the Stars and Stripes
 Is as cheerful as the heavean's beautiful, varied expanse;
Beneath it sits the old Guardian Angel
 Of the Union, his appearance serious and amazed –
His clothing is torn – his gaze majestic,
 And his lips whisper a line like this:'

Ionoron might have found inspiration in the popular iconography of the time; one of the patriotic images used to decorate envelopes, stationery, and other wartime paper goods was that of a martial (often sword-brandishing) angel guarding the United States flag. While these iconic angels are often female, and might be interpreted as personified Liberty or 'Lady Liberty', Ionoron's angel is male. This is not surprising given the fact that Welsh nouns have a gender and that the noun *angel*, 'angel', is masculine (the female form in Welsh is *angyles*, the word used by Cymro Tawel in his description of Gweni Davies). Biblical angels were masculine, and, more to the point, understood as such by nineteenth-century Welsh Protestants. The visual image which Ionoron presents in his opening verse, this flag-and-angel tableau, would surely have resonated with Welsh-Americans in a number of ways. If it reflected the popular patriotic imagery of the wartime United States, it also evoked Old Testament images central to the religious imagination of nineteenth-century Welsh readers.

Whatever the ultimate source or sources from which Ionoron derived this image, what is important here is that the body of the poem, framed by the opening and closing stanzas, is placed in the mouth of this angel. The last line of this opening stanza ensures that the reader – or listener, remembering that this poem was commissioned, most likely for public performance – interprets the following four stanzas as the words of the Union's Guardian Angel. His lips are said to 'whisper' not simple 'words' (*geiriau*) but *rhyw linell*, 'a line' or 'a kind of line'; the word 'line' (*llinell*) tells us that the angel of the poet's conceit is speaking – like the poet himself – in verse. As so many other patriotic anthems in both English and Welsh centred on the visual image of the flag alone, it is worth exploring this Welsh poet's decision to present this particular tableau. In leading our mind's eye from the 'Stars and Stripes' to the Guardian Angel sitting beneath it, the poet is taking us from the Union's abstract metonymical symbol (the flag) to a figure imagined as having human form and the power of speech. The poet moves from the abstracted representation of the United States (each star representing a state in the Union) to an individual character who recites a personalized exhortation. The plight of the nation is linked to the struggle of the individual, as each reader or member of the audience is asked to empathize with the war-torn angel, said to be shocked or 'amazed' (*syn*) by the conflict engulfing the land which he guards.

Except for the crucial difference that these lines are in Welsh, the first of the four stanzas placed in the mouth of the Guardian Angel is similar to a great many patriotic poems written in English during the Civil War.

'Ah! feibion Columbia, derchafwyd ein Baner
 Gan lu ein henafiaid trwy afon o waed,
Diweiniwyd eu cleddyf, oedd gleddyf cyfiawnder,
 A'u gelyn cadarnaf a gwympodd tan draed;
Ac ar ol hir ryfel, teyrnasodd maith heddwch[.]'[113]

' "Ah! sons of Columbia, our banner was raised
 By a host of our ancestors through a river of blood,
Their sword was unsheathed, it was the sword of justice,
And their stoutest enemy fell beneath their feet;
After a long war, expansive peace reigned[.]" '

The Welsh readers or listeners are addressed as Americans, called 'Columbia's sons' (*feibion Columbia*), and they are asked to consider the Revolutionary heritage of the United States. During the Civil War writers and propagandists on both sides depicted their respective causes as an extension of the Revolutionary War, portraying Union or Confederate soldiers as the 'sons' of the heroic 'fathers' who had fought for freedom from Britain less than a century before. In the words of James McPherson:

> The patriotism of Civil War soldiers existed in a specific historical context. Americans of the Civil War generation revered their Revolutionary forebears. Every schoolboy and schoolgirl knew how they had fought against the odds to forge a new republic conceived in liberty. Northerners and Southerners alike believed themselves custodians of the legacy of 1776. The crisis of 1861 was the great test of their worthiness of that heritage. On *their* shoulders rode the fate of the great experiment of republican government launched in 1776.[114]

If this was true of native-born Americans (including Welsh-speaking native-born Americans), it was also true of a great many immigrants who adopted this ideological interpretation of their new country's history. The poetry competitions of nineteenth-century American *eisteddfodau* often included odes to George Washington and other Revolutionary heroes, and the Fourth of July 1861 was not the first time that Welsh immigrants had celebrated Independence Day with patriotic songs and recitals.

The poet defines his audience in the first of the Angel's stanzas. Obviously Welsh-speaking, they are also sons of Columbia, heirs to those Revolutionary American heroes who carried 'the sword of justice' through the past war's 'river of blood'. The Angel then proceeds to 'read' the flag for them, interpreting the abstract symbol for the benefit of Columbia's Welsh sons.

'Ni cheir ar ein Baner un eilun o ryfel,
Nac unrhyw feddylrith o'r fidog na'r cledd;
A phan y mae'n derbyn cusanau yr awel,
Nis gellir gwneyd allan un trais yn ei gwedd;
Mae'n eilun o Ryddid, Cyfiawnder a Heddwch
Lle bynnag mae'r wybr yn ymledu uwch ben –
Gwneyd allan Gaethiwed o'n Banner na cheisiwch
Tra byddo'r ser dysglaer yn britho y nen.'

'"No image of war is to be found on our Banner,
Nor any representation of the bayonet or the sword;
And when it receives the kisses of the breeze,
No violence can be made out in its form;
It is an image of Freedom, Justice and Peace
Wherever the sky extends overhead –
Do not attempt to make Slavery out of our Banner
As long as the bright stars adorn the heavens."'

The apparent contradiction between the violent birth of the nation ('a river of blood') and the supposedly peaceful nature of that nation's banner is elided here; it is the symbol of an idealized Union, free from war and slavery. Like the poems by Ab Morydd interpreting the freedom which the flag represents explicitly in terms of fighting slavery, Ionoron Glan Dwyryd has the Union's Guardian Angel read slavery out of the Stars and Stripes. He presents a closed interpretation of the symbol, one including 'Freedom, Justice and Peace' while ruling out 'Slavery' once and for all. This is the meaning of the flag which the Angel presents to those Welsh-American volunteers marching off to war.

While the Angel begins by addressing the nation's 'sons', the next verse includes the women of Welsh America, if only elliptically. Another reason why the Banner is so sacred is that it protects the *aelwyd* or 'hearth', a charged word in Welsh which for nineteenth-century readers indexed a constellation of concepts relating to the role and importance of the wife, mother, home and family.

'Mae cysur yr aelwyd i filoedd yn eistedd
 Dan aden ein Baner heb ddychryn na braw,
Pwy bynag a'i tyno i lawr mewn gorphwylledd,
 Fel corsen wywedig disgyned ei law[.]'

'"The comfort of the hearth for thousands sits
 Beneath the wing of our Banner without fear or fright,
Whoever shall take it down in rage,
 May his hand fall like a withered stalk."'

Like so many other pro-Union texts, this poem invokes the bonds of family in the same context as the bonds of Union. Having defined that for which these soldiers are fighting as Freedom (including that of the slaves), Justice and Peace as well as 'the comfort of the hearth', the Angel uses his final verse to again address them directly as 'Columbia's sons'.

'O glogwyn i glogwyn, yr udgorn dadseinied
 I alw dewr feibion Columba i'r gâd
I ymladd â phleidwyr gwrthnysig Caethiwed
 Sy'n ymladd yn erbyn hoff Faner ein gwlad;
Diweinier y cleddyf – y fagnel fo'n rhuo,
 A rhengau y gleyn yn ddarnau tan draed;
Hen Dalaeth Virginia, ei glaswellt fo'n rhuddo,
 A South Carolina yn afon o waed.'

'"From cliff to cliff, let the trumpet sound
 Calling the brave sons of Columbia to war
To fight with the rebellious supporters of Slavery
 Who are fighting against the dear Banner of our county;
Unsheath the sword – let the cannon roar,
 And let the enemy's ranks lie in pieces under foot;

Old Virginia State, may its grass grow red,
And may South Carolina become a river of blood.'"

The phrase *afon o waed*, appearing at the poem's start, is repeated here. As the Revolutionary fathers unleashed their river of British blood in pursuit of 'justice', so these 'sons' are commanded to transform the rebellious, slave-owning South into 'a river of blood'. If the poet's reading of the Stars and Stripes rules out all bloody images – 'war', 'bayonet', 'sword' and 'violence' – he nonetheless revels in the violence which will be wrought upon the Confederacy, willing the bloody subjugation of Virginia and South Carolina. The editors and writers who informed much of Welsh America's public culture had indeed turned their backs on pacifism by the end of 1861.

Ionoron Glan Dwyryd ends the Angel's address with this vengeful exhortation. The final stanza of the poem, like the opening one, is part of the frame which he uses to contain and present the Angel's direct speech:

Fan yma terfynodd yr Angel Gwarcheidiol,
A'i drem yn melltenu eiddigedd ei fron;
A chan ei ddigofaint, mae cefnfor ymchwyddol
Dros wyneb Columbia yn gwthio ei don;
I chwyddo y fyddin, awn ninau, feib Gwalia,
Gan gofio Caradog ac Arthur ein tad;
Trywaner â'r fidog frâd luoedd Virginia,
A buan daw heddwch i lwyddo y wlad.

'It is here that the Guardian Angel ended,
And his gaze flashed the lightning of his heart's jealous passion;
And because of his wrath, a swelling sea
Is throwing its waves across the face of Columbia;
In order to swell the army, let us go, sons of Gwalia,
Remembering Caradog and Arthur our father;
Let the treacherous hosts of Virginia be struck with the bayonet,
And soon peace will come to rule the land.'

Gwalia is one of the popular names for Wales found in the romantic literature of the nineteenth century. The simple fact that this poem was written and printed in Welsh defines the audience as *Welsh*-American from the beginning. However, the bard's fanciful conceit – the Union's Guardian Angel addressing 'Columbia's sons' – can also be taken as a reference to all of the patriotic and loyal sons of America. These final lines, on the other hand, stress in an unmistakable fashion that it is the Welsh sons of Columbia who must answer the Angel's call.

This poem's combination of specifically Welsh and American images reveals how the Civil War sharpened the focus of a particular kind of expression of Welsh-American identity. Potential volunteers targeted by this poem would have been immigrants as well as the Welsh-speaking children of immigrants; very few if any of them would have had literal ancestors who fought in the American army during the Revolution. While employing the father–son imagery of family descent, this poem is concerned with an ideological lineage rather than a literal blood-line. It describes how immigrants and their children can *become* a part of America's metaphorical family; the act of 'unsheathing the sword' in defence of Union and Freedom makes them 'sons of Columbia', the spiritual descendants of the nation's Revolutionary forefathers. The poet states that Welsh volunteers can become 'sons of Columbia' by recalling the simple fact that they are in fact sons of Wales. Like many other Welsh-language texts written and published before, during and after the Civil War, this poem suggests that it is the very essence of their Welsh heritage which, paradoxically, allows immigrants and their children to become good Americans. If this seems paradoxical to us today, it was a logical and accepted part – indeed, even a cornerstone – of nineteenth-century Welsh-American identity.

While civilian poets like Ionoron Glan Dwyryd interpreted the identity of Welsh-American volunteers in this manner, some of the volunteers themselves took an active part in the same process. Thomas D. Thomas, a soldier serving near Memphis, Tennessee, published a letter in *Y Seren Orllewinol* in September 1862 urging the 'sons of Wales' to fight for the Union. He did so by invoking Llywelyn, the last native Prince of Wales, killed in 1282 while fighting against the English king's invading army: 'Fechgyn Cymru, dangoswch eich bod yn perthyn i'r gorenwog Dywysog Llywely[n], yr hwn dros ryddid a gollodd y dafn diweddaf o'i waed. Edrychwch ar ein baner, a dywedwch, *It shall wave.*' ('Sons of Wales, show that you are related to the most famous Prince Llywelyn, who for freedom lost the last drop of his blood. Look at our flag, and say, *It shall wave.*')[115]

Ionoron urges Welshmen to become spiritual heirs to the American Revolution by 'remembering Caradog and Arthur'. As they aspire to be 'sons' of the 1776 heroes, so they are explicitly described as the 'sons' of Arthur, called by the poet *ein tad* ('our father'). Like King Arthur, Caradog was one of the heroic figures inhabiting that strand of medieval Welsh pseudo-history which was still so popular in nineteenth-century Wales (and Welsh America).[116] Both were characters entrenched in popular tradition as heroic war-leaders of the Welsh people. In taking up the bayonet in order to strike 'the treacherous hosts of Virginia', Welsh volunteers are said to exhibit the martial spirit of their own great 'father', Arthur, who fought against the Anglo-Saxons in order to secure the freedom of the Welsh (or 'Ancient Britons', *yr hen Frytaniaid*, as they were often called). Taken as a whole, the poem equates the ancient struggles of the Welsh against oppression with the Union's war against rebellion and slavery. As the sons of Wales become sons of Columbia, the descendants of Arthur add the Revolutionary fathers of the United States to their conceptual genealogy. While presenting a distinct interpretation of the Union and its 'Banner', Ionoron's poetic call to arms also presents a distinct interpretation of the identity of those Welsh-American volunteers who were fighting for that Union. This interpretation – charged ideologically as pro-Union, pro-war and anti-slavery – is coloured with references drawn from the cultural history of both Wales and the United States.

Ionoron Glan Dwyryd worked as a quarryman in the 'Slate Valley' straddling Vermont and New York, and Ab Morydd used his poetry to support the wartime activities of the Welsh community of Floyd, New York. Some poems addressing the new volunteers and their families came from farther a field. When D. W. Jones – or 'Dewi Morgannwg', a poet living in Merthyr Tydfil, south Wales – learned that the son of his American friends had enlisted in the Union army, he sent them encouragement by way of a poem. The young soldier's family in Tuscarora, Pennsylvania, sent it on to the editor of *Y Seren Orllewinol* in Pottsville, who published it under the title 'Thomas yn Filwr', 'Thomas a Soldier'.[117] As it crossed the sea from Wales to America, so this poem also travelled from the personal letter's private realm to the public sphere of the printed text. Dewi Morgannwg addresses Thomas's mother and father directly, providing what is in part a meditation on the parents' feelings at seeing their son volunteer.

Mae codi'r gwn neu'r cleddyf
 I ymladd dros y gwir
Yn fraint ac yn anrhydedd
 I bawb o fewn eich tir.

Ac os yw Thomas chwithau
 Yn filwr yn y gad,
Yn ymladd dros iawnderau,
 Yn erbyn trais a brad,

Ar allor egwyddorion
 Aberthwch deimlad brau,
A sugnwch eich cysuron
 O'r gwir ac nid o'r gau.[118]

'Taking up the gun or sword
 To fight for truth
Is a privilege and an honour
 For everybody within your land.

And if your Thomas
 Is a soldier in the battle,
Fighting for rights,
 Against violence and treachery,

On the altar of principles
  Sacrifice fragile feeling
And take your comfort
  From the truth and not the lie.'

The poet originally wrote these lines for a very specific audience, Evan and Mary Williams, the very real parents of a very real volunteer. Unlike the steel-like Republican mothers constructed by other poets, these are not literary abstractions; Dewi Morgannwg was addressing people whom he knew, and the poem was part of a very personal kind of communication. He offered them solace in several forms, first and foremost by praising the cause for which Thomas was fighting. The fact that the poem moves from the private context of the parents' fears to the national context of the Union cause surely helped speed its journey from manuscript letter to printed page. While the personal origins of this poem differ greatly from the public-performative contexts for which the songs of Ab Morydd and Ionoron Glan Dwyryd were composed, Dewi Morgannwg's address to Thomas's parents also asks them to accept the sacrifice of their son. He tells them that, just as their son has offered himself for service, so they should 'sacrifice' their own concerns on 'the altar of principles'. These principles are defined in terms of fighting for [*y*] *gwir*, 'the truth', defeating *brad*, 'treachery', and ending an otherwise undefined *trais*, 'violence'.

In the final three of the poem's six stanzas Dewi Morgannwg joins the parents in prayer, asking for the safe return of their son:

Gwnawn â chwi gyd ddymuno
  I Dduw fod iddo'n ran,
I'w gynnal a'i gysuro,
  A'i noddi yn mhob man.

Ac ar ol darfod brwydro
  Dychwelyd yn ddinam
Yn iach, heb gael ei g'wyfo,
  I dŷ ei dad a'i fam.

A choron buddugoliaeth
  Fo ar ei goryn mad;
Ar ol cael goruchafiaeth
  Ar dreiswyr brwnt ei wlad.

'We will join with you in asking
God to accompany him,
  To protect and comfort him,
And support him everywhere.

'And after the fighting ends
Let him return unhurt,
Healthy, without being wounded,
To the house of his father and mother.

'And may the crown of victory
 Sit on his good brow;
After gaining supremacy
 Over the nasty oppressors of his country.'

If this bard, writing thousands of miles away in Merthyr Tydfil, voices ideological support for the Union, he also draws attention to the geographical gulf which separates him from the Pennsylvania family. The printed version of the text is signed, 'Dewi Morgannwg, Merthyr, D[e] C[ymru]' ('Dewi Morgannwg, Merthyr, South Wales), and the poem itself foregrounds the difference between their nation and his, using phrases such *eich tir* ('your land') and *[e]i wlad* ('his country') which emphasize the fact that their country is not his. This text, both in the form of personal letter sent from Wales to America and as a published poem offered to the wider community of Welsh America on the pages of *Y Seren Orllewinol*, represents an act of trans-Atlantic Welsh solidarity.

The Welsh poet's prayer for the volunteer addresses the feelings of loss which his parents experience at seeing their son enlist, yet it does not treat directly the possibility that he might die in the war. This is hinted at only elliptically in that the prayer calls for God's protection; there is no direct mention of death in battle or by disease. The poet instead concentrates on positive aspects of the war, describing the volunteer's situation as 'an honour and a privilege', and interpreting the battle to which he marches as an opportunity for gaining a 'crown of victory'.[119]

A very different meditation on the volunteers' departure was published by *Y Cyfaill o'r Hen Wlad* in November 1861. This poem, composed by one of Oneida County's many bards, Ab Ioan, bears the title 'Y Rhyfel Presenol', 'The Present War'. It begins by portraying the 'brave sons' who answer the call of the drums:

Mae'r tabyrddau'n dechreu curo,
Meibion dewrion sydd yn 'listio,
I fyn'd i gario'r cleddyf caled
O flaen y tân heb gael eu harbed.[120]

'The drums begin to beat,
Brave sons are enlisting,
To go to bear the hard sword
Before the fire without being saved.'

While these volunteers are depicted carrying the sentimental symbol of past wars, the sword which they bear is no romantic image meant to distance readers from the reality of modern warfare. Unlike the glorified 'sword of justice' of Ionoron Glan Dwyryd's poem, Ab Ioan simply describes it as *caled*, 'hard'. This is the nature of the weapon which they carry into the 'fire' of the guns.

The word *tân*, 'fire', suggests several interconnected meanings; while conjuring up the literal gunfire of the Civil War battlefield, it also asks the reader to consider another kind of fire.[121] The final line of this stanza reworks what was surely familiar imagery to the *Cyfaill*'s readers; by linking the noun *tân*, 'fire', with the verb *arbed*, 'to save' or 'to spare', Ab Ioan echoes the kind of language which Welsh Calvinistic Methodists would have heard from the pulpit on occasion (remembering that the *Cyfaill* was published in order to serve that denomination). In addition to the fire spouted by cannon and rifle, the poet is calling to mind the fire of hell from which sinners might or might not be 'saved' ([c]*ael eu harbed*). The fact that these volunteers are not 'saved' from the war's earthly fire is presented here as a manifestation of their virtue, offered as an assurance of their preservation from the unearthly fires of hell. The volunteers go willingly into battle for their country, proving their patriotism as well as their Christian virtue by casting themselves into the fire.

The suggestion of self-sacrifice is expanded in the next stanza, as the volunteers are described leaving their homes for Southern battlefields:

Dynion ieuanc swydd Oneida
Sydd yn cychwyn yn ugeinia,
Heb feddwl unwaith na gorbwyso,
Y deuant byth yn ol oddiyno[.][122]

'Young men of Oneida county
Are leaving by the score,
Without once considering or placing too much weight
On whether they will ever come back from there.'

Unpublished writings by some Oneida County Welsh volunteers show how idealized this poet's portrait really is; for example, rather than heading for war 'without once considering' his possible death, David Davies, ever the honest diarist, confessed that he had grave misgivings shortly after enlisting.[123]

Far from being an honest record of real soldiers' feelings, Ab Ioan's poem is an example of a particular kind of meditation on the volunteers' heroism, one spun through the fire, brimstone and sacrificial imagery of the Welsh Nonconformist chapel. The poet's idealized soldiers are abstracted from reality, inhabiting a realm defined only by bravery, loyalty and Christian self-sacrifice. However, rather than painting a sentimental or sanitized picture removed from the realities of war, Ab Ioan's interpretation of the conflict stresses its horrible nature. While Dewi Morgannwg's prayer for the young soldier skirts around his possible death, this poet emphasizes the violence and danger which await the Welsh volunteers of Oneida County; they march to meet the Red Horse of the Apocalypse, whose rider, according to Revelation 6.4, 'was given power . . . to make men slaughter one another.'[124]

Y march coch sy'n dechreu symud,
A barnau Duw sy'n goddiweddyd
Ar ein gwlad am iddi bechu,
Yn ngwyneb cymaint o oleuni.

'The red horse begins to move,
And God's judgments are overtaking
Our land because it has sinned,
In the face of so much light.'

Instead of blaming only a demonized Confederacy, a simplified version of the 'evil South' so common in the wartime literature of the North, Ab Ioan states clearly that the entire county has brought the war on itself by sinning. It is *ein gwlad*, 'our country', the United States to which this poet and the Union soldiers whom he praises owe allegiance, which has sinned. The self-sacrifice of the volunteers is placed within a wider moral (and historical) context; they go willingly to face the Red Horse of war in order to rid their country of the sin which has unleashed this apocalyptical destruction. And that sin is slavery. The poem's final six stanzas expound the relationship between slavery, the war and the soldiers' battlefield sacrifice:

Dacw'r negro yn dechreu synu,
A chyda hyn yn gorfoleddu,
Fod ei ddyddiau wedi dwad
I fyned o'i gaethiwed caled.

Y rhyfeloedd er eu dechreu
Dros gaethiwed yn y Dehau,
Pleidir 'nawr gan ddynion gwynion
Yn y Gogledd ar eu hunion

Dydd a ddaw a phethau i'r gola,
A chaethiwed oll i'r ddalfa;
A'r meistriaid gwaith eu goddiweddyd,
Fel hen Phar'o hwnw foddwyd

Trwm yw clywed am ryfela
Sy'n llenwi y wlad y dyddiau yma;
Trymach eto yw bod yno,
O flaen bwledi fydd yn rhwygo.

Trwm yw clywed am y milwyr
Yn cael eu tori i lawr yn brysur,
A'u cyrff fydd yno yn fwyd i bryfed,
A'u heneidiau yn nhrag'wyddoldeb.

Bod yn barod yw'r peth cynta'
A ddylai fod ar ein meddylia';
A gwell fydd eto mewn canlyniad
Golli'r byd na cholli'r enaid.

'There is the negro looking up with surprise,
And beginning to rejoice at this,
That the day has come
To leave his cruel enslavement.

'Since their start, the battles have been
Over slavery in the South;
Now they are fought openly
By white men in the North.

'Day will bring things into the light,
And all of slavery arrested;
And the overseers overtaken,
Like that old Pharaoh who was drowned.

'It is difficult to hear about the warfare
Which is filling the country these days;
It is yet more difficult to be there,
Before the bullets which rend.

'It is difficult to hear about the soldiers
Being cut down rapidly,
And their bodies will be food for worms there,
And their souls will be in eternity.

'Being ready is the first thing
Which should be on our minds;
And yet better a thing
Is losing the world instead of losing one's soul.'

The third stanza from the end casts the reader's mind to a place called simply *yno*, 'there': this is the Southern battlefield, a reference to the '*(oddi)yno*' of the poem's first stanza, the field of war from which the volunteers might not return. In these lines the theological abstractions of apocalyptical horse and hell-fire yield to a terror which is grounded more closely in the reality of war; the mind's eye is forced to see the soldiers being 'cut down rapidly' by the 'bullets' of the Rebels. The souls of the dead volunteers are accorded 'eternity', yet we are not allowed to forget the physicality of the war and its effects; instead of the flower-covered graves described in more sentimental poems, Ab Ioan gives us the worm-eaten corpses of the sacrificed soldiers.

Like the poetic tributes to volunteers composed by Ab Morydd and Ionoron Glan Dwyryd, this poem is simple metrically. It is in a 'free metre' according to the traditional Welsh way of discussing metrics, that is, while it follows a regular rhythm and rhyme pattern, it does not use one of the complex strict metres codified in the bardic grammars of the late Middle Ages.[125] The kind of free metre employed by Ab Ioan, however, is nonetheless a traditional form; it is a *pennill*, a type of four-line stanza associated with various kinds of folk poetry and singing. Poems of this type appear in Welsh manuscripts as early as the sixteenth century,[126] and the form was used by churchmen to circulate Christian teaching among the poorer levels of Welsh society during the early modern period.[127] The tradition to which this kind of *pennill* belonged thus suited the religious message which Ab Ioan was presenting to Welsh-Americans.

In the case of this particular poem, the formal simplicitly hides a complex assemblage of moral and theological arguments. The final stanza states that 'being ready should be the first thing', and the phrase 'the first thing' (*y peth cynta*) also calls to mind 'the last things' (*y petha diwetha*); the words *y peth cynta* occur in the *last* lines of a poem which has been describing the *last* experiences of the self-sacrificing soldiers. The expression *y petha diwetha* ('the last things'), sometimes rendered as *y pedwar peth diwetha[f]* ('the four last things'), was used to refer to the final experiences for which a Christian must ready himself or herself: death, judgement, heaven and hell. Texts circulating in manuscript and in print, often in the form of didactic poetry using simple free metres like the *pennill* used by Ab Ioan, were extremely popular in early modern Wales.[128] In fact, one of America's first Welsh-language books was a treatise on this very subject, printed in Philadelphia in 1735: *Myfyrdodau Bucheddol ar y Pedwar Peth Diwethaf, sef Angau, Barn, Nef ac Uffern* ('Devout Meditations on the Last Four Things, namely Death, Judgement, Heavan and Hell').[129] Several aspects of Ab Ioan's poem reflect a range of earlier Welsh texts dealing with these 'last things'; its use of specific imagery gleaned from the Book of Revelation, the application of such imagery to contemporary events, and the emphasis on preparing one's soul for final judgement all allow us to locate this Welsh-American poem within that older tradition of didactic literature.[130]

According to Ab Ioan's meditation on the fate of the Union volunteers, preparing oneself spiritually was 'the first thing' which should be done in order to face the last things, that is, death, God's judgement, and the result of that judgement. This reading of the poem's final stanza deepens the apocalyptical tone set by earlier references to the Red Horse and the fires from which none are saved; the poet draws upon traditional Welsh Christian discourse involving the end of all things and God's ultimate judgement, and he does so in order to present a specific interpretation of the Union volunteers' sacrifice. Ab Ioan tells his readers (and, possibly, listeners) that readying themselves for these 'last things' is 'the first thing / which should be on [their] minds', adding that it is better to lose – or sacrifice – one's body and worldly possessions than to 'lose one's soul'. This is the lesson provided by his idealized volunteer's decision to throw himself before the fire and bullets of the battlefield; the sin of the United States has unleashed the forces of destruction, and it is only the willing self-sacrifice of the Union volunteers which can stop the hellish process. They give up their lives in this world in order that the soul of the nation, endangered by the sin of slavery, be saved.

Ab Ioan's poem is a meditation on the moral decisiveness of the volunteers, yet it is aimed directly at the civilians who stay at home. The succession of lines beginning *trwm*, 'heavy' or 'difficult' (or *trymach*, 'more difficult') lead the civilian closer to an understanding of the volunteer's sacrifice on the battlefield. While it might be 'difficult' for those who stay behind to see all these young 'sons' leaving for war, it is much more difficult to do what they do and go 'before the bullets'. And, if it is difficult for people at home to hear or read about the soldiers being 'cut down' on Southern battlefields, it is nonetheless everybody's duty to consider the meaning of their death. The poet suggests that their own death is the means by which these volunteers teach those who stay at home, and the lesson which they teach is that such self-sacrifice is better than allowing the nation to lose its soul to the sin of slavery. The idealized Christian soldier constructed by Ab Ioan dies in order to cleanse the nation of sin, and he also dies in order to teach those who stay behind that this sacrifice is the 'first thing' which they should be thinking about as they prepare themselves for the rest of the war.

Rather than indulging in the patriotic clichés which drive so many other poetic tributes to the volunteers, Ab Ioan's meditation on the self-sacrificing soldiers is bound up with a specific theological interpretation of the Civil War and its ultimate causes. Despite the poem's simple metrical structure, it is a complex piece of literature which melds the genre of the recruiting song with a millennarian discourse, thus interpreting the war and its causes within broader moral, theological and historical contexts. Its contents in part recall many of the simpler Welsh-language recruiting songs of the early war years, yet it also resembles the more complex kinds of religious prose being published by Welsh America's religious leaders at the time. Ab Ioan's poem has as much in common with the writings of Iorthryn Gwynedd, Robert Everett and Erasmus Jones as it does with the patriotic anthems composed by poets such as Ab Morydd and Ionoron Glan Dwyryd.

In July 1861 Iorthryn Gwynedd suggested that the war be viewed as God's 'scourge', set upon the nation in order to draw blood in penance for its sins. Erasmus Jones would later use similar language, interpreting the conflict as 'Jehovah's chastising rod'. Like the poet Ab Ioan, both these Welsh-American writers had ties with Oneida County, having served there as ministers in the years before the war. However, when Erasmus Jones composed and published his theological interpretation of the war he was stationed on Morris Island, South Carolina, serving as chaplain to the 21st United States Coloured Regiment. The soldiers of his regiment had been slaves a short time before; when he wrote to *Y Cenhdawr Americanaidd* echoing Ab Ioan's description of the volunteers' blood sacrifice, Jones was witnessing with his own eyes the freedom which the war was bringing to hundreds of thousands of enslaved African Americans. If the violent times were indeed 'God's chastisements', then He was to be thanked for them:

> Diolch iddo, hyd yn oed am *geryddon*! Credaf fod ein 'hymwared yn agoshau.' Caiff ein gwlad ei 'hadgenedlu drachefn i obaith bywiol. O'r bedydd gwaed, cawn "gyfodi i newydd-deb buchedd.' Ar ol y gwyntyllio ofnadwy ceir ni yn wenith mwy pur, a deuwn allan o'r "ffwrn danllyd boeth" fel aur wedi ei buro trwy dân.[131]

> 'Thank Him, even for *chastisements*! I believe that our "deliverance is growing near." Our land will be "born again to living hope". From this baptism of blood, we will be able "to awaken to the newness of life". After this horrible winnowing we will be found to be purer wheat, and we will come out of the "hot fiery furnace" like gold purified by fire.'

Like Ab Ioan's meditation on the fate of the volunteers leaving Oneida County, Revd Jones described the battlefield sacrifice as a 'baptism of blood' which promised new life for a nation stained by the sin of slavery. Ab Ioan's poem appeared in November 1861, three years before Erasmus Jones would publish his fiery sermon of a letter. In November 1861 the Union army was a long way from authorizing the formation of 'coloured' regiments like the one Jones was to serve, and Lincoln's government was a long way from making the formal declaration which would link the Union war effort more closely to the fight against slavery. However, poems published early in the war by Ab Ioan, Ab Morydd, Ionoron Glan Dwyryd and others show that, from the very start, the Welsh-language literature which praised and encouraged the volunteers was bound up with a specific interpretation of the war as a struggle against slavery. For these Welsh-American poets and writers, the march of Union volunteers to battle was a purposeful journey into the fiery furnace of war, a sacrificial venture which would cleanse the nation of its original sin.

NOTES

1 *Y Cenhadwr Americanaidd*, November 1861.

2 *Y Cenhadwr Americanaidd*, January 1862. Judging by the surviving print record, Dewi Glyn Ebbw's protest apparently gained little support, and it seems to have had little or no effect on the activities of Dewi Emlyn and others during the war.

3 In addition to caring for several chapels in Ohio, Benjamin Chidlaw became the first missionary employed by the American Sunday School Union, and in this capacity he did much to connect the Welsh-speaking chapels of the United States with the larger English-language denominations of the country. He went on a widely-publicized preaching tour of Wales in 1839 which was said to spark a revival in at least one area which he visited. Chidlaw's various activities received much attention in the pre-war Welsh-American press, and he himself published articles regularly; see John Edward Lloyd, R. T. Jenkins and William Llewelyn Davies (eds), *Y Bywgraffiadur Cymreig Hyd 1940* (London, 1953), pp. 69–70. In addition to being a popular minister in Ohio, Dewi Emlyn (or David Davies) published a great deal of poetry and prose in the Welsh-language press of America, before and during the war. He was often called upon to adjudicate the literary competitions of the country's various *eisteddfodau*; see Chapter One, pages 4–5.

4 According to *Y Seren Orllewinol*, June 1861, the Revd D. L. Davies preached a pro-war sermon in Blakely on Sunday, 5 May 1861.

5 The piece is actually signed *I. G.*, and Iorthryn Gwynedd is the only known author publishing at the time in Welsh-American journals whose name fits the initials. Initials were often used for familiar names; Robert Everett, for example, frequently signed his pieces with a simple *E.* Iorthryn did indeed publish frequently in *Y Cenhadwr Americanaidd*, and he would have been well known to its readers.

6 *Y Cenhadwr Americanaidd*, July 1861.

7 The entire message was written and punctuated as follows: 'I John Brown am now quite *certain* that the crimes of this *guilty, land*: *will* never be purged *away*; but with Blood. I had *as I now think*: *vainly* flattered myself that without *very much* blooshed; it might be done.' Stephen B. Oates, *To Purge This Land With Blood* [:] *A Biography of John Brown* (Amherst, 1970), p. 351.

8 See Chapter Two, pages 82–3.

9 For example, the Revd R. L. Herbert, a Welsh-American Wesleyan minister, also published material presenting a similar interpretation of the war and its causes. As America's Welsh-speaking Wesleyans did not have their own journal, Herbert published these in the denomination's publication in the Old Country; see, for example, *Yr Eurgrawn Wesleyaidd*, February 1862 and February 1863.

10 In addition to the fact that he as editor published the writings of R. D. Thomas, Erasmus Jones and other similar writers, the fact that Robert Everett himself felt that the United States was being punished for the sin of slavery is evident in a number of his own published writings. For example, in *Y Cenhadwr Americanaidd*, September 1861, Everett published an essay on the evils of slavery which concludes, 'Ac onid yw yn drueni meddwl fod y fath ddrygau yn cael eu cyflawni . . . a thrwy y cyfan Duw yn cael ei ddigio, a'i ddigofaint yn gawodydd o farnedigaethau ar ddisgyn ar ein gwlad' ('And is it not a pity to think that such evils are being committed . . . and that through all of it God is angered, and his anger falling in showers of judgements upon our country').

11 *The Morning Star* was published in New London, Connecticut between 1845 and 1881.

12 *Y Cenhadwr Americanaidd*, May 1861.
13 Ibid.
14 *Y Seren Orllewinol*, June 1861.
15 Ibid.
16 T. E. Hughes and D. Edwards (eds), *Hanes Cymry Minnesota* (Mankato, 1895), p. 117.
17 Ibid.
18 Bell Irvin Wiley, *The Life of Billy Yank* [:] *The Common Soldier of the Union* (Baton Rouge and London, 1952), p. 24.
19 Ibid.
20 *Baner ac Amserau Cymru*, 25 September 1861. This is a reprint of a letter originally published in *Y Drych*; no known copies of this edition of *Y Drych* have survived.
21 Ibid.
22 Ibid.
23 *Y Seren Orllewinol*, August 1863.
24 Ibid.
25 *Y Drych*, 31 January 1863.
26 On 'the American children of Dic Siôn Dafydd', see Chapter One, pages 22–7.
27 *Y Cyfaill o'r Hen Wlad*, December 1862.
28 *Y Drych*, 11 July 1863.
29 *Y Cenhadwr Americanaidd*, September 1865.
30 *Y Cyfaill o'r Hen Wlad*, June 1864; Thomas J. Davies was this soldier's name.
31 Eugene Walter Leach, *The Racine County Militant* (Racine, 1915), p. 81. Company F, like all of the 22nd Wisconsin's ten companies, was originally recruited during July 1862, and joined the regiment at Camp Utley, Racine, on 25 August 1862. The 'war meeting' described by the *Racine County Militant* must have been an event organized in order to fill out the company's ranks and held mid-way between the initial recruiting drive in July and the company's final rendez-vous with the regiment. See Frank J. Welcher and Larry G. Ligget, *Coburn's Brigade* (Carmel [Indiana], 1999), p. 11.
32 Several soldiers mention in letters home that they had learned English since enlisting. For example, John Griffth Jones letters, National Library of Wales 22421D, letter dated 27 July 1863.
33 Reid Mitchell, *The Vacant Chair* [:] *The Northern Soldier Leaves Home* (New York and Oxford, 1993), p. 25.
34 *The Racine County Militant*, pp. 81–2.
35 See the discussion in Chapter 10, pages 395–401.
36 Mitchell, *The Vacant Chair*, p. 25.
37 *Y Cenhadwr Americanaidd*, June 1863.
38 Mitchell, *The Vacant Chair*, p. 5.
39 Ibid., p. 4.
40 Ibid., p. 73.
41 *Y Cenhadwr Americanaidd*, December 1861.
42 *Y Drych*, 24 January 1863.
43 *Y Drych*, 28 March 1863.
44 For those not familiar with Welsh grammar, it is worth noting that *gwlad*, 'country', is a feminine noun, and thus mutated after the definite article, *y*, 'the', giving *y wlad*, 'the country'. Similarly, when put into the compound with the prefix *cyd-*, the initial *g-* disappears.
45 See, for example, Chapter One, page 13.
46 *Y Cenhadwr Americanaidd*, July 1863.

47 Dean B. Mahin, *The Blessed Place of Freedom* [:] *Europeans in Civil War America* (Washington, 2002), p. 2. All the statistics quoted in this paragraph are discussed by Mahin, pp. 1–3.

48 William L. Burton, *Melting Pot Soldiers* [:] *The Union's Ethnic Regiments* (New York, 1998), p. 48.

49 While my use of the word 'neighbour' is in part metaphorical, meaning simply 'fellow citizens of the United States', in some cases it can be applied literally. Welsh and Irish immigrants worked together in Pennsylvania's coal fields, and in rural Wisconsin Welsh farms at times bordered those of German-speaking immigrants. In cities such as Cincinnati, New York and Utica, Welsh-speaking Americans often lived a short walk away from German and Irish neighbourhoods.

50 Burton, *Melting Pot Soliders*, p. 11.

51 See, for example, Burton, *Melting Pot Soliders*, p. 53.

52 As noted in Chapter Two, a kind of proto-pacificism was espoused by many of Welsh America's religious leaders; while it is impossible to assess to what degree these ideas were embraced by the community as a whole, the fact that not one essay or letter taking issue with pacifistic ideas was published in the press *before* the Civil War is suggestive.

53 Another rare example of a Welsh officer who climbed high in the army is Joshua T. Owen. After serving as colonel with two successive Pennsylvania regiments (the 24th and the 69th), he was promoted to brigadier. However, he did not correspond with any of the Welsh-American publications, and, as far as surviving evidence shows, he was never acknowledged or praised by the Welsh-language American press. For a short biography of Owen, see Dean B. Mahin, *The Blessed Place of Freedom* [:] *Europeans in Civil War America* (Washington, 2002), pp. 226–7. *Y Cyfaill o'r Hen Wlad*, October 1861, mentions a Capt. Williams who was promoted to an unspecified higher rank, but nothing more is known about him.

54 *Y Cenhadwr Americanaidd*, September 1861.

55 Even studies devoted to what is usually called the 'ethnic' element in the Union army give very little if any attention to the Welsh. William L. Burton's book-length study, *Melting Pot Soliders*, has only a few isolated sentences which mention the Welsh, and Ella Lonn's massive volume, *Foreigners in the Union Army and Navy* (New York, 1969), does not have much more. One exception is Dean Mahin's recent book, yet he still only includes the Welsh in a short chapter which lumps them in with other 'Britons' (i.e. English and Scots); see Mahin, *The Blessed Place of Freedom*, pp. 29–37. Two short articles on the subject have been published: Alan Conway, 'Welshmen in the Union Armies', *Civil War History*, 4 (1958), and Robert Roser, 'Give them cold steel: The Welsh in the Civil War,' *Cambria* (October 1998).

56 *Y Seren Orllewinol*, June 1861. Note that, while cross-indexing census information on Welsh immigrants with army enlistment records may help future researchers work out exactly how many Welsh-born soldiers were in the Union army, it will be impossible to determine how many American-born Welsh-speaking soldiers enlisted (remembering that the children, and sometimes grandchildren, of immigrants were raised speaking Welsh in the United States).

57 *Y Cenhadwr Americanaidd*, October 1862.

58 A number of Welsh-speaking chaplains published letters, sermons and essays during the war. In addition to the three mentioned in this chapter (Erasmus Jones, Benjamin Chidlaw and John M. Thomas), examples include Robert Littler of the 74th New York Infantry (who will be discussed Chapter Five) and J. D. Jones of the 117th New York Infantry (whose prose is treated in Chapter Nine).

59 The manuscript letters of Elias J. Prichard are in Emory University Library; I have used copies in the National Library of Wales (NLW 17673D).
60 *Y Cenhadwr Americanaidd*, June 1861.
61 *Y Drych*, 11 July 1863.
62 These words are italicized in the original text.
63 *Y Cyfaill o'r Hen Wlad*, January 1862. This same vocabulary list was also published in *Y Cenhadwr Americanaidd*, August 1861.
64 *Y Cyfaill o'r Hen Wlad*, January 1862.
65 *Y Cenhadwr Americanaidd*, April 1862.
66 *Y Cenhadwr Americanaidd*, January 1862.
67 Robert Everett published such statements several times. See, for example, *Y Cenhadwr Americanaidd*, October 1862: 'Pe caem y cyfarwyddyd priodol at ein milwyr Cymreig danfonem rifynau o'r Cenhadwr iddynt yn awr ac eilwaith, mor aml ag y gallem fforddio i wneud hyny.' ('If we had the proper addresses for our Welsh soldiers we would send them numbers of the Cenhadwr now and again, as often as we could afford to do that.')
68 *Y Cenhadwr Americanaidd*, October 1862.
69 Ibid.
70 See, for example, J. P. Thomas, writing in *Y Drych*, 11 July 1863, and using the same title as the piece which Evan Griffiths published in the *Cenhadwr* eight months earlier, 'Coffadwriaeth y Dewrion'.
71 *Y Cenhadwr Americanaidd*, May 1862.
72 *Y Cenhadwr Americanaidd*, December 1861.
73 Ibid. The first line of the poem has been amended, as it was misprinted in the original as *pwy'n yw medd rhyw un oddi draw*.
74 Mitchell, *The Vacant Chair*, p. 72.
75 Alice Fahs, *The Imagined Civil War* [:] *Popular Literature of the North and South 1861–1865* (Chapel Hill and London, 2001), p. 121.
76 'The Feminized War' is used by Alice Fahs for the title of her fourth chapter; ibid., pages 120–49.
77 For the 'Blue Books', see Chapter One, pages 11–12.
78 Jane Aaron, *Pur Fel y Dur* [:] *Y Gymraes yn Llên Menywod y Bedwaredd Ganrif ar Bymtheg* (Cardiff, 1998), p. 10.
79 Ibid., p. 11.
80 That the responsibility for maintaining the Welsh language was conceived of as being invested specifically in the women is made manifest in the common phrase 'mother tongue' (*mam iaith* or *mamiaith*). In this piece, the writer states specifically that Welsh was the language of his mother; in other words, he draws attention to the fact that Welsh, spoken by this young American woman, is the language which his mother gave to him back in Wales.
81 *Y Drych*, 11 July 1863.
82 *Y Cenhadwr Americanaidd*, October 1861.
83 This might have been Josiah D. Jones, who would later enlist and become a corporal with the 94th Illinois Infantry, and who published some Welsh-language poetry during the middle years of the war. The 94th Illinois Infantry, however, was not mustered into service until 20 August 1862, ten months after this poem was published, and thus, if the poet was indeed Josiah D. Jones, then the poem was composed at a time before he himself enlisted in the army.
84 *Y Cenhadwr Americanaidd*, October 1861.

85 John Rowlands's diary, in the collection of Albert Gregorovich, entry for 6 October 1862.

86 T. Islwyn Walters's unpublished transcription of David Davies's diary, in the collection of Carol Mills, entries for 5 and 6 January 1862.

87 'Rebeca' from Nelson, New York, published a great deal of poetry during the war years. As her identity has not been discovered, it is theoretically possible that the poet was a man using a female voice for dramatic effect. There is, however, no good reason for not taking Rebeca to be a woman. There were many Welsh-speaking women who published poetry in the United States before and during the Civil War, and there is no internal evidence suggesting that Rebeca was not one of them.

88 *Y Cenhadwr Americanaidd*, October 1862.

89 Ibid.

90 *Y Cenhadwr Americanaidd*, October 1861.

91 As the real name of the poet 'Ab Morydd' is not at present known, it is possible that he and the Revd Evans were, in fact, the same person.

92 Fahs, *The Imagined Civil War*, p. 62.

93 Richard Marius, 'Introduction', p. xiii, in Richard Marius (ed.) and Keith Frome (associate ed.), *The Columbia Book of Civil War Poetry* (New York, 1994).

94 Hywel Teifi Edwards, *Ceiriog* (Caernarfon, 1987), p. 23.

95 The words 'speech act' constitute a theoretically-charged phrase. The classic formulation of 'speech act theory' is J. L. Austin, *How to do things with Words* (Oxford, 1962).

96 On the role of the press in helping Welsh-speaking Americans to 'imagine' their nation, see the discussion in Chapter One, pages 12–13.

97 Fahs, *The Imagined Civil War*, p. 121.

98 Linda Kerber is cited by Reid Mitchaell, *Vacant Chair*, p. xii. The fact that Welsh-language American writers adopted much of the Revolutionary imagery, romance and rhetoric of the United States can be supported by a substantial body of writing. For another example from the Civil War period, see a letter which Benjamin Chidlaw published in *Y Cenhadwr Americanaidd* in November 1861, linking those who signed the Declaration of Independence to the young Welsh-Americans enlisting in the Union army. Welsh-language literature praising the Revolution and its 'heroes' was appearing long before the Civil War; for example, during the early 1850s the Welsh-American press published a considerable amount of material stemming from a campaign calling for a stone commemorating the Welsh to be placed in the Washington Memorial, and much of this material seeks to connect the Welsh and Welsh-Americans to Washington and the Revolutionary heroes. At least one anonymous writer published against the campaign, as he viewed the monument as *dyn-addoliaeth* ('man-worship') and an unseemly glorification of war; *Y Cyfaill o'r Hen Wlad*, May 1851.

99 Mitchell, *Vacant Chair*, p. xii. The image of the 'Republican Mother' was not simply a way for male writers to portray an idealized soldier's mother; as Elizabeth Young suggests, women also employed the traditional rhetoric for their own ends, including leaders of the Abolition movement, Elizabeth Cady Stanton and Susan B. Anthony, who used 'the rhetorical tradition of "republican motherhood" developed during the Revolutionary War era' while petitioning Congress in 1863. See Elizabeth Young, *Disarming the Nation* [:] *Women's Writing and the American Civil War* (Chicago and London, 1999), p. 14.

[100] Aaron, *Pur fel y Dur*, p. 11.
[101] Ibid., pp. 8–19.
[102] Ibid, p. 20.
[103] Judges 4.4–16.
[104] *Y gaethglud*, translated here as 'those enslaved', more literally means 'the captivity'. This biblical term, referring to the captivity of Israel in Egypt, was commonly adopted by Welsh-American abolitionists in referring to the collective body of enslaved African Americans. In imagining the triumphant end of the Union's war to free the slaves, this poet imagines *y gaethglud* singing its 'song', an image perhaps underpinned by more specific biblical references to the people of Israel thanking their God for freedom, or to specific texts such as Psalm 137 presented as songs about captivity. The spirituals of African Americans were mentioned and praised in the Welsh-American press at the time, and the link between the religious songs of those enslaved in their American captivity and the ancient songs stemming from the captivity of Israel was always implied, and sometimes made explicit, by these writers.
[105] Fahs, *The Imagined Civil War*, p. 62.
[106] Mitchell, *The Vacant Chair*, p. xiii.
[107] *Y Cenhadwr Americanaidd*, May 1862.
[108] By 'superficial patriotic' literature I mean the vast body of American writing which presents an unproblematic picture of the United States as the perfect or ideal nation. It should be noted that these propagandistic and often two-dimensional constructions often stem from more complex cultural processes. See, for example, Lauren Berlant's discussion of 'the way [America] has politically exploited its privileged relation to utopian discourse'; Lauren Berlant, *The Anatomy of National Fantasy: Hawthorne, Utopia and Everyday Life* (Chicago and London, 1991), p. 31.
[109] This poem was composed in November 1861, four months after the first battle of Bull Run. As earlier lines refer to that engagement ('A'r fyddin, yn unair d'wed, "Myn / Abe Lincoln nid mwyach daw damwain Bull Run." '; 'And the army says as one "Abe Lincoln declares that the accident of Bull Run will never again take place" '), the battle field described in this verse might be taken as referring specifically to Bull Run.
[110] The religious journals of Welsh America would publish the occasional piece by a few dissenting pacifists during the war, but these were very rare exceptions to the general rule. See Chapter 7, pages 291–311.
[111] *Y Cyfaill o'r Hen Wlad*, December 1861.
[112] Ibid.
[113] Ibid.
[114] James M. McPherson, *For Cause and Comrades* [:] *Why Men Fought in the Civil War* (Oxford and New York, 1997), p. 104.
[115] *Y Seren Orllewinol*, September 1862.
[116] There are in fact several characters named Caradog appearing in medieval literature, for example: Caradog fab Brân, mentioned in the Second Branch of the Mabinogi; and Caradog Freichfras, described in 'the Dream of Rhonabwy' and other Arthurian texts; See Rachel Bromwich (ed.), *Trioedd Ynys Prydein* [:] *The Welsh Triads* (Cardiff, 1978), pp. 297–300.
[117] *Y Seren Orllewinol*, September 1862.
[118] Ibid.

[119] It is possible to read this reference to the soldier's 'crown of victory' as an elliptical reference to his (possible) death; reading the phrase in terms of common Christian imagery suggests the crown of Christ, gained by crucifixion and death, yet turned into a crown of victory by his resurrection and ultimate triumph.

[120] *Y Cyfaill o'r Hen Wlad*, November 1861.

[121] The wide circulation of such images in the North was achieved through popular publications such as *Frank Leslie's Illustrated Newspaper* and *Harper's Weekly*, both of which included frequent illustrations of battles. See Fahs, *The Imagined Civil War*, p. 13.

[122] *Y Cyfaill o'r Hen Wlad*, November 1861.

[123] David Davies first joined an infantry regiment before being persuaded by friends that the work of a foot soldier was too dangerous and that he should disappear and then re-enlist with the artillery. (T. Islwyn Walters's unpublished transcription of David Davies's diary, in the collection of Carol Mills, entries for 2 January 1862 and 4 January 1862).

[124] Revelation 6.4: 'And out came another horse, all red. To its rider was given power to make men slaughter one another; and he was given a great sword'; quoted from *The New English Bible* (New York, 1972).

[125] In addition to the rules defining each individual metre, the strict metres as a group are defined by the presence of *cynghanedd*, the complex system of internal line ornamentation which was developed by medieval Welsh bards and codified in the bardic grammars of the late Middle Ages and early modern period. The poems discussed here do not use *cynghanedd*; despite their regular rhyme patterns, they are free metres according to the Welsh way of assessing metrics. This does not mean that these three poets did not use *cynghanedd* and the strict metres; on the contrary, all of them also published poems in the *englyn unodl union* form, one of the traditional strict metres, and Ionoron Glan Dwyryd composed and published several *awdlau*, or long poems using a combination of the strict metres.

[126] This kind of *pennill* can be defined as a four-line stanza, following an aa-bb rhyme scheme. It has four main accents in each line, with lines usually containing eight or nine syllables. While the word *pennill* is used loosely to mean 'verse' or 'stanza', the term is also used to refer to this specific kind of free verse (sometimes the phrase *hen benillion*, 'old stanzas', is used; these poems are also at times called *penillion telyn*, 'harp stanzas'). See T. H. Parry-Williams, *Hen Benillion* (Llandysul, 1940), pp. 7–17.

[127] The best-known example is the work of Rhys Prichard (1579–1644), vicar of Llanymddyfri. His religious *penillion* were published posthumously, the most complete collection being the volume *Canwyll y Cymru*, published by Stephen Hughes in 1681. See Siwan Non Richards, *Y Ficer Prichard* (Caernarfon, 1994).

[128] Cathryn Charnell-White, 'Y Pedwar Peth Diwethaf – Marwolaeth, Nefoedd, Uffern a'r Farn – yn Llenyddiaeth Gymraeg y Ddeunawfed Ganrif' (unpublished PhD thesis, University of Wales, Aberystwyth, 2000).

[129] Griffith Hughes, *Myfyrdodau Bucheddol ar y Pedwar Peth Diwethaf, sef Angau, Barn, Nef ac Uffern* (Philadelphia, 1735). According to Hywel Roberts, this was the fourth Welsh-language book printed in America; in his bibliography, Henry Blackwell describes this as the third Welsh-American publication. See D. Hywel E. Roberts, 'The Printing of Welsh Books in the United States: An Introductory Survey,' *The Journal of the Welsh Bibliographical Society* (183/4, vol. XII, no. 1), p. 5, and Henry Blackwell, *A Bibliography of Welsh Americana* (Aberystwyth, 1942), p. 37.

[130] I am extremely grateful to Cathryn Charnell-White for reading this poem and confirming my impression that it follows the tradition of *y pethau diwethaf*. In this sentence I draw upon her observations; personal communications with author, August 2004.

[131] *Y Cenhadwr Americanaidd*, November 1864.

4

'For Freedom, Union and Order'

On 2 May 1863 a seventeen-year-old soldier named Benjamin F. Thomas wrote a letter to his mother in Gallia County, Ohio. Although his family had left Llangeitho in south-west Wales when Benjamin was only two years old, he was raised in one of Ohio's Welsh-speaking communities, with the institutions of chapel and Sunday school ensuring that the Welsh which the children of immigrants learned at home was augmented by the sturdy literary language of biblical Welsh. As in Wales, the high literacy rates among even the poorest of immigrants were in part a result of the radical Nonconformist Protestantism which dominated the life of Welsh America. Benjamin Jones carried the religious beliefs of his family and community with him to war, and he did so both figuratively and literally; he enlisted in the 91st Ohio Infantry a few months after his seventeenth birthday, and left home with a parting gift from his mother, a small Welsh Bible. He was to carry it throughout the war. Benjamin survived three years of military service and, according to his own testimony, this Bible was the only personal possession which he brought home from the army when he mustered out in 1865.[1] At some point after the war – perhaps following the death of his mother – the original manuscript letter which he had written to her in May 1863 was placed inside the Bible, where it remained until the twenty-first century. Benjamin Thomas became a minister later in life, and these two coinciding texts – (published) Bible and (unpublished) letter – were kept safe by him for obvious reasons; both are concrete manifestations of the way in which religious belief informed the close mother-son relationship. Both texts are also potent reminders of the way in which different kinds of (often overlapping) discourses – public, personal, religious and political – were carried on through the medium of Welsh in this Ohio community.

Because Mrs Thomas had trouble with her eyes, Benjamin wrote the letter using an unusually careful and clear large block print. This special form of handwriting was apparently developed by the teenager before the war in order to help his mother with her Sunday school *pynciau* ('subjects' or 'texts'), as the first part of the letter demonstrates.

> Fy Anwyl Fam
> Yr ydwyf yn danfon hyn o linellau attoch chwi Mam er mwyn i chwi darllain hyn eich hunan (os nad ydych wedi anghofio darllain print or fath hyn)

Yr ydwyf yn Iach a chysurus o fawr ddaioni yr ARGLWYDD tuag ataf hyd yn hyn, gobeithio eich bod chwi yn mwynhau yr unrhyw fendith gobeithiaf fod John ag Evan au teuluoedd yn Iach

Carwn wybod yn eich nesaf pa fodd yr ydych chwi yn dyfod yn y blaen gyda'r pynciau yn yr Ysgol Sabbothol? pwy sydd yn eu printio i chwi nawr? ac hefyd yn mhwy cllass yr ydych chwi nawr? Pwy Claaes yr ydych wedi bod wedi i m'i'ch g'adael chwi?

Mam rhaid I chwi fy esgusodu am y fath Lythyr swta. mae yn cymeryd llawer i m'i Printio fel hyn[.][2]

'My Dear Mother,
I am sending these lines to you, Mother, for you to read for yourself (if you have not forgotten how to read print of this type).

I am well and comfortable by the great goodness of the LORD towards me so far, in the hope that you are enjoying the same blessing [and] I hope that John and Evan and their families are well.

I would like to know in your next [letter] how you are coming along with your subjects in Sunday School? who is printing them for you now? and also in whose class are you now? in which class have you been since I left you?

Mother, you must excuse me for [writing] such a short letter; it takes me a lot of time to print like this.'

Not only is this an unpublished manuscript letter, it is a letter of an extremely personal kind. It was written using a special kind of writing which a devoted son developed in order to help his vision-impaired mother. It is not a long letter; as Benjamin says in the last sentence, writing in this fashion took a lot of time. However, before finishing the 'short' letter, the young soldier set out for his mother – using this special, meticulous hand – his reasons for fighting in the Civil War.

Ond dywedaf hyn cyn terfyny sef fy nheimlad yma yr ydwyf yn caru'r 'Service', yn gampus cyhyd ag y caf Bywyd ag Iechyd, yr hyn fendith yr ydwyf wedi gael yn hynod hyd yn hyn o fawr ddaionu DUW Naf gellwch fod yn esmwyth yn fy nghylch.

Ni chymerwn un arian am 'dessertio'. na wnaf byth! sylwch y pwysfawrogrwydd or weithred Dyma fi wedi myned ar fy Llw! gerbron DUW y gwnaw fod yn ffyddlon ac amddiffyn y LLYWODRAETH yn erbyn brâdwyr!

Mae genym 3 dyledswydd iw chyflawni. ein dyledswydda tuag Dduw ein dyledswydd tuag at ein LLYWODRAETH, a'n dyledswydd tuag ein teuluoedd (a'n) cartrefu. A dylau pob Dyn wneuthur ei orau tuag at ein Gwlad. Gellwch fod yn sicr yn eich meddwl Mam na fuasai dim yn fy arwain oddicartref na dim yn fy mherswadio I aros (nid am yr arian) ond tra byddo y Llywodraeth a fy anghen yr ydwyf am aros.

Wel Mam rhaid i mi derfynu Cofiwch fi at fy nghyfeillion Fy serch atoch fil o weithuau Cofiwch fi o flaen gorsedd Grass ac yn eich gwjddiâu bob amser Eich Mab Benjamin F. Thomas[3]

'But I will say this, that is, relate my feelings, here before finishing: I love the Service exceedingly, as long as I have Life and Health, which blessing I have received

> wondrously by the great goodness of GOD the Lord – you can be assured concerning me.
> I would not take any amount of money to desert. I never will! Take note of the importance of the act: Here I am, having given my Oath before GOD that I will be faithful and defend the GOVERNMENT against the traitors!
> We have three duties to fulfil: our duty to God, our duty to our GOVERNMENT, and our duty to our families and our homes. And every Man should do his best for our Country. You can put your mind at ease, Mother, that nothing would lead me away from home nor would anything persuade me to stay [in the army] (not for the money), except that as long as the Government happens to need me I am going to stay.
> Well, Mother, I must finish. Remember me to my friends. I send you my love a thousand times. Remember me before the throne of Grace in your prayers each time. Your Son, Benjamin F. Thomas.

In spelling out his reasons for enlisting – and staying – in the Union army, Benjamin Thomas cites 'duty to . . . government', also described as remaining 'faithful in defending the government against traitors'. He was fighting to preserve the United States government against the Rebels, and this was for him a holy duty, placed in a trinity with duty to God and duty to home and family.

THE CAUSES EMBRACED BY WELSH-AMERICAN SOLDIERS: AN OVERVIEW OF THE SOURCES

War-time print culture gives the impression that the vast majority of Welsh-speaking Americans were pro-Union, anti-slavery and pro-war (in the sense that the war was seen as a necessary struggle to preserve the Union and/or to end slavery). As was seen in the last chapter, many of the poets, writers and religious leaders of Welsh America, as well as the editors who published their writings, described the Welsh volunteers as selfless individuals marching off to save the Union and to cleanse the nation of the sin of slavery. To what extent was this interpretation – or these interpretations – of the war and its causes embraced by the soldiers themselves? We know that thousands of Welsh-speaking Americans volunteered for the Union army; what do we know about the beliefs of individual soldiers and their reasons for enlisting? How many of them would have seen their military service in a manner similar to young Benjamin Thomas? What other reasons did Welsh soldiers give for fighting?

Recent research has yielded a data base which includes over 400 individual Welsh-speaking soldiers in the Union army. These are individual soldiers whom we know something about because texts written by or about them have survived.[4] These sources range from unpublished manuscripts written by soldiers and their families (letters and diaries) to a wide variety of published material (epistles by soldiers published either in the United States or in Wales; poetic tributes; obituaries and funeral sermons). Statistically speaking, this data base constitutes a good sample, containing somewhere between 3 and 10 per cent of all of the Welsh-speaking soldiers in the Union army.[5] However, while the size of this data base (over 400 individuals) represents a good sample, the range and variety of sources poses a number of interpretative problems.

Even unpublished manuscript sources have come down to us by means of selective processes. While not as formal as the kind of editing and censorship which can affect printed texts, each individual or family's collection of personal papers nonetheless has been formed by a kind of unofficial editorial or selective process (or by a series of such processes). Put simply, people decide what letters, diaries and personal papers they want to keep.

Benjamin Thomas's letter and the circumstances which have allowed it to survive over the years are evidence of such a process. The letter which the seventeen-year-old private sent back to his mother in Ohio suggests that there was a regular correspondence between them (Benjamin asks his mother for specific information in her 'next' letter). He also draws attention to the fact that he is using his special handwriting for this particular letter, suggesting that he wrote other, more hasty letters in his normal hand, which were then read to his partially blind mother by a third person. It is also likely that she, in turn, dictated her letters to somebody else, who then sent them to Benjamin on her behalf. It is perhaps no surprise that this one letter has survived; the young soldier took an inordinate amount of time to write it so that his mother could read his words for herself without the help of a third party and, in addition to referring to the deep religious beliefs which were held by both, he used this special letter to spell out for his mother his reasons for fighting. Its very nature has ensured that this letter – of all of the correspondence which presumably travelled between Mrs Thomas and her son during the war – has survived. Because of what it represented, it was this epistle which was preserved as a textual souvenir of Benjamin's military service, placed within the Bible which he carried while serving with the 91st Ohio Volunteer Infantry. If processes which we might describe loosely as editing and censoring affected texts printed during the war, it is also clear that, at least in some cases, a conscious selective process has decided which unpublished texts are handed down to us from the Civil War period.

However, some families have preserved the entire body of letters which their soldier sent home during the war. And in such cases, the great bulk of surviving correspondence often contains nothing whatsoever about the volunteer's reasons for enlisting and fighting. A great many surviving manuscript letters written by soldiers chronicle everyday life in the army and ask after the health and circumstances of friends and family at home; they do not on the whole contain ideological treatises on the soldier's reasons for enlisting and fighting. The same can be said for surviving manuscript diaries; more attention is given to the changing weather and the details of the soldier's diet than to ideological questions.[6]

On the other hand, published letters tend to contain more about the soldiers' reasons for enlisting and their views on the cause or causes for which they were fighting. This fact can usually be explained by the history of their publication. A soldier's letter had two ways of reaching the press, the first of which involved what we might call direct correspondence: the soldier himself wrote directly to the editor of the newspaper or journal. The second path leading to publication can be described as indirect correspondence: a soldier wrote a personal letter to a friend or family member at home, and the civilian recipient then forwarded the epistle to the press for publication *because* of the information and/or uplifting sentiments contained. We can take these published letters as a more or less accurate reflection of what the soldiers themselves actually wrote; there is little or no evidence of editorial interference with individual texts.[7] However, this does not mean that a selective process did not take place; the text was often chosen for publication because of the fact that the feelings expressed by the soldier supported the dominant view of the war being promulgated by the Welsh-American press. In other words, had a soldier written a private letter to a friend despairing over the war and damning the Union cause and/or the abolitionists, it is highly unlikely that such correspondence would be sent to the press for publication. Moreover, even were such a letter to be sent to *Y Drych* or one of the journals, it is extremely unlikely that the editor would have published it (given what we know about the political agenda pursued by these Welsh-American editors during the war).

Similarly, obituaries and funeral sermons by their very nature tend to eulogize the deceased soldier; had the departed soul been known for voicing opinions generally thought to be immoral by the religious leaders of Welsh America, it is unlikely that they would have found a place in print. On the other hand, the religious practices of Nonconformist Welsh chapels included *torri allan*, a very public 'excluding' or 'excommunicating' of (perceived) sinners from the religious community, and this aspect of public religious culture might have mitigated in favour of a more honest treatment of departed souls. Indeed, the authors of some memorial pieces refer to the urge to speak overly well of the dead, insisting that they, in contrast, are trying to present an 'honest' picture. To what extent such claims are merely part of a rhetorical strategy designed to increase the effect of the individual tribute, and to what extent they reflect the actual relationship between text and reality, we will, in most cases, never know.

The sources which tell us about individual soldiers' beliefs are literary texts, and they are subject to the full range of forces and circumstances which separate literature from 'real' experience, including literary artifice, censorship, and the selective processes (both intentional and unintentional) which have allowed specific manuscripts to survive.[8] However, despite this rather complex caveat, we do have a variety of texts, both published and unpublished, which give us information regarding a large sample of individual Union soldiers. It goes without saying that the following discussion can by no means be taken as the final analysis of Welsh-speaking soldiers and their reasons for fighting; however, this body of material can be taken as a reasonably sound reflection of the ways in which these soldiers and their acquaintances described their motives *in writing*.

MANUSCRIPT SOURCES

It is perhaps useful to start with some more evidence gleaned from unpublished letters and diaries. Several letters by Elias J. Prichard, a musician with the 22nd Wisconsin Infantry, have survived in manuscript. In one of these, sent back to his family in Wisconsin, he touches upon the 'cause' of the war and how he saw his reasons for enlisting.

> yr ydwyf yn gobeithio gweled y dydd y byddaf yn dyfod i Chicago a Jeff. Davis ai clever crew wedi ei dymchwel or wlad a garem oreu ai taflu i riw le da hefo ei dad Satan a Ball & Chain wrtho rhag iddo Seceshio.[9]

> 'I hope to see the day when I'll be coming to Chicago with Jeff Davis and his clever crew cast out of the country we love the best and thrown to some fitting place with his father Satan and a Ball & Chain on him to keep him from seceding.'

Like Benjamin Thomas, Elias Prichard described the war as a struggle to preserve the Union and defeat the rebellious secessionists, though he did it in less uplifting language than the religious soldier from Ohio. If Pvt Thomas saw preserving the Union as a near-holy duty, the musician from Wisconsin described the war in terms of fighting Satan's secessionist son, Jefferson Davis.

A manuscript letter written by John Davies, a blacksmith serving with a battery of artillery, set out for his relatives back in Wales his reasons for enlisting in the Union army: 'mae bron bob dyn ag sydd yn teimlo ychydig gynesrwydd tua ag rhyddid wedi enlistio ag yr wyf inau yn ei plith'; 'just about every man who feels a little warmth towards freedom has enlisted and I am among them'.[10] He does not expand upon this statement; it is impossible to know whether he saw himself as fighting for 'freedom' because he was against slavery or whether he was describing the fight to preserve the Union in terms of preserving freedom (or a combination of both).

The diary of Evan Davies, a private with the 21st Wisconsin Infantry, contains a dramatic and eloquent description of the volunteer's first experience of combat during the Battle of Perryville. As will be seen in Chapter Nine, in addition to presenting a detailed description of the realities of battle, this part of the diary contains a meditation on the difference between second-hand literary accounts of combat and experiencing the real thing – what Anglophone soldiers called 'seeing the elephant'. However, Davies refers to the Confederate army in passing as 'byddin lladron rhyddid,' 'the army of freedom's thieves', echoing the phrases *lladron dynion* ('thieves of men') and *lladron rhyddid* ('thieves of freedom') which punctuate Welsh-language abolitionist literature from the period. This, of course, does not mean that Davies was an abolitionist, but rather that he had internalised the abolitionist language of the Welsh-American press.

Thomas H. Jones, a Welsh soldier from Ohio, kept a diary while serving in Kentucky. On 30 April 1863 a slave was sold near where Jones was encamped, and he recorded his feelings in writing.

> Heddyw cymerodd golygfa e[r]chyll o effeithiau caethiwed le yma; cafodd merch ieuanc hardd bron yn wyn ei gwerthu, ac er ei chri ei hun a'i mam, gorfu iddi fyned [,] teimlwn yn grac o ngho – wrth y dynion creulon sydd yn prynu a gwerthu dynion, fe ddaw terfyn ar hyn, cyn hir, neu fo ein distryw fel gwlad.[11]
>
> 'Today a horrible scene of the effects of slavery took place here; a beautiful young girl, nearly white, was sold, and despite her own cry and that of her mother, she had to go; I feel out of my mind with anger at the cruel men who buy and sell men; this will stop, before long, or it will be our destruction as a country.'

Thomas H. Jones's diary is macaronic; it is written in both English and Welsh. What is interesting is that Jones turned to his native tongue in order to express his anti-slavery feelings.[12] Moreover, this record of his views on slavery and the relationship between the Southern institution and the crises threatening to 'destroy [the] country' is one of the more elaborate and emotional parts of the diary. An otherwise bald chronicle of events gives way to a passionate aside here, as the soldier from Ohio punctuates his simple narrative of army life with a rhetorical assault upon the slave system.

PRINT SOURCES

The views expressed in manuscript sources such as these are echoed and amplified in the much greater body of surviving print material. Like Benjamin Thomas, Dafydd Owen was born in south Wales before emigrating at a young age with his family. Also like Benjamin Jones, Dafydd enlisted in a regiment of the Ohio Infantry while he was still a teenager. After more than two years of service which included some of the western theatre's bloodiest engagements, Dafydd was killed during the assault on Missionary Ridge at Chattanooga, Tennessee.[13] A short biography was published in both *Y Cenhadwr Americanaidd* and *Y Seren Orllewinol*, presumably because the family had friends and relatives who were Congregationalists (and thus read the *Cenhadwr*) as well as ones who were Baptists (who would have turned first to the pages of the *Seren* for their information).[14]

The biographical piece is imbued with a degree of tragic drama; the writer emphasizes the young soldier's self-sacrifice, portraying him as being deeply religious and unflinchingly patriotic. This published text thus provides an image of the soldier's commitment to the 'cause' which, however stylized, reflects the way in which Benjamin Thomas described his own feelings in that private letter which he wrote to his mother. Dafydd Owen's biographer – most likely the family's minister – intensifies the piece's tragic drama by stressing early on that Dafydd was his parents' only child:

> . . . daeth Cyhoeddeb allan oddiwrth yr Arlywydd yn gofyn am chwech can' mil o filwyr. Teimlodd ein cyfaill ieuanc gwladgarol dros ei wlad, ac wele ef yn awr am y tro cyntaf yn ei fywyd yn dweyd 'na' wrth ei rieni. Pan ddeisyfasant arno beidio ymrestru, atebodd yntau nas gallasai gydsynio â'i cais yn y peth hwn. 'Fy ngwlad i yw hi, ebe fe, ac y mae hi yn ddyledswydd arnaf ei hamddiffyn hyd y mae ynof, ac yr wyf yn penderfynu gwneud.'[15]

> '. . . an Announcement came from the President asking for 600,000 soldiers. Our patriotic young friend felt for his country, and for the first time in his life he said "no" to his parents. When they pleaded with him not to enlist, he answered that he could not comply with their request in this matter. "It is my country," he said, "and it is my duty to defend it as long as I can, and I am resolved to do [that]." '

The published record of this young Ohioan's reasons for fighting reflects the unpublished personal letter penned by that other Welsh soldier from Ohio, Benjamin Jones; both describe their decision in terms of *dyledswydd*, 'duty', although one refers specifically to duty to 'government' (*llywodraeth*) and the other to 'country' (*gwlad*). In both cases, the expression of patriotic motivation is also set in conjunction with duty and loyalty to family; while Benjamin Thomas attempted to ease his mother's worrying by placing his duty to her within a sacred trinity which included duty to the government, Dafydd Owen's biographer claims that this young Welsh-American cited his duty to country as the express reason for going against his parents' wishes. Similar expressions of patriotism are found in numerous other biographies and death notices. To give but one example, Richard M. Jones, killed near Petersburg, Virginia, on 17 June 1864, was described on the pages of *Y Seren Orllewinol* as fulfilling what he saw as his patriotic duty: 'Credai mai ei ddyledswydd oedd amddiffyn ei wlad'; 'he believed that his duty was to defend his country'.[16]

Soldiers' letters were often presented in their own special column by the various Welsh-language publications. As noted above, some of these were sent directly to the editor by the writers, while others originated as personal letters that were then forwarded by the recipients to the journal or paper. In the case of this kind of indirect correspondence between soldiers and the press, the civilian intermediaries often state in a prefatory note that they are sending the epistle for publication because of the fact that it contains (what were seen as) uplifting moral sentiments which would benefit the wider Welsh-American reading public. For example, M. A. Ellis sent a soldier's letter to the editor of *Y Drych* along with the following note of explanation:

> Mr. Golygydd, – Rhoddwyd yn fy llaw y llythyr canlynol a dderbyniwyd gan gyfeillion i'r ysgrifenydd; ac wedi ei ddarllen tybiais fod y naws grefyddol, y teimlad dwfn, y tarawiadau bywiog, a'r penderfyniad gwrol a amlygir ynddo yn ddigon o reswm dros roddi cyhoeddusrwydd iddo yn y DRYCH.[17]
>
> 'Mr. Editor, – The following letter, which was received by friends of the writer, was placed in my hand; and after reading it, I thought that the religious nature, the deep feeling, the lively turns, and the heroic determination which are expressed in it are enough of a reason for publishing it in the DRYCH.'

This letter was selected for its content ('religious' and 'heroic') as well as for its literary characteristics, its 'lively turns' of phrase.

One letter published by *Y Drych* on 4 April 1863 is described as 'Talfyriad o Lythyr oddiwrth Filwr Cymreig', 'An Abridgement of a Letter from a Welsh Soldier'. As the published epistle is in fact quite long, if it is indeed an 'abridgement' of a lost original, then that original personal letter must have been extremely lengthy indeed. However, the fact that the newspaper's editor describes it as 'an abridgement', coupled with the religious and ideological slant of the published extract, demonstrates the way in which private correspondence forwarded to the press was mined for material which suited the editor's moral and political agenda. This soldier signed his letter 'John W. Rowlands, Sergeant, Com[pany] H, U. S. A.', and no further details as to his identity and service record are given. In the central section of this long piece Sgt Rowlands articulates his reasons for fighting and details the nature of his commitment to the Union cause. This ideological treatise is framed by a religious discussion, ensuring that the letter when taken as a whole presents commitment to the Union cause within the context of religious faith and duty, much the same as Benjamin Thomas does in his unpublished letter. Like Benjamin Thomas, John W. Rowlands also discusses his Christian faith in connection with his mother. Towards the end of the letter he describes how as a boy he was given biblical instruction back in Wales:

> Cefais fy nysgu yn foreu ar liniau fy mam, ger yr hen Ddyfi ddolenog, i ddywedyd – 'Gwneler dy ewyllys ar y ddaiar, megys y mae yn y nefoedd.' Ychydig oedd hi yn ei feddwl y pryd hwnw mai ar feusydd gwaedlyd Virginia y buasai meddwl ei phlentyn yn plygu o'i fodd i ewyllys 'Ein Tad.'[18]
>
> 'I was taught at a young age on my mother's knee, by the old winding Dyfi [River], to say – "Let your will be done on earth, as it is in heaven." Little did she

think at that time that it would be on the bloody fields of Virginia that her child's thoughts would yield willingly to the will of "Our Father." '

While Benjamin Thomas described duty to country as one of three holy or near-holy duties alongside duty to God and duty to home and family, John Rowlands's interpretation of 'the will of "Our Father"' held that he was fighting for a patriotic trinity:

mae anrhydedd y milwr yn fawr; y mae mewn *struggle* dros Ryddid, Uniondeb a Threfn; mae yn rhoddi ei ysgwydd i ddal i fyny deml Llywodraeth ryddgarol; mae yn codi ei fraich yn erbyn bradwriaeth gelynion a therfysgwyr, ac yn myned allan a'i fywyd yn ei law i'w aberthu ar allor llwyddiant ei Wlad.[19]

'the soldier's honor is great; he is in a struggle for Freedom, Union and Order; he gives his shoulder to support the temple of a freedom-loving Government; he raises his arm against the treachery of enemies and trouble-makers, and takes his life in his hand to sacrifice at the altar of his Country's well-being.'

This Welsh soldier wrote that he was willing to 'sacrifice' himself for 'Freedom, Union and Order', all presented as qualities of the United States government which he was serving. The reference to 'Freedom' and the 'freedom-loving Government' might mean that he saw the war in part as a struggle against slavery, and, as will be seen below, this interpretation would certainly be supported by the writings of many other Welsh soldiers as well as by the activities of the Welsh-American press in general. John Rowlands, however, does not give any further details as to the exact nature of the 'freedom' for which he was fighting.

He does, however, expand upon his religious interpretation of the service provided to a Government struggling to preserve 'Freedom, Union and Order'. The 'soldier's honor' is gained by lending his individual 'shoulder' in the support of the collective 'temple' of the United States Government. Similarly, by risking his life in a struggle against the Rebels' 'treachery' he is taking his own 'life . . . to sacrifice at the altar of his Country's well-being.' In this one sentence John Rowlands uses three terms laden with biblical meaning, [*t*]*eml* ('temple'), *aberthu* ('to sacrifice') and *allor* ('altar'). He would have become familiar with these words and concepts at a young age, perhaps during that biblical instruction which he received from his mother on the banks of the Dyfi back in Wales. Like Benjamin Thomas, he is equating service to country with service to God, and John Rowlands does this by re-inscribing these biblical terms with a specific patriotic meaning.[20]

Sgt Rowlands was appropriating the biblical Welsh vocabulary which came to him by means of Nonconformist chapel culture. However, while his religious culture was in many ways uniquely Welsh, John Rowlands's use of these Old Testament concepts was by no means unique to Welsh-speaking Americans;

many English-speaking soldiers in the Union army were interpreting the war in a similar fashion. Steven E. Woodworth stresses the significance of the way in which these soldiers used the combination of the words 'sacrifice' and 'altar':

> Things sacrificed on an altar were offered directly to the deity whose altar that was, for the purpose of propitiating that god or atoning for wrongdoing. The Old Testament Scriptures spoke of sacrificing animals to the God of Israel as a token of the final sacrifice that God would provide Himself . . . The ultimate sacrifice in the Bible has been Christ[.][21]

Woodworth examines this kind of discourse against the background of what he calls 'orthodox Protestant Christianity'.[22] His conclusions are that 'the resulting theology was not that of Christianity.'

> What was happening was that the pressure, pain, and enthusiasm of war were leading some Northerners to create a form of civil religion, a twisted version of Christianity in which the nation was god and rewarded those who sacrificed themselves in its cause. Significantly, however, it was a concept which seemed to have most resonance with persons who had only a passing acquaintance with the concepts and terminology of Christianity. A number of Northerners did begin to talk in such terms, but it is important to remember that they remained a minority and that the teachings of orthodox Christianity remained predominant.[23]

While this analysis helps us get to grips with the ways in which some northern Protestants were using religious terminology to discuss their allegiance to country, describing these Welsh-speaking soldiers' appropriation of biblical terminology for patriotic uses as evidence of 'a twisted form of Christianity' would be imposing a particular twenty-first-century version of what constitutes 'orthodox Christianity' on the complex intersection of religious and patriotic feelings which characterizes the writings of these Welsh-American soldiers. To be more exact, rather than viewing such expressions of patriotism as a 'civil religion', it would be better to describe these texts as presenting a kind of discourse which re-inscribes the terminology of the Old Testament for patriotic purposes but which, rather than constructing a new 'civil religion' which is set against or used to displace any previous Christian faith, is rather harmonized by the writer (and believer) with that faith.

Whatever the religious background of the English-speaking northerners described by Woodworth, the statement that this 'concept seemed to have most resonance with persons who had only a passing acquaintance with the concepts and terminology of Christianity' is certainly not applicable to Welsh-American writers. The abridged version of John Rowlands's letter published by *Y Drych* in April 1863 reveals a profound acquaintance with the kinds of

Christian doctrine and modes of analysis conveyed by the Welsh Nonconformist chapel's services and Sunday school education, whether Methodist (either Calvinistic or Wesleyan), Baptist, or Congregationalist. In addition to the specific reference to learning Scripture at his mother's knee, the piece is punctuated by biblical quotations.[24] It also exhibits the confessional nature of the chapel's *seiat*, a discussion of the inner workings of personal faith combined with a self-examination of the individual's sins and shortcomings: 'Yr wyf yn ofni, ar ol y cwbl, mai Cristion gwael ydwyf – rhy anniolchgar o lawer i Dduw'; 'I fear that, after all, I am a poor Christian – too unthankful by far to God'.[25] Quite the opposite of having 'only a passing acquaintance' with Christian teachings, John Rowlands, like so many Welsh-speaking Americans, had been totally immersed in such teachings from the earliest possible age. Indeed, such religious instruction formed the main educational horizons of people like John Rowlands in Wales and in the United States. The lower economic strata of nineteenth-century Welsh society were often more literate than their English counterparts because of the intense nature of religious instruction in the Nonconformist chapels with their attendant Sunday school systems.

Rather than presenting some kind of 'heretical' version of 'twisted' Christianity, when Welsh soldiers like John Rowlands used Christian terms and concepts to describe their commitment to the Union cause they were simply doing what came naturally to them; they were describing the subject at hand using the linguistic and conceptual resources which they had at their disposal. Biblical Welsh provided them with the most heightened linguistic register available to them, and their religious education provided them with a range of terms and concepts on which to draw. This biblical language was used in constructing written expressions of patriotism, a fact which attests to the central role of that language in Welsh-language culture. It does not mean that worship of the Union was being substituted for worship of the Christian God.

Moreover, like Benjamin Thomas, John Rowlands emphasized that he had sworn an oath to serve the United States government faithfully. In his letter to his mother, the young Ohioan called her attention to the sacred nature of his oath: 'take note of the importance of the act: here I am, having given my Oath before GOD that I will be faithful and defend the GOVERNMENT against the traitors!' ('sylwch y pwysfawrogrwydd o'r weithred: Dyma fi wedi myned ar fy Llw! gerbron DUW y gwnaw fod yn ffyddlon ac amddiffyn y LLYWODRAETH yn erbyn brâdwyr!').[26] The published letter by John Rowlands contains a similar emphasis on the religious aspect of the military oath. And, like the personal manuscript letter written by Benjamin Thomas, the published epistle draws the intended audience's attention to the religious question at stake by using the word *sylwch*, the imperative form of the verb *sylw* ('to notice something' or 'to take note of something'):

> Sylwch, yr wyf wedi myned ar fy llw, yn wirfoddol o flaen Duw a dyn yr aberthwn fy mywyd ar allor milwriaeth fy Ngwlad os byddai eisiau – y cai fy ngwaed ei dywallt, bob dyferyn i'r llawr os byddai hyny yn angenrheidiol er cadw i fyny urddas fy Ngwlad yn ei holl gyfreithiau, ei Chyfansoddiad a'i Hundeb – aethum ar fy llw mwyaf cysegredig a difrifol y rhoddwn fy nerth, fy ngofal, fy meddwl a fy mywyd i lawr er galluogi fy Ngwlad i ddarostwng y gwrthryfel drwg presenol.[27]

> 'Take note, I have sworn an oath, willingly before God and man that I would if need be sacrifice my life on the altar of my Country's military service – that my blood would be spilled, every drop on the ground, if that should be necessary in order to preserve the dignity of my Country and all its laws, its Constitution and its Union – I gave my most sacred and serious oath that I would lay down my strength, my charge, my mind and my life in order to enable my Country to put down the present evil rebellion.'

The Union army, like many armies in many periods of history, did in fact require new volunteers to swear a religious oath. In inducting new soldiers into its army, the government was asking them to galvanize their commitment with religious conviction and the evidence provided by the writings of these Welsh-speaking northerners is that they took that oath seriously. The very act of being a Union soldier brought their religious beliefs into a close alliance with their service to the United States government, and these written texts which re-inscribe biblical terms with patriotic meanings are logical literary extensions of the way in which religious commitment was melded with military service during the swearing in of new soldiers. In describing his oath of service, John Rowlands employs two of those terms which he later uses in describing his service to country: the verb *aberthu* ('to sacrifice') and the noun *allor* ('altar').

Whether or not one accepts Steven Woodworth's conclusion that those (Anglophone) Northerners who described their military service in these terms were only 'a minority', the use of biblical language and imagery to describe support for the Union cause was one of the main strains characterizing Welsh writing about the war. As was seen in the last chapter, a number of Welsh-American poets described the volunteers' march to war in terms of a willing *aberth* or 'sacrifice', presented in explicitly Christian terms. And these texts, rather than being composed by writers 'who had only a passing acquaintance with the concepts and terminology of Christianity', often on the contrary exhibit a profound knowledge of the kinds of Christian teachings which characterized Welsh religious culture before the Civil War. Remember, for example, that Ab Ioan's poetic meditation on the self-sacrificing Union soldiers draws upon the complex traditions involving spiritual preparation for *y pethau diwetha*, 'the last things'. The idealized Christian soldier constructed by that Welsh-language poet sacrifices himself for two reasons: to purify the nation of sin and to teach others that the 'first thing' which should be on their minds is just this kind of sacrifice. A considerable amount of the prose published by

Welsh-speaking Northerners during the war reflects the poet's theological interpretation of the soldiers' sacrifice: R. D. Thomas described the war as God's 'scourge' (*fflangell*); Erasmus Jones portrayed the conflict as 'Jehovah's chastising rod' (*gwialen ceryddol Jehofah*); and Robert Everett in several different essays and editorials described the war as a way of cleansing the nation of its past sins. All three of these writers were Congregational ministers, and intensely learned ones at that; all three wrote various theological tracts, and Robert Everett was awarded an honorary Doctor of Divinity by an American college.[28] In other words, they were the exact opposite of individuals who had 'only a passing acquaintance' with Christian teaching; they were the intellectual, moral and religious leaders of Welsh America. And, primarily because they interpreted slavery as a sin against God, they saw the war as an opportunity provided by Him to cleanse the United States of that sin.

Given the fact that poems describing the soldiers' sacrifice in Christian terms were published in the same journals used by these minister-writers to present their theological interpretations of the war, we can suggest that all of these published texts provided a field of related discourses which held a specific theological interpretation of the war and its causes in association with a specific theological interpretation of the service and sacrifice rendered by the Union soldiers. John Rowlands wrote that he was willing to 'sacrifice' his life on the 'altar' of his country in order to support the 'temple of a freedom-loving Government', adding that he was doing this consequent to taking a 'sacred oath before God'. His personal letter – made into a very public text when published on the pages of *Y Drych* – must be read in the context of other theological interpretations of the war published by the Welsh-language press in the United States. He certainly appropriates biblical language in order to construct an expression of patriotic sentiment, yet he does so – according to his own statement – not to displace Christianity with a new 'civil religion' but rather because his military service and support for the Union cause were subsumed within the Christian world-view which had informed his life from his childhood in Wales to his soldiering on the battlefields of Virginia. The 'real' feelings entertained by this soldier are of course lost and ultimately unknowable to us; what we do have is his published epistle, a text presenting a complex constellation of beliefs in which an intense Nonconformist Protestant Christianity is asserted in relationship to an assertion of faith in the Union cause.

The religious and patriotic discourses which characterize this text are coloured by at least one other theme. In addition to referring repeatedly to *fy Ngwlad*, 'my Country', John Rowlands writes *fy Ngwlad fabwysiedig*, 'my adopted Country', at two different places. His commitment to the Union cause is presented explicitly in terms of an immigrant's resolve to serve his new country faithfully. The second and last time that John Rowlands uses this expression is in the context of his possible death.

> . . . os aberthir fy mywyd yn yr ymdrechfa galed hon ca fyned yn ewyllysgar. Y cwbl a ofynwyf ydyw ystyllen uwch ben fy medd gyd a'r geiriau hyn arni: *Gwnaeth ei ddyledswydd yn anrhydeddus; bu farw yn achos ei Wlad Fabwysiedig; ac ni throdd ei gefn yn nydd y frwydr. Huned ei lwch mewn heddwch.*[29]

> '. . . if my life is sacrificed in this difficult struggle, I will go willingly. All that I ask is a plank above my grave with these words on it: *He did his duty honourably; he died in the cause of this Adopted Country; and he did not turn his back on the day of battle. Let his dust sleep in peace.*'

There is thus another strand in this text's complex weave of the religious and the patriotic, one running from the heart of the immigrant's experience. John Rowlands, like so many of his fellow Welsh-American soldiers, had emigrated under the shadow of the 'Blue Books' and all of the condescension which that very public insult to Welsh national pride had symbolized.[30] Immigrants like John Rowlands had left British Wales for Welsh America, and in the Civil War they had the ultimate opportunity to prove that they were worthy of their United States citizenship. As was seen in the last chapter (and as will be seen again in Chapter Seven), many of the United States' Welsh-language writers and editors were pointing to the fact that so many young Welsh-Americans were enlisting in the Union army as proof of their patriotism; though none would have asked for it, the war gave these immigrants and their children the ultimate opportunity to prove themselves to be good Americans. As is seen in John Rowlands's published letter, this interpretation of the war was widely embraced by the soldiers themselves. Rowlands writes his own epitaph, drawing attention to this short yet highly significant text within the larger text of the letter. The significance of this text-within-a-text is stressed in several ways; it comes as a dramatic high-point in this carefully-constructed piece of prose, and the use of italic print emphasizes its importance. Forming the thematic centre of the letter, the epitaph's message is supported by all the surrounding discussion of the intersecting religious and patriotic duties of the soldier. Presented quite literally as the last words about this particular Welsh-American, the epitaph states in simple terms that he was totally committed to his *adopted* country, and that he proved this ideological commitment by serving in the Union army.

While most published letters by Welsh-speaking soldiers make at least passing reference to religion, the majority of them do not engage in a detailed theological interpretation of their commitment to the Union cause. Thomas D. Thomas, a Northern soldier stationed in Memphis, Tennessee, published a letter in the September 1862 issue of *Y Seren Orllewinol*.[31] He had heard that his regiment was going to be sent to fight in Arkansas, and while writing to inform the journal's readers of this development he also engaged in a moralistic description of the enemy he was preparing to face in combat:

> Mae yn debyg ein bod ni i fyned i Helena, Arkansas – gwlad a'i dynion yn farbaraidd – gwlad a'i thrigolion yn sychedu am ein gwaed – gwlad fydd a'i daear yn feddau i amryw ohonom – gwlad lle y dangoswn ein gwroldeb – gwlad lle yr ymdrechwn dros ryddid a chyfiawnder[.][32]

> 'It is likely that we will go to Helena, Arkansas – a land with men who are barbaric – a land with inhabitants who thirst for our blood – a land with earth which will become graves for a number of us – a land where we will show our bravery – a land where we will struggle for freedom and justice.'

Thomas writes here that the army to which he belonged was 'struggl[ing] for freedom and justice'. Earlier in this same letter he states that he had marched to war in order to do his 'part for justice and freedom' as well as to fight 'violence, oppression and slavery': 'Teimlwn fy nghalon fach yn curo yn erbyn trais, gormes, a chaethiwed, ac yn chwyddo gan awydd i wneud fy ran dros gyfiawnder a rhyddid' ('I felt my little heart beating against violence, oppression and slavery, and swelling with a desire to do my part for justice and freedom').[33]

In another letter which *Y Seren Orllewinol* published in May 1862, this same soldier presents a slightly different articulation of his reasons for fighting. Having described his regiment's role in the battle of Fort Donelson, Thomas, a military musician, concludes by affirming his faith in the righteousness of his cause.

> Rhaid tynu i ben gyda dweyd fy mod yn gorfod chwythu yn y fife ar rai amgylchiadau nes y byddaf bron allan o wynt; ond ar y cyfan teimlwyf wrth fy modd o herwydd credwyf fy mod yn pleidio achos ag y mae Duw y nefoedd o'i blaid, sef rhyddid, ac mae ni sydd i fod yn fuddugoliaethus.

> 'I must conclude by saying that I had to blow my fife on some occasions until I was nearly out of wind; but on the whole I feel pleased because I believe that I am supporting the cause that the God of heaven is supporting, namely freedom, and that it is we who are to be victorious'.

Like John W. Rowlands, Thomas D. Thomas was sure that his fight for 'freedom' was justified by his religious faith. Some letters, like the one which Thomas D. Thomas published in September 1862, coupled 'freedom' with 'justice'. And some, like a letter which John W. Jones of Company G, 23rd Wisconsin Volunteers, published in *Y Cyfaill o'r Hen Wlad* in January 1863, mention only 'justice': 'Prysured yr amser y byddo y rhyfel yma yn cael ei ddarostwng, a chyfiawnder i lywodraethu dros ein gwlad unwaith eto'; 'Speed the time when this war will be put down, and justice rule our land once again.'[34]

Stating that they were fighting for an otherwise unspecified 'freedom' characterizes a great many of these soldiers' writings. In January 1863 *Y Drych* published a letter by Gwilym ab Ioan, a volunteer serving with the 154th New

York Infantry. He belonged to a group of eleven Welsh-Americans serving together in the regiment, all from the same community (and, apparently, the same chapel) in Freedom, Cattaraugus County, New York. The purpose of this letter was to inform friends and family at home in Freedom how the Welsh soldiers had spent their Christmas, and it gives details of the food cooked and consumed as part of their 'Christmas dinner on the hills of the Rappahannock' ('ciniaw Nadolig ar fryniau'r Rappahanock').[35] In concluding his letter, Gwilym ab Ioan gave the names of all the eleven Welsh soldiers, finishing with a play on the name of their home town: 'O Freedom y daethom, a thros Ryddid ac Undeb yr ydym yn ymladd'; 'It is from Freedom that we have come, and it is for Freedom and Union that we are fighting.'[36]

A letter written by Frederick K. Jones while stationed near White House, Virginia, and describing his part in the Peninsula campaign, was published by *Y Cyfaill o'r Hen Wlad* in June 1862. While the main purpose of this epistle was to provide news about the army's movements and actions, Jones includes a pointed interjection as he draws to a close: 'Yr ydwyf yn gobeithio, ac yn gweddio, am i'r amser ddyfod ar frys i'r rhyfel hwn gael ei ddarostwng, ac y byddo trigolion ein gwlad eto yn genedl unawl, ddedwydd, a llwyddiannus'; 'I hope, and I pray, that the time will come soon for this war to be put down, that the inhabitants of our land may be a united, happy and prosperous nation.'[37] He says nothing more about his reasons for serving in the Union army, but in this isolated sentence Frederick Jones states that he was fighting to make the 'land' (*gwlad*) into a united 'nation' (*cenedl*) again. Put simply, he was fighting to preserve the Union.

James Thomas, serving with the 3rd Pennsylvania Heavy Artillery, wrote a letter directly to the editor of *Y Drych* in order to accomplish several things at once. Like many other Welsh-Americans before, during and after the war, he hoped that his published letter would eventually reach his family back in Wales and inform them as to his whereabouts and his recent history.[38] He also took the opportunity to tease a brother who had gone west before the war to search for gold in the region of Pike's Peak: 'Y mae ef yn dewis cloddio aur a minau yn dewis wastio plwm a phowdr'; 'He chooses to dig for gold and I choose to waste lead and powder.'[39] The way in which he contrasts the two occupations, prospecting and soldiering, is then taken out of the personal realm of the brother's jest and turned into a patriotic lecture aimed at the newspaper's readers in general.

> Y mae yr ychydig linellau hyn i'r neb a ddarlleno i ystyried, a ystyrio gwnaed, a wnelo, parhaed. Wel, gyfaill, mi leiciwn gael gwybod genyt, pa ddaioni yw aur ac arian, a thai a thiroedd i ddyn ar ol iddo eu colli. 'Dim,' meddai y cyfaill. Wel, cymer dy ddryll yn dy law a lladd bob *rebel* ag alli, ac un dyn arall a ddywedo un sill yn erbyn y *Stars and Strips* [sic], fel y caffom heddwch yn ein gwlad un waith eto.[40]

'These few lines are for those who read them to consider, and those who consider to act upon, and those who act to continue to do so. Well, friend, I'd like for you to tell me, what good is gold and silver and houses and lands to a man after he has lost them? "None," says the friend. Well, take your gun in your hand and kill every rebel that you can, and any other man who happens to say one syllable against the Stars and Stripes, so that we might have peace in our country once again.'

The patriotic message is introduced by means of a proverbial formula which had been employed by several centuries' worth of Welsh moralistic literature. For example, the Dantean depiction of sinners and their punishments which Ellis Wynne published in 1703 begins with virtually the same words used by this Union soldier:

A Ddarllenno, ystyried;
A ystyrio, cofied;
A gofio, gwnaed;
A wnêl, parhaed.[41]

'Let he [or she] who Reads, consider;
He who considers, remember;
He who remembers, act;
He who acts, continue.'

While other Welsh-American soldiers and civilians were appropriating biblical language in order to describe their commitment to the Union cause, James Thomas used an age-old didactic formula in constructing a lesson in patriotic morality; these words informed Welsh readers that the following sentences contained a message which the author considered to be of the utmost moral significance. And this moral lesson tells us something of how James Thomas viewed his own military service (and his apparent willingness to shed blood in pursuit of that service); it is described as a necessary duty rendered to the nation ('our country'), a duty described also in terms of defending the nation's symbol, the Stars and Stripes, with the ultimate goal of returning 'peace' to the land. The moral imparted by this text involves service to country and that alone. Unlike the prose and poetry composed by so many other Welsh writers during the war, this service is described without any attendant religious discourse. There is no mention of Christianity or an oath to God, only loyalty to the collective community of the nation.

This nation is imagined in terms of a community of 'friends' and it is also described as a family of 'brothers' coming together to fight the rebels.[42] Immediately following the jovial exhortation to 'kill every rebel' (directed to *cyfaill*, 'a friend', constructed for rhetorical purposes), James Thomas ends his open letter in a simple and pointed manner: 'Yn awr, mi derfynaf gan gofio at bob darllenwr y DRYCH fel brawd. Hyn yn fyr oddiwrth eich ffyddlon gyfaill, James Thomas, Co. E, 3rd P. V.'; 'Now, I will finish by greeting every one of *Y Drych*'s readers as a brother. This from your faithful friend, James Thomas, Co. E, 3rd P. V.'[43] If he began his patriotic moralizing by addressing his own 'brother' (*brawd*) directly, Thomas now uses the term to describe a metaphorical family of patriotic Welsh-speaking Americans (defined explicitly as readers of *Y Drych* as well as by their inclusion in the patriotic discourse). Similarly, having earlier addressed a 'friend' (*cyfaill*) as part of the literary construct designed to impart the pro-Union message, he now describes himself as the 'friend' of all who follow his advice. While the tone of this published text is in places light-hearted, and even humorous, it is also a direct assertion of devotion to the Union cause. And that assertion of personal devotion is combined with an exhortation to the national community of Welsh America, a community imagined and defined as fellow readers of the Welsh-language newspaper and as friends and brothers united in their willingness to fight in defence of their country.[44]

Unlike John W. Rowlands, who describes the country which he was fighting to defend as his 'adopted country' (*gwlad fabwysiedig*), James Thomas refers simply to 'our country' (*ein gwlad*). However, Thomas does describe himself explicitly as an immigrant; in addition to noting in the body of his letter that he hopes it will reach his family back in Wales, he begins the published epistle by stating that he is 'an old bachelor from South Wales' ('Hen lanc ydwyf o Ddeheubarth Cymru'), and that he has been in the United States for ten years.[45] What Rowlands's letter does explicitly this letter does implicitly, suggesting that service in the Union army was a manifest symbol of the immigrant's loyalty to his new country.

A great number of other soldier-writers also describe the United States as their country, using either the singular *fy ngwlad* ('my country') or the plural *ein gwlad* ('our country'). These include the Revd Benjamin Chidlaw, and this is no surprise given what we know of his life. Having emigrated from Wales with his parents at the age of ten, Chidlaw was fifty years old and serving as chaplain to the 39th Ohio Infantry when he wrote to *Y Cenhadwr Americanaidd* in October 1861. The letter, which was published immediately, begins by describing his regiment's experiences in Missouri.[46] In addition to informing readers as to the nature of the war in the west, Chidlaw's letter also includes a personal reflection upon his own military service:

> Mae fy amser yn cael ei gymeryd i fyny yn darllen, ysgrifenu, ymweled â'r claf, ac ymddyddan â'r milwyr ar y maes, neu yn eu gwersyll. Mae genyf gyfeillion wrth fodd fy nghalon, ac yr ydwyf yn lled gysurus, ac yn ddiolchgar am y fraint o wasanaethu fy ngwlad yn amse[r] ei chyfyngder, ac i bregethu Crist a'i groes i'w hamddiffynwyr ar faes y rhyfel.[47]

> 'My time is taken up reading, writing, visiting the sick, and conversing with the soldiers on the field, or in their camp. I have friends to my heart's liking, and I am

fairly comfortable, and thankful for the privilege of serving my country in the time of its need, and to preach Christ and his cross to its defenders on the field of battle.'

The Union soldiers whom the Revd Chidlaw serves are described as the 'defenders' of '[his] country'. The fact that he had lived for forty years in the United States might have mitigated against echoing John Rowlands's phrase *gwlad fabwysiedig*, 'adopted country'. However, the very next sentence in Benjamin Chidlaw's letter does in fact introduce a mediation on his status as an immigrant.

> Mae yn dod i fy meddwl y cof cyntaf sydd genyf am America. Pan yn fachgen 6 neu 7 oed, gyda fy nhad ar ochr bryn yn agos i'r Bala, cododd fy hybarch dad ei fraich a chadach yn ei law, a thra yr oedd y gwynt yn chwythu y cadach, dywedodd, 'Dyma wynt teg i fyn'd â phobl i'r America.' Gofynais iddo, 'Beth oedd America?' Atebodd; 'Gwlad bell, – ond lle da i bobl i fyw, a lle da i blant gael ysgol a chodi i fod yn ddynion da.' Cafodd hyn effaith ddwys ar fy meddwl, ac o'r dydd hwnw hyd heddyw credais mai lle da i bobl i fyw ynddo yw America, ac am hyny gwnaf fy ngoreu i gynal y Llywodraeth sydd yn gwneud yr Unol Dalaethau y peth ydynt. Mae Cymry Ohio o'r un meddwl, mae eu plant gwladgarol yn brysio i'r fyddin, ac yn ddewr dros eu gwlad.[48]

> 'The first memory which I have about America comes to my mind. As a boy of 6 or 7 years old, with my father on the side of a hill near Bala, my most respected father raised his arm with a handkerchief in his hand, and while the wind was blowing the handkerchief, he said, "Here is a fine wind to take people to America." I asked him, "What was America?" He answered, "A far country, – but a good place for people to live, and a good place for children to get schooling and grow up to be good men." This had a deep effect upon my mind, and from that day to this I have believed that America is a good place for people to live, and because of that I am doing my best to maintain the Government which makes the United States that which it is. The Welsh of Ohio are of the same mind, their patriotic children are hurrying to the army, and [standing] bravely in defence of their country.'

James Thomas addressed readers whom he defined as Welsh-speaking American patriots; similarly, Benjamin Chidlaw describes the Ohio community of which he was a part as being both Welsh and patriotic. His personal narrative provides a romantic version of the reasons why Chidlaw's own family had emigrated forty years before the start of the Civil War, yet its message is extended to apply to the entire community of Welsh-speaking Ohioans; they are 'of the same mind' as Chidlaw and his father regarding the virtues of the United States and its government, and volunteering to serve in the Union army is proof of their American patriotism.

Like so many other texts published by the Welsh-American press during the war, Chidlaw connects the Welshness of his neighbours in Ohio with that which makes them such good Americans.[49] He concludes his letter by noting that several Welshmen had signed the Declaration of Independence, before linking this historical fact to the patriotism of the Union soldiers from Ohio's Welsh communities: 'Nid rhyfedd fod ein cenedl yn ymwneud â'u holl egni i amddiffyn egwyddorion eu tadau, llwyddiant y nefoedd fyddo ar eu gwladgarwch a'u gwroldeb'; 'No wonder that our nation is working with all of its energy to defend the principles of their fathers, may their patriotism and their heroism receive the success of the heavens.'[50] Although referring to the United States earlier in this same letter as *fy ngwlad*, 'my country', Chidlaw refers in this last sentence to *ein cenedl*, 'our nation', meaning 'the Welsh nation'. We can take the word *cenedl* here to refer to Welsh America, a 'nation' of people defined culturally as Welsh (and Welsh-speaking) just as they are defined politically as loyal citizens of the United States and supporters of the Union cause.

Earlier in this same letter Benjamin Chidlaw presents a meditation on the connection between slavery and the war. In describing the Confederates fighting his regiment in Missouri, he claims that they are motivated by the slave powers.

> Mae y *rebels* bron oll yn gaethfeistriaid, neu yn ddarostyngedig i awdurdod a dylanwad caethfeistri; hwy sydd wedi rheoli y wlad. Ond mae eu nerth wedi ei wanhau; ac os bydd gwrthgaethiwyr yn ffyddlon a gwrol, mae *slavery* yn Missouri o dan ergydion angeuol, a dydd ei ddiddymiaeth wedi gwawrio.[51]

> 'The rebels are almost all slave owners, or subjugated to the authority and the influence of the slave owners; they are the ones who rule the country. But their strength is weakening; and if the abolitionists are faithful and heroic, then slavery in Missouri is receiving mortal blows, and the day of its abolition has dawned.'

Chidlaw published a number of anti-slavery pieces before and during the war.[52] While he does not give the fight against slavery as the reason why he himself enlisted as an army chaplain, he nonetheless makes the connection between the two causes, Union and Abolition, explicit here.

Other soldiers published letters which presented the defeat of slavery as a reason for joining the army and fighting in the war. D. M. Williams of the 18th Wisconsin Infantry was one of many Welsh volunteers who wrote directly to the editor of *Y Drych*.[53] Like other unofficial military correspondents, he wanted to inform readers as to his regiment's activities, as well as to impart an uplifting message regarding the cause(s) for which he was fighting. In drawing his letter to a close, Williams writes of the uncertainties facing his regiment:

> Nid ydym yn gwybod i ba le yr ydym i fyned, ond gobeithiwn gael ein hanfon i ryw le y gallom gynorthwyo i lethu gwrthryfel lladron dynion. Buan y gwawrio y bore i wasgaru y rhai sydd *dda* ganddynt ryfel, a phob caeth fyddo yn cael ei ryddid.[54]

> 'We do not know where we are to go [next], but we hope to get sent to some place where me might help to stop the rebellion of the thieves of men. Soon may the day dawn when those who *like* war are scattered, and may every slave have his freedom.'

This Union soldier's Confederate enemies are described using one of the Welsh abolitionists' favourite phrases, *lladron dynion*, 'thieves of men'. Williams also writes that, in addition to putting down the 'rebellion', he is fighting to bring freedom to 'every slave'. In a piece published in *Y Cyfaill o'r Hen Wlad*, David M. Hughes of the 118th Ohio Infantry exclaimed 'Oh! na ddarfyddai caethiwed o'r tir, ac na ddelai heddwch a thangnefedd i deyrnasu eto!' ('Oh! that slavery would disappear from the land, and that peace and tranquillity would reign again!').[55]

Y Drych published a letter by another Northern soldier, Thomas Griffiths, describing the disastrous battle of Fredericksburg. While the body of the piece presents a vivid description of the engagement and the horrible massacre which was wrought upon the Union army there, Griffiths ends on a positive note.

> . . . nis gallant feddalhau dim ar yspryd gwrol a phenderfynol milwyr yr Undeb, a phlant eu hen dad, Abraham Lincoln, y rhai sydd wedi llyncu ei ysbryd rhydd a dyngarol, a phenderfyniad i golli y diferyn olaf o waed dros ryddid dynoliaeth, a darostyngiad caethiwed, trais a gormes – un wlad yw eu *motto*[.][56]

> 'They [i.e. the Southerners] cannot diminish any of the heroic and determined spirit of the Union's soldiers, children of their old father, Abraham Lincoln, who have imbibed his free and humane spirit, and are determined to spill the last drop of blood for the freedom of humanity, and the defeat of slavery, violence and oppression – one country is their motto.'

Like James Thomas's exhortation to all 'brothers' willing to pick up a gun and fight rebels, Thomas Griffiths's idealized description of the Union army portrays it as a family, described as the collective children of one father, Abraham Lincoln. And those brothers-in-arms are described explicitly as fighting to end slavery as well as to preserve the Union.

Some Welsh soldiers and sailors stated that, while they had always opposed slavery, military service had strengthened their views on the subject. One of these, John W. Hughes, wrote a letter to a friend which was then forwarded for publication in *Y Drych*:

> Wel, fe allai eich bod yn meddwl fy mod wedi edifarhau dyfod i'r fath le: Ddim o gwbl. Mae gwrando ar y Negroaid yn siarad am y triniaethau y maent hwy yn ei gael yn ddigon a pheri i bawb fyned yn *soldiers*. Mae yn well genyf fi farw ar y maes yn anrhydeddus na chael dyfod adref. Y mae ar y Democratiaid eisiau cadw y Negro druan yn gaeth yn ei dywyllwch tan ddydd mawr y farn ddiweddaf. O! gresyn, onide? Yr wyf yn ceisio gweddio ar yr hwn sydd yn goruwch-lywodraethu dynion ddyrysu eu hamcanion.[57]

> 'Well, perhaps you are thinking that I regret coming to such a place: Not at all. Listening to the Negroes talk about the treatment they receive is enough to make everybody become soldiers. I prefer to die honourably on the field than to come home. The Democrats want to keep the poor Negro enslaved in his darkness until

the great day of the final judgement. O! isn't it a shame? I try to pray to him who rules over men to confound their plans.'

Another letter published in *Y Drych* was written by John Morgan, a Welshman from Ohio serving on board a Union warship. This sailor gave ending slavery as his main reason for enlisting in the US Navy.

> Yr oeddwn yn rhyfedd dros ryddhad y caeth cyn myned o Newport; mewn gwirionedd, dyna oedd fwyaf ar fy meddwl i'm tueddu i godi arfau yn erbyn y *rebels*; ond er cymaint yr oeddwn yn dymuno eu rhyddhad y pryd hwnw, yr ydwyf yn dymuno eu rhyddhad yn fwy heddiw.[58]

> 'I was remarkably in favour of freeing the slave before leaving Newport [Ohio]; in truth, that was what was foremost on my mind driving me to take up arms against the rebels; yet however much I desired their freedom at that time, I desire their freedom even more today.'

In his ambitious study of all of the European immigrant populations in the United States during the war, Dean B. Mahin concludes that '[t]here is very little evidence that immigrants . . . were thinking about the abolition of slavery when they enlisted.'[59] The testimony of soldiers and sailors like John Morgan suggests, however, that many of these Welsh immigrants were ideologically motivated in ways very different from other immigrant groups: according to their own testimony, many Welsh immigrants did enlist entirely or partially because they wanted to abolish slavery.

Towards the end of the war, David T. Evans, a cavalryman serving with Sheridan's battle-seasoned forces, published a letter in *Y Cenhadwr Americanaidd*. This letter, while obviously aimed at the larger community of Welsh America, was also directed to a friend back in Troed-yr-aur, south Wales. In the epistle Evans draws attention to the fact that he had been praying for the end of slavery back in Wales before emigrating, and that by fighting in the Union army he had helped to bring about the fulfilment of those prayers.

> Yr wyf wedi bod mewn 26 o ysgarmesoedd a brwydrau, rhai o honynt yn dra phoeth. Cwympodd amryw o'm dewrion gyfeillion wrth fy ymyl, rhai o honynt i beidio codi mwy. Saethwyd fy ngheffyl danaf 3 gwaith, a lladdwyd ceffyl arall danaf, eto darfu i mi gael fy nghadw yn ddiogel trwy y cyfan, pan yn y peryglon mwyaf; ac yr wyf yn priodoli y cyfan i ofal tyner y Nef am danaf. . . . Ychydig oeddwn i a thithau yn feddwl pan yn sir Aberteifi, yn y cyfarfodydd gweddio tua Hawen a manau eraill, gyda y brodyr yn anfon ein herfyniadau am ddilead caethiwed yn y 'Gorllewin pell;' ychydig oeddwn i yn feddwl y buasai yn rhaid gwneud rhywbeth hefyd i dynu y cledd er dwyn hyny i ben.[60]

> 'I have been in 26 skirmishes and battles, some of them fairly hot. A number of my brave friends fell at my side, some of them to arise no more. My horse was shot beneath me 3 times, and another horse was killed beneath me, yet I managed to be

kept safe through all of it, when in the greatest dangers; and I attribute all of it to the gentle care of the Lord for me. . . . Little did you and I think when we where in Cardiganshire, in the prayer meetings in the district of Hawen and other places, sending our entreaties with the brothers for the abolition of slavery in the 'far West'; little did I think that I would have to do something as well [and] draw the sword in order to bring that about.'

As was seen earlier in this chapter, other soldiers published letters which discussed their commitment to the Union cause in relation to their status as immigrants. This published letter by David Evans describes his life before and after emigrating in terms of his commitment to the cause of abolition; the Welshman who prayed for the end of slavery while living in south Wales becomes a Welsh-American soldier who 'draws the sword' in order to bring about the end of that immoral institution.

As will be discussed in detail in Chapter Ten, Company F of the 22nd Wisconsin Infantry contained a large group of Welsh soldiers who made a name for themselves as abolitionists early in the war, contravening the orders of their own commanding general in order to help fugitive slaves. One of them, Thomas J. Davies, sent a letter to his uncle in 1864 who then forwarded it for publication in *Y Cyfaill o'r Hen Wlad*. Davies told his uncle (and the readers of the *Cyfaill*), that his opinion on the relationship between slavery and the war had, if anything, been strengthened during his two years of service.[61]

. . . nid edifarhëais erioed ddyfod allan i wneyd fy ngoreu dros fy ngwlad. Ond yr wyf wedi cyfnewid fy marn ychydig o barthed achos ag effaith y rhyfel. Bum yn meddwl achosi[d] yr anghyfod yma gan ben-boethder a brwdfrydedd *politicians* y De, am iddynt gael eu gwrthod gan eu gwrthwynebwyr eofn i'r Gogledd; ac mae asgwrn y gynhen oedd y *caeth* druan. Ond bellach amlwg iawn ydyw mae chwyldroad anocheladwy ydyw ymdrechfa anwrthwynebol rhwng cyfiawnder ac anghyfiawnder. Nid yw yn natur pethau i ryddid a chaethiwed fy[w] ynghyd, mwy nag ydyw i ddwfr a than. Yr oedd yn anmhosibl gochelyd y gwrthdrawiad yma, heb i ryddid ostwng ei phen dan iau ormesol y caeth-ddeilwyr. A gwell na ph[e]chu cymaint a hyny yn erbyn dynoliaeth, sefyll dros gyfiawnder a rhyddid, er y coller llawer o waed gwerthfawr[,] ydoedd y ffordd mwyaf anrhydeddus. Gwell fyddai genyf i'r rhyfel bara dair flynedd eto, os rhaid nag i'r Undeb gael eu sefydlu a'r gair lleiaf o gaethiwed o fewn i'n cyfansoddiad.

'. . . I have never regretted coming out to do my best for my country. But I have changed my opinion a little concerning the cause and effect of the war. I used to think that this contention was caused by the hot-headedness and eagerness of the South's politicians, because they were defeated by their fearless opponents in the North, and that the bone of contention was the poor *slave*. But it is now quite obvious that an unchecked struggle between justice and injustice is an unavoidable revolution. It is not in the nature of things for freedom and slavery to live together, more than it is for water and fire. It was impossible to avoid this conflict, without having freedom bow its head beneath the oppressive yoke of the slave-owners.

> And standing up for justice and freedom is better than committing such a sin against humanity, even though much valuable blood be lost, it was the most honourable course of action. I would prefer the war to last for three more years if need be, than to let the Union be established with the slightest word about slavery existing within our constitution.'

What this Wisconsin soldier is saying in these long and complex sentences is that, while he had always viewed slavery as the cause of the war, the nature of his analysis has changed. Davies tells us that he used to view the cause of the war in concrete political terms, as a struggle initiated by Southern pro-slavery politicians who resented losing the 1860 election. However, his analysis has now shifted from the world of practical politics to a more metaphysical realm; rather than describing the war as being caused by politicians feuding over slavery, by 1864 Thomas Davies was viewing it as a struggle between the very essences of freedom and slavery. Like those religious writers discussed in the last chapter who described the soldiers' march to war as a sacrificial act designed to cleanse the nation of the sin of slavery, this soldier tells his uncle (and readers of the *Cyfaill*) that the conflict is an unavoidable bath of blood which will rid the nation of 'such a sin against humanity'.

While not stating specifically that they joined the army in order to end slavery, many Welsh-speaking soldiers nonetheless wrote that they saw their military service as a chance to help the slaves. Early in the war the Revd Franklin Jones, chaplain to the 1st New York Volunteers, published a letter in *Y Cenhadwr Americanaidd*. Although he was writing less than six months after the fall of Fort Sumter, he already felt that the war had opened his eyes regarding the degree to which Christians like himself could help the slaves. In describing 'y boblogaeth gaeth yn Virginia', 'the enslaved population in Virginia', he wrote that:

> . . . [p]rin yr ymddangosodd erioed i lygad y dyngarwr a'r Christion olgyfa fwy toddedig na chynulliad y trueniaid didŷ a di-gartref hyn o feibion Affrica, yn estyn eu dwylaw erfyniol yn brysur at Dduw, yn nghanol y ddiffeithfa arswydol bresenol. Mae eu sefyllfa yn un a'r sydd yn galw yn uchel am sylw a chydymdeimlad y byd Cristionogol.[62]

> '. . . scarcely has a more heart-melting scene appeared to the eyes of the humanitarian and the Christian than this congregation of poor houseless and homeless sons of Africa, lifting their entreating hands busily to God, in the midst of the current horrible devastation. Their situation is one which calls loudly for the attention and sympathy of the Christian world.'

As will be seen in Chapter Ten, the writings of civilian ministers and army chaplains like the Revd Jones were often coupled with calls to support various charities founded in order to help former slaves.

Other letters, both published and unpublished, contain statements about slaves and former slaves which exhibit sympathy and voice a desire to help them, without stating explicitly that defeating slavery was the individual soldier's reason for enlisting and fighting. One of these, a letter published by John E. Roberts in *Y Cenhadwr Americanaidd*, chronicles the northern soldier's experiences in Virginia during the Spring of 1862.[63] The soldier's views on slavery are suggested by the way in which he describes two individuals encountered in the context of burying the Union dead. The first of these is a former slave who was welcomed into the army camp:

> Ychydig ddyddiau yn ol daeth hen gaethwas i mewn i'n gwersyll. Y mae yn 63 ml. oed – ac wedi bod yn gaethwas trwy ei oes ac wedi gweithio yn bur galed. Yr holl arian fu ganddo erioedd oedd $1.50 am ail gladdu milwyr yr Undeb, a syrthiasant yn Leeburg. Yr oedd yn dweyd fod y gelynion wedi eu claddu yn gyntaf, gan daflu dim ond ychydig o bridd drostynt – y moch oedd wedi eu turio i fyny a'u hanffurfio yn arswydol.[64]
>
> 'A few days ago an old slave came into our camp. He is 63 yrs. old – and has been a slave all his life and has worked quite hard. All the money which he ever had was $1.50 [which he received for] re-burying the Union soldiers who had fallen at Leeburg. He said the enemies had buried them first, throwing naught but a little soil over them – the pigs had dug them up and had deformed them horribly.'

Next John Roberts describes a man from Philadelphia who came to the same camp looking for the body of his son, presumably one of those soldiers recently buried or re-buried by the ex-slave:

> Rhoddais i'r hen wr fara a chig a choffi, a dywedai y truanddyn na welsai bobl mor garedig yn ei fywyd. Ymadawodd i fyned i Alexandria, ac fel yr oedd yn cychwyn dywedai ei fod yn gobeithio y byddai i'r Arglwydd ein bendithio a'n gwneud yn fuddugoliaethus, ac y gwnaem ninnau ddaioni i'r caethion druain.[65]
>
> 'I gave the old man bread and meat and coffee, and the poor creature said he had never seen people as kind in his life. He left to go to Alexandria, and as he was starting he said he hoped the Lord would bless us and make us victorious, and that we for our part would do good to the poor slaves.'

Soldiers like John E. Roberts came into increasing contact with freed slaves as the conflict wore on. Indeed, before the end of the war tens of thousands of former slaves would become Union soldiers. As will be seen in Chapter Eleven, the writings of many Welsh soldiers (and civilians) demonstrate that they welcomed these African-American soldiers enthusiastically.

While a considerable number of Welsh-speaking soldiers expressed anti-slavery sentiments in writing, the negative evidence is just as revealing. By negative evidence is meant that which is conspicuous by its absence. Of the more than 400 individual Welsh soldiers and sailors in our data base, not one said (or is recorded as saying) that he was *not* fighting to free the slaves.[66] Whether the final tally of Welsh-speaking soldiers in the Union army and navy be set at the last chapter's most conservative estimate, around 3,000, or whether it is placed as high as 9,000 or even 10,000, our survey of 400 individuals represents a substantial sample. And there is no evidence that any of these 400 soldiers or sailors ever said that they were opposed to describing the war as a struggle against slavery. There is no record that any of them ever complained about the Emancipation Proclamation and what it meant in terms of the direction and interpretation of the Union war effort.

This negative evidence is significant, especially given the range of feelings expressed by (non-Welsh) soldiers in the Union army. In his 1997 study, *For Cause and Comrades [:] Why Men Fought in the Civil War*, James McPherson provides a detailed discussion of this subject. Except for African-American soldiers, who comprised around 10 per cent of the Union army by the end of the war, most English-speaking speaking Northern soldiers saw the conflict as a war for Union, and for Union alone. According to McPherson, 'The cause of Union united Northern soldiers; the cause of slavery divided them. Letters and diaries mention vigorous campfire arguments about slavery.'[67] These feelings intensified during the winter of 1862–3 as news of Lincoln's Emancipation Proclamation reached the soldiers. McPherson quotes a number of letters, including one by a 'German-born' soldier from New York which exemplifies an opinion common in the camps: 'I don't want to fire another shot for the negroes and I wish that all the abolitionists were in hell.'[68] A private from Indiana, also cited by McPherson, wrote of his fellow soldiers that they would 'not fight to free the nigger', adding that a number of his comrades were planning to desert because of the Emancipation Proclamation.[69]

Also revealing is the way in which Oliver Wendell Holmes, Jr., described his fellow soldiers in the 20th Massachusetts Infantry, many of them students at Harvard before enlisting. Although New England was widely regarded by Americans, both north and south, as the home of abolitionism, in the words of Louis Menand, 'many of Holmes's comrades in the Twentieth despised the abolitionists and thought the war a mistake.'[70] The negative feelings which Irish immigrants expressed concerning the Emancipation Proclamation have been well documented; this hostility was exhibited most violently by Irish civilians in the New York Draft riots, but such feelings were also voiced by Irish Americans serving in the Union army. According to William L. Burton, partly because 'Irishmen tended to link abolitionists with anti-foreign and anti-Catholic elements in America', their 'enthusiasm for the war declined sharply after the Emancipation Proclamation'.[71] Anti-abolitionist attitudes were thus embraced by a considerable cross-section of the Union army, ranging from the wealthy Boston Brahmins of the 20th Massachusetts Infantry, to recent Irish immigrants, to farmers from the western states. Given the prevalence of these feelings in the Union army and the North in general, the fact that not one of the Welsh-speaking soldiers in our data base voices a similar attitude is remarkable.

As will be seen in Chapter Six, there were a few Welsh copperheads in south-eastern Ohio by 1863, individuals whose support for the anti-war Democrats clashed with the ideology which was otherwise embraced so publicly by Welsh-American society. It is safe to assume that there were a few more people sharing this view (including, perhaps, a few soldiers) who did not come to the attention of the press. Indeed, when one considers the hold which a pronounced kind of pro-Lincoln, pro-Union, pro-war and anti-slavery ideology had on the Welsh-language press in the United States, it is unlikely that Welsh-Americans who held anti-abolitionist views would have been given much of an opportunity to express them publicly.[72] However, the unpublished manuscript sources which have come to light do not contradict the picture provided by the surviving print record. New primary source material is turning up regularly, and, given the range of diverse feelings expressed by (non-Welsh) Union soldiers on the subject of slavery, it is extremely likely that a dissenting Welsh soldier or two will emerge at some point. However, a few dissenting voices, were they to be found, would not change the picture substantially; the thousands of pages written in Welsh which have survived in print and in manuscript allow us to conclude that the vast majority of Welsh-Americans, including those who volunteered to serve in the Union forces, were united in their views on the evils of slavery. The considerable body of surviving texts suggests strongly that most of the Union's Welsh-speaking soldiers would have said with John W. Rowlands that they were taking part in a struggle 'dros Ryddid, Uniondeb a Threfn', 'for Freedom, Union and Order'.[73] The same body of evidence also suggests that they would have interpreted the Freedom for which they were fighting as including that of the slaves.

This chapter began by examining the very personal letter which Benjamin Thomas sent to his mother in May 1863. That seventeen-year-old soldier, it will be remembered, wrote that he saw his service in the Union army in terms of 'being faithful and defending the government against traitors' ('fod yn ffyddlon ac amddiffyn y llywodraeth yn erbyn brâdwyr').[74] Nearly a year later, one of Benjamin's fellow-soldiers published a letter in *Y Cyfaill o'r Hen Wlad*.[75] This writer, William G. Jones, noted that there were eighteen Welsh-Americans serving together in the 91st Ohio Volunteer Infantry, and he listed their names, including 'Benj. Thomas'.[76] Jones claimed to be writing on behalf of all the regiment's Welsh volunteers, and he described the cause for which they were fighting.

> Yr ydym wedi treulio oddeutu 18 mis yn myddin 'Newythr Sam, ac nid ydym wedi blino ar y gwasanaeth hyd yn hyn; yr ydym yn ystyried ein bod gyd ag achos da, ac yr yr ydym yn foddlon i'r gwaith, ne bo'r annuwioldeb o brynu a gwerthu dynion, a'u gormesu, sydd yn blino y Talaethau Unedig, wedi ei lwyr lanhau o'u plith.[77]

> 'We have spent about 18 months in the army of Uncle Sam, and we have not tired of the service yet; we consider that we have a good cause, and we are content to do the work, until the ungodliness of buying and selling men, and oppressing them, which troubles the United States, has been completely cleansed from them [i.e. the States].'

If Benjamin Thomas's unpublished manuscript letter refers only to serving the government by fighting 'traitors,' William Jones, who claimed to be speaking for Thomas as well, interpreted their 'service' (*gwasanaeth*) as bringing an end to slavery.

NOTES

1 The present owner of Thomas's Bible, Charlene Dixon Hutcheson, provided photocopies of the relevant pages to the University of Wales Bangor archive. The book contains English inscriptions in two places: 'Aug 26 1862 – Aug 1865 This Bible I carried during the three years I was in the Army from 1862 to 1865 and the only thing I took home'; 'My dear mother's present. This Bible mother gave to me when going away to the war. Only book I brought home through the war.'

2 Benjamin F. Thomas letter, copy in University of Wales Bangor archive. This document, a photocopy of the original manuscript letter, was donated by Charlene Dixon Hutcheson, who discovered the letter inside Thomas's Bible. The spelling (for example, the variations *cllass* and *claaes*) follows the original.

3 Benjamin Thomas letter.

4 The number of individual soldiers contained in the data base at present is between 407 and 434. This number is not exact because there is a degree of uncertainty regarding texts by or about some soldiers with common names (for example, John Jones). As there are a number of soldiers with such names who did not sign letters or publications with further personal details (company and regiment; place of residence before enlisting), there are questions as to whether we have multiple texts written by the same soldier or writings by different individuals.

5 See Chapter Three, page 112.

6 Compare Bell Irvin Wiley's study of English-language material: 'One searches most letters and diaries in vain for soldiers' comment on why they were in the war or for what they were fighting.' Bell Irvin Wiley, *The Life of Billy Yank* [:] *The Common Soldier of the Union* (Baton Rouge and London, 1952), p. 39.

7 The only direct evidence of editorial interference with soldiers' letters involves abridging. See, for example, the abridged letter by John W. Rowlands discussed below in this chapter.

8 'Intentional' selective processes are defined above. By 'unintentional selective processes' I mean accidents leading to the destruction of manuscript material over time (fire, water damage).

9 National Library of Wales Ms 17673D, letter 1, folio 1a. A copy of the original, which is in Emory University Library.

10 National Library of Wales Ms 16098C, folios 54–5.

11 The Diary of Thomas H. Jones; photocopy provided by Pedr Lewis from private collection.

12 According to Pedr Lewis who provided a copy of this diary, the original manuscript was transcribed by Thomas H. Jones's grandson at some point during the middle of the twentieth century. It is thus possible that more (or, indeed, all) of the original diary was written in Welsh, and that the grandson translated some of it into English as he copied the text. However, as no other information as to the history of the original manuscript is available, we must assume that Thomas H. Jones wrote his diary in both English and Welsh.

13 Dafydd Owen served with the 97th Ohio Infantry. While this published biographical sketch says that he died on Lookout Mountain, details regarding his regiment's service record force us to conclude that he in fact died on the other side of Chattanooga, on Missionary Ridge. The biographer was most likely misled by all the attention which the battle of Lookout Mountain received. See Jerry Hunter, *Llwch Cenhedloedd [:] Y Cymry a Rhyfel Cartref America* (Llanrwst, 2003), pp. 159–62.

14 *Y Seren Orllewinol*, March 1864; *Y Cenhadwr Americanaidd*, March 1864.

15 *Y Seren Orllewinol*, March 1864; *Y Cenhadwr Americanaidd*, March 1864.

16 *Y Seren Orllewinol*, April 1865.

17 *Y Drych*, 10 January 1863. The letter was written by a soldier named John Rowlands, and it describes the battle of Fredericksburg. See Chapter Nine, pages 365–77, for more details. It is not known whether this is the John W. Rowlands who is discussed below in this chapter; there were at least ten Welsh soldiers in the Union army with the name John Rowlands of whom something is known.

18 *Y Drych*, 4 April 1863.

19 Ibid.

20 Melinda Lawson suggests that a particular kind of American discourse, originating in 'the mid-seventeenth century [and stemming from the fact that] Americans had embraced the idea of an elect nation', became applied to ideas of nationhood during the Civil War: 'Over time, the blending of the secular and the sacred in religious and political tracts became commonplace'. Melinda Lawson, *Patriot Fires [:] Forging a New American Nationalism in the Civil War North* (Lawrence [Kansas], 2002), p. 6.

21 Steven E. Woodworth, *While God is Marching On* [:] *The Religious World of Civil War Soldiers* (Lawrence, Kansas, 2001), p. 106.

22 See, for example, Steven Woodworth, *While God is Marching On*, p. 107. Given that the history of Protestantism involves divergences from pre-existing Christian practice, it is my view that describing a variety of Protestant churches, sects and religious practices as 'orthodox Christianity' is extremely problematic.

23 Steven Woodworth, *While God is Marching On*, p. 107.

24 *Y Drych*, 4 April 1863. Biblical quotations and paraphrases used in the letter include: 'Gwneler dy ewyllys ar y ddaiar, megys y mae yn y nefoedd'; 'yr Hwn sydd a'i "lywodraeth ar bob peth" '; 'cymylau a thywyllwch o amgylch ei orseddfainc Ef'; 'cyfiawnder a barn yw ei thrigfa'.

25 *Y Drych*, 4 April 1863.

26 Benjamin Thomas letter.

27 *Y Drych*, 4 April 1863.

28 Robert Everett was awarded an honorary Doctor of Divinity by Hamilton College in July 1861. The original certificate is part of the Michael Everett collection.

29 *Y Drych*, 4 April 1863. The italics appear in the original.

30 For the Blue Books, see Chapter One, pages 11–12.

31 *Y Seren Orllewinol*, September 1862.

32 Ibid.
33 Ibid.
34 *Y Cyfaill o'r Hen Wlad*, January 1863.
35 *Y Drych*, 24 January 1863.
36 Ibid.
37 *Y Cyfaill o'r Hen Wlad*, June 1862.
38 James Thomas refers to his family thus: 'Os digwydd yr ychydig linellau hyn ddyfod dan sylw rhai o'm cyfeillion yn y wlad hon neu yr Hen Wlad: mae tad, a mam wedi bod genyf, a brodyr a chwiorydd, ond nid wyf ddim wedi clywed oddiwrthynt er's dwy flynedd a hanner'; 'If these few lines happen to come to the attention of some of my friends in this country or the Old Country: I had a father, and a mother, and brothers and sisters, but I have not heard from them for two and a half years'. *Y Drych*, 11 July 1863.
39 *Y Drych*, 11 July 1863.
40 Ibid.
41 Ellis Wynne, *Gweledigaetheu y Bardd Cwsc* (London, 1703).
42 My use of the verb 'to imagine', combined with a description of the nation as a 'community', invokes the theory of Benedict Anderson; see Benedict Anderson, *Imagined Communities [:] Reflections on the Origin and Spread of Nationalism* (London, 1983).
43 *Y Drych*, 11 July 1863.
44 For the relationship between print culture and the act of 'imagining' the national community, see Chapter One, pages 12–13.
45 *Y Drych*, 11 July 1863: 'Yr ydwyf yn y wlad hon er's deg mlynedd'; 'I have been in this country for ten years.'
46 *Y Cenhadwr Americanaidd*, November 1861.
47 Ibid.
48 Ibid.
49 See Chapter Three, pages 141–2.
50 *Y Cenhadwr Americanaidd*, November 1861.
51 Ibid.
52 For example, in January 1861 Chidlaw published a piece in *Y Cenhadwr Americanaidd* describing his visit to the slave ship *Cora*, recently captured by the United States navy: 'Braidd y gallwn gredu fod 705 o blant, gwyr a gwragedd, wedi cael eu gwthio rhwng ei *decks*, ei dwyn o'u gwlad, ac ar eu ffordd i gaethwasanaeth bythol. Ond gwir oedd.' ('I could hardly believe that 705 children, men and women were stuffed between its *decks*, stolen from their country, and on their way to eternal slavery. But it was true').
53 *Y Drych*, 18 April 1863.
54 Ibid.
55 *Y Cyfaill o'r Hen Wlad*, December 1862.
56 *Y Drych*, 31 January 1863.
57 *Y Drych*, 11 April 1863.
58 Ibid.
59 Dean B. Mahin, *The Blessed Place of Freedom* [:] *Europeans in Civil War America* (Washington, DC], 2002), p. 9.
60 *Y Cenhadwr Americanaidd*, May 1865.
61 *Y Cyfaill o'r Hen Wlad*, June 1864.
62 *Y Cenhadwr Americanaidd*, October 1861.

63 There were (at least) two Welsh soldiers named John E. Roberts who published material during the war. One was the poet known as 'Cymro Brith' who served as wagon master with the 5th Pennsylvania Cavalry. The one quoted here is the other John E. Roberts, also a poet, who apparently worked in the Slate Valley straddling Vermont and Upstate New York before the war, and who served with a New York regiment. (It is even possible that the Vermont civilian and the New York soldier were, in fact, separate individuals; if that proves to be the case, then we have three different Welsh-American writers from the period named John E. Roberts.)

64 *Y Cenhadwr Americanaidd*, June 1862.

65 Ibid.

66 An obvious exception is Henry Morton Stanley, one of the dozen or so Welshmen who fought for the Confederacy. As is discussed in Chapter Six, pages 256–7, Stanley published his own very negative feelings regarding the way in which some Northerners connected the cause of abolition to the war.

67 James McPherson, *For Cause and Comrades [:] Why Men Fought in the Civil War* (New York and Oxford, 1997), p. 121.

68 Ibid., p. 122.

69 Ibid., p. 123.

70 Louis Menand, *The Metaphysical Club* [:] *A Story of Ideas in America* (New York, 2001), pp. 30–40. See also Richard F. Miller, 'The Trouble with Brahmins: Ethnic Tensions in Massachusetts's "Harvard Regiment"', *New England Quarterly*, vol. 76, No. 1 (March, 2003), 38–72.

71 William L. Burton, *Melting Pot Solidiers*, p. 152. See also Dean B. Mahin, *The Blessed Place of Freedom*, pp. 26–7.

72 See Chapter Six, pages 273–41, for a discussion of the short-lived paper, *Yr Amserau*, produced by Democrats in Oneida County for a few months during the war.

73 *Y Drych*, 4 April 1863.

74 Benjamin Thomas letter.

75 *Y Cyfaill o'r Hen Wlad*, April 1864.

76 In addition to himself, William G. Jones gives the names of John James, James Davis, Benj. Thomas, Thos. Lloyd, Thos. Hughes, Thos. T. Richards, Thos. Roberts, Moses . . . David Edwards, Evan Lloyd, John Lloyd, David Evans, Solomon Evans, Daniel J. Davis, John S. Davis, Thos. Davis, and Wm. J. Davis. *Y Cyfaill o'r Hen Wlad*, April 1864.

77 *Y Cyfaill o'r Hen Wlad*, April 1864.

5

'We, the Welsh of the Regiment'

In examining the war-time transformation of Welsh America, the last two chapters have focused on the ways in which different kinds of writing were used to articulate a number of associated interpretations of the conflict. Chapter Three suggested that the period's Welsh-language writing was characterized by a field of related discourses which promoted and linked the causes of Union and Abolition while also offering a specific theological interpretation of the service and sacrifice rendered by Union soldiers to those causes. Chapter Four's analysis of a range of texts written by Welsh-American volunteers suggests that they embraced this interpretation of the war in which they were fighting. While continuing to concentrate on these volunteers, this chapter will shift the focus, leaving the study of overt expressions of ideology in order to examine the everyday lives of the Union's Welsh-speaking soldiers. If the coming of war ensured that many aspects of Welsh-American society were militarized, to what extent did Welsh-speaking volunteers take their language and culture with them into the ranks of the Union army?

Some Welsh soldiers would go to a great deal of trouble in order to have a conversation in their native language. James R. Jones, who read widely in both Welsh and English, was led by a series of published letters to believe that a well-known Welsh writer was – like himself – serving with the Union army in Arkansas.

> Lluaws o lythyrau a ddarllenais o waith un Mr. Pierce, mewn newyddiaduron yn y wlad hon a'r hen wlad, ond heb ddeall mai yr un yw yr awdwr hwn ag sydd yn ysgrifenu i'r newyddiaduron Saesneg o'r rhan hyn o'r De, hyd yr wythnos ddiweddaf, pryd y derbyniais ddau Ddrych oddiwrth gyfaill, yn cynws llythyr oddiwrth Mr. P. ar daith Cad. Steele i Camden ac yn ol i'r lle hwn.[1]

> 'I have read many letters by one Mr. Pierce, in the newspapers in this country and the old country, without understanding that this author is the same one who writes for the English newspapers from this part of the South, until I received two copies of *Y Drych* from a friend, including a letter by Mr. P. concerning Gen. Steele's journey to Camden and back again to this place [Little Rock, Arkansas].'

After being posted to Little Rock in the summer of 1864, Jones began hunting for Pierce, literally stopping other soldiers in the street in order to ask for information.

> Fel yr oeddwn yn myned i lawr cyfarfum â milwr yn perthyn i un o gyflegrau *Merrill's Horse*; gofynais a oedd yn adnabod dyn o'r enw Pierce yn ei gatrawd? Atebodd ei fod yn adnabod un o'r enw yn Quartermasters Department of M. H.; pryd y gofynais drachefn, pa fath ddyn o edrychiad yw? Atebodd mai llanc o gylch 22 neu 23ain oed, cyffredin ei edrychiad, siriol ei wedd ar bob amgylchiadau. Gan fy mod wedi ffurfio barn wahanol am Mr. P., yr oeddwn yn meddwl fy mod wedi camgymeryd yn y peson. Gofynais a oedd yn Gymro?[2]
>
> 'As I was going down [to town from the camp] I met a soldier attached to one of the artillery pieces belonging to Merrill's Horse. I asked if he knew a man by the name of Pierce in his regiment. He answered that he knew one by the name in the Quartermaster's Department of M[errill's] H[orse]. When I then asked what kind of man he was in appearance, he answered that he was a lad of 22 or 23 years, common of appearance, cheerful of manner at all times. As I had formed a different opinion about Mr. P., I thought I had mistaken the person. I asked if he was a Welshman.'

Jones, having read articles and letters by Mr Pierce during the previous few years, had formed a mental picture of him, and he was sure that the author whom he was seeking was a mature man of experience, not a 'cheerful lad' of twenty-three. However, having gone this far, he was not going to give up. He persisted in his search, eventually finding Pierce, as directed, in the Quartermaster's Department. The writer was indeed a young man, but otherwise he was everything Jones had hoped for.

> Cyfeiriwyd fi gan y milwr at ystafell Mr. P., pryd yr oedd yn eistedd y tu allan i'r ddor yn y cysgod, ac newydd dderbyn lluaws o newyddiaduron Gogleddol, ac yn eu mysg y Cenhadwr a'r Drych. Pan y gwelais y cyfryw, gofynais yn yr hen Omeraeg am y tro cyntaf er pan y daethum i'r fyddin, pa fodd yr oedd ei iechyd? Gydag ychydig o syndod gan edrych ataf yn graff atebodd ei fod yn iach, ond nad oedd yn fy adnabod yn bersonol, ond nad oedd hyny o bwys, fy mod yn Gymro a bod hyny yn ddigon yn awr, gan erfyn arnaf gymeryd eisteddle gerllaw, pryd y mynegais pwy oeddwn, a pha fodd y daethum o hyd iddo.[3]
>
> 'I was directed by the soldier to Mr. P.'s room, where he was sitting outside the doorway in the shade, having just received a number of Northern newspapers, amongst them *Y Cenhadwr* and *Y Dyrch*. When I saw these, I asked in the old Gomeric for the first time since I joined the army, how was his health? With a little surprise, looking at me carefully, he answered that he was well, but that he did not know me personally, yet that was of no importance, that I was a Welshman and that was enough for now, and he asked me to take a seat near by, at which time I told him who I was, and how I had come to find him.'

This was the first time that James Jones had spoken Welsh – or 'the old Gomeric' – since joining the army, and the event carried great importance for him personally. Having pursued a considerable amount of detective work and having tracked down Humphrey Pierce successfully, Jones had his reward; he was able to sit down and enjoy a long conversation in Welsh.

As was discussed in Chapter Three, there were several thousand Welsh-speaking soldiers in the Union army, yet only a few hundred of these served in Welsh or mostly Welsh companies. The number of Welsh soldiers varied considerably from regiment to regiment, depending upon the population of the local Welsh community where the unit was formed and the abilities of that community's leaders when it came to recruiting and organizing. John E. Roberts, or Cymro Brith ('Motley Welshman'), was one of the bards slated by *Y Drych*'s self-appointed poetry critic back in 1859; he joined the 5th Pennsylvania Cavalry, becoming the regiment's wagon master. Despite the way in which the paper had slighted his poetry a few short years before, he corresponded with *Y Drych*, providing reports on his unit's service in Virginia for Welsh readers across the northern United States. In describing the 5th Pa. Cavalry, he noted that 'there is not in our regiment but myself and one other Welshman, namely William Roberts, Corporal, Company H, from Pottsville . . . This man is an honour to his nation.' ('Nid oes yn ein catrawd ond un Cymro a finau, sef William Roberts, *Corporal*, Co[mpany] H, un o Pottsville . . . Mae hwn yn anrhydedd i'w genedl').[4] His use of the word 'nation' (*cenedl*) reflects many other writings by Welsh-speaking Union soldiers; while taking pride in the fact that they were part of an army which was fighting to defend the Union of their adopted country, these soldiers also took pride in the separate identity and unique character of Welsh America. However, this particular regiment had a minority of two Welsh-speaking soldiers; while he was better off than James Jones in Arkansas, the Welsh conversations which John Roberts had while in uniform were seriously constricted.

John Davies was in a similar situation after enlisting with an artillery battery and being stationed in Washington, DC. According to a letter which he sent back to his family in Wales, his new circumstances did not bother him at all:

> Dymunaf arnoch chwi fy mam beidio poeni eich meddwl . . . yr wyf i . . . mor foddlawn a llo, heb ddim ond un Cymro yn agos ataf. Mae yma dros bum can mil ohonom, yn Wyddelod a Saeson a Yankys a Dutch a bron pob cenedl dan yr haul, ag yr wyf fi yn teimlo fy hyn mor gysurys yn eu canol a phe buaswn ynghanol lot o Gymry, os nad yn fwy felly.[5]
>
> 'I beseech you my mother not to trouble your mind . . . I am . . . as content as a calf, without but one Welshman near to me. There are over five thousand of us here, Irish and English and Yankees and Dutch and just about every nation under the sun, and I feel myself as comfortable in their midst as if I were in the middle of a lot of Welsh people, if not more so.'

The Union army was a melting pot for this Welshman, and it appears that John Davies was more than willing to forgo Welsh companionship in order to serve his new multi-ethnic and multi-lingual nation.

On the other hand, a considerable number of Union soldiers boasted of the fact that they could speak Welsh every day in the army. Those regiments discussed in Chapter Three with a Welsh or mostly Welsh company were characterized by a lively Welsh sub-culture within the larger culture of the regiment's camp life. The 56th Ohio, it will be remembered, had, in addition to two mostly Welsh companies complete with Welsh-speaking captains, a Welsh adjutant and chaplain. John Thomas, the chaplain from Pennsylvania, boasted that he provided his Welsh soldiers with 'a preacher who can socialize with them in Welsh' ('pregethwr a all gymdeithasu â hwynt yn Gymraeg').[6] The editor of *Y Seren Orllewnol* informed his readers that he was 'assured by a friend who visited "Camp Curtin" in Harrisburg . . . that one could hear Welsh being spoken in just about every part of the camp' ('Sicrhawyd ni gan gyfaill a ymwelodd â "Camp Curtin," yn Harrisburg, ddechreu y mis diweddaf, y gallesid clywed y Gymraeg yn cael ei siarad yno braidd yn mhob rhan o'r gwersyll').[7]

Thomas J. Owens, 'late of Newark, Ohio' ('diweddar o Newark, Ohio'), enlisted in a company which was later made part of the 26th Regiment of Ohio Volunteers. There were 16 other Welshmen with him, and the new regiment's Welsh population was increased as companies from other parts of Ohio joined it: 'Yr oeddwn . . . yn teimlo yn llawen wrth gyfarfod â'm cydgenedl yn y lle hwn. Daeth cwmni arall yma ddydd Sadwrn, o swyddi Jackson a Galia, Ohio. Y mae yn eu plith 26 o Gymry' ('I felt joyous . . . at meeting my fellow countrymen in this place. Another company came here Saturday, from Jackson and Gallia Counties, Ohio. There are among them 26 Welshmen').[8] John Griffith Jones also found that his Welsh social circle expanded during his first few months as a soldier; he enlisted with eleven Welsh-speaking friends in Company G of the 23rd Wisconsin Infantry, and there were more Welsh soldiers in other companies in the same regiment. They were placed in the same brigade as the 118th Ohio, which had a Welsh company, and the 22nd Wisconsin with its 'Cambrian Guards' was quartered in the same camp: 'Y may y 22 Wisconsin wedi dyfod yma heddiw; y may ynddi Gymry ond nid wyf yn gwybod pa faint eto' ('The 22 Wisconsin has come here today; there are Welshmen in it but I do not yet know how many').[9] Jones took pride in the fact that the Welsh subculture of which he was a part constituted a visible – or audible – part of the army camp's life, noting that 'may yma gryn lawer o gany hefo yr holl Gymry', 'there is a lot of singing here with all of the Welsh'.[10]

Many Northern regiments had between ten and twenty-five Welsh-speaking soldiers. A letter sent by James J. Jones to *Y Drych* describing his regiment, the 31st Wisconsin Infantry, shows the degree to which these Welsh soldiers formed a kind of sub-culture within the larger societies of the company and regiment:

> Yr ydym yn rhifo o ugain i bump ar hugain, i gyd yn perthyn i'r un cwmni. . . . Y mae chwech o honom yn mhob pabell, ac mae dwy babell yn ein cwmni ni yn cael

> eu dal gan Gymry yn hollol, ac os deui di, gyfaill, y *Drych*, i ymweld a ni ryw dro i Fort Halleck, cei afael yn yr ysgrifenydd yn South Wales ar Iowa Street. Y mae yma Gymry eraill yn y babell hon heblaw fi sydd yn gyfeillion cywir i ti[.][11]

> 'We number from twenty to twenty-five, all belonging to the same company. . . . There are six of us in each tent, and two tents in our company are held entirely by Welshmen, and if you, friend, the *Drych*, come to visit us some time at Fort Halleck, you will find the writer in 'South Wales' on Iowa Street. There are other Welshmen in this tent besides myself who are true friends of yours.'

Unlike James R. Jones, who was posted in Arkansas, James J. Jones was able to speak a lot of Welsh every day while in the army. He states that the Welsh soldiers of his company numbered 'from twenty to twenty-five'; it is possible that the uncertainty regarding the exact population is to be attributed to the fact that sick soldiers had fallen out of the company temporarily, thus making an exact count difficult. Whatever the case, this letter demonstrates that this Wisconsin regiment's camp life had a Welsh component; a sign reading 'South Wales' was placed outside one of its tents on 'Iowa Street' in the regimental camp, and inside that tent there were six soldiers who looked forward to receiving and reading the Welsh-language newspaper.

While much of the bustle of daily camp life went on about them in English, small groups of Welsh soldiers like those of the 31st Wisconsin could at least meet together while off duty to read and discuss *Y Drych* in their native language. By the way, it should be remembered that English was by no means the only other language which many of these Welsh soldiers would have heard while in camp. For example, Company F of the 46th Pennsylvania Infantry had seven Welsh immigrants who served alongside eleven Irishmen, four Scotsmen, and two Germans. And, while seventy-eight of the company's soldiers were listed as natives of Pennsylvania, it is quite possible that they spoke German or Welsh as a first language (or, perhaps less likely, Irish or Scots Gaelic).[12]

John H. Williams was one of a small group of Welsh soldiers in the 14th Vermont Infantry.[13] All of them immigrants from the North Wales slate communities, they had been employed in the quarries around Fairhaven, Vermont, before the war. They had been friends and co-workers in peace time, and they stayed together while in military service, as the record of daily camp life in Williams's diary demonstrates.

> Tachwedd 4ydd 1862. Daeth ein Tents yma heddyw a chawsom le da i'w gosod, yr ydym ni fel Cymry yn y Squad a berthyn i Joel Hamilton. Cawsom Dent dda a phlanasom goed ffawydd tlysion o'i chwmpas.[14]

> 'November 4th 1862. Our Tents came here today and we got a good place to set them up[;] we the Welsh are in the squad belonging to Joel Hamilton. We got a good tent and planted pretty pine trees around it.'

The 14th Vermont Infantry was to stay in this Virginia camp throughout the winter, and Williams and the other Welsh-Americans who bunked with him went about improving their quarters, 'stockading' the lower part of their tent with wood and building a brick chimney and fire place.[15] The tents which most soldiers customized for winter habitation had wooden chimneys, often made by joining several barrels together.[16] However, as one of John Williams's friends, Richard Lewis, was a stone mason by trade, the peace-time skills of the Welsh volunteers were utilized to ensure that they enjoyed a better standard of winter residence; these Welsh soldiers had a real brick chimney, more efficient and less likely to catch fire.

The daily chronicle of camp life contained in Williams's diary refers continually to the small group of Welsh soldiers which clearly operated as a tight social unit within the broader society of the Vermont regiment. For example, on 28 October 1862, John Williams wrote that '[c]efais i a'r Cymry le mewn adeilad newydd', 'I and the Welsh got a place in a new building', and three days later he recorded that 'yn y prydnawn aethom fel Cymry i chwilio am le i olchi ein dillad', 'in the afternoon we the Welsh went to look for a place to wash our clothes.'[17] As the Welsh were not only in the same company but also in the same squad, the social circle which they formed of their own accord also extended to their official duties; time and again we find Williams recording that he went on picket duty with one or more of his fellow Welsh soldiers.

> Aethom ar y Picket chwech or gloch y nos, W. E. Williams a finau hefo ein gilydd yr oeddym yn nganol y coed ac yr oedd hi yn niwl a gwlaw mawr drwy nos, a ninau heb ddim tân ac allan yn gwylio heb gysgu dim o gwbl.[18]
>
> 'We went on Picket [duty] six o'clock at night, W. E. Williams and myself together; we were in the middle of the woods and it was foggy and raining heavily all night, and we without any fire out watching without sleeping any at all.'

Those regiments which had groups of Welsh soldiers serving together often witnessed separate Welsh celebrations on occasions such as Christmas and New Year's Day. The Welsh of the 14th Vermont were no exception.

> Calan. 1863. Ionawr 1af 1863. Diwrnod braf ond y gwynt yn oer, cawsom giniaw da fel Cymry, aethom i'r coed at y tân, ar ol ffrio ysglisan o Pork a Beef bob un, rhoisom yr Hard tacks i ffrio yn y toddion, ac ar ol berwi cwpanaid o goffi, cawsom wledda ar damaid o giniaw blasus.[19]
>
> 'New Years. 1863. January 1st, 1863. A nice day but the wind is cold. We the Welsh had a good dinner; we went to the woods to the fire, [and] after frying a slice of Pork and Beef each, we put our Hard tacks to fry in the drippings, and after boiling a cup of coffee, we feasted on a bit of tasty dinner.'

Typical also is the Christmas dinner enjoyed by Welsh soldiers of the 154th New York Infantry. One of them, Gwilym ab Ioan, published an account of the feast which they had 'ar fryniau'r Rappahanock' – 'on the hills of the Rappahannock' – in *Y Drych*.

> Boreu Nadolig, cynigiodd un o honom ni, sef o'r ychydig Gymry sydd yma (11 mewn nifer), fod i ni gael ciniaw gyd a'n gilydd, a bod i ni gael rhyw beth gwahanol i'r cyffredin. Felly cytunwyd fod i ni gael cyflawnder o gloron, a chig eidion a moch, ac hefyd siwgr a choffi, a chacenau caledion. Ar ol cael pethau at eu gilydd, aethom ychydig ffordd o'r gwersyll i'w coginio, ac ar ol ffeindio lle cyfaddas, cyneuwyd tân. Y peth nesaf oedd apwyntio *cook*. Penderfynwyd fod i dri o'r rhai mwyaf medrus fyned ati i ffrïo y cig, a'r gweddill o honom i gymeryd gofal y cloron a'r coffi. . . . Ar ol cael pob peth yn barod, eisteddwyd i lawr, a bwytaodd pawb hyd ddigon . . . Ar ol bwyta, rhoddwyd amryw lwnc destynau, y rhai nis gallaf eu cofio i'w geirio yn awr.[20]
>
> 'Christmas morning, one of us, that is the few Welshmen who are here (numbering 11), suggested that we have dinner together, and that we have something different to the usual. Thus we agreed that we were to have a sufficiency of potatoes, beef and pork, and also sugar and coffee, and hard cakes. After getting everything ready, we went a little ways from the camp to cook, and after finding a suitable place, a fire was kindled. The next thing was to appoint a cook. It was decided that three of the most capable ones were to get to work frying the meat, and that the rest of us were to take care of the potatoes and coffee. . . . After getting everything ready, we sat down, and everybody ate satisfactorily . . . After eating, several toasts were offered, the words of which I can't remember now.'

Although they do not usually give as much detail as Gwilym ab Ioan does here, a number of other published and unpublished letters and diaries show that Welsh-speaking soldiers tended to eat – and, when possible, celebrate – together.

Around seventy of the letters which Corporal John Griffith Jones sent back to his family in Wisconsin have survived in manuscript. As noted above, Jones was one of twelve Welsh-speaking soldiers in Company G, 23rd Wisconsin infantry, and other small groups of Welsh soldiers were sprinkled in other companies throughout the regiment. According to his correspondence, Jones and his Welsh friends ate together, prayed together, sang together and marched together.

> Y mae y Cymry yn cael canmoliaeth gora gin y swyddogion. Mi ddaru ni martsio oddeutu 20 milltir dydd Mawrth, yr oeddym yn mynd tan ganu braidd ar hyd y ffordd. . . . Nid oes yr un o'r hogia Cymreig wedi syrthio allan eto pan oeddym yn martsio.[21]
>
> 'The Welsh receive the best praise from the officers. We marched 20 miles on Tuesday, [and] we sang as we marched nearly all the way. . . . Not one of the Welsh lads fell out while we were marching.'

This collection of letters also contains written manifestations of the emotional bond which linked the small community of soldiers serving together to the community at home. John Griffiths Jones constantly informs his mother back in Wisconsin as to the health of his fellow-Welsh soldiers. He reported to her early in the war that, more than simply being in good health, both he and his friend Thomas Hughes had gained weight: 'the lads have never looked as good as they do at present' ('ni welais i erioed yr hogia yn edrach cystal ag y maent yn bresenol').[22] One of his other friends in Company G, John W. Jones, published letters in *Y Cyfaill o'r Hen Wlad* which provided similar reports for the wider Welsh-American community: 'Y mae ein iechyd fel Cymry yn hynod o dda . . . i'n Tad nefol y byddo y diolch am ei ofal a'i amddiffyn drosom ni fechgyn y Cymry' ('Our health, the Welsh, is remarkably good . . . thanks be to our heavenly Father for his care and his watching over us, the sons of the Welsh').[23] This picture soon changed as John Griffiths Jones's letters began to catalogue a series of illnesses and deaths.

> Y mae yn debyg eich bod wedi clywad fod Edwart Parry wedi cael ei gladdu. Am hynny byddwn innau barod. Yr ydym wedi colli un bachgen o Gymro eto o'n catrawd, sef John Williams, Co. C. Yr oedd yn fachgen symala, cymwynasgar; yr oedd yn sal ers amser maith; cafodd gystudd trwm. Y mae Hugh Hughes, Co. K, yn bur sal yn yr ysbyty, a William Robarts, Co. C; y clwy' rhwydd yw ei salwch. Y mae John Owen yn cwyno ei fod yn wael heddiw. Yr wyf yn iach, ac yn teimlo yn bur dda.[24]
>
> 'It's likely that you've heard that Edwart Parry has been buried. For that let us all be ready. We have lost yet another Welsh boy from our regiment, namely John Williams, Co. C. He was a fun-loving boy, and helpful; he had been sick for a long time; he had a great affliction. Hugh Hughes, Co. K, is very sick in the hospital, as is William Robarts, Co. C; diarrhoea is his illness. John Owen is complaining that he is poorly today. I am healthy, and felling fairly well.'

When describing a battle in which his regiment took part, John always takes care to inform his mother whether or not his fellow-Welshmen were injured. And, when possible, he also reports on the fate of Welshmen in other Wisconsin regiments serving in the same area.

> Yr ydwyf wedi bod mewn brwydr ofnadwy arall y dyddiau diwethaf, enw y lle yw Grand Gulf, Mississippi. Daeth y bechgyn Cymreig allan yn fyw ac yn iach ei gyd. Buom yn siarad efo Richard Owans ar ol y frwydr; cafodd y 29th ei thorri yn bur ddrwg; aeth pelan trwy cartrig bocs Richard Owan.[25]
>
> 'I have been in another awful battle these past days; the name of the place is Grand Gulf, Mississippi. All the Welsh boys came out alive and healthy. I spoke with Richard Owans after the battle; the 29th got cut up fairly badly; a bullet went through Richard Owans's cartridge box.'

After serving in Grant's Vicksburg campaign, the 23rd Wisconsin was sent to southern Louisiana where a series of small battles and skirmishes, combined with the ever-present diseases, took an increasing toll.

> Y mae W. Jones, Co. B, wedi marw ers wythnos oddi wrth ei goes. Y mae bechgyn Co. B wedi marw ei gyd: W. Jones, David Jones, Hugh Hughes. Yn Co. C. mae tri wedi marw: W. Jones, John Williams, a William Robarts. Nid oes ond Rhys Cook a John W. Jones a minnau allan o'r bechgyn Cymreig.[26]
>
> 'W[illiam] Jones, Co. B, died a week ago because of his leg. All the boys in Co. B have died: W. Jones, David Jones, Hugh Hughes. In Co. C three have died: W. Jones, John Williams, and William Robarts. There is nobody left except Rhys Cook and myself out of the Welsh boys.'

While his regiment suffered terrible losses in general, it was the loss of his fellow Welsh soldiers which left John Griffith Jones feeling most isolated as the fighting wore on: 'Ni feddyliais y buaswn yn cael fy ngadael wrth fy hun pan oeddwn yn Kentucky pan oedd 12 ohonom hefo ein gilydd'; 'I never thought that I would be left all by myself when we were in Kentucky and there were 12 of us together.'[27] One of John's friends who had been sent to the hospital because of sickness, Thomas Hughes, did eventually return to the regiment. However, John Griffith Jones himself was soon killed in a skirmish in Louisiana. It was Thomas Hughes who wrote to John's family in Wisconsin informing them of the manner in which he was buried.

> Rhaid imi ddweud na chawsom amser i'w gladdu, ond cafwyd amser i'w gario i fin y ffordd. Peidiwch a bod yn anesmwyth ynghylch hynny; fe gafodd ei gladdu gan y gelynion, a dywedaf wrthych pa fodd yr wyf yn gwybod. Daeth Major Head C. S. A. i fewn gyda flag of truce at Col Guppy . . . Gofynodd C. G. iddo a oedd wedi claddu ein meirwon, atebodd yntau iddynt gladdu pedwar o'n dynion ni, felly claddwyd John, canys pedwar o'n dynion a laddwyd. Maddeuwch fy ysgrifen wael . . . a derbyniwch ein cofion gwresocaf a'n cydymdeimlad. Gras i chwi, Amen.[28]
>
> 'I must say that we did not have time to bury him, but there was time to carry him to the side of the road. Do not be uneasy about this; he was buried by the enemy, and I will tell you how I know. Major Head, C. S. A., came to Col. Guppey under a flag of truce . . . [The colonel] asked him if he had buried our dead, and he answered that they had buried four of our men, thus John was buried, as four of our men were killed. Excuse my poor handwriting . . . and accept our warmest regards and condolences. Grace be unto you, Amen.'

Before the war, Thomas Hughes had attended the same Methodist chapel in Wisconsin as John and his family. In addition to writing this personal letter to his dead friend's family, Hughes also published a short biographical sketch in

Y Cyfaill o'r Hen Wlad, the monthly journal produced for America's Welsh-speaking Methodists.[29] This published tribute to John Griffith Jones echoes the ways in which John's own letters to his family describe life in the 23rd Wisconsin, portraying John as one of a group of soldiers who were 'hoff iawn o ganu emynau Cymraeg' – 'very fond of singing Welsh hymns' – while marching or in the camp.[30]

Like the personal letters of John Griffith Jones, epistles which soldiers published in the Welsh-American press also recorded the fate of fellow Welsh soldiers with care. In addition to being newsworthy information, this was part of the process of making a public record of Welsh America's service and sacrifice during the war.[31] For example, one the 56th Ohio Infantry's many Welsh-speaking soldiers published an account of the part the regiment played in Grant's Vicksburg Campaign. He finished his account of the battle of Port Gibson with a tally of the casualties: 'Colled ein catrawd ni oedd 26ain. Lladd 4, clwyfo 22; Cymry – lladd: 1, clwyfo 4 yn ysgafn'; 'Our regiment lost 26. 4 Killed, 22 wounded; Welsh – 1 killed, 4 wounded lightly.'[32] And, after describing the hard-fought battle of Champion's Hill: 'Ein colled o hyn oedd 1,340; colled ein catrawd oedd 175 o gwbl; colled ein cwmni oedd tri wedi eu lladd a 15 wedi clwyfo; 3 Cymro wedi eu lladd ac 8 wedi eu clwyfo'; 'Our loss from this was 1,340; our regiment's loss was 175; our company's loss was three killed and 15 wounded; 3 Welshmen killed and 8 wounded.'[33] The Union dead are counted and described in terms of a telescoping series of meaningful units: first, the losses suffered by Grant's entire army are given, then come the individual regiment's losses followed by those of the writer's own company. Last of all, he lists the losses sustained by that sub-set of the 56th Ohio Infantry which was most significant to the writer and his readers: the regiment's Welsh soldiers. The manner in which these numbers are presented is in itself an articulation of this Welsh soldier's multi-layered identity within the army; he defined himself as part of a telescoping series of military units, beginning with the largest unit, Grant's army, and ending with the group of Welsh soldiers to which he belonged.[34]

The tightly-knit social groups formed by Welsh soldiers serving together can be seen as interpretative communities which helped individual soldiers assess and understand the varying experiences which befell them during their time in uniform.[35] Discussions which these soldiers had amongst themselves in their native language provided a framework for analysing and understanding a great number of experiences, ranging from the more mundane aspects of camp life to the extreme horrors of the battlefield. In his study of the ways in which Union soldiers reacted to the experience of battle, Earl J. Hess suggests that the kind of tactics commonly used by Civil War armies, which focused on a long 'battle line' of soldiers standing together, intensified the social interpretation of combat.

> Every group of soldiers in every war develops a special relationship that transcends explanation. It ties individuals together with invisible cords forged by their common experiences under extreme conditions of death and suffering. The near presence of these special companions enabled soldiers to endure much. The linear tactical formations used in the Civil War grouped them together on the battlefield in intimate ways. They stood next to their comrades, shoulder touching shoulder, forming an unbroken chain across the contested and deadly field. They shared the same dangers, stood the same chances of getting hit, fired their muskets in unison . . . They accepted the task of helping one another through the most exciting, demanding, and passionate experience of their lives.[36]

Evan Davies's diary describes how, during their first experience of battle at Perryville, he and his fellow Welsh soldiers stood side by side in the line, conversing in their native language while in the midst of battle. Davies returns to this image in another part of the diary, written while recovering in hospital after receiving the news that one of these Welsh comrades, Ben Morris, had died.

> Yr oedd ein cyfaill yn filwr dewr a Christion cywyr – yr oeddwn wrth ei ochr yn y Battl at Perryville. Siaradais ag ef pan oedd y bwledau yn chwythu heibio ein penau dewaf; yr oedd yn ymddangos yn dawel a digyffro. Hefyd wrth ei ochr yn ysgarmes ac *cavalry* y gelyn at Muphressboro. . . . Ar ein *long marches* trwy Ky. a Tenn. a'n mynych gyfarfyddiad a'r gelyn, yr oedd Ben bob amser yn barod, hefyd yn ewyllysgar i gyflawnu ei ddyledswydd. Yr oedd ei ymddiddanion . . . bob amser yn werth [eu clywed]. Yr oedd yn un o anwylion y nefoedd, mae yn ddiamau genyf. Collasom ni y Cymry gyfaill gwych.[37]

> 'Our friend was a brave soldier and a true Christian – I was at his side in the Battle at Perryville. I talked with him when the bullets were flying thickest past our heads; he appeared quiet and calm. Also at his side in the skirmish with the enemy's cavalry at Murfreesboro. . . . On our long marches through Kentucky and Tennessee and our frequent encounters with the enemy, Ben was always ready, and also willing to fulfil his duty. His conversation . . . was always worth hearing. He was one of heaven's dear ones, I am certain. We the Welsh lost an excellent friend.'

Published death notices often present a similar image, with the writer describing a fellow-soldier who fell, literally, at his side in combat. While a great many surviving texts depict groups of Welsh-speaking soldiers bunking together, eating together, marching together and standing guard together, some also depict them fighting – and at times, dying – side by side.

It was not only within the context of their own regiments that soldiers found opportunities to speak their native language. In addition to the small Welsh communities which existed within some companies and regiments, there were social networks within the army which extended beyond the immediate boundaries of these units. Letters written by Elias J. Prichard of the 22nd Wisconsin record a social network which extended far beyond the regimental lines.

> Yr ydwyf newydd ddyfod yn ol o Chattanooga yn edrych am fy ffrindia. Yno buas yn edrych am Capt. J. R. Davies, a chefais amser *first rate*. Y mae ganddo le *first rate – quarters, etc*. Y mae yn comandio pob peth yna ac o gwmpas y *fort*.[38]

> 'I have just come back from Chattanooga looking for my friends. There I looked in on Capt. J. R. Davies, and I had a first rate time. He has a first rate place – quarters, etc. He commands everything there and within the fort.'

In his diary, John Williams of the 14th Vermont notes that, on 19 December 1862, 'daeth Davey Humphrey, ac Ellis Williams, o Fairfax Station i edrych am danom'; 'Davey Humphrey and Ellis Williams came from Fairfax Station to look for us.'[39] The 'us' surely refers to the small group of Welsh soldiers with whom William served; like the two visitors (who were serving in another Vermont regiment), all had lived and worked in Vermont's slate district before the war. This entry in Williams's private diary echoes an account of military life published by an unnamed Vermont Welshman in *Y Cyfaill o'r Hen Wlad*.

> Daeth y 4edd a'r 5ed Gatrodau Vermont yma yr wythnos ddiw[e]ddaf; mae wedi ffurfio Brigade o Vermonters, ac y mae pedwar o Gymry yn y 4edd Vermont, sef Robert Roberts (Bob Maine), a Robert Jones arall, (yr oedd ef yn gweithio yn Chwarel Copland flwyddyn yn ol), ac Owen Jones, hen was Evan Jones, y Ffarm (yr oedd yn canlyn y ceffyl yn y Chwarel iddo yn Scotch Hill), a bachgen ieuanc arall. Yr oeddent yn gweithio yn Gillfort, Vt., ac aethant o'r Chwarel mewn gwaed oer, meddent, a darfu iddynt ymrestru heb fod yn feddw na dim, meddant hwy. Gwelais Bob Maine nos Sadwrn . . .[40]

> 'The 4th and 5th Vermont Regiments came here last week; they have formed a Brigade of Vermonters, and there are four Welshmen in the 4th Vermont, namely Robert Jones (Bob Maine), and another Robert Jones (he was working in the Copland Quarry a year ago), and Owen Jones, Evan Jones's former worker (who drove the horse for him in the Quarry at Scotch Hill), and another boy. They were working in Gilford, Vermont, and they went from the Quarry in cold blood, they said, and they enlisted without being drunk or anything. I saw Bob Maine Saturday night.'

Not only do texts like these show soldiers seeking out fellow-Welshmen in other regiments, they also hint at the way in which the social networks of their former civilian existence were transposed upon the new structures of army life. These former quarrymen were used to associating fellow-slate-workers with the quarries where they worked (the Copland Quarry, Scotch Hill, Gilford), and they were now redrawing their identities in terms of the military units in which they served (the 4th Vermont Infantry, the 5th Vermont Infantry).

James Griffiths of Cincinnati wrote to his mother in South Wales, giving news of three members of the family all serving in the Union army during the

Confederate advance through Kentucky in 1862. He detailed the nature of his own his work as a sharp-shooter: 'Yr oedd yn fy meddiant i y dryll goreu, gallaswn saethu 12 gwaith bob mynyd, ac yr oedd genyf 100 ergyd wrth fy ochr, ac yr oeddwn yn cael fy ystyried yn ergydiwr da iawn ar ben 600 o latheni'; 'I had in my possession the best gun, I could shoot twelve times each minute, and I had 100 rounds by my side, and I was considered to be a good shot at 600 yards.'[41] James added also that, while his brother John was away working as an army sapper, the two kept in contact. Finally, he reported on a meeting with his nephew:

> Yr oedd Theophilus Davies, mab Mary ein chwaer yma yr wythnos ddiweddaf, ac y mae yn dychwelyd at ei fyddin i Loisoille [sic] . . . y mae yn iach yn bresenol, ac yn fachgen cryf a gwrol. Buoedd yn *marchio* yn ddiweddar am 300 o filldiroedd yn ddiaros.[42]
>
> 'Theophilus Davies, the son of Mary our sister, was here last week, and he is returning to his regiment in Louisville[.][43] . . . He is healthy at present, and he's a strong and brave boy. He recently marched 300 miles without pause.'

Similarly, while Joseph R. Davies's cousin was serving in a different regiment, they kept each other informed of their movements and took advantage of opportunities to visit each other. As Davies noted in a letter: 'Mae yr 8fed New York yn rhyw le yn y gymydogaeth, a bwriadaf geisio cael pass i fyned i weled fy ngefender John'; 'The 8th New York is somewhere in the neighbourhood, and I intend to get a pass to go to see my cousin John.'[44]

In addition to generic references to 'seeing' (*gweld*), 'meeting' (*cyfarfod*) and 'talking with' (*siarad gyda*) friends, many texts written by Welsh-speaking soldiers describe in detail how they spent their free time. They also remark frequently on the ways in which other (non-Welsh) soldiers amused themselves. Mention has already been made of John H. Williams, one of several Welsh quarrymen who served together in the 14th Vermont Infantry. Another of them, John Rowlands, also kept a diary, and he chronicled the various ways in which the regiment's soldiers passed the time, describing a range of activities with a mixture of amusement, admiration and condemnation.

> Mae yn y Barics hwnn canu a dawnsio – rhai campus eraill yn lled wael am y celfyddid hwn; mae eraill yn canu cerddi, eraill yn cario naill llall ar ysgwyddau eu gilydd, eraill yn neido tros pen naill a'r llall, eraill yn cario dwr, eraill yn baratoi y boreufwyd, eraill chwara cardau, eraill yn darllen, eraill yn gwenud rhiw bethau eraill, yn ysgrifenu. Fel hyn mae pethau yn myned yn mlaen yma ac yn wir mae yma lle hynod iawn yn ein mysg – tyngu a rhegi a caplu y Duw mawr yr hwn wnaeth Daear a'r Nefoedd, dyn ac anifail, ac ni parchant ddyn ac ni ofnant Dduw. Fel hyn mae bethau yn mynd heibio.[45]

'In this Barracks there is singing and dancing – some excellently, others rather badly in respect to that art; others sing songs, others carry each other on their shoulders, others playing leap-frog, other carrying water, others preparing breakfast, others playing cards, others reading, others doing other sorts of things, [like] writing. It is like this that things go on here, and truly it is a strange sight here amongst us – swearing and cursing and blaspheming the great God who made Earth and Heavens, man and animal, and they do not respect man and they do not fear God. It is like this that things proceed.'

Many aspects of life in the army camp worried religious Welsh-Americans, soldiers and civilians alike. *Y Cenhadwr Americanaidd* published a letter which a fifteen-year-old girl had written to her brother, a Union volunteer: 'Anwyl Frawd . . . paid a chwareu cardiau, paid a rhegi, paid ag yfed diodydd meddwol, ac uwchlaw pobpeth, paid ag anghofio dy Dduw'; 'Dear Brother . . . don't play cards, don't swear, don't drink intoxicating refreshments, and above all else, don't forget your God.'[46] This girl had good reason to worry; camp life was indeed characterized by a range of these 'immoral' activities. The Revd Ben Chidlaw, serving as chaplain with the 39th Ohio Infantry, worried about the soldiers' worldly pursuits.

Mae yma lawer o anystyriaeth a phechod yn ein plith, a llu o demtasiynau i ddifa ein milwyr, eto rhaid ymdrechu er eu bendithio â dylanwadau efengyl gras ein Duw, a gallaf ddweyd o waelod fy enaid, 'O frodyr, gweddiwch drosom!'[47]

'There is much inconsideration and sin amongst us, with a host of temptations destroying our soldiers; yet one must strive to bless them with the influences of the gospel of our God's grace, and I can say from the bottom of my heart, 'O brothers, pray for us!'

Like abolition, temperance was one of the radical causes which had a strong hold on the public life of Welsh America before and during the war. Given the fact that various kinds of alcohol played a prominent part in the social life of the army, teetotal Nonconformists who volunteered for service were faced with considerable problems. While Chidlaw often complained about the 'drunkenness' (*meddwdod*) which in his view plagued the Union army, he was at least lucky in that the officers of his regiment agreed with him. As another Welsh soldier in the 39th Ohio Infantry noted:

'I lawr a'r fasnach feddwol' yw arwyddair yr wrol '39ain', ac y mae ein swyddwyr o un meddwl am ddarostwng cynhyrfydd i'r fath anfoesgarwch. Bydd ein gwragedd, ein mamau a'n chwiorydd yn ateb yn y modd mwyaf canolog i hyn, ac i bob ymdrech arall i amddiffyn ein moesau, cynal ein hiechyd, a'n parotoi at y gwasanaeth a'r treialon sydd yn ein haros.[48]

'"Down with the trade in intoxication" is the motto of the heroic "39th," and our officers are of the same mind regarding the suppression of something which drives people to such immorality. Our wives, our mothers and our sisters will respond in a most enthusiastic manner to this, and to every other effort to defend our morals, maintain our health, and prepare us for the service and the trials which await us.'

This soldier refers to the wives, mothers and sisters of Welsh America in order to help temper the moral fibre of Welsh-speaking soldiers in the Union army. He is fashioning a morally charged link between the soldiers and the civilian life they have left behind, and that link is forged by invoking the women of the community. War-time writings usually use the verb *amddiffyn* ('to defend') when describing the duty of the soldier who volunteers 'in order to defend' the Union. This soldier's moral exhortation inverts the common patriotic formula; instead of calling upon men to volunteer and fight in defence of country, Union, home or family, the women of the community are enlisted metaphorically to serve alongside the regiment's chaplain and officers in 'defending' the soldiers' morality.

In publishing this soldier's letter, and in publishing the girl's letter asking her soldier brother not to indulge in a range of 'sins' (which included drinking), the *Cenhadwr*'s editor, Robert Everett, was promoting a conceptual link between the women of the community and the community's morality. As was seen in Chapter Three, a number of Welsh texts published during the war emphasize the roles which women (and girls) played in supporting their communities' volunteers. These writings can be located within a broader American tradition of domestic imagery, a tradition which during the Civil War helped to generate a range of texts presenting 'feminized' aspects of the conflict.[49] They can also be read in terms of a broader Welsh historical context, a tradition of writing which, in the words of Jane Aaron, sought to portray the 'pure' Welsh woman who is entrusted with upholding the 'honour of her religion'.[50] Women played a central role in the temperance movement in both Wales and Welsh America, both directly as speakers, organizers and campaigners, and indirectly as a point of moral reference for (male) writers and preachers.[51] Robert Everett had used *Y Cenhadwr Americanaidd* to promote temperance since the journal's establishment in 1840. After April 1861, that aspect of his journal's moral agenda was adapted to war-time circumstances, and he published a number of texts like these which encouraged volunteers to carry the cause with them into the army. By publishing letters such as the two cited here, Everett was using his role as editor to encourage women to exert moral influence over their sons, brothers, husbands and fathers, and he was similarly encouraging men to adhere to temperance while in uniform by invoking the women they had left behind. A great many Welsh soldiers did write that they were adhering to *dirwest* ('temperance') while in uniform, but there were also many others who chose not to follow the advice of teetotallers like the chaplain Benjamin Chidlaw.

David Davies, an artilleryman from Nelson, New York, apparently left a considerable number of women behind when he enlisted. His diary records the great number of letters which this soldier sent and received, and much of this correspondence appears to have been with potential girlfriends. For example, after receiving a letter from Mag Davis on 28 May 1862, Davies confided to his diary that he was 'teimlo yn falch o'i gael ac awydd ei gweled', 'feeling glad to have it and had a desire to see her'.[52] On 20 June he received a letter from an Angeline and wrote a letter to a Mary, and three days later a letter from an Alis reached him in camp.[53] After protracted correspondence with Angeline, this aspiring Lothario decided early in 1863 that he had to 'finish' (*darfod*) with her, but he was consoling himself that same week with letters from a Jane, as well as Alis and Mary.[54] Other than noting that Angeline's epistles were 'rhy ddifrifol' – 'too serious' – for him, David Davies failed to record the contents of these women's letters in his diary, and it is thus impossible to know if they offered moral advice similar to the kinds of things being published by the Welsh-American press.[55] However, if they did offer him moral advice similar to that which the fifteen-year-old girl sent to her brother, their admonishments failed to influence this Welsh soldier's behaviour. On 5 April 1862 Davies wrote that, after target practice in the morning, he 'went to town to get a glass or two of beer in the afternoon' ('mynd i'r dre i gael glasied neu ddau o gwrw yn y prynhawn').[56] One pay-day when he was posted in a nearby town and charged with keeping order, Davies used his position of authority to procure a great deal of drink.

> 11 Ebrill. Diwrnod teg. Cael ein tal heddiw. Cael fy 'ordro' allan gan y Capten ar 'patrol' y prynhawn i gasglu y Bois i fewn. Corporal Titus 'in charge.' Cael fy 'mhostio' ganddo wrth ymyl 'Saloon' ond cefais bedwar glasied llawn o 'whisky' gan y perchennog am beidio bod yn frwnt wrth y bois. Cael 'Good Time.' . . . Buom i lawr yn y dref a thrwy y 'Saloons' heb ofyn cennad neb. Erbyn 8 p.m. yr oeddem wedi cychwyn . . . Gorfu arnom gario un, (6 ohonom mewn nifer). Cawsom ddigon o beth yfed am ddim.[57]

> '11 April. A fine day. Got paid today. Got ordered out on patrol by the Captain in the afternoon to bring the Boys in. Corporal Titus in charge. I got posted by him near a Saloon but I got four full glasses of whisky from the owner for not being too nasty to the boys. Had a Good Time. . . . We went down to town and through the Saloons without asking anybody's permission. By 8 p.m. we had started . . . Had to carry one (we numbered 6). He had enough to drink for free.'

Another time, Davies notes that he was appointed as the procurer of whisky for his group of friends: 'a minnau yn ei brynu a'i gadw. Ni thrystiwn neb arall'; 'me myself buying it and keeping it. I wouldn't trust anybody else.'[58] He was also drinking 'cryn dipyn o whisky' – 'quite a lot of whisky' – on the Fourth of July, and he celebrated New Year in a similar fashion. In one of his more outrageous diary entries, Davies confesses that he and a friend impersonated – *chwarae*, 'to play', is the verb he uses – a lieutenant and his 'orderly' in order to get beer and whisky.[59] David Davies was by no means the only Welsh-speaking soldier who was fond of a drink. That unnamed quarryman-turned-soldier cited earlier in this chapter quoted several other Welsh volunteers from Vermont as saying that 'they enlisted without being drunk or anything' ('darfu iddynt ymrestru heb fod yn feddw na dim'), a casual comment which suggests that they could easily have been drunk at another time.[60] In one of the many letters which John Griffith Jones sent back to his family in Wisconsin he remarks on the price of beer in New Orleans, and Thomas James of the 3rd Pennsylvania Heavy Artillery noted without hesitation in *Y Drych* that he had owned a tavern before enlisting.[61]

Among other things, the diary of David Davies proves that the temperance movement did not have a universal hold upon the religious life of Welsh-speaking Americans. In addition to drinking whatever came to hand, this Welsh artilleryman also read his Bible from cover to cover and he greatly appreciated those sermons and prayer meetings he was able to attend. According to the evidence of his diary, Davies's public profession of religion, combined with his bravery while under fire, had an influence upon his comrades.

> Sul, Ebrill 1. Diwrnod teg a hyfryd iawn. Ar 'Sunday Morning Inspection' . . . y bore. Yn gwrando pregeth ar y Psalm 119, Adnod 116, ac efallai mai dyma y bregeth olaf a glywaf am byth. Yr oedd yn deffro teimladau cysegredig yn fy mynwes ac yn codi rhyw awydd dwys yn fy ysbryd am gartref a hen gapel Nelson (O!! Enw annwyl) ac am gael mwynhau'r Efengyl yn fy hen iaith felys ac annwyl fy hun. Yr ydym wedi bod yn cael moddion crefyddol yn lled gyson ar y Sabbath ers wythnosau bellach a cyfarfodydd gweddi yn ystod yr wythnos ac wedi cael llawer o fwynhad ynddynt. Robertson, Ropes a Briggs wedi cael eu hennill at grefydd y tri (fel y mae ein pabell o ddedwyddwch ers amser). A'u tystiolaeth wrthyf oedd eu bod wedi dod i'r penderfynniad bod rhywbeth mewn crefydd (Ac y gwnaent broffes gyhoeddus ohoni y cyfle cyntaf a gaent i wneud hyny) pan welsant fi mor dawel a digyffro pan o dan y tan dychrynllyd o 'shells.'[62]

> 'Sunday, April 1st [1864]. A fine and a very lovely day. On Sunday Morning Inspection . . . in the morning. Listened to a sermon on Psalm 119, Verse 116, and it's possible that this is the last sermon I will ever hear. It awakened sacred feelings within my breast and brought a deep longing in my spirit for home and the old chapel in Nelson (Oh!! Dear name) and for being able to enjoy the Gospel in my own sweet and dear language. We have been having religious services fairly regularly on the Sabbath for some weeks now as well as prayer meetings during the week and have had much benefit from them. Robertson, Ropes and Briggs all three have been won over to religion (and so our tent has been [one] of happiness for some time). Their testimony to me was that they had come to the decision that there was something in religion (And that they would make a public profession of

> it the first opportunity that they had to do that) when they saw me so quiet and calm when enduring the horrible fire of shells.'

David Davies writes that a sermon on Psalm 119.116 had an especially powerful effect upon him. That verse begins 'Preserve me according to your promise, that I may live'; whoever the chaplain or minister was who preached to Davies and his comrades that Sunday morning, he chose an extremely appropriate text. By April 1864 David Davies and his comrades had been through some of the biggest battles of the war, including Gettysburg, and these horrific experiences informed the religious mediations which Davies records in his diary. If his conduct in battle made his fellow-soliders believe that there was 'something in religion', his own battle experience also led him to muse upon the possibility that he might soon die.

David Davies seems to have been the only Welshman in his unit, and the sermons which he heard while in uniform were delivered in English. His longing for his native language and culture is manifest in the parts of the diary which discuss religion; in the entry quoted above Davies writes that hearing the English-language sermon engendered 'a deep desire in [his] spirit for home and the old chapel in Nelson . . . and for being able to enjoy the Gospel in [his] own sweet and dear language.' Many other soldiers wrote in their diaries and letters that they longed to hear sermons in Welsh. One of them, Thomas J. Owen, described his feelings in a letter to a minister at home in Newark, Ohio:

> Nid oes yn y Cwmni hwn yn awr ond un Cymro, sef fy hunan. Y mae Edward Jones yn gweithio gwaith yn Corinth; nid wyf yn gwybod pa bryd y daw yn ol i'r Cwmni, ond bydd iddo weithio gwaith gof tra y bydd y gwaith yn para . . . Nid wyf wedi cael y fraint i wrando pregeth Gymreig er pan fum yn gwrando arnoch chwi y Sabboth diweddaf a dreuliais yn Newark, ac y mae hiraeth mawr arnaf am gael eich gweled, eich clywed yn pregethu, a chael ymddyddan â chwi am wahanol bethau.[63]

> 'There is not but one Welshman in this Company now, namely myself. Edward Jones is doing work in Corinth; I don't know when he will come back to the Company, but he'll be working as a blacksmith as long as the work lasts . . . I have not had the honour of listening to a Welsh sermon since I listened to you the last Sabbath I spent in Newark, and I have a great longing for seeing you, hearing you preach, and discussing various things with you.'

As will be seen below, many other soldiers corresponded with ministers from their home communities. And, like this letter – which appeared in *Y Cenhadwr Americanaidd* – many of those ministers then forwarded the soldiers' letters to the Welsh-American press for publication. As Thomas Owen suggests here, the soldiers' desire to correspond with Welsh ministers was in part fuelled by the fact that they did not have access to Welsh-language sermons while in the army.

Some Welsh soldiers were lucky enough to have chaplains who spoke their native language. One of these, the Reverend J. D. Jones, wrote to Robert Everett asking for help with his ministry.

> Anwyl frawd Everett: Teimlwn yn hynod ddiolchgar i chwi, pe medrech sicrhau tua dwsin o Destamentau Cymreig at wasanaeth y Cymry sydd yn y Bedwaredd Oneida, o ba un yr wyf yn Gaplan. Gallwn gael digon o rai Seisnig yma, ond anmhosibl cael rhai Cymraeg, ond drwy gyfeillion gartref.[64]

> 'Dear brother Everett: I would feel especially thankful to you if you could secure about a dozen Welsh Testaments for the use of the Welsh who are in the Fourth Oneida [the 117th N. Y.], of which I am Chaplain. I can get enough English ones here, but it's impossible to get Welsh ones, except from friends at home.'

The 117th (or 'Fourth Oneida') was not the only New York regiment with a Welsh chaplain; Robert Littler, a Baptist minister who published in *Y Seren Orllewinol*, was chaplain with the 74th New York Infantry. Welsh soldiers serving with the 39th Ohio were extremely fortunate in that they had one of the most famous Welsh-American ministers as a chaplain, Ben Chidlaw, and the 56th Ohio's 150 Welsh volunteers had a chaplain, Jonathan J. Thomas, who could preach to them in their native language. Chapter Three discussed the letter which John M. Thomas published, noting that he offered Welsh-language services to the soldiers of several different Pennsylvania regiments.[65]

However, most Welsh soldiers were, like David Davies, only afforded the opportunity of hearing sermons in English. Although he longed for Welsh religious services, Davies was apparently fluent in English. This was by no means the case for all Welsh volunteers; many had little command of English upon enlisting in the Union army, and the lack of Welsh chaplains thus posed acute problems for religious monoglot Welsh speakers. John Griffiths Jones's mother asked in a letter if he had learned any English while in the army, and he replied that, after a year's service, he had indeed become quite fluent (though some of the English sentences he included by way of a boast suggest that his mastery of the language was far from perfect).[66] He learned enough English to appreciate, and even criticize, sermons he heard in that language. His favourite ones were delivered by African-American preachers.

> Y mau yma amryw o colerd regiments, ac y mae ganddynt hwy bregethwyr 'run lliw. Yn wir, y maunt yn pregethu yn ardderchog; y maunt yn tynu sylw'r milwyr yn fwy na'n pregethwyr ni ein hunain. Y mau ganddynt ddoniau mawr. Y mau cystal genyf welad y milwyr duon a gwelad y rhai gwynion.[67]

> 'There are many coloured regiments here, and they have preachers of the same colour. Indeed, they preach wonderfully; they attract the attention of the soldiers

better than our own preachers. They have great talents. I am just as happy to see the black soldiers as I am the white ones.'

John Griffith Jones wrote this letter after about two years in the army, and by that time his command of English must have become very good. In his earlier letters he describes how, in the absence of a Welsh chaplain, he and his fellow-soldiers went about organizing their own religious services in their native language. In addition to holding their own Sunday school, the Welsh volunteers of the 23rd Wisconsin Infantry held nightly singing sessions. This information is presented in conjunction with a statement found elsewhere in his letters that he regularly studied the Welsh Bible which he received as a gift before leaving Wisconsin.

> Yr ydwyf wedi cael pleser mawr wrth ddarllen y testament gefais gin Ann Jones Glan yr Afon. Mi fyddwn yn mynd at ein gilydd i gadw ysgol, mi fyddwn yn cael cyfarfod canu bron bob nos. Mi fyddwn wedi dysgy cany yn lled berffaith erbyn y down adra os cawn fyw.[68]

> 'I have great pleasure reading the Bible which I received from Ann Jones, Glan yr Afon. We get together to keep school, [and] we hold a singing meeting just about every night. I will have learned to sing fairly perfectly by the time I come home if I live.'

The kinds of books used by John and his comrades are sometimes described in his correspondence. In another letter to his family he notes that he has a book of *psalmau*, 'psalms', and in yet another he asks them to send him a *hyfforddwr*, a 'catechism'.[69] Although lacking a Welsh chaplain, John Griffith Jones was clearly better off than David Davies in that he could at least conduct Bible study and Sunday school with a group of other Welsh-speaking soldiers.

In the Spring of 1863, twenty-three Welsh residents of Gomer, Ohio, volunteered together. According to their civilian minister, who published an account in *Y Cenhadwr Americanaidd*, sixteen of the volunteers had been members of the same chapel before enlisting. They began organizing their own religious services even before leaving home, and the 'church' which they established within their military unit attracted more members as the Welsh population in the new regiment increased.

> Ymunasant â'u gilydd mewn cyfamod cyn cychwyn i ddwyn yr iau yn ffyddlon ar y maes . . . Ymunodd 4 eraill a hwy y noson hono. Yr oedd 20 yn ymadael dan faner Iesu. . . . Tra yn y camp yn Lima enillasant sylw eraill trwy eu hymddygiad rhagorol. Eu cadben a ganmola eu hymddygiad gweddaidd yn fawr. Pump neu chwech o Gymry crefyddol o eglwys Vanwert a unasant gyda hwy fel eglwys fechan i gario ymlaen moddion gras.[70]

'They joined together in a covenant before starting to bear the yoke faithfully on the field . . . 4 others joined them that same night. There were 20 departing under the banner of Jesus. . . . While in the Camp at Lima they gained the attention of others through their exemplary behaviour. Their captain praised their seemly behaviour greatly. Five or six religious Welshmen from Vanwert's church joined together with them forming a little church to carry on the means of grace.'

These new volunteers did not have a Welsh-speaking chaplain, but the author of this piece, the Revd John Parry, visited them in their camp at Lima and preached to them there.

Bum yn pregethu yn eu camp y Sabboth diweddaf – nid anghofiaf byth yr odfa hono – ychydig oedd yno heb wylo. Gallaf ddweyd na theimlais erioed gymaint o eiddigedd yn erbyn y gallu caethiwol a phan y mae eglwysi yn gorfod aberthu eu goreuon er attal eu cynddaredd i'n llethu yn y Gogledd.[71]

'I preached in their camp last Sabbath – I will never forget that prayer meeting – few were there who were not crying. I can say that I have never felt so much anger at the slave powers as when the churches have to sacrifice their best members in order to keep their madness from afflicting the North.'

This minister published his description of the Welsh army church in order to provide the *Cenhadwr*'s readers with a series of interlocking moral lessons. Revd Parry's description of the soldiers' religious activities is bound up with an interpretation of the war's meaning; the fact that such committed Christians had to go to war in order to defeat the 'slave powers' fuels his hatred of the slave system. However, the piece was first and foremost designed to inspire other Welsh soldiers to follow the example of these Ohioans and organize their own churches in camp.

As has been seen already, Thomas J. Owen sought to mitigate the lack of Welsh-language religious services which army life forced upon him by writing to his minister in Newark, Ohio. This appears to have been a fairly common practice. Another soldier from Ohio, Theophilus Davies, wrote several letters to his minister, the Reverend Thomas Edwards of Cincinnati, who then forwarded them to *Y Cenhadwr Americanaidd* for publication. During the first months of the war Davies's regiment, the 6th Ohio Volunteer Infantry, was sent from Camp Dennison near Cincinnati to fight in the mountains of (what was to become) West Virginia, and he wrote to the Revd Edwards, mixing complaint with confession: 'Yr ydym yn gorfod teithio bob Sabboth, ac nid oes yn ein plith yr un math o addoliad crefyddol'; 'we have to travel every Sabbath, and there is in our midst no kind of religious worship'.[72] The young soldier tempered this bad news with some comments meant to reassure his civilian pastor: 'Mae genyf Destament, yr hwn wyf yn darllen yn yr amser y bydd adeg i hyny, ac nid wyf wedi gweled cymaint gwerth mewn Testament o'r blaen. Ni feddaf yr un llyfr arall'; 'I have a Testament, which I read when there is time for that, and I have never seen so much worth in a Testament before. I do not own any other book.'[73]

Corresponding with Edwards clearly worked as a surrogate for the Welsh chapel which Theophilus Davies had left behind in Cincinnati, a point made clear in another letter: 'Dymunaf arnoch oll weddio droswyf, oblegid mae yn galondid mawr i fy meddwl i glywed bod fy nghyfeillion yn gweddio ar fy rhan. Cyflwynaf fy nghofion at yr holl eglwys'; 'I beseech you to pray for me, because it is a great boost to my thoughts to hear that my friends are praying for me. Give my regards to the whole church.'[74] These letters often turn to confession and self-examination, providing a literary substitute for the spiritual discussions of the Welsh chapel's *seiat*.[75] One such example is the manner in which Davies recounts his experiences while on picket duty in the wooded mountains of West Virginia:

> Mae fy meddwl yn aml yn crwydro pan y byddaf gyda'r ysbïw[y]r mewn unigedd yn y mynyddau, heb ddim i'w glywed ond oernadau y dulluanod, a gwichiadau y cathod gwylltion . . . Byddaf yn meddwl am fy ngyfeillion gartref, ac am fy anwyl fam yr hon sydd tu draw i'r môr, ac yr ydwyf yn ymholi yn aml a ydwyf yn barod i gyfarfod â Duw. Rhaid i mi gyfaddef fy mod yn bechadur mawr, ac ofnaf nad ydwyf yn gwybod pa fynud y caf fy saethu yn farw gan un o'r gelnynion, yr hyn a wneir yn ddyddiol i ryw rai o'r yspïwyr. Yn nghanol myfyrdod clywaf swn ergydiau o rych-ddrylliau o'm cwmpas, yna mi a gollaf y cwbl. Yr ydwyf yn treio gweddio ar Dduw am ei ras a'i gymhorth i'm cadw rhag y temtasiynau pechadurus a'm hamgylchant.[76]
>
> 'My thoughts often wander when I am with the pickets alone in the mountains, with nothing to hear except the cries of the owls and the screams of the wild cats . . . I think of my friends at home, and of my dear mother who is on the other side of the sea, and ask myself often if I am ready to meet God. I must confess that I am a great sinner, and I am afraid because I do no know what minute I will be shot dead by one of the enemy, which happens daily to some of the pickets. In the midst of meditation I hear the sound of rifle shots around me, and then I lose it all. I try to pray to God for his grace and his help to keep me from the sinful temptations which surround me.'

Theophilus Davies describes his attempts at 'praying' (*gweddio*), 'meditation' (*myfyrdod*) and spiritual 'self-examination' (*ymholi*). This soldier, deprived of the kind of religious fellowship to which he was accustomed, attempted to carry out the practice of worship alone. In doing so, he turned to the fundamental mechanisms of literature – reading and writing – for help; no longer able to meet regularly with other Welsh-speaking Christians, he replaced the regular experience of community (and communion) with the solitary acts of reading (his Bible, and, presumably, his minister's letters) and writing. The very act of writing these letters helped take the place of the spiritual discussion, confession and examination which would have been a regular part of his religious life at home; Theophilus Davies created literary texts which allowed writer and reader to fill the roles which they would otherwise have occupied in the chapel's *seiat* or 'fellowship meeting' (*cyfeillach*). The literary move towards communion of writer and reader was extended to include a wider community of readers; like a number of other ministers who received such letters, the Revd Edwards published Theophilus Davies's letters, thus expanding the congregation of his textual *seiat*.[77]

Even John Griffith Jones, who was able to participate in regular prayer meetings and Sunday school sessions with other Welsh-speaking soldiers, missed his old chapel. He stated in one of the letters written after joining the army that he did not feel *hiraeth* – an intense longing or homesickness – for anything at home other than his old Methodist chapel: 'Cofiwch fi i bawb o'm cyfeillion yn Salem; nid oys arnaff hiraeth ar ol dim ond y capal'; 'Remember me to all of my friends at Salem; I do not have *hiraeth* for anything except the chapel.'[78] This same word was used by Thomas J. Owen, who told his minister back in Ohio that he had a 'great' *hiraeth* 'for seeing [him], hearing [him] preach, and discussing various things with [him].'[79] The *hiraeth* which John Griffith Jones felt for his old chapel was apparently intense, and in later letters he asked for details regarding Salem's religious, cultural and social events:

> Dywedwch wrthyf y tro nesaf pa fath o gyfarfodydd geusoch ddydd Nadolig a New Years. A ous cyfarfodydd canu a gweddi a llenyddol ac felly yn mlaun yn y capal y gaeaf yma?[80]
>
> 'Tell me next time what kind of meetings you had Christmas Day and New Year's Day. Are there singing meetings and prayer meetings and literary meetings and the like being held in the chapel this winter?'

As seen in Chapter One, the chapel was the epicentre of social life in Welsh-American communities, holding the religious observances of the community in productive association with literary events – competitions and small *eisteddfodau* – and other kinds of social and cultural activities. This young soldier was trying to present a brave face to his mother in writing that he did not miss anything other than the chapel, yet by confessing that he felt *hiraeth* for the chapel he was using short-hand to refer to a whole network of Welsh-language religious, social and cultural practices.

While solitary Welsh volunteers such as Theophilus Davies and Benjamin Owen wrote to their ministers, groups of Welsh soldiers serving together at times corresponded as a group with their home chapel. Company F of the 22nd Wisconsin Infantry – 'the Cambrian Guards' – was for the most part made up of Welsh-speaking soldiers from Racine, and many of them had attended the same Calvinistic Methodist chapel before enlisting. The two religious communities, civilian and military – perhaps best described as the two halves of a congregation temporarily severed by war – kept in touch by means of the postal service as well as the printing press. One of the company's lieutenants, Robert Blair Jones, wrote on behalf of the soldiers, and the Wisconsin minister, William Hughes, replied. Both forwarded the letters which they received for publication in the Methodists' monthly journal, *Y Cyfaill o'r Hen Wlad*.[81] Lt. Jones appended a note to one of the Revd Hughes's letters which he was forwarding for publication, spelling out the soldiers' reasons for enlisting the aid of the printing press.

> Mr. Golygydd. – Yn unol â chais llawer, yr ydym yn danfon yr anerchiad hwn i chwi i'w argraffu, am ein bod yn dal perthynas â'r Eglwys, ac â'r awdwr, ac am y gwyddom fod llawer o'n perthynasau a'n cyfeillion yn eiddigeddus i'w weled a'i gadw, yr hyn drwy ei argraffu yn eich misolyn clodwiw a gânt; a gwybod fod rhai o fechgyn Gwalia ar y maes yn amddiffyn y Llywodraeth yma a thraw; ac nid ydyw eu mam Eglwys wedi eu hanghofio, er eu bod yn mhell oddiwrth eu cartrefleoedd, a breintiau moddion gras. Dros y cyfeillion, R. Blair Jones, Co. F, 22nd Regt. Wis. Vol. Infantry.[82]

> 'Mr. Editor. – In keeping with the request of many, we are sending this exhortation to you to be printed, because we maintain a relationship with the Church, and with the author, and because we know that many of our relations and friends are eager to see it and to keep it, which they will be able to do through printing it in your praiseworthy monthly; and [because we] know that some of the sons of Wales are on the field defending the Government here and there, and that their mother Church has not forgotten them, even though they are far from their homes and the privileges of the means of grace. On behalf of the friends, R. Blair Jones, Co. F, 22nd Regt. Wis. Vol. Infantry.'

Although two individuals, the lieutenant and the civilian minister, did the actual writing, it is clear that they are acting on behalf of the communities which they were representing. Jones stresses that 'many' of his fellow-soldiers had asked him to forward the minister's letter for publication, adding that this request stemmed from the fact that they knew that 'many' of their civilian friends and relations wanted to read it. He notes that these people want to 'keep' a copy of the printed letter; the published correspondence was transformed into a textual monument to the bonds of fellowship and religious communion which these Methodists maintained despite the hundreds of miles which separated them.[83]

The Revd Hughes's letter also makes it clear that he was writing on behalf of the collective body of his chapel's congregation. He details the significance of the group communications between soldiers and civilians, providing what the *Cyfaill*'s readers might have taken as a model for maintaining connections between their chapels and the volunteers who had left them for war.

> Anwyl Gyfeillion. – Mewn cyfarfod Eglwysig a gadawsom ar yr ail noswaith o'r flwyddyn hon, penderfynwyd yn unfrydol anfon anerchiad eglwysig atoch, i amlygu i chwi ein cydymdeimlad â chwi, a'n pryder parhaus yn eich helynt bwysig. Dymunem eich cydnabod yn ddiolchgar am anfon cymaint o'ch hanes i ni yn barhaus er pan y gadawsoch . . . Mae eich gohebiaeth â ni fel Eglwys wedi rhoddi prawf boddhaol ini o'ch teimladau caredig atom, ac yn foddion effeithiol i feithrin y serchawgrwydd hwnw sydd yn hanfodi mewn Cristnogion gwir tu ag at eu gilydd.[84]

> 'Dear Friends. – In a Church meeting which we held on the second evening of this year, we decided unanimously to send a religious exhortation to you, in order to make manifest to you our sympathy for you, and our continual concern during your present trial. We desire to acknowledge thankfully the sending of so much of your news to us continually since you left us . . . Your correspondence with us as a Church has given us satisfactory proof of your kind feelings for us, and it is an effective means of nurturing that affection which is of essential importance in the feelings of true Christians towards each other.'

As seen above, the letters written by John Griffith Jones show that the small group of Welsh soldiers serving together in the 23rd Wisconsin Infantry held their own religious services. The much larger Welsh contingent of the 22nd Wisconsin did likewise, and their home chapel congratulated them on their efforts.

> Llawenychwyd ni yn fawr aml dro wrth ddarllen eich hanes yn cadw cyfarfodydd gweddio, Ysgol Sabbothol, &c., yn y Camp, a byddem yn dywedyd wrthom ein hunain bob tro bod ein plant yn 'rhodio mewn gwirionedd,' ar ol gadael aelwyd eu mam, ac ymdeithio y'mhlith cenedloedd lled ddienwaededig.[85]

> 'We were made extremely joyful many a time by reading your news about holding prayer meetings, Sunday School, &c., in the Camp, and we can say to ourselves constantly that our children our "walking in the truth" after leaving their mother's hearth, and journeying amongst rather heathen peoples.'

This final sentence refers directly to the fact the Welsh soldiers must now conduct their social and religious lives in close association with men from other cultural and religious backgrounds. The adjective *dienwaededig*, originally meaning 'uncircumcised', was used to refer to people not initiated into the Christian community (and thus translated as 'heathen' here).[86]

These soldiers, who conducted their own Sunday school and Bible study in camp, would have been extremely familiar with this kind of term. When the Revd Hughes, speaking on behalf of the chapel, praised them for 'walking in the truth' amongst peoples who were 'uncircumcised' (*dienwaededig*), they surely would have thought of passages such as Genesis 17.9–14, where circumcision is given as the sign of the covenant between God and Abraham's descendants. The word translated above as 'peoples' is *cenedloedd*, which can also be rendered as 'nations'. In fact, the singular form of this noun, *cenedl*, was the word most commonly used by Welsh-American writers during the Civil War to describe the 'nation' of the Welsh as a separate group existing within the larger community of the United States.[87] The cultural currency of this word was enhanced by the resources of biblical Welsh, where *cenedl* is used in the context of 'the nation of Israel' and *cen[h]edloedd* is used to refer to the different 'nations' which are set apart from Israel. The linguistic and cultural identity of this community's soldiers was being articulated together with their religious identity. They are portrayed as a separate *cenedl*, 'nation', set apart from other 'nations' by their separate language and culture as well as by their profession of religion. If the bond linking the civilian Methodists to those serving in the army was expressed in terms of religious identity, the community to which both groups belonged was also explicitly defined as Welsh; the minister's letter was published under the title 'Eglwys y Trefnyddion Calfinaidd yn Racine, Wis., yn anfon anerch at eu cyfeillion Cymreig yn y Gatrawd 22ain Wisconsin'; 'The Church of the Calvinistic Methodists in Racine, Wis., send greetings to their *Welsh* friends in the 22nd Wisconsin Regiment.'[88] The Wisconsin minister, who claims to be writing on behalf of their chapel, hearths and mothers, praises these Welsh soldiers for maintaining their own identity within the melting-pot of the army.

The last chapter began by discussing a letter which Benjamin Thomas sent to his mother in Ohio, a personal text which made manifest the son–mother bond within the context of the Christian world-view which both shared. After the war, that letter was placed in the Welsh Bible which the soldier's mother had given him upon departing for the army; it was preserved within the family as a textual monument to the personal bonds which helped support soldier and civilian alike during the war years. Similarly, the correspondence between the Welsh soldiers of the 22nd Wisconsin and their home chapel was a literary expression of the religious, cultural and social bonds connecting them, and for that reason Lt. Jones asked the editor of the *Cyfaill* to print it in order to aid those 'many . . . relations and friends [who] are eager to see it and to keep it'. And, like that letter which Benjamin Thomas sent his mother, the expression of personal affection and religious communion is bound up with a discourse on the nature of patriotism: the soldiers define themselves (by means of Jones's letter) as 'sons of Wales . . . [who are] defending the [US] Government.' The writer defines himself and his comrades as *Welsh* soldiers who are fighting to affirm their status as loyal *American* citizens.

The letters which Lt Jones sent to *Y Cyfaill o'r Hen Wlad* are thus textual expressions of these Wisconsin soldiers' group identity; as he claims to be writing on behalf of the entire group, the community of Welsh soldiers which formed the background for many other texts is brought to the foreground in Jones's writing. As has been seen in detail in this chapter, the published and unpublished letters and diaries of Welsh soldiers make frequent reference to the presence (or lack) of other Welshmen within the writer's company and regiment. The blacksmith John Davies, it will be remembered, did not mind turning his back on Welsh companionship in order to follow a new life in the Union's multi-ethnic and multi-lingual army. However, as also seen above, most soldiers in this situation complained about the lack of Welsh conversation, and many also complained about the lack of religious services in their mother tongue. Those who could recreated their own society within the larger social contexts of company and regiment; as we find soldiers of the 31st Wisconsin Infantry gathering in their tent while off duty to read and discuss the latest issue of *Y Drych*, so we also find soldiers of the 22nd and 23rd Wisconsin organizing their own prayer meetings, singing sessions and Sunday schools. Whether solitary Welsh volunteers like Thomas J. Owen of Newark, Ohio, or serving together in large groups such as the Welshmen of the 22nd Wisconsin, these soldiers often sought to expand the sphere of their Welsh-language religious practice by corresponding with their minister and chapel at home.

Indeed, the very act of writing and reading letters can be viewed as a literary extension of the soldier's social life. Bell Irvin Wiley noted that 'letter writing was one of the most pervasive of camp diversions,' and this was certainly true for the Welsh soldiers within the Union army.[89] John Griffith Jones's letters stress his commitment to maintaining a steady stream of correspondence: 'Yr ydym wedi bod yn trafaelio er pan adawsom Memphis ac felly ni chefais ddim cyfleustra i ysgrifenu dim cynt. Mi ysgrifenaf bob cyfla a allaf gaul; mi fuaswn wedi ysgrifenu ers talwm bytaswn yn gallu'; 'We have been travelling since we left Memphis and thus I have not had an opportunity to write any earlier. I write every chance I can get; I would like to have written a while ago if I could have.'[90] Even when fighting during the siege of Vicksburg kept him from writing, he felt the need to explain the break in correspondence to his family back in Wisconsin: 'Gobeithio y gwnewch fy esgusodi am fod mor hir heb ysgrifenu y tro hwn; treiaf fod yn fwy cyson. Yr ydym wedi bod yn ymladd ers 10 diwrnod o flaun muriau Vicks'; 'I hope that you will excuse me for being so long without writing this time; I will try to be more constant. We have been fighting for 10 days before the walls of Vicksburg.'[91] Excuses were also made for the lack in quality and legibility of individual letters. John Griffith Jones referred to the difficult writing conditions experienced while travelling on a steamboat: 'Y mae yn rhaid imi derfynu; y mau yr hen gwch yn crynu cymaint nad ous dim posib gwneud dim llun o ysgrifenu' ; 'I must end; this old boat is shaking so much that I cannot make any form of writing.'[92] One New York soldier worried about the faint marks made by his pencil: 'Y mae yn ddrwg genyf na fuasai genyf inc i ysgrifenu'; 'I am sorry that I did not have ink with which to write.'[93] Jenkin Lloyd Jones finished a long letter scribbled with frozen fingers in a snow-covered January camp by apologizing for his handwriting: 'Terfynaf yn nawr yn ofni nac allwch ddarllen; cofion oddy wrth eich anwyl fab, Jenk'; 'I finish now fearing that you will not able to read [this]; regards from your dear son, Jenk.'[94]

Fifty years after writing this letter, Jenkin Lloyd Jones published his English-language diary. The entry for 24 February 1865 refers to the letters which he received that day: 'Mail came, bringing me four splendid letters, one from my father in the good old Welsh tongue. I prize it above all others.'[95] As the published letters which some ministers sent to soldiers remind us, correspondence flowed both ways. However, for obvious reasons not as many manuscript letters sent to soldiers have survived. David Davies, that New York artilleryman who wrote to a large number of women, chronicled in his diary the considerable amount of post which he received. The diary, which has survived in manuscript, also tells us why this massive collection of letters did not come home with Davies from the war.

> 16 Ebrill. Diwrnod teg braf. Yn pacio llafur ar y 'carriages' erbyn martsio . . . Yn llosgi fy llythyron heddiw, 112 mewn nifer. Teimlo yn ddrwg iawn wrth wneud hyny ac yn teimlo hiraeth yn fy mynwes am rai o'r rhai a ysgrifennodd ond gwell gennyf eu llosgi nac iddynt syrthio i ddwylo dieithriaid, yn neilltuol y gelyn.[96]

> '16 April [1863]. A fine, fair day. Packing grain on the carriages in preparation for marching . . . Burnt my letters today, 112 in number. Feel very bad at doing this and feel *hiraeth* [intense longing] in my breast for some of those who wrote them, but I prefer to burn them than that they should fall into the hands of strangers, especially the enemy.'

While most soldiers do not record the intentional destruction of their letters, many mention the fact that their knapsacks and personal items were lost in battle or during travel (for example, while crossing rivers). The considerable body of manuscript letters which have survived present a one-sided picture in that they tend to be ones which the soldiers sent home, a fact easily explained by reference to the material circumstances of army life.

David Davies also received a number of pictures through the mail, and he makes no mention of burning them. Like all kinds of soldiers and civilians both North and South, Welsh soldiers in the Union army exchanged a considerable number of portraits with families and friends by means of the post. John Griffith Jones asked for a picture of one or both of his younger brothers: 'Mi faswn yn lecio caul llun Richard, er fy mod yn bell mi fyddaf yn meddwl y baswn yn lecio ei welad, neu Owan'; 'I would like to have a picture of Richard; even though I am far away I would like to see him, or Owen.'[97] Although John maintained in other letters that he did not miss anything from home 'other than the chapel', his request for family pictures suggests otherwise. And, as he apologized for breaks in his stream of letters, so he also made excuses when he could not send his picture: 'Nid oydd geni ddim cyfla i dynu fy ll[u]n, mi gyraf cynta y gallaf'; 'I have not yet had any opportunity to have my picture taken; I will send one the first chance I get.'[98] When he did get the chance, John had more than one picture made: 'Yr wyf wedi anfon llythur dyddiedig Ebrill 6 yr oudd fy ll[u]n ynddo, yr wyf yn anfon un yn hwn hefyd rhag ofn i un golli. Yr ydwyf yn cyfri hwn yn well arlun na'r llall o lawer'; 'I have sent a letter dated April 6 [and] my picture was in it; I am sending another one in this letter as well in case one gets lost. I consider this one to be a better portrait than the other by far.'[99] The letter quoted above which Jenkin Lloyd Jones wrote with shaking fingers also contained a picture. He had walked through ten miles of deep snow in order to send his *wyneb*, 'face', home to Wisconsin.

> Ddoe fy fyon – hynny iw y rhai sydd yn byw yn y shanty – yn Memphis. Fe ddechreion ein taith am 8 o'r gloch y bore a fe ddaithom yn ol erbyn machlydiad haul, 10 milltair a cerddad trw yr eira gwedy blino peth. Cefais fy Wyneb yr hwn yr wyf yn hala; gallwch weled pa effaith y mae milwra yn gwneyd arnaf i[.][100]
>
> 'Yesterday we – that is those who live in the shanty – were in Memphis. We started our journey at 8 o'clock in the morning and we came back by sunset, 10 miles and walking through snow [had] tired [us] a bit. I got my Face, which I am sending; you can see what effect military life is having upon me.'

If this soldier had to go to heroic efforts in order to send his 'face' back home to his family, other soldiers were fortunate enough to have professional photographers following their camps or to be stationed near towns with photographic studios.

The act of having one's picture taken was often a social activity. Whether trudging with friends through snow to town like Jenkin Lloyd Jones or standing in line outside a camp photographer's tent, getting a portrait made to send back home was something which soldiers often did together in their free time. Such a social context is suggested by an English riddle which John Williams of the 14th Vermont recorded in his diary: 'Question: What is taken from you before you get it? Ans[wer]: Your Portrait.'[101] Williams's diary is otherwise written in Welsh; even the words of English-speaking officers are recorded in Welsh translation. However this riddle, heard in English, would have lost its impact in translation; the English phrases 'taking [i.e. stealing] something' and 'taking a portrait' would have to be rendered with different verbs in Welsh, *dwyn*, 'to take' or 'to steal', and *tynnu llun*, 'taking' or 'making a picture' (or some other collocation). As noted above, the diaries of John Williams and John Rowlands attest to the fact that these two soldiers moved within a small, tightly-knit group of Welsh-speaking soldiers within the wider community of the 14th Vermont Infantry. However, the riddle which Williams scribbled in his diary also tells us that this (obviously bilingual) soldier was also attuned to the English-language conversations surrounding him while in camp.

Taken together, the surviving writings of John Williams provide an important case study, as published correspondence which he sent directly to *Y*

Drych as well as his unpublished manuscript diary have survived. Both published and unpublished texts provide evidence as to the way in which the soldier maintained a connection with his civilian community back in Vermont; he wrote personal letters to friends and acquaintances and he also published open letters in the newspaper in order to address the community at large. Like other soldiers, Williams used his diary to record carefully the correspondence which he carried on with relatives, friends and acquaintances at home, including his old minister. For example, on 3 November 1862 he wrote to the Reverend R. L. Herbert and he also sent five 'songs' to his uncle Robert J. Williams (the exact nature of these 'songs' – whether in English or Welsh, whether works of his own composition or printed broadsides which he had obtained – is not described).[102] In less than two weeks he had received replies from both his uncle and the minister. The Revd Herbert – who was also well-known as a poet and writer – also sent a note to John Williams's regimental chaplain, though the nature of the message (if it was even known to Williams) was not recorded in his diary.[103]

To this record of personal correspondence we can add the slightly different tones expressed in a letter which Williams published in *Y Drych*. Rumour had reached him in his regiment's Virginia camp that civilians back 'yn nhaleth y Bryn Gwyrdd', 'the Green Mountain state', were joking about the fact that the 14th Vermont had not yet seen combat.[104] The former quarryman's open letter defended his regiment, noting that they were performing many services in Virginia, including potentially dangerous picket and patrol duties, adding that it was not their fault that they had not yet been sent into battle. Williams also went on the offensive, making fun of civilians who stayed at home only to criticize the soldiers from the safe distance afforded by several hundreds of miles: 'Pobl y *coesau meinion* yr wyf yn feddwl wyddoch, y rhai sydd yn ceisio rhoi y *rebellion* i lawr yn y Stores, a'r Offices, hefo eu tafodau llithrig'; 'I mean the people with *thin legs*, you know, the ones who try to put the rebellion down in the Stores and Offices with their slippery tongues.'[105] While the dialogues which most soldiers conducted with their home communities by means of letters and printing press were expressions of mutual support and affection, that was clearly not always the case!

When *Y Drych* published John Williams's letter he duly noted the event in his diary.[106] In fact, Williams's daily record of camp life makes frequent mention of the papers and journals which he read. In addition to receiving *Y Drych* on numerous occasions, he also notes that civilian friends sent him *Y Cenhadwr Americanaidd*: 'Sul Rhagfyr 14eg, 1862. . . . Cefais lythyr oddiwrth W. Herbert a *Chenhadwr*, a llythyr oddiwrth Jane; yr oedd yn dda gennyf eu cael'; 'Sunday, December 14, 1862. . . . Received a letter from W. Herbert with a [copy of the] *Cenhadwr*, and a letter from Jane; I was very glad to get them.'[107] Other soldiers similarly record in diary or letter the fact that they received – or failed to receive – a particular publication.[108] John Griffith Jones noted with concern in one letter to his mother that *Y Drych* had not reached him: 'Nid wyf wedi caul y Drych diwethaf'; 'I have not received the latest *Drych*.' He added that, by way of consolation, a friend had passed on a copy of *Y Cyfaill o'r Hen Wlad* to him: 'cefais y Cyfaill a oedd rhiwin wedi i anfon i J. W. J'; 'I got the *Cyfaill* that somebody had sent to J. W. J.'[109] When John did receive his copy of the Welsh-language weekly, he wrote to thank his mother: 'yr wyf yn diolch o galon i chwi am anfon y Drych'; 'I thank you heartily for sending *Y Drych*.'[110] One cavalryman from Ohio, Howell Hopkins, noted that he would like 'to see *Y Drych*, a Bible and a preacher before dying' ('gweld Y DRYCH, Beibl a phregethwr cyn marw').[111]

As was noted in Chapter Three, Robert Everett sent free copies of *Y Cenhadwr Americanaidd* to Union volunteers and he urged his readers to join him in providing Welsh-speaking soldiers with reading material in their native language. One recipient – who signed his letter 'Milwr mewn Hysbyty', 'A soldier in Hospital' – wrote to thank the *Cenhadwr*'s editor.

> Barch. Gyfaill, – Teimlwyf yn dra diolchgar i chwi am ddanfon rhifyn[a]u Ebrill a Mai o'r Cenhadwr i mi yn y lle anhysbell yma. Yr ydwyf wedi bod yn ddarllenydd cyson o'r Cenhadwr er's blynyddau bellach. Cefais lawer o ddyddordeb a bendith i'm henaid wrth ei ddarllen, a theimlais y golled yn fawr ar ol fy ymddifadu o hono yr Hydref diweddaf. Gan hyny gellwch amgyffred i raddau fy llawenydd wrth gyfarfod â hen gyfaill yr hwn a fedrai siarad â mi yn iaith fy mam yma yn mhlith dyeithriaid, ac yn glaf hefyd yn yr Hysbytty. Derbyniwch fy niolch mwyaf cynhes. Ar ol darllen y rhifenau yn ofalus, danfonais hwy i'm cyd-filwyr Cymreig yn Tennessee, canys yr wyf yn gwybod trwy brofiad beth yw ymddifadrwydd o ddefnyddiau darllen yn mhlith ein cenedl yn y fyddin.[112]
>
> 'Respected Friend, – I feel extremely thankful to you for sending the April and May numbers of the *Cenhadwr* to me in this distant place. I have been a regular reader of the *Cenhadwr* for years. Reading it both held my interest and was a blessing for my soul, and I felt the loss greatly after I was deprived of it last October. Because of that, you can comprehend to a degree my joy at meeting an old friend who could speak with me in the language of my mother here amongst strangers, and [me being] sick as well in the Hospital. Please accept my warmest thanks. After reading the [back] numbers carefully, I sent them to my fellow Welsh soldiers in Tennessee, since I know from experience that there is a lack of reading materials among our nation in the army.'

This soldier described the journal's appearance metaphorically as 'an old friend' visiting him in hospital, and the particular turn of phrase which he employed was solidly anchored in the history of the Welsh-American press. As was discussed in Chapter One, the oldest of America's Welsh-language monthly publications, *Y Cyfaill o'r Hen Wlad*, was presented to its readers in January 1838 by means of a dialogue between the personified journal – the *Cyfaill* or 'Friend' – and a *Cymro* or 'Welshman'.[113] The fact that the *Cenhadwr* is here described as a friend who 'speaks' the reader's mother-tongue is also similar to the claim put forward by the *Cyfaill*'s title that it was 'The Friend from the Old Country.'

For more than two decades before the start of the Civil War, the printing press had been one of the main engines of Welsh-American identity; 'friends' like *Y Cyfaill o'r Hen Wlad* and *Y Cenhadwr Americanaidd* 'visited' Welsh families and communities across the United States, keeping them in touch with one another and helping them to construct and maintain a Welsh-language American culture. With the coming of war there was a new call for this kind of service, and print culture helped to keep soldiers in southern camps and hospitals in contact with their home communities in the northern states as well as with the broader community of Welsh-speaking America. James Jones of the 31st Wisconsin described the Welshmen with whom he shared a tent as 'true friends' (*cyfeillion cywir*) of *Y Drych*. John E. Roberts – or 'Cymro Brith', one of the poets beaten with John Bunnau's bardic 'measuring stick' on the pages of the newspaper before the war – corresponded with *Y Drych* while serving as wagon master of the 5th Pennsylvania Cavalry. In one letter he described the Welsh paper metaphorically as a gentleman visiting the soldier's camp.

> Mr Golygydd: Mae rhyw awydd arnaf i anfon gair o'n hanes i'w osod yn rhyw gongl o'th Ddrych clodwiw. Yn wir, mae arnaf hiraeth am dy weled, ond er pob peth, nid gwiw gwingo dim. Pan oeddyt yn ymweled a mi nid oedd un boneddwr yn cael mwy o roesaw. Bu Lincoln . . . yn ein gweled, ond yr oedd yn hoffusach genyf dy weled ti; ond anfynych iawn yr oeddyt yn cael chwarae teg, gan fod y ffordd mor bell rhyngom ni ag Utica [.][114]
>
> 'Mr Editor: I have a desire to send a bit of our history to put in some corner of your praiseworthy *Drych* ['Mirror']. Indeed, I long to see you, yet despite everything, it is not fit to complain. When you visited me there was no gentleman who received more of a welcome. Lincoln came . . . to see us, but seeing you was more pleasing to me; yet it is very infrequently that you receive fair play, as the road between us and Utica is so long.'

The personified newspaper's visit to the soldier's camp was even more welcome an occasion than a visit from the president of the United States himself! While John Roberts cast *Y Drych* as a *bonheddwr*, a civilian 'gentleman' who visited the army camp from time to time, the chaplain Robert Littler used another metaphor to describe the appearance of *Y Seren Orllewinol* in his regiment's camp:

> . . . a mi yn eistedd yn fy milwrol babell ar lwmfryn yn nhalaeth Virginia, yngwyneb y gelyn, yn mwynhau fy hwyr-bryd ar fin nos . . . llewyrchodd y 'Seren (siriol) Orllewinol', a synwyd fi gan nad oeddwn wedi gweled unrhyw hysbysiad am ei hymaddangosiad yn yr ardal hon. . . . Wel, meddwn i, henffych well iti, Seren wib; ar daith yr wyt ti, mae'n debyg, ar draws y wlad . . . Croeso, croeso i ti, i lewyrchu ar fy mhabell, ac i ddenu'm sylw oddiwrth oleuadau eraill am enyd[.][115]

> '. . . as I was sitting in my military tent on a bare hill in the state of Virginia, facing the enemy, enjoying my evening meal at nightfall . . . the cheerful "Western Star" [*Seren Orllewinol*] shone, and I was surprised as I had not seen any sign of its appearance in this region. . . . Well, said I, greetings to you, shooting Star; you are on a journey, most likely, across the country . . . Welcome, welcome to you, to shine on my tent, and draw my attention away from other lights [i.e. stars] for a moment.'

Many of the personal letters and diaries which survive in manuscript make frequent mention of one or more of the Welsh-American publications, and in published texts like the ones quoted here the importance which Welsh-speaking soldiers placed in them is often translated in flowery praise. Whether personifying *Y Drych* as the soldier's 'friend' or praising one of the journals using another extended metaphor, literary-minded volunteers such as John E. Roberts, Robert Littler and the unnamed 'Milwr mewn Hysbyty' drew upon a range of tropes in constructing literary tributes to their country's Welsh-language press.

As has been seen already in this chapter, writing and receiving personal letters played a central role in the weekly lives of Welsh-Americans serving in the Union army, and in this they were no different from other soldiers during the Civil War (and, indeed, any other war in which a high percentage of the soldiers were literate and had access to a developed postal system). These private texts, travelling back and forth between northern home and southern camp, hospital or battlefield, helped soldiers to interpret the experiences which came their way during the war in terms of their home communities' culture and belief systems. As Reid Mitchell has remarked, 'This nexus of personal communication was a context in which men experienced the more purely military aspects of the war. Furthermore, it provided much of the motivation that kept men in the service of their country and their homes.'[116] One of the functions fulfilled by the press during the war can be seen in terms of extending the personal letter's private realm of discourse into the public sphere. If personal letters let individual soldiers maintain contact with friends and family at home, publications allowed soldiers to maintain contact with the entire community which they had left behind as well as to address the broader community of Welsh-speaking America in general.

Several examples of this kind of letter have been cited already, and in many cases these texts offer clues as to their own genesis which help us to understand more clearly the Welsh-language sub-culture which existed within some Union companies and regiments. As they sometimes organized their own Sunday schools, singing schools and prayer meetings, so Welsh-speaking soldiers also formed what we might call loosely organized literary societies, gathering when off duty to read and discuss *Y Drych* or one of the other Welsh publications and then elect one soldier to correspond with the press on behalf of the group.[117] When large numbers of Welsh-speaking soldiers were serving together in the same military units, the correspondent at times seems to have won this role because of rank. This, surely, was true in the case of Lt Robert Blair Jones, who wrote to the soldiers' home chapel as well as *Y Cyfaill o'r Hen Wlad* on behalf of the 22nd Wisconsin's 'Cambrian Guards'.[118] These soldiers' captain, Owen Griffiths, also wrote to *Y Drych* on their behalf. At other times correspondents were apparently 'appointed' because of their literary talents, as seems to have been the case with Gwilym ap Ioan who wrote to *Y Drych* on behalf of ten other soldiers with whom he served in the 154th New York Infantry.[119] When William G. Jones corresponded with *Y Cyfaill o'r Hen Wlad* he claimed to be doing so at the request of the seventeen other Welsh-Americans serving in the 91st Ohio Volunteer Infantry.[120]

Whether chosen by their comrades or self-appointed, these correspondents often sought to legitimize their own bids for publication by referring to the popularity of soldiers' letters. Several of the 56th Ohio's more than 150 Welsh soldiers wrote to the press; one of them, William S. Jones, opened his letter to *Y Drych* by noting that Welsh-American readers were fond of such things: 'Gwelais trwy y Drych rai milwyr Cymreig yn ysgrifenu ychydig hanes eu catrodau, eu sefyllfa, a'u gweithredoedd, a bod hynny yn dra chymeradwy gan y Cymry yn gyffredin'; 'I've seen in the *Drych* some Welsh soldiers writing the history of their regiments, their situation, and their deeds, and that this is very acceptable in the eyes of the Welsh in general.'[121] The popularity of these published letters is confirmed by internal evidence such as William Jones's assertion as well as by the simple fact that all the major publications devoted entire columns at times to 'Llythyrau oddi wrth Filwyr Cymreig', 'Letters from Welsh Soldiers'. This is one of the more obvious ways in which the Welsh-American press was transformed by the coming of war; a new type of popular literature, the soldier's letter, became *tra chymeradwy*, 'extremely acceptable', overnight.

Obviously, soldiers' letters became a regular feature of all kinds of publications across the country; this trend can also be seen as one of the ways in which the war-time reading tastes and habits of Welsh-Americans paralleled those of their Anglophone neighbours. However, the manner in which *Y Drych* and the three monthly journals presents soldiers' letters often draws attention to the fact that the writers are Welsh: while headings such as 'Llythyr o Faes y Gwaed', 'A Letter from the Field of Blood', appear as well, the editors frequently tell their readers that they are presenting the letters of soldiers who are specifically *Cymreig*, 'Welsh'. Since the start of *Y Cyfaill o'r Hen Wlad* in 1838, all the Welsh-American publications had at times translated material from the English-language popular press of the United States, and that trend continued during the war years. By noting that Welsh soldiers had written letters directly to the press (or that one of the soldier's acquaintances had forwarded the letter for publication), editors were stressing the fact that they were publishing original material produced by members of the community which they served. Almost all these writers also draw attention to their own Welshness (and, at times, to that of the community of which they were a part), and thus in most cases the writer and editor work together in stressing the fact that the text was produced by a member of that same Welsh-American community to which its readers belonged. These published letters affirmed the common culture shared by writer and reader while simultaneously making a statement, either explicitly or implicitly, regarding the commitment of Welsh America to the Union cause. This emphasis on the cultural and linguistic identity of the writer gave a unique character to a new kind of popular literature which was otherwise part of a much broader American trend.

If the content of the Welsh-American publications changed with the coming of war, one of the most basic and essential functions of the war-time press can be seen as an extension of its pre-war mission. Three years before the start of the Civil War, a Welshman from Cattaraugus County, New York, described *Y Drych* as a metaphorical 'field' on which Welsh-speaking Americans from all over the country could meet and get to know each other:

> Yn mhlith yr amrywiol a'r lluosog bethau sydd yn gwneyd eich cyhoeddiad mor dderbyniol gan bob Cymry o chwaeth, nid y lleiaf ydyw, fod y Cymry, er mor wasgaredig ydynt ar hyd a lled y Cyfandir mawr hwn, yn cael cydgyfarfod i ysgwyd llaw â'u gilydd ar faes y *Drych*[.][122]

> 'Amongst the various and numerous things which make your publication so acceptable to all Welsh people of taste, not the least is that the Welsh, however spread-out they may be across this great Continent, can meet together and shake hands with each other on the field of the *Drych*.'

The kind of 'field' described here is a village green, a communal common space where the national village of Welsh America could meet and maintain its own society and culture through the medium of its native language. The fact that thousands of Welsh-speaking Americans were serving in the Union army meant that the real geographical space occupied by members of this community was extended substantially; many of them were scattered in far-flung camps across the southern states, thus making the 'field' provided by the country's Welsh-language press even more important. This surrogate communal space kept soldiers – whether as individuals or as groups – in touch with their communities at home in northern states, just is it allowed the whole of Welsh-speaking America to partake of the new hold on the rights of citizenship which their soldiers were earning by serving in the Union army.

As has been seen repeatedly in this chapter, the articulation of group identity is in itself one of the main themes characterizing the writings of Welsh-speaking soldiers. The first person plural pronoun *ni*, 'we', accrues a new, specific meaning in these texts; it comes to mean 'we, the Welsh of the regiment'. The pronoun often appears as part of a phrase which stresses the fact that it refers to the *Cymry* or 'Welsh' with whom the writer was serving. John Williams recorded in his diary that: 'yr ydym ni fel Cymry yn y Squad a berthyn i Joel Hamilton; 'we the Welsh are in the squad which belongs to Joel Hamilton.'[123] John W. Jones used the same collocation in his published letter: 'mae ein iechyd fel Cymry yn hynod o dda . . . i'n Tad nefol y byddo y diolch am ei ofal a'i amddiffyn drosom ni fechgyn y Cymry'; 'our health, the Welsh, is remarkably good . . . thanks be to our heavenly Father for his care and his watching over us, the sons of the Welsh.'[124] Gwilym ab Ioan published his letter in order to inform *Y Drych*'s readers as to the Christmas dinner enjoyed by his small social circle, a group which he defined as 'ni, sef o'r ychydig Gymry'; 'we, that is the few Welshmen [who are here]'.[125] In recording the death of a friend in his diary, Evans Davies wrote: 'Collasom ni y Cymry gyfaill gwych'; 'We the Welsh lost an excellent friend.'[126]

Texts like the ones quoted here attest to the fact that Welsh-speaking soldiers formed lively social groups within many Union regiments. For soldiers who served without the companionship of others who spoke their native language, the Welsh-American press offered a kind of literary substitute. A great many soldiers could describe the Welsh social life which they experienced in the Union army by writing *ni . . . Cymry'r gatrawd*, 'we . . . the Welsh of the regiment'. However, Welsh-American print culture marshalled its own kind of literary regiment, a community of readers and writers which provided a surrogate society for isolated Welsh-speaking soldiers.

NOTES

1 *Y Cenhadwr Americanaidd*, November 1864.
2 Ibid.
3 Ibid.
4 *Y Drych*, 24 January 1863.
5 National Library of Wales Ms 16098C, folios 54–5.
6 *Baner ac Amserau Cymru*, 25 September 1861. Reprint of a letter originally published in *Y Drych*; no known copies that edition of *Y Drych* have survived.
7 *Y Seren Orllewinol*, June 1861.
8 *Baner ac Amserau Cymru*, 11 September 1861.
9 National Library of Wales Manuscript 22421D.
10 Ibid.
11 *Y Drych*, 11 April 1863.
12 Bell Irvin Wiley, *The Life of Billy Yank* [:] *The Common Soldier of the Union* (Baton Rouge, 1952), p. 311.
13 Diary of John H. Williams, manuscript in the collection of the Vermont Historical Society. Williams lists his fellow-Welshmen in several places; for example, p. 51: J[ohn] Rowlands, R[ichard] Lewis, W[illiam] J[ones], and L[ewis] Roberts.
14 Diary of John H. Williams, p. 17.
15 Ibid., p. 50: 'Mercher, Ionawer 14eg 1863. Gwnaethom y Stockade a chodasom y Dent i fynu cariasom Bricks i wneyd fire place, daeth R. Lewis atom yn y

prydnawn a dechreuodd yn ddioed adeiladu y fire place' ('Wednesday, 14 January 1863. We made the Stockade and we put up the Tent[;] we carried Bricks to make a fire place, R. Lewis came to us in the afternoon and started without delay to build the fire place').

16 Bell Irvin Wiley, *The Life of Billy Yank*, p. 57: 'Perhaps the most common type of winter quarters was a hybrid structure, part wood and part fabric, made by superimposing wedge or shelter tents on log bases. These "winterized," "stockaded" or "barricaded" tents . . . were usually designed for the accommodation of four men. . . . [W]interized tents were commonly heated by fireplaces . . . Chimneys were usually of sticks and daubing topped by one or more barrels. The advantage . . . was offset to some extent by the tendency of the barrels to catch fire.'

17 Diary of John H. Williams, pp. 12 and 14.

18 Ibid., p. 22.

19 Ibid., p. 36.

20 *Y Drych*, 24 January 1863.

21 National Library of Wales Ms 22421D.

22 Ibid.

23 *Y Cyfaill o'r Hen Wlad*, January 1863.

24 National Library of Wales Ms 22421D.

25 Ibid.

26 Ibid.

27 Ibid.

28 Ibid.

29 *Y Cyfaill o'r Hen Wlad*, January 1865.

30 Ibid.

31 See the discussion in Chapter Three, pages 117–18.

32 *Y Drych*, 25 July 1863.

33 Ibid.

34 These kinds of casualty lists were included in many published soldiers' letters. See, for example, William G. Jones of the 91st Ohio Infantry who, after describing a heavy skirmish in West Virginia, wrote: 'Colled y 91st O., rhwng llad a chlwyfo, yw 27; pump o'n cwmni ni wedi eu clwyfo, ond ni laddwyd neb – dau o ohonynt yn Gymry, sef T. Hughes a James Davies' ('The loss of the 91st O[hio], counting killed and injured, is 27; five from our company were injured, but nobody was killed – two of them Welsh, namely T. Hughes and James Davies'); *Y Cyfaill o'r Hen Wlad*, July 1864. Compare the letter published by the chaplain J. D. Jones: 'Mae gan y Bedwaredd Oneida i alaru am y Cadben Thomas, Cymro o Trenton, yr hwn a saethwyd drwy ei galon tra yn arwain ei wyr yn mlaen. Collodd Ed. Jones o Trenton ei goes, a chlwyfwyd Ed. Williams, o York Mills, yn dost drwy ei fynwes' ('The Fourth Oneida have to grieve for the Captain Thomas, a Welshman from Trenton, who was shot through his heart while leading his men forward. Ed. Jones of Trenton lost his leg, and Ed. Williams, of York Mills, was wounded seriously in his chest'). *Y Cenhadwr Americanidd*, March 1865.

35 My use of the term 'interpretive community', coupled with the fact that this study is concerned in general with the processes of writing and reading, recalls Fish's concept; see Stanley Fish, *Is There a Text in This Class? The Authority of Interpretive Communities* (Cambridge, Massachusetts and London, 1980). However, my use of the term here does not follow Fish's formulation of the concept exactly; I am referring first and foremost to the discussions and 'informal' social behavior

which would have characterized these groups of people, and ways in which those closed-group discussions would have provided a framework for analysing and interpreting specific experiences.

36 Earl J. Hess, *The Union Soldier in Battle* [:] *Enduring the Ordeal of Combat* (Lawrence, Kansas, 1997), pp. 111–2.
37 The diary of Evan Davis, National Library of Wales fac. 647.
38 National Library of Wales 17673D, 2; copy of original manuscript in Emory University Library.
39 Diary of John Williams.
40 *Y Cyfaill o'r Hen Wlad*, November 1861.
41 The letter which James Griffiths sent to his mother was published in a Welsh paper, *Y Byd Cymreig*, 15 January 1863.
42 *Y Byd Cymreig*, 15 January 1863.
43 The original phrase *ei fyddin* could be translated as 'his army'. However, the noun *byddin* was sometimes used by Welsh writers during the American Civil War to mean regiment (instead of the more common *catrawd*).
44 *Y Drych*, 28 March 1863.
45 John Rowlands's diary, in the collection of Albert Gregorovich. Note that the John Rowlands of the 14th Vermont Infantry is not the John W. Rowlands quoted in Chapter Three.
46 This is apparently a Welsh translation of an English original which appeared in *The American Messenger; Y Cenhadwr Americanaidd*, October 1862.
47 *Y Cenhadwr Americanaidd*, October 1861.
48 This soldier simply signed his name 'T.'; he also praises Chidlaw directly for having a positive moral influence upon the regiment. *Y Cenhadwr Americanaidd*, October 1861.
49 See Alice Fahs, *The Imagined Civil War* [:] *Popular Literature of the North and South 1861–1865* (Chapel Hill and London, 2001), pp. 120–49, and Reid Mitchell, *The Vacant Chair* [:] *The Northern Soldier Leaves Home* (New York and Oxford, 1993), p. 73.
50 Jane Aaron, *Pur Fel y Dur* [:] *Y Gymraes yn Llên Menywod y Bedwaredd Ganrif ar Bymtheg* (Cardiff, 1998), p. 11. See Chapter Three, pages 130–1.
51 The best-known example is Sarah Jane Rees, known by her bardic name, Cranogwen (1839–1916); poet, editor, teacher, temperance campaigner and lay preacher. See D. G. Jones, *Cofiant Cranogwen* (Caernarfon, 1932) and Gerallt Jones, *Cranogwen: Portread Newydd* (Llandysul, 1981).
52 The Diary of David Davies, in the collection of Carol Mills; transcription by T. Islwyn Walters.
53 Ibid.
54 Ibid.
55 Ibid.
56 Ibid.
57 Ibid.
58 Ibid.
59 Ibid.
60 *Y Cyfaill o'r Hen Wlad*, November 1861.
61 National Library of Wales Ms 22421D. *Y Drych*, 11 July 1863.
62 The diary of David Davies.
63 *Y Cenhadwr Americanaidd*, June 1863.
64 *Y Cenhadwr Americanaidd*, October 1864.

65 Chapter Three.
66 National Library of Wales Ms 22421D.
67 Ibid.
68 Ibid.
69 Ibid.
70 *Y Cenhadwr Americanaidd*, July 1863.
71 Ibid.
72 *Y Cenhadwr Americanaidd*, September 1861.
73 Ibid.
74 *Y Cenhadwr Americanaidd*, November 1861.
75 This writer and his minister were Congregationalists. While Welsh Congregationalists often held a kind of meeting which they called *seiat*, the concept was most rigorously formulated in the Calvinistic Methodists' system of worship. This particular kind of meeting, focusing on the spiritual experiences of members, was sometimes held by Congregationalists under the name of *cyfeillach*, or 'fellowship meeting'. See R. Tudur Jones, *Congregationalism in Wales* (Cardiff, 2004), p. 151.
76 *Y Cenhadwr Americanaidd*, November 1861.
77 For another example of this kind of 'literary *seiat*', see the letter which Thomas E. Hughes, a Calvinistic Methodist, wrote to his home minister; the correspondence was published *Y Cyfaill o'r Hen Wlad*, August 1864.
78 National Library of Wales Ms 22421D; this letter is undated, and is fourth in the order in which they are filed in the National Library of Wales.
79 *Y Cenhadwr Americanaidd*, June 1863.
80 National Library of Wales Ms 22421D.
81 See, for example, *Y Cyfaill o'r Hen Wlad*, April 1863 and 1864.
82 *Y Cyfaill o'r Hen Wlad*, April 1863.
83 The 22nd Wisconsin was serving in Tennessee at the time; this letter is marked 'Gwersyllfa ger ["camp near"] Brentwood, 10 mill. o ["ten miles from"] Nashville, Tenn.' *Y Cyfaill o'r Hen Wlad*, April 1863.
84 *Y Cyfaill o'r Hen Wlad*, April 1863.
85 Ibid.
86 The University of Wales Dictionary gives 'pagan', 'heathen' and 'unregenerate' as figurative meanings. The word has been used in Welsh since at least the 1567 translation of the New Testament, and the 1588 translation of the entire Bible provided even more examples of the word for Welsh readers. *Geiriadur Prifysgol Cymru* (Cardiff, 1950–2002), p. 974.
87 For discussions of the word *cenedl*, 'nation', see pages 13, 39, 79, 217, 270, 467 and 486.
88 *Y Cyfaill o'r Hen Wlad*, April 1863. Italics added to the translation for emphasis.
89 Bell Irvin Wiley, *The Life of Billy Yank*, p. 183.
90 National Library of Wales Ms 22421D.
91 Ibid.
92 Ibid.
93 *Y Drych*, 18 July 1863.
94 Jenkin Lloyd Jones letter, in the collection of Georgia Snokes.
95 Jenkin Lloyd Jones, *An Artilleryman's Diary* (Tower Hill, Wisconsin, 1913), p. 307.
96 The diary of David Davies.
97 National Library of Wales Ms 22421D.
98 Ibid.
99 Ibid.

[100] Jenkin Lloyd Jones letter.
[101] The diary of John Williams.
[102] Ibid.
[103] Ibid.
[104] *Y Drych*, 16 May 1863.
[105] Ibid.
[106] The diary of John Williams.
[107] Ibid.
[108] See, for example, F. K. Jones of the 1st New Jersey Infantry, who finished one letter: 'Mae yn llon iawn genyf gael y CYFAILL, a'i drysorau gwir werthfawr a chyfeillgar, bob mis pan y'm cyrhaeddo'; 'I am very happy to get the CYFAILL, with its (or 'his') truly valuable and amiable treasures, every month when it reaches me'. *Y Cyfaill o'r Hen Wlad*, August 1862.
[109] National Library of Wales Ms 22421D.
[110] Ibid.
[111] *Y Drych*, 28 March 1863.
[112] *Y Cenhadwr Americanaidd*, June 1863.
[113] See Chapter One, pages 17–18.
[114] *Y Drych*, 24 January 1863.
[115] *Y Seren Orllewinol*, September 1863.
[116] Reid Mitchell, *The Vacant Chair*, p. 20.
[117] See James Jones of the 31st Wisconsin, who describes his tent-mates as a group of readers looking forward to receiving the Welsh-language newspaper; *Y Drych*, 11 April 1863.
[118] See the discussion above; one of the company's soldiers, Thomas J. Davies, noted in a letter to the press that two thirds of the company were Welsh (roughly sixty men); *Y Cyfaill o'r Hen Wlad*, June 1864.
[119] *Y Drych*, 24 January 1863.
[120] *Y Cyfaill o'r Hen Wlad*, April 1864.
[121] *Y Drych*, 31 January 1863.
[122] *Y Drych*, 13 March 1858.
[123] The diary of John H. Williams. What is in italics here is underlined in the original manuscript.
[124] Ibid.; *Y Cyfaill o'r Hen Wlad*, January 1863.
[125] *Y Drych*, 24 January 1863.
[126] The diary of Evan Davis.

6

The Moles Beneath Welsh America's Political Landscape: Exceptions to the Union Rule

In examining various aspects of Welsh America's involvement in the Union war effort, the last three chapters have been concerned with a specific part of Welsh America, defined geographically in terms of the Northern states and identified ideologically as being Republican, pro-Union, anti-slavery and pro-war. Surviving sources indicate that this included the vast majority of Welsh-speaking Americans. However, like most rules, this one has its exceptions. There were small groups of Welsh immigrants living in Southern slave states when the war started, and there were also a few Welsh-American Democrats in the North, some of whom allied themselves with the anti-war wing of that party. Given the ideological uniformity which characterized Welsh America's war-time press, it is worth asking whether or not such individuals were even allowed a public forum for their views. What means do we have of detecting dissenting voices in war-time Welsh America?

To begin in the realm of speculation, it is surely true that had any hypothetical writers produced pro-Confederate pieces in Welsh, neither *Y Drych* nor any of the three denominational journals would have published them. On the other hand, American writers did publish in journals and newspapers in Wales, and these publications were not subject to the same ideological pressures as the Welsh-American press. The Old Country's press was pro-Union and anti-slavery to a great extent, yet there were also Welsh publications which criticized Lincoln and the Union war effort, and at least one popular Welsh paper sometimes translated or paraphrased anti-Union pieces published by the *London Times*.[1] This did anger a great many of the cultural and religious leaders in Wales, yet there were Welsh editors who were willing to take that step nonetheless. After all, the hegemonic force of English-British culture and the fact that the *London Times* and other English papers were attacking Lincoln and his war aims allowed, and even invited, some Welsh editors to publish similar material. Thus, should any writer be censored by the Welsh-language press of the United States, he or she could always turn to the press in the Old Country. In addition, it should be remembered that a great amount of manuscript material has survived, including many private letters and diaries which record the personal views of soldiers and civilians.

Moreover, the ideological uniformity which characterized the press was accompanied by an attendant policing of Welsh-American society. Rather than trying to hide or ignore those people who did not adopt the pro-Union, pro-Lincoln, anti-slavery and pro-war stance of the majority, a number of Welsh-American writers and editors hunted out individuals thought to be 'traitors'. One of *Y Drych*'s writers described this process succinctly, noting 'that the Welsh papers expose the *Welsh Democrats*' ('bod y papyrau Cymreig yn dynoethi y *Democrats Cymreig*').[2] Another asked the paper's vigilant readers to help: 'let us know the names, &c, of those base, lowly and despised Welsh people who belong to "The Copperhead Party" ' ('gadewch i ni wybod enwau, &c., y Cymry iselwael, dirmygus hyny ydynt yn perthyn i'r "Copperhead Party" ').[3] The policy can be summarized using a phrase popular with modern tabloid journalism: 'name and shame'. While this editorial strategy did not give anti-war Democrats a voice in the press, it did ensure that their names and alleged 'crimes' were recorded. Like those Calvinistic Methodist ministers who 'excommunicated' or 'excluded' (*torri allan*) sinners from their chapels in a very public fashion, writers and editors searched for individuals thought to have violated the moral and political standards of Welsh America in order to chastise them in print. As will be seen below, the pursuit of this aggressive agenda did at times lead to false or exaggerated accusations.

In addition to the English word 'copperhead', various Welsh translations of that pejorative term were in use by the end of 1862. The word was, for the most part, employed to describe anti-war Democrats. James McPherson has traced the history of this 'political label':

> Like most political labels, "copperhead" was originally an epithet invented by opponents. Ohio Republicans seem to have used it as early as the fall of 1861 to liken antiwar Democrats to the venomous snake of that name. By the fall of 1862 the term had gained wide usage and was often applied by Republicans to the whole Democratic party. By 1863 some Peace Democrats proudly accepted the label and began wearing badges bearing the likenesses of the Goddess of Liberty from the copper penny . . .[4]

In July 1863 *Y Drych* carried a piece entitled 'Credo y Pennau-copr', 'The Copperheads' Credo'. It was heavy-handed satire, beginning: 'Nid oes gan neb hawl i fod yn Arlywydd ond Democrat caethbleidiol'; 'Nobody has a right to be President except a pro-slavery Democrat'.[5] Like the country's English-language Republican press, *Y Drych* and other Welsh-American publications railed incessantly against the 'copperheads', denouncing them as 'traitors', 'criminals' and 'spies'.

As well as vilifying the North's anti-war Democrats in general, specific attacks were aimed at individual Welsh-Americans as the press went about the business of rooting what were seen as subversive moles out of Welsh America's Republican landscape. The largest pocket of Welsh copperheads was apparently found in Ohio, perhaps no surprise given the fact that Clement Vallandigham, the leader of the movement, had his power base in that state. One Welsh-speaking Ohioan, Michael Jones, was serving with the Union army in the west when news reached him concerning the activities of the anti-war faction in his home community. He immediately sent a vitriolic letter to *Y Drych*.

> Drwg iawn gennyf ddeall fod Cymry, fy nghyd-genedl, trigolion Paris a Palmyra, lawer o honynt yn fradwyr i'r Undeb – yn bleidwyr gwrthryfelwyr melltigedig, y rhai sydd wedi achosi cymaint o anrhefn yn ein gwlad, y rhai sydd wedi achosi cymaint o rwygiadau mewn teuluoedd cysurus, y rhai sydd wedi peri neu achosi anrhrefn a gwarth ar ein gwlad rydd Republicanaidd. . . . Dyben y *Copperheads* yn ddiamhau yw ein digaloni ni sydd yn y gwasanaeth, a'n tueddu i ddesertio . . . ond . . . pell ydynt o gyrhaedd eu hamcan, mor isel yw, nid ydynt ond yn ein cynddeiriogi i ymladd yn fwy gwrol pan fydd galwad, a mwynhau ein casineb at yr achos isel y maent yn ei bledio.[6]

> 'I am very sorry to understand that there are Welsh people, my own countrymen, inhabitants of Paris and Palmyra [Ohio], who are, many of them, traitors to the Union – supporters of accursed rebels who have caused so much disorder in our country, who have instigated or caused disorder and [brought] shame to our free Republican country. . . . The aim of the Copperheads without doubt is to dishearten those of us who are in the service, and to induce us to desert . . . but . . . they are far from reaching their goal, it is so base that they only enrage us [and drive us] to fight more heroically when there is need, and to enjoy our hatred for the base cause which they support.'

An anonymous writer published a similar attack in an open letter entitled 'Oddiwrth Filwr Cymreig at ei Gyd-Genedl', 'From a Welsh Soldier to his Fellow Countrymen'. Like Michael Jones, he drew attention to his own status as a Union volunteer, thus hoping to intensify the 'shame' which he has heaping upon the anti-war agitators.

> er gwarth a dirmyg . . . i'n cenedl, yr wyf yn deall trwy lythyrau a thystiolaethau rhai o'm cydfilwyr a fu gartref fod lluaws o Gymry uchel eu dylanwad fel dinasyddion a chrefyddwyr yn Nhalaeth Ohio wedi troi yn gopperheads o'r fath waethaf a mwyaf pigog[.] . . . Cofiwch ein bod wedi gadael ein cartrefi hoff, a rhieni, perthynasau, a chyfeillion tirion, ac wedi gwynebu maes y rhyfel, ac hefyd wedi aberthu ein galwedigaethau; ïe, er hyny yr ydym yn foddlon i aberthu ein bywydau gwerthfawr os bydd achos, er mwyn cael y gwrthryfelwyr dan draed[.][7]

> 'to the shame and derision . . . of our nation, I understand by means of letters and the testimonies of some of my fellow soldiers who were home that a number of Welsh people of great influence as citizens and religious people in the State of Ohio have turned into copperheads of the worst and most prickly sort. . . . Remember that we have left our dear homes, and parents, relatives, and kind friends, and have faced the field of war, and have sacrificed our vocations; yes, despite that we are content to sacrifice our valuable lives if need be, in order to set the rebels under foot[.]'

Both these writers were soldiers serving hundreds of miles away from Ohio and their information is, by their own admission, second hand. It is difficult to support the claim that were 'many' ([*ll*]*awer*) Welsh copperheads in Ohio with other evidence. The editor of *Y Drych* could, however, name at least one of them: 'y Copperheads wedi ffurfio Cymdeithas yn Palmyra, Ohio . . . dywedir . . . bod boneddwr o Gymro, o'r enw John Breeze, yn gadeirydd i'r cyfryw gymdeithas, a Chymro arall yn ysgrifenydd iddi'; 'the Copperheads have formed a Society in Palmyra, Ohio . . . it is said . . . that a Welsh gentleman by the name of John Breeze is chairman of said society, and another Welshman is its secretary'.[8]

Y Drych was also able to name and shame a couple of Wisconsin's copperheads. Thomas D. Jones of Prairieville, Wisconsin, was described as one of Welsh America's 'few Democratic traitors' ('ambell i fradwr Democrataidd').[9] William G. Roberts of Racine named another one in an extended piece on 'The Politics of War' ('Gwleidyddiaeth Rhyfel'):

> Ychydig wythnosau yn ol, ymgasglodd un o Eglwysi Waukesha i gyfarfod eglwysig yn eu haddoldy. Cyn myned i mewn, aeth yn ddadl rhwng y Parch. Mr. Jenkins, gwladgarwr gonest, ag un David Roberts, sydd yn gweini y swydd urddasol (?) o fraich gynalydd i Jeff. Davis.[10]
>
> 'A few weeks ago [April 1863], one of Waukesha's Churches came together to hold a church meeting in their house of worship. Before going inside, an argument started between the Revd Mr Jenkins, an honest patriot, and one David Roberts, who is fulfilling the dignified (?) occupation of Jeff Davis's supporter.'

In an essay on 'The Patriotism of the Welsh' ('Gwladgarwch y Cymry') one anonymous writer claimed that the Welsh copperhead was a rare creature: 'Diolch i'r nef, mae nifer y rhai hyn o honom yn llai nag eiddo unrhyw genedl arall yn America'; 'Thank heavens, the number of them amongst us is fewer than any other nation in America'.[11]

This writer used the pen-name 'Undebwr', meaning 'Unionist'. While research to date has not uncovered his real name, he wrote as if he expected his readers to know who he was, for he imbued his political writings with a number of personal references. This literary 'Unionist' claimed to be extremely familiar with the Union's Welsh communities; indeed, he noted in this particular essay that, having travelled widely throughout Welsh America, he had only counted a small number of Welsh Democrats: 'Yn fy holl deithiau yn mysg y gwahanol sefydliadau Cymreig yn y wlad hon, nid wyf wedi cwrddyd a mwy na dau ddwsin o Ddemocratiaid caethwasiol'; 'In all my travels through the different Welsh settlements in this country, I have not met more than two dozen slave Democrats.'[12] While the soldier Michael Jones had heard that some of Ohio's Welsh copperheads were 'religious people of great influence', this writer described them in rather different terms:

> yr oedd pob un ohonynt yn ddieithriaid yn rhai digymeriad; cadwent ystordai tafarnol bychain, er budd y Gwyddelod a'r Ellmyn, neu yr oeddent yn swyddgeiswyr. Ni chwrddais ag un dyn *respectable* o honynt. Y mae un o honynt – a dim ond un – yn ninas bresenol fy nhrigfod – a lleiaf a dywedir am dano, gorau yw.[13]
>
> 'they were, every one of them without exception, characterless types; they kept small tavern stores for the benefit of the Irish and Germans, or they were people hungry for office. I did not meet one respectable man amongst them. One of them – and only one – lives in the city where I dwell at present – and the less which is said about him, the better.'

The term *swyddgeiswyr* can be rendered literally as 'job-seekers'. It was at times employed in reference to political 'candidates' and was more often than not used pejoratively to describe individuals who 'were hungry for office'.[14] Undebwr portrays these 'two dozen' copperheads as individuals residing beyond Welsh America's moral pale; in addition to earning money by selling alcohol to 'Irish and Germans', they were in his estimation willing to sell any principles they might have had in order to obtain political office.

Having described the nation's small group of Welsh copperheads in these terms, this writer then brought his critical gaze to focus upon the place where *Y Drych* was published – the city of Utica in Oneida County, New York. Undebwr stated that he wanted the whole of Welsh America to know who these copperheads were, thus providing us with a good example of the process of naming and shaming:

> Mae genych chwithau *dri* o leiaf o honynt yn Utica; gwyr Cymry Oneida am danynt yn dda, ac ni raid i mi eu henwi iddynt hwy; ond gadawer i eraill wybod pwy ydynt. Cyfeiriwyf at eich dau Aldermen, John Griffiths, ac Evan Roberts (diweddar olygydd yr *Amserau*) a'r cysgod bychan hwnw o eiddo Horatio Seymour, John O. Pritchard[.][15]
>
> 'You have *three* at least in Utica; the Welsh of Oneida know about them well enough, and I don't need to name them for them; but let others know who they are. I am referring to your two Aldermen, John Griffiths, and Evan Roberts (lately the editor of the *Amserau*) and that little shadow belonging to Horatio Seymour, John O. Pritchard.'

After providing these names to Welsh readers across the United States, Undebwr finishes by drawing attention to the newspaper's central role in this process: 'Lle bynag y mae eu cyffelyb tafler hwynt o flaen gwyneb y DRYCH, fel y byddo i'r byd Cymreig oll eu gweled'; 'Wherever their like are, let them be thrown before the face of the *DRYCH* [Mirror], so that all of the Welsh world can see them.'[16]

The three Utica residents named by Undebwr were what he would have described as *swyddgeiswyr*. Moreover, they were successful *swyddgeiswyr*; two had become Aldermen in the city of Utica and one was part of Horatio Seymour's entourage. An influential Democrat, Seymour was a 'conservative veteran of thirty years in New York politics.'[17] He was elected governor of New York in November 1862, one of several blows delivered to Lincoln's Republicans during those mid-term elections. Back in 1856 the Democrats had produced an abortive Welsh paper, *Y Gwron Democrataidd* ('The Democratic Hero'). Having appeared for two issues only before disappearing for ever, it was described in Chapter Two as pre-election propaganda masquerading as a newspaper. The Democrats repeated this stunt during the 1862 election. This new paper, *Yr Amserau* ('The Times'), lasted for only one or two issues, and no known copies have survived. The fact that Undebwr, writing in April 1863, described Evan Roberts as the paper's *diweddar olygydd* – 'late' or 'former' editor – suggests that the publication was already being considered as history half a year after it first appeared. When Paul Evans was researching this subject for his 1914 MA thesis, one of his informants, an elderly Oneida County Welsh speaker, could only remember that *Yr Amserau* supported Seymour and that 'this was enough to make it unpopular with the Welsh'.[18] That the paper was primarily designed to support Seymour's bid for office is born out by an assault upon *Yr Amserau* which was published in *Y Drych*. Evan Roberts and his colleagues were described as 'Democrats [who] love "the Union as it was, and the constitution as it is" ' ('Democratiaid ydynt yn caru "yr Undeb fel yr oedd, a'r cyfansoddiad fel y mae" '); this was one of Horatio Seymour's own campaign slogans, and *Y Drych* turned it on its head, using it to condemn those responsible for *Yr Amserau*.[19]

TURNING THE NIGHTINGALE INTO A MOLE

Evan Roberts was no newcomer to the realm of Welsh-American print culture, and some of his earlier publishing ventures were much more successful than the shortlived political paper which he edited in 1862. In 1854 he published a volume of poetry by John Edwards, that bard known as Eos Glan Twrch who was one of the most popular and best known of America's Welsh poets.[20] The literary alliance between Evan Roberts and Eos Glan Twrch was apparently extended onto the pages of *Yr Amserau*.[21] Since the publication itself has not survived, it is difficult to know what services the Eos rendered, but it seems that he was named as either co-editor, poetry editor or as a featured columnist for the Democrats' short-lived paper. Whatever his role, he was – according to *Y Drych* – on *Yr Amserau*'s payroll and thus had 'sold his principles for five dollars a week!' ('Wedi gwerthu ei egwyddorion am bum dolar yr wythnos!').[22] Thus accusing him of exchanging his beliefs for an editor's salary, *Y Drych* portrayed Eos Glan Twrch as a Welsh-American Judas, suggesting that the deficiencies which led him to sell out politically extended to all aspects of his moral character: 'y mae yr hwn a wertha ei wleidyddiaeth am bum dolar yr wythnos, yn ddigon salw ei egwyddorion i werthu ei grefydd am lai na phum dolar y Sabath!'; 'he who sells his politics for five dollars a week has weak enough principles to sell his religion for less than five dollars a Sabbath!'[23]

The characterization of the Eos as a copperhead does not sit comfortably with the poet's surviving writings. He had worked as poetry editor for *Yr Arweinydd*, a fortnightly paper which first appeared on 10 January 1858 and which lasted a little over three years. Eos Glan Twrch made his own anti-slavery feelings known on the pages of *Yr Arweinydd*, urging Welsh-Americans 'to vote in favour of freedom and justice, and against the violence and oppression of slavery in all of its tyranny and infamy' ('i bleidleisio o du rhyddid a chyfiawnder, ac yn erbyn trais a gormes caethiwed yn ei holl orthrwm a'i ysgelerder').[24] He had won a competition in the Utica *Eisteddfod* with a poem canonizing John Brown as 'a martyr at freedom's gate' ('merthyr . . . ym mhorth rhyddid'), subsequently making sure that the piece appeared in more than one Welsh-American publication. Moreover, Eos Glan Twrch composed and published poetry during the war praising Union soldiers for their service on the battlefield. A discussion of this poet's political career cannot avoid several unanswered questions: what did he actually do for the Democrats' abortive paper, and to what extent do the accusations levelled against him by *Y Drych* reflect his actual actions? The fact that no copies of *Yr Amserau* are extant, compounded by the fact that not all the relevant editions of *Y Drych* have survived, makes speculating about Eos Glan Twrch's war-time activities an extremely frustrating enterprise.

As the Union's losses mounted during the first half of the war did the Eos, like many Northerners, become disillusioned with Lincoln's war and decide to change parties? Had he in fact always been a Democrat, one who, judging by his writings, was also anti-slavery and pro-war? Or did he, as *Y Drych* suggested, simply sell his political principles for five dollars a week? It seems that Eos Glan Twrch tried to earn a living as a professional Welsh-language writer in America, and thus it is possible that his political trajectory was conditioned (by what he saw as) economic necessity.[25] Is it possible, then, that his search for a paying job as a Welsh-American journalist was the main impetus? In addition to experiencing *Yr Arweinydd*'s failure a few years before, he had been part of another abortive Welsh-American publishing venture back in the 1840s.[26] Moreover, he did not succeed in securing a regular paying job with any of the country's main Welsh publications. Any combination of these factors might have played a part in his decision to work for the Democrats' newspaper. Unless the lost publications are discovered, we may never know.

What we do know is that at least two – and possibly three – writers were ready to denounce the Eos in no uncertain terms.[27] In addition to the editorial piece cited above, William G. Roberts's essay on 'The Politics of War' ('Gwleidyddiaeth Rhyfel') also attacked the staff of the Democrats' paper, and he focused his fire for the most part on Eos Glan Twrch. The rhetorical hinge of this assault was fashioned out of the poet's bardic name; he called himself the *Eos* or 'Nightingale' from *Glan Twrch*, 'the banks of the Twrch river', yet William Roberts focused on the fact that the common noun *twrch* translates simply as 'mole'. Play upon the word *twrch* also informs Roberts's use of the phrase *dod i lan*, which means 'coming ashore' (or 'to the bank') in addition to 'coming into view' or 'appearing'.

> Mr. Golygydd: – Yn gymaint a bod ambell faldorddyn i'w gael yma a thraw, ar hyd a lled y Talaethau Gogleddol, a'r rhai hyny wedi eu geni a'u magu yn anamserol, a'u bod yn bleidiol i Jeff. Davis a'i ganlynwyr gwaedlyd, megys E- ac E- G- T-, a lliaws eraill; ambell un o honynt wedi dynoethi ei Goperheadism yn y DRYCH, a diameu yr ewyllysiai llawer yn ychwaneg wneyd hyny pe caffent eu rhwysg. – Rhoddwch le iddynt weithiau, Mr. Golygydd, cânt eu tal yn ddiarbed. Ai nid mwy gweddus fyddai newid enw y 'Twrch'? Yn lle ei alw yn 'Glan Twrch,' ymddengys i mi mai mwy teilwng a mwy cydunol a'i ymddygiad gwleidyddol a fyddai ei alw, nid 'Glan Twrch,' ond 'Y Twrch tanddaiarol'; oblegid mae y gair *Glan* yn rhyw awgrymu ei fod wedi gweled goleu haul, pan mae rhai o'i anturiaethau diweddar yn profi na all ei lygaid sylwi ar y goleuni mwy na'i frodyr tanddaiarol.
>
> 'Mr. Editor: – Considering that the occasional babbler is to be had here and there throughout the United States, and that these people have been born and raised in the wrong time, and that they support Jeff Davis and his bloody followers, such as E- and E- G- T-, and many others; an occasional one having revealed his Copperheadism in the DRYCH, and it is certain that many others would desire to do that if they were to find their boldness. – Give them space sometimes, Mr. Editor, [for] they will be repaid without delay. Would it not be more fitting to change the name of the "Twrch"? Instead of calling him "Glan Twrch," it seems to me that it would be more fitting and more in keeping with his political behaviour to call him, not "Glan Twrch," but rather "The underground Mole [*Twrch*]"; for the word *Glan* suggests in a way that he has seen the sun's light, when some of his recent adventures prove that his eyes cannot see the light any more than his underground brothers.'

There is much about this passage which bears detailed analysis. First of all, as every edition of *Y Drych* is not available, it is difficult to know exactly which 'copperheads' had 'revealed' themselves in the paper. As will be seen below, at least one writer from Wisconsin wrote in to complain about the draft and it is possible that Roberts is referring to this individual. It is also possible that one of the lost issues of the newspaper contained a piece by Eos Glan Twrch answering his accusers; once again, there are many things about this subject which must remain in the realm of speculation.

Also of direct concern here is the way in which William Roberts vilifies the poet. He attacks John Edwards's good name by assaulting his bardic name, Eos Glan Twrch. By means of word-play he transforms the 'Nightingale' (*Eos*) into a 'mole' (*twrch*), and Roberts thus generates an extended metaphor which allows him to do several things at once. He draws attention to (what he considered to be) the poet's moral blindness, saying that the mole 'cannot see the light'. Furthermore, calling him 'an underground mole' was a way of chiding the Eos for joining what was thought to be a secret or 'underground' movement. Thus William Roberts implies that Eos Glan Twrch and his 'underground brothers' are operating in a network of secret tunnels constructed beneath the landscape of Welsh America.

This same metaphor informed a poem published by an anonymous bard who used the name 'Sant y Dyddiau Diweddaf' ('The Saint of the Last [or 'Recent'] Days'). Entitled 'Adgyfodiad yr "Eos"' ('the Resurrection of the "Eos"'), this verse also suggests that the 'Nightingale' had been 'resurrected' as a 'Mole'. The self-styled 'Saint' used a variation of *toddaid*, one of the categories of the traditional strict metres, and he apparently had trouble expressing himself while also fulfilling the metrical demands of that complicated verse form; if he accused the Eos of hiding in the dark earth, the poem is in itself opaque in many ways. The following translation is less than satisfactory; it follows the original as closely as possible, yet the relationships connecting various parts of the verse are at times unclear.

Eos Glan Twrch, roes y gelyn tan – ro,
Na allai hwn wingo llaw, neu yngan;
Ond o'i roi mewn du raian – gyda'r gair,
Er twrw a chellwair, dyma'r Twrch allan.[28]

'Eos Glan Twrch, he placed the enemy under ground,
So that he could neither move a hand, nor speak;
But by placing him within black earth – with the word,
Despite commotion and joking, here the Mole is out.'

The references to the mole's inability to 'speak' and to the 'word' being buried in the earth with him, coupled with the coming 'out' described at the end of the last line, might be intended to refer to Eos Glan Twrch's work with *Yr Amserau*. If that is indeed the proper reading of this part of the poem, then the poet is saying that the Eos, after some time suppressing or hiding the things he wanted to say, was finally bringing them into the open on the pages of the Democrats' newspaper. One of the few things which is certain about this puzzling poem is that it refers twice to being 'under ground.'[29] It is also clear that, despite failing to convey some of the attendant nuances, this poet is describing a transformation; in order to understand this, the reader need only to focus on the capitalized words – that is, the two names – which open and close this short poem. Like William Roberts, this poet is concerned first and foremost with turning the Nightingale into a Mole.

Other Welsh-American writers did not join in and accuse Eos Glan Twrch of being a copperhead, and this fact is perhaps significant. In that piece quoted above, Undebwr referred by name to Evan Roberts, describing him specifically as former editor of *Yr Amserau*, yet he made no mention whatsoever of Eos Glan Twrch. Given the emphatic way in which Undebwr expressed his desire to name and shame all Welsh copperheads, the fact that he did not name the Eos tells us that there was no consensus of opinion regarding the poet's political status. It is also clear that he remained at the centre of Welsh-American literary culture; rather than going 'underground', Eos Glan Twrch continued to publish poetry throughout the war. For example, two short weeks after that anonymous bard published his verse claiming that the Nightingale had become a Mole, the Eos published a poem boasting of his friendship with the poet Ieuan Ddu.[30] Otherwise known as the Revd J. P. Harris, Ieuan Ddu was one of Welsh America's most seasoned abolitionists, having contributed anti-slavery pieces to Robert Everett's *Dyngarwr* back in 1843, and having ensured that his own journal, *Y Seren Orllewinol*, maintained a solidly abolitionist stance. Whatever Eos Glan Twrch had done by way of service to the Democratic party, he was not ostracized by this prominent Welsh-American abolitionist.

'A SHAME TO THE WELSH NATION': DRAFT DODGERS AND DESERTERS

Whether or not we accept the opinion of his accusers and count Eos Glan Twrch as a copperhead, the published assaults upon him reveal much about the nature of Welsh America's war-time print culture. Just as poetry and prose was used to turn this Nightingale into a Mole, so other writers searched relentlessly for dissident moles tunnelling beneath the foundations of the Union. One issue which helped bring anti-war Democrats out of their tunnels and into the light of public scrutiny was the draft. That piece from *Y Drych* quoted above 'outing' John Breeze of Palmyra, Ohio, as a copperhead specifically accused the 'society' (*cymdeithas*) to which he belonged of striving to undermine the draft: 'dywedir fod ei hamcan i wrthwynebu gweinyddiad deddf y rhestriad milwrol'; 'it is said that its purpose is to oppose the administration of the military conscription.'[31]

One of the nests of copperheads uncovered by *Y Drych* was in Waukesha, Wisconsin. This area experienced considerable tensions when, during the second half of 1862, the state began implementing the militia act, a 'quasi-draft' which was soon followed by the national conscription act of 1863.[32] A Welsh-speaking soldier from Waukesha, David Williams, heard that some of his former neighbours were avoiding the draft, and he published a fiery letter denouncing them.

> Yn niwedd mis Awst diweddaf daeth y newydd allan fod y *drafftio* i fod y 15fed o Fedi, a mawr oedd yr ofnau a gynyrchwyd gan yr hysbysiad. Yr oedd rhai bron yn methu cysgu yn eu gwely y nos. . . . Pan ddaeth y drafftio, y 10fed o Tachwedd, ciliasant i bob cyfeiriad, a rhedasant gan ofn megys defaid yn myned ar gyfrgoll.[33]
>
> 'At the end of last August the news came out that the *draft* was to take place on the 15th of September, and great were the fears which were produced by the announcement. Some people could hardly sleep in their beds at night. . . . When the draft came, on the 10th of November, they fled in every direction, and they ran in fear like sheep scattering.'

This soldier added that 'scores' (*ugeiniau*) of Waukesha's Welshmen visited the doctor in hopes of being excused for medical reasons, and that those who were judged to be healthy enough for service decided 'to escape away to Canada, or the Old Country' ('ddianc ymaith i Canada, neu yr Hen Wlad').[34]

David Williams was answered by a civilian from the area, Thomas D. Jones. He defended Waukesha's Welsh community, claiming that the young soldier had distorted the truth.

> Ni wyddom ar hyn o bryd pa nifer a ymddangosodd yn mhentref Waukesha, eithr hyn a wyddom, ei fod ef yn eu cyhuddo yn anwireddus; ni ymddangosodd ugeiniau o honynt o flaen y meddyg; a gwyddom hefyd fod y rhan fwyaf o'r rhai a wnaeth hyny, wedi cael eu hesgusodi, ac nid heb achos.[35]
>
> 'We do not know at this time what number appeared [before the doctor] in the village of Waukesha, but we do know this, that he accuses them falsely; scores of them did not appear before the doctor; and we know also that the majority of those who did so were excused, and not without reason.'

He added that the Welsh behaved exactly like other people in the region: 'Onid oedd gan y Cymry gystal hawl i hyn a chenedloedd eraill? Cafodd bron bob *Yankee* eu rhyddhau, ar ba dir nis gwyddom'; 'Did the Welsh not have an equal right to this as other nations? Just about every Yankee was released [from service], on what grounds we do not know.'[36]

This argument raged on the pages of *Y Drych* for several months, with various writers contributing to the debate over 'Cymry Swydd Waukesha a'r Ddrafft', 'The Welsh of Waukesha County and the Draft'. Evan Williams wrote in from Milwaukee to defend his nephew, the soldier who had initiated the contention.

> Mr. Golygydd: Canfyddais yn y *Drych* am Mawrth 21, ysgrif o waith un a eilw ei hun, Thomas D. Jones, yn ymosod ar fy nai, David Williams, sydd ar faes y gwaed, yn filwr gwirfoddol yn ymladd dros lywodraeth ei wlad, yn nghwmni F, 28ain Gat. Gwirfoddlu Wis. Gan fod D. W. mewn lle mor anfanteisiol i amddiffyn ei hun yn wyneb cyhuddiadau maleisus T. D. Jones, ymddiriedaf yn eich egwyddor y gwelwch mai teg i mi roddi fy mys ar rai o'r camddarluniadau[.][37]

'Mr. Editor: I noticed in the *Drych* on March 21 an essay by one who calls himself Thomas D. Jones, attacking my nephew, David Williams, who is on the field of blood, a volunteer soldier fighting for the government of his country, in company F, 28th Regiment of Wis. Volunteers. Since D. W. is in such a disadvantageous place to defend himself in the face of the malicious accusations of T. D. Jones, I trust in your principles and that you will see that it is fair for me to put my finger on some of the misrepresentations.'

Rather than answering Jones point by point, the soldier's uncle paraded a series of indignant exclamations before the eyes of readers, preaching on the evils of slavery and accusing his nephew's critic of bringing shame to Welsh America: 'A ydych yn meddwl nad ydych yn warth i genedl y Cymry yn eich ymddygiadau at Lywodraeth dirion ein gwlad?'; 'Do you think that you are not a shame to the nation of the Welsh in your behaviour towards the kind government of our country?'[38] Evan Williams suggested that the volunteer soldier was in a moral category which placed him beyond the reach of people like Thomas Jones, referring more than once to his nephew's service 'on the field of blood'. To this end, he concluded his rant of a letter by quoting a traditional Welsh proverb: 'Cofied T. D. J. yn y dyfodol fod y fath beth a "Fflangell i gorgi am gyfarth ei well" '; 'Let T. D. J. remember in the future that there is such a thing as "Whipping a corgi for barking at his better."'[39] The Welsh word *corgi* – which has become the universal term for that particular breed of dog – is a compound noun formed from *cor*, meaning 'dwarf' or 'little', and *ci*, meaning 'dog'. Evan Williams finished his assault upon Thomas Jones with a particularly nasty *ad hominem* attack, describing him as a 'little dog' whom he was 'whipping' for barking at his 'superior'.

John Griffith Jones, one of several Welsh volunteers serving with the 23rd Wisconsin Infantry, received *Y Drych* on occasion, and it was apparently by means of the newspaper that he and his comrades learned about the controversy erupting back in their home state. In a letter to his family, the young soldier commented on the issue:

Yr ydym yn clowad fod cryn gynwrf yn yr hen dalayth Ws hefo y drafftio. Gair at Richard a Owan fy mrodur, yr ydych chwi eich dau yn rhy ifanc i'r dra[ff]t, peidiwch a listio tra y cewch aros gartra. Gwnewch fel yr wyf i yn dweud, peidiwch a gwneud fel yr wyf i yn gwneud.[40]

'We hear that there is quite a stir in the old state of Wisconsin with the drafting. A word to Richard and Owen my brothers: you two are too young for the draft, [so] don't enlist as long as you can stay home. Do as I say, do not do as I do.'

Drawing attention to his own hypocrisy, the soldier who had volunteered while still a teenager was telling his younger brothers *not* to follow his example.

A considerable body of his personal letters have survived in manuscript, and in other places John Griffith Jones expresses support for the Union cause in a manner akin to many of the patriotic pro-war texts published by the Welsh-American press. However, while some soldiers relished the thought of seeing civilians drafted into the army, he remarked that conscripts were not treated well by the old volunteers and that he would not like to see old friends from his chapel in Wisconsin, Salem, in that situation: 'Yr ydwyf i wedi gwelad rhai wedi cayl ei gyru i lenwi yr hen regiments, dyna beth na leiciwn i welad un o fechgyn Cymru ardal Salem'; 'I have seen some sent down to fill out the old regiments, that is something which I would not like to see happening to one of the Welsh boys from the Salem area'.[41] In addition to telling his brothers to stay out of the army and harm's way for as long as possible, he also advised friends at home how to avoid the difficult life of the draftee: 'os cei rhai ei dra[ff]tio y may yn well iddynt ddengid a listio os gallant'; 'if some are drafted, it is better for them to escape and [then] enlist if they can'.[42]

In addition to being used as an instrument for digging out Welsh America's anti-war moles and shaming draft dodgers, *Y Drych* was used on at least one occasion to record the names of deserters. An anonymous writer from the 22nd Wisconsin Infantry noted in a letter published in January 1863 that 'several have fled from the regiment . . . and I am sorry to say that three of these men are Welsh' ('diangodd amryw o'r gatrawd . . . a drwg genyf ddweud fod tri o'r rhai hyn yn Gymry').[43] Adopting the stance of a minister 'excluding' (*torri allan*) sinners from his chapel, this writer went on to reveal the identities of these three deserters, providing enough details to ensure that people would know exactly who they were:

> enwau y Cymry yw Evan G. Roberts, gynt o Nelson Flats, N.Y., ond yn ddiweddar o Gambria, Wis.; Thomas Hall, bu yn gweithio yr haf diweddar i Mr. W.G. Roberts, Racine, Wis.; a Samuel I. Thomas, mab Thomas Thomas, o Berlin, Grenn Lake Co., Wis. Nid hoff genyf gyhoeddi ffaeleddau y Cymry, ond yr wyf o'r farn fod cyfiawnder yn galw am roddi enwau yr uchod o flaen y cyhoedd yn y modd mwyaf amlwg . . . fel y gallai pob Cymro, ac yn enwedig pob Cymraes, gael gweled pwy ymhlith y Cymry sydd yn gallu iselu eu hunain gymaint[.][44]
>
> 'the names of the Welsh are Evan G. Roberts, formerly of Nelson Flats, N. Y., but lately of Cambria, Wis.; Thomas Hall, who was working last summer for Mr. W. G. Roberts, Racine, Wis.; and Samuel I. Thomas, son of Thomas Thomas, from Berlin, Green Lake Co., Wis. I do not enjoy publishing the faults of the Welsh, but I am of the opinion that justice demands the placing of the above names before the public in the most obvious way . . . so that every Welshman, and especially every Welsh woman, can see who amongst the Welsh can lower themselves so much.'

Significantly, this writer does not bother to record the names of the regiment's non-Welsh deserters. Just as the country's Welsh-language press was used to record the sacrifice and service of Welsh America's soldiers, so it was also used as a whipping-post to punish individuals who were perceived as bringing shame to that community.

This passage is in many ways a negative mirror image of the kinds of texts discussed in Chapter Three. While other writers said that it was their moral duty to record the valour of their community's soldiers, so this one states that 'justice demands' the recording of deserters' names. The focus on women also mirrors a substantial body of patriotic texts praising soldiers. As Alice Fahs has suggested, popular literature of the Civil War often 'stressed the central importance of women in supporting men's enlistment', a fact born out by several of the Welsh examples analysed earlier in this study.[45] Thus this writer rubs salt into the wounds by noting that the shameful roll-call is being published 'especially [so that] every Welsh woman' in America can read it. He also had an even more severe punishment in mind:

> Nid oes neb (*os nad yw Copperheads y Gogledd*) yn fwy dirmygedig yn fy ngolwg na *Deserter*, y mae wedi fforffedio ei hawl i'w fywyd ei hun, nid yw yn teilyngu na haeddu y parch lleiaf gan ei gyd ddyn, a dylai pob gwladgarwr ei ysgoi fel gelyn personol iddo ei hun, a gobeithio y bydd y Cadf. Hooker yn rhoddi y ddedfryd o farwolaeth mewn grym yn erbyn y rhai a gaed yn euog o ddesertio.[46]

> 'There is nobody (*if not the Copperheads of the North*) who are more despised in my sight than the *Deserter*; he has forfeited his right to his own life, he does not deserve the least respect from his fellow man, and every patriot should avoid him like a personal enemy to himself, and it is hoped that Gen. Hooker will put the death sentence into effect against those found guilty of deserting.'

While this soldier's letter was not answered by other writers supporting his opinions, neither was it criticized in print by individuals who disagreed with his harsh verdict. The first fact suggests that this writer was relatively isolated in his extremism, yet the second fact also reveals much about the war-time transformation of Welsh-American print culture.

This text presents a vision of the national Welsh-American community which differs profoundly from the image conveyed by the pre-war press. As was seen in Part One of this study, a great deal of Welsh-language literature published in the United States for more than twenty years before the start of the Civil War suggests that Welsh America was a tightly-woven community characterized by a great amount of solidarity within the group. It was also a community relatively unexposed to war and military life, and several of Welsh America's leading ministers and writers had even voiced direct support for pacifism in the 1850s. This soldier's letter marks a drastic move away from that orientation; this Welsh-American was, quite literally, using *Y Drych* to sentence other members of his community to death. In addition to expressing his hope that the commanding general would use execution as a punishment for deserters, he was publishing the exact identities of his three former comrades and thus enabling readers to identify and report them should they appear back home in the North. Print culture was still defining Welsh America as a tightly-woven community, yet the penalty for transgressing against the moral lines used to draw that community's boundaries was, at least in some cases, apparently as severe as the penalty prescribed by the army's court martial. The simple fact that this letter did not provoke horrified reactions is a potent suggestion as to the degree to which Welsh-American culture had been militarized by 1863.

'WE THE WELSH HAVE TO BE QUIET ON THAT MATTER': THE WRITINGS OF WELSH-SPEAKING SOUTHERNERS

Copperheads and other ideological 'moles' rooted out by the Welsh-American press represent a small number of exceptions to the rule that Welsh-speaking Northerners defined themselves as Republican, pro-Union, anti-slavery and pro-war (in the sense that the war was seen as a necessary struggle to preserve the Union and/or end slavery). With the important exception of the war's effect upon the pacifism which some sectors of the community had embraced before 1861, war-time Welsh America reacted to the war in a way which one might have expected given the ideological orientation of the pre-war community. As was seen in Chapter Two, most Welsh-Americans were Republicans by the 1860 election, a political allegiance predicated to a great extent upon their opposition to slavery. Predisposed ideologically in this manner, Welsh America was also predisposed geographically to support the North; well over 90 per cent of the country's Welsh immigrants were living in Northern states in 1860.[47]

According to 1860 census figures, out of the 45,763 Welsh immigrants residing in the United States, only 950 were living in what were to become the Confederate States of America.[48] There were others living in Maryland, a slave state which did not secede from the Union. James McPherson has succinctly described the tension which dominated life in that state during the early months of the war:

> Like the lower South, Maryland had voted for Breckinridge in the presidential election. South-Rights Democrats controlled the legislature; only the stubborn refusal of unionist Governor Thomas Hicks to call the legislature into session forestalled action by that body. The tobacco counties of southern Maryland and the eastern shore . . . were secessionist. . . . [T]he loyalty of Baltimore, with a third of the state's population, was suspect.[49]

A number of Maryland's Welshmen were employed in Baltimore's metal works when the war broke out. In June 1861 *Y Seren Orllewinol* published a story by an anonymous writer who, as he or she refers to the city as *y lle hwn* – 'this place' – appears to have been a member of Baltimore's Welsh community.

> Cymry Baltimore. Mae amryw Gymry yn gweithio yn y gweithfeydd copr yn y lle hwn. Secessionists yw y perchnogion, a throisant yr adeilad yn fagnelfa yn amser y terfysg diweddar. Yr oedd hyn nid yn unig yn troi ein cydwladwyr allan o waith, ond hefyd yn [eu] gosod mewn perygl i amlygu eu meddyliau a'u hegwyddorion ar y mater. Ffodd rhai o hononynt ymaith ar hyd y nos, ac arosodd eraill yno mewn ofnau a chaethiwed. . . . Mae y Cymry yn dra thrallodedig hefyd mewn rhanau eraill o Maryland. . . . Y mae yn annymunol bod yn mhlith pleidwyr cathiwed[.]'[50]

> 'The Welsh of Baltimore. Several Welsh people work in the copper works in this place. The owners are secessionists, and they have turned the building into a battery during the recent unrest. This not only put our fellow-countrymen out of work, but it also placed them in danger should they reveal their thoughts and their principles on the matter. Some of them fled during the night, and others stayed there in a state of fear and captivity. . . . The Welsh are sorely afflicted in other parts of Maryland as well. . . . It is unpleasant to be surrounded by slavery's supporters.'[51]

Though living and working in a slave state, these Welsh-Americans are described as opponents of slavery, an uncomfortable situation which was intensified with the coming of war. Surrounded by pro-slavery secessionists, they are forced to choose between flight (presumably over the border to Washington, DC, or to Pennsylvania) and remaining in a state of 'captivity' where their pro-Union and anti-slavery sentiments place them in constant 'danger'.

One of these Welsh metal workers was a man named Henry Davies. Four days after the fall of Fort Sumter he wrote a letter to his father in Wales, who had it published immediately in *Seren Cymru*, one of the Old Country's newspapers. Like that anonymous writer who published in *Y Seren Orllewinol*, Davies described Baltimore's Welsh population as being anti-slavery and pro-Union.

> os bydd i ryw un ddweyd gair yn erbyn caethwasiaeth yma, peth rhyfedd os na cha'r gŵr hwnw belen neu ddwy idd ei fol; o ganlyniad, y mae'n rhaid i ni y Cymry fod yn ddystaw ar y pen hwnw, yn enwedig y dyddiau hyn. . . . Y mae'n amser prysur yn y dref hon y dyddiau hyn ac nid ydys yn gwybod etto pa beth a wna y dalaeth hon, myned allan o'r undeb ai peidio; bu dau ddyn trwy y gwaith yma echdoe yn gofyn am enw pob un ag oedd am gadw yn yr undeb; rhoddodd pob Cymro sydd yma eu henwau iddynt, ond yr ydym yn gorfod bod yn ddystaw.[52]

> 'if somebody says one word against slavery here, it's a strange thing if that man does not receive a bullet or two in his stomach; as a result, we the Welsh have to be quiet on that matter, especially these days. . . . It's a busy time in this town these days and it is not yet known what this state will do, go out of the union or not; two men were here the day before yesterday going through the works asking for the

> name of everybody who was in favour of preserving the Union; every Welshman who is here gave his name to them, but we have to be quiet.'

Welsh-language material published in the United States during the war was subject to an ideological filter which was markedly pro-Union, anti-slavery and pro-war. This letter, however, originated as a piece of private correspondence between father and son and, when it was published, it appeared in a newspaper in Wales. As was discussed at the start of this chapter, the newspapers and journals of the Old Country were not subject to the same ideological pressures as the Welsh-American press. Thus, despite the very different context in which this Baltimore Welshman's letter was published, the text itself supports the view that Welsh residents of Maryland remained anti-slavery and pro-Union after the start of the Civil War.

Covington, in the slave state of Kentucky, had a small Welsh population by the start of the war. One member of this community, a writer who used the pen-name 'Cyfeiliog', published a letter in *Y Cyfaill o'r Hen Wlad* in July 1864 welcoming the end of slavery.

> Da genyf eich hysbysu fod yr hen ddelw felldigedig, caethiwed Negroaidd, yn dadfeilio yn gyflym yn y Dalaeth hon, dymchwela yn ddarnau y naill ddydd ar ol y llall. Dywedasom yn gyhoeddus ychydig gyda thair blynedd yn ol, fod ei dynged wedi ei selio, a bod ei bleidwyr wedi ei ddinystrio a'u dwylaw eu hunian. Yr oeddym yn credu ein bod yn gweled ei gysgod yn "arwyddion yr amserau," a dywedem felly, er nad oedd genym sicrwydd nad côt o dar a phlu, a'n bwrw o'r ddinas fyddai ein tynged. Ond mawr yw y cyfnewidiad yn awr.[53]

> 'I am pleased to inform you that the old accursed idol, Negro slavery, is crumbling quickly in this State; it falls down in pieces day by day. We said publicly nearly three years ago that its fate was sealed, and that its supporters had destroyed it with their own hands. We thought we had seen its shadow in "the signs of the times," and we spoke thus, though we had no certainty that a coat of tar and feathers and being run out of the city would not be our fate.'

The Ohio river is all that separates Covington from the city of Cincinnati, and the small Welsh community of Covington in many ways operated as a satellite of the larger community located across the river in the free state of Ohio. While it is thus no surprise that the abolitionist sentiments being preached by some of Cincinnati's Welsh ministers were also embraced by people like 'Cyfeiliog' in Covington, the simple fact that they were living in a slave state meant that the tar and feathers referred to here were a very real threat before and during the war.

However difficult things were at times for the Welsh of Kentucky and Maryland, those slave states did not secede from the Union. William Pierce was in a very different situation; he had moved with his wife and children to New Canton, Virginia, some time before 1861. In a letter which Pierce sent back to his brothers and sisters in Wales he described the pressures placed upon him and his sons, Richard and David, by their Confederate neighbours.

> [Bu] yn galed arnom yn y dechreu – eisiau i mi ymuno â'r fyddin. Ychydig o dramorwyr oedd yn New Canton . . . ni thalent ein cyflog i ni, ni werthent flawd na dim, er treio pob ffordd ein cael ond yr oeddwn mor benderfynol nas awn i byth i ymladd dros yr hen gaethfasnach. Gwrthsefais bob bygythiad – cawsom rybydd i ymadel â'r wlad yn mhen ychydig ddiwrnodau, felly cychwynais yn y fan, ond gan na allwn groesi y llinell i'r Gogledd bu raid aros yn y fan hon. . . . Cyn hir daethant am Richard a David i'r fyddin, ond sefais i'w gwrthwynebu fel llew a chan i mi ddadcan fy marn am Lincoln taflwyd fi i garchar[.][54]

> 'It was hard on us at the start – [they] wanted me to join the army. There were only a few foreigners in New Canton . . . they would not pay us our salary, they would not sell us flour or anything, in order to try every way to get us, but I was so determined that I would never go to fight for the old slave trade. I withstood every threat – we were warned to leave the region within a few days, thus I started immediately, but as I could not cross the line to the North [we] had to stay in this place. . . . Before long they came for Richard and David for the army, but I stood and opposed them like a lion, and as I declared my opinion about Lincoln I was thrown into prison.'

This letter survived only in manuscript and was not published until 1997; like Henry Davies's correspondence with his father, it was a personal letter sent to close family members in Wales. Both texts reveal that, despite considerable pressures placed upon these Welsh people living in slave states during the war, they maintained their pro-Union, pro-Lincoln and anti-slavery beliefs. Henry Davies and his co-workers did so secretly, holding their tongues and, it seems, only expressing their true feelings in writing or in clandestine meetings with other Unionists. William Pierce, apparently brave to the point of recklessness, expressed himself openly, resisting Confederate conscription agents while lecturing them about the virtues of Lincoln's government! Both print and manuscript sources show that the ideological uniformity of Welsh America also encompassed individuals living in Southern slave states.

The western Confederacy also contained isolated pockets of Welsh-Americans. D. M. Williams, a soldier serving with the 18th Wisconsin Infantry, was surprised to find a small group of people who spoke his native language living near Lake Providence on the banks of the Mississippi River in northern Louisiana. He published an account of his discovery in *Y Drych*:

> mae yma rai o'n cenedl yn byw, ac yn y fynwent gerllaw, yn ymyl y pentref, mae rhan farwol llawer Cymro yn pydru yn llwch y pentwr. Un o'r cyfryw o'r enw Hugh Hughes, gynt o Swydd Fon . . . yr hwn fu farw dair blynedd a dau fis yn ol; a dywed Mr. Griffith, hen dderbyniwr y *Drych*, a'r *Cenhadwr*, sydd wedi bod yn byw yma er's agos i bymtheg mlynedd, ac i'r hwn yr oedd Hughes yn gweithio cyn ei farw, fod yn agos i ddau cant o ddoleri yn ddyledus i'r trancedig, oddiwrth

> wahanol bersonau yn yr ardal hon, a bod cefnder i'r trancedig yn byw yn Wisconsin, a byddai dda iawn gan Mr. Griffith iddo ddyfod yma i dderbyn yr hyn oedd ddyledus i Hughes.[55]
>
> 'some of our nation are living here, and in the graveyard nearby, next to the village, the mortal remains of many a Welshman are rotting in the dust of the mound. One of them by the name of Hugh Hughes, formerly of Anglesey . . . who died three years and two months ago; and Mr Griffith, an old subscriber to the *Drych* and the *Cenhadwr* who has been living here for close to fifteen years, and for whom Hughes was working before his death, says that nearly 200 dollars are owed to the deceased, from various people in this region, and that a cousin of the deceased is living in Wisconsin, and that Mr Griffiths would like him to come here to receive that which was owed to Hughes.'

As this Wisconsin soldier describes Mr Griffiths as 'an old subscriber' to *Y Drych* and *Y Cenhadwr Americanaidd*, it is extremely unlikely that this Welsh-American Southerner supported the Confederates; both publications were solidly pro-Lincoln and anti-slavery, and the *Cenhadwr* had preached abolition since its inception in 1840. As if to support this point, the Welsh-speaking soldier recorded the joy with which Mr Griffiths and his family received copies of the pro-Union Welsh newspaper: 'Mae yn dda ryfeddol ganddynt weled y *Drych*, ac yr wyf wedi gadael pedwar rhifyn iddynt'; 'They are wondrously happy to see the *Drych*, and I have left four copies with them.'[56]

Perhaps the best-known Welsh community south of the Ohio river was the settlement which Samuel Roberts of Llanbrynmair had founded in Tennessee in 1857.[57] Samuel Roberts, known simply as 'S. R.' to Welsh people on both sides of the Atlantic, was by the 1850s a well-known minister, writer, and thinker. Long before 1861 he had published stirring essays in support of a number of radical causes, including abolition, pacifism, women's rights and agricultural reform. Thus when S. R. purchased land for settlement in the hill country of eastern Tennessee he surprised – and even shocked – sections of Welsh society both in Wales and the United States; in addition to moving to a place far from other Welsh communities, the outspoken abolitionist was leading his followers to a slave state. Samuel Roberts, however, was as stubborn as he was principled, and, ignoring advice to the contrary, he proceeded to move to eastern Tennessee, naming his new home Brynffynon ('well-hill' or 'fountain-hill').

The new community was beset by problems even before the start of the Civil War. The Welsh immigrants had been cheated by property dealers, and as a result the farm land which they had purchased was neither as extensive nor as fertile as they had been led to believe. However, there were signs that the settlement might flourish despite these economic difficulties. For one thing, it had a number of famous writers; in addition to S. R. himself, Roberts's brother Richard had moved to Tennessee with his family. Known as Gruffydd Rhisiart, he had published a great deal of prose and poetry in Wales before emigrating. Another literary talent was added to the small community in 1859 when the poet Cadwgan Fardd moved from south Wales to eastern Tennessee. One of the poets assessed by *Y Drych*'s 'bardic measuring stick' before the war (and discussed in Chapter One), Cadwgan was a well-known poet in both Wales and Welsh America.[58] His new neighbour, Gruffydd Rhisiart, published a boastful letter in *Y Cenhadwr Americanaidd*, using a joke to draw attention to the settlement's cultural clout: 'Gobeithio na fyddwn yn ormod o lenorion yma i wneud ffarmwyr'; 'I hope that we will not be too many writers here to make farmers.'[59] Indulging in an ancient bardic tradition, Gruffydd Rhisiart and Cadwgan Fardd entered into a playful poetic contest, using strict-metre poetry to discuss the agricultural enterprise in which they were engaged. Before long, Welsh publications on both sides of the Atlantic were presenting readers with poetry stemming from this interchange, offering them a bardic view of Brynffynon, Tennessee.[60]

Like S. R., these other Welsh settlers were opponents of slavery. And, like the majority of their Welsh-American compatriots in the North – as well as many of their non-Welsh neighbours in eastern Tennessee's hill country – they supported the Republican party. When the Civil War came, Samuel Roberts, Gruffydd Rhisiart and Cadwgan Fardd remained pro-Union, pro-Lincoln and anti-slavery. Some time between Lincoln's election in November 1860 and the start of the war in April 1861 Cadwgan composed a satire on Jefferson Davis, using the strict-metre *englyn* form. He predicted that the arch-secessionist would be punished: 'Jeff. Davis gaiff . . . wae / Am ei waith, yr adyn'; 'Jeff. Davis will receive . . . woe / For his doings, the wretch.'[61] The long poem also devotes several stanzas to unmitigated vilification of Davis's Confederate followers, beginning with an *englyn* which describes them as 'hell's children':

Yn Richmond does ond y swn – anifyr,
  Gan ufudd blant anwn,
 I'w glywed – rhagddynt gwyliwn,
 Gwnant ladd ac ymladd mal cwn.[62]

'In Richmond there is nothing but the nasty sound
  Of hell's obedient children
 To be heard – let us watch them carefully,
 They will kill and fight like dogs.'

The word translated here as 'hell' is *annwn* (often spelled *anwn* in the nineteenth century, and sometimes spelled more archaically as *annwfn*); while often used as a synonym for the Christian hell, it was originally used to describe the 'otherworld' of early Welsh legend. Up through the twentieth century, living Welsh folklore told of *cŵn annwn* or 'the dogs of annwn', supernatural beasts who wander the land at night carrying omens of impending death. The main rhyme of this englyn is *-wn*, and the fact that the second and third lines end respectively with *annwn* and *cŵn* is no coincidence; Cadwgan Fardd is describing the blood-thirsty followers of Jefferson Davis as the hell hounds of Welsh folklore, roaming the land and crying out for human blood. Their frightening 'sound' (*sŵn*) is also tied into this image by the main rhyme; the poet makes good use of the *englyn*'s metrical constraints, combining this ancient bardic metre with an image drawn from equally ancient Welsh tradition in order to portray the southern Rebels as blood-thirsty bringers of death.

Whether we translate *annwn* as a Christian 'hell' or envision it as a Celtic 'otherworld', Cadwgan Fardd found himself wandering in his own kind of Hades for a while, sleeping rough in the wilderness of eastern Tennessee and hiding from Confederate raiders. He was joined by Gruffydd Rhisiart; both of these Welsh poets were made fugitives during the war because of their pro-Union and anti-slavery sentiments. Samuel Roberts, the older of the two brothers, was sixty-one years old when the war started, and he chose not to flee. The old radical stuck bravely to his anti-slavery and anti-war principles, and he was harassed by Confederate guerrillas while also suffering the wrath of Welsh-Americans in the North who were angered by his printed criticism of 'ysbryd rhyfel y Gogledd', 'the North's spirit of war'. An uncompromising pacifist, S. R. despised 'the South's spirit of war' as well, yet refusal to support the Union war effort was enough to make him a traitor in the eyes of many Northerners. Yet, while trying to sooth the wrath of the Northern 'brothers' who attacked him, he refused to retract any of his anti-war declarations, a point made clear by a piece published in *Y Cenhadwr Americanaidd* in September 1861:

> Yr wyf fi yn teimlo yn serchog ac yn gynes at y brodyr yn y Gogledd sydd wedi fy nghondemnio drymaf am i mi feio ysbryd rhyfel y Gogledd. Yr oeddwn yn bur gydwybodol, ac yn lled bwyllog yn ysgrifenu hyny a ysgrifenais ar bwnc y rhyfel.[63]
>
> 'I feel friendly and warmly towards the brothers in the North who have condemned me most harshly for criticizing the North's spirit of war. I was acting very conscientiously, and fairly reasonably when writing what I wrote on the subject of the war.'

Although the war at times isolated the small community of Brynffynon, Tennessee, from the Welsh press of the North, several letters written by Samuel Roberts succeeded in reaching Robert Everett, editor of *Y Cenhadwr Americanaidd*. Both were Congregational ministers, yet Everett had himself taken issue with some of Roberts's comments.[64] However, while *Y Drych* and other publications were vilifying Samuel Roberts, falsely accusing him of supporting the Confederacy and slavery, Everett ensured that his *Cenhadwr* treated S. R. with a greater degree of fairness, and he published a number of long protestations written by the long-suffering Welsh minister from Tennessee. At times these writings reached Everett's press in Oneida County, New York, via *Y Cronicl*, a journal which Roberts's brother edited back in Wales, and at other times S. R. managed to send personal letters through the Union lines from Tennessee to New York.

In June 1863 the *Cenhadwr* published a piece by Samuel Roberts describing the hardships which the community's pro-Union Welsh people had endured.

> Peth cyfyng ydoedd bod mewn ofn parhaus am bron ddwy flynedd, rhag i'r anrheithwyr oeddynt yn gwibio ar bob llaw ddyfod heibio i ni. Peth cyfyng ydoedd bod bron fel carcharorion rhyfel drwy yr holl amser, na feiddiem symud oddicartref heb fyned i ddanedd rhyw beryglon. . . . Peth cyfyng oedd gweled fy mrawd, a'r Bardd Cadwgan, ar frys gwyllt yn taflu ychydig luniaeth a chorn . . . i'r wagen, ac yn gyru ymaith dros ugain milldir o ffordd arw, i gadw allan o'r golwg am amryw ddyddiau, pan oedd mintai gref o'r anrheithwyr o fewn pedair milldir i ni yn cymeryd y *dynion* a fedrent ddal, yn gystal a'r eiddo[.][65]

> 'It was a difficult thing to live in continual fear for nearly two years, from the raiders who were rushing through on either side of us. It was a difficult thing to live almost as prisoners of war all of the time, so that we did not dare to leave home lest we go into the jaws of some danger. . . . It was a difficult thing to see my brother and the Bard Cadwgan in wild haste throwing a little sustenance and corn . . . into the wagon, and driving off across more than twenty miles of difficult road, to keep out of sight for some days, when a strong band of the raiders were within four miles of us, taking the men whom they could catch, in addition to the possessions.'

S. R. was an accomplished writer, and this passage conveys the nature of his distress extremely effectively. By repeating the phrase 'peth cyfyng (yd)oedd' – 'it was a difficult thing' – at the start of each sentence, he suggests the desperation engulfing the isolated Unionists living inside the Confederacy. Readers would have encountered these emotional sentences with knowledge of what might be described as a charged sub-text, the fact that Roberts, while suffering this series of hardships, was also being (falsely) accused by some sectors in the North of supporting the South. Samuel Roberts provides a clear example of an individual who fell foul of the Welsh-American press because he did not conform completely to the pro-war, pro-Union and anti-slavery ideology which it espoused. However, he and his neighbours also provide equally clear examples of Welsh Southerners who did not support the Confederacy. Like Henry Davies of Maryland, 'Cyfeiliog' of Kentucky, and William Pierce of Virginia, the Welsh of Brynffynon, Tennessee, continued to be pro-Union and anti-slavery throughout the war.

These letters failed to win the sympathy of *Y Drych*'s editor, J. W. Jones, and Welsh America's weekly newspaper would continue to attack Samuel Roberts right up to the end of the war. For example, in November 1865 the paper addressed S. R.'s constant (and, it seems, very justifiable) complaints that he did not receive fair play at the hands of *Y Drych*:

> mae genym ni resymau i gredu fod S. R. yn euog o'r hyn y cwyna gymaint yn ei gylch, trwy ei fod yn treio dylanwadu ar ddynion i goelio ei haeriadau am anhegwch y *Drych*. Nid oes genym ond tosturio wrth y cyfryw a fynant eu camarwain gan ymadroddion dichellgar a thwyllodrus Mr. Roberts.[66]
>
> 'we have reason to believe that S. R. is guilty of that which he complains so much about, because he tries to influence men to believe his claims about the unfairness of *Y Drych*. We have nothing but pity for those who want to be mislead by the crafty and deceitful utterances of Mr. Roberts.'

Shortly after the end of the Civil War, Samuel Roberts moved back to Wales. The settlement which he had tried to establish in Tennessee had turned into an economic disaster and his good name was severely stained. Welsh America's press, in the grips of its pro-war hysteria, had thrown enough mud at him to ensure that some of it would stick for a long time. When S. R. produced an autobiographical volume in 1875 he was still defending his war-time stance, echoing the protestations he had offered on the pages of *Y Cenhadwr Americanaidd* more than ten years earlier. Appropriately enough, Roberts published this autobiography under the title *Crynodeb o Helyntion Bywyd S. R.* – 'A Summary of the Troubles of S. R.'s Life.'[67]

WELSH CONFEDERATES

Not every Welsh immigrant living in Tennessee was a part of Samuel Roberts's community. According to William S. Jones, a soldier with the 56th Ohio Infantry, another Welshman was residing near Memphis, one whose politics differed substantially from those other Welsh-speaking residents of Tennessee. The encounter which Jones described in a letter to *Y Drych* was surely a remarkable one: the 56th Ohio, the unit with what was most likely the highest percentage of Welsh-speaking soldiers of all Union regiments, was, by sheer chance, sent to work on a farm owned by a Welsh immigrant.

> Wedi i ni gyraedd Memphis, gorchymynwyd ein milwyr yn y gatrawd hon i fyned allan tua 28 milltir o'r dref i adgyweirio pontydd ar y gledrffordd, y rhai a losgasid gan y gwrthryfelwyr. Wedi ein myned allan yno, digwyddodd er ein syndod ein bod yn gweithio ar ffarm hen Gymro o'r enw, Davis, yn enedigol o Sir Gaerfyrddin, yn Nghymru. Ymddiddanai yn yr hen iaith o'r goreu, dywedodd nad oedd neb o'i berthynasau yn y rhyfel, nac wedi rhoddi un cynorthwy i fyddin y Deheuwyr; ond hawdd oedd deall fod ei egwyddor . . . yn *secesh*. Carai ni fel Cymry, ond fel milwyr Gogleddol, mynai ein bod wedi cael ein twyllo gan ein blaenoriaid i wneyd yr hyn oedd anghyfiawn.[68]
>
> 'After we reached Memphis, our soldiers in this regiment were ordered to go out about 28 miles from the town in order to repair bridges on the railroad, which had been burned by the rebels. After we went out there, it happened to our surprise

> that we were working on the farm of an old Welshman by the name of Davis, originally from Carmarthenshire in Wales. He spoke the old language as well as anybody: he said that none of his relatives were in the war, and that he had not given any help to the Southerners; but it was easy to see that his principles . . . were secesh. He loved us as Welshmen, but as Northern soldiers, he insisted that we had been tricked by our leaders into doing that which was unjust.'

Mr Davis told the Welsh soldiers from Ohio that none of his relatives were in the army and that he had not helped the Confederates in any way. However, given the fact there were dozens of Welsh-speaking soldiers wearing the Union uniform working on his farm when this conversation took place, would he have admitted it if he did in fact have a son or two in the Rebel army? And, given that these soldiers were working to repair damage done by Confederate raiders – and that civilians who helped the enemy were often summarily executed as spies – it is highly unlikely that the old Carmarthenshire man would've admitted 'giv[ing] any help to the Southerners' even if he had done so. It is impossible to know how far his support for the Confederacy extended, but Mr Davis gives us one example of a Welsh-speaking American who was definitely *not* pro-Union. It is safe to assume that there were a few more like him who have gone unrecorded.

Whether or not Davis had any sons, and whether or not they served in the Confederate army, one prominent Welsh-American did have a son fighting for the Rebels. Even though the Reverend Jenkin Jenkins lived in the North, his son David had been working on a Mississippi river boat before the war. When war came, David Jenkins went with some of his Southern friends to enlist in the Confederate army. He died in Virginia in October 1862, and his father, suspended somewhere between grief and shame, published the following verse in *Y Cenhadwr Americanaidd:*

> O pwy all ddwey'd ar eiriau deimladau mam a thad,
> Ar ol eu mab anwylgu, yn trengu yn ei waed.
> Fe aeth i dir y gelyn roedd hyn yn wrthyn llawn,
> Er hynny 'rym ni'n wylo am dano'n aml iawn.[69]
>
> 'Oh who can relate in words the feelings of mother and father,
> After their dear son, dying in his blood.
> He went to the land of the enemy; that was completely repugnant,
> Yet despite that we now often cry for him.'

A considerable number of Welsh-language elegies were composed for soldiers who died in the American Civil War. This short poem, however, is unique; in addition to the fact that it was written for a Confederate soldier, the father-poet actually apologizes for his dead son's actions, stressing that David's decision was *wrthyn llawn*, 'totally' (or 'completely') 'repugnant' (or 'offensive'). However, we know very little about David Jenkins other than what can be gleaned from the apologetic words of his father's short elegy.

There is one Welshman who fought for the Confederacy about whom a great deal is known. Indeed, while present research has revealed thousands of Welsh soldiers in the Union army as opposed to only a very small handful who served the Confederacy, it is, ironically, one of the Confederates about whom the greatest amount of published material is available. Henry Morton Stanley, the adventurer who would 'find' Dr Livingstone in Africa, in fact claimed to have served both the North and the South during the American Civil War. This claim in itself points up a lack of ideological commitment to either side; H. M. Stanley was, by his own admission, a mercenary. In the words of Ella Lonn, Stanley's 'record as a Confederate soldier . . . [was] quite in character with his love of adventure and his history':

> As a warrior he was strictly a free lance and fought under many flags – that of the United States, the Confederacy, England, and Belgium, and commanded thousands of King M'tesa's followers as allies during . . . his march through Africa.[70]

It is also difficult to know when Stanley was telling the truth; he was prone to exaggerating his own adventures, and more than one writer in both Britain and the United States would later accuse him of lying about the events of his incredible life.[71] However, all sources agree with Stanley's autobiography on a few points, including the fact that he landed in New Orleans in 1859, thirteen years before he would finally achieve the fame he so craved. It also appears to be true that Stanley enlisted with the 6th Arkansas Infantry during his time in America and that he fought at Shiloh, where he was taken prisoner.

Stanley discussed his experiences in the American Civil War in the *Autobiography* which he began writing in 1893.[72] He touched only briefly upon the causes for which his former comrades on both sides had been fighting, including some passing comments on the subject while discussing his time as a prisoner of war.

> The only official connected with Camp Douglas whom I remember with pleasure is Mr. Shipman, the commissary. . . . After some two days' acquaintance . . . he sounded me as to my intentions. I scarcely comprehended him at the outset, for Camp Douglas was not a place to foster intentions. He explained that, if I were tired of being a prisoner, I could be released by enrolling myself as a Unionist, that is, becoming a Union soldier . . . it was useless to try and influence me by political reasons. In the first place, I was too ignorant in politics, and too slow of comprehension, to follow his reasonings; in the second place, every American friend of mine was a Southerner . . . and, in the third place, I had a secret scorn for people who could kill one another for the sake of African slaves. There were no blackies in Wales, and why a sooty-faced nigger from a distant land should be an

> element of disturbance between white brothers, was a puzzle to me. I should have to learn a great deal about him, ascertain his wrongs and his rights, and wherein his enslavement was unjust and his liberty was desirable, before I could venture upon giving an opinion adverse to 20,000,000 Southerners.[73]

According to his own recollections, Stanley was eventually persuaded by Mr. Shipman, and he gained his freedom by enrolling 'in the U. S. Artillery Service'.[74] He soon deserted, later to rejoin the Union war effort by enlisting as a sailor with the United States navy. His lack of commitment to the Southern cause is also made clear at an early point in his *Autobiography* where he notes in passing that 'enlisting in the Confederate service . . . was certainly a grave blunder.'[75]

Stanley also produced a different, more colourful account of the way in which he secured his freedom. In this version, he has himself escaping by swimming across a river 'under a hail of bullets'.[76] One of his more recent biographers, Emyr Wyn Jones, has shown convincingly that the adventurer made up this particular story in order to impress a woman he was courting at the time.[77] What is most significant here is not the facts surrounding Stanley's escape from prison, but rather the fact that, decades after the war, Stanley would later employ overtly racist language in questioning the abolitionists' interpretation of the Civil War. His *Autobiography* provides a rare example of a Welshman who, in addition to serving the Confederacy, expressed an opinion counter to the anti-slavery ideology being promulgated by the Welsh-American press during the war.

H. M. Stanley wrote his autobiography in English, and he was what his contemporaries would have called a 'Dic Siôn Dafydd', a Welshman who turned his back on his native language in order to fashion a new, English identity. An exceptional character in more ways than one, he can in fact be seen as an exception which proves the rule; obsessed with changing his identity and re-writing his past, Stanley was by no means typical of nineteenth-century Wales (or Welsh America). Indeed, he changed his own name from the Welsh John Rowlands to the English Henry Morton Stanley. Stanley did not seek out any of America's Welsh communities. By the same token, he did not commit himself ideologically to any particular vision of either the United States or the Confederate States of America. Rather than allying himself with the interests of any community, Stanley appears to have served only himself in seeking money and fame. Moreover, as his American adventures took place a number of years before Stanley was to make a name for himself as an explorer, he was apparently completely unknown to the rest of Welsh America during the Civil War and thus he was not mentioned in the country's Welsh-language publications during the war years.

The short list of Welsh-speaking Confederate soldiers provided here can be lengthened slightly, for at least one more name can be added to those of David Jenkins and H. M. Stanley. Humphrey Pierce, the soldier-writer known as 'Wmffra o Faldwyn' discussed in Chapter Five, published a letter in *Y Cyfaill o'r Hen Wlad* which discussed a remarkable encounter he had while serving in Missouri. Pierce described how, in the middle of a battle, he was sent to converse with the Confederates under a flag of truce: 'Aethum gyda lluman wen ac ymborth i'n carcharorion un tro, o dan swyddog gwrthryfelgar o Gymro, o'r enw Lewis; 'Once I went with a white flag and sustenance for our prisoners, [who were] under a Welsh rebel officer, by the name of Lewis.'[78] Pierce tells us nothing else about this man other than that he was Welsh, that his name was Lewis, and that he was a 'rebel officer' fighting in Missouri.

Given the brief conversation conducted under the white flag, Pierce apparently had little time to learn more about this Welsh Confederate. However, he was most immediately concerned not with Lewis but rather with his commanding officer, Sterling Price. A Confederate general who had won a number of victories in Missouri, Price was a hot topic of conversation in Welsh America. The Revd Edward Jones, a prominent minister in Cincinnati, had been saying that Price was a Welshman, and the rumour had reached Humphrey Pierce's ears. Because of his service with the Union army in Arkansas and Missouri, Pierce had been able to learn a great deal about Price, and he published his letter in *Y Cyfaill o'r Hen Wlad* in order to put an end to the speculation:

> Mr. Gol. – Gan fod chwedl wedi cael ei chyfodi yn mysg y Cymry yn y wlad hon, fod y gwrthryfelwr Price yn Gymro, ac yn cael ei chredu gan luaws, ac yn debygol ei bod wedi dyfod o enau y Parch. Edward Jones, Cincinnati. Mae yn sicr i Mr. Jones gam-ddeall y person: nid yr un yw hwn ag un y mae efe yn ei feddwl sydd o Gymru. Deheuwr Americanaidd o'i enedigaeth yw y Price hwn[.][79]
>
> 'Mr. Ed[itor] – [I write] because a story has sprung up among the Welsh in this country that the rebel Price is a Welshman, [a story which is] believed by many, and likely to have come from the mouth of the Revd Edward Jones, Cincinnati. It is certain that Mr. Jones has mistaken the person: this man is not the same one whom he thinks is from Wales. This Price is a Southern American by birth.'

Humphrey Pierce elaborated on the sources and nature of his knowledge, discussing the Confederate general's supposed Welshness in detail. He had even met his family and slept in his house (at an unspecified time, either before the war or when the Union army occupied the rebel General's home).

> bum yn nghartref Price, ac fe gysgasom yno am un noson . . . Nid oedd yno un llyfr Cymraeg o fewn ei dŷ. Gall pob dyn fod yn gadarn na welodd Price Gymru erioed, ac na all lefaru gair o'r hen Omeraeg; ac os ydyw o waedoliaeth, nid yw am arddel hyny, efe na'i deulu.[80]
>
> 'I was in Price's home, and we slept there one night . . . There was not one Welsh book in his house. Every man can say with certainty that Price has never seen Wales, and that he can not speak one word of the old Gomeric [i.e. Welsh language]; and if he is of [Welsh] heritage, he does not claim it, neither he nor his family.'

It is in this context that Humphrey Pierce mentions the Welsh-speaking Rebel discussed above, citing the testimony given by Lewis as further evidence as to the fact that Sterling Price was not Welsh.

> Fe ymladdais â Price o frwydr Wilson Creek hyd y frwydr ar lan Saline, yn 1864. Aethum gyda lluman wen ac ymborth i'n carcharorion un tro, o dan swyddog gwrthryfelgar o Gymro, o'r enw Lewis, yr hwn a ddywedodd yn gadar[n]haol nad yw Price yn Gymro, nac o'n hachau, oddieithr yn mhell.[81]

> 'I fought with Price from the battle of Wilson Creek to the battle on the banks of the Saline in 1864. I went with a white flag and sustenance for our prisoners one time, under a Welsh rebel by the name of Lewis, who said with certainty that Price is not a Welshman, neither [is he] of our heritage, except only distantly.'

As has been stressed repeatedly, while there were many Southern Americans of distant Welsh descent (including Jefferson Davis himself), Welsh-American writers differentiated between such individuals and those who spoke Welsh. This study has from the outset used language as a way of assessing Welsh identity because that was the most common factor used by writers in the 1860s. Humphrey Pierce's discussion of the Confederate general's cultural identity provides a vivid example of that process of definition; Sterling Price could 'not speak one word of the old Gomeric', he owned no Welsh books and he was thus – according to both Pierce (a Welsh-speaking Union soldier) and Lewis (a Welsh-speaking Confederate) – 'not a Welshman'.

David Jenkins, H. M. Stanley and Lewis of Missouri: present research has uncovered only three examples of Welsh speakers who joined the Confederate army. This small group can be increased by moving the focus from North America to Britain while also shifting attention from the army to the navy. The Confederacy made considerable use of British ports, constructing ships in the safety of the 'neutral' environment which they afforded and recruiting British sailors to help fill out their crews. Port cities such as Bristol and Liverpool were full of Welsh sailors looking for work, and it is certain that a number of them signed on to serve on Confederate blockade runners and even warships. In fact, it is possible that there were more Welshmen serving on one Confederate ship, the *C. S. S. Alabama*, than there were in the entire Confederate army.

One of these sailors, James Evans, had been residing in the American South before the war. His family had moved from Wales to Ireland soon after his birth, before relocating again to Charleston, South Carolina, when Evans was about five years old. The small settlement which Welsh immigrants had established in South Carolina in the eighteenth century had long been assimilated by this time; Evans was raised outside the orbit of Welsh-speaking America and it is not known whether or not he spoke the language.[82] However, his parents would have most certainly been Welsh speakers and he must have had at least some knowledge of things Welsh.[83] Already an experienced sailor before the start of the Civil War, Evans served on several Confederate ships in 1861 before sailing for Liverpool, England, where Captain Raphael Semmes enrolled him to serve as pilot and Master's Mate on the *C.S.S. Alabama*. This ship, which was launched on 15 May 1862, was built across the Mersey from Liverpool in Birkenhead.[84]

Shortly after beginning her maiden voyage, the new ship anchored near Traeth Coch, Anglesey, in North Wales. There the crew captured a local man, John Roberts, presumably because the Confederates suspected that he would inform US naval agents as to the movements of the *Alabama*.[85] The ship sailed with Roberts on board, the first of many prisoners who would be held in her hold. As the Confederate vessel began capturing American merchant ships, Roberts was eventually joined by four other Welshmen: one named Hughes, from Holyhead, Anglesey, as well as Thomas Williams, Samuel Roberts and a 'Lieutenant Morris', all from Caernarfon. These five sailors were eventually freed on condition that they join the *Alabama*'s crew. Several of them would serve on the Confederate ship until she was sunk in June 1864 by the *U. S. S. Kearsage*.[86] Samuel Roberts managed to escape several months before this final battle, jumping ship in Capetown, South Africa, and eventually working his way back to Wales. When he died on 12 April 1916, it would be claimed that Roberts was the last surviving sailor who had served on the famous Confederate ship.[87] While providing definite examples of Welshmen who fought for the Confederacy, these sailors must also be described as exceptions which prove the rule. They served under duress, after being offered a choice between joining the crew and remaining in chains. Moreover, at least one of them, Samuel Roberts, would later escape. Despite his obvious lack of commitment to the Confederate cause, this sailor appears to have enjoyed basking in the romance which the ship's history was to accrue after the war. Living the rest of his life in Caernarfon and the nearby village of Groeslon, this colourful character became known as 'Sam yr Alabama' ('Sam of the Alabama').[88]

One man who joined the ship's crew voluntarily was David Herbert Llewelyn, the *Alabama*'s doctor. Described as 'holding a close connection with Pembrokeshire' ('yn dal cysylltiad agos â Sir Benfro'), he was the son of the Revd David Llewelyn, a well-known Welsh churchman who held a prestigious curacy in England. The young doctor died when the ship was sunk, and one Welsh newspaper, *Yr Herald*, published a laudatory obituary.

> Yr oedd David Herbert Llewelyn, yr hwn a drengodd yn y cyflawniad ardderchog o'i ddyledswydd yn ystod y frwydr ddiweddar gyferbyn a Cherbourg, yn fab i'r Parch. David Llewelyn, curad parchus Euston Royal, Wilts. . . . Bu gyda'r Alabama yn ystod ei holl fordeithiau hynod; a pherchid ef yn fawr gan bawb oedd ar ei bwrdd.[89]

> 'David Herbert Llewelyn, who died in the excellent fulfilment of his duty during the recent battle near Cherbourg, was son to the Revd David Llewelyn, the

respectable curate of Euston Royal, Wiltshire. . . . He was with the Alabama during all its remarkable voyages, and he was respected greatly by everybody who was on board.'

By virtue of his job, David Llewelyn would have come into contact with the *Alabama*'s prisoners, and it is entirely possible that he played a role in convincing those captive Welshmen to join the crew. Such speculation, however, must be put aside at present; the writer who praised Llewelyn on the pages of *Yr Herald* said nothing about the presence of other Welsh sailors on the Confederate ship.

The author of the doctor's obituary referred to the ship's 'remarkable voyages'; indeed, stories of the *Alabama*'s adventures and victories were apparently popular in Wales. Nearly a year before she was sunk, a poet named John Evans published a short verse praising the ship on the pages of the same newspaper which was to record Llewelyn's death. Evans – called 'Y Bardd Cocos', or the 'Cockle Poet', because he earned his living by collecting shellfish on the Anglesey coast – was the unwitting clown of nineteenth-century Welsh bardic culture. Considered by many to be 'simple-minded', he was known for his naive antics and for producing poetry which contained 'neither sense nor metre nor rhyme'.[90] A kinder critic would note that he composed some humorous rhymes which became so popular that they entered into oral tradition, earning him an enduring place in the folklore of north Wales. The short verse praising the *Alabama* can in fact be considered as one of his better compositions (although, characteristic of the ignorance which would make his name a by-word in Wales for shoddy verse, he called this composition an *englyn* even though it does not follow the rules of that strict metre).

Englyn i'r Alabama gan y Bardd Cocos

Mae'r Alabama hyd y tona,
Fel cath yn nhraed ei sana,
Yn dwfflo ac yn dafflo'r llonga,
Yn eu watchio a'u catchio ar eu siwrna,
A dau gylch gogor un bob ochor,
Yn rhwygo'r lli, a ffwrdd â hi.[91]

'An *Englyn* to the Alabama by the Bardd Cocos

The Alabama is all over the waves,
Like a cat in its stocking feet,
Duffeling and daffeling the ships,
Watching them and catching them while they travel,
With two sieve circles, one on either side [i.e. the ship's swirling wake?],
Tearing the sea, and away she goes.'

At some time after the *Alabama*'s demise another Welsh poet praised her in verse, romanticizing the ship's voyages in a ballad which was printed and most likely sold in fairs and other public gatherings.

Roedd ynddi fechgyn Cymru, rhai dewis o Ynys Fôn,
 Ac hefyd rhai o Arfon yn hwylus ar frig y don.
A mawr a fu'r llawenydd eu gweld gan fam a thad . . .
 Wel, diwedd a ddaeth arni, ei hamser ddaeth i ben.
Ni chlywir mwy mo'i gynnau fel t'rannau'n dod i'r nen,
 A'i shels fel mellt yn hollti pob peth a ddaeth o'r blaen
Nes iddi gwrdd a'r 'Kearsage' a'i gynnau mawr a'i thân.[92]

'There were within her boys from Wales, some select ones from Anglesey,
 And also some from Arfon, easily [sailing] upon the crest of the wave.
And great was the joy of mother and father at seeing them . . .
 Well, she came to be finished, her time was up.
No more will her guns be heard, like thunder coming from heaven,
 With her shells like lightning splitting everything which came before [her]
Until she met with the "Kearsage" with her big guns and her fire.'

This ballad, together with David Llewelyn's obituary and the verse by Y Bardd Cocos, is one of a trio of texts glorifying the adventures of the *Alabama*. Two of them, it should be stressed, make specific reference to the fact that Welshmen served on the ship. Remembering that Stanley wrote in English, these writings about the *Alabama* provide rare examples of Welsh texts written from a Confederate perspective. It is safe to assume that a detailed study of Confederate sailors recruited in British ports would turn up more Welshmen, ones who – unlike Samuel Roberts and those four other men from north Wales – enlisted of their own free will. Whatever the actual number of Welshmen serving on Confederate ships, they have left no known literary record other than these three texts.

It must be noted that the normal bounds of this study have been exceeded in order to include the literature of the *C. S. S. Alabama* here. This book is otherwise concerned with Welsh writing stemming directly from the American Civil War, that is with texts written by Welsh-speaking Americans who lived through the war. Moreover, almost all the print sources analysed in this study were published in the United States; other than these three exceptions, the only texts published in Wales included here are letters which Welsh immigrants sent back from America or articles reprinted from Welsh-American publications which have not otherwise survived. A study of the Welsh press and the American Civil War is in itself a complicated and fascinating subject, but one which lies beyond the scope of this book. Quoting these three texts in isolation in fact gives a false impression as to the ways in which Welsh writers reacted to the American Civil War. As was noted above, while Welsh (-British) publications were not subject to the same ideological pressures as the Welsh-American press, and while some editors and writers in the Old Country were extremely critical of Lincoln's war aims, the majority of the Welsh press was solidly anti-slavery, and many publications were also markedly pro-Union.

Unless the anonymous ballad monger turns out to have been a Confederate sailor (highly unlikely given the fact that he does not use the first person in discussing the ship's crew), then we can conclude that, in addition to being published in Wales, all three of these texts were composed by Welsh writers who had no direct experience of the war. Significantly, all three are devoid of ideological interpretations of the conflict; they praise the valour of the ship's crew while saying nothing about the reasons why those Confederate sailors were fighting. David Llewelyn is lauded for fulfilling his 'duty' (*dyledswydd*), yet the writer is silent regarding the cause or causes which the doctor was serving by performing that duty. It is the adventure of military service which is of main concern, and in that respect the Welsh literature of the *Alabama* resembles the main thrust of Stanley's writings.

Except for Stanley's English-language *Autobiography*, it is difficult to give voices to the handful of Welsh Confederates uncovered by present research. While Humphrey Pierce offers us a brief encounter with that Confederate officer named Lewis, we do not know his reasons for fighting, his history, or even his first name. We can consider David Jenkins – who died 'in his blood' in Virginia while wearing a Rebel uniform – through the lens provided by his father's apologetic elegy, yet this tells us very little about the views which David himself held. Similarly, we can view the exploits of the *Alabama*'s sailors from the second-hand remove provided by two romantic poems composed and published in Wales, yet this tells us nothing about how Samuel Roberts of Caernarfon felt when he agreed to serve on the Confederate ship or when he later decided to escape from that enforced service. If the Welsh-language press of the United States was used to bring subversive moles out into the light of public scrutiny, the history of those few Welshmen who did serve the Confederacy remains for the most part in the dark.

NOTES

1 The paper was *Baner ac Amserau Cymru*. See Jerry Hunter, *Llwch Cenhedloedd* [:] *Y Cymry a Rhyfel Cartref America* (Llanrwst, 2003), pp. 62–4.

2 *Y Drych*, 9 May 1863.

3 *Y Drych*, 4 April 1863.

4 James M. McPherson, *Battle Cry of Freedom* [:] *The American Civil War* (Oxford, 1988), p. 494, note 8.

5 *Y Drych*, 25 July 1863.

6 *Y Drych*, 18 July 1863.

7 Ibid.

8 *Y Drych*, 4 April 1863.
9 *Y Drych*, 23 May 1863.
10 *Y Drych*, 9 May 1863.
11 *Y Drych*, 4 April 1863.
12 Ibid.
13 Ibid.
14 *Geiriadur Prifysgol Cymru* (Cardiff, 1950–2002), p. 3371.
15 *Y Drych*, 4 April 1863.
16 Ibid.
17 James McPherson, *Battle Cry of Freedom*, p. 561.
18 Paul D. Evans, 'The Welsh in Oneida County, New York' (MA thesis: Cornell University, 1914). Published online by Siloam Road Enterprises (2001): *http://members.aol.com.siloamroad/oneidawelsh.*
19 This editorial was originally published in an edition of *Y Drych* which is not extant; it was reprinted in *Baner ac Amserau Cymru*, 12 November 1862.
20 John Edwards (Eos Glan Twrch), *Llais o'r Llwyn; sef Barddoniaeth ar Amryfal Destynau* (Utica, 1854). Evan E. Roberts of 2 Heol Seneca (Seneca Street), Utica, is listed as the printer.
21 Evan Roberts and Eos Glan Twrch had also worked together on another abortive paper, *Haul Gomer* (Gomer's Sun), which ran to eighteen numbers between December 1847 and September 1848.
22 *Y Drych*, reprinted in *Baner ac Amserau Cymru*, 12 November 1862.
23 Ibid.
24 *Yr Arweinydd*, 25 February 1858. The piece was signed 'J. Edwards (Eos Glan Twrch)'.
25 It seems that Eos Glan Twrch otherwise earned his living by farming; his home in Oneida County was described as a *tyddyn*, a 'small holding'. It thus appears that he was a farmer of modest means and that he turned towards the press in an attempt to supplement his income. See R. D. Thomas, *Cyflawn Olygfa ar Gymry America* (Utica, 1872), p. 153.
26 See note 21 above.
27 The phrase 'at least two and possibly three' refers to the fact that the identity of the anonymous poet who called himself 'Sant y Dyddiau Diwethaf' is not known.
28 *Y Drych*, 4 July 1863.
29 Both words translated here as 'ground', *gro* and *graian*, can be rendered more literally as 'gravel' or 'coarse sand'. Since at least the Middle Ages they have been used by poets to refer to 'ground' or 'earth', specifically in the case of elegies (referring to the deceased being buried in the ground).
30 *Y Drych*, 18 July 1863: 'Englynion Gwahodd "Ieuan Ddu" ar Ddydd Cymanfa Floyd, Meh. 22, 1863 (by the poet 'Ab Morydd', followed by:) "Eto" gan E.G.T'. See also *Y Drych*, 8 August 1863, 'Englyn Byrfyfyr Pan oedd Ieuan Ddu ar ei daeth yn Floyd, yr haf hwn, ac yn aros dros noson gyda'r "Eos".'
31 *Y Drych*, 4 April 1863.
32 James McPherson, *Battle Cry of Freedom*, pp. 492–3.
33 *Y Drych*, 10 January 1863.
34 Ibid.
35 *Y Drych*, 21 March 1863.
36 Ibid.
37 *Y Drych*, 25 April 1863.

38 Ibid.
39 Ibid.
40 National Library of Wales Manuscript 22421D.
41 Ibid.
42 Ibid.
43 *Y Drych*, 24 January 1863. Owen Griffiths, captain of the 22nd Wisconsin's Welsh Company, 'the Cambrian Guards', published his own short notice in *Y Drych* publicizing the names of these same three men.
44 *Y Drych*, 24 January 1863.
45 Alice Fahs, *The Imagined Civil War* [:] *Popular Literature of the North and South 1861–1865* (Chapel Hill and London, 2001), p. 121.
46 *Y Drych*, 24 January 1863.
47 See Anne Kelly Knowles, *Calvinists Incorporated* [:] *Welsh Immigrants on Ohio's Industrial Frontier* (Chicago and London, 1997), p. 4.
48 Dean B. Mahin, *The Blessed Place of Freedom* (Washington, 2002), p. 85.
49 James McPherson, *Battle Cry of Freedom*, p. 285.
50 *Y Seren Orllewinol*, June 1861.
51 While one might read this as a description of the way in which a peacetime copper foundry was turned into a facility for producing Confederate guns, the word [*m*]*agnelfa* used here means 'battery'; the writer is apparently saying that, during the chaos of April 1861 when Union troops marching through Baltimore were attacked, the foundry building was used to house – or as an emplacement for – Secessionist guns. The important thing is that the foundry's community of workers, engulfed by the owners' anti-Union sentiments, forced the Welshmen to either flee in secrecy or remain in a state of confinement. And the specific experience of those Welsh workers is extended to described the fate of Maryland's Welsh population in general.
52 *Seren Cymru*, 24 May 1861.
53 *Y Cyfaill o'r Hen Wlad*, July 1864.
54 William Pierce letter, collection of Gareth Griffith. It was also published in T. Alun Williams, *Atgofion Uncle Tomos* (Caernarfon, 1997).
55 *Y Drych*, 18 April 1863.
56 Ibid.
57 For a detailed treatment of this subject, see Wilbur S. Shepperson, *Samuel Roberts* [:] *a Welsh Colonizer in Civil War Tennessee* (Knoxville, 1961).
58 See Chapter One, pages 31–4.
59 *Y Cenhadwr Americanaidd*, October 1861. This same piece was also published in *Y Cronicl*.
60 Ibid.
61 Cadwgan's poem was sent by Samuel Roberts for publication in *Y Drych*, perhaps as a conscious move intended to demonstrate his community's continued support for Lincoln and the Union. Although it did not appear until 1863, S. R.'s note suggests that it was composed much earlier.
62 Ibid.
63 *Y Cenhadwr Americanaidd*, September 1861.
64 *Y Cenhadwr Americanaidd*, June 1861.
65 Ibid.
66 *Y Drych*, 23 November 1865.
67 Samuel Roberts, *Crynodeb o Helyntion Bywyd S. R.* (Y Bala, 1875).

68 *Y Drych*, 31 January 1863.
69 Robert Roser, 'Give them Cold Steel: The Welsh in the Civil War', *Cambria* (October, 1998), 11.
70 Ella Lonn, *Foreigners in the Confederacy* (Chapel Hill, 1940), p. 198.
71 For a detailed discussion of the complex sides of Stanley's character, see Emyr Wyn Jones, *Sir Henry M. Stanley: The Enigma* (Denbigh, 1989) and John Bierman, *Dark Safari: The Life Behind the Legend of Henry Morton Stanley* (New York, 1990).
72 The book did not appear in print until five years after Stanley's death, and the final version was heavily edited by his wife; Henry Morton Stanley, *The Autobiography of Sir Henry Morton Stanley*, (ed.) Dorothy T. Stanley (New York, 1909).
73 Nathaniel Cheairs Hughes, Jr. (ed.), *Sir Henry Morton Stanley* [:] *Confederate* (Baton Rouge, 2000), p. 148. This text contains the portion of Stanley's *Autobiography* dealing with the Civil War.
74 *Sir Henry Morton Stanley* [:] *Confederate*, pp. 148–9.
75 *Sir Henry Morton Stanley* [:] *Confederate*, p. 97.
76 Emyr Wyn Jones, *Sir Henry M. Stanley: The Enigma*, p. 128.
77 Ibid.
78 *Y Cyfaill o'r Hen Wlad*, March 1865.
79 Ibid.
80 Ibid.
81 Ibid.
82 D. Hugh Matthews, 'Bedyddwyr Cymraeg a Chaethwasiaeth', *Y Traethodydd* (April, 2004).
83 See 'When Liverpool Was Dixie', www.csa-dixie.com/liverpool_dixie/alabama.htm.
84 The *Alabama* was originally named the *Enrica*; Dean B. Mahin, *One War at a Time* [:] *The International Dimensions of the American Civil War* (Washington, 1999), p. 146.
85 See T. Meirion Hughes, 'Sam yr Alabama', *Caernarfon 2000* (Caernarfon, 2000).
86 Ibid.
87 *The Caernarfon Herald*, 21 April 1916.
88 See T. Meirion Hughes, 'Sam yr Alabama'.
89 *Yr Herald*, 9 July 1864.
90 *Y Bywgraffiadur Cymreig Hyd 1940* (London, 1953), John Edward Lloyd, R. T. Jenkins and William Llewelyn Davies (eds.), p. 229: 'hanfod y peth yw bod y 'bardd' bron yn gwbl anllythrennog, ac na bo na synnwyr na mydr nac odl yn ei waith. Yn wir, prin ei fod yn "llawn llathen".'
91 *Yr Herald*, 5 September 1863.
92 Ben Bowen Thomas, *Drych y Baledwr* (Llandysul, 1958), p. 53.

Part Three

Writing War, Writing Peace

7

Writing on the Home Front

In the spring of 1863 Harry H. Davis brought his paintings to Pennsylvania. The young Welsh-American artist, recently released from service in the Union army for medical reasons, was touring the North with an ambitious panorama depicting the Civil War. Having experienced the war as a soldier, Davis was now taking his artistic representation of the conflict to the doorsteps of civilians in the North.[1] *Y Seren Orllewinol* – published in Pottsville, Pennsylvania – urged readers to support the artist.

> Mae ein cydwladwr ieuang Harry H. Davis wedi ei ryddhau yn anrhydeddus o'r fyddin, oherwydd diffyg iechyd, yn awr yn arddangos ei ddarluniau o'r gwrthryfel yn y swydd hon. Gan fod y brwdyrau diweddaraf wedi eu hychwanegu at *y panorama*, mae yr adran hanesyddol yn cael ei gadael allan yn bresennol, canys byddai dangos y cwbl yn cymeryd gormod o amser; ac felly y mae y dyddordeb yn cynyddu, a phawb yn ymdyru i'w weled. Yr ydym eisoes wedi dangos y gymeradwyaeth a dderbynia gan y rhai a'i gwelsant, a chan ei fod Mr. Davis yn debyg o ymweled ag amryw o'r sefydlfeydd Cymreig yn y dalaeth hon, hyderwn y bydd i'r Cymry yn gyffredinol beth bynag ei gefnogi â'u presenoldeb, a sicrhawn na na [sic] bydd yn edifar ganddynt, ac na byddant yn ystyried gorchestwaith y bachgen o sir Fynwy yn un dianrhydedd iddynt fel cenedl.[2]

> 'Our young fellow-countryman Harry H. Davis, released honourably from the army because of failing health, is now displaying his pictures of the rebellion in this county. As the most recent battles have been added to the panorama, the historical section has been left out at present, for showing the whole would take too much time; and thus interest is increasing, and everybody is thronging to see it. We have already attested to the approval which he has received from those who have seen it, and since Mr. Davis is likely to visit a number of the Welsh settlements in this state, we are confident that the Welsh in general will support him with their presence, and we assure them that they will not regret it, and that they will not consider the masterpiece by the boy from Monmouthshire to be one which does them dishonour as a nation.'

Painting is an art which should be able to transcend the boundaries of language, ethnicity and nationality. However, in his praise of Harry Davis's work the *Seren*'s editor refers repeatedly to the Welshness of both artist and (potential) audience. Davis is described as *ein cydwladwr*, 'our fellow countryman', and the editor assures his readers that the Welsh artist's work will uphold their honour *fel cenedl*, 'as a nation', and that [*y*] *Cymry yn gyffredinol*, 'the Welsh in general', will support the artist's tour by turning out to view the panorama. Apparently counting on the patronage of his 'fellow countrymen', Harry Davis ensured that his tour stops included a number of Pennsylvania's *sefydlfeydd Cymreig* or 'Welsh settlements'. While Davis's artwork was presumably viewed by other Northerners during (and perhaps after) the war, the editor of this Welsh-language journal describes the work as one Welshman's attempt to bring an illustration of the war home to Welsh-speaking civilians in the North.

If Harry H. Davis used painting to bring the war home to Welsh-American civilians, the Welsh-American press had been doing the same thing with words since the start of the conflict. In addition to more prosaic news items describing battles and troop movements, readers were at times provided with bardic meditations on specific engagements, such as Ieuan Ddu's *englyn* on Chickamauga, referred to by the poet in his preface as 'y frwydr waedlyd yn Georgia Ogleddol rhwng Bragg a Rosecrans', 'the bloody battle in Northern Georgia between Bragg and Rosecrans':[3]

Afradwr farch coch ddifrada! – sathrwyd
  Ar faes uthr yr aerfa
 Lawer dewr o'n milwyr da
 Yn agos i Chattanooga

'The wasteful red horse destroys! – trampled
  On the awful field of struggle
 Were many a brave one of our good soldiers
 Near to Chattanooga.'

While civilian writers and poets used poetry and prose to interpret recent military events, the Welsh-American press also published a range of material which reflected the war's effect upon civilian life. The feelings and concerns of the Welsh communities living in the North's 'front line cities' were expressed at length; for example, when two Confederate armies pushed north threatening Pennsylvania and Ohio during the autumn of 1862, the editor of *Y Seren Orllewinol* addressed what he called 'Y Teimlad Cartrefol', 'The Feeling at Home'.[4]

> Y mae dynesiad y gelyn i'n gororau wedi enyn gwladgarwch pleidwyr yr Undeb yn fflam angherddol trwy y wlad. Y mae y cwmwl a ganfyddid gynt yn mhell, yn awr yn dechreu ymdaenu uwch ein penau, a phawb yn dyfod yn ystyriol o'r perygl ydym ynddo, ac yn ymysgwyd o'r llwch, mewn modd difrifol a chyffredinol.[5]

> 'The enemy's advance to our borders has fanned the patriotism of the Union's supporters into a passionate flame throughout the land. The cloud which was

perceived from afar before is now starting to spread over our heads, and everyone is becoming aware of the danger we are in, [all are] bestirring themselves from the dust in a serious and general manner.'

Fear grew at this time that Washington would be attacked, and an anonymous correspondent in that city conveyed his or her impressions to the readers of *Y Cenhadwr Americanaidd*.

> Mae yr wythnos hon wedi bod yn un o gyffröad a phryder mawr yn y brif ddinas, ac mae yn rhaid ei bod felly dros yr holl wlad. Ond yr ydym yn teimlo pobpeth cysylltiedig â'r rhyfel yn ddwysach yma nag yn y wlad. Mae rhyfel yn golygu rhywbeth arswydus yma. Yr ydym yn clywed rhuad y cyflegrau pa fo yr ymladd yn ymgreuloni. Y clwyfedigion a ddygir yma wrth y miloedd at ein drysau, ychydig oriau wedi i'r maes gael ei enill neu ei golli. . . . I unrhyw un nad yw ei galon wedi ei gwneyd megys o haiarn, y mae yn lle difrifol. Mae dirboenau y wladwriaeth i'w gweled a'u teimlo megys yn ei chalon – yma.[6]
>
> 'This week has been one of great agitations and concern in the capital city, and it must be thus throughout the entire country. Yet we feel that everything connected with the war is somehow more serious here than it is in the countryside. We hear the roar of the cannon when the fighting grows fierce. The wounded are brought here by the thousands to our doors, a few hours after the field has been won or lost. . . . To anybody whose heart is not made as if of iron, it is a serious place. The tortures of the country are to be seen and felt in its heart – here.'

And in October 1862 the same journal published a piece by the Revd Thomas Edwards of Cincinnati, voicing the fears of that city's Welsh population.

> Yr ydym yn credu i raddau helaeth y treiant feddiannu y ddinas gyfoethog hon. Mae Cincinnati, Covington, a Newport o dan y gyfraith filwrol, ac y mae pob dyn galluog i wisgo arfau yn y lleoedd uchod wedi ei galw allan. . . . Mae y Cymry dan arfau yn y lleoedd a enwyd, a meddylir y codir ugain mil o filwyr o bob cenedl, yn Cincinnati.[7]
>
> 'We for the most part believe that they [e.g. the Confederate army in Kentucky] will try to take possession of this wealthy city. Cincinnati, Covington and Newport are under martial law, and every man who can bear arms in the places noted above has been called out. . . . The Welsh are under arms in the places named, and it is thought that twenty thousand soldiers of every nation will be raised in Cincinnati.'

Once a vehicle for spreading the beliefs of the Peace Movement throughout Welsh America, *Y Cenhadwr Americanaidd* was now acknowledging the fact that a large portion of its readers were under arms. The *Cenhadwr*'s editor, Robert Everett, also published a dramatic letter which his daughter-in-law Sarah had sent from Kansas.

> Boreu ddoe cawsom gryn ddychryn. Rhwng 4 a 5 yn y boreu . . . daeth Charley Mendanhall, bachgen i un o'r Crynwyr tua 12 oed, i mewn i'r ty . . . a deffrodd ni gan waeddi yn frawychus, 'O Sarah! Sarah! mae arnaf eisiau dweud rhywbeth wrthych. . . . Mae y rebels wedi gnweud ruthriad i'r dalaeth – wedi cymeryd yr arfau oedd yn Olathe . . . wedi lladd rhywun – cymeryd Shipley, y *recruiting officer*, yn garcharwr.' . . . Cododd fy mhriod a brysiodd un ffordd, a minau ffordd arall, i geisio rhybuddio y cymydogion; ond deallasom cyn y nos nad oedd dim perygl uniongyrchol.[8]

> 'Yesterday morning we got quite a fright. Between 4 and 5 in the morning . . . Charley Mendanhall, a boy of one of the Quakers about 12 years old, came into the house . . . and he woke us up, calling fearfully, "Oh Sarah! Sarah! I have to tell you something. . . . The rebels have made an attack on the state – they have taken the arms which were in Olathe . . . they've killed somebody – [and] taken Shipley, the recruiting officer, as a prisoner." . . . My husband got up and hurried off in one direction, and I went in the other, in order to try to warn the neighbours; but we came to understand before the night that there was no immediate danger.'

Having used correspondence from the Kansas branch of the Everett family to provide readers with a personal view of 'bleeding Kansas' a few years before the war, Robert Everett now used Sarah Everett's letter in order to give them a taste of the precarious circumstances which the Civil War had brought to the civilians of that state.

Of course, not everybody was affected by the war in equal measures. Some surviving manuscript diaries and letters written by Welsh-American farmers in New York and Ohio, for example, suggest that they were more concerned with the weather and the yield of their crops than with the events unfolding on Southern battlefields. One Welsh civilian from Oneida County, Robert Pugh of Pen-y-graig, published a poem in *Y Cyfaill o'r Hen Wlad* describing 'The Influence of the War' ('Dylanwad y Rhyfel'), ordering the forces of industry to stand still and take stock of the conflict.

> O sefwch olwynion masnachau,
> A'r holl wyllt elfennau yn lân
> Dystewi eich twrf a ddymunwyf,
> Tra byddwyf yn traethu fy nghân.[9]

> 'O stand still the wheels of business,
> And all the wild elements
> Silencing your noise is what I desire,
> While I present my song.'

In reality, the wheels of the North's industry did anything but stand still during the war, and growing numbers of Welsh workers contributed to the Union's war-time economy. While some historians have assumed that the Civil War slowed emigration from Wales to the United States, recent research by Huw Griffiths has proven conclusively that the opposite was in fact true: 'Welsh migration to the United States actually increased during the Civil War.'[10] Despite attempts by the press in Wales to discourage emigration, the labour-hungry Northern states succeeded in attracting growing numbers of workers from the coalfields and iron furnaces of South Wales.[11]

This aspect of war-time Welsh America is also chronicled in detail on the pages of the country's Welsh-language press. One anonymous writer attempted to divert *Y Cenhadwr Americanaidd*'s readers from the horrors of war by praising what he called 'Our Mineral Wealth' ('Ein Cyfoeth Mwnawl').

> Mae swn y rhyfel a'i drallodion alaethus bron yn boddi pob swn arall, bydded mor hyfryd a dymunol ag y byddo. Ond ni byddai niwed i ni sylwi ychydig ar bethau eraill. . . . erbyn hyn ceir fod mwn aur a mwnau gwerfawr eraill yn cael eu cloddio ar lanau pob afon bron ag a red i'r Missouri, i'r Colorado a'r Columbia[.][12]

> 'The sound of war with its sorrowful tribulations is nearly drowning every other sound, however nice and desirable it may be. Yet it would do no harm for us to take a little note of other things. . . . by now it is learned that gold ore and other kinds of valuable ore are being mined on the banks of nearly every river which runs into the Missouri, the Colorado and the Columbia.'

Considerable numbers of Welsh workers did join the western gold rush.[13] However, the vast majority of these new immigrants found work in the North's coalfields. A writer using the pen-name 'Coal Digger' published a letter in *Y Drych* in January 1863 describing the situation in Coal Valley, Illinois: 'Cymry ydyw y rhan luosocaf o breswylwyr y lle hwn, a'r glo ydyw ein prif nwydd masnachol'; 'The Welsh are the greater part of the inhabitants of this place, and coal is our main commercial commodity.'[14] He concludes his letter by describing the cultural life of Coal Valley's Welsh miners: 'Mae llenyddiaeth yn ein plith fel pe byddai yn blaguro, Dirwest yn codi ei phen, a chrefydd yn ei blodeu'; 'Literature among us appears to be growing, Temperance is raising its head, and religion is in flower.'[15]

In the same edition of *Y Drych*, Joseph Prosser of Minersville, Pennsylvania, described the influx of Welsh workers into his community: 'Mae y gymdogaeth mor llawn o ddynion ag y gwelais hi erioed, o herwydd dyfodiad cynifer o ddyeithriaid i'r lle – y rhan fwyaf o Gymry, wedi tirio yn ddiweddar o'r Hen Wlad; 'this area is as full of men as I ever saw it before, because of the coming of so many newcomers to the place – the majority of them Welsh, recently landed from the Old Country.'[16] If the temperance movement was 'raising its head' among Coal Valley's Welsh miners, Joseph Prosser suggested that economic, rather than moral concerns, were keeping Minersville's Welsh workers sober: 'Clywais gyfaill i mi yn dweyd fod y cwrw wedi codi yn 15 sent y chwart. Ah! Rhaid byw yn sobr bellach, pe bae dim ond o ran *spite*'; 'I heard one of my friends say that beer has gone up to 15 cents a quart. Ah! Must live sober now, if only out of spite'.[17] However, while many new immigrants came to work in the coal fields, Prosser also noted that a considerable number of Minersville's men had left the mines for the army: 'Gofidus genyf ddweyd fod aml un o'r dref a'r gymydogaeth wedi cael beddrod milwr a lluaws wedi eu clwyfo . . . O, Amerig! Daeth y farn arnynt yn ddiau'; 'It is sad for me to say that many from this town and region have received a soldier's grave and that many have been injured . . . Oh, America! Your judgement is surely upon you.'[18] Unlike Coal Digger's boast that literature was flourishing among Illinois's Welsh miners, Joseph Prosser remarked in passing that 'there was nothing outstanding here in the literary circle last Christmas' ('Ni fu dim neillduol yma yn y cylch llenyddol ddydd Nadolig diweddaf').[19]

THE WAR AND THE *EISTEDDFOD*

Indeed, the Civil War had an immediate effect upon that most public expression of Welsh literary culture, the *eisteddfod*. California's annual gathering was held in North San Juan on 4 July 1861, less than three months after the start of the war. The subjects for the literary competitions had been set before the fall of Fort Sumter, and included titles such as 'twelve stanzas to George Washington' ('deuddeg pennill i George Washington'). Despite this fact, one contestant – Sam ab Dewi of Port Wein, Sierra County, California – moulded the subject to fit his own bardic agenda, bringing it to bear upon the present conflict.[20] After devoting the first half of his composition to George Washington, he turned his final six stanzas to a discussion of the Civil War, complaining that the democracy established under Washington was now being undermined: 'Gresynol fod bradwyr am blanu unbenaeth, / Trwy ddichell a gormes ar weryd gwlad rydd' ('It's a pity that traitors would plant a dictatorship / By means of treachery and oppression in the soil of a free country').[21] Ignoring (or perhaps ignorant of) the fact that Washington himself owned slaves, the poet moves from the Revolutionary hero's struggle against England to the newly initiated war between the Union and the Southern 'slave masters':

Banerau caethiwed trwy drais am lywyddu,
 'Gael bwrw teml Rhyddid uchelwych i'r llawr;
Ymroddant i dori y fodrwy undebawl,
 Fe rua magnelau, mae'r cleddyf yn noeth,
Pa beth yw dechreuad y stormydd aruthrawl?
 Anghofio cynghorion ein Washington doeth.[22]

'The banners of slavery by violence would rule,
 And pull the temple of noble Freedom to the ground;

They strive to break the union ring,
  The cannons roar, and the sword is naked,
What was the start of the awesome storms?
  Forgetting the councils of our wise Washington.'

Sam ab Dewi then elaborates on his interpretation of the war, praising the 'thousands' ('[m]iloedd') who answer Lincoln's call to arms, rushing to place 'offerings at the altar of patriotism' ('ebyrth at allor gwladgarwch').[23] The final verse addresses a personified Union directly, willing a return of the stars which the Confederates had removed from the United States flag.

Undeb, O Undeb, i'r lan a'th fanerau,
  Mae'r byd yn blodeuo yn llewyrch dy sêr;
Pwy feiddia anharddu gorchestwaith ein tadau
  Sy 'nawr yn ymorphwys yn mynwes eu Ner?
Gwobrwyau cyfiawnder trysorfa'n llywodraeth,
  Yr hyn sy ddyledus 'i ffurfwyr y brad;
Fe glywir pêr adsain y gair buddugoliaeth,
  Heb seren yn ddiffyg ar wybren fy ngwlad.[24]

'Union, Oh Union, up with your banners,
  The world is flourishing in the shine of your stars;
Who dares to disfigure the masterful work of our fathers
  Who now rest in the bosom of their Lord?
The rewards of justice from our government's treasure hoard,
  This is what is owed to the organizers of treachery;
The sweet echo of the word victory will be heard,
  Without one star missing from my country's firmament.'

While this poem begins as a paean of praise to George Washington, it ends in that same pro-Union and pro-war register which characterizes those Welsh recruiting songs discussed in Chapter Three.[25]

One poet who was not victorious in this California *eisteddfod* wrote to *Y Seren Orllewinol* in order to complain, criticizing the entire proceedings in addition to voicing indignation over the way in which he had been 'mistreated' by the poetry judges. Using the pen-name *Pererin*, 'Pilgrim', this disgruntled bard presented a negative view of the war's effects on the Welsh cultural festival, attributing what he saw as the *eisteddfod*'s failings to the presence of so many soldiers: 'Nid wyf yn beio neb ond rhai o swyddau, y *belts* a'r *regimental dresses*'; 'I do not blame anybody expect those holding offices, the belts and the regimental dresses'.[26] Since the middle of the 1850s American *eisteddfodau* had been sites of conflict between the temperance movement and those Welsh-Americans who enjoyed a drink with their poetry. This 'Pilgrim' from California complained bitterly about the soldiers who tipped the balance of power in favour of the latter, noting that 'the men of uniform' ('[g]wyr yr *uniform*') who attended the *eisteddfod* indulged in 'feasting . . . drinking and . . . getting drunk' ('gwledda . . . yfed a . . . meddwi').[27]

Utica's first war-time *eisteddfod* was held on 1 January 1862. As if competing consciously with the distraction of war, the organizers placed advertisements in the Welsh-American press assuring readers that the occasion would be a memorable one.

> Gwneir darpariadau mawrion ar gyfer yr wyl . . . nid yw y pwyllgor wedi arbed traul a thrafferth er gwneud yr Eisteddfod eleni i ragori ar ei rhagflaenyddion mewn dyddordeb a daioni cyffredinol, a sicrheir gwledd i bawb a ddeuant iddi.[28]
>
> 'Great preparations are being made for the festival . . . the committee has spared no expense and trouble in order to ensure that the Eisteddfod this year exceeds its predecessors in interest and general good, and all who come are ensured a feast.'

Moreover, several aspects of the event seem to have been designed to meet the patriotic expectations of the time. The festival's president was the Revd Robert Littler, an influential Baptist minister from the area who had enlisted as a chaplain with the 74th New York Infantry. The *eisteddfod* hall was decorated with 'two beautiful American flags' ('dwy faner Americanaidd hardd') in addition to 'two mistletoe plants from Wales' ('dau uchelwydd o Gymry').[29]

The proceedings were opened by a popular Welsh-American bard, 'Callestr' Roberts, and the poem which he recited in praise of the *eisteddfod* and its president was deemed fit to print.[30] According to one published report, the organizers who had 'spared no expense and trouble' were not disappointed: 'Yr oedd y neuadd wedi eu llenwi â Chymry hardd a chalonog; 'The hall was filled with beautiful and hearty Welsh people.'[31] However, not everybody agreed that the event was a success. Eos Glan Twrch, an enthusiastic supporter of Utica's *eisteddfod* since the festival's inception, felt that the war had undermined the cultural celebration. Chapter One, it will be remembered, opened by discussing the *englyn* which he composed on this theme:

> Llonyddodd ein llenyddiaeth – a rhyfel
> Arafodd Farddoniaeth,
> Diwrnod Eisteddfod os daeth,
> Mae hwn i mi'n amheuaeth.[32]
>
> 'Our literature has grown still – and war
> Has slowed the pace of poetry,
> If the *Eisteddfod* day has come,
> This is for me an uncertainty.'

As these lines sit so uneasily with the report that the hall was 'filled' with 'hearty' people, it is hard to know exactly what the atmosphere was really like in Utica on 1 January 1862. Despite claims to the contrary, Eos Glan Twrch's sombre assessment must have contained more than a grain of truth: when the committee met the following September to plan the next year's event it was decided that, because of the war, Utica would have no *eisteddfod* at all in 1863.

When January 1863 came, a writer describing himself as 'one of her [or its] sons' ('un o'i meibion'), published a piece in *Y Drych*'s obituary column.[33] He employed all the trappings of a real obituary, starting with the formulaic title 'Bu Farw' – 'Deceased' or 'Died' – and proceeding to name the departed as 'Eisteddfod Utica.' Continuing the mock obituary, the place and time of death are given as 'Utica, Medi, 1862' ('Utica, Medi, 1862'). For the cause of death, the 'son' listed 'terror' (*arswyd*), describing it further as a fear of 'trusting America's Poets and Writers' ('ymddiried Beirdd a Llenorion America') to 'keep up' the *eisteddfod*'s 'ancient splendour' in the face of 'the effects of the present war upon the public's thoughts' ('i gadw i fynu ei gogoniant cyntefig . . . effeithiau y rhyfel presenol ar feddwl y cyhoedd').[34] As one might expect of a writer claiming to be an *eisteddfod*'s son, he included two *englyn* by way of an elegy.

Hunodd y dduwies heini – yn llawn nwyf,
    Llen y nos aeth drosti;
  O bair y byd sy'n berwi,
  Yn mro hedd marw yw hi.

Ei halawon mwyn 'leni a'i hawen,
    A'i hyawdl farddoni;
  A'i holynol ysgrifeni,
  Nid oes son na dystaw si.[35]

'The sturdy goddess has slept – full of energy,
    The shroud of night went over her;
  [Far] from the boiling cauldron of the world,
  She is dead in the land of peace.

'There is no mention nor quiet rumour this year
    Of her dear tunes, her *awen*,
  Her eloquent poetry and
  Her productive writings.'[36]

These verses provide a striking example of the way in which Welsh-American writers brought their ancient literary inheritance to bear upon war-time America. This Utica poet personifies the town's *eisteddfod*, describing her as a 'goddess' who has forsaken the world's 'boiling cauldron' for the peaceful slumber of death. The prose obituary accompanying this elegy expresses hope that this death is only temporary, and that she will soon be reborn: 'Gorph wysed enyd bach mewn llawn obaith o adgyfodiad mwy gogoneddus'; 'May she rest for a short while in full hope of a more glorious resurrection.'[37] While the word *adgyfodiad*, 'resurrection,' suggests a Christian image, the word [*d*]*uwies*, 'goddess,' ensures that the poem also occupies a different referential field as well. Medieval Welsh literature contains numerous references to the origins of *awen* or poetic inspiration, and this complex constellation of traditions includes the narrative of Taliesin, the archetypal Welsh bard. Taliesin's supernatural origins involve Ceridwen – often described as a 'witch', though also interpreted by nineteenth-century antiquarians as a 'goddess' – and her magic cauldron.[38] In addition to obtaining poetic knowledge from this cauldron, Taliesin gains the ability to transform himself physically and thus be reborn anew in every age.[39] Thus the 'goddess' of poetry described in these verses goes to the sleep of death 'full of energy' ('yn llawn nwyf'), ready for the *eisteddfod*'s phoenix-like resurrection from the ashes of Civil War.[40]

It is perhaps no surprise that Utica's *eisteddfod* committee decided that 'the present war's effects' were too much of a strain upon 'the public's thoughts'. They had met in September 1862, shortly after the Union's disastrous defeat in the Second Battle of Bull Run.[41] And, while the exact date of the meeting is not known, it is possible that it took place after the Battle of Antietam (17 September 1862), 'the bloodiest day' in American history. Whatever the exact circumstances surrounding the decision, Utica was the most important Welsh cultural centre in the United States, and the effect of the Civil War upon its *eisteddfod* is surely indicative of the deep way in which the conflict touched different parts of Welsh America.

Despite the temporary 'death' of Utica's *eisteddfod*, not all the country's festivals became casualties of war.[42] The Welsh of Fairhaven, Vermont, held their annual literary gathering on Christmas Day 1862, a week before Utica's residents were to mark with sadness the absence of their *eisteddfod*. Describing the event as 'Diwrnod Difyr' ('An Entertaining Day'), John E. Roberts, the Fairhaven festival's secretary, published a report in *Y Drych*. The 'entertaining' proceedings of the day, he claimed, were too numerous to recount in detail: 'Oni bai fod y papyr mor ddrud yn awr, a ninau yn bobl wylaidd yma, ac arnom ofn cymeryd gormod o'ch gofod, rhoisem adroddiad manwl o hanes ein gwyl Lenyddol'; 'If only paper were not so expensive now, and if we were not modest people here, afraid of taking up too much of your space, we would give a detailed report of the history of our Literary festival.'[43] However, Roberts did provide what he called a 'summary' ('[c]rynodeb') of the day's high points, listing the traditional Welsh songs which were performed and describing the various literary competitions.

While the organizers of the Utica *eisteddfod* felt that the pressures of war left them with no choice but to cancel the event, the Welsh people of Fairhaven reacted very differently, using their literary festival to inspire a series of reflections on various aspects of the conflict. One competition involved composing and delivering a speech on 'Patriotism' ('Gwladgarwch'), and John Roberts insisted that all of them were 'very good [and] worth publishing' ('da iawn; gwerth eu hargraffu').[44] For another competition, contestants had to compose 'extemporaneous speeches' ('Areithiau byrfyfyr') on the subject of Jefferson Davis, and these, the secretary insisted, were 'brilliant, considering the shortness of time in which they were composed' ('yn wych ac ystyried byrder yr amser i'w gwneyd'). R. O. Pritchard won the essay competition for a piece on 'Politics' ('Gwleidyddiaeth'), and the festival's secretary, John E. Roberts, won one of the poetry competitions by composing an *englyn* on the martial subject of 'Y Cleddyf', 'The Sword'.[45]

FEASTS, FAIRS AND BOXES

The war clearly affected different American *eisteddfodau* in different ways. Or, to rephrase the point, different Welsh-American communities reacted to the war in different ways; while some allowed the conflict to 'slow the pace of poetry', others used the war as a means of 'quickening' the literary resources of their community. Whatever the fate of various *eisteddfodau*, many other public celebrations went on as usual. As might be expected, explicitly patriotic events flourished in response to the challenges of war. For example, the Welsh Baptists of Pittston, Pennsylvania, held their Fourth of July 'Feast and Concert' ('Gwestfa a Chyngherdd') in 1863, and it was – according to the surviving print record – a memorable occasion. While 'recitals and singing' ('adrodd a chanu') took place inside the chapel, tables were set up in an adjacent yard; the preparations were said to 'display the taste, skill, and comeliness of the Welsh nation' ('arddangos chwaethusrwydd, medrusrwydd, a glanweithdra y genedl Gymreig'), and 'the Welsh ladies of Pittston' ('[b]oneddigesau Cymreig Pittston') were praised for their efforts in staging the event.[46]

In March 1863 one Welsh Sunday school in Nebo, Ohio, transformed its yearly 'competitive meeting' (*cyfarfod cystadleuol*) into a display of support for the Union's Welsh soldiers. As in years before the war, the 'young people' (*pobl ieuanc*) gathered to recite quotations from the Welsh Bible, debate points of Scripture, and perform 'old Welsh tunes' (*hen Alawon Cymreig*). However, the event was now being called 'Cwrdd y Milwyr Cymreig' ('The Welsh Soldier's Meeting').[47] The explicit link between the religious institution and the Union war effort was also manifest in the choice of guest speaker: the Revd Benjamin Chidlaw. Known for his energetic support of the Sunday School Movement before the war, Chidlaw was by 1863 famous throughout Welsh America for his work with the Union army; his experiences as chaplain with the 39th Ohio Infantry, his work as missionary among the soldiers, and his efforts on behalf of the Christian Commission had all been well publicized by the Welsh-American press.[48]

As the activities of Ben Chidlaw demonstrate, many of Welsh America's religious leaders drew upon the resources of their chapels and denominations in order to support the Christian Commission's work on behalf of Union soldiers. A great many Welsh-Americans also did volunteer work for the United States Sanitary Commission and the Women's Central Association of Relief, which together formed an impressive network of civilians 'which took much responsibility for the state of military hospitals and the health of the troops'.[49] According to James McPherson, the 'national officers and most of the five hundred paid agents of the Commission were men; most of the tens of thousands of volunteer workers were women'.[50] Separate Welsh-speaking branches of these national organizations were formed, and surviving records show that they were run almost entirely by women. The Welsh women of Remsen, in Oneida County, New York, published an account of their activities in *Y Cenhadwr Americanaidd* under the heading 'Cymdeithas er Cynorthwyo y Milwyr, y Claf a'r Clwyfus' ('the Society for Aiding the Soldiers, the Sick and the Injured').[51]

> Ffurfiwyd y gymdeithas hon yn Remsen, gan foneddigesau y Pentref a'r amgylchoedd. Trefnasant i ymgyfarfod yn wythnosol i barotoi defnyddiau, gwau a gwnio, ac er cael gwahanol bethau yn nghyd ac i drefn i'w danfon ymaith. Buont yn ymdrechgar a gweithiasant yn unfrydol, a llwyddiasant tu hwnt i'w disgwyliad, fel y gorphenasant un box, ac anfonwyd ef i Washington[.][52]

> 'This society was formed in Remsen by the ladies of the Village and the environs. They decided to gather together weekly to prepare materials, to knit and to sow, and to get various things together and organized for sending off. They have been dedicated and they have worked harmoniously, and they have succeeded beyond their expectations, so that they have finished one box and sent it to Washington.'

The box – which contained bandages, clothing and bed clothes – was sent to a Washington hospital. In addition to producing and posting these kinds of materials, the Welsh women of Remsen also collected money for the cause.[53] A sub-group within the society was formed by 'merched bychain Remsen o 10 i 15 ml oed,' 'the little girls of Remsen from 10 to 15 years old,' and they sent their own 'sypan bychan' or 'small package' to Washington, including twenty-three pairs of woollen mittens, eight towels and two sets of bed clothes.[54]

This local organization was formed along the pre-existing lines of the community's religious infrastructure, with the Remsen society acting as a network connecting a number of the area's Welsh-speaking chapels. While the differences between the different denominations were an extremely important part of nineteenth-century Welsh (and Welsh-American) religious culture, the work of these women ensured that they crossed those boundaries; the chapels of Ebenezer,

Sion, Peniel, Capel Ceryg and Pen y Graig are listed by name, proving that Calvinistic Methodists, Congregationalists and Baptists worked together in providing aid for the soldiers. However, it appears that the women of each chapel also had their own sub-committee. For example, the names of the Calvinistic Methodist women who comprised 'Pwyllgor Pen y Graig', 'The Committee of [the Chapel of] Pen y Graig', were also published: Mrs Jane Pugh, Mrs E. Salisbury, Miss Ann Jones and Miss Ellen Lewis. They were led by what seems to have been a mother-daughter team, with Mrs M. Griffiths acting as 'President' (*Llywyddes*) and Miss Sarah A. Griffiths taking on the role of 'Secretary' (*Ysgrifenyddes*).[55] As if to stress the ecumenical nature of the enterprise, the work of these Methodists was praised on the pages of the Congregationalists' journal, *Y Cenhadwr Americanaidd*.

Similarly, volunteers from one of Utica's Congregational chapels published a record of their proceedings in the non-denominational paper, *Y Drych*. Though living only a few miles from Remsen, these women formed their own separate society, described in print as 'Cymdeithas y Boneddigesau, Ail Eglwys Gynulleidfaol Utica at gynorthwyo milwyr afiach a chlwyfedig', 'The Ladies' Society, Second Congregationalist Church of Utica, for helping sick and injured soldiers'.[56] Jane Isaac, who described herself as the society's 'Treasurer' (*Trysores*), noted that they were working with the 'New York Sanitary Commission' ('[D]irpwyaeth Iechyddol New York').[57] In addition to collecting material which they sent to the Sanitary Commission's office, these women from Utica also sent clothing and food directly to the 26th New York Infantry, a regiment which included a number of Welsh volunteers from their area, providing yet another example of the close bonds which connected civilian communities with the soldiers recruited from among them.[58]

According to the diary of John H. Williams, the 'young women' of West Brattleboro, Vermont, sent a box of much appreciated food stuffs to the small group of Welsh soldiers who served together in the 14th Vermont Infantry.[59]

> Sul, Rhagfyr 7ed, 1862. . . . Yn yr hwyr daeth *Box* i ni yn anrheg oddiwrth ferched ieuainc West Brattleboro; yr oedd yn llawn o bob math o drugareddau, sef, ymenyn, caws, gwin, pies, tea, siwgr, cakes, penwaig cochion, a phob peth o'r defnyddiau goreu; ni welais erioed ferched mor garedig a'r rhai hyn.[60]

> 'Sunday, December 7th, 1862. . . . Tonight a Box came as a present from the young women of West Brattleboro; it was full of all kinds of delicacies, namely, butter, cheese, wine, pies, tea, sugar, cakes, herrings, and every thing of the best sort; I never saw women as kind as these.'

While such 'delicacies' were perhaps not as essential as the kinds of basic materials sent by women's groups to hospitals, they were nonetheless a sure way of boosting the soldiers' morale. For John Williams and his comrades, food was a potent manifestation of the civilian community's support, and he thus finished his diary entry by emphasizing the value of this culinary connection between the Northern state and the Southern army camp: 'Yr oedd yn dda cael tamaid o flasus fwyd Vermont yn Virginia ryfelgar'; 'It was good to get a bit of Vermont's tasty food in warlike Virginia.'[61]

Civilians found numerous ways of obtaining food, clothing and other needed goods for their men 'in warlike Virginia' and other Southern states. Welsh-Americans held their own versions of what Melinda Lawson calls 'Union love feast[s]', organizing fairs in order to boost the morale at home while simultaneously collecting money and goods to help the soldiers.[62] When the US Sanitary Commission organized its great national fair in Washington, DC, the Welsh of New York City held a meeting in order to co-ordinate their contribution to the event. They published a report in *Y Cyfaill o'r Hen Wlad*, holding their actions up as a model for the rest of Welsh America:

> Galwad ar Ddinasyddion Cymreig America.
>
> Ar Ran Ffair Brif Ddinasawl Cennadaeth Iechyddawl (Sanitary Commission) Y T. U. Dyben y Ffair yma yw cynnorthwyo ein milwyr, a fyddont yn dyoddef trwy glefyd neu glwyfau, yn achos amddiffyniad ein gwlad. Cymry gwladgarawl ac elusengarawl New York a alwasant gyfarfod . . . yn nghapel y Bedyddwyr Cymreig ar hëol Chrystie, Ion. 25ain diweddaf, i amlygu eu cydymdeimlad, a threfnu moddion i gydweithredu yn yr amcan haelfrydig.[63]
>
> 'A Call to America's Welsh Citizens.
>
> On Behalf of the Sanitary Commission of the United States's Capital City Fair. The purpose of this Fair is to assist our soldiers, who may suffer sickness or wounds, in the cause of our country's defence. The patriotic and charitable Welsh people of New York called a meeting . . . in the Welsh Baptists' chapel on Chrystie street, Jan. 25th the last, to express their sympathy, and to organize the means of cooperating in the generous endeavour.'

The journal's editor voiced his own support for what he called 'yr achos teilwng hwn', 'this worthy cause', urging other Welsh communities to hold their own meetings 'i gydweithredu â'n brodyr yn New York', 'in order to co-operate with our brothers in New York'.[64] His use of the word *brodyr*, 'brothers', is unfortunate, given all the evidence which testifies to the central roles played by women in planning and running these kinds of events.

While the *Cyfaill*'s editor ignored the Welsh 'sisters' of New York in his note, many other Welsh-Americans praised the charitable work of a host of Northern women. For example, one volunteer from Oneida County published a letter in *Y Cenhadwr Americanaidd* chronicling his journey through Philadelphia to Virginia.

> Gadawsom Ynys Staten y 12fed o'r mis diweddaf, a chyrhaeddasom Philadelphia am 12, y noson hono. Yno cawsom swper da yn y *Soldier's Refreshment Saloon.*

Cedwir y Saloon hwn gan foneddigesau Philadelphia, y rhai ydynt ar bob awr, ddydd a nos, yn barod i groesawu pob milwr o'r Undeb. Bydded i'r Arglwydd eu bendithio am eu caredigrwydd.[65]

'We left Staten Island on the 12th of the last month, and we reached Philadelphia at 12.00 that night. There we had a good supper in the Soldier's Refreshment Saloon. This Saloon is kept by the ladies of Philadelphia, who are ready at every hour, night and day, to welcome every soldier of the Union. May the Lord bless them for their kindness.'

Philadelphia was by no means the only city which could boast of such kindnesses. Following the disastrous battle of Fredericksburg, a writer whom *Y Drych* identified simply as 'ein Gohebydd yn y Brif Ddinas' – 'our Correspondent in the Capital City' – described the situation in Washington, DC

Yr ysbytai. – Yn y boreu, llawer o'r rhai oedd wedi eu clwyfo waethaf yn y frwydr ddiweddaf ger Fredericksbu[r]g a ddaeth i fewn i'r gwahanol ysbytai. Golygfa dor calonus dros ben . . . Amser ciniaw diwallwyd angenrhediau corphorol y clwyfedigion mewn tua deugain o ysbytai trwy giniaw ardderchog wedi ei ddarparu gan foneddigesau o wahanol ranau o'r wlad yn awr yn triganu yn Washington. Gweithred anghydmarol ydoedd hon; cydymdeimlad na welwyd ei fath mewn un wlad nac mewn un oes o'r byd – teimlad tuag at y rhai sydd mewn ystyr wedi ei halltudio oddicartref. Os y wlad a sudda i ebargofiant tragwyddol, y weithred hon a ddysgleiria, ac a fydd fel cof-adail am yr oesoedd dyfodol. Mynegiad perffaith rydd ydoedd o gydymdeimlad oddiwrth y rhai sydd yn caru lles dynoliaeth a rhyddid.[66]

'The hospitals. – In the morning, many of those who had been wounded worst in the recent battle near Fredericksburg came into the various hospitals. An extremely heartbreaking sight . . . At dinner time the bodily needs of the wounded were provided for in about forty hospitals in the form of a splendid lunch prepared by ladies from different parts of the country now residing in Washington. This was an unparalleled act; sympathy the likes of which has never been seen in any country or any of the world's ages – feeling for those who are in a sense exiled from home. If the country should sink to eternal oblivion, this act will shine, and it will remain as a monument for the future ages. It was a perfectly free expression of sympathy by those who love the good of humanity and freedom.'

During the dark days following Fredericksburg, many Northerners were contemplating what seemed like a very real possibility at the time – the possibility that they might in fact lose the war. The Welsh newspaper's Washington correspondent attempts to lighten the oppressive weight of defeat by trumpeting the moral triumph of the Union's women. Stressing the fact that they came to the Capital 'from all over the country', he emphasizes the connection between this group of women and the entire civilian population of the United States. Just as Northern soldiers were praised by the Welsh-American press for supporting 'freedom and Union', so Northern women were lauded for their commitment to 'the good of humanity and freedom'. This writer suggests that the powers of domesticity help ease the wound of defeat; the women's 'unparalleled' display of 'sympathy' is directed towards men who are 'exiled from home'. Even should the Union's men fail on the battlefield, the triumph of the country's women on the home front will 'shine' for all time.

RACHEL'S WEEPING

While Welsh-American women such as Sarah Griffiths of Remsen and Jane Isaac of Utica published unadorned records of their societies' charitable activities, *Y Drych*'s Washington correspondent presented readers with an interpretation of the meaning of that kind of volunteer work. Many of the country's Welsh-speaking women were also writers and poets who, like their male counterparts, put pen to paper in an attempt to interpret the war's effect upon their communities. They at times fulfilled the same literary roles as men, publishing patriotic songs and poems in support of the Union war effort. When a son was lost in the war, it was common for the father to publish a tribute in prose and/or verse, often signing the piece *y tad galarus*, 'the grieving father'. More than one *mam alarus* or 'grieving mother' also published a public expression of her family's grief. For example, Catherine Jones sent a prose piece to *Y Cenhadwr Americanaidd* describing the loss of her son, Lt Robert Williams of the 40th Iowa Infantry.[67] During the last months of 1864 Jane Jones lost both her sons, Josiah and Jonadab Jones of the 94th Illinois Infantry. She turned to verse, publishing an elegy in the *Cenhadwr*.[68] When John D. Jones of Jefferson Furnace, Ohio, died in uniform, his cousin published a 'Galar-Gân' or 'Elegy' which she had composed on behalf of the family.[69] In addition to helping their family's grieving process, some women poets put their talents at the service of the wider community. Fifteen Welsh-Americans serving with Company F of the 133rd Pennsylvania Infantry were killed on the same day at Fredericksburg, including the captain, John J. Jones. They were all from Ebensburg, Pennsylvania, and a poet using only the name *Cymraes* or 'Welsh Woman' published an elegy which, though concentrating on Cpt Jones, memorialised all the community's dead.[70]

While real women like these used writing to express the grief of their families or communities, these grieving women were also reflected by a number of literary constructs, the most common of which was the figure of *y fam alarus* or 'the grieving mother'. This character hovered in the background of many poems and songs which focused on the soldier's plight, providing an emotional contrast between the horrors of war and the mother's love. A typical example, 'Y Milwr Archolledig' ('The Wounded Soldier'), was published in *Y Cenhadwr Americanaidd* in June 1863. The poet used the pen-name 'Benoni', and research to date has revealed no more about this writer's identity (including whether the poet was a woman or a man). The piece depicts a scene common to the popular literature of the Civil War, a young soldier who lies dying on the battlefield, turning his last thoughts to his mother. It begins in the opening lines with the soldier addressing the instrument of his death directly: 'O gleddyf! O gleddyf! archollaist fy mynwes, / Ymsuddaist yn ddwfn tan waelod fy mron'; 'Oh sword! Oh sword! you have wounded my chest, / You have sunk deep beneath my breast.'[71] Although this piece is steeped in melodrama, Benoni's use of sentimental cliché yields an interesting observation. The soldier attempts to personify the sword (manifest in the repeated direct address, *O gleddyf!*, 'Oh sword!'), yet this literary device is soon undermined.

> Pe byddai it' galon, O gleddyf! hi doddai
> Wrth weled y mamau a'u dagrau yn lli
> Yn ochain fel Rachel am blant eu mynwesau
> Rhai fagwyd yn anwyl a thyner fel fi.[72]

> 'If you had a heart, Oh sword!, it would melt
> At seeing the mothers with their flood of tears
> Crying like Rachel for the children of their bosoms,
> Ones who were raised dearly and tenderly like me.'

The verbs in the first line of this stanza are conditional ('If you had a heart . . . it would melt'), emphasizing the imaginary nature of the soldier's address to the sword. By reminding readers or listeners of the obvious fact that the metal weapon does not have a person's 'heart' (*calon*), the poet invites us to consider the difference between this kind of literary construct and the reality of war. However, this meditation occurs on the margins of the stanza; its main purpose is to invoke a host of mourning mothers. The reference to Rachel is biblical short-hand, a move meant to conjure the mother described in Jeremiah 31.15: 'Hark, lamentation is heard in Ramah, and bitter weeping, Rachel weeping for her sons. She refuses to be comforted: they are no more.'[73] References to Rachel's grief characterize a considerable body of Welsh-language Civil War literature, just as they also punctuate a great many English-language texts from the same period.[74] While part of a field of biblical imagery which nineteenth-century Welsh-Americans shared with their non-Welsh neighbours, this biblical character would have resonated and melded with other traditional Welsh constructions of motherhood, deepening the religious connotations of *y fam Gymreig* ('the Welsh mother').[75]

Thus this Welsh-American poet conjures up the Rachel of Scripture, the archetypal grieving mother of Christian tradition, employing her to characterize the plurality of mothers whose combined tears form a 'flood'. Benoni then moves from these mothers' collective grief to the prayer which this individual soldier uses to focus attention on his own mother. Asking Jesus to receive his spirit, the final lines echo a great number of other Civil War poems in their description of the soldier's view of heaven: 'Ac yna caf eto yn iach o bob archoll / I edrych yn siriol yn ngwyneb fy mam'; 'And there, healed of every wound, I will be able / To look cheerfully in my mother's face.'[76]

Welsh-speaking soldiers and civilians alike would have been exposed to English-language songs dealing with this exact subject. As Alice Fahs notes:

> from early in the war numerous popular songs imagined a soldier's dying thoughts turning to his mother, including Charles Carroll Sawyer's 'Who Will Care for Mother Now?' . . . 'The Dying Volunteer' . . . 'The Dying Soldier or Kiss Me Good Night Mother' . . . 'Is That Mother Bending o'er Me?' . . . and Henry C. Work's 'Our Captain's Last Words'. . .[77]

Benoni's poem could have been put to music as well, providing Welsh-speaking Americans with their own answer to these English songs. At times, the connection between the English-language popular songs of the war-time North and the output of the Welsh-American press is even more apparent. A composition entitled 'Pwy Ofala am fy Mam?' – 'Who Will Care for my Mother?' – was published by Jonathan J. Nicholas in the April 1864 issue of *Y Seren Orllewinol*. The piece was meant to be sung, a point emphasized by the identification of 'the chorus' (*y gytgan*) in the printed text.

> Pwy ofala am fy mam?
> Ar fy mhen caf flodau gwynfa,
> Yn mhlith engyl pur dinam,
> Dros fy ngwlad 'rwyf wedi syrthio,
> Pwy ofala am fy mam?[78]
>
> 'Who will care for my mother?
> On my head I'll have the flowers of paradise,
> Among pure perfect angels,
> For my country I have fallen,
> Who will care for my mother?'

These lines are in fact a loose translation of the chorus of Charles Carroll Sawyer's popular song, 'Who Will Care for Mother Now?':

> Soon with angels I'll be marching,
> With bright laurels on my brow,
> I have for my country fallen,
> Who will care for mother now?[79]

In addition to modifying some details of Sawyer's original – for example, substituting 'the flowers of paradise' ([*b*]*lodau gwynfa*) for the 'laurel' (which was readily available to him in Welsh as *llawryf*) – Jonathan Nicholas presented his Welsh version of the song to *Y Seren Orllewinol*'s readers with a prose preface.

This introduction attempts to ground the sentiment of the song's stylized grieving in reality, making a claim for the authenticity of the experience which it treats. It describes the field as 'un o'r brwydrau diweddar rhwng milwyr yr Unol Dalaethau â'r gwrthryfelwyr' – 'one of the recent battles between the soldiers of the United States and the rebels' – and claims that the words which give the song its title were actually spoken by a dying Northerner. He seems to know a considerable amount about this dying soldier, for the poet adds that he was 'dyn ieuangc, unig ymddibynydd ei fam oedranus am ei chynnaliaeth' ('a young man, the only one on whom his elderly mother could depend for her sustenance').[80]

In addition to invoking the soldier's mother in this manner, some poems were placed directly in the mother's mouth. Thomas Edwards, a Congregational minister residing in Cincinnati, published one such piece in *Y Cenhadwr Americanaidd* in April 1864, giving it the simple title, 'Galar Mam' ('A Mother's Grief'). This poet turned the mother's voice into a vehicle for presenting an elaborate narrative, a family tragedy which he locates at the very heart of the Welsh-American experience. The fictitious mother of the poem begins her tale of sorrow by referring to her family's former home in Wales:

Ni fuom gynt yn Nghymru'n byw,
  Ein genedigol wlad,
Mewn lle wrth odrau uchel fryn,
  Y man bu'm mam a'm tad[.][81]

'We used to live in Wales,
  Our native country,
In a place by the foot of a high hill,
  The place where my mother and father had lived.'

Continuing her monologue, this mother then describes the crucial moment when she and her husband decided to emigrate:

O gylch y tân ar noswaith oer,
  Yn nghanol gauaf hir,
Ymddiddan am y trethi wnaem
  A'r rhent oedd ar y tir;
Y gwr ddywedai, 'Hi ddaw'n well,
  Ni awn yn bell i fyw,
Mae yn Americ', dir yn rhad,
  Na fydd gwynfanus[,] clyw.[82]

'Around the fire one cold evening,
  In the middle of a long winter,
We conversed about the taxes
  And the rent which was due for the land;
My husband said, 'It will get better,
  We'll go far away to live,
Land is cheap in America,
  Listen, be not sad.'

She then adds that they decided to emigrate 'er mwyn y plant' – 'for the sake of the children'; like her husband's injunction that they not be sad, these words foreshadow ironically the tragedy which comes with the end of the story. The versified narrative proceeds apace, moving through the start of the war and the decision of her *meibion dewr* or 'brave sons' to enlist in the army. Then, after an exposition of the mother's worries and reference to a letter reassuring her that her sons were still alive, the tragedy promised by the poem's title is related:

Ond buan daeth y newydd blin,
  Do am y frwydr fawr;
Fy nghalon aeth yn oer fel plwm,
  Mi wylais lawer awr[.][83]

'Yet before long the sore news came,
  Yes, about the great battle;
My heart went cold like lead,
  And I cried for many an hour.'

In the closing verse of his poem, Thomas Edwards has his grieving mother describe her condition. Like so many other poets and writers, he employs the biblical character of Rachel.

Mewn galar dwys a'm gwisg yn ddu
  Yr af hyd ben fy nhaith,
Ac mi feddyliaf lawer awr,
  Nad yw y ffordd yn faith;
Ac megis Rachel wylo wnaf,
  A hawdd yw gwybod pa'm.
Trwy brofiad gwn rwy'n tystio nawr,
  Mai mawr yw galar mam.[84]

'In deep grief with my clothes black
  I will go until the end of my journey,
And I often think

That the road is not long;
And like Rachel I will weep,
And it's easy to know why.
I know through experience, I can testify now
That a mother's grief is great.'

The mother of Edwards's poem asks us to meditate on the difference between second-hand knowledge of grief (such as was provided by this kind of literature) and the reality of experience. Though herself a literary construct, this Welsh-American Rachel asks readers to consider the 'great . . . mother's grief' which is only knowable 'through experience.'

This literary construction of 'A Mother's Grief' can be set within the context of the poet's activities on the home front of Cincinnati, Ohio. Edwards was a minister, and his war-time duties included performing funeral sermons for members of his chapel who died in the war and consoling their families. As was discussed in Chapter Five, the Revd Edwards also corresponded with at least one of Cincinnati's Welsh soldiers; it will be remembered that Theophilus Davies of the 6th Ohio Infantry sent letters to Edwards who in turn forwarded them for publication in *Y Cenhadwr Americanaidd*, the same journal which published this poem. In one of those published letters the young soldier described for his minister the thoughts and fears which gripped him while standing picket duty in the mountains of western Virginia, including the fact that he often 'thought . . . about [his] dear mother' ('yn meddwl am . . . fy anwyl fam').[85] This versified meditation on 'A Mother's Grief' can thus be set within a wider context of Welsh-American writing, one which connects personal letters with public texts just as it also connects the home front with soldiers serving in the field. Moreover, if his work as minister helped his own immediate community face the hardships of war, the prose and poetry which Edwards published interpreted aspects of the conflict for the broader community of Welsh America.

Given this, it is worth noting that Edwards's poem on 'A Mother's Grief' is concerned solely with the sorrow of war. Like so many other Welsh-American ministers he was an ardent abolitionist, and he also lent public support to the Union's war effort. However, in this poem Edwards avoids the patriotic rhetoric of so much of the war-time poetry published by the country's Welsh-language press, focussing instead on the tragedy of war; while those recruiting songs discussed in Chapter Three asked the Welsh mothers of America to offer up their sons for the cause(s) of Union and Freedom, this poem concentrates on the grief resulting from that sacrifice.

The increased emigration from Wales to the United States discussed above was the source of some tension between the Welsh in Wales and those in America, and some Welsh-American writers published propaganda encouraging this emigration.[86] However, Edwards does something entirely different in this poem, forcing his readers to focus on the fact that the Civil War brought tragedy to many Welsh families who emigrated 'for the sake of the children'. While the 'grieving mother' was a character whom the Union's Welsh poets shared with numerous Anglophone writers, the circumstances of the immigrant family presented bards like Thomas Edwards with a subject outside the experience of native-born Americans. As has been seen throughout this study, those Welsh people who emigrated – who *decided* to become Americans – had in the Civil War an unparalleled opportunity to prove themselves worthy of their new citizenship. However, the reality of war could also make parents like the mother imagined by Edwards wish they had never left the Old Country in the first place. The harsh contrast between the mother's nurturing domesticity and the lonely battlefield death is intensified by another contrast, that between the hopes of the immigrant family and the cruel mockery which war makes of those hopes.

Poets could also make this dual contrast manifest by focusing on the figure of the grieving wife or fiancée. Rowland Walters, that quarryman from the 'slate valley' known in bardic circles as Ionoron Glan Dwyryd, put his poetry at the service of his Vermont community by composing elegies for local boys killed on Southern battlefields. He also interpreted the war's meaning by means of abstracted meditations on fictitious soldiers. One of these, 'Bedd y Milwr Cymreig yn America' ('The Welsh Soldier's Grave in America'), depicts a Welsh woman who travels to the United States only to find her lover buried in a soldier's grave.[87] As has been seen at other points in this study, many Welsh-American writers described the soaking of American ground with Welsh blood or the interring of Welsh soldiers in American soil as a potent symbol of the immigrant's unquestionable hold on American citizenship. This poem, however, finds only sadness in the combination of Welsh soldier and American grave. It was common practice for young Welsh couples to emigrate in stages, with the man crossing the sea first in order to find work before being joined by his fiancée or wife. This familiar pattern forms the background for the story which Ionoron weaves in his poem, a narrative which takes as its dramatic centre the lament which the young woman utters over the grave of Ioan, her intended husband:

Ar ol d'od dros donau y dw'r,
I'th wnethur yn ol fy nymuniad,
O Ioan! yn gariad a gwr;
Ond yma yn dawel gorweddi[.][88]

'After coming across the water's waves,
To make you, Oh Ioan!,
According to my desire, a lover and a husband;
Yet here quietly you lie.'

Like Thomas Edwards, Ionoron Glan Dwyryd also published poetry in keeping with the anti-slavery, pro-Union and pro-war stance which so characterized Welsh-American print culture during the Civil War.[89] However, both poets also used verse to examine the special kind of tragedy which the war brought for many immigrants.

THE 'SOLDIER'S WIFE' AND HER SISTERS

Needless to say, while the immigrant's situation added different inflections to the ways in which this sorrow was felt, the plight of the grieving wife or lover was examined by a wide range of Civil War authors. As Elizabeth Young notes, Elizabeth Stuart Phelps produced a memorable (English-language) treatment of this theme:

> The works of Elizabeth Stuart Phelps . . . repeatedly interweave female rebellions against civility with the Civil War itself. Phelps's first published story, 'A Sacrifice Consumed' (1864), focuses on the grief of a woman whose lover, a Union soldier, dies at Antietam; as she later recalled in her memoir, she was inspired to write it by 'the women, – the helpless, outnumbering, unconsulted women; they whom war trampled down, without a choice or protest . . . to them I would have spoken.'[90]

The grieving women depicted by Thomas Edwards and Ionoron Glan Dwyryd occupy a slightly different register from the one described by Phelps. While focusing attention on the tragedy of war, it is not necessarily the tragedy of 'unconsulted women . . . without a choice' in the matter. Rather, these male poets use sentimentalized constructs of women in order to contrast the hallowed realm of domesticity with the soldier's violent death (while also employing them to bring the harsh reality of war to bear upon the immigrant's American dream).

One Welsh-American poet who provided a voice for the war's 'unconsulted women' was Margaret Watkins of Racine, Wisconsin. In September 1863 *Y Cenhadwr Americanaidd* published her poem 'Gwraig y Milwr', 'The Soldier's Wife', an examination of the war's effect on the woman left at home. While this text ends as a religious meditation, with the troubled wife discovering that God is her only comfort, it begins with an emotional description of the woman's plight. Like a label on a picture, the poem's title tells the reader exactly what he or she is meant to see in the first stanza:

Gwraig y Milwr

Ymwasgai yn dawel yn ochr yr aelwyd
 Cofleidiai y baban yn dyn at ei bron,

Ymneidiai ochenaid o'i chalon hiraethus
  Pwy wyr y fath drallod sy'n gorphwys ar hon?[91]

'The Soldier's Wife

She snuggled up quietly to the side of the hearth,
  She embraced the baby tightly at her breast,
A sigh came forth from her longing heart,
  Who knows what affliction rests upon this woman?'

The scene which Margaret Watkins draws in her opening line depicts the soldier's wife at the family 'hearth', using that charged word, *aelwyd*, which would have conjured up a constellation of concepts in readers' minds relating to the roles and importance of the wife, mother, home and family. As was seen in Chapter Three, one of those recruiting songs published early in the war urged Welsh-Americans to fight for the Union banner by stating that the flag protected the family's *aelwyd* or 'hearth'.[92] As if offering a critique of that literary call to arms, Margaret Watkins portrays an *aelwyd* which is 'afflicted' because a man answered that call.

Every one of the poem's first three lines begins with a verb in the third person imperfect (ending in *-ai*). The poet is describing continual past action; in other words, readers are made to see a woman in a protracted state of affliction. The first two of these verbs, *ymwasgu* – meaning 'to press close' or 'to snuggle up' – and *cofleidio* – meaning 'to embrace' – intensify the force of the word *aelwyd*, conveying a sense of domestic comfort and warmth. The third line twists violently away from the tone of the opening couplet, as the verb *ymneidio* – meaning 'to come forth', or, more literally, 'to jump forth' or 'start' – introduces the 'affliction' which 'rests' heavily upon both wife and hearth.

Like those poems by Thomas Edwards and Ionoron Glan Dwyryd discussed above, the emotional force of this text emanates in part from the clash between the wife's domestic sphere and the world of battle which has consumed her husband. However, while the women constructed by those male poets function first and foremost as vessels for grief, Margaret Watkins portrays a soldier's wife who actively embarks on an inward journey. The poem's second stanza runs the domestic sphere against the world of war by describing the woman's attempt to divine the fate of her husband.

A'i mheddwl a sylla ar faes yr ymdrechfa
  I edrych ganfydda ei phriod mewn grym.
Yn fyw heb ddim clwyfau nac ol y bwledau
  Er's 'chydig chwyrnellai o'i amgylch mor chwim.[93]

'With her mind she gazes upon the field of struggle
To see if she can find her husband in health,
Alive without wounds nor trace of the bullets
Which lately had whirled so swiftly about him.'

As the poet uses her imagination to create this vision of the afflicted hearth, so the woman she depicts uses her imagination in an effort to transcend the distance between home and battlefield. The first line of the next stanza grounds this flight of fancy in the reality of recent events, referring to one of the Union's most important victories.

Os Vicksburg a gwympodd, pa beth os fy mhriod
A orphwys yn dawel yn nyfnder y bedd
Tramwyaf dros erchyll glogwyni'r magnelau
I dremio a ydyw fy anwylyd mewn hedd.[94]

'So what if Vicksburg has fallen if my husband
Lies quietly in the bottom of a grave;
I travel back and forth over the horrible cannon-studded cliffs
To see if my dear one is in peace.'

While the first two verses are in the third person, these lines are spoken by the first-person voice of the soldier's wife; her act of imagination is accompanied by speech as she actively interprets her situation for the reader.

This poem was published in September 1863, two months after the long siege of Vicksburg came to an end. When 'the Gibraltar of the West' finally fell to the Union army on 4 July 1863, the Confederates lost their last hold on the Mississippi river. Like the Northern press in general, the Welsh-American publications made much of this victory. *Y Drych*'s editor included all his readers in a collective congratulation ('Gallwn longyfarch ein darllenwyr yr wythnos hon'; 'we can congratulate our readers this week'), also asking them 'to lift up their hearts in thanks' ('i ddyrchafu eu calonau mewn diolchgarwch').[95] The monthly journals published letters written by victorious soldiers; for example, *Y Cyfaill o'r Hen Wlad* offered John W. Jones of the 23rd Wisconsin Infantry a platform for boasting to all of Welsh America that 'never had an army been seen feeling so much joy anywhere as the excellent army of . . . U. S. Grant before Vicksburg on the morning of the 4th of July, 1863.' ('Ni welwyd erioed fyddin yn teimlo mwy o lawenydd mewn un man ag oedd yn myddin ardderchog . . . U. S. Grant o flaen Vicksburg ar forau'r 4ydd o Orphenaf, 1863').[96] Other soldiers published letters describing their joy at spotting 'the white flag . . . being raised above the enemy works' ('y faner wen . . . yn cael ei derchafu uwch y gweithiau gelynol') or their pride at seeing the Stars and Stripes flying over Vicksburg again.[97] Against all this militaristic bluster and self-congratulating, Margaret Watkins sets the rhetorical question posed by the soldier's wife: 'so what if Vicksburg has fallen' if her husband has died in the process? The rejoicing of the kind recorded by the Welsh-American press is dismissed with a few short words as the woman's personal grief is set against the community's public celebrations.

The poem's next verse provides the transition from this examination of the wife's 'affliction' to her search for solace in religion.

Y meddwl ddaeth adref heb wasgar cysuron
 Ei hysbryd cystuddiol a'i theimlad mor syn,
Ac yna syn sylla ar weithredoedd Jehofa,
 Canfydda mai ef ydyw noddwr pob dyn.[98]

'The mind came home without the embrace of reassurances,
 Her spirit was stricken and her feelings so stunned,
And then she gazes in wonder upon the works of Jehovah,
 Perceiving that he is every man's protector.'

Her mind must return 'without the embrace' which knowledge of her husband's fate would provide, and the poet uses the word [*g*]*wasgar* ('embrace,' 'press') to echo the manner in which the very first line employs the verb *ymwasgu* ('to press' or 'to snuggle up'). The reader is brought back to the poem's initial scene and reminded that, rather than travelling to the 'horrible cliffs' of Vicksburg, this woman is confined to a hearth afflicted by war. Though failing 'to gaze' upon the battlefield, she now 'gazes' successfully upon 'the works of Jehovah'. Just as the verb *sylla* ('she gazes') is used both times, so the verb *canfydda* ('she perceives') is repeated; while failing earlier 'to perceive' her husband at Vicksburg, she now succeeds in 'perceiving' the comfort derived from knowledge of God's protection.

The poem returns to the first-person voice of the wife as the reader is made privy to her prayer. She asks God 'to take pity . . . on lowly man's boasting' ('Tosturia . . . wrth ymffrost gwael ddyn') and 'destroy the cannons and break the bayonets' ('dryllia'r magnelau a thor y bidogau').[99] Recalling the 'so what' voiced earlier, the word *ymffrost*, 'boast', again brings the woman's critical scrutiny to bear upon the Vicksburg celebrations. And, while soldiers were publishing letters in the Welsh-American press which boasted of the fact that the white flag of surrender and the Stars and Stripes were waving above Vicksburg, Margaret Watkins longed to see a different kind of banner raised on high:

Prysura y dyddiau bydd baner odidog
 Brawdgarwch a chariad yn chwifio uwch ben
Pob adail fawreddog a'r tyrau godidog
 A rhyddid yn mhob man i'r du fel y gwyn.[100]

'Speed the day when the splendid banner
  Of brotherliness and love waves over
Every imposing building and [all] the splendid towers,
  With freedom everywhere for black as for white.'

These words follow the wife's address to God and are to be taken as part of her prayer. However, with these lines Margaret Watkins is also asking her readers to join her in prayer. Her poem is an examination of the afflicted woman's condition, and it ends by describing how such a woman finds both voice and spiritual empowerment in the face of war's oppression. If the newspaper headlines celebrated the heroes who travelled to Vicksburg, this poet suggests that a woman confined to the domestic sphere of the hearth can undergo her own equally heroic internal journey. If the husband's journey ends with victory (and, it seems, death) at Vicksburg, the wife's journey takes her to knowledge. A comforting knowledge of God's power is accompanied by a realization that peace, and not the defeat of the enemy, is the ultimate victory and that the baner of love is the only flag that should be planted on earth.

Set against the huge weight of pro-war literature which the Welsh-American press was publishing, this poem represents a rare example of what we might call a pro-peace poem. The peace which Margaret Watkins prayed for, however, was not that which Northern 'Peace Democrats' were suggesting by the time of the 1864 election. Rather than desiring peace on any terms, the peace which this poet imagines is conceptualized in reference to part of that ideological constellation which characterized war-time Welsh America. Put simply, the end of war is to be accompanied by the end of slavery. If the bulk of Welsh America's war-time print culture can be characterized as pro-Union, pro-Lincoln, anti-slavery and pro-war, this poem's ideological charge runs along anti-slavery and pro-peace lines.

As was seen in Part One of this study, pacifism, or at least a kind of proto-pacifism, was not uncommon in pre-war Welsh America. Is it possible, then, to read Margaret Watkins's poem as a pacifist declaration? What else did this woman from Racine, Wisconsin, have to say about the Civil War? In fact, the same issue of *Y Cenhadwr Americanaidd* which published 'The Soldier's Wife' also carried another poetic examination of the conflict by Margaret Watkins. Simply entitled 'Y Rhyfel!' ('The War!'), this composition uses phrases which echo lines from her other poem; for example, it expresses a desire to see 'y faner o hedd' ('the flag of peace') while also criticizing the *ymffrost* or 'boasting' of the men who started the war. Her first stanza describes 'The War' as a 'horrible excitement' which turns 'the earth' into one vast military 'camp':

Pa beth yw y cynhwrf dychrynllyd a welaf
  Ar wersyll y ddaear rhwng dynion ein gwlad,
Pob un yn sychedu am waed ei gydymaith
  A rhyfedd yr anrhaith ysgeler a wnaed.[101]

'What is the horrible excitement that I see
Upon the camp of the earth between men of our country,
Each one thirsting for his companion's blood
And strange is the atrocious destruction which was wrought.'

Unlike that vast body of pro-war literature which casts the conflict as one of righteous Northerners defending the Union and fighting the evil slave-owners of the South, this poem's opening lines occupy a different register; like so many (Anglophone) Americans who would resort to the trope of the 'brothers' war', Margaret Watkins focuses here on the way in which the national family is split by civil war. Rather than seeing a sacrificial journey to righteousness, this poet finds the 'atrocious destruction' to be 'strange', for it pits citizens of the same country against each other. The noun *cydymaith*, meaning 'fellow', 'friend' or, literally, 'travelling companion', is used to undermine the tragedy of a situation which finds 'every man' of her country seeking the blood of 'his companion'.

However, if the war is imagined as a struggle between (former) 'companions', the two sides in that struggle are interpreted in strikingly different terms. In her second stanza Watkins blames the 'traitors' (*bradwyr*) for the violence, adding that they are 'Enemies of the Negro' ('Gelynion y Negro').[102] The poem then continues to develop both of these discourses, expressing horror at war's destruction while also criticizing the Southern 'traitors'. Watkins sees the unstoppable 'hurricane of war' ('corwynt y rhyfel') ravaging the land, 'sweeping within its turning some thousands before it' ('Ysguba'n ei gylchdro ryw filoedd o'i flaen'), while also foreseeing the ultimate destruction of the Confederates on the battlefield: 'Daw cwpan o chwerwedd at fin y gelynion, / Dan bwysau heiarnaidd y fagnel a'r cledd'; 'A cup of bitterness will come to the enemy's mouth, / Under the iron-like weight of the cannon and the sword.'[103] This poem's hero is 'the true and faithful Abe Lincoln' ('y ffyddlon a'r cywir Abe Lincoln'), characterized as an American David pitted against Jefferson Davis's 'boastful Goliath' ('Jeff Davis fel ffrostgar Goliath').[104]

In these meditations on 'The Soldier's Wife' and 'The War!' we have two poems by the same woman which were published in the same poetry column of the same issue of *Y Cenhadwr Americanaidd*. And yet they present strikingly different views on the war. If the soldier's wife imagined in the first poem finds no joy in Vicksburg's fall, Margaret Watkins's second poem looks forward to the defeat of the Southern 'traitors'. Both poems recoil at the horrors of war, and both express hatred for the institution of slavery, yet the second poem describes the destruction of the Confederate forces as the means of achieving both 'peace' and 'freedom'. While Margaret Watkins used her verse to provide what Elizabeth Young Phelps called 'unconsulted women' with a voice, placing the nation's militaristic boasting beneath the critical gaze of 'The Soldier's Wife', her poem on 'The War!' shows clearly that she also partook of the same pro-Union, pro-war and anti-slavery discourse as the majority of her fellow Welsh-American writers. If Welsh-speaking soldiers could describe themselves as 'children of their old father, Abraham Lincoln', this daughter of Lincoln accompanied her Christian meditation on war's evils with a biblical tribute to the president, transforming him into the heroic (and future king) David.

Anne A. Williams of Steuben, Oneida County, New York, was another Welsh daughter of Lincoln who published poetry during the war. Her poem on 'Y Rhyfel Cartrefol', 'The Civil War', appeared in May 1863, a few months *before* the dual Union victories at Vicksburg and Gettysburg.[105] Like Margaret Watkins's poem on 'The War!', this composition combines a condemnation of bloodshed with a wish for the Confederacy's defeat. In her final stanza, Anne Williams laments all the 'relatives placed by war in the grave' ('[p]erthynasau / roed gan ryfel yn y bedd'), while also praying for a peace marked by restoration of the Union:

Arglwydd Dduw rho ini heddwch,
 Ac Undeb eto dros ein tir.
Onide bydd gwlad Americ
 Heb 'r un enw cyn bo hir.[105]

'Lord God give us peace,
 And Union again over our land.
If not then the land of America
 Will be nameless before long.'

While the end of this poem addresses the concerns of her fellow Northern Unionists, Williams's opening stanza is in part addressed to the Welsh back in the Old Country:

Beth yw'r cyffro sydd i'w weled,
 Heddyw drwy holl wledydd cred?
Y gwrthryfel sy'n Americ
 Yw'r newyddion sydd ar lêd,
Am y bechgyn ieuainc gwrol
 A syrthiasant yma i lawr.
Am y brwydrau erchyll gwaedlyd,
 Y mae son yn Mrydain Fawr.[107]

'What is the excitement which is to be seen,
 Today throughout all of creation's lands?
The rebellion which is in America
 Is the news which is abroad,

About the heroic young boys
  Who have fallen here.
About the horrible bloody battles,
  There is talk in Great Britain.'

She interprets the magnitude of the conflict in international terms while simultaneously acknowledging the fact that many of the 'brave young boys' killed in the war – described as 'relatives' before the end of the piece – were related to people in Wales. Like those poems by Thomas Edwards and Ionoron Glan Dwyryd, this text also partakes of the discourse on the immigrant's situation.

If the opening lines refer to the international dimension of the tragedy, the body of the poem concentrates on the battles disfiguring the American landscape. Anne Williams laments the 'colouring' of American ground with the blood of 'boys', many of them killed shortly before their term of enlistment was due to end.

Yr oedd llawer bachgen heinif
  Am ddo'd adref cyn bo hir,
Erbyn heddyw trwm yw dywedyd,
  Fod eu gwaed hwy'n lliwio'r tir,
O Americ! O Americ!
  Gelli wylo'r dagrau'n lli,
Am y miloedd a syrthiasant
  Ar dy feysydd gwyrddion di.[108]

'There were many sturdy boys
  Ready to come home before long;
By today it is sad to say
  That their blood is colouring the land,
Oh America! Oh America!
  You can cry a flood of tears,
For the thousands who have fallen
  Upon your green fields.'

Anne Williams then takes the flowers of the bloodied fields and turns them into a metaphor for the slain soldiers. Like that song by Pete Seeger which would become popular more than a hundred years later as Americans went off to fight a very different war, this poem's impact stems from the simple yet powerful image of flowers which are made to represent young soldiers as well as the growth which covers their graves.[109]

Blodau'r wlad sy'n cael ei difa
 Gan y fagnel gyda grym,
Blodau'r wlad sy'n gorfod myned
 I wynebu'r cleddyf llym,
Blodau'r wlad sydd wrth y miloedd,
 Dan garnau'r meirch yn cael eu lladd,
Blodau'r wlad sy'n cael e[u] galw,
 Yn fechgyn ieuainc o bob gradd.[110]

'It is the country's flowers which are being exterminated
 By the cannon with force,
It is the country's flowers which must go
 To face the harsh sword,
It is the country's flowers which, by the thousands,
 Are being killed beneath the horses' hooves,
It is the country's flowers which are called,
 Young boys of every class.'

Representing freshness and young life, these flowers emphasize the youth of the 'boys' called up and slaughtered 'by the thousands'. The next stanza, however, widens the panorama of destruction to take in older men as well, fathers whose deaths leave many an *aelwyd* or 'hearth' in ruins.

O mae llawer aelwyd gynhes
 Wedi ei gwneud yn ddarnau mân,
Trwy i'r tad oedd fwyn a hawddgar,
 Orfod myn'd o flaen y tân,
Ac mae'i weddw fwyn a thyner
 Heddyw'n wylo'r dagrau'n lli,
Am ei phriod hoff anwylgu.
 Och or chwerw yw ei chri!

'Oh many a warm hearth
 Has been shattered into little pieces,
Because the father who was kind and amiable,
 Had to go before the fire,
And his kind and tender widow
 Today is crying a flood of tears,
For her dear beloved spouse.
 Oh, how bitter is her lament!'

While the weeping widows of these lines recall those grieving women depicted in poems such as 'Gwraig y Milwr' ('The Soldier's Wife') and 'Bedd y Milwr

Cymreig yn America' ('The Welsh Soldier's Grave in America'), it is significant that the word *milwr*, 'soldier', is completely absent from this text. Every stanza in Anne William's meditation on 'Y Rhyfel Cartrefol' ('The Civil War') refers in unmistakable terms to the soldiers being killed, yet the word 'soldier', *milwr*, is not used in any of the poem's forty-eight lines.

The dead are called 'relatives' (*perthynasau*) in the concluding stanza. They are referred to repeatedly as 'boys' (*bechgyn*) and once as 'fathers' (*tad*[*au*]), and they are also described metaphorically as 'the country's flowers' (*blodau'r wlad*). Yet not once are they called *milwyr*, 'soldiers'. In her final lines Anne Williams prays for peace and Union, adding that, without a Union victory, the country which these 'flowers' are called upon to serve would cease to exist. However, while praying for the Union cause, she takes no joy in the Union's feats of arms. This woman focuses instead on the human cost of the conflict, describing the dead in domestic terms, as 'sons', 'fathers' and 'relatives', while totally refusing the military terminology which would label her 'flowers' as 'soldiers'.

OTHER MEDITATIONS ON PEACE

Several other Welsh-Americans produced versified meditations on the war's human cost which echoed the work of these women. Jonathan J. Nicholas, who wrote that Welsh version of 'Who Will Care for Mother Now', published one such piece in *Y Seren Orllewinol* in December 1863, using the simple title 'Myfyrdod' – 'Meditation' – to emphasize the contemplative tone of his poem. Nicholas begins by assuming the persona of a *prydydd* or 'poet' who seeks refuge in the wilderness, enjoying the tranquillity of his 'glade of contemplation' (*llanerch myfyrdod*).[111] He revels in the sounds of nature, inviting the reader to join him as he lifts his eyes to gaze at 'the sheep which can be seen quietly grazing' – 'Y defaid yn dawel a welir yn pori' – on the mountain slopes which frame this woodland scene.[112] Here the poet finds what he seeks, and the governing experience is described as one of *heddwch* or 'peace'. This reverie is soon disturbed as human noise shatters the serenity of nature. The pace of the poem quickens, and the reader is soon immersed in a meditation on the Civil War.

Ond dynion a welir yn prysur ymdyrru,
Pa beth yw eu dyben? ow! ymladd yn nghyd!
Amerig fawr eang, sydd uchel mewn breintiau,
Ei meusydd ffrwythlonog a gochwyd gan waed;
Palasau ardderchog osodwyd yn fflamiau,
Gwroniaid dros ryddid a fathrwyd dan draed.[113]

'But men are seen busily mustering,
What is their purpose? Oh! to fight together!

Great expansive America, which is great in privileges,
Her fertile fields have been stained with blood;
Splendid palaces have been set aflame,
Heroes [fighting] for freedom have been trampled under foot.'

The peaceful world of nature is completely displaced by these man-made horrors, as the poet's woodland clearing disappears in 'the smoke which gathers like fat clouds' ('y mwg sydd yn dyrchu, / Fel tewion gymylau').[114]

Nicholas then describes a *bwthyn* or 'cottage', asking the reader to draw near and examine the scene in detail. Ostensibly a part of the pastoral scene presented earlier, this modest rural home is suited to the sloping pastures with their grazing sheep. It has, however, become a home disfigured by war.

De'wch heibio i'r bwthyn, ceir yno wraig weddw,
Ei phriod a syrthiodd yn aberth i'r cledd;
O'i hamgylch ymddifaid sy'n cwyno yn arw,
Eu tad sydd yn gorwedd yn ngwaelod y bedd.[115]

'Come by the cottage, there you'll find a widow,
Her husband has fallen in sacrifice to the sword;
Around her orphans are lamenting bitterly,
Their father is lying in the bottom of a grave.'

This, then, is Jonathan J. Nicholas's depiction of the soldier's wife. The ruined domestic scene which he reveals within the cottage mirrors the way in which the beauty of nature has been wrecked by the destructive forces of battle.

This compounded destruction forces the poet to ask a simple question: 'Pa beth ydyw'r achos?' – 'What is the cause?'[116] He then rephrases this query, searching for an answer which might restore peace to the country: 'I'r echres gyflafan pa fodd ceir terfyniad, / A thynu y cleddyf niweidiol o'n tir?'; 'How can an end to the horrible slaughter be achieved, / And [how can] the wounding sword be drawn from our land?'[117] This poem, labelled a 'Meditation' by the poet, becomes a meditation on this specific question, as Nicholas examines it from several different angles, trying to imagine the answers which other people might offer.

Fe ddichon fod llawer yn barod i ateb,
Nad oes ond un llwybr 'gael diwedd i hyn,
Er cadw hoff rhyddid, a phleidio yr undeb,
Rhaid gosod pob gelyn yn ngwaelod y glyn[.][118]

'It's likely that many are ready to answer
That there is only one way to put an end to this:

In order to maintain dear freedom, and support the Union,
Every enemy must be interred in the bottom of the valley.'

With these lines Nicholas is imagining the kind of answer that many of his fellow Welsh-Americans would surely provide; he is referring to the rhetoric of those Welsh recruiting songs – like the ones discussed in Chapter Three – which asked volunteers to turn the South into 'a river of blood' ('afon o waed').

Having meditated on the possible answers which others might give, this poet provides his own answer, one that echoes the religious turn of Margaret Watkins's 'Gwraig y Milwr' ('The Soldier's Wife'):

Ond diolch i'r Nefoedd am ffordd sydd amgenach
I ladd yr elyniaeth, a'r gelyn yn fyw;
Yn ofer y chwilid am lwybr ragorach,
Pa elyn all sefyll o flaen nerthoedd Duw?

Tyr'd allan, O! Seion, y dyddiau drwg yma,
Ymnertha yn wrol, mae'r angen yn fawr;
Ymostwng yn ffyddiog wrth orsedd Jehofa,
A gofyn am daflu y fflangell i lawr,
O ateb ein gweddi, y Duwdod trag'wyddol,
Trwy haeddiant yr Iesu, O arbed yn awr,
A deled y dyddiau a'r amser hyfrydol
Pan dderfydd rhyfeloedd, O brysied yr awr.[119]

'Yet thank Heavens for a better way
Of killing the animosity, and [keeping] the enemy alive;
In vain would one search for a superior path,
What enemy can stand before the powers of God?

'Come out, Oh! Zion, these evil days,
Gather your strength bravely, the need is great;
Submitting faithfully at Jehovah's throne,
And asking for the whip to be thrown down,
Oh answer our prayers, eternal Deity,
By the merit of Jesus, Oh save [us] now,
And let the days and the lovely time come
When wars will end, Oh speed the hour.'

This poem resembles Margaret Watkins's 'The Soldier's Wife' in more ways than one; both poets ask God to speed the day when the war will end, and both also state that they desire peace to be accompanied by an end to slavery. Many Northern Democrats were arguing that ending the war was more important than freeing the slaves, while other Northerners – including the majority of Welsh America's public figures – were maintaining that no peace with a slave-owning Confederacy was possible. While numerous, often violently opposed, viewpoints were being fielded in the political arenas of the North, the public opinion of Welsh America was relatively uniform. Jonathan Nicholas's 'Meditation', like Margaret Watkins's 'The Soldier's Wife,' is a text which attempts to situate a plea for peace within the pro-Union, anti-slavery and pro-war arena of the Welsh-American press. Moreover, both poets employ the same strategy in pursuing this goal; they invoke an omnipotent God, stating that He can bring peace, Union and freedom to all Americans without resorting to the death of 'every last enemy'.

All the poems discussed in this chapter were published during the second half of the Civil War. The naiveté which characterized the early months of the conflict was by this time a distant memory, and the civilians who wrote these texts would have been painfully aware of the huge casualties which the war was inflicting on both sides. However, these poems were also composed and published after Lincoln signed the Emancipation Proclamation on 1 January 1863. As one would expect, and as will be discussed in detail in Chapter Ten, that step linking the Union's war aims directly to the emancipation of the slaves was greeted with great enthusiasm by Welsh America's writers, poets and community leaders. While these poets reject the concept of war, they could not reject the Union's war effort in its entirety without undermining the abolitionism which so many Welsh-Americans passionately embraced. Thus their meditations end with a religious turn, a move which leaves the worldly realm of politics, looking instead to the metaphysical realm of an omnipotent God.

This religious turn was enacted by means of several different authorial strategies. As is seen in the work of the poets discussed above, the most obvious method involved invoking God directly, praying for a just peace accompanied by emancipation. Samuel Williams, a poet from Pennsylvania who used the bardic name Gwentydd, employed a different strategy, praying instead to a personified Peace. This 'heavenly handmaiden' ('[ll]awforwyn nefolaidd') occupies the foreground of his prayer, yet she in turn is motivated by God, called her 'Creator' ([C]*rewr*) by the poet.[120] Gwentydd's poem, appropriately entitled 'Heddwch' ('Peace'), appeared in the April 1864 issue of *Y Cyfaill o'r Hen Wlad*. Like those other pleas for peace being published during the second half of the war, this poet qualified his prayer, demanding that Peace bring justice as well ('Gwna derfyn ar orthrwm a thrais'; 'Put an end to oppression and violence').[121]

Obviously, these Welsh-language poets were not the only Americans who were offering up prayers for peace. By the same token, the tension between a desire for peace and a desire to see slavery ended was by no means unique to Welsh America. To cite but one example, Severn Teackle Wallis was a Quaker who embraced pacifism and abolition equally. In his powerful poem 'A Prayer for Peace', Wallis condemns all who fight, equating the 'curse of war' with 'greed', 'hate', 'ambition' and 'vanity'.[122] He asks the 'God of our fathers' to fashion an all-inclusive peace, extending it to encompass all sectors of society, both oppressed and oppressor:

> Peace for the captive on his weary way,
> And the mad crowds who jeer his helplessness;
> For them that suffer, them that do the wrong
> Sinning and sinned against. O God! for all[.][123]

The manner in which these Welsh-American poets turned to God in seeking a just peace for all was by no means unique. However, in addition to the obvious difference of language, the versified prayer offered by Gwentydd is characterized by a distinctly Welsh inflection.

Having introduced personified Peace in his first line, characterizing her as God's 'heavenly handmaiden', this Welsh poet concludes his poem by describing the heavenly realm in which she dwells:

> Y Corau cerubaidd dysglaerwych,
> I ti y pêrseiniant eu ceirdd;
> Cymhlethant gynghanedd bêrleisiol
> Yn gymysg ag odlau y Beirdd.[124]

> 'The brilliantly shinning Choirs of cherubs,
> It is to you that they sweetly sing their songs;
> They will weave a sweet-voiced harmony
> Mixed together with the Poets' rhymes.'

The words *Corau cerubaidd* are easily translated as 'Choirs of cherubs' (or, more literally, 'cherub-like Choirs'), and the image which this Welsh phrase presents is also a part of Anglo-American Christianity's conceptual framework. However, the words *ceirdd* and [c]*ynghanedd*, translated here as 'songs' and 'harmony', evoke a complex constellation of concepts which cannot be rendered easily in English. Along with the more common *cerddi, ceirdd* is a plural form of the noun *cerdd*, a word which since at least the Middle Ages has been used to refer to 'music' as well as 'poetry'. The bardic poetry of medieval Wales was recited or sung to the accompaniment of a harp, and the art forms employed by poets and harpers are referred to traditionally as *cerdd dafod* – literally 'tongue craft', but usually rendered simply as 'poetry' or 'the art of poetry' – and *cerdd dant* – 'string craft' or 'the art of playing stringed instruments'.[125] *Cynghanedd* is also a term which can refer to both music and poetry. While meaning 'harmony' in the sense of that English word, it is also a technical term describing the internal line ornamentation which is mandatory in Welsh strict-metre poetry.

This description of the Heavenly chorus is bound up with the Welsh vocabulary used to describe music, poetry and the connection between the two. To further emphasize this theme, the word *Beirdd* – 'poets' or 'bards' – is capitalized in the final line; like the common noun *heddwch*, 'peace', which is transformed into a personified 'Peace' (*Heddwch*), so the 'Poets' of this poem are presented as actors with a specific role to play in the scenario. The 'songs' (*ceirdd*) of the angels, which can also be interpreted as 'poems', are woven with the *cynghanedd* of the Welsh bardic tradition, and as such they meld with praise poems composed by (presumably earthly) 'Poets'. While the poem is not a strict-metre composition (although this stanza's first line gestures towards *cynghanedd*: 'Y Corau cerubaidd'), it is a rhyming form of free verse and thus an example of what Gwentydd calls 'odlau y Beirdd', 'the rhymes of the Poets'. This text operates on what we might call a metapoetic level; it is a poem about poetry in which the poet refers to the nature and value of his own bardic composition. He weaves his own invocation to Peace, making himself a member of that throng of angels and Poets which praises the 'heavenly handmaiden', asking her to end war and oppression.

These poets' search for a just peace – an immediate end to war accompanied by the freedom of the slaves – led them to what I have been calling a religious turn, an invocation of the powers of heaven. However, Samuel Williams also published a very different kind of meditation on war and peace, a series of strict-metre *englynion* presented on the pages of *Y Cyfaill o'r Hen Wlad* under the title 'Drygedd Rhyfel', 'War's Evil'.

A rifir drygau Rhyfel – a'r dinystr
    Mawr daena y magnel,
  Tan boerydd cafodydd fel
  Llosg afar genllusg ufel.

Gyra o'i ymysgaroedd – ei filfil
    Ufelfyllt drwy'r glynoedd;
  Yn nghol ei flin ingawl floedd,
  I angeu y dyg rengoedd.

Drwy oesau y dyrysir – trefn odiaeth
    Trafnidol y frodir,
  A blin ynt holl bobl ein tir,
  I drist ing ein darostyngir.[126]

'Can war's evils be numbered – and the great destruction
    Which the cannon spreads,

Fiery spitter of showers like
The burning sorrow of hailstone sparks?

'It drives from its entrails – its thousand
bolts of sparks through the valleys;
In the sting of his angry anguished cry,
It carries ranks [of soldiers] to death.

'Through the ages – the most commercial order
of the country will be confounded,
And all our land's people are worried,
We are subjected to sorrowful anguish.'

Though referring directly to neither Union nor Confederacy, the poet's condemnation of war is nonetheless brought to bear upon the American Civil War. This bard from Scranton, Pennsylvania, refers in his closing couplet to the collective nation of which he was a part ('our land', 'we are subjugated'). Samuel Williams laments the evils which the Civil War wrought on both people and 'commerce,' and in doing so he neither turns his poem towards religion nor foresees the coming of peace. However, this text does not contradict all the ideological parameters which defined most of the Welsh-American press' war-time literature. It is decidedly anti-war, yet it makes no comment whatsoever on the causes of Union and freedom.

However, we should be careful that we are not forced by the ideological stance of Welsh America's war-time press (and the aggressive manner in which that stance was often maintained) into an interpretive strategy which has us interrogating every poem by means of a pro-Union, pro-Lincoln, pro-war and anti-slavery 'tick list'. This is, after all, a work of literature and not an oath of political allegiance. Neither is it intended to be a testimony of religious faith. While not following the propagandistic cues of Welsh America's pro-Union, pro-war and anti-slavery press – or, rather, *because* it eschewed the realm of propaganda – this is, in fact, one of the more interesting Welsh poems produced during the Civil War. Samuel Williams puts the compact *englyn* metre to the use to which it is best suited, composing an epigrammatic meditation on one subject. That subject, as his title proclaims, is 'Drygau Rhyfel', 'War's Evils', and not the causes of the American Civil War. He avoids all mention of religion, not because he is rejecting Christianity, but rather because the subject of his poem is war's destruction and not the spiritual aid which religion provides in time of war. Samuel Williams was, in fact, a minister, and, as will be seen in the final chapter, he published material which attested to his religious faith while also demonstrating his support for Lincoln and the Union.[127]

ANTI-WAR PROSE

As was seen in Chapter Six, Samuel Roberts of Tennessee stayed true to his pacifism throughout the Civil War, condemning the Union's war efforts directly (while also condemning the Confederacy twice over, for pursuing the war and for maintaining slavery). This, it will be remembered, made Roberts a pariah on the pages of the North's Welsh-language press, as several writers, and *Y Drych*'s editor in particular, strove unfairly to imply a link between his anti-war stance and the slave system. As was also seen in Chapter Six, Roberts did manage to publish a few letters in *Y Cenhadwr Americanaidd*, thus proving that the press' pro-war stance did not completely preclude the publication of pacifistic material. Indeed, like the letters of protestation which Roberts presented on the pages of the *Cenhadwr*, the other two denominational journals published a few isolated pieces of anti-war prose. In June 1862 *Y Cyfaill o'r Hen Wlad* published an essay by an anonymous author bearing the title 'Ac Ni Ddysgant Ryfel Mwyach', 'And They Will No Longer Learn [or 'Teach'] War'. The title's quotation of Isaiah 2.4 is repeated in the piece's opening sentence, as the writer invokes his (or her) version of personified peace: '"Ni ddysgant ryfel," ond bydd *heddwch* yn eistedd ar yr orsedd, a'r deyrnwialen aur yn ei llaw, yn llywodraethu yr holl genedloedd'; '"They will not learn war", but peace will sit on the throne, with the golden sceptre in her hand, governing all the nations.'[128] Unlike some of the prose which Samuel Roberts published, this pacifist's essay says nothing specifically about the spirit of war which as gripping Welsh-American society. Indeed, the Civil War itself is only mentioned parenthetically, as the writer attempts to offer a tally of those killed by all of history's wars:

> Y mae dros bedair mil ar ddeg o filiynau o'n cydgreaduriaid . . . wedi syrthio yn ysglyfaeth i'r anghenfil rheibus hwn er pan y daeth i fod (yn flaenorol i ryfel cartrefol Talaethau Unedig America yn 1861–2) . . . Y mae rhyfel yn difa teimladau gwerthfawrocaf y natur ddynol, ac yn gwneyd y byd yn anghyfanedd, ac y mae y draul i'w gadw yn fyw, o'r bron, tu hwnt i'n hamgyffred.[129]

> 'More than fourteen million of our fellow creatures . . . have fallen as prey to this rabid monster since it first came into being (before the civil war of the United States of America in 1861–2) . . . War destroys human nature's most valuable feelings, and it makes the world desolate, and the cost of keeping it alive is nearly beyond our reckoning.'

Although not addressing the ideological claims which other writers were advancing on behalf of the Union's war effort, this writer leaves no room for moral equivocation: 'a beth a *enillwyd* i ni . . . mewn *rhyfel*? Enill yn wir! Y mae hyny allan o'r cwestiwn; nid oes anrhydedd, na gogoniant, na chyfoeth i'w gael trwy ryfel'; 'and what has been *won* for us . . . in *war*? To win indeed! That is out of the question; there is no honour, nor glory, nor wealth to be achieved through war.'[130]

Two pieces of anti-war prose were published in *Y Seren Orllewinol* in 1865, one in February, two months before the end of the war, and one in August, after the last Confederate army had surrendered. The first one, written by a writer simply identified as 'T. D.', attempts to describe what its title calls 'Echryslonrwydd Rhyfel,' 'War's Horror'.[131]

> I gael golwg ar erchryslonrwydd rhyfel, ni a ddyneswn ychydig yn nes yn mlaen, fel y byddom yn fwy agos at y frwydr, a gwelwn olygfeydd dychrynllyd. Gwelwn fintai fawr o ddynion nerthol, eu cerddediad yn gyflym a rheolaidd, yr olwg arnynt yn ysblenydd, a phob peth yn ymddangos yn orwych a rhwysgfawr. Ond A! yn mhen ychydig amser canfyddir golygfa wahanol i'r un flaenorol. Clywir trwst carlamiad meirch yn rhuthro allan i'r gad, cyflegrau yn rhuo, tân yn wasgaredig, pelenau tân (bombshells) yn gwau ac yn chwyrnellu yr awyr, y mwg yn esgyn yn gaddug gorchuddiedig, fel na allasid canfod y ddaear ar ba un y safasant, a'r ysgrechfeydd mwyaf truenus yn esgyn i'r clyw, nes trywanu y galon. Dyna ddigon. Na! safwn ychydig eto. Dyma yr awel yn chwythu, y mwg yn myned ymaith, a rhyw olygfa ddychrynllyd a thorcalonus yn ymddangos: y ddaear wedi ei gorchuddio â gwaed dynol; a channoedd ïe, miloedd ar filoedd o fodau dynol yn gorwedd yn gelaneddau meirwon yn eu gwaed: tra y mae eraill yn dyoddef y poenau mwyaf arteithiol wedi eu clwyfo ar y maes, fel y maent yn boen i'r byw eu gweled![132]

> 'In order to get a glimpse of war's horror, let us draw a little nearer, so that we might be closer to the battle, and see the frightening scenes. We see a great host of powerful men, their walk quick and regular, their appearance splendid, and everything appearing superb and ostentatious. But Ah! In a short time a scene different to the previous one is perceived. The tumult of horses rushing out to battle is heard, cannons roaring, dispersed fire, bombshells weaving and whirling in the air, the smoke ascending in a concealing mist, so that it is not possible to perceive the earth on which they stood, and the most pitiful screams ascending to the ear, so that the heart is smitten. That is enough. No! We will linger yet for a while. There the breeze is blowing, the smoke is going away, and a frightening and heart-rending scene is appearing: the earth covered with human blood; and hundreds, yes, thousands upon thousands of human beings, dead bodies laid low in their own blood: while others suffer the most torturous pains after being wounded on the field, so that it is painful for the living to see them!'

Having painted this prose picture of the battlefield's horrors, the writer then lists some of recent history's more famous battles, naming 'Austerlitz . . . Bauntzen. . . . Dresden . . . Waterloo . . . [and] Borodino'.[133] Then, after referring in less precise terms to the bloody battles fought in India, he turns to the American Civil War:[134] 'Ofer i ni fyddai cynnyg roddi darluniad . . . o'r brwydrau ofnadwy yn y wlad hon. Y mae iaith yn pallu'; 'It would be vain for us to attempt to present a picture . . . of the fearful battles in this country.

Language fails.'[135] The end of this didactic essay echoes its opening sentence, as the author quotes from Isaiah's prophecy of peace, asking the 'dear Reader' ('Darllenydd hoff') to join him in praying for the time when 'swords will be turned into ploughshares, and the spears into scythes' ('troir y cleddyfau yn sychau, a'r gwaewffyn yn bladuriau').[136]

The piece which the *Seren* published in August 1865 was most likely composed during the final weeks of the war. Echoing T. D.'s picture of 'war's horror', this anonymous author labels his or her prose painting as 'Golygfa Ddychrynllyd Rhyfel', 'War's Frightening Vista'. The noun *golygfa* can mean 'scene', 'view' or 'vista', yet this short piece of powerful prose is perhaps best described as a 'panoramic view'. This writer piles together a series of short, urgent clauses, barely containing them within three loosely-constructed sentences. The result is a disturbing survey of war's horrors which jolts the reader from one frightening scene to the next. It is worth quoting in its entirety:

> Rhoddais iddo ddesgrifiad o fagnelau, (meddai un ysgrifenwr dienw,) drulliau, magnelau, cleddyfau, drulliau blaenfiniog, gwarchaeoedd, ymosodiadau, cloddio, a gwrth-gloddio, a thân-dafliadau: o ryfeloedd ar dir a môr, llongau yn suddo gyda mil o ddynion, deuddeg mil yn cael eu lladd o bob tu, griddfanau marwol, aelodau yn ehedeg yn yr awyr, mwg, twrw, sathru i farwolaeth dan garnau meirch: ffoedigaeth, erlyniad, buddugoliaeth, caeau wedi eu gorchuddio â chyrff meirw wedi eu gadael yn ymborth i gwn a chreaduriaid rheibus. Ac yn mhellach, gwelais anrheithio, diosg dillad, llosgi, a dinystrio. Sicrheais iddo i mi weled cant o elynion yn cael eu chwythu i fyny mewn gwarchaead, a chynifer a hyny mewn llong; a gwelais y calaneddau yn syrthio i lawr yn ddarnau o'r cymylau, er difyrwch mawr yr edrychwyr.[137]

> 'I gave him a description of projectiles, (said one anonymous writer,) rifles, cannons, swords, rifles with bayonets affixed, sieges, attacks, entrenching, and digging counter-trenches, and cannonades: of wars upon land and sea, ships sinking with a thousand men, twelve thousand being killed on every side, the cries of the dying, limbs flying through the air, smoke, noise, trampling to death beneath horses' hooves: a route, pursuit, victory, fields covered with dead bodies left as fodder for dogs and rabid animals. And, moreover, I saw pillaging, shedding clothes, burning, and destroying. I assured him that I had seen one hundred enemies being blown up in a siege, and as many in a ship; and I saw the bodies falling down in pieces from the clouds, to the great amusement of the observers.'

This striking piece of prose appears in isolation on the page; other than the title, there is nothing else printed with it which offers any meaningful context to which a reader might turn in interpreting these sentences. It is a fiction, and presents an interaction between the speaker and an unspecified man (the word *iddo*, 'to him,' appears twice).

While appearing at first to be a dialogue between a soldier and a civilian, with the former 'assuring' (*sicrhau*) the later that he has seen the horrors of war at first hand, the dizzying breadth of this panoramic vision of war moves into the patently fictional realm of the surreal; the speaker claims to have witnessed battles on land and on sea, and the way in which he tallies the dead suggests the all-seeing eye of a supernatural observer. Like Samuel Williams's strict-metre poem condemning war, the force of this text is derived from its brevity, and the author does not provide details as to the exact nature of his narrator. Given the kinds of Welsh prose published in Wales and the United States before and during the Civil War, it is possible that readers would have read this fantastical piece as an (albeit experimental or unorthodox) example of the dream vision genre; they would have been familiar with other texts in which angels or supernatural guides were employed by authors as devices for presenting vistas which would otherwise be denied to mortals.[138]

The means by which this text's speaker is able to view the panorama of war, however, are not important here. Rather than drawing attention to the fictional characters who inhabit his (or her) text, the writer instead concentrates on constructing the vision of war's horrors. The effect is cumulative, with the bald references to weapons ('cannons', 'guns', 'swords') yielding to words describing the ways in which these arms are employed ('sieges', 'attacks', 'cannonades'). At the start of the war Welsh-American publications provided readers with lists of military vocabulary; as was suggested in Chapter Three, these glossaries helped readers unaccustomed to war follow the stories in the country's English papers as well as adapt their own native Welsh to the circumstances of war. This piece of prose reads like an ironic comment on those vocabulary lists, for it moves quickly from an emotionless list of those military terms to a description of the actual purpose for which these weapons exist, as 'body parts fly in the air' and 'fields are covered with dead bodies left as food for dogs and rabid animals'.

If the critique of war begins with the first sentence's accumulation of military terminology, it is heightened by several other subtle details. The word *buddugoliaeth*, 'victory', had appeared hundreds of times in the Welsh-American press during the four years preceding this piece's publication in August 1865, and it was almost always presented in terms of celebrating a Union victory (or regretting the failure to achieve one). Here it is tossed into a list of words which presents 'victory' in an off-hand manner, following *ffoedigaeth* ('rout') and *erlyniad* ('pursuit'). The author has devised a technique which robs the word *buddugoliaeth* of the glory normally associated with 'victory', and this helps to sharpen the text's critical edge.

This chapter began by discussing the paintings which Henry H. Davis brought to Pennsylvania in the spring of 1863. The editor of *Y Seren Orllewinol*, it will be remembered, urged the state's Welsh citizens to turn out and view the artist's 'panorama'. This is the same journal which, in August 1865, published our anonymous writer's panoramic view of the horrors of war. Davis was a former soldier, and he used visual art as a way of bringing the war – or his representation of the war – home to civilians in the North. On the other hand, nothing is known about that Welsh-American who used words to paint 'Golygfa Ddychrynllyd Rhyfel', 'War's Frightening Vista'. Whoever this writer was, he or she ventured beyond the bounds of literary convention in order to fashion a unique piece of experimental prose.

Despite its originality, this urgent piece of writing is similar to the other works of anti-war prose discussed here in two important ways: it condemns war unconditionally while also avoiding any direct comment on the causes of Union and freedom for which other Welsh-Americans claimed to be fighting. Samuel Roberts criticized what he called 'Ysbryd Rhyfel y Gogledd', 'The War Spirit of the North', placing blame squarely at the door of those Welsh-speaking Americans who wrote and published pro-war literature. When examined against the background of Welsh America's substantial body of war-time writing, Samuel Roberts's aggressively honest pacifism is startlingly unique. However, while not criticizing their fellow-countrymen directly, these three prose-writers, like several of the poets discussed in this chapter, produced memorable condemnations of war itself. These texts constitute isolated islands of pacifism in the sea of pro-war literature which poured forth from the Welsh-American press during the Civil War. However, that which isolates them also makes them unique; free from the conventions of patriotic propaganda, these anti-war writers and poets produced some of the war's most memorable works of Welsh-language literature.

NOTES

1 I have not been able to learn whether Davis's panorama has survived. Ambitious paintings of this type were not uncommon, whether panoramic illustrations of single battles (such as the one which General Joseph Hooker commissioned to commemorate his victory at Lookout Mountain) or series of pictures which provided extended pictorial narratives. Perhaps the best-known example of this kind of panorama is the one by William Travis, a '528-foot Civil War panorama celebrating the Federal Army of the Cumberland'; also like Davis, Travis took his panorama on tour: 'Travis mounted his work on rollers and toured with it in the Midwest after the war.' Richard M. Ketchum (ed.), *The American Heritage Picture History of the Civil War* (New York, 1960), p. 72. Similarly, while Davis's panorama contained what *Y Seren Orllewinol*'s editor described as *yr Adran hanesyddol* ('the historical section'), Travis' massive work opens with a painting entitled 'Going to war'.

2 *Y Seren Orllewinol*, April 1863.

3 *Y Cenhadwr Americanaidd*, November 1863.

4 The adjective *cartrefol* could also be translated as 'homely' or 'comfortable'; however, in the present context the phrase *y teimlad cartrefol* must be rendered as 'the feeling at home'.

5 *Y Seren Orllewinol*, October 1862.

6 *Y Cenhadwr Americanaidd*, October 1862. The article is entitled 'Gohebiaeth o Washington' ('Correspondence from Washington').
7 *Y Cenhadwr Americanaidd*, October 1862. This piece, entitled 'Y Trallod yn Cincinnati' ('The Tribulation in Cincinnati'), was by the Revd Thomas Edwards.
8 Ibid.
9 *Y Cyfaill o'r Hen Wlad*, May 1865.
10 Robert Huw Griffiths, 'The Welsh and the American Civil War c.1840–1865' (unpublished PhD thesis, Cardiff University, 2004), p. 234. See in general Chapter 6, 'Welsh Emigration During the American Civil War'.
11 Ibid.
12 *Y Cenhadwr Americanaidd*, October 1863.
13 For the history of Welsh gold miners in Colorado, see Eirug Davies, *Y Cymry ac Aur Colorado* (Llanrwst, 2001).
14 *Y Drych*, 24 January 1863. The pen-name is in English, 'Coal Digger'.
15 Ibid.
16 *Y Drych*, 24 January 1863. The piece on Minersville is by Joseph Prosser (Penfelyn).
17 Ibid.
18 Ibid.
19 Ibid.
20 It is not clear whether this poem actually won the competition. As with so many nineteenth-century American *eisteddfodau*, the records are incomplete.
21 The poem was not published until a year after the event; *Y Seren Orllewinol*, July 1862.
22 Ibid.
23 For a discussion of this kind of 'altar' imagery, see Chapter Four, pages 169–71.
24 *Y Seren Orllewinol*, July 1862.
25 Chapter Three, pages 127–42.
26 *Y Seren Orllewinol*, July 1862.
27 *Y Seren Orllewinol*, July 1862.
28 *Y Seren Orllewinol*, January 1862. Note that the January issue of this journal was produced early, before the end of December.
29 Littler was serving in South Trenton, New York, before enlisting in the army. *Y Seren Orllewinol*, January 1862.
30 *Y Seren Orllewinol*, April 1862.
31 *Y Seren Orllewinol*, January 1861.
32 *Y Cenhadwr Americanaidd*, February 1862.
33 *Y Drych*, 31 January 1863.
34 Ibid.
35 Ibid.
36 For the translation I have re-arranged the order of the lines in order to achieve a more fluid syntax in English. I have taken the phrase *ei holynol ysgrifeni*, literally 'her [i.e. the *eisteddfod*'s or the goddess's] consecutive writings' to mean the stream of literature or writings produced for the *eisteddfod*, and published subsequently by the Welsh-American press.
37 *Y Drych*, 31 January 1863.
38 See Marged Haycock, 'Llyfr Taliesin: Astudiaethau ar Rai Agweddau' (unpublished PhD thesis, University of Wales, Aberystwyth, 1983); Patrick Ford, 'Introduction,' *Ystoria Taliesin* (Cardiff, 1992).
39 In most versions of the narrative, it is Taliesin's earlier incarnation as Gwion Bach

who actually steals the contents of Ceridwen's cauldron. See Patrick Ford, *Ystoria Taliesin*.

40 This image – the 'goddess' going to sleep in 'the peace of death's land' even though she is 'sturdy' (*heini*) and 'full of energy' (*yn llawn nwyf*) – suggests two things at once; in addition to evoking the supernatural triumph over death found in the Ceridwen-Taliesin story, it also suggests that this 'son of the Utica Eisteddfod' disagreed with those committee members who cancelled the event. Echoing his fake obituary's sarcastic comment that the organizers were afraid of trusting the Welsh poets and writers of America to hold an *eisteddfod* in the face of war, the poem suggests that, though put to rest temporarily, the *eisteddfod* had enough 'vitality' or 'energy' (*nwyf*) to continue.

41 The Battle of Second Bull Run: 29 August 1862.

42 *Y Drych*, 24 January 1863.

43 *Y Drych*, 17 January 1863.

44 Ibid.

45 Ibid.

46 *Y Seren Orllewinol*, August 1863.

47 *Y Drych*, 10 January 1863. While the meeting was held in March, it was advertised the previous January, a fact which suggests that the local Sunday school expected to attract competitors who travelled from other communities. The word *cwrdd*, translated here as 'meeting', is used to mean 'prayer meeting' or 'religious gathering'.

48 According to James McPherson, 'the Christian Commission [was] founded by YMCA leaders in November 1861 to provide blankets, clothing, books, and physical as well as spiritual nurture to Union soldiers.' James M. McPherson, *Battle Cry of Freedom* [:] *The American Civil War* (Oxford, 1988), p. 483.

49 Stuart Murray, *A Time of War* [:] *A Northern Chronicle of the Civil War* (Lee [Mass.], 2001), p. 95.

50 James McPherson, *Battle Cry of Freedom*, p. 481.

51 This appears to have been a branch of the Women's Central Association of Relief; however, different Welsh names were used for local branches of the various national organizations, and it is at times difficult to tell whether they working directly with the US Sanitary Commission or the Women's Central Association of Relief (or, indeed, with one of the other smaller charities which were organized during the war).

52 *Y Cenhadwr Americanaidd*, January 1862.

53 Ibid.

54 Ibid.

55 Ibid.

56 *Y Drych*, 10 January 1863.

57 Ibid.

58 Ibid. Compare James McPherson, *Battle Cry of Freedom*, p. 481: 'Because of the close ties between Commission leaders and the citizen volunteers who became officers of regiments, the Sanitary helped shape the hygienic conditions of army camps.'

59 Diary of John H. Williams, manuscript in the collection of the Vermont Historical Society. The fact that this box was sent specifically to the regiment's group of Welsh soldiers is borne out by later passages in the diary, where it is specified that Williams stayed behind to guard the food while some of the other Welsh soldiers were performing their duties.

60 Diary of John H. Williams.

61 Ibid.
62 Melinda Lawson, *Patriot Fires [:] Forging a New American Nationalism in the Civil War North* (Lawrence [Kansas], 2002), 15–39.
63 *Y Cyfaill o'r Hen Wlad*, March 1864.
64 Ibid. These comments, placed after the main text, are followed by the abbreviation '-Gol.', '-Ed[itor]'.
65 *Y Cenhadwr Americanaidd*, March 1863.
66 *Y Drych*, 17 January 1863.
67 *Y Cenhadwr Americanaidd*, January 1863. She signed the obituary letter 'Ei anwyl fam alarus, Catherine Williams' ('His dear grieving mother, Catherine Williams').
68 *Y Cenhadwr Americanaidd*, January 1865.
69 *Y Cyfaill o'r Hen Wlad*, February 1865.
70 *Y Cenhadwr Americanaidd*, June 1863.
71 Ibid.
72 Ibid.
73 *New English Bible* (Oxford, 1976), p. 846.
74 For example, Robert Everett used the image in addressing his journal's readers: 'Ceir llawer yn ein hoff wlad y dyddiau hyn yn nyffryn trallod a galar – ac nid hawdd sychu y dagrau. Collasant eu hanwyliaid ar faes yr ymdrechfa fawr, ac fel Rahel ni fynant eu cysuro am nad ydynt.' *Y Cenhadwr Americanaidd*, January 1865.
75 For *y fam Gymreig* ('the Welsh Mother'), see Chapter Three, pages 130–1.
76 *Y Cenhadwr Americanaidd*, June 1863.
77 Alice Fahs, *The Imagined Civil War* [:] *Popular Literature of the North and South 1861–1865* (Chapel Hill and London, 2001), p. 108.
78 *Y Seren Orllewinol*, April 1864.
79 Quoted by Alice Fahs, *The Imagined Civil War*, p. 108.
80 *Y Seren Orllewinol*, April 1864.
81 Ibid.
82 Ibid.
83 Ibid.
84 Ibid.
85 *Y Cenhadwr Americanaidd*, November 1861.
86 Robert Huw Griffiths, 'The Welsh and the American Civil War c.1840–1865', Chapter 6.
87 Rowland Walter, *Caniadau Ionoron* (Utica, 1872), p. 303. This was published during the war in *Y Cenhadwr Americanaidd*.
88 Ibid., pp. 303–4.
89 See, for example, the poems by Ionoron discussed in Chapter Three, pages 136–42.
90 Elizabeth Young, *Disarming the Nation* [:] *Women's Writing and the American Civil War* (Chicago, 1999), p. 69.
91 *Y Cenhadwr Americanaidd*, September 1863.
92 See Chapter Three, page 140.
93 *Y Cenhadwr Americanaidd*, September 1863.
94 Ibid.
95 *Y Drych*, 11 July 1863.
96 *Y Cyfaill o'r Hen Wlad*, September 1863.
97 J. D. Jones of the 94th Illinois; *Y Cenhadwr Americanaidd*, October 1863.
98 *Y Cenhadwr Americanaidd*, September 1863.
99 Ibid.

[100] Ibid.
[101] Ibid.
[102] Ibid.
[103] Ibid.
[104] Ibid.
[105] *Y Cenhadwr Americanaidd*, May 1863.
[106] Ibid.
[107] Ibid.
[108] Ibid.
[109] Pete Seeger, 'Where Have All the Flowers Gone?' The song was composed during the late 1950s, and became a favourite protest piece during the Vietnam War of the 1960s. See Tom Glazer (ed.), *Songs of Peace, Freedom and Protest* (New York, 1970), pp. 338–40.
[110] *Y Cenhadwr Americanaidd*, May 1863.
[111] *Y Seren Orllewinol*, December 1863; 'Mor hyfryd i brydydd yw llanerch myfyrdod, / O afael helbulon a'r trafferth i gyd'.
[112] *Y Seren Orllewinol*, December 1863.
[113] Ibid.
[114] Ibid.
[115] Ibid.
[116] Ibid.
[117] Ibid.
[118] Ibid.
[119] Ibid.
[120] *Y Cyfaill o'r Hen Wlad*, April 1864.
[121] Ibid.
[122] Richard Marius (ed.) and Keith Frome (associate ed.), *The Columbia Book of Civil War Poetry* (New York, 1994), pp. 3–4.
[123] Ibid., p. 5.
[124] *Y Cyfaill o'r Hen Wlad*, April 1864.
[125] *Geiriadur Prifysgol Cymru* (Cardiff, 1950–2002), p. 465.
[126] *Y Cyfaill o'r Hen Wlad*, March 1864.
[127] *Y Cyfaill o'r Hen Wlad*, July 1865.
[128] Isaiah 2.4 is echoed by Micah 4.3. The rest of this sentence, though not an exact quotation, reflects Isaiah 2.4's reference to a situation in which 'nation shall not lift sword against nation.'
[129] *Y Cyfaill o'r Hen Wlad*, June 1862.
[130] Ibid.
[131] *Y Seren Orllewinol*, February 1865.
[132] Ibid.
[133] Ibid.
[134] I am using the masculine pronoun in referring to this writer because the initials 'T. D.' suggest a man's name, most likely Thomas Davies (or Davis). A less likely possibility, Theophilus, is also a man's name. No known Welsh-American women writers from this period had a first name beginning with 'T'.
[135] *Y Seren Orllewinol*, February 1865.
[136] Ibid.
[137] Ibid.
[138] See Chapter Two's discussion on Ieuan Ddu's dream vision, pages 63–5.

8

Turning Pens into Swords: Soldiers' Poetry

As was seen in the last chapter, one of wartime Welsh America's more successful literary festivals was the event which took place on Christmas Day 1862 in Fairhaven, Vermont. It will be remembered that, while the pressures of war forced Utica's Welsh community to cancel their 1 January 1863 *eisteddfod*, the Fairhaven festival went on as planned, and that it was described in print by John E. Roberts as 'Diwrnod Difyr', 'An Entertaining Day'. Roberts had his own reasons for finding the day 'entertaining'; he himself won the *englyn* competition with his strict-metre stanza on the 'Y Cleddyf' ('The Sword').

> Llunio clwy sy'n lloni cledd – a'i afiaeth
> yw yfed creulonedd;
> Gelyn hallt i galon hedd
> yw a fwrir o'i fawredd.[1]

> 'Crafting a wound is what delights a sword – and its mirth
> is drinking cruelty;
> A severe enemy of the very heart of peace
> is he who is drawn by its majesty.'

This *englyn* was saved for posterity by one of the poet's friends, John H. Williams; he copied it into his diary sometime after being mustered into the 14th Vermont Infantry.[2] Williams corresponded with several poets while in uniform; in addition to his friend John E. Roberts, he also wrote to the Revd R. L. Herbert, one of the country's better known Welsh bards.[3] The soldier also noted in his diary that publications such as *Y Drych* reached him in his Virginia camp, and he would thus have been exposed to a considerable amount of new verse in his native language dealing with various aspects of the war. However, this *englyn* on 'The Sword' was the only poem which Williams took the trouble of recording in his diary. He would carry Roberts's words with him during his first and only experience of combat, when he and his fellow-Vermonters were among the first Union soliders to face Picket's Charge on the final day of the Battle of Gettysburg.

John Williams did not carry a sword himself, let alone use one in combat, and in this he was like the vast majority of soldiers on both sides. The image central to Roberts's verse was in many ways an anachronistic one; by the time he composed his *englyn* the carnage on numerous Civil War battlefields had made it horrifically clear that the age of the rifled musket had arrived. Nevertheless, most Civil War poets were still using the sword to represent the soldier's weaponry. It was a highly charged symbol, easily employed to evoke romanticized tales of past wars as well as a range of biblical images. For example, one of the best-known compositions of the war, Julia Ward Howe's 'The Battle Hymn of the Republic', describes in its first verse a vengeful Lord who 'hath loosed the fateful lightning of his terrible swift sword'.[4] Popular iconography of the period – appearing in a variety of contexts ranging from magazine prints to the decorated envelopes sold to soldiers and their families – often featured an idealized soldier defiantly brandishing a blade.

However, the poem which John Williams copied into his diary was neither a meditation on God's sword of judgement nor an ode to a romanticized swordsman. While its central image is the romantic weapon of the past, Roberts's *englyn* occupies an entirely different realm from the one inhabited by the sword-raising cartoon hero of popular iconography. It is, in fact, much closer to another war-time *englyn* composed by another poet from Vermont, Ionoron Glan Dwyryd's stanza on 'The Cannon':

Offeryn ing o ffwrn angau – â thân
A thwrf rhwng ei weflau;
O'i mîn hyll, dinistr mae'n hau –
Gwae! yw anadl ei genau.[5]

'An instrument of agony from death's furnace – with fire
And tumult between its lips;
From its ugly orifice it sows destruction –
Woe! is the breath from its mouth.'

Both poets personify the weapon in question. While Ionoron's cannon has lips and a mouth, an 'ugly orifice' from which it can 'sow destruction', John Roberts's sword 'delights' in wounding and 'drinking' cruelty. Similarly, both are characterized in diabolical terms, as opposites of the peaceful (and heavenly) forces which should govern life; the cannon is 'an instrument of pain from death's furnace' and the sword turns those whom it possesses into enemies of the very 'heart of peace'. Roberts makes good use of the internal line ornamentation mandatory in this strict metre, ensuring that form works hand in hand with content; the *cynghanedd* of the line 'Gelyn hallt i galon hedd' links the 'heart of peace' and its 'severe enemy' together in a tightly woven phrase which brings vanquisher and vanquished into an unnerving proximity.

If these lines differ substantially from the sword imagery which characterized much of America's war-time popular culture, they were not without precedent within the Welsh literary tradition. There was a vast body of medieval Welsh poetry dealing with the experience of warfare, some of which was made available to nineteenth-century readers by means of published collections and bardic primers. However, it is likely that a Victorian Welsh reader coming across this American poem for the first time would have been reminded first and foremost of a more recent composition, an extremely popular *englyn* by William Ambrose (1813–73):

Celfyddyd o hyd mewn hedd – aed yn uwch
    O dan nawdd tangnefedd;
  Segurdod yw clod y cledd,
  A'i rwd yw ei anrhydedd.[6]

'Art eternal in peace – may it prosper
    Under amity's patronage;
  Idleness is the sword's praise,
  And its rust is its honour.'

According to William Ambrose's oft-anthologized poem, the sword was only to be praised for being idle, displaying rust instead of blood as its badge of honour. The American *englyn*, while taking the same moral standpoint regarding the act of blood-letting, describes the reverse of the idle, honourable sword; John Roberts focuses on the active weapon, personifying it as a bloodthirsty monster which sustains itself by 'drinking cruelty'.

While focusing on the sword instead of the rifle which John Williams was himself carrying into battle, this verse presents anything but a sentimental construction of romanticized war. It is a darkly meditative piece which, unlike so much sentimental poetry being composed at the time, does in fact take the reader towards an honest appraisal of the weapon's purpose. Like William Ambrose's popular *englyn*, this stanza reminds the reader that, rather than being the accoutrements of glory, weapons exist for killing and for killing alone. Although the Welsh-American press provided John Williams with a range of more romantic and morale-boosting war poems from which to choose a potential inscription for his soldier's diary, he chose – for whatever reason – this grim meditation on 'the enemy of the heart of peace'. Indeed, this *englyn* sits comfortably with those pieces of anti-war literature discussed at the end of the last chapter.

If John Williams carried his friend's poem with him into battle, other Welsh-speaking soldiers composed verse of their own. These poems are for the most part virtually indistinguishable from the poetry which was produced by civilians. Direct references to the poet's experience of the war are – if they are included at all – often only incidental to the main thrust of the poem. Rather than basing an entire composition on first-hand experience of military life, these poets tend to use such references in a secondary manner, adding them on to works which otherwise occupy the same registers which dominate the civilians' literature.

In the previous chapter, mention was made of Jane Jones, that mother who used verse to mourn her sons Josiah and Jonadab, both of whom died while serving in the 94th Illinois Infantry. Jonadab was the first to die, and Josiah composed an elegy for him, 'Ymson Milwr ar Ol Brawd', 'A Soldier's Soliloquy after a Brother'. While the title identifies the poet as 'a soldier', the poem itself contains few direct references to the fact that both the brothers were serving in the army. At one point, Josiah claims that he can still hear his brother's voice, coming to him as clear as 'when [we were] still standing together beneath the strange storms / of the cold world' ('Pan eto'n cyd-sefyll is stormydd dïeithriawl / Yr oeraidd fyd').[7] However, other Victorian Welsh elegies use the image of the storm in referring to the troubles of this world, and these lines are not grounded overtly in an attempt to evoke the military service which took Jonadab's life. Josiah Jones included only one direct reference to the war, weaving it into a description of his brother's grave: 'Caf yna ail ddychwel o'r cymysg gyffröad / Sy'n siglo sylfeini ein hoff wlad yn awr'; 'I will be able to return there from the confusing tumult / Which is now shaking the foundations of our dear country.'[8] There is no further discussion of the conflict in which both brothers were embroiled.

By the time this poem was published in *Y Cenhadwr Americanaidd* Josiah too had died and the brothers' mother, Jane Jones, was left to mourn them both. She employed a device which was used by many other civilians who composed elegies for soldiers, describing heaven as a land where her boys can be free from the pains of war: 'Ni raid yna gario'r cledde' / Ofni 'r gelyn ni raid mwy / Pob peryglon wedi darfod'; 'No need to carry the sword there, / No need to fear the enemy any more, / All dangers have ended.'[9] While her soldier-son devoted only two lines of his elegy to the conflict, Jane Jones devotes three. Rather than being separated by any protracted mediation on the soldier's life, both poems actually occupy the same mournful register; both concentrate on the closeness of the tie that death has severed, and both meditate on attempts to remember the deceased.

'THIS LITTLE LIGHT': THE POETICS OF PICKET DUTY

One of the few Welsh poems published during the war which is grounded directly in the soldier's experience was published in *Y Cyfaill o'r Hen Wlad* in November 1864 under the title 'Gobaith y Vidette', 'The Hope of the Vidette' or 'Picket-guard'. Calling himself 'Omicron' (and thus, for reasons which are unclear, fashioning a bardic name from the fifteenth letter in the Greek Alphabet), this poet described himself as a member of 'Co. K., 3ydd Gat. Wisc. Vol. Infantry', Company K of the 3rd Regiment of Wisconsin Volunteer Infantry.[10]

Although the plight of the solitary picket – the soldier stationed alone to watch for advancing enemies – inspired a number of poems, this seems to be the only one composed by a poet who had himself been in that situation. A poet from Gomer, Ohio, using the name 'Eiddil o'r Coed' ('The Weak One from the Woods'), published a meditation on 'Marwolaeth y Gwylwyr' or 'The Death of the Watchers' in *Y Cenhadwr Americanaidd*. Beginning 'Lleoedd gwag rhai milwyr dewrion, / Heddyw ar furiau Seion sydd' ('The empty places of some brave soldiers / Are today on Zion's walls'), this poet prayed God to 'fill the gaps again' ('llanw 'r bylchau eto'), drawing a comparison between the holes which the dead guards left in the army's picket line and the empty places in the religious community at home created by the death of Welsh-American volunteers.[11] A popular English-language song composed by Ethel Lynn Beers, 'All Quiet along the Potomac Tonight', contrasted what is described ironically as the 'insignificant' killing of a lone soldier with the effect which his death will have on his family at home: ' "All quiet along the Potomac to-night!" / Except here and there a stray picket / Is shot, as he walks on his beat, to and fro, / By a rifleman hid in the thicket.'[12]

It is fear of a similar fate which drives Omicron's Welsh poem. He appended a prose explanation assuring readers that his verse was grounded in the reality of war-time experience.

Chattahoochie, Ga., Awst 31, 1864
OMICRON, Co. K., 3ydd Gat. Wis. Vol. Inf'ty.
BARCHUS OLYGYDD. – Tra yn sefyll yn rhagwyliwr (*Vidette*) ar drum o dir uchel, mewn coed tewion, ar noson dywyll, rhwng 12 ac 1 ar gloch boreu y dydd uchod, wrth edrych o'm cwmpas drwy y tywyllwch, gwelwn oleuni tân y *Picket Reserve* yn llewyrchu fel seren fach drwy y coed, yn groes i'r nant ddofn oedd rhyngwyf fi â hwy, trwy ba un yr oedd yn rhaid i mi groesi pe buasai y gelyn yn dyfod yn mlaen. Wrth sylwi ar y 'goleu bach', llonai fy meddwl, a rhedodd y llinellau uchod drwy fy meddwl, pa rai, os gadewch iddynt ymddangos yn y CYFAILL, fydd yn destun llawenydd i amryw o'm cyfeillion a'm perthynasau yn y wlad hon a'r Hen Wlad. Yr eiddoch yn ostyngedig, &c., O.[13]

'Chattahoochee, Ga., August 31, 1864
OMICRON, Co. K, 3rd Regiment, Wisconsin Volunteer Infantry.
RESPECTED EDITOR. – While standing as a picket (*Vidette*) on the ridge of some high ground, within a thick wood, on a dark night, between 12 and 1 o'clock in the morning on the day noted above, and while looking around me through the darkness, I saw the fire of the Picket Reserve shining like a little star through the woods, across a deep ravine which was between me and them, which I had to cross should the enemy come forward. At noticing the 'little light', my mind grew calm, and the above lines ran through my mind, which, if you allow them to

appear in the CYFAILL, will be a source of joy for various friends and relatives of mine in this country and the Old Country. Yours humbly, &c., O[micron].

The scene described in the soldier's explanatory prose is also presented in the poem's first two stanzas.

Tu cefn dwfn geunant sy',
 Llawn d'rysni du a dŵr;
Tu blaen mae'r gelyn cry',
 Yn saethu ddigon siwr:
Ond wele'r goleu bach sydd draw,
Mae'n d'weyd fod gwylwyr byw ger llaw.

Yn nyfnder tywyll nos,
 Rwy'n sefyll wrtho'm hun;
Un cwmni im' nid oes,
 Yn agos, unrhyw ddyn,
Ond wele'r goleu bach sydd draw,
Mae'n d'weyd fod gwylwyr byw ger llaw.[14]

'Behind lies a deep ravine,
 Full of dark thickets and water;
In front is the strong enemy,
 Shooting sure enough:
Yet see the little light which is there,
It is saying that living watchers are near by.

'In the dark depths of night,
 I stand by myself;
There is no company for me
 Near by, not a man,
Yet see the little light which is there,
It is saying that living watchers are near by.'

The geographical barrier separating the lone soldier from his comrades, like the camp fire which he sees on the other side, becomes heavily invested with layers of meaning. This verse resembles so many other poems discussed in this study in that it ends by shifting from the worldly war which is its starting-point to a consideration of heaven, described by Omicron as a 'land' ([*b*]*ro*) existing 'above tumult and every plague' ('uwch cyffro a phob pla').[15] If in the first stanza the soldier fixes his worried gaze on the 'deep ravine' separating him from his fellow soldiers, by the last stanza he is moved to contemplate God's triumphant passage 'through the coldness of the water and the gravel'

('Drwy oerni'r dŵr a'r gro'), suggesting a flight through the parted waters of the Red Sea to salvation.[16] The refrain repeated at the end of every stanza is by the end used to refer to an assurance of God's presence: 'Mae'r goleu bach a welaf draw, / Yn dyst ei fod E'r ochr draw'; 'The little light I see yonder, / Is a witness to His existence on the other side.'[17] The 'ravine' thus comes to represent a challenge to the soldier's faith, that vale of uncertainty which must be traversed in order to reach a state where knowledge of God's presence is assured.

Moving from the worldly to the spiritual, Omicron guides the reader from his initial description of the soldier's experiences to the concluding stanza's acknowledgement of God's presence. The ideational ravine which must be crossed in order to reach this conclusion includes a protracted meditation on the causes of the war, and the first step in that act of crossing is taken as the soldier attempts to dispel his own fears by turning his thoughts to people who suffer a 'worse fate'.

Ow! 'r Negro du sy'n gaeth,
  Faint gwaeth dy dynged di,
Dan greulawn feistr ffraeth,
  I'm clustiau daeth dy gri:
Ond gwel y goleu bach sydd draw,
Mae'n d'weyd fod gobaith it' ger llaw.

Do, aeth dy lef uwch ben,
  I'r nefoedd wen at Dduw,
Disgyn gan rwygo'r llen,
  Ef wnaeth wahaniaeth lliw:
Ond gwel y goleu bach sydd draw
Mae'n d'weyd fod gobaith it' ger llaw.

Dros fryniau Georgia falch,
  Y seinir arch y Llyw;
Trech ERYR nag un *gwalch*,
  A'r caeth gaiff ryddid gwiw:
A thystia'r goleu bach sydd draw,
Mae'n d'weyd fod gobaith it' ger llaw.[18]

'Oh! the black Negro who is enslaved,
  How much worse your fate,
Beneath a cruel and impudent master,
  To my ears your cry has come:
Yet see the little light which is there,
It says that there is hope for you near at hand.

'Yes, your cry went overhead,
Through the blessed heavens to God,
He descends while rending the veil,
It is He who made differences of colour:
Yet see the little light which is there,
It says that there is hope for you near at hand.

'Over the hills of proud Georgia
The President's demand is sounded,
An EAGLE is mightier than any *hawk*,
And the slave will have his deserved freedom:
And the little light which is there testifies,
It says that there is hope for you near at hand.'

The word italicized in the original, *gwalch*, means 'rascal' or 'scoundrel' as well as 'hawk'. Rejoicing in the role which he is playing by helping to ensure that the President's writ runs through 'proud Georgia', the poet describes what he has already defined as a struggle for freedom in terms of the American Eagle triumphing over the Confederate hawk/scoundrel.

The emotional pitch rises as the reader, having been guided away from the frightening predicament of the picket guard, is led to a series of revelations concerning the nature of the war in which the soldier is fighting. Having first stressed the fact that he fights for freedom, the poet-soldier then asks his readers to support the Union army: 'Ond hoff gyfeillion llon, / Na foed eich bron yn brudd; / Rho'wch nerth i'r fyddin hon'; 'Yet, dear happy friends, / Let not your breast be troubled; / Give strength to this army.' The succour which civilians provide thus becomes another light of hope, cheering lonely soldiers all across the South: 'Gadewch i'n wel'd eich goleu draw / Yn d'weyd fod cymhorth i'n wrth law'; 'Let us see your light over there / Saying that there is help for us at hand.'[19] Fear is conquered by the various kinds of hope which the 'little light' is made to represent, and this triumph is accompanied by renewed faith in the soldier's purpose.

Mae'r gwaith yn fawr ei werth,
Ac ynddo anferth fri:
Myn Duw ei wneyd mewn nerth,
Gan ryw rai – Onid ni?
Gadewch i'n wel'd eich goleu draw
Yn d'weyd fod cymhorth i'n wrth law.[20]

'The work is of great worth,
And it contains great honour:

God desires that it be undertaken mightily
 By somebody – Why not us?
Let us see your light over there
Saying that there is help for us at hand.'

Like those Welsh-American writers who provided theological interpretations of the war, this soldier is sure that God expects people to take up arms in order to free the slaves. The emotional coercion applied to readers can be interpreted as an appeal for volunteers: the time is now, he says, and who will do the job at hand, if not us? This poem, then, can also be interpreted in the context of those recruiting songs discussed in Chapter Three; among other things, it is an appeal for others to join the lonely soldier serving in the Southern wilderness.

Omicron grounds his verse solidly in the soldier's very real experiences (or what we are asked to accept as such). The title, the first two verses, the long prose explanation, and the fact that the poet described himself as a volunteer serving with Company K of the 3rd Wisconsin Infantry all work together to assure the reader as to the context in which this text was composed. However, rather than being fashioned so as to provide readers with a detailed glimpse of this experience, the text is concerned with the same ideological goals which were pursued by so many of Welsh America's other writers and poets. Rather than being a work of what we might call military realism, this piece was published in order to provide readers with a specific interpretation of the war's causes and the role of the volunteer in pursuing those causes; the poet strove so hard to (re)create the experiential grounding of his text in order to add moral weight to this interpretation. The prose appended to the poem tells readers that the lines which they have just read 'ran through [the poet's] mind' at a precise time in a specific place – while the soldier was standing picket duty on a wooded hill near Chattahoochee, Georgia, on 31 August 1864. We are asked to imagine the exact moment of poetic inspiration, a moment which – bound up so closely in the soldier's experience – forges a powerful link between text and context. Rather than being an end in itself, this note of authenticity is used to validate the poet's ideological agenda.

AWENYDD: A SOLDIER SEEKING INSPIRATION

Another poet who used his status as a soldier to authenticate his verse was Edward Thomas, or 'Awenydd'. When he published his long poem 'Y Milwr' – 'The Soldier' – in *Y Cenhadwr Americanaidd* in December 1864, Thomas noted that he was serving with Company E of the 2nd Minnesota Cavalry; like Omicron's composition, this text was presented as a poem about a soldier written by a soldier. Edward Thomas provides an example of Welsh America at the height of its cultural vibrancy. Never even seeing Wales, he was born in

Centreville, Ohio, in 1839, and moved to Minnesota with his parents six years later. Like the children of so many other immigrants, Thomas was raised speaking Welsh in Ohio and Minnesota, and at a young age he began composing poetry in his mother-tongue. He delved deeply into the Welsh bardic tradition's complexities, mastering several kinds of strict-metre poetry, and before the end of the war he was to win the main poetry competition in the Minersville *eisteddfod*, one of the largest Welsh festivals in Pennsylvania, and, indeed, the entire country.[21] Before enlisting in the Union army, Thomas had followed in his father's footsteps by working as a schoolteacher. His father, Edward Thomas, Sr, was also a remarkable man; although he was self-taught, receiving no formal education outside of Sunday school, he became noted for his learning and was a popular teacher in both Ohio and Minnesota. He was also a singing instructor, and in this capacity he played his part in maintaining America's *eisteddfod* culture. Moreover, Edward Thomas Sr was active politically, being described by one writer as 'a free soiler in politics . . . and a friend to every moral and social reform'.[22] If the son followed the same career as his father, he also followed his moral and political lead; the anti-slavery poetry published by 'Awenydd' during the war suggests that it was to fight slavery that he volunteered for the Union army.[23]

By the end of the nineteenth century Edward Thomas was to become one of Welsh America's most noted poets, yet the bardic name which he adopted in his youth suggests that a hint of this literary success was manifest at a young age. Often translated simply as 'poet', the noun *awenydd* is formed from the word for bardic inspiration, *awen*, and can thus also be rendered as 'inspired one'. Thomas played consciously with his public bardic persona, publishing a short strict-metre poem on the subject of *awen* in the same poetry column which contained his longer poem on 'The Soldier'.

Englyn a gant yr Awenydd iddo ei hun pan yn ceisio prydyddu heb gynhorthwy yr Awen.

> O'r yni! gwelwch 'r awenydd, – pan
>   Yn poeni wrth gywydd;
> O flaen byd fel hyn y bydd,
> Yn y man, heb ymenydd![24]

'An *englyn* which the *Awenydd* sang to himself while trying to compose poetry without the help of the *Awen*.

> 'Oh the distress![25] – see the *awenydd*, – while
>   Worrying at a *cywydd*;
> Like this he will go before the world,
> Before long, without a brain!'

Awenydd is, of course, describing a phenomenon recognizable to modern English speakers as 'writer's block'. However, he does so using terms which had been bound up with Welsh bardic practice since at least the early medieval period. For centuries Welsh poets had contemplated *awen*, its source, and the manifestations of its presence; this twenty-five-year-old poet was continuing that tradition, meditating on the *awen*'s failure to visit him in his army camp.

This is an *englyn*, that popular strict metre used for short, epigrammatic meditations, and it refers to another of the traditional Welsh strict metres, the *cywydd* (plural *cywyddau*).[26] The *cywydd* was, in fact, the form which Awenydd used for his long composition on 'The Soldier'. In addition to his choice of metre, the Welsh-American poet's diction resonates with numerous *cywyddau* composed over several centuries, a point evident in the opening lines.

Milwr wyf fi a'm helynt
Yw hel, a gwasgar ar hynt,
Gelynion, gwael eu henw,
Dreisient y wlad – dor'sant lw, –
Anffyddlon i'w gwlad lonydd,
O ran ei hegwyddor rydd,
Tua'r llawr, o hyd i'r llwch,
Eu darostwng i dristwch;
I fynu codi'r faner,
Y sŷdd, wedi'i britho â ser,
Yn awr, ac amddiffyn hon,
Yw amod fy ymrywmion.[27]

'I am a solider and my course
Is to drive, and send dispersed on [their] way,
Enemies, poor their name,
Who ravage the country – they broke an oath –
Unfaithful to their peaceful country,
In terms of its free principle,
To the ground, steadily into the dust,
Subject them to sorrow;
In order to raise up the banner,
Which, (spangled with stars),
Is now, (and to defend it),
The condition of my pledges.'

The words giving the opening couplet its rhyme, *helynt* and *hynt*, also anchor the first lines of a poem by Goronwy Owen which was popular at the time, 'Cywydd y Farn' ('*Cywydd* on The Judgement').[28] Taken as the most proficient strict-metre poet of the eighteenth century, Goronwy Owen's poetry was considered as the gold standard for the eisteddfodic verse of the nineteenth century, and it is safe to assume that more than one reader who encountered Awenydd's *cywydd* on the pages of *Y Cenhadwr Americanaidd* would have known at least the opening lines of Goronwy's popular composition by heart.[29]

The Union cavalryman's opening line also resonates with much older *cywyddau*. Dafydd ap Gwilym, the fourteenth-century poet credited with popularizing the *cywydd* metre, often opened his dramatic compositions with first-person declarations set in the mouth of the poem's persona. Whereas the soldier of Awenydd's poem begins by identifying himself as such ('I am soldier and my course / is to . . .'), the amorous persona of Dafydd's love poetry usually begins with a similar act of self-introduction. To cite but a few examples: 'Prydydd i Forfudd wyf fi' ('I am Morfudd's poet'); 'Caru 'ddwyf, gwaith hynwyf gwyllt' ('I am loving, wild passionate work'); 'Gorllwyn ydd wyf ddyn geirllaes' ('I am pursuing a person of comely word'); 'Plygu rhag llid yr ydwyf' ('I am bent with rage').[30] Furthermore, the way in which this Welsh-American poet takes the grammatical structure of the Welsh sentence and explodes it creatively within the rigorous metrical confines of the *cywydd* also echoes medieval compositions by Dafydd ap Gwilym and other masters of the form. Edward Thomas runs one long sentence over a number of couplets, using the bardic technique of *sangiad* to forestall the sentence's grammatical conclusion, creating insertions or asides which fill out the line metrically while also enforcing the layers of meaning which the poet is constructing (for example, *dors'ant lw*, 'they broke an oath').[31]

Formal aspects of this poem are in keeping with a tradition which was more than five hundred years old by 1864. However, despite the antiquity of the form, Awenydd grounded his poem in his own recent experiences. The *cywydd* is divided into three sections, the first of which is devoted entirely to describing the soldier whose 'pledges' have him fighting 'enemies' described as 'ravaging' the 'free principle' of the country. Having set out the reasons why he has volunteered, the second half of this opening section is used to expand upon the hazardous nature of his occupation.

Heibio hêd y bwledi,
Bron, fel y cenllysg heb ri!
Mil a syrth fawr a mân!
Drwy oll rhaid brwydro allan,
Dyma alwad y milwr,
A gwaith y dewrfrydig wr.[32]

'The bullets fly past,
Almost, like hailstones without number!
A thousand fall both large and small!

Through everything one must battle on,
That is the soldier's calling,
And the work of the brave-minded man.'

In a recent discussion of ways in which Civil War soldiers 'shaped the battle experience' by drawing upon other familiar experiences, Earl J. Hess notes that veterans often used metaphors drawn from the world of nature to describe what had been previously an unknown experience, the 'rain' or 'hail' of bullets and shells on the battlefield.[33] Awenydd's metaphorical hailstones are drawn in terms which resemble the imagery used by many other soldiers, both Welsh- and English-speaking, to describe the same phenomenon.[34]

While the poem's first section attempts to present a realistic description of the dangers which Edward Thomas and his comrades had enlisted to face, the entire poem is not concerned with expounding upon this theme. The second section examines the concept of 'doing battle', removing it from the realm of the literal Civil War battlefield and turning it into the backbone of a didactic lecture which casts 'every man' as a 'soldier' fighting against life's troubles.

Pob gwr sydd filwr i fod
O hyd oes tra'i fod isod;
Brwydr, bâr i'w hedrych,
I'w oes-ran y gwan a'r gwych:
Brwydro sy'n bod â thlodi,
A rhan ryw luaws diri',
Yw afiechyd, – y fuchedd
Hon sy'n ymddifad o hedd;
Brwydro am gyfoeth, moethau,
Bery o hyd i barhau,
Am enw mawr a mwyniant,
Brwydro a cwyno mae cant[.][35]

'Every man is to be a soldier
Throughout life as long as he is on earth;
A battle, it is adversity to see it,
Is the part in life of [both] the weak and the great:
There is doing battle with poverty,
And the part of some unnumbered host
Is illness, – this life
Is bereft of peace;
Battling for wealth, luxuries,
Causing it always to continue,
For a great name and for benefit,
Hundreds are battling and complaining.'

The earnest tone which rings through this versified sermon recalls the early fourteenth-century *cywyddau* of Siôn Cent (a poet who was, incidentally, known to Welsh-American writers at the time, for at least one of them took his name as a pen-name). The metaphorical 'soldier' at the centre of the poem's moralistic middle section is later defined as 'Y Cristion gwirion, gwrol', 'The innocent, heroic Christian'. This heroic everyman 'has his enemies to trouble him' – 'A'i elynion i'w flino' – and these foes are described as internal forces ('Oddifewn iddo fynant / Orthrechu, ei nychu wnant'; 'Inside of him they desire / to overcome, they vex him'). Finally, he must fight with his own heart: 'His heart is hard' ('Ei galon sydd yn galed'), for 'its nature runs / away from God to mischief' ('ei thueddiad red / Oddiwrth Iôn at ddrygioni').[36] This strict-metre sermon thus concludes with a rhetorical question, as the poet asks 'Does one not have to battle against [the heart]?' ('Onid rhaid yw brwydro â hi?').

This elaboration on the perils, both external and internal, which plague the Christian's life sets the stage for the poem's short concluding section. Edward Thomas ends with a prayer, asking for strength.

> Nerth i mi a chynorthwy,
> Sy raid, methiantus yr wy,
> Duw fy Iôr, tyrd i arwain,
> A rhwydd orchfygaf y rhain[.][37]

> 'Strength and aid for me
> Is what's needed, I am weak,
> My Lord God, come to lead,
> And easily I will overcome these.'

Like that poet serving with the 3rd Wisconsin Infantry in Georgia, Edward Thomas grounded his poem soundly in references to his own military service. However, also like that other soldier-poet, Thomas uses this contextual grounding as a platform to pursue another agenda. Rather than focusing entirely on the realities of army life, both of these soldier's poems are ultimately concerned with other things.

'LOVING THE FIELD OF BLOOD'

A very different kind of soldier's poem was published by G. O. Jones in *Y Cenhadwr Americanaidd* under the title 'Y Rhyfel' ('The War'). Although all the biographical details are not clear, it seems that this man, whose full name was apparently George Owen Jones, served either with the 12th Pennsylvania Cavalry or with the 80th New York Infantry.[38] Whatever the real circumstances of the poet's life, he delivered his meditation on 'The War' by means of a soldier persona, and his words can be read as an answer to those anti-war voices discussed in the last chapter. This poem begins as a stylized confession, with the soldier-poet admitting that he has 'started loving the field of blood'. In the first verse he characterizes himself in a way which seems to play into the hands of the peace protesters. Like that anonymous prose-writer who described soldiers taking joy at watching 'bodies falling down in pieces' ('calaneddau yn syrthio i lawr yn ddarnau'), this poet presents himself as a soldier who has come to 'love' his bloody work.[39]

Rwy' wedi dechreu *caru maes y gwaed!*
 Os tybia neb yn addas gwaeddi 'ffol'
Ac 'yspryd dial' a 'gwag ymffrost,' gwnaed –
 Mae nghalon yno ac ni ddaw yn ol!
Mae'r teimlad wedi ymgymysgu â 'ngwaed,
 Nes rhed drwy nghalon fel toddedig ddur,
Nes ffero'r olaf ddafn ar faes y gâd![40]

'I have started *to love the field of blood!*
 If anyone thinks it fitting to scream "foolish"
And "spirit of revenge" and "vain boasting," let him do so –
 My heart is there and will not come back!
The feeling is mixed together with my blood,
 Until it runs through my heart like molten steel,
Until the last drop shall congeal upon the battle field!'

The words which Jones sets in quotation marks are in fact some of the exact phrases used by contemporary anti-war authors. He – or rather the soldier-persona who speaks in his poem – is apparently pleading guilty to the pacifists' charges.

However, this soldier's 'confession' is in reality a rhetorical ploy, part of an arsenal of authorial weapons which G. O. Jones deploys in order to persuade the reader that the Union's war is a just war. In fact, *Y Cenhadwr Americanaidd*'s readers were subjected to this ideological thrust even before encountering the poet's opening line. Jones prefaced his composition with a tribute to the *Cenhadwr*, and these words asked readers to consider the stance which the journal's editor had taken on the war: 'Cyflwynir y llinellau hyn i ofal y CENHADWR fel arwydd syml o barch i un sydd wedi codi ei lais mor hyf o blaid ei Wlad; a hyny heb lychwino ei gymeriad â *blagardiaeth* ac anfoneddigeiddrwydd'; 'These lines are presented to the CENHADWR's care as a simple symbol of respect for one who has raised his voice so boldly in support of his Country; and that without besmirching his character with *blackguardism* and ungentlemanliness.'[41] To further ensure that his reader was ideologically predisposed in a favourable manner, Jones introduced his own poem with an English quotation, a short extract from 'Table Talk', the long political satire which William Cowper published in 1782.

"When a country (one that I could name)
In prostitution sinks the sense of shame;
When Perjury, that Heaven-defying vice,
Yells oaths by tales, and at the lowest price,
Stamps God's own name upon a lie just made
To turn a penny in the way of trade;
When Av'rice starves, (and never hides his face)
Two or three millions of the human race,
What follows next –
But Providence himself will intervene,
And throw his dark displeasure o'er the scene.[42]

Cowper described his own poem as a 'moral satire', and it was aimed directly at the political situation which obtained in England at the time of its composition, including the growing debate over that country's involvement in the slave trade.[43] Jones adapts the eighteenth-century English poet's lines, applying them to the pre-Civil War United States, a country prostituted by slavery which had 'in the way of trade' hidden 'millions of the human race'.

The first line of G. O. Jones's own poem follows hard on the heels of this quotation. The soldier confesses 'to loving the field of blood' and then proceeds to quote those anti-war voices, pleading guilty to what they call 'vain boasting' and a 'foolish' indulgence in 'the spirit of revenge'. In his second verse Jones conjures a very different chorus of voices.

'R areithfa a 'ngwlad yn fy nhaer gymell sydd –
'Dos,' medd Dyngarwch, a phryderus lef,
'Mae'r caeth yn awr yn dysgwyl dod yn rhydd,'
'Dos,' medd Cyfiawnder llidiog, 'dial ef!'
Dychrynllyd drem dialedd sy yn ei wedd,
Awdurdod deddfau Duw sydd yn ei lais –
Cyfeiria yn ddigofus at y cledd;
'Dos,' meddai, 'dial orthrwm brad a thrais.'[44]

'The orator's platform and my country earnestly urge me –
"Go," says Humanitarianism, with a worried cry,
"The slave is now waiting to become free,"
"Go," says enraged Justice, "revenge him!"
The frightening look of revenge is upon his countenance,
The authority of God's laws is in his voice –
He gestures indignantly towards the sword;
"Go," he says, "revenge the oppression of treachery and violence." '

These voices urge the soldier to fight for what the poet is presenting as a just cause, and the instrument of Justice constructed by Jones is more akin to the 'terrible swift sword' which Julia Ward Howe placed in the hand of God than the bloodthirsty monster described in John E. Roberts's *englyn* (and discussed at the start of this chapter).

In his third verse the soldier continues to cross-examine the pacifist's protestations, placing the tension between war and peace within a moral context supplied by his interpretation of the Civil War's causes.

Gall gelyn Rhyfel alw am weinio'r cledd,
A gwaeddi, 'Dychwel Heddwch' – y gwir yw, –
Nid mewn budreddi a llaid y triga Hedd
Nid ar y domen bydd y duwiau'n byw;
Ni adeilada Hedd ei gorsedd hi,
Wrth draed gorseddau trais, a chestyll brad;
Tra anhyfiawnder bery'n gwmwl du,
Ni th'wyna haulwen Heddwch ar y wlad.[45]

'The enemy of War can call for sheathing the sword,
And scream, "Return Peace" – [but] the truth is, –
It is not in filth and mud that Peace resides
It is not on the dung-heap that the gods live;
Peace does not construct her throne
At the feet of violence's thrones and treachery's castles;
As long as injustice remains a black cloud,
The sunshine of Peace will not shine upon the country.'

This soldier does not reject Peace, but rather the possibility of building a 'throne' for her in a land corrupted by slavery. Like so many other Civil War writers, Jones invokes a personified Peace, asking his readers rhetorically whether or not this 'pure' creature could survive in the morally polluted climate of a slave-owning nation.

Pa le'r anadlai Heddwch pe bai'n dod,
P'le mae'r elfennau gadwai'i bywyd hi?
'R elfennau pur ddarparwyd iddi erioed?
Nid yn awyrgylch ein gwlad fostgar ni
Mae gwenwyn tawch Caethiwed – waeth pa le,
Yn gyfryw na all Rhinwedd ynddo fyw;
Gwnai ladd Archangel pura' cryfa'r Ne',
Neu'i droi yn gythraul o aflanaf ryw.[46]

'Where would Peace breathe should she come,
Where are the elements that would sustain her life?
The pure elements which were always provided for her?
Not in the climate of our boastful country;
The poison of Slavery's haze – no matter where,
Is such that no Virtue can live within it;
It would kill the purest and strongest Archangel of Heaven,
Or turn him into a devil of the basest sort.'

G. O. Jones follows these lines with a verse describing how 'a land of slavery' ('[g]wlad caethiwed') has perverted the very Bible that pacifists quote in defence of peace, turning 'the old Gospel' ('[y]r hen Efengyl') into 'a steel chain, / and a cruel whip for oppressing the Slave' ('yn gadwn ddur, / A chreulon fflangell i orthrymu'r Caeth').[47] This in turn is followed by a stanza which echoes those millennialistic texts discussed elsewhere in this study, those pieces of prose and poetry which interpreted the war as God's vengeance for sin ('Fy Ngwlad, fy ngwlad, mae Duw yn ddig – beth ddaw / O'th blant? mae'u hymddygiadau'n warth i'w byd'; 'My Country, my country, God is angry – what will come / Of your children? their behaviour is a shame to the world').[48] Using the slave master's perversion of Christianity as yet one more justification for the conflict, Jones finishes his penultimate stanza by stating that 'the Heavens' ('y Nefoedd') are left with no choice in such a situation but to use 'the judging sword' ('y barnol gledd').[49]

The poem's concluding stanza continues this millennialistic discourse, arguing that Heaven's judgement cannot now be avoided. The poet of the 3rd Wisconsin Infantry, it will be remembered, asked rhetorically why the work which God was demanding should not be done by 'us'. G. O. Jones lets his theological interpretation of the conflict run well beyond the realm of human agency, for he suggests that, should 'man' (*dyn*) refuse to wield God's 'judging sword', He will ensure that other forces wreak the violence required to cleanse the country of sin.

Nid *gweinio'r cledd* adfera Hedd i wlad
Lle byddo Rhyddid a Dyngarwch wedi eu lladd,
Cyfiawnder a gwirionedd o dan draed,
Heb neb a faidd dosturio mewn un grâdd
Os na ddaw dyn i'r maes o blaid y rhai'n –
O blaid yr egwyddorion mwyaf pur;
Fe naid y cledd o hono'i hun o'r wain,
A thyf y glaswellt yn fidogau dur![50]

'It is not *sheathing the sword* which will return Peace to a country
Where Freedom and Humanitarianism have been killed, [and]
Justice and truth [have been trampled] under foot,

Without anybody who dares to take pity in any way.
If man comes not to the field in support of these ones –
In support of the purest principles;
Then the sword will jump by itself from the sheath,
And the blades of grass will grow into steel bayonets!'

Several of those poems discussed in the last chapter which are both anti-war and anti-slavery resolve the tension between the two stances by enacting a religious turn, that is, by invoking an omnipotent God who can stop the fighting immediately while also ending slavery. In this poem G. O. Jones employs a very different kind of religious turn, countering the pacifist's accusations by claiming that the soldier's work on 'the field of blood' is a divinely dictated necessity. Rather than denying the charge that he is gripped by the 'spirit of revenge', he counters it with an aggressively creative strategy, first admitting to the allegation before re-interpreting it in morally positive terms.

Although Jones answers the anti-war voices with an overwhelming assault of fire and brimstone, he leaves one important question unanswered for the reader. After confessing in his opening stanza to 'loving the field of blood', the soldier adds that he cannot extract himself from that bloodthirsty state: *'Mae nghalon yno ac ni ddaw yn ol!* / Mae'r teimlad wedi ymgymysgu â 'ngwaed'; *'My heart is there and will not come back!* / The feeling is mixed together with my blood.' The warrior whom Jones constructed for the *Cenhadwr*'s readers was one possessed entirely by that 'spirit of revenge'; while he claims that his bloody sword is motivated by 'the authority of God's laws', there is no trace of that biblical verse which points the way from 'the field of blood' to a peace signalled by beating swords into ploughshares. While many civilian writers were looking hopefully towards the conflict's end, this text is located entirely in the here and now of the war's bloodshed.

The shocking confession of the opening stanza, in which Jones admits to 'loving the field of blood', gestures towards the harshest realties of the soldier's life. However, the soldier-poet *confesses* to the pacifists' accusations in order to *possess* their reproving words and turn them to suit his own purposes. This soldier's poem, though expressing a mindset which finds the carnage of the battlefield to be justifiable, is no more concerned with describing the realties of the soldier's life than are the other poems discussed here. Like the picket guard's anti-slavery recruiting song, and like Awenydd's meditation on the Christian's worldly struggles, the bloodythirsty confession of G. O. Jones's soldier is intended ultimately not to describe the acts to which he is 'confessing', but rather to interpret them in political, moral and theological terms. Like the swords which other soldier-poets fashioned with their pens, the weapons of this poem are literary constructs. Instead of reflecting the real weapons being carried into battle, they were designed first and foremost as rhetorical tools to be employed in a series of religious, moral and political arguments.

NOTES

1 Diary of John H. Williams, manuscript in the collection of the Vermont Historical Society. The *englyn* is inscribed on one of the opening pages, before the chronicle of daily life begins.

2 John Williams notes in his diary that he corresponded with his friend John E. Roberts; for example, one 6 January 1863: 'anfonais lythyr at Jane, ac at John E. Roberts'; 26 January 1863: 'yn y prydnawn daeth Billy Williams i edrych am danaf a daeth a llythyr i mi oddiwrth John E. Roberts.'

3 See Chapter Five, pages 220–2.

4 Richard Marius (ed.) and Keith Frome (associate ed.), *The Columbia Book of Civil War Poetry* (New York, 1994), pp. 55–6.

5 *Y Cenhadwr Americanaidd*, April 1862. See Chapter Three, pages 115–16.

6 Different anthologies present different versions of this *englyn*; the text quoted here is from Thomas Parry (ed.), *The Oxford Book of Welsh Verse* (Oxford, 1962), p. 531. Other anthologies present the stanza under the title 'Heddwch' ('Peace'); for example, W. J. Gruffydd, *Blodeuglwm o Englynion* (Cardiff, no date).

7 *Y Cenhadwr Americanaidd*, January 1865.

8 Ibid.

9 Ibid.

10 It seems that Richard H. Williams, Hugh Williams and William F. Harris were its only surviving Welsh soldiers by August 1864, and one of these three must have been 'Omicron'.

11 *Y Cenhadwr Americanaidd*, August 1863.

12 Richard Marius (ed.) and Keith Frome (associate ed.), *The Columbia Book*, p. 20.

13 *Y Cyfaill o'r Hen Wlad*, November 1864.

14 Ibid.

15 Ibid.

16 Ibid.

17 Ibid.

18 Ibid.

19 Ibid.

20 Ibid.

21 See, for example, T. E. Hughes, David Edwards, Hugh Roberts and Thomas Hughes (eds.), *Hanes Cymry Minnesota [:] History of the Welsh in Minnesota* (Mankato, 1895), p. 273.

22 Edward Thomas, Sr, was born in Llanidloes, Wales in 1807; *Hanes Cymry Minnesota*, p. 273.

23 See the discussion in Chapter Ten, pages 395–6.

24 *Y Cenhadwr Americanaidd*, December 1864.

25 I have taken the word *yni* to be a twice-mutated from of the noun, *cyni*, meaning 'distress' or 'anguish'. A reading which is more grammatically correct, though less pleasing in terms of sense, would take this as the noun *ynni*, meaning 'energy' or 'vigour', with the poet referring to the 'vigour' which *awen* normally brings him, now absent.

26 The *cywydd* (more formally called *cywydd deuair hirion*) is a couplet-based form. The couplet consists of two seven-syllable lines, one ending in an accented rhyme, the other in an unaccented rhyme. *Cynghanedd* is mandatory in both lines. A *cywydd* can contain any number of these couplets.

27 *Y Cenhadwr Americanaidd*, December 1864.

28 The first couplet of Goronwy Owen's *cywydd* is 'Dod im Dy nawdd a hawdd hynt, / Duw hael, a deau helynt'. A. Cynfael Lake (ed.), *Blodeugerdd Barddas o Ganu Caeth y Ddeunawfed Ganrif* (Llandybïe, 1993), p. 93.

29 The *cywydd* was first published by Huw Jones in *Dewisol Ganiadau yr Oes Hon* (1759). Numerous other editions of Goronwy Owen's work were produced during the eighteenth and nineteenth centuries. His poems were also widely circulated in manuscript. For the publication history, see Alan Llwyd, *Gronwy Ddiafael, Gronwy Ddu* [:] *Cofiant Goronwy Owen 1723–1769* (Llandybïe, 1997), pp. 275–303.

30 Thomas Parry (ed.), *Gwaith Dafydd ap Gwilym* (Cardiff, 1979), pp. 285, 236, 114, and 130. The poet-lover persona of Dafydd ap Gwilym's poetry is also frequently presented in the past (or imperfect) tense in the *cywydd*'s opening line, for example: 'Doe yr oeddwn, dioer eddyl'; 'Fal yr oeddwn, gwyddwn gêl'; 'Fal yr oeddwn ymannos'; 'Fal yr oeddwn yn myned'. *Gwaith Dafydd ap Gwilym*, pp. 107, 110 and 112.

31 Rachel Bromwich has provided a useful description of the *sangiad* (plural *sangiadau*) or 'parenthetical phrase': 'In their simplest forms such phrases occupy part of a line only (most frequently the second half) . . . [and they] run parallel to the poet's main statement, underlining or giving emphasis to it, but always subordinated. *Sangiadau* are usually of an exclamatory or descriptive nature, their linguistic constituents being conditioned by the requirements of the *cynghanedd*.' Rachel Bromwich, *Selected Poems of Dafydd ap Gwilym* (New York, 1985), p. xviii.

32 *Y Cenhadwr Americanaidd*, December 1864.

33 Earl J. Hess, *The Union Soldier in Battle [:] Enduring the Ordeal of Combat* (Lawrence, 1997), p. 130.

34 To cite but one of many examples, Robert J. Thomas of the 14th Wisconsin Infantry described his regiment's experiences at Shiloh thus: 'buom yn y frwydur hud y diwedd yn nghanol y tân a'r bwledi, y rhai a chwifiant o'n cwmpas fel cenllus'; 'we were in the battle until the end in the middle of the fire and bullets, which swirled about us like hailstones.' Unpublished manuscript letter in the collection of Nadine Thomas.

35 *Y Cenhadwr Americanaidd*, December 1864.

36 *Y Cenhadwr Americanaidd*, December 1864.

37 Ibid.

38 All the biographical details of this poet are not known, though present research suggests that he was one of two individuals, both named George O. Jones: one served with the 80th New York Infantry, and the other with the 12th Pennsylvania Cavalry. There was also a George O. Jones who belonged to the unassigned Illinois Volunteers.

39 See Chapter Seven, pages 309–11.

40 *Y Cenhadwr Americanaidd*, January 1862.

41 Ibid.

42 The quotation is not exact, and it is impossible to know whether Jones was intentionally rewording Cowper's lines, quoting (incorrectly) from memory, or quoting from another text which itself presented an alternate wording of the original poem. Compare the lines 413–23 in John D. Baird and Charles Ryskamp (eds), *The Poems of William Cowper Volume I: 1748–1782* (Oxford, 1980): 'But when a country, (one that I could name) / In prostitution sinks the sense of shame, / When infamous venality grown bold, / Writes on his bosom, *to be let or sold*; /

When perjury, that heav'n defying vice, / Sells oaths by tale, and at the lowest price, / Stamps God's own name upon a lie just made, / To turn a penny in the way of trade; / When av'rice starves, and never hides his face, / Two or three millions of the human race[.]' The final couplet in Jones's text is of unexplained origin, and may be the Welsh poet's own way of adapting the quotation to his own ends.

43 See John D. Baird and Charles Ryskamp, 'Commentary', in *The Poems of William Cowper Volume I*, p. 507.

44 *Y Cenhadwr Americanaidd*, January 1862.

45 Ibid.

46 Ibid.

47 Ibid.

48 Ibid.

49 Ibid.

50 Ibid.

9

'Ink made from Gunpowder': Prose of the Battlefield

As we have seen, some of the Union's soldiers published Welsh poems which were grounded to varying degrees in their own experience of the war. However, rather than striving to represent the reality of battle, all these compositions are ultimately concerned with other enterprises. In all three of the poems examined in detail in the last chapter, references to the poets' military service are used to add weight to the moral, political and religious discourses which lie at the centre of these texts. As one might expect, the substantial body of war-time prose is in many ways strikingly different. Many Welsh-speaking soldiers used their native language to create an account of the most horrible events which they experienced while in uniform, using the act of writing to record, and sometimes to analyse, that thing which was to separate them forever from the civilians whom they had left at home – the experience of battle.

Some, however, were more sparing with their words than others. After surviving ten hours of fierce fighting on the final day of the battle of Shiloh, Robert J. Thomas of the 14th Wisconsin Infantry sat down and wrote a letter to his brother in Oneida County, New York. He did not record the details of his role in the battle, and was content to express his joy at being alive:

> Fe ges y fraint o fod yn y frwydur ynwaith a dod allan yn fyw heb glwu nac archoll, ond fe roedd miloedd yn feirwon ar hud wyneb y maes – nis gallaf ddywedud pa faint a glwyfwyd ac a laddwy[d].[1]
>
> 'I had the honour of being in the battle once and come out alive with neither injury nor wound, but thousands were dead all over the field – I cannot say how many were killed and wounded.'

Shiloh was his regiment's first taste of combat, and despite their inexperience the 14th Wisconsin distinguished themselves, earning the sobriquet 'the Wisconsin Regulars'. However, rather than boasting of his unit's performance that day, Robert Thomas confessed that he hoped never to see a battlefield again.

Gallaf fina ddywedud fod y nifer yn fawr a'r olygfa yn druenus ei gweled – wedi ei toru yn ddarna bob dull a modd. Nid oes arnaf eisio gweled maes y frwydur eto: rwyf wedi cael llwyr fy modloni yn awr.[2]

'I can say that the number is great and that the scene is pitiful to see – torn up in pieces in every way and manner. I never want to see the battlefield again: I have been completely satisfied now.'

The only other information he provided to his brother about the battle was a brief tally of the 14th Wisconsin's losses: 'Fe laddwyd o'n Regiment ni 15, ac fe glwyfwyd tia 70'; '15 from our Regiment were killed, and about 70 were injured.'[3]

Three Welsh diaries have survived in manuscript which provide first-hand accounts of the battle of Gettysburg, two written by those former quarrymen of the 14th Vermont Infantry who are discussed elsewhere in this study, John H. Williams and John Rowlands.[4] Their regiment had been recruited to serve for nine months only, and they had spent almost all that time without seeing any combat. However, a few short weeks before they were due to be mustered out of military service, the 14th Vermont were sent to Gettysburg. By the time they reached the field, two days of fighting had already taken place. On 3 July 1863 they were posted in a thin skirmish line positioned in advance of the main body of Union forces, and they were thus among the first Northerners to meet Picket's Charge on the third and final day of the battle.

John Rowlands wrote a short account of the day's fighting in his diary, and scrawled the heading *Maes y Frwydr*, 'The Battle Field', across the top of the page. Like the brief reflections which Robert J. Thomas recorded after fighting on the field of Shiloh, this quarryman from Vermont confided that he hoped never to see battle again.

dyma y bora wedi wawrio, mae y Brigade a squads yn dechra dyma ini order i fyned yn mellach ir maes ac i fyny a ni ar ein traed ac yn cychwin ac gyda hyn dyma y Rebels yn dechra ein sellio ni ond ffwrdd a ni a gorweddasom i lawr ar ol hyn cawsom dawelwch am hir amser ond yr oedd sgarmesau yn myned yn mlaen ac yr oedd yr haul yn boeth a llaweroedd yn cael eu taro gan yr haul Wel, wel, dyma hi wedi myned arnom. Mae ygynau mawr y *Rebels* yn dechra tan pelanu ni dychrynllyd a nina ar ein gwynebau ar lawr ond dyma y Rebels allan ac yn dechra tanio arnom ond ni fuont yn hir heb dderbyn eu tâl am hyny yr oedd y Rebes [sic] yn llichio canesters atom wrth inni fyned yn mlaen wel dyma y diwrnod mwya ofnadwy a fu ar fy mhen yrioed ac nid wyf yn dymuno weled rhun oi fath eto. Cafodd Luteuant Boswerth ei frifo yn ei goes a G. Meuling ei ladd.[5]

'here the morning has dawned, the Brigade and squads are starting [to move], here is an order for us to go farther into the field, and we are up on our feet and starting and at this the Rebels start shelling us, but away with us, and we lie [down]. After this, we had peace for a long time but there were skirmishes going

> on and the sun was hot and many were affected by the sun. Well, well, here it has come upon us. The big guns of the Rebels are starting to shell us with a fearful fire and we are on our faces on the ground, but then the Rebels are out and starting to shoot at us, but they were not long before receiving their payment for that. The Rebels were tossing canister at us as we went on; well this is the most terrible day that has ever been upon me and I do not wish to see another of its sort again. Lieutenant Bosworth was injured and G. Meuling was killed.'[6]

The account which John H. Williams recorded in his diary is almost the same length as the one written by John Rowlands (both are around 150 words). While both diaries concur as to the details of the 14th Vermont's actions that day, Williams included less commentary, noting simply that the 'fighting' (*ymladdfa*) was as [*b*]*rwd* ('hot', 'heated' or 'enthusiastic') and [*c*]*aled* ('hard').[7] However, this section of his diary has one detail which bears some analysis:

> o'r diwedd daeth eu *Infantry* ymlaen am danom, rhuthrasom arnynt, syrthiasom yn ol, a'r ailwaith yn mlaen a ni a gwnaethom hwynt i Skeddadlio, eu lladd, a chymeryd eu *Colors*, a channoedd yn garcharorion.[8]

> 'at last their Infantry came on towards us, we charged them, we fell back, and, for the second time, on we went and we made them Skedaddle, killed them, and took their Colours, and hundreds as prisoners.'

Despite the staccato nature of this short passage, John Williams's description of the rout of Picket's Charge tells us something about the linguistic and literary dimensions of this soldier's war-time experiences. Even though Welsh-American journals were publishing military vocabulary lists, Williams uses many English terms in his diary. For example, this sentence contains the words 'Infantry' and 'Colours', whereas a great many other writers from the period used the Welsh words *traed-filwyr* and *baneri*.[9] While the passages from these diaries discussed in Chapter Five show that Williams and Rowlands associated as much as possible with the other Welsh-speaking soldiers in the 14th Vermont, the military terminology which their commanding officers used on the drill field – and on the Gettysburg battlefield – found its way into this soldier's personal account of the battle.

The use of English terms is not the only noteworthy linguistic feature of this diary. Like several writers who published in the Welsh-American press, John Williams uses the verb *Skedadlio,* a Welsh word which was created by adding the verbal ending *-io* to the English 'skedaddle'. Since the Union's defeat at Bull Run in July 1861, after which the Northern army was derided for its 'great skedaddle', the word had punctuated the war reports and commentaries of English-language newspapers both North and South. The Welsh-American press was soon to adopt the Welsh version of this word, and the fact that John

Williams uses *skedadlio* in the hasty narrative which he wrote on the day of battle suggests the degree to which this kind of new war-time vocabulary was adopted by Welsh-speaking soldiers. Welsh *skedadlio* (or *scadadlio*), like the English word on which it was based, was often used in slightly humorous or satirical contexts.[10] This writer, however, uses it in referring to his army's triumph in the only battle which he was to experience during the war, a day of fighting which his comrade John Rowlands described as 'the most terrible day of his life'.

EVAN DAVIS AND 'THE DOGS OF DEATH'

The battle narratives recorded in these two diaries, like Robert J. Thomas's short description of Shiloh, were written on the day of battle. It goes without saying that the staccato nature of their prose and the brevity of their accounts must be attributed in part – and perhaps to a very great extent – to the circumstances in which these soldiers were writing. As John Rowlands makes clear in his diary they were literally writing on 'The Battle Field'. The manuscript diary of Evan Davis includes several similar records of battles, including Perryville and Murfreesboro. However, what is surely the most interesting passage in the diary is a meditation on the battle of Perryville which Davis wrote a year later, while recuperating from a protracted illness in hospital. This battle was extremely significant for the Welsh-American because it was his first experience of combat.

Having volunteered during the summer of 1862, Davis was mustered into the 21st Wisconsin Infantry. By the second week of September the new regiment was heading for war, despite the fact that they had received little more than a month's training. On 8 October these poorly prepared volunteers were thrown into their first battle at Perryville, Kentucky. Sitting in an Indiana hospital a year later, Davis's thoughts turned back to the events of that day.

> Ac yn cofio mai blwddin i heddyw ar Fryniau Perryville y gwelais y Battle gyntaf imi erioed. Yno y daethum i wybodaeth o'r brofiad o sefyll i eraill saethu ataf. Yr oeddwn wedi darllen llawer am frwydrau ac am wrolder rhai dynion yn nydd y frwydr, ond yno y gwelais yr olygfa yn wirioneddol, heb gymorth dychymig, a gallaf ddweyd, er cymaint a fynegwyd trwy lyfrau a phapurau, na fyn[e]gwyd mo'r haner; rhyw deimlad rhyfedd a'n meddianai wrth glywed cŵn angau yn cyfarth o bell, a phob cam a roddem yn ein dwyn yn nes atynt. Ac o nis gallaf ddarlunio yr olygfa . . . a welais oddiar fryn bychan, cyn cyrraedd maes y gwaed, ond mae ei argraph yn annileadwy yn s[ylff] lyfr fy meddwl.[11]

> 'And remembering that it is a year ago today that I saw my first ever battle on the hills of Perryville. There I came to have knowledge of the experience of standing for others to shoot at me. I had read much about battles and about the courage of some men on the day of battle, but there I saw the scene for real, without the aid of

> imagination, and I can say, despite however much has been expressed by means of books and papers, that not half of it has been related; such a strange feeling possessed us as we heard the dogs of death barking from afar, while every step that we took was bringing us closer to them. And, oh!, I cannot describe the scene . . . which I saw from the top of a small hill before reaching the field of blood, yet it has made on indelible impression upon the book shelf of my memory.'

This text is an unpublished manuscript. It is a personal record of this soldier's experiences, and it also includes a record of Evan Davis's reflections and meditations on those experiences. Davis's diary is, in fact, one of the most complex and introspective pieces of Welsh prose written during the American Civil War, and these qualities are exemplified by the section dealing with the battle of Perryville. Prior to 8 October 1862, battle had been a foreign concept to Evan Davis, a fact which he stresses in several ways. Although he used his native language in describing (or attempting to describe) his first experience of combat, Evan Davis presents that experience using a word foreign to Welsh, 'battle'. Later on in this same passage he uses the Welsh word for 'battle,' *brwydr*, twice (once in the plural, [*b*]*rwydrau* – 'battles' – and once in the singular, *y frwydr* – 'the battle'), yet the first sentence employs the English word 'battle': '[a]r fryniau Perryville y gwelais y *Battle* gyntaf imi erioed' ('On the hills of Perryville I saw my first ever Battle').[12] The concept, originally presented by means of an English word, is possessed by the writer and re-written using the vocabulary of his native language. By means of these sentences Evan Davis meditates on what was surely one of the most significant moments in his life, the point in time when a strange and distant concept, 'battle', became something which he had experienced first-hand.

A gifted writer, Davis uses this description of his own baptism of fire to present a meditation on the difference between literary artifice and actual experience, between reading (and writing) about war and the actual experience of it. After witnessing the aftermath of a Civil War battle, Walt Whitman wrote in his diary that '[w]e already talk of Histories of War', asking rhetorically 'shall we ever get histories of the real things?'[13] This Welsh writer used his diary to explore the gulf between the literature of war and the reality of it. He describes his first battle as the 'experience' – [*p*]*rofiad* – which brought him actual 'knowledge' – [*g*]*wybodaeth* – of something hitherto unknown. Other parts of his diary show that this Welsh-American was an avid reader, and this passage states that Davis had, as a civilian, 'read much about battles and about the courage of some men on the day of battle'. He sets seeing and experiencing battle first-hand against the faculties of 'imagination' – *dychymig* – which help readers to experience (or imagine) battle from a distance.

However, while the efforts of writers and the attempts made by 'books and papers' to describe this indescribable experience are found to be deficient, Evan Davis cannot help but to use a literary frame of reference while interpreting his own experience of battle: he describes that experience as an 'indelible impression' upon 'the book shelf of [his] memory'. The word translated here as 'impression', *argraph* (spelt *argraff* today), is like the English word 'imprint' in that it can be used to describe the printing of a book in addition to the impression made upon a person. Davis writes that literature cannot treat the real experience of war adequately, yet he himself describes that experience metaphorically as a newly printed book which will rest for ever on the bookshelf of his memory. Despite concluding that 'not half of [the reality of combat] had been related' by previous writers, he nonetheless uses the realm of literature as a field of reference for constructing his own metaphorical description of the experience's effect upon him.

Like other soldiers in other wars, many of the Union army's Welsh-speaking volunteers wrote home saying that they could not describe adequately the experience of battle. Even the sights left on the field after fighting had ceased often proved too much for their descriptive abilities. For example, one soldier wrote to his mother following the battle of Shiloh, saying of the field that: 'Mae yr olwg yn ofnadwy o ddychrynllyd. Yn wir mae ei darlunio yn ormod gorchwyl i mi'; 'The appearance is horribly frightening. Truly, describing it is too much of a task for me.'[14] While a great many soldiers exhibited a need to write about their experiences, that act of describing is often cut short. The inadequacies of language (and/or the writer's inadequate powers of description) are cited by way of excuse, and the civilian reader is left only with a reference to something which is horrible, yet ultimately unknowable in the second-hand manner presented through the remove of reading. Unlike letters sent to civilians at home or pieces which soldiers published, Evan Davis was using the most private kind of text, a diary, in order to create a literary record of his personal meditations. Yet even when writing for an intended audience which included only himself (a person who, by the time of writing, had actually experienced combat), he still had to emphasize the gulf between the literary imagination and the reality of experience. Yet the urge to *write* about it is present nonetheless.

Evan Davies writes about the 'strange feeling' ([*t*]*eimlad rhyfedd*) which 'possessed' (*meddianai*) the raw recruits as they heard 'the dogs of death barking' (*cŵn angau yn cyfarth*) for the first time. This might be taken on one level as referring to the cannon fire which the soldiers heard as they marched towards their first battle. However, given the fact that this entire passage is concerned with the writer's first experience of battle and the difference between the reality of that experience and the remove of literary descriptions, hearing 'the dogs of death' can also be taken as a more abstract reference to that experience in general. English-speaking soldiers often described their first battle in terms of 'seeing the elephant', a phrase which presumably referred to the experience of seeing a live elephant in a travelling circus and thus gaining first-hand knowledge of a strange thing which was otherwise known only through the remove of stories or books.[15] Interestingly, none of the Welsh-language texts surveyed during this study use this phrase (or a Welsh translation of it).

Evan Davis comes up with his own metaphor, *cŵn angau*, 'the dogs of death', one which seems to be grounded in Welsh tradition. Tales of – and, it seems, expressions of belief in – *cŵn Annwn* were common in nineteenth-century Wales.[16] Often translated as 'dogs of the otherworld' or 'hounds of hell', these supernatural creatures were said to roam the night skies in search of the souls of the recently departed. Narratives transmitted orally in Wales throughout the twentieth century depict *cŵn Annwn* as tokens of death, appearing as a sign that somebody is about to die. *Angau*, the word for 'death' used by Evan Davis, and *Annwn* echo each other acoustically in that they are both two-syllable words beginning with *a-*. They also bear a semantic relationship in that 'the otherworld' of *Annwn* was seen as a place distinguished from (and even opposed to) the world of the living, thus allowing the term to be applied to the Christian 'hell', a place for dead souls. In other words, *cŵn angau* was a logical rewording of the phrase *cŵn Annwn*.

While numerous Civil War soldiers described their first experience of battle as 'seeing the elephant', this volunteer from Wisconsin chose a very different kind of image, one which resonated with the folk traditions of his native Wales. Earl J. Hess has analysed the ways in which (Anglophone) soldiers went about 'shaping the battle experience', suggesting that describing war in terms of familiar metaphors and experiences was a way of 'taming' it.

> As they became familiar with the nature of combat, soldiers also began to realize that they did not have to be passive victims of war. Each of them had the chance to deal with battle by shaping their perception of it. They gained a handle on the experience by using models or metaphors. It was a conscious effort to make battle familiar by comparing it to experiences in their civilian lives. Through this process, soldiers tamed battle. They relied on romantic literary conceptions of war, on nature, and on the familiar habits of their working-class lives to serve as models of behavior and thought. This was a workable strategy for mastering a unique, unprecedented part of their lives.[17]

Dozens of Welsh-language texts provide examples of what Hess describes as 'mak[ing] battle familiar by comparing it to experiences in . . . civilian [life]'. As was seen in the last chapter, some Welsh-Americans echoed their English-speaking comrades by describing bullets as 'rain' or 'hailstones'. Similarly, many Welsh-speaking soldiers used the familiar language of agriculture in describing battle, writing that trees or men 'had been mowed down like hay' (*wedi'u medi fel gwair*), or that they had 'pursued [the enemy] like partridge' (*wedi'u erlid fel petris*).[18]

Like many other Union soldiers whose writings have been examined as part of this study, Evan Davis took that first step towards making war more familiar by writing about it, using not the language of the officers who commanded him on the field of battle, but rather his own native Welsh. Another way of interpreting the experience was by drawing on traditional metaphors, sayings and images which were transmitted by means of that native language. Even in the passage quoted above, where Evan Davis emphasizes the horrible strangeness of battle, he draws upon traditional imagery involving the frightening and unworldly nature of death. For generations Welsh speakers had talked about *cŵn Annwn* chasing the souls of the dead or referred to the appearance supernatural dogs as a sign that death was near, and such traditions were surely a way of dealing with the unknown nature of the journey between this world and the otherworld, between life and death. Evan Davis used a similar image to describe the strangeness and horribleness of the forces of death which rampaged on the field at Perryville.

Davis recounts his actual encounter with 'the dogs of death' in great detail. He describes how, even before reaching the field, the raw recruits were forced to face an increasing array of the horrors of war.

> Ar fryn bychan o'n blaenau, gwelem fwg du las yn ymgodi . . . tua'r nefoedd, ac yn cael ei gario yn arafaidd ar edyn yr awel. . . . Gwelwn ddynion, ceffyla, mulod a'r gwageni mewn prysurdeb cymysgaidd, yn symud eu sefyllfa o ein ffrynt, ac yn gosod eu hunain mewn trefn mewn [ffrynt] arall, ac yn y man wele y canons yn rhuo drostyn, *grape* a *canister* yn medi rhengau y gelyn, a buledau y gelyn yn suo heibio ein clustiau ac yn disgyn wrth ein traed. Roedd yn ddigon dealladwy wrthym am gadw draw, fod perygl o'n blaen, ac er ceisio ein dychryn yn fwy, gwelem ddynion yn amddifad o freichiau ac yn orchuddiedig gan waed a cheffylau heb farchogion yn carlamu i'r goriwaered i'n cyfarfod. Ond er hyn oll, nid oedd dim yn tyccio, neu'n ein digaloni. Ymlaen yr awn ar *double quick*, dros geryg, trwy dyllau a thrwy gorn cyn uwch a'n penau[.][19]

> 'On a small hill before us we saw blue-black smoke ascending . . . towards the heavens, being carried slowly on the wings of the breeze. . . . We saw men, horses, mules and wagons in a state of confused haste, moving their position from our front, and placing themselves in order in another front, and there we saw the cannons roaring over them, grape and canister harvesting the ranks of the enemy, while the enemy's bullets whizzed past our ears and fell at our feet. It was well understood by us that we should keep away, that there was danger before us, and in order to scare us more, we saw men deprived of arms and covered with blood and horses without riders galloping to the rear to meet us. Yet despite all this, nothing was working nor disheartening us. On we went at the double quick, over rocks, through depressions and through corn as high as our heads.'

According to Hess, writing was a way of 'shaping the battle experience'; soldiers employed literary models and processes in order to 'tame' the horrific and chaotic experience of combat.[20] In his diary Evan Davis sets the frightening chaos of battle against the courage displayed by himself and his comrades.

The 'dogs of death' are still felt as a presence in these sentences; Davis suggests there is an agency at work, a sentient force which tries to make it 'well understood' by the soldiers that they 'should keep away'. They are actively assaulted with sights designed to 'scare' them. However, none of it succeeds in 'work[ing]' or 'dishearten[ing]' them; they proceed, making unswerving progress ('over rocks and through depressions') towards the very source of these horrors.

While Evan Davis does not 'tame' the experience of battle by romanticizing or domesticating it, he does 'shape the battle experience' in writing; in his diary he ordered his own interactions with the chaos of battle by writing what we might call a tale of triumph. His personal narrative describes how the untried Wisconsin soldiers defeat, by means of their resolve, an armoury of horrors designed to 'dishearten' them and dissuade them from closing with 'the dogs of death'. The linear movement of the soldiers towards battle is set against the unorganized chaos of war ('confused haste'). And this linear progression ends when Davis and his comrades start killing the enemy, a point emphasized by the fact that Davis describes the minutes proceeding this final release as 'the most painful and bitter' moments of his life.

> Cawsom orchymin i orwedd lawr am ychydig fynudau. Ac o, mynudau ofnadwy oedd y rhai hyny, y mynudau mwyaf poenus a chwerw o'm hoes oeddynt – yno yn gorwedd ar ein hwynebau yn gwrando chwyrnillio y *shells* a suad y *rifel balls* dros ein penau, ie, ac yn gwrando gruddfan y clwyfedigion yn ein hymyl a screchiadau dieflig y gelynion ar y bryn gyferbyn â ni. Yn fuan, rhyddhawyd ni o'r sefyllfa boenus hon trwy gael gorchymin i godi a thanio cynhwysiad ein gynau i wynebau y gelyn . . . yr hyn a wnaethom gyda chalon.[21]
>
> 'We received an order to lie down for a few minutes. And oh, what horrible minutes were those, they were the most painful and bitter minutes of my life – lying there on our faces listening to the hum of the shells and the whiz of the rifle balls over our heads, yes, and listening to the moaning of the injured ones at our side and the devilish screaming of the enemies on the hill opposite us. Shortly, we were released from this painful situation by being given the order to stand and fire the contents of our guns into the faces of the enemy . . . which we did heartily.'

After the soldiers' progression through the horrors of war into the heart of combat brings them to the act of killing itself, the mood changes entirely.

> Ar ol ysgafnhau ein gynau y waeth gyntaf, ysgafnhaodd ein calonau hefyd. Gweithiai ein bysedd yn gyflym, ein breichiau heb grynu, ac anelai ein llygaid heb wyro at fyddin lladron rhyddid ag einioes. Yr oedd y gwaith yn ymddangos yn blesurus, ac edrych ar y corph yn cycio wrth ffarwelio â'r enaid yn . . . felys. Crochfloeddiem o lawenydd, wrth weled llinell y gelyn yn gwingo o flaen tân ein gynau ac yn ffoi heb drefn i wyneb eu cyfeillion.[22]

> 'After discharging our guns the first time, our hearts grew light as well. Our fingers worked quickly, our arms without shaking, and our eyes aimed without swerving at the army of the thieves of freedom and life. The work appeared pleasant, and looking at the body kicking as it bade farewell to the soul was . . . sweet. We shouted with joy at seeing the line of the enemy flinch before the fire of our guns and flee in disorder into their friends.'

Rather than romanticizing or domesticating the horrors of war, Evan Davis details the bloody nature of combat, focusing on the experience of killing others. In introducing the narrative of his first battle experience, he highlights the gulf between the remove of literature and the reality of experience, and in detailing that experience he does not spare the gruesome details.

The bravery which carries Evan Davis and his comrades into combat is transformed into joy in death. In other parts of his diary this writer professes a kind of Christianity characterized by what we might call a peace-loving humanity, yet here he confesses to enjoying the 'pleasant' work of killing, finding the 'kicking' bodies of the men he has shot down to be a 'sweet' sight. While other Union soldiers at times recorded similar feelings, the grizzly honesty found in Evan Davis's battle narrative is unique as far as Welsh-language Civil War writing is concerned.[23] The fact that it is an unpublished diary certainly allowed for a kind of confessional honesty which would surely have been omitted from pieces designed for publication, yet other manuscript diaries by Welsh-speaking soldiers do not record similar feelings. Indeed, this passage is all the more striking when read in the wider context of modern Welsh literature; despite the huge body of Welsh writing generated by a series of nineteenth- and twentieth-century wars, Evan Davis's description of the Battle of Perryville is unique.[24]

'THE FIELD OF BLOOD'

Given that the text concerned is a private diary which exists only in manuscript, we can but guess as to the reasons why Evan Davis wrote this extended meditation on his experiences at Perryville. As with most diaries, a range of psychological explanations can be offered, yet the context in which the text was written remains a personal (and ultimately unknowable) one. On the other hand, a number of extant Welsh prose-works dealing directly with the experience of battle were published during the war. As was seen in Chapter Three, a variety of literary calls to arms were published by the Welsh-American press after the fall of Fort Sumter, marking its emergence as a pro-war press. These 'recruitment songs' soon had to share space on the printed page with other kinds of war writing, as more and more Welsh-Americans came to experience the realities of battle. As one anonymous writer suggested in a piece published by *Y Drych* in April 1863, the fact that the Union's Welsh soldiers were experiencing battle was altering the very nature of the public discourse on Welsh-American identity.

> Cochwyd aml i lanerch y De â gwaed meibion goreu ein cenedl o fryniau Steuben, yn Efrog Newydd, ac o drumau cribog yr Alleghannies, yn swydd Cambria, Pennsylvania, yn nghyda manau eraill ellid nodi yn y ddwy Dalaeth hon yn gystal a Thalaethau Wisconsin, Ohio, Minnesota a Kansas. Nid oes braidd frwdyr o bwys wedi cymeryd lle o lanau yr afonydd James, Potomac, a'r Rappahannock yn y Dwyrain, hyd yr afon byth-gofiadwy Stono gerllaw Murfreesboro yn Tennessee, ac oddiyno hyd New Orleans yn eithaf y Deorllewin, nad yw ein cydwladwyr wedi bod yn bresenol, mewn rhifedi mwy neu lai, ac wedi gwneyd eu hol ar y gelyn na blotir ymaith ar frys.[25]

> 'Many of the South's pastures have been stained with the blood of the best sons of our nation from the hills of Steuben in New York and from the crested peaks of the Alleghenies in Cambria County, Pennsylvania, along with other places which could be noted in these two states as well as the states of Wisconsin, Ohio, Minnesota and Kansas. There is scarcely an important battle which has taken place, from the banks of the James, Potomac and Rappahannock rivers in the East, to the memorable Stone's River near Murfreesboro, Tennessee, and from there to New Orleans in the farthest reaches of the South-West, in which our fellow countrymen have not been present, in some number for the most part, and have left a mark on the enemy which will not be removed in a hurry.'

This author used the pen-name *Undebwr*, 'Unionist', and his essay presents an interpretation of the meaning of Welsh soldiers' service to the Union in terms of their American citizenship. For years before the start of the war, *Y Drych* and other Welsh-American publications had provided a national forum for articulating a distinct Welsh-American identity. While supporting a passionate cultural nationalism and roundly criticizing those 'children of Dic Siôn Dafydd' who denied their native language, the print culture of pre-war Welsh America also harmonized this confident Welshness with a fiery American patriotism. Thus *Undebwr* refers to the Union's Welsh soldiers as his *cydwladwyr*, 'fellow countrymen', meaning 'fellow Welshmen', yet these sentences were written (and published) in order to declare that those Welshmen had proven themselves to be exemplary Americans. And they did that by spilling their blood on Southern soil.[26]

This Unionist describes the loss of the lives of his 'countrymen' with a mixture of registers, combing public grieving with a kind of sombre rejoicing. The spilling of Welsh blood is presented as a sacrificial act which marks the geography of the United States, thus proving that immigrants and their descendants are inextricably bound forever with the physical existence of their new country. This symbolic soaking of American ground with Welsh blood became one of the salient images of the war for some Welsh-American writers.

As has been seen at other junctures in this study, some of Welsh America's poets and writers described the march of Welsh volunteers to war as an act of sacrifice which would help cleanse the nation of the sin of slavery. Here the battlefield sacrifice is seen as a way of ensuring that Welsh America could lay its own irrefutable claim to American patriotism. The realities of battle experience and the attendant spilling of Welsh-American blood provided the Union's Welsh writers with a new way of expressing their identity as Welsh-Americans.

Like the Welsh blood staining 'many of the South's pastures', texts were written and published using language and imagery which were grounded in those Southern battlefields. As was seen in Chapter Five, the Welsh-American press often published soldiers' letters under titles such as *Llythyrau Oddi Wrth Filwyr Cymreig* – 'Letters from Welsh Soldiers' – which drew attention to the Welshness of the authors. Such texts were also presented to readers as 'Letters from the Battle Field'. While the expression was sometimes rendered as *Llythyr o Faes y Frwydr* – literally, 'A Letter from the Battle Field' (or 'Field of the Battle') – this kind of epistle was also described by editors as *Llythyr o Faes y Gwaed* – 'A Letter from the Field of Blood'. Like many aspects of the texts themselves, this title shows that the intermingling of earth and blood became a prominent part of the field of images used by Welsh-American writers to discuss and interpret the war.

The Southern landscape became a literary subject for soldier-writers even before it was stained by blood spilt in battle. Service in the Union army ensured that a great many Welsh-speaking Americans visited the Southern states for the first time, and even before the Welsh-American press began publishing pieces in which soldiers attempted to describe (or described their failure to describe) their first experience of battle, *Y Drych* and the Welsh monthly journals were publishing letters by Welsh-speaking Americans from places such as Racine, Wisconsin, and Oneida County, New York, which presented their impressions of the American South. In his social history of the Civil War soldier, Reid Mitchell notes that, 'for the most part, the Union soldier found the South ugly and dreary', adding that many Northern soldiers had been expecting a 'tropical Elysium' when they travelled south for the first time.[27]

> Northerners . . . expected to find the legendary South that figured so prominently in minstrel songs and plantation myths. Even before the Civil War, the notion that the South was exotic and foreign, a region removed from Yankee norms, was widespread among Northerners; the golden vision of the South served as a counterpoint to the savage vision of the South – both were embodied in books like *Uncle Tom's Cabin*. The romantic south was an integral part of American popular culture.[28]

Remembering that two different Welsh translations of *Uncle Tom's Cabin* were published in the United States in the early 1850s, it is certainly true that many Welsh-Americans (including ones with little command of English) had been exposed to literary constructions of this 'legendary South' during the pre-war years.[29] However, given the fact that literature published by America's Welsh-language press during the two decades before the war tended to paint a negative, even demonic, picture of the slave-holding South, it is hard to know to what extent young Welsh-Americans would have expected to find 'a tropical Elysium'. What they actually found, or at least what they chose to write about, varied greatly and depended upon the individual writer's reactions to specific places and circumstances.

D. M. Williams of the 18th Wisconsin Infantry described different parts of the South in strikingly different ways. In one letter which he published in *Y Drych* Williams bemoans the fact that his regiment had spent 'close to a year in the wilderness of Tennessee and Mississippi' ('agos flwyddyn yn anialwch Tennessee [a] Mississippi') before reaching Lake Providence, on the banks of the Mississippi in northern Louisiana, an area which pleased him greatly.

> . . . wedi bod yn teithio ac yn gwersyllu agos flwyddyn yn anialwch Tennessee [a] Mississippi, wedi cyrhaedd o'r diwedd i'r ochr arall i'r afon, ac yr ydym yn awr mewn . . . gwlad lawn o bob rhyw ffrwythau . . . ac mae ar lan y Llyn hwn, sef Lake Providence, rai palasau gyda'r harddaf a welais erioed, ac mae'r coed bythol wyrdd . . . yn addurno y llwybrau a'r gerddi o amgylch ogylch iddynt. Ac ar foreu teg, fel heddyw, tua diwedd Mawrth – pan mae natur yn ymddangos mewn gwisg mor ogoneddus ag ydyw yn nghanol Mai yn Wisconsin – gwelir yr adar ar frigau y coed, a chlywir hwynt yn dyrchafu llais clodforedd am y bendithion a dderbyniant. Mae yr olwg yn hardd ac effeithiol mewn gwirionedd, ac yn arwain ein meddwl yn ol at amser plentyndod, pan y chwareuwn yn bennoeth ar gopa'r twyni, yn Nghwm Nedd, yn Swydd Forganwg, a gallwn dybied weithiau fy mod yn clywed yr un aderyn yn pyncio yn y llwyni cylchynol ar lanau y Mississippi, ag a glywais yn Ngwalia draw er's tua phymtheg mlynedd yn ol. Ac i wneyd y lle fyth yn fwy anwyl i mi, mae yma rai o'n cenedl yn byw[.][30]

> '. . . after travelling and camping for close to a year in the wilderness of Tennessee and Mississippi, [and] after finally reaching the other side of the river, we are now in . . . a land full of all kinds of fruits . . . and there are on the banks of this Lake, namely Lake Providence, some of the most beautiful mansions that I have ever seen, and the evergreen trees . . . adorn the paths and the gardens all around them. And on a fair morning, like today, about the end of March – when nature appears in as splendid a dress as it does in the middle of May in Wisconsin – the birds can be seen on the trees' branches and they can be heard lifting a voice of praise for the blessings which they receive. The scene is in truth beautiful and moving, and takes our mind back to the time of childhood, when we used to play bare-headed on top of the hills of Cwm Nedd, in Glamorgan, and I could suppose at times that I was hearing the same bird singing in the bushes around the banks of the Mississippi as I heard yonder in Wales around fifteen years ago. And to make the place even more dear to me, there are some of our nation living here.'

This letter then proceeds to discuss a small community of elderly Welsh settlers whom Williams found living there, a passage quoted and discussed in Chapter Six. His glowing description of this Southern landscape thus ends by introducing Welsh residents of the area who were, like the soldier-writer himself, avid readers of *Y Drych* and *Y Cenhadwr Americanaidd* (and thus, as was suggested in Chapter Six, also pro-Union and anti-slavery despite the fact that they had been living for so long in a slave state).[31] It could be argued that in this passage Williams is in effect describing what Reid Mitchell calls 'the peopled landscape,' and that his description of the region is influenced by the author's attitude towards the people inhabiting it.[32]

Williams says that the Lake Providence region compares favourably with his home in Wisconsin, and it reminds him – and by means of his literary artifice, is made to 'remind' the reader – of the writer's boyhood home in Wales. His style is informed by the biblical language of the Welsh chapel; he uses the phrase *llais gorfoledd* – 'a voice of praise' – in suggesting that birds (and, by extension, the writer) give thanks for the *bendithion* – 'blessings' – received. It also appears that this piece of prose was composed under the influence of a kind of imagery which had characterized Welsh poetry for centuries, one in which birds are described metaphorically as priests, poets or minstrels singing praises to God.[33] However, that which makes this American landscape so praiseworthy in Williams's eyes is that it resembles Wales (a resemblance which seems to have been suggested to him by the fact that he found Welsh speakers living in the area).

D. M. Williams refers to both Wisconsin and Wales while describing the Southern landscape for readers in the North, and both kinds of comparison appear in the prose writings of a number of other soldiers. R. C. Roberts, a soldier from Oneida County, New York, wrote that he had crossed 'the two branches of the Shenandoah' ('[d]wy gainc y Shenandoah'), adding that 'each one was greater than the Mohawk river near Utica ('y mae pob un o honynt yn fwy nag afon y Mohawk wrth Utica').[34] In describing the warm weather which he experienced in Tennessee during February 1864, Thomas J. Davies referred to summer in Oneida County: 'allem gyffelybu y dyddiau hyn i lawer a dreuliais yn *Oneida Co.* yn mis Mehefin'; 'we could compare these days to many which I spent in Oneida Co. during the month of June'.[35] When John W. Jones's service with the 23rd Wisconsin Volunteer Infantry took him to Kentucky, he wrote that, 'the roads were cobbled like the Old Country' ('[y] ffyrdd wedi eu creigio fel yr Hen Wlad').[36] Immigrants had a wider range of geographical experiences on which to draw than did native-born Americans, a fact which meant that they sometimes reacted to Southern landscapes in ways different from their non-Welsh comrades. One of the most famous writers to emerge from the American Civil War, Ambrose Bierce, described the experience of seeing Cheat Mountain in western Virginia in a manner which would have resonated with a great many of the Union's native-born soldiers:

'It was a strange country. Nine in ten of us had never seen a mountain, nor a hill as high as a church spire, until we had crossed the Ohio River.'[37] Welsh immigrants were in a very different situation, for their familiarity with the hills and mountains of Wales meant that the transition from the flat lands of Ohio or Wisconsin to the mountains of western Virginia was much less of a shock.

While many soldiers drew comparisons with their home in the North or with the landscape of Wales, others found parts of the South to be exotic, a place totally unlike anything previously encountered by them on either side of the Atlantic. In a series of letters which he sent back to his family in Wisconsin, John Griffth Jones marvelled at the swamps in Louisiana: 'mau yma lefydd mor wlyb i'w trafaelio, weithiau trwy ddwr 'that y penglin, a'r tro arall at ei haner'; 'there are here places so wet to traverse, at times [we must go] through water to the knee, at other times to the waist.'[38] He also described the animals inhabiting that exotic landscape: 'mau yma y nadroedd mwyaf a welais erioed'; 'here there are the largest snakes that I have ever seen'.[39] John also told his family that he and his fellow-soldiers had killed a number of alligators, 'some of which were 12 feet in length' ('rhai ohonynt yn 12 troedfedd o hyd').[40] The young Welshman from Wisconsin also commented on the houses and towns which he saw in the deep South, praising the beauty of New Orleans and recording the fact that his regiment was encamped near a plantation owned by Jefferson Davis.[41]

The abolitionist literature published before the war ensured that the word *planhigfa* – 'plantation' – had become a normal part of Welsh America's vocabulary. Visiting real plantations was thus worthy of comment, a chance for the soldier to demonstrate to readers at home that he had now anchored a concept previously known only through the remove of literature in the reality of experience. While in Virginia, Frederick K. Jones saw a plantation which held special significance, namely:

> ... White House, planigfa berthynol i'r Milwriad Wm. Lee, mab i'r Cadfridog Lee, pa rai sydd yn myddin y gwrthryfelwyr. Y mae y lle yn cynnwys oddeutu 2,000 o erwau o dir, ac o ddeutu 300 o Negroaid, oll yn perthyn i'r lle hwn. Dyma y nifer fwyaf yn perthyn i'r un lle a welais eto yn Virginia.[42]
>
> '. . . White House, a plantation belonging to the Colonel William Lee, son to General Lee, both of whom are in the rebels' army. The place contains around 2,000 acres of land, and about 300 Negroes, all belonging to this place. This is the greatest number belonging to one place which I have seen so far in Virginia.'

A year later another Welsh-speaking Northerner, W. H. Jones, remarked (apparently without regret) that his Union comrades had destroyed Lee's plantation: 'nid oes yn awr o hono ond carnedd o fricks; llosgwyd ef'; 'there is now nothing left of it but a pile of bricks; it was burned.'[43] In the words of Reid Mitchell:

> . . . some Northern soldiers came to think of the war itself as a war against the Southern way of life. Burning plantations were only the concrete manifestation of the desire to remake the South in the North's image. That desire too could be justified only by a belief in the South's cultural and moral inferiority.[44]

As was seen in Chapter Two, a whole generation of young Welsh-Americans were brought up with an abolitionist literature which demonised the slave-holding South.[45] Given the extent to which anti-slavery sentiments permeated the religious discourses of Welsh America, it is safe to say that Welsh-speaking Union soldiers in particular were instilled with what Mitchell describes as 'a belief in the South's . . . moral inferiority'.

This belief in the South's moral failings, while preconditioned by the prevalence of abolitionist sentiments before the war, was also strengthened by the war-time experiences of many soldiers. One of the 56th Ohio's numerous Welsh volunteers, William S. Jones, attempted to excuse the way in which his regiment took food from Southern civilians by referring to their (perceived) culpability: 'Rhaid ystyried mai gwrthryfelwyr a dinystrwyr Llywodraeth ydyw yr oll braidd o'r Deheuwyr; onide buasai y fath ymddygiad yn gywylidd i ni'; 'one must consider nearly all of the Southerners as rebels and the destroyers of government; otherwise, such conduct would be a shame to us.'[46] This same text implies that the writer's attitude towards the Southern population was in part conditioned by what he saw as a fluid border between unarmed civilians and armed guerrillas. While in Arkansas, the 56th Ohio came into repeated contact with the latter:

> Y guerilliaid ydyw yr unig elynion sydd yn y parthau hyn, a'r gelynion gwaethaf a chreulonaf o bawb ydynt. Maent yn peri llawer o aflonyddwch i ni yma, ac yn cyflawni y gweithredoedd mwyaf ysgeler i ddynoliaeth. . . . nid ydynt ond lladron cyhoeddus, yspeilwyr a llofruddion a hyny i'r graddau gwaethaf.[47]

> 'The guerrillas are the only enemies who are in these parts, and they are the worst and cruellest enemies of all. They cause much disturbance here, and commit the most hideous acts known to humanity. . . . they are nothing but public thieves, despoilers and murderers, and that of the worst sort.'

Similar feelings might account for the fact that other writers record the destruction of Southern property without any discussion of the morality of such actions. An anonymous comrade of William Jones's published a letter describing the 56th Ohio's service in Mississippi, noting that they were 'like a plague of locusts'; 'fel pla o locustiaid.' John Griffith Jones's (unpublished) letters record the manner in which his regiment travelled through the same state: 'Yr oeddym yn dwyn gwydda a moch a defaid a bob math o betha i'w fwyta. Caswom boxiad o fêl y noson'; 'we were stealing geese and pigs and sheep and all kinds of things to eat. We had a box of honey every night.'[48] In recounting his experiences during Grant's Vicksburg campaign, this young Wisconsin soldier noted without comment that they had burned the town of Port Gibson: 'Yr ydym wedi llosgi Port Gibson bob cwt i lawr *by the order of U. S. Grant, Major General*'; 'we have burned down Port Gibson, every shed, by the order of U. S. Grant, Major General').[49] The cavalryman Jonathan Davies wrote a letter to his brother in Utica, New York, boasting of his unit's looting in Virginia:

> . . . cofiwch fod genym ni fel meirchfilwyr mewn gwlad enciliadol y fraint o'n helpu ein hunain at beth bynag a ddymunom, a gellwch feddwl ein bod yn cael amser da . . . ymosodasom ar yr ymborth yn ddidrugaredd. Oh! Pe buasech gyda ni yn ein gweled yn ymosod ar y *pies* o bob math, y *fowls* wedi eu coginio, teisenau &c., a bron bob peth y gallech feddwl am danynt. . . . Cefais i ar y daith hono, bar da o fotasau, menyg, blancet o *rubber*, &c, &c., a nifer o bethau eraill rhy luosog i'w henwi. Cymerasom tua 7 o *sutlers* a 150 o geffylau, a dychwelasom i'r gwersyll.[50]
>
> '. . . remember that as cavalrymen in a secessionist country we have the privilege of helping ourselves to whatever we wish, and you can imagine that we have a good time . . . we attacked the provisions without mercy. Oh! If you were only with us seeing us attack the pies of every sort, the cooked fowls, cakes, &c., and just about everything else that you could think of. . . . On that journey I gained a good pair of boots, gloves, a rubber blanket, &c, &c., and a number of other things too numerous to name. We took about 7 sutlers and 150 horses, and we returned to camp.'

Originating as a personal letter, this text was later published in *Y Drych*, the same paper which carried descriptions of the 56th Ohio's conduct in Mississippi and Arkansas. Needless to say, the North's English-language press presented its readers with similar letters. However, the fact that the honest confessions of looting soldiers were being published in Welsh invites further discussion. Although military experience was foreign to almost all Welsh-Americans prior to 1861, and despite the fact that a kind of proto-pacifism had been supported by many of their religious leaders during the pre-war years, *Y Drych*'s readers apparently accepted (and even welcomed) texts describing how soldiers from their own communities were plundering Southern civilians. The pro-war and anti-slavery ideology which had engulfed war-time Welsh America created a context in which the violent treatment of the morally 'inferior' Southerner was accepted, and even expected.

Except for the rare case of Southerners who were Welsh-speaking and pro-Union, these soldiers' reactions to the (white) people of the South were more uniformly negative than their reactions to the Southern scenery. If memories of Welsh landscape at times made parts of the South seem less foreign, a shared humanity failed to mitigate their negative responses to the Confederacy's white population. Although Welsh America's commitment to abolition clearly influenced reactions to the South's wealthy plantation owners, poor whites who did not own slaves often received similar treatment at the hands of these soldier-writers. To again quote Reid Mitchell:

> . . . popular imagination divided the white South into planters and poor whites. Northern soldiers sought evidence of the degradation and ignorance of the non-slave-holding portion of the white population. The Northern interpretation of the war's causes required that the masses of Southern whites be pitiable slaves to aristocratic domination. In the wartime South the soldiers frequently found the evidence they needed.[51]

Even the most thoughtful of soldiers indulged in this kind of classification. Theophilus Davies was cited in Chapter Five as an example of a Welsh soldier who corresponded regularly with the minister of his home chapel.[52] It will be remembered that the letters which this member of the 6th Ohio Infantry sent to the Revd Thomas Edwards in Cincinnati were later forwarded by Edwards for publication in *Y Cenhadwr Americanaidd*, and that Davies used these texts to present his minister (and the journal's readers) with prolonged mediations on spiritual subjects. However, when the 6th Ohio crossed into western Virginia in order to engage the enemy, the young Welsh-American wrote to the Revd Edwards, dismissing the residents of the mountainous area as 'half civilized' (*haner gwareiddiedig*).[53] This contrasts with Davies's varied reactions to the landscape. While filling one letter with a description of the fear and doubt which assailed him while standing picket duty at night, in another epistle he describes the town of Beverley as 'a beautiful place, surrounded by mountains' ('lle hardd, yn cael ei gylchu gan fynyddau'), while saying of Rich Mountain that 'a splendid view is to be had from here' ('Golygfa ardderchog a geir yma').[54]

The campaign which took Theophilus Davies into western Virginia also gave him his first taste of battle. Despite experiencing violent contact with the enemy over a period of several days, the event is described only sparsely in his letter, and aspects of the terrain and their effect upon the soldiers' ability to travel receive as much attention as does the fighting itself.

> Gor. 10, cawsom ymladdfa, ac yr oeddem y dydd a'r nos allan yn chwilio, ac yn gwylio rhag y gelynion. Gor. 12, ni a giliasom yn ol. Gor. 13, ni a gychwynasom ar ol y gelynion, pa rai oeddynt wedi cilio yn y nos cyn hyny, taith galed o 34 o filltiroedd trwy y llaid a'r gwlaw. Yr oeddem yn teithio dros fynyddau, ac aethom dair gwaith trwy Cheat River, yr hon oedd tua thair troedfedd o ddyfnder ac ni a'u goddiweddasom; yr oeddynt yn bedair mil mewn rhifedi, a chymerodd ymladdfa le mewn dyffryn rhwng dau fynydd; parhaodd y frwydr ugain mynud; collasom ninau trwy farwolaeth 5, a chlwyfwyd 6 neu 7. Ni a laddasom eu pen-swyddog yn yr afon.[55]

'July 10 [1861], we had a fight, and we were out day and night searching, and watching for the enemy. July 12, we retreated back. July 13, we started after the enemy, who had retreated during the night before, a hard journey of 34 miles through the mud and the rain. We were travelling over mountains, and we went three times through the Cheat River, which was three feet deep, and we overtook them [i.e. the enemy]; they were four thousand in number, and a fight took place in a valley between two mountains; the battle lasted twenty minutes; we for our part lost 5 dead, and 6 or 7 were wounded. We killed their commanding officer in the river.'

While not detailing the nature of his own experience during the fighting, Theophilus Davies does give attention to the battle's aftermath and the effect of combat on an otherwise pleasing landscape.

Yr oedd yr olygfa yn arswydus i weled y meirw yn cael eu taflu ar eu gilydd ac i glywed cwynfanau y clwyfedigion. Cysgasom y nos hono ar faes y gwaed, ac yr oedd y ddaear lle y gorweddem yn wlyb odditanom.[56]

'The scene was horrible, to see the dead being piled on each other and to hear the complaints of the wounded. We slept that night on the field of blood, and the earth where we lay was wet beneath us.'

Similarly, while describing the Rich Mountain area as 'beautiful' (*hardd*), Davies also found it blemished by the stench of slaughter: 'Mae yr awyr yn ddrewedig yma, am fod llawer o gyrph heb eu claddu yn y coed'; 'The air stinks here, because many unburied bodies are in the woods.'[57]

Other soldiers' letters published by the Welsh-American press are like the epistles of Theophilus Davies in that they avoid detailed descriptions of fighting, focusing instead on the horrors arrayed on 'the field of blood' after the battle. This included writers who reached the field after the fighting had ended. The chaplain Ben Chidlaw, for example, wrote to *Y Cenhadwr Americanaidd* after visiting the field at Perryville.

Yr oedd golwg ar faes y gwaed, ddyddiau ar ol y frwydr, yn ddigon i ddryllio y galon. O erchyllfeydd rhyfel! Nid allaf ddarlunio y golygfeydd alaethus. Dyma o 15 i 20 o geffylau yn eu gwaed ac yn eu hymyl o 30 i 40 o feddau. Dyma 35 yn un rhes, marwolion y 75th Ill[inois]. Dacw restr hir o feddau y 10fed a'r 3edd Ohio, ac yma un arall o feibion Wisconsin ac Indiana. Ar ochr arall y mae dros fil o'r Deheuwyr wedi eu claddu, o leiaf wedi eu priddo, ond mae y moch wedi turio y pridd, a gwelais ugeiniau o gyrff wedi eu di-briddo, golygfa byth, gobeithio, i'w gweled eto.[58]

'The appearance of the field of blood, days after the battle, was enough to shatter the heart. Oh, horrors of war! I cannot describe the sorrowful scenes. Here are 15 to 20 horses in their blood and beside them 30 or 40 graves. Here are 35 in one row, the dead of the 75th Illinois. Over yonder is a long line of graves of the 10th and

> 3rd Ohio, and here is another of the sons of Wisconsin and Indiana. On the other side more than a thousand of the Southerners have been buried, at least put in the earth, only the pigs have dug in the earth, and I saw scores of unearthed bodies, a scene never, I hope, to see again.'

By the same token, William Jones of the 56th Ohio Infantry did not fight at Shiloh, but he reached the field soon after the battle had ended. Using one of those agricultural metaphors discussed by Earl Hess, he told *Y Drych*'s readers that trees had been 'mowed like hay': 'Gwelais rhai parthau o hono wedi ei orchuddio bron gan gyrff dynol a cheffylau, a'r coed wedi eu medi fel gwellt'; 'I saw some parts of it covered almost completely by human bodies and horses, and the trees were mowed like hay.'[59]

Other soldiers published pieces which avoided these kinds of domesticating or familiarizing metaphors, choosing instead to offer more meditative discussions on the transformative experience of war. The Revd J. D. Jones, chaplain of the 117th New York Infantry, wrote directly to *Y Cenhadwr Americanaidd*'s editor with a description of the hardships endured by his regiment during the siege of Petersburg.

> Y mae ein catrawd wedi cael amser lled galed y pymthegnos diweddaf. . . . Nid oes braidd ddiwrnod yn myned heibio . . . heb fod rhai yn cael ei clywfo gan danbelenau y gelyn. . . . Nos Sabboth diweddaf, tarawyd un o'n gwyr gan un o'r *shells* hyn, tra yn cysgu yn ymyl y gwarchglawdd. Aeth y *shell* yn nghyntaf drwy ei ben i'w fynwes, yna ymffrwydrodd, gan ei rwygo yn fil o ddarnau. Casglwyd ei weddillion mewn cwrlyd, goreu y gellid, a chladdwyd hwynt gerllaw y fan y cwympodd.[60]
>
> 'Our regiment has had a fairly hard time the last fortnight. . . . Hardly a day goes by . . . without some [of us] being injured by the enemy's shells. . . . Last Sunday night, one of our men was struck by one of these shells, while sleeping near the defences. The shell went first through his head into his chest, and then exploded, ripping him into a thousand pieces. We collected his remains in a blanket, the best as could be done, and buried them near the place where he fell.'

This horrific account resembles Benjamin Chidlaw's description of the field at Perryville. Both men were army chaplains, and both published their detailed depictions of the horrors of battle in one of Welsh America's denominational journals, *Y Cenhadwr Americanaidd*. Neither of these religious writers shielded their readers from the horrible reality of warfare; to the contrary, they describe the grizzly effects of battle in more detail than did many other soldier-writers. The *Cenhadwr*'s editor, Robert Everett, was at the forefront of the campaign to portray the war as a struggle against slavery, and he also published many pieces championing the cause of Union. However, despite striving tirelessly to encourage support for the Northern war effort, Everett did not shield his readers from pieces like these which offered a more sobering view of the conflict. *Y Cenhadwr Americanaidd* published a range of prose and poetry encouraging young Welsh-Americans to enlist in the Union army, yet it also printed letters which presented potential volunteers with vivid pictures of the terror awaiting them on the battlefield. This strain of war-time prose can be considered one of the main ways in which America's Welsh writers faced the reality of war in as honest – or at least as realistic – a way as possible.

If these two texts are similar in their candid descriptions of war's carnage, they are also separated by an important difference: whereas Chidlaw reached the field of Perryville after the fighting had stopped, Jones lived through the siege of Petersburg. Indeed, the Revd J. D. Jones used his detailed account of his regiment's experiences in order to offer readers a meditation on the relationship between the exterior circumstances of battle and the interior state of those who live through it.

> Fel hyn y mae ein dyddiau yn pasio yn y fyddin – yn nghanol peryglon ddydd a nos. Ni wyddom wrth fyned i'n gorphwysleoedd y nos, nac wrth gyfodi yn y boreu, beth sydd o'n blaen am gymaint â moment. . . . Pethau cyffredin yw golygfeydd fel hyn, fodd bynag, yn y fyddin, ac y mae un rywfodd yn ymarfer â hwynt. Pan ddaeth eich gohebydd o tan dân am y tro cyntaf, teimlai ei holl gyfansoddiad fel pe dan ergydion trydanol; ond erbyn hyn, y mae mynych ymarfer â'r swn a'r dryllio wedi ei allugoi i gysgu yn lled dawel yn nghanol y tanbeleniad trymaf. Mae yn ysgrifenu atoch yn awr mewn ceunant bychan, wedi ei dori yn y bryn, tra y mae *shells* yr Undebwyr a'r Cyngreirwyr yn pasio dros ei ben. Gallwch ddyfalu yn hawdd mai nid pleserus yw peth fel hyn; canys gall y naill neu'r llall o honynt ymdori drwy ddamwain neu yn bwrpasol, gan ei glwyfo neu ei ladd mewn eiliad.[61]

> 'It is like this that our days pass in the army – in the middle of dangers day and night. We do not know when we go to our resting places at night, nor when we get up in the morning, what is ahead of us for so much as a moment. . . . Sights like these are common things in the army, however, and one somehow gets used to them. When your correspondent came under fire for the first time, his whole composition felt as if it were undergoing electrical shocks; but by now, frequent acquaintance with the sound and the destruction has enabled him to sleep fairly quietly in the middle of the heaviest shelling. He is writing to you now from a small ravine that has been cut in the hill, while the shells of the Unionists and the Confederates pass over his head. You can guess easily that a thing such as this is not pleasant; for any of them can fall by accident or by intention, injuring or killing him in a second.'

This piece of battlefield prose invites readers to empathize with its author, describing as it does the exact circumstances in which it was written. Although the letter was addressed directly to the *Cenhadwr*'s editor, the 'you' (*chwi*) of the published piece speaks to the journal's readers as well. After asking them to imagine the time 'when [their] correspondent came under fire for the first time', Jones foregrounds the here and now of the text's composition, describing how he wrote the very words they are reading 'while the shells . . . pass overhead'. Though prefacing this address to the reader with a discussion of the way in which a person becomes accustomed to such things, he ends this passage by again focusing attention on the fearful nature of the situation. The words they are reading were written by a man who might be 'injured or killed' any 'second', and this dramatic address to the journal's readers thus emphasizes the fact that they are reading a text which has come to them through the uncertainties of battle. While Evan Davis used his diary to meditate on the gulf which separated writing about war from experiencing it, this army chaplain composed a letter which tries to bring the civilian reader closer to the battlefield experiences which it describes.

THOMAS D. THOMAS AND THE JOURNEY TO WAR

While the epistles discussed above were sent directly to the press, letters which friends and family members forwarded for publication at times offered readers a similar kind of battlefield prose.[62] In May 1862 *Y Seren Orllewinol* published a letter which Thomas D. Thomas had sent to his parents in Wales, Ohio.

> Llythyr Oddiwrth Gymro o Fort Donelson, Tenn.
> Ysgrifenwyd y llythyr canlynol o'r amddiffynfa uchod gan Thomas D. Thomas, mab i'r Parch. D. C. Thomas, at ei rieni, yn Wales, O.
>
> *Fy anwyl dad a mam,* – Yr wyf yn teimlo yn rhwymedig i Dduw am y fraint hon, sef cael eich cyfarch o faes y gwaed. Yr wyf yn iach, ac yn gobeithio eich bod chwithau felly hefyd. Rhoddaf ychydig o hanes ein taith o Porstmouth, O., i'r fan gwaedlyd hwn.[63]

> 'A Letter from a Welshman from Fort Donelson, Tenn.
> The following letter was written from the above fortress by Thomas D. Thomas, son of the Revd D. C. Thomas, to his parents, in Wales, Ohio.
>
> *My dear father and mother,* – I feel beholden to God for this privilege, namely being able to greet you from the field of blood. I am healthy, and hope that you are thus as well. I'll give a little history of our journey from Portsmouth, Ohio, to this bloody place.'

Like the emphasis which J. D. Jones placed on the fact that he was writing as shells passed over his head, this young soldier opens his letter by defining his own act of writing as a 'greeting' (*cyfarch*) sent 'from the field of blood' (*o faes y gwaed*). While the writer's parents were the original intended readers, the letter's transformation into a public text on the pages of *Y Seren Orllewinol* redirected this greeting from the battlefield to the whole of Welsh America. The journal's editor included a prefatory note which drew *his* readers' attention to the fact that he was presenting them with a soldier's narrative written on the field of battle; the title and subtitle stress that Thomas D. Thomas had composed the epistle at Fort Donelson, the 'fortress' (*amddiffynfa*) described in the ensuing battle narrative.

Like the personal reflections which Evan Davis confided to his diary, this letter deals with Thomas D. Thomas's first experience of combat. His 'little history' describes the soldier's battlefield initiation; it is a narrative which recounts his journey from the Northern state of Ohio (where he had lived as a civilian) to what he calls 'this bloody place', the Southern battlefield. The word *taith*, 'journey', is used repeatedly, and the people encountered on that journey southwards become increasingly hostile as the new recruits leave 'the supporters of freedom' behind and move closer towards their first experience of warfare.

> Gwelsom garedigrwydd nid bychan ar ein hymawiad o Portsmouth. . . . Teimlwn fy nghalon fach yn curo yn erbyn trais, gormes, a chaethiwed, ac yn chwyddo gan awydd i wneud fy ran dros gyfiawnder a ryddid; ar ein ymadawiad llon-gyfarchwyd ni gan y miloedd. Yna cychwynasom i'r daith, o ba un ni ddychwel llawer o honom. Ni ddygwyddodd dim yn annymunol ar hyd y ffordd; ond aethom rhagom yn dra llwyddiannus: llon-gyfar[ch]wyd ni gan bleidwyr rhyddid nes myned o honom islaw Lewisville ac wedi hyn, O! y fath gyfnewidiad. Edrychai y *Secesh* bradychlyd yn wgus arnom. Cymrhaeddasom Padducah Chwef. 14, am 7 o'r gloch y boreu. . . . Daeth gorchymyn am i ni frysio tua *Fort Donelson*. Yn ddioed wele ni yn gwynebu i fynu i'r Cumberland; ac ar ein taith dros yr afon hon ni chawsom ond tri theulu i'n llon-gyfarch. Cododd rhyw fradwr ei fawd at ei drwyn, a gwnaeth ryw glemiau rhyfedd arnom. – Dyna'r tro cyntaf erioed i mi deimlo tuedd i ladd dyn.[64]

> 'We experienced considerable kindness as we left Portsmouth, [Ohio]. . . . I could feel my little heart beating against violence, oppression, and slavery, and swelling with a desire to do my part for justice and freedom; during our departure we were cheered by thousands. Then we set out on the journey, from which many of us would never return. Nothing unpleasant happened along the way, but rather we made progress fairly successfully: we were cheered by the supporters of freedom until we went below Louisville and after this, Oh! what a transformation! The traitorous Secesh looked frowningly upon us. We reached Paducah February 14th, about 7 o'clock in the morning. . . . An order came for us to hurry towards Fort Donelson. Without delay we were directed up the Cumberland; and on our journey over the river we had but three families to cheer us. One traitor raised his thumb to his nose, and made some strange gestures towards us. – That was the first time ever I felt inclined to kill a man.'

While surely a (more or less) honest description of the facts surrounding this soldier's journey towards war, Thomas's text nonetheless displays a kind of thematic structuring which can be interpreted in terms of literary artifice.[65]

The soldier's journey southward towards his first experience of battle is accompanied by a transformation in his interior state. Despite having volunteered for the Union army, Thomas D. Thomas had never before felt a desire to kill; now, having come into increasing contact with people who are hostile to the cause which he supports (defined as 'freedom' and the defeat of 'violence, oppression and slavery'), he confesses to feeling that desire 'for the first time'.[66] Thomas is using his narrative to guide readers towards a description of his first experience of battle, and the emotional sea-change which occurs along the way can be seen as preparation for the encounter which awaits him at Fort Donelson. As both writer and editor emphasize at the start, this 'little history' was composed *after* the battle itself, and the pre-battle portion of the text is constructed so as to lead the reader to that dramatic point in more ways than one.

There is yet another development in Thomas's description of the increasingly hostile Southern population; after arriving at the place where the fighting is about to take place, the young soldier has an opportunity to see enemy soldiers before his regiment encounters them on the field. The Union soldiers, who had been travelling on river boats, disembark, and the writer is thus afforded a close first-hand look at the 'frightening scene' which awaits them there.

> Cyrhaeddasom o fewn dwy filldir i'r *Fort*, erbyn 4 o'r gloch boreu Sabboth. Cawsom orchymyn i fyned allan o'r badau: wedi glanio, awd yn nghyd a gwneud trefniadau er cael lluniaeth. – Cymerais yr hyfdra o fyned i fynu yr afon, nes myned o fewn milldir i'r gaerfa. Pryd hyn gwelwn yn amlwg ein gwnfadau, ac hefyd y gelynion. Safasom yn syn, o herwydd yr oedd yn olygfa ofnadwy. Arosai Grant yn bryderus am atebiad oddiwrth Buckner; ond buan y daeth yr amser pennodedig, sef naw o'r gloch, pryd y dechreuodd ein gwnfadau nesau at y *fort*, gwelwn y *shells* yn cael eu chwythu, nes y gorfu i'r gelynion ffoi yn mhob cyfeiriad. Mae yn anmhosibl i mi ddarlunio yr olygfa hon. Ond O y llawenydd a'r gwaeddi a fu wedi cael y fuddugoliaeth. Rhuthrai miloedd ar filoedd o'n milwyr i mewn i'r gaerfa.[67]

> 'We had come within two miles of the Fort by 4 o'clock Sunday morning. We received an order to get out of the boats: after landing, we were called together and plans were made to get food. – I was so bold as to travel up river, until I came within a mile of the fortress. At this time I could see easily our gunboats, and also the enemy. I stood in awe, for the scene was frightening. Grant was waiting nervously for an answer from Buckner, yet the appointed time came soon enough, namely 9 o'clock, when our gunboats started approaching the fort; I could see the shells being fired, until the enemy was forced to flee in every direction. It is impossible for me to describe this scene. But, Oh, the joy and the shouting which took place once victory was won. Thousands and thousands of our soldiers rushed into the fortress.'

One of the interesting aspects of this personal narrative is the way in which Thomas characterizes himself. While other aspects of this letter stress his loyalty to the Union army and the cause(s) for which it was fighting, he also describes himself as an individualist who acts alone, outside the orbit of the army with which he was serving. Calling himself 'bold', he confesses to wandering away from his regiment in order to satisfy his curiosity and better survey the 'frightening' sight of the enemy fortifications.

Like several other writers discussed in this chapter, Thomas D. Thomas refers to the incommunicable nature of battle; he writes that 'it is impossible' for him 'to describe this scene' for his civilian readers. He focuses instead on the 'frightening' nature of the sights which he sees before and after the battle, describing the Confederates' huge siege guns as horrible creatures with gaping mouths.

> Wrth fyned gwelem y cyflegrau mawrion, a'u safnau yn agored. Yr oedd yr olwg arnynt yn ofnadwy. Wedi ein myned heibio, o fewn milldir i dref Dover, cawsom fyned ar y tir eilwaith; aeth llawer iawn o'n milwyr i fynu y dref, er *plundro*. Ond meddyliais y gallaswn dreulio fy amser i well dyben na hyny, ac felly aethum dros faes yr ymdrechfa, a rhoddaf i chwi yma ddarluniad o'r golygfeydd mor gywir ag y medraf.[68]
>
> 'As we travelled [along the river on their boats] we could see the great cannons, with their mouths open. Their appearance was frightening. After we went past [the fort], travelling to within a mile of the town of Dover, we got to go upon land once again; many of our soldiers went up to the town, in order to plunder. But I thought that I could spend my time pursuing a better goal than that, and thus I went over the field of struggle, and I will provide you here with a depiction of the scenes as accurately as I can.'

While the battle itself is indescribable, Thomas does attempt to describe its aftermath in as much detail as possible. The young soldier again presents himself as an individualist, acting apart from the rest of his regiment. Like the 'bold' excursion along the river bank which he took before the battle, his movements are motivated by a desire to study the effects of battle. And, having viewed the carnage in detail, he describes it for his readers, conveying the horrors of warfare by detailing the sights which he found on the 'field of blood' after the actual fighting had ended.

> Y peth cyntaf a dynodd fy sylw oedd pumtheg o'n milwyr ni yn gorwedd ar draws eu gilydd wedi cael eu lladd. Teimlwn yn rhyfedd. Wedi hyn aethum yn mhellach: a gwelwn ddyn ieuangc, tua 19 oed, yn claddu ei dad, ac yn gwlchu y fan â'i ddagrau: rwygodd hyn fy nheimladau. Yr oedd yn dda genyf eich bod chwi yn mhell o'r fath le. Aethum rhag fy mlaen drachefn, a gwelais olygfeydd nad anghofiaf 'mo honynt. Yr oedd ein milwyr dewrion wedi cael eu medi yn mhob dull a modd, a'u dwylaw wedi eu gwasgu yn eu gilydd, yn edrych tua i

> fynu am dderbyniad i'r llys gwyn; eraill fel yn cysgu yn dawel yn nghanol y tawelwch rhyfeddaf; y gwahaniaeth oedd yn yr olwg arnynt. Rhaid i mi addef fod teimladau cymysgedig yn fy meddianu wrth eu gweled – gallaswn wylo y dagrau uwchben ein gwroniaid, ond teimlwn yn barod i sathru pleidwyr caethiwed dan fy nhraed. Gwelais driugain a phump o'n milwyr ni yn cael eu claddu yn yr un bedd. Credwch fi yr oedd yn olygfa ddifrifol iawn.
>
> 'The first thing that drew my attention was fifteen of our soldiers lying across each other, killed. I felt strange. After this I went farther: and I saw a young man, about 19 years old, burying his father and making the spot wet with his tears: this rent my feelings. I was glad that you are far from such a place. I went on again, and I saw sights that I will never forget. Our brave soldiers had been reaped in every fashion and manner, with their hands pressed together, looking up to be received by the blessed court; others as if sleeping quietly in the midst of the strangest tranquillity; there was such a difference in their appearance. I must admit that mixed feelings ran through my mind as I saw them – I could weep tears over our heroes, yet I felt ready to trample the supporters of slavery beneath my feet. I saw sixty-five of our soldiers being buried in the same grave. Believe me, it was a very sobering sight.'

Thomas D. Thomas gives considerable attention to the relationship between the external experience of war and the interior state of the individual soldier. Having already remarked that he 'felt strange' when viewing dead soldiers, he then attempts to describe 'the mixed feelings' which possessed him, as grief for the Union dead spilled over into a vengeful desire to destroy the enemy.

This is the second time that Thomas expresses a desire to kill Confederates, defined here as 'the supporters of slavery'. It is worth stressing the simple fact that this text was published on the pages of *Y Seren Orllewinol*, a journal serving the Welsh Baptists of the United States. Before the war the *Seren* had published material supporting the principle of pacifism; as was discussed in Chapter Two, it presented its readers with 'The Peace Society's Address' ('Anerchiad Cymdeithas Heddwch'), a text which stated in plain terms that 'all sorts of wars were inconsistent with the spirit of Christianity and the well-being of humanity' ('fod pob math o ryfeloedd yn anghysson ag ysbryd Cristionogaeth a daioni dynolryw').[69] Welsh-American print culture was transformed during the Civil War, and the publication of this kind of battlefield prose was one of the more dramatic aspects of that transformation.

The *Seren*'s editor highlighted the fact that the original letter was sent to the soldier's parents, and at this point in the narrative the journal's readers are made privy to an emotional interjection directed to the writer's father ('I was glad that you are far from such a place'). The manner in which Civil War regiments were recruited ensured that brothers and, at times, fathers and sons, served side by side on the battlefield, a fact which led to the kind of tragedy described in this letter. As was discussed in Chapter Three, the popular literary traditions of both Wales and the United States placed great emphasis on the concepts of family and hearth, and this part of Thomas's letter should be read within the context of that domestic imagery. The soldier provides an extended meditation on the tragic collision between family life and the horrors of battle: 'Mae galarnadau brodyr a chwiorydd, gwragedd a phlant . . . yn dorcalonus i[a]wn, ac yn effeithio arnom i'n cynhyrfu i ymddial ar y llofruddion'; 'the lamentations of brothers and sisters, wives and children . . . are extremely heart-breaking, affecting us so as to inspire us to take revenge upon the murderers'. Referring thus to the burial of fathers, brothers, sons and husbands on the field near Fort Donelson, Thomas stresses the emotional nature of the experience by adding: 'Mae fy nghalon yn gwaedu uwchben yr olygfa'; 'my heart bleeds at the sight.'[70] This is the second time that the writer's 'heart' is used to describe his feelings. Looking back on the interior state which he had experienced while leaving for war, Thomas wrote that he 'could feel [his] little heart beating against violence, oppression, and slavery, and swelling with a desire to do [his] part for justice and freedom'. Now, having witnessed the immediate results of war, that same heart 'bleeds.'

Ignoring the simple fact that soldiers on both sides were trying to kill each other, this Welsh-American characterizes the Confederates as *llofruddion*, 'murderers'. Having turned his readers' attention to the Southern soldiers, he than expands upon his characterization of them, describing the actions of the captured Rebels.

> Cymerasom o ddeuddeg i bumtheg mil o garcharorion. Pan oedd bâd wedi ei lwytho o'r carcharorion hyn ar gychwyn, dywedodd rai o'n bechgyn ni, *'Good-bye, boys,'* wrthynt. Yr ateb a gawsant oedd, *'Go to h-ll, you yellow bellied Yankees. Jeff. Davis forever.'*[71]

> 'We took from twelve to fifteen thousand prisoners. When the boat were loaded with these prisoners and ready to depart, some of our lads sad, "Good-bye, boys," to them. The answer they received was, "Go to h-ll, you yellow bellied Yankees. Jeff Davis for ever."'

Thomas's next sentence moves from these Southern prisoners to material items which the Northerners had taken from them: 'Ysgrifenais y llythyr hwn ag inc wedi ei wneud o bylor y gelyn a dwfr; ac y mae genym ddigonedd o fwydydd da ar eu hol'; 'I wrote this letter with ink made from the enemy's gunpowder and water; and we have obtained a sufficiency of good food from them.'[72]

This sentence introduces the text's closing paragraph. As the letter's opening sentence refers directly to the fact that Thomas was writing 'from the field of blood', so he brings his epistle to an end by referring directly to the circumstances in which his words were written. By telling his readers that he used ink made from the defeated enemy's gunpowder, Thomas D. Thomas was telling them that he was, quite literally, writing with the stuff of war. This curious detail enforces the thematic thrust of the entire narrative, a 'little history' intended to describe a soldier's introduction to the experience of combat. While Evan Davis meditated on the difference between experiencing the enemy's gunfire and writing about it, this soldier-writer drew attention to the authenticity of his battlefield experience by telling his civilian readers that he wrote with ink made from the enemy's gunpowder.

Thomas ends this final paragraph by appending a kind of coda to his narrative. He again states that he was fighting for 'freedom' (*rhyddid*), adding that this 'cause is supported by the God of the heavens' ('achos ag y mae Duw y nefoedd o'i blaid').[73] Having interpreted the Union cause as a struggle against slavery, and having justified this cause in religious terms, he ends by asking for the support of prayer: 'Yr ydym yn dymuno rhan yn eich gweddiau, a gweddiau holl bleidwyr breiniau dyn yn mhob man'; 'We desire a place in your prayers, as well as the prayers of all of the supporters of the rights of man everywhere.'[74] This writer points to an emotional link between himself and his readers, a connection which is charged with the combined energies of ideology and religion. And by ending with this authorial move he forces his readers to again consider the ideological fabric of the entire text. As the description of the regiment's departure from Ohio refers to the 'supporters of freedom' who cheered them on, so the letter's conclusion asks 'all the supporters of the rights of man everywhere' to pray for the soldiers who fight for 'freedom'. While Thomas sent this letter to his parents before they in turn forwarded it to *Y Seren Orllewinol* for publication, he nonetheless addresses an imagined audience which extends far beyond the boundaries of his parent's home. His father was a minister, the Revd D. C. Thomas, and thus in a position to ask the entire congregation of his chapel to pray for the Union soldiers. However, Thomas D. Thomas addresses the friends of freedom 'everywhere', suggesting that he knew, or at least hoped, that his letter would be read by a much wider audience. While the Revd Thomas may well have asked his congregation of Baptists to pray for his son and his comrades, he also ensured that the narrative which his son wrote with the enemy's gunpowder reached the pages of the Baptists' Welsh journal.

JOHN ROWLANDS AND 'THE DIRTY STENCH OF DEATH'S BREATH'

The suggestion that Thomas D. Thomas hoped to see his description of the field of Fort Donelson in print is supported by the fact that he sent other letters directly to the editor of *Y Seren Orllewinol*.[75] The dramatic value of soldiers' letters such as those published by Thomas had to off-set the fact that any 'news' which they contained was often out of date. Unlike those stories which reached the press by means of the telegraph, the vagaries of a war-time postal system often ensured that soldiers' letters reached journals weeks, and at times, months, after they were actually written. Despite the time-lag separating published battlefield prose from the battles they described, all evidence suggests that such texts were extremely popular with Welsh-American readers.[76] As this status cannot be attributed to the 'breaking' of news, the popularity of battlefield prose should rather be located in the realm of aesthetics; though descriptions of battles and life in the hostile South may have been out of date, these letters carried the authenticity of prose written on the field of blood with ink made of gunpowder. In other words, these kinds of texts were valued because they provided readers with a unique kind of reading experience.

At times, the delay between the composing and publishing of a letter enshrouded the printed text with a poignant dramatic aura. Such was the case with a letter which John W. Rowlands wrote while in 'Camp near Fredericksburg' on 6 December 1862.[77] It was sent originally to a friend – Mrs Jane Parry of Slate Hill, Pennsylvania – who then passed it on to a mutual acquaintance – M. A. Ellis of Peter's Creek – who in turn forwarded it to *Y Drych*. Mr Ellis included a note to the paper's editor, indicating that he was sending the soldier's letter on 15 December 1862, two days *after* the disastrous battle of Fredericksburg. The text was not published in *Y Drych* until 10 January 1863, nearly a month after the Union army's defeat in that bloody battle. As John Rowlands, writing a week *before* the battle, refers in his letter to the fact that he is about to fight at Fredericksburg, *Y Drych*'s readers would have come to the text with a kind of dramatic irony. In other words, they knew things about the battle's outcome which the writer did not know at the time when he was writing. The paper published the text under the heading *Llythyr oddiwrth Filwr Cymreig*, 'A Letter from a Welsh Soldier', prefacing it with M. A. Ellis's note.

Peter's Creek, Rhag. 15, 1862.

Mr. Golygydd, – rhoddwyd yn fy llaw y llythyr canlynol a dderbyniwyd gan gyfeillion i'r ysgrifenydd; ac wedi ei ddarllen tybiais fod y naws grefyddol, y teimlad dwfn, y tarawiadau bywiog, a'r penderfyniad gwrol a amlygir ynddo yn ddigon o reswm dros roddi cyhoeddusrwydd iddo yn y DRYCH. Mae y berthynas naturiol sydd rhwng ei ysgrifenydd â minau, yr hirfaith amser er pan glywais oddiwrtho, yr ofnau am ei ddiogelwch, hollol anwybodaeth am ei sefyllfa, a'r meddyliau bywiog am yr amseroedd gynt a redasant trwy fy meddwl tra yn darllen y llythyr, yr adgyfodiad mawr a gymerodd le yn mysg hunedigion meddyliol cyfnod y myned i'r ysgol a'r chwareu, yn peri i mi deimlo dyddordeb mawr ynddo; gan hyny wele ef i chwi.

Yr eiddoch yn wir, M. A. Ellis[78]

'Peter's Creek, Dec. 15, 1862.

Mr. Editor, – the following letter which was received by friends of the writer was placed in my hand; and, after reading it, I supposed that the religious nature, the deep feeling, the lively turns and the courageous determination which are expressed in it are enough of a reason for giving it publicity in the DRYCH. The natural relationship which exists between its writer and myself, the long time which has passed since I have heard from him, the fears concerning his safety, complete ignorance of his situation, and the lively thoughts concerning former times ran through my mind as I read the letter, the great stirring which took place amongst sleeping memories from the days of school and playing, have caused me to take a great interest in it; at that, here it is for you.

Yours truly, M. A. Ellis'

The words 'Mrs Jane Parry Slate Hill, Pa.' were printed at the very end of the published text, allowing us to put a name to one of the 'friends' referred to by Ellis in his introductory comments. Like Thomas D. Thomas's letter to his parents, the details published along with John Rowlands's text invite readers to place his battlefield meditations within a telescoping series of personal relationships. As the act of publishing presented the soldier's personal reflections to the wider community of Welsh America, so *Y Drych*'s readers were also introduced to the network of friends responsible for bringing this text from the camp at Fredericksburg to the printed page.

As has been stressed already, readers did not turn to these kinds of soldiers' letters for 'news', but rather to satisfy other reading needs or desires. In describing the virtues which make John Rowlands's letter worthy of publication, M. A. Ellis provides us with what is in essence a poetics of this literary genre, the soldier's letter. He draws the attention of potential readers to those qualities which, in his opinion, make the text a piece of literature worth reading. Ellis praises both form and content, referring to the piece's 'lively turns' (*tarawiadau bywiog*) of phrase as well as that which John Rowlands expresses by means of his 'lively' prose. This soldier's letter is said to express 'courageous determination' (*penderfyniad gwrol*), a martial characteristic one would expect to be praised on the pages of this pro-war newspaper. Ellis also draws attention to 'the religious nature' (*y naws grefyddol*) of Rowlands's letter, adding similarly that it exhibits 'deep feeling' (*teimlad dwfn*).

A kind of Romanticism was gaining popularity with Welsh readers and writers on both sides of the Atlantic at this time, and the expression of 'feeling' was seen increasingly as one of literature's main goals. While some critics have worried about what they see as a clash between this Romanticism and the chapel society of nineteenth-century Wales, others have suggested that Welsh literary culture harmonized the Romantic cult of feeling with the demands which Nonconformist Protestantism placed upon its writers and poets.[79] As E. G. Millward has remarked in his study of the singing culture of Victorian Wales: 'Yr oedd sentiment y canu Victoraidd yn ffenomen grefyddol a chymdeithasol yn ogystal â llenyddol'; 'the sentiment of Victorian song was a religious and social phenomenon as well as a literary one.'[80] (One could also note that similar processes were taking place in the United States at this time; perhaps the most notable example being the Romanticism adopted by New England's Unitarian writers.[81]) In commending John Rowlands's letter to *Y*

Drych's readers, M. A. Ellis suggested that it would fulfil a number of their literary expectations. He implied that it was the proper kind of battlefield prose (exhibiting 'courageous determination'), while also suggesting that it fulfilled the aesthetic expectations of Welsh readers, combining 'deep feeling' with a 'religious nature.'

Having first primed readers with Ellis's critical appraisal of the text, *Y Drych* then presents John Rowlands's letter complete with the writer's original heading. These extremely significant details – the place of writing and the date – convey the dramatic impact discussed above. Like so many letters written during the war, the first paragraph begins by describing the importance of correspondence to the soldier. John Rowlands then moves from thanking his friend for her letter to thanking God, introducing the religious tone praised by M. A. Ellis.

Gwersyllfa ger Fredericksbug,
Rhagfyr 6, 1862

Anwyl Gyfeilles – Daeth eich llythyr i'm llaw neithiwr, yr oedd yn dda iawn genyf ei gael. O mor ddedwydd yw derbyn llythyr oddiwrth hen gydnabyddion! Mae yn rhoddi bywyd newydd hyd yn nod yn y milwr mwyaf bywiog – yn gwroli y milwr mwyaf gwrol, ac yn gwasgaru llawenydd trwy ei holl galon. Da genyf ddeall eich bod chwi a'r plant a'ch priod yn iach. Nid ydym yn haner digon diolchgar i Dduw am y drugaredd hon. Meddyliwyf yn aml pa mor anniolchgar yr wyf wedi bod iddo ef am ei amddiffyn droswyf yn nghanol yr holl dân, y peleni, y trychineb a'r galanastra arswydus ar faes y frwydr, tra y syrthiai lluaws o'm cydfilwyr yn fy ymyl yn eu gwaed. Mae erchyllterau'r brwydr-faes yn ddigon i arswydo y meddwl mwyaf gwrol ac anystyriol. Yma y gwelir angau yn difrodi yn ei elfen – yma y mae yn rhwygo yn rhwysg ac egni ei gynddaredd – yma y mae wrth ei *fodd*. O elyn bywyd! Yr wyf yn dy gasau â chasineb perffaith, – saethwn belen farwol i'th galon pe medrwn. Dyna sydd yn fy mhoeni: Fy mod yn dy wasanaethu wrth ladd Sesesiaeth uffernol Jeff. Davis.[82]

'Camp near Fredericksburg,
December 6, 1862

Dear Friend – Your letter came into my possession last night, [and] I was very glad to get it. Oh what joy it is to receive a letter from old acquaintances! It gives new life to even the liveliest soldier – brings courage to the most courageous soldier, and spreads happiness through his whole heart. I am pleased to learn that you and your children and your spouse are healthy. We are not half thankful enough to God for this blessing. I think often how unthankful I have been to him for his watching over me in the middle of all of the fire, the bullets, the calamity and the dreadful carnage on the field of battle, wile a host of my fellow soldiers fell at my side in their blood. The horrors of the battle field are enough to frighten the most courageous and unheeding mind. Here death is seen ravaging in his element –

> here he rends in the pomp and energy of his fury – here he is *happy*. Oh enemy of life! I hate you with perfect hatred, – I would shoot a fatal bullet into your heart if I could. That is what worries me: that I serve you by killing the hellish Secessionism of Jeff. Davis.'

The soldier's meditations on God's 'blessing' lead him to describe 'the horrors of the battlefield', a point which he emphasizes by introducing a personified 'death' (*angau*). While numerous parallels can be found in the folklore and literature of many different cultures, the manner in which John Rowlands characterizes death resonates particularly with the masterpiece of Welsh prose which Ellis Wynne published in 1703, *Gweledigaetheu y Bardd Cwsc* ('The Visions of the Sleeping Bard').[83] The second of Wynne's three visions is entitled *Gweledigaeth Angeu yn ei Frenhinllys isa*, 'The Vision of Death in his lower Royal Court'. Unlike those traditions which portray the 'Grim Reaper' as a solitary figure in the modest attire of peasant or monk, Ellis Wynne's 'Death' is a pompous king who wallows in the adoration of a sycophant court while gorging himself on the bodies of the dead.

The 'Sleeping Bard' of Wynne's grotesque vision first encounters 'King Death' (*Brenin Angeu*) beside 'a huge, terrible Altar' (*Allor fawr arswydus*), where he is busy 'devouring the flesh and blood of men' (*yn traflyncu cîg a gwaed dynion*).[84] John Rowlands portrays death 'rend[ing] in the pomp and energy of his fury' ('yn rhwygo yn rhwysg ac egni ei gynddaredd'), endowing the phrase with an alliteration (*rhwygo – rhwysg*) which draws attention to that which is taking place in this sentence. While I have here translated the word *rhwysg* as 'pomp', it also carries a range of connotations relating to power, rule and authority.[85] If we read this 'Death' as a version of Ellis Wynne's *Brenin Angeu*, then we must conclude that he has left his 'court' for another environment which suits him equally – the Civil War battlefield. The connection between personified Death and the physical location being described is emphasized repeatedly, as Rowlands tells his friend (and readers of *Y Drych*) that Death is 'in his element' on the battlefield and that he is 'happy' or 'thrilled' (*wrth ei fodd*) there.

Having thus characterized Death, John Rowlands then addresses him directly, calling him 'enemy of life' ([*g*]*elyn bywyd*). This Union soldier professes 'perfect hatred' for personified death; although he himself was poised to attack the Confederate enemy on the field at Fredericksburg, it is the 'enemy of life' whom he wants to kill with 'a fatal bullet.' Unlike the hatred which Thomas D. Thomas expresses for 'the supporters of slavery' and his repeated claims to be fighting 'for freedom', John Rowlands does not pay much attention to the cause or causes for which he was fighting. He does, however, refer to 'the hellish Secessionism of Jeff Davis' in passing, thus making it clear (if such clarification were needed) how he felt about his other 'enemy'.

The use of the adjective *uffernol*, 'hellish', might be significant in light of the suggestion that John Rowlands is echoing Ellis Wynne's dream visions. Wynne's third and final vision is entitled *Gweledigaeth Uffern*, 'the Vision of Hell', and it describes both Satan and Hell in depth. Despite the grotesque unreality of Wynne's moralistic tale, all three visions are located in a well-defined (though fantastical) geography. Wynne locates Hell, complete with Satan's 'royal court' (*brenhinllys*), near to Death's 'lower royal court' (*brenhinllys isa*). This connection is further stressed by stating that Satan and Death are 'relatives'. John Rowlands's writing can be read productively against the background of Ellis Wynne's allegory, for a similar field of associations informs his battlefield meditations. In order to 'kill' the 'hellish' Secessionism of Jefferson Davis, the Union soldier is forced to serve that other 'enemy', death. In other words, he is caught in a moral trap which the allied forces of Hell and Death have set for him.

Reference has been made earlier in this chapter to Earl J. Hess's pioneering study, *The Union Soldier in Battle*. According to Hess, soldiers went about 'shaping the battle experience', employing metaphors and comparisons familiar to them from civilian life. 'This,' Hess concludes, 'was a workable strategy for mastering a unique, unprecedented part of their lives'; it was one way in which soldier-writers attempted to 'tame' the horrible knowledge of war.[86] While John Rowlands shapes his experience of battle in a rather unique fashion, he nonetheless drew upon a range of literary devices and images which would have been familiar to him before enlisting in the army. Ellis Wynne's *Gweledigaetheu* enjoyed a long-lived popularity with Welsh readers, and at least one edition was printed in the United States during the nineteenth century. It is impossible to prove whether John Rowlands echoed Ellis Wynne's text intentionally, and the question of intention is ultimately unimportant; Wynne's book is in itself part of a rich vein of Welsh prose writing which combined moralistic allegory with grotesque imagery, a textual field which included the Welsh Bible, particularly the Book of Revelation.[87] Whatever the ultimate sources informing this soldier's battlefield prose, we can conclude that he shaped his experiences by drawing upon the literary resources which would have been available to him in a range of texts. While other soldiers applied agricultural metaphors to war as they 'tamed' it in writing, John Rowlands used the familiar literary registers of grotesque and moral allegory to shape his battle experience.

Having presented his abstracted meditations on the nature of warfare, Rowlands then focuses more closely on the specific feelings which he had experienced during combat. The following paragraph thus provides a narrative delineating the movement to and across the field of battle, combining (as do other texts discussed in this chapter) a description of war's physical sensations with an attempt to discuss the soldier's interior state. In examining this subject, Rowlands details the soldier's feelings before, during and after battle, thus outlining the emotional transformations which mark different stages of the experience.

> Pan y byddys yn *marchio* i'r frwydr, bydd pawb, ond y llwfr, yn wrol ei galon, ac uchel ei yspryd – gwrhydri yn frenin ei natur, a gwroniaeth yn sylfaen ei orsedd. Yn awr, llenwir y milwyr â math o ysprydoliaeth yn dal buddugoliaeth o flaen y meddwl i'w dynu yn mlaen yn erbyn y gelyn, i'r chwareufa ddychrynllyd. Daw math o swyn i'w meddyliau yn eu sugno i'r tân a'r mwg, trwy bortreadu gogoniant buddugoliaeth a'i ddal yn uchel o flaen uchelgais yr enaid. Mae y swyn hwn yn codi ei ddwrn ar bob rhwystr, ac yn agor ei lygaid tanbaid, awyddus am ddarostyngiad y gelyn. Hyrddia yn mlaen, ac atega rhag myned yn ol. Try wg angau yn wên plentyn, a chwardda yn awgrymol mewn hyder angerddol am ben cythruddedd awdurdodol brenin y dychryniadau. Clywch! Dyna'r *'Charge'* ofnadwy! Dacw y *mass* byw yn rhuthro yn mlaen heibio i drwyn un o lewod mawrion y glyn, gan uchel floeddio mewn hyder gwronol, a damsang, mewn moment, filoedd o feirwon a chlwyfedigion dan eu traed, ac yn mhen ychydig fynydau bydd y maes yn eiddo i ni, a'r twrf tinciadau y dur gloyw wedi ei suo i gwsg yn mreichiau'r tawelwch. Mr. Hush yw llywodraethwr difrifol y chwareufa yn awr. Yn y fan gwisga y dynion haiarn gymeriad y plentyn tyner, a gwelir hwynt yn chwilied, mewn pryder, am frawd, neu gyfaill yn mysg y meirwon a'r clwyfedigion a orweddent yn eu gwaed. Tynant y naill oddiar gefn y llall tra y cura y galon gan brudd-der, a thra y treigla y deigryn gloyw yn ddistaw dros y rudd. O ddifrifoldeb! O bryder! O ddifrod ar fywyd! Ow Ryfel! Pa dad mor greulon a'th genedlodd?[88]
>
> 'When marching to battle, everybody, except the coward, is courageous of heart and of high spirits – valour is the king of his nature, and heroism the foundation of his throne. At this time, the soldiers are filled with a kind of inspiration which keeps victory before their thoughts in order to pull them onwards against the enemy, to the frightful arena. A kind of charm comes to their minds which draws them to the fire and the smoke by depicting the splendour of victory and holding it high before the soul's ambition. This charm raises up his fist at every obstacle, and opens his fiery eyes, eager to defeat the enemy. He rushes on, and offers support lest one should fall back. The frown of death turns into a child's smile, and he laughs suggestively in passionate confidence at the king of fright's authoritative provocations. Listen! There is the frightful "Charge"! Yonder is the living mass rushing on past the nose of one of the valley's great lions, shouting loudly in courageous confidence, and trampling, in a moment, thousands of the dead and injured beneath their feet, and in a few minutes the field will belong to us, and the noise of the bright steel's clanking will be sung to sleep in the arms of silence. Mr Hush is the sombre ruler of the arena now. Suddenly the men of iron take on the character of the tender child, and they can be seen searching, worried, for a brother or friend among the dead and the wounded who lie in their blood. They take the one from on top of the other while the heart beats with sadness, and while the bright tear travels quietly over the cheek. Oh the earnestness! Oh the anxiety! Oh the destruction of life! Alas War! What father so cruel conceived you?'

Death personified stalks through this paragraph as well. John Rowlands characterizes him here as 'the king of frights' (*brenin y dychryniadau*), recalling 'the King of Fright' (*Brenin y Dychryn*) who inhabits Ellis Wynne's vision.[89]

The 'authoritative provocation' (*cythruddedd awdurdodol*) of this frightful monarch is offset temporarily by the power of another 'king' ([*b*]*renin*), the 'valour' (*gwrhydri*) which commands the soldier from a throne of 'heroism' (*gwroniaeth*). While Evan Davis presented the soldier's courage as a positive force which offsets the horrors arrayed by the 'dogs of death', John Rowlands suggests that the forces of heroism work together with the spirit of war in order to deceive the soldier. They create a 'charm' (*swyn*) which 'sucks' (*sugno*) men into battle, momentarily transforming the 'frown' of personified death into a 'child's smile'. Much of this text's force stems from the way in which John Rowlands reworks his imagery, using the same descriptive language in different contexts as he takes his readers through the emotional changes marking the soldier's battlefield experience. Thus the false child's smile conjured by the charm of war is made to contrast with the temperament which possesses the soldiers after battle, as 'the men of iron take on the character of the tender child'. The transformation of the soldier's internal state is enforced by introducing a new character, 'Mr Hush'.[90] Having personified the forces of death and war in the first half of his epistle, Rowlands now personifies the soft force of reverent grief.

John Rowlands finishes this paragraph by grounding his elaborate literary construction in the reality of war, reminding his readers that his meditations are based upon actual experience.

> Oh, fe welais fwy mewn awr nag a ddymunwn weled mewn oes eto. Y trugarog Ior a atalio rwysg y march gwaedlyd hwn. Wel, dichon eich bod chwi yn meddwl fy mod yn myned yn *sentimental*. Na, yr wyf yn dweud ffeithiau difrifol prawf. – Gwelais hyn, filoedd fwy na hyn – yn yr *Antietam*, er enghraifft.[91]
>
> 'Oh, I have seen more in an hour than I care to see again in a lifetime. May the merciful Lord restrain this bloody horse. Well, perhaps you think that I am becoming sentimental. No, I am relating the serious facts of experience. – I have seen this, a thousand times more than this – at Antietam, for example.'

This writer presents a construction of two different – yet interconnected – fields. John Rowlands asks the reader to consider real battlefields, referring directly to Antietam and stressing the fact that he has 'seen' these things with his own eyes (and before the end of the letter he will tell us that he has lived through every major engagement 'in the east'). However, these real fields of battle are covered with a literary palimpsest, a supernatural field where the personified forces of death, war, valour and grief are set in motion. Despite stressing the difference between literary constructions of war and the reality of battle, Evan Davis nonetheless resorted to an intensely literary image, describing the experience as an 'imprint' upon the 'book shelf' of his memory. John Rowlands negotiates the gulf separating literature from reality in a different way, employing the elaborate literary registers of grotesque and moral allegory while at the same time insisting that his text is grounded in the authority of experience. He asks the reader to interpret his literary construct within the framework of experience, reading his sentences as reflections of the 'serious facts' with which the soldier was intimately familiar.

This writer thus guides the reader's interpretation of his text, citing the reality of his experience to authenticate what might otherwise be taken as sentimentality. Whereas M. A. Ellis's introductory note praises the letter for its 'deep feelings' (*teimladau dwfn*), the writer himself uses the English word 'sentimental' here, a fact highlighted by *Y Drych*'s editor, who has placed it in italics ('dichon eich bod chwi yn meddwl fy mod yn myned yn *sentimental*'). As was suggested above, Ellis's words can be taken as an appeal to the aesthetics of the newspaper's Welsh readers, a configuration of literary tastes which included a Romantic emphasis on the primacy of feeling. On the other hand, John Rowlands's use of the word 'sentimental' invites us to consider the influence of the country's English-language literature upon the Welsh writers of the United States. According to Alice Fahs, 'the sentimental soldier' was an extremely popular literary construct during the Civil War.[92]

> The sentimental soldiers of this popular literature were not 'realistic' in the modes later developed by late-nineteenth-century social realism, with its insistence on the primacy of 'fact' and a mimetic depiction of social conditions. Rather, these literary soldiers were highly conventionalized and typologized, presented within a framework of sentimentalism that insisted on the primacy of emotion and sentiment as a form of 'reality.'[93]

It is of course impossible to know exactly how any individual reader would have regarded the relationship between reality and literary constructions of emotion. However, when this letter was transformed into a public text by the newspaper it was offered up to a large community of readers which surely included a range of overlapping literary tastes and experiences. It is safe to assume that many of *Y Drych* 's readers would have interpreted John Rowlands's text using overlapping Welsh and American fields of reference, drawing upon modes of writing popular in the Old Country (including the elaborate imagery of Ellis Wynne and the emerging Welsh Romanticism) as well as 'the sentimental soldier' of popular American literature. Whatever interpretive framework readers might have had at hand, John Rowlands insists that they *not* interpret his words as 'sentimental', insisting rather on the authenticity of his experience.

M. A. Ellis also noted the 'religious nature' (*naws grefyddol*) of this epistle. As the writer grounds his elaborate meditations on the essence of war and death in the reality of experience, so he anchors his religious meditations in present reality by stressing the fact that he was writing the letter on a Sunday.

> Y Sabboth yw heddyw. Yr ydych chwi yn cael rhyddid i fyned i *le* o addoliad cyhoeddus. Ond nid felly yma. Heddyw fel pob dydd arall gyda ni. O, fe fydd gorphwysdra yn hyfryd i'r milwr. Mor dda fuasai genyf gael myned i Dy Dduw ambell dro, eithr ofer yw disgwyl hyny – nid yw y wledd hono yn perthyn i'n bwrdd ni. Modd bynag, y mae genyf un Cyfaill cywir – ni ddywedodd anwir erioed; mae yn ffyddlon – ni chilia yn nydd y frwydr. Dyma pwy ydyw – Y TESTAMENT CYMRAEG. Yr wyf yn ei ddarllen bob dydd – yn ei fyfyrio bob nos hyd yn nod pan yn cyweirio fy ngwely ar fy arfau. A ydych chwi yn meddwl ei fod yn sarhad i filwr yn llawn o wrhydri i ystwytho i gymeryd cyngor gan 'Air ein Duw ni'? Y milwr dewraf yn achos cyfiawnder ac uniondeb yw yr hwn sydd yn deall egwyddorion cyfiawnhad trwy ffyrdd oreu. Pondrwch hwnyna. Good night. O, ïe, dywedaf hyny eto. Yr wyf wedi bod yn mhob brwydr yn y Dwyrain. Bu aden Duw yn darian i mi ynddynt oll. Syrthiodd miloedd o flaen fy llygaid, ac o dan fy nhraed. Rhwyd-dwyllwyd fy nillad. Bum yn arogl brwnt anadl angau. Ond, ond, byw ydwyf, ac iach ydwyf! I Dduw y byddo y diolch, Efe oedd y *fortification* mwyaf *impregnable* o'r un y bum ynddi erioed. Pa fodd y byddaf yn ddigon diolchgar iddo![94]

> 'Today is Sunday. You are free to go to a *place* of public worship. But it is not thus here. Today is like every other day for us. Oh, the soldier finds rest pleasant. How much I would like to go to God's House once in a while, yet it is in vain that one waits for that – that feast does not belong to our table. However, I have one true Friend – he has never told me a lie; he is faithful – he never flees on the day of battle. This is who it is – THE WELSH TESTAMENT. I read it every day – study it every night even when I make my bed upon my weapons. Do you think that it is an insult for a soldier full of valour to bend and take council from "our God's Word?" The bravest soldier [fighting for] the cause of justice and union is he who best understands the principles of justification by faith. Ponder that. Good night. Oh, yes, I will say that again. I have been in every battle in the East. God's wing was a shield to me in all of them. Thousands fell before my eyes, and under my feet. My clothes were shot full of holes. I have been in the dirty stench of death's breath. Yet, yet, I am alive, and I am healthy! To God be the thanks, He was the most impregnable fortification of all the ones in which I have ever been. How will I be thankful enough to him!'

Like those soldiers discussed in Chapter Five, John Rowlands refers to the succour which he derives from his Welsh 'Testament'.[95] Having already personified the forces of war, death, valour and grief, he now employs that literary strategy for the last time, describing his Bible as his 'one true Friend'. Unlike the deceitful charm conjured jointly by valour and war, this Friend offers support 'on the day of battle' which is honest and 'faithful'.

Having drawn upon a number of literary registers up to this point, John Rowlands now turns to the language of the Calvinistic Methodist *seiat*, asking his audience to 'ponder' his testimony of belief.[96] 'The bravest soldier', he writes, is the one 'who best understands the principles of justification by faith'. While the principle of *sole fide* can be traced back to early Protestant reformers, the exact words which Rowlands uses – *egwyddorion cyfiawnhad trwy ffydd* ('the principles of justification through faith') – constitute a specific formulation of that religious tenet which is bound up with the history of Welsh Methodism. The earliest known example of the phrase *cyfiawnhad trwy ffydd* is found in Howel Harris's 1742 publication, *Sail, Dibenion, a Rheolau* ('Foundation, Purposes and Rules'), a handbook produced for the first Methodist societies in Wales.[97] By the middle of the nineteenth century, the kinds of 'rules' established by Harris had become soundly embedded in the very heart of Welsh Calvinistic Methodism, informing individual belief as well as the public examination of that belief.[98]

The 'principles of justification through faith' which this soldier cites were part of the process by which Welsh Calvinistic Methodists defined the membership of their religious community.[99] Howel Harris presented the phrase *cyfiawnhad trwy ffydd* in that section of his 'rules' dealing with the questions which were used to define the believer's faith. Welsh Methodists were instructed to ask themselves as well as fellow members: 'a ydych yn credu'r gwirioneddau sylfaenol am . . . Cyfiawnhad trwy Ffydd'; 'do you believe the essential truths concerning . . . Justification through Faith?'[100] John Rowlands presents this point following his own rhetorical question – 'Do you think that it is an insult for a soldier . . . to take council from "our God's Word?" ' – and, having expressed his own belief in the importance of 'justification through faith', he asks his reader to 'ponder' his avowal of faith. Moreover, this spiritual examination comes near the end of a letter in which the soldier confesses to 'serving' death. The relationship between writer and reader is made to reflect the relationship existing between members of the chapel's *seiat*, a community of Christians who come together in order to confirm their belief by rigorously cross-examining the nature and foundations of each individual member's faith. If John Rowlands 'shaped' his experience of battle by drawing upon the literary resources of dream vision and moral allegory, he shapes his meditations on what it meant to be a soldier by employing the language and concepts of the Welsh Calvinistic Methodist chapel.

Rowlands concludes this paragraph by thanking God for protecting him on the battlefield. Once again, he anchors his writing in the reality of experience: 'thousands fell before my eyes, and under my feet. My clothes were shot full of holes' ('Syrthiodd miloedd o flaen fy llygaid, ac o dan fy nhraed. Rhwyd-dwyllwyd fy nillad'). At the same time, he employs an ornate mode of personification in order to elaborate upon the experience, describing these real battlefield experiences in terms of living 'in the dirty stench of death's breath' ('yn arogl brwnt anadl angau').

The published epistle contains one final paragraph; like the coda which Thomas D. Thomas appended to his battlefield narrative, John Rowlands ends his letter by asking the reader to pray for him. Consistent with the entire fabric of his text, he again grounds his sentences in a real battlefield. This time, however, it is not one on which he has fought, but rather one on which he is about to fight.

> Dacw Fredricksburg. Byddaf yn gorwedd yn fy ngwaed yno, neu yn *marchio* trwy waed ereill yno, yn union deg. O ddrychfeddwl ofnadwy! A gaf fi fy mywyd? Duw yn unig a wyr. Gweddiwch droswyf. Eich hen gyfaill dros byth, John W. Rowlands.

> 'Behold Fredericksburg. There I will be lying in my blood, or there I will be marching through the blood of others, shortly enough. Oh horrible thought! Will I be spared? God alone knows. Pray for me. Your old friend for ever, John W. Rowlands.'

While various discourses and literary registers are woven together in this letter, it is above all else a description of what the Welsh-American press called *maes y gwaed*, 'the field of blood'. No image is more central to this text than the soldiers' blood soaking the battlefield. Rowlands's opening paragraph states that 'hosts of [his] fellow soldiers had fallen beside [him] in their blood' ('syrthiai lluaws o'm cydfilwyr yn fy ymyl yn eu gwaed'), and he later describes the 'brothers' and 'friends' discovered 'among the dead and the wounded who lie in their blood' ('yn mysg y meirwon a'r clwyfedigion a orweddent yn eu gwaed'). The cruel reality of warfare is emphasized by referring repeatedly to the manner in which soldiers march over the fallen, treating their own comrades as part of the bloody field on which they walk; he writes that they 'trample, in a moment, thousands of the dead and injured beneath their feet' ('damsang, mewn moment, filoedd o feirwon a chlwyfedigion dan eu traed'), confessing later that 'thousands have fallen . . . beneath [his own] feet' ('Syrthiodd miloedd . . . ac o dan fy nhraed'). This writer's concluding sentences thus stem from his epistle's central image; John Rowlands ends by gesturing towards the battlefield which awaited him near Fredericksburg, writing with poignant frankness that 'there I will be lying in my blood, or there I will be marching through the blood of others, shortly enough' ('Byddaf yn gorwedd yn fy ngwaed yno, neu yn *marchio* trwy waed ereill yno, yn union deg').

This letter was presented to readers on the pages of *Y Drych*, the same newspaper which published Undebwr's discussion of Welsh America's battlefield service. That writer, it will be remembered, focused on the soaking of American ground with Welsh blood, using that image to imply that people of his 'nation' had earned their American citizenship in the hardest possible way: 'Cochwyd aml i lanerch y De â gwaed meibion goreu ein cenedl'; 'Many of the South's pastures have been stained with the blood of the best sons of our nation.'[101] In the hands of writers like Undebwr, the image of the blood-soaked battleground became a new way of articulating Welsh-American identity. However, the war-time press presented Welsh-Americans with a wide range of battlefield prose, as different writers found different ways of grounding their language and imagery in the soil of Southern battlefields. John Rowlands says in passing that the struggle against 'hellish Secessionism' placed him in death's 'service', yet he does not elaborate upon the connection between his battlefield service and the causes for which he was fighting. He chose instead to pursue other themes, constructing a series of personifications which help him focus his literary imagination on the forces of death, war, valour and grief, while also evoking the contemplative space of the chapel's *seiat* in order to work through religious questions stemming from his encounter with death. He also created a piece of prose which leaves the reader with a feeling for the horrible physicality of the battlefield, a place where soldiers march over the dead bodies of friends and enemies alike, churning the 'blood of others' into the field beneath their feet.

NOTES

1 Robert J. Thomas letters, 3, in the collection of Nadine Thomas.
2 Ibid.
3 Ibid.
4 See Chapter Five, 197–8. The third diary, not discussed in this chapter, is that of the artilleryman David Davies.
5 John Rowlands's diary, in the collection of Albert Gregorovich.
6 I have added punctuation and capitalization in the translation to facilitate reading.
7 The Diary of John H. Williams, Vermont Historical Society Library.
8 Ibid.
9 Note that, while several of his more specific military terms are English, this Vermont soldier also employs his native Welsh vocabulary in describing the battle; he writes *tân* ('fire') as well as [c]*archarorion* ('prisoners'), and he uses the verbs *rhuthro* ('to charge') and *syrthio* ('to fall back') to describe his regiment's movements.
10 See, for example, *Y Seren Orllewinol*, September 1862.
11 The diary of Evan Davis, National Library of Wales fac. 647.
12 In addition to the more commonly used word *brwydr*, the English word 'battle' (or rather, a Middle English form such as *batayle* or *batel*) was borrowed into Welsh at least as early as the fourteenth century. However, this was spelt as *batel*, *batl* or *batail* in Welsh. See *Geiriadur Prifysgol Cymru* (Cardiff, 1950–2002), p. 264. Evan Davis spells the word 'battle'; it is the English word which he is using.
13 Walt Whitman, *Memoranda During the War* (1875; reprint Bedford, MA, no date), p. 15.
14 This was a personal letter sent by two brothers, David and Benjamin Thomas, to their mother in Wales; she then forwarded it to a Welsh paper, *Y Gwladgarwr*, for publication (*Y Gwladgarwr*, May 1862). While both brothers signed the letter, the

singular form (*imi*, 'for me') is used here; it is impossible to know which of the two brothers actually wrote the letter (or this part of it). Many examples of this statement (using the same words *darlunio* and [*g*]*ormod*) are found in other letters; for example, manuscript letters in the collections of Mary Jones, Alan Williams and David R. Smith.

15 See Gerald Conti, 'Seeing the Elephant', *Civil War Times Illustrated* (June 1984) and Joseph Allan Frank and George A. Reaves, *'Seeing the Elephant'* [:] *Raw Recruits at the Battle of Shiloh* (Champaign [Illinois], 2003).

16 For the expression *cŵn Annwn, Geiriadur Prifysgol Cymru* gives 'hounds of hell, reputed to be supernatural hunting dogs traversing the skies at dead of night (lit. hounds of Annwn or the underworld)', and notes that the earliest recorded example of the phrase is an eighteenth-century ballad; *Geiriadur Prifysgol Cymru* (Cardiff, 1950–2002), p. 474. *Annwfn* or *Annwn*, however, occurs in a number of medieval texts, and it is clear that the history of this tradition (or these associated traditions) is much older.

17 Earl J. Hess, *The Union Soldier in Battle* [:] *Enduring the Ordeal of Combat* (Lawrence, 1997), pp. 127–8.

18 For example, *Y Drych*, 25 July 1863.

19 The diary of Evan Davis.

20 Earl J. Hess, *The Union Soldier in Battle*, pp. 127–8.

21 The diary of Evan Davis.

22 Ibid.

23 Compare Earl J. Hess, *The Union Soldier in Battle*, p. 105.

24 See, for example, Gerwyn Williams, *Tir Neb* [:] *Rhyddiaith Gymraeg a'r Rhyfel Byd Cyntaf* (Cardiff, 1996), pp. 165–6.

25 *Y Drych*, 4 April 1863.

26 Compare 'Bugail', writing in *Y Seren Orllewinol*, July 1862: 'EIN MILWYR. Mae y dosbarth hwn o'r genedl ar y maes y dyddiau hyn yn profi eu gwladgarwch.'

27 Reid Mitchell, *Civil War Soldiers* (New York, 1988), p. 95.

28 Ibid.

29 See Chapter Two, pages 55–6.

30 *Y Drych*, 18 April 1863.

31 See Chapter Six, pages 249–50.

32 Reid Mitchell, *Civil War Soldiers*, p. 108. Mitchell's analysis of the 'peopled landscape', however, focuses on Northern soldiers' negative reactions to the people inhabiting the Southern landscape. D. M. Williams's discovery of (apparently pro-Union) Welsh people, it might be suggested, reverses the trend described by Mitchell, leading the Welsh-speaking Northerner to view the Southern landscape as a welcoming and comforting environment.

33 One of the best examples is the fourteenth-century poem by Dafydd ap Gwilym, 'Offeren y Llwyn'; Thomas Parry (ed.), *Gwaith Dafydd ap Gwilym* (Cardiff, 1979), pp. 323–4. See also Huw M. Edwards, *Dafydd ap Gwilym* [:] *Influences and Analogues* (Oxford, 1996), p. 32.

34 *Y Cyfaill o'r Hen Wlad*, July 1862. The writer, R. C. Roberts, sent this letter to relatives in Holland Patent; they subsequently had it published in the *Cyfaill*.

35 *Y Cyfaill o'r Hen Wlad*, June 1864. This same letter describes the winter snows and ice of Tennessee in a memorable fashion: 'a bod ein cartrefleoedd y pryd yma wedi eu hamgylchu ag anferth luwchfeydd o eira, a phob aber, afonig a llyn, yn y cyffiniau wedi eu cau dan sel brenin y Rhew' ('and our dwellings at this time were

surrounded by gigantic drifts of snow, and every river, stream and lake in the area was closed under the lock of the king of Ice'). The letter was dated 11 February 1864. Though serving with Co. F., 22nd Wisconsin Infantry, Thomas J. Davies had lived in Oneida County, New York, before moving to Wisconsin, a pattern followed by many other Welsh immigrants.

36 *Y Cyfaill o'r Hen Wlad*, January 1863. The verb *creigio* describes the process of lining a road with rocks; while it is translated here as 'cobbled', the description is not of the cobbled streets of the town but rather of rural roads which have been macadamised. This soldier also praised the Kentucky landscape, describing it as being 'even and beautiful' ('[g]wastad a hardd') and noting that the farms boasted 'splendid buildings' ('adeiladau ysplenydd'). However, when he got to Island No. 10 in the Mississippi, he echoed those soldiers whom, according to Reid Mitchell, saw it as 'dreary and ugly': 'mae y lle hwn yn anghyfanedd iawn yn bresenol; mae y coed wedi crino, a phob peth yn edrych yn anial iawn'; 'this place is very much unsettled at the moment; the trees have wilted, and everything looks very wild.'

37 Ambrose Bierce, 'On a Mountain'; reprinted in (ed.) William McCann, *Ambrose Bierce's Civil War* (Washington, DC, 1956), p. 4.

38 The letters of John Griffith Jones, National Library of Wales Manuscript 22421D.

39 Ibid.

40 Ibid.

41 Ibid.

42 *Y Cyfaill o'r Hen Wlad*, June 1862.

43 *Y Drych*, 11 July 1863.

44 Reid Mitchell, *Civil War Soldiers* (New York, 1988), p. 91.

45 See especially Chapter Two, pages 61–3.

46 *Y Drych*, 31 January 1863.

47 Ibid.

48 National Library of Wales Manuscript 22421D.

49 Ibid.

50 *Y Drych*, 21 March 1863.

51 Reid Mitchell, *Civil War Soldiers*, p. 109.

52 See Chapter Five, pages 212–14.

53 *Y Cenhadwr Americanaidd*, September 1861.

54 Ibid.

55 Ibid.

56 Ibid.

57 Ibid.

58 *Y Cenhadwr Americanaidd*, January 1863.

59 *Y Drych*, 31 January 1863.

60 *Y Cenhadwr Americanaidd*, October 1864.

61 Ibid.

62 See Chapter Four, page 164, for a discussion of the different channels which carried soldiers' letters to the printed page.

63 *Y Seren Orllewinol*, May 1862.

64 Ibid.

65 The suggestion that writers of factual prose rely upon thematic structuring and literary artifice can be explored in connection with (what has been called) 'post-modern' historiographical theory. See Hayden White, *Metahistory* (Baltimore,

1973) and *The Content of Form* (Baltimore, 1987); Keith Jenkins, *On 'What is History'* (London, 1995).

66 Note that, while Thomas D. Thomas was a military musician and thus not issued with a weapon, he states in another letter that he later acquired a rifle. *Y Seren Orllewinol*, July 1862: 'Ni chefais i ddim ond y *fife* – ond . . . daethum o hyd i *Enfield Rifle* – yr wyf yn cadw hwn, ac yn bwriadu gwneud'; 'I received nothing but the fife – but . . . I came across an Enfield Rife – I am keeping this, and intend to do so.'

67 *Y Seren Orllewinol*, May 1862.

68 *Y Seren Orllewinol*, May 1862.

69 *Y Seren Orllewinol*, June 1850.

70 *Y Seren Orllewinol*, May 1862.

71 Ibid.

72 Ibid.

73 See Chapter Four, pages 165–88.

74 *Y Seren Orllewinol*, May 1862.

75 This suggestion is supported by the fact that Thomas D. Thomas also sent letters directly to *Y Seren Orllewinol* for publication. See for example, *Y Seren Orllewinol*, September 1862: 'Llythyr Oddiwrth Filwr Cymreig. *At Olygydd y Seren Orllewinol*,' which begins: 'Anwyl Edwards, – Dymunol yw genyf gael cyfleusdra i anfon gair atoch o'r ddinas hon (Memphis)'.

76 See Chapter Five, page 225, on attestations as to the popularity of soldiers' letters.

77 This John W. Rowlands is not the John Rowlands discussed earlier in this chapter who wrote a diary while serving with the 14th Vermont Infantry. It is not known whether this is the same John Rowlands who is discussed in Chapter Four, as neither provided the name of the regiment with which he was serving.

78 *Y Drych*, 10 January 1863.

79 For example, in discussing one of the centrepieces of the traditional canon of nineteenth-century Welsh literature – the poem *Y Storm* by William Thomas (Islwyn) – Glyn Tegai Hughes refers to the fact that a number of critics have called the poem a 'muddle' because it is marred by 'the struggle between Romanticism and Calvinism'; Glyn Tegai Hughes, 'Islwyn and *Y Storm*', in Hywel Teifi Edwards (ed.), *A Guide to Welsh Literature c.1800–1900* (Cardiff, 2000), p. 93.

80 E. G. Millward, *Cenedl o Bobl Ddewrion* [:] *Agweddau ar Lenyddiaeth Oes Victoria* (Llandysul, 1991), p. 19.

81 See Lawrence Buell, *New England Literary Culture From Revolution Through Renaissance* (Cambridge, 1986), pp. 44–5 and 69–73.

82 *Y Drych*, 10 January 1863.

83 For suggestions as to other ways in which Ellis Wynne's work may have influenced Welsh-American writing, see pages 63–6 and 448 in this study.

84 Ellis Wynne, *Gweledigaetheu y Bardd Cwsc* (London, 1703), p. 65.

85 *Geiriadur Prifysgol Cymru* (Cardiff, 1950–2002), p. 3120: 'power, authority, ruel, dominion, influence; majesty, dignity, glory, splendour, pomp, ostentation; pride, presumption'. The word *rhwysg* also carried another range of meanings, which GPC gives as 'rush, attack, (fast) course, path; force, might.' The later also applies to the battlefield context described by John Rowlands, and a combination of both fields of meaning is also possible.

86 Earl J. Hess, *The Union Soldier in Battle*, pp. 127–8.

87 See the discussion on Ieuan Ddu's 'Vision'; Chapter Two, pages 63–6.

88 *Y Drych*, 10 January 1863.

89 Ellis Wynne, *Gweledigaetheu*, for example, p. 71.

90 This 'Mr Hush' might also be read in terms of Ellis Wynne's personified sleep, *Cwsc*, the character who guides the 'sleeping bard' through a series of dream visions. The interplay between different supernatural forces, most of them personified, in this text makes the resemblance to Ellis Wynne's work all the stronger; the manner in which 'death', 'war', 'hellish secessionism' and 'Mr Hush' work in John Rowlands's epistle can be seen to reflect the interplay between 'Sleep', 'Death', and Lucifer in Wynne's text.

91 *Y Drych*, 10 January 1863.

92 Alice Fahs, *The Imagined Civil War* [:] *Popular Literature of the North and South 1861–1865* (Chapel Hill, 2001), pp. 93–119.

93 Ibid., p. 94.

94 *Y Drych*, 10 January 1863.

95 For the religion of Welsh soldiers, see Chapter Five, pages 208–18.

96 For a definition of *seiat*, see Chapter Five, pages 00–00.

97 Howell Harris, *Sail, Dibenion, a Rheolau'r Societies Neu'r cyfarfodydd Neullduol a ddechreuassant ymgynnull yn ddiweddar yn Nghymru. At y rhai y chwanegwyd Rhai Hymne Yw canu yn y cyfarfodydd Neulltuol, gan Wyr o Eglwys Loegr* (Bristol, 1742). See also *Geiriadur Prifysgol Cymru*, p. 694.

98 Of course, other texts were added by later generations of Welsh Calvinistic Methodists. Of extreme importance in this respect is the *Cyffes Ffydd* ('Confession of Faith') which they adopted in 1823. For the influence of this publication upon nineteenth-century Welsh prose, see R. Tudur Jones, 'Rhyddiaith Grefyddol y Bedwaredd Ganrif ar Bymtheg', in Geraint Bowen (ed.), *Y Traddodiad Rhyddiaith* [:] *Darlithiau Rhydychen* (Llandysul, 1970) pp. 336–7.

99 Geraint Tudur, *Howell Harris* [:] *From Conversion to Separation* (Cardiff, 2000), pp. 85–6: 'The Welsh societies were . . . exclusive assemblies; not only was faith a condition of acceptance, but the applicant was also expected to subscribe to Calvinism'; 'This doctrinal emphasis in the rules formally established the Calvinistic nature of the Welsh Methodist movement[.]'

100 Howel Harris, *Sail, Dibenion a Rheolau . . . Holiadau* ('Questions'), number 5.i. See Gomer Morgan Roberts (ed.), *Hanes Methodistiaeth Galfinaidd Cymru* (Caernarfon, 1973), vol. 1, p. 177.

101 *Y Drych*, 4 April 1863.

Part Four

Writing Freedom

10

Star over Washington: The Literature of Emancipation

One of Welsh America's more prolific war-time writers was the Revd David Davies, a Congregational minister serving Ohio's large Welsh-speaking population. Known by the bardic name Dewi Emlyn, Davies contributed a considerable body of prose and poetry to the pages of his denomination's journal, *Y Cenhadwr Americanaidd*. In the November 1862 issue of the *Cenhadwr* he published one of his more ambitious pieces under the title 'Gwersi Rhyfel', 'War's Lessons'. This impressive essay is a powerful piece of Welsh prose, combining the force of astute political reasoning with the emotional impact of an evangelical sermon. Like Morgan Llwyd, the seventeenth-century Welsh Puritan who turned the preacher's verbal techniques into a powerful literary medium, this Welsh-American writer generated a fresh literary language by reworking the rhetorical resources of the Welsh pulpit.

While Dewi Emlyn's prose style owes much to his experience in crafting and delivering oral sermons, this essay is self-consciously literary. It is presented by its author as a kind of moral historiography, a point emphasized in the opening paragraph:

> Y mae llawer o ryfeloedd wedi ffaglu yn y byd hwn erioed. Cofnoda tudalenau Hanesiaeth lawer o honynt; ond nid yw rhyfeloedd eraill wedi cael neb i'w hanesyddu; nid ydynt wedi cael un Herodotus, Thucydides, na Josephus i gofnodi eu helytnion; nac un Homer awenyddol i ganmol gorchestion eu gwroniaid. . . . At holl ryfeloedd adnabyddus ac erbargofiedig yr oesau, wele ryfel yn America; rhyfel yn y wlad lle yr ydym yn byw; a rhyfel yn ei achosion, a'i ddadblygiadau, a'i effeithiau, sy'n dal cysylltiad pwysig a phawb o honom; ac yn cyflwyno i ni wersi teilwng o'n sylw manylaf. Nodwn rai o honynt[.][1]

> 'Ever have many wars flamed in this world. The pages of Historiography record many of them; yet other wars have had nobody to write their history; they have not had one Herodotus, Thucydides, or Josephus to record their course; nor one inspired Homer to praise the feats of their heroes. . . . Added to all of the wars [both] known and forgotten of the ages, here is a war in America; a war in the country where we live; a war which in its causes, and its developments, and its effects, holds an important connection with every one of us; and presents us with lessons worthy of our most acute attention. We will note some of them.'

The body of the essay is structured around a number of sub-headings, each dealing with one of the 'lessons' which Dewi Emlyn is 'noting' for the reader. The first of these makes the writer's views on the relationship between the war and slavery clear: 'Bod gormes a chaethiwed yn cymhwyso dynion i gyflawni pob drygioni ac ysgelerder'; 'That oppression and slavery adapt men to perform every evil and villainy.'[2] Staying true to the line of historiographical inquiry promised in his introduction, Dewi Emlyn then suggests that the killing on Civil War battlefields was an extension of the violence which had characterized the antebellum South:

> Yr oedd y defnyddiad parhaus o ddeddf Lynch, y gyllell hir a'r llawddryll, yn y Talaethau Deheuol, yn arddangos er ys blynyddau eu bod yn cael eu barbareiddio yn gyflym; ac yn awr mae y gwrthryfel, yn holl echryslonrwydd ei hanes, yn rhoddi y prawf gorphenol o hyny ger bron y byd.[3]
>
> 'The continual use of the Lynch law, the long knife and the pistol in the Southern States has demonstrated for years that they were being speedily barbarised; and now the rebellion, in the entire horribleness of its history, gives the final proof of this before the world.'

Continuing in this vein, he then describes the actions of Jefferson Davis and other Southern politicians before 1861 as prefiguring their role in the war, concluding that promoting slavery was always at the forefront of their agenda: 'Nid rhanu y wlad, ond ei gwneud i gyd yn wlad gaeth. Bradwriaeth ffiaidd a Satanaidd yn erbyn Rhyddid ydoedd'; 'Not dividing the country, but making all of it a slave country. It was a disgusting and Satanic treachery against Freedom.'[4]

This analysis of the relationship between slavery and the war is then followed by an address which Dewi Emlyn aims at the pacifists: 'Tra yn credu am ddrygedd rhyfel cystal a neb, credwn ar yr un pryd ei fod yn gyfreithlawn, pan y rhaid ei ddefnyddio er mwyn gochelyd drygau o fwy'; 'While believing in the evil of war as much as anybody, I believe at the same time that it is legal when it must be used in order to avoid greater evils.'[5] Samuel Roberts of Tennessee, Welsh America's most vocal pacifist, had accused the North in print of embracing *yspryd rhyfel*, 'the spirit of war'; while not naming Roberts, Dewi Emlyn uses that same phrase, examining the associated moral implications.[6]

> Nid yw yr yspryd rhyfelgar sydd yn y wlad yn beth i'w ddymuno, ond eto dan yr amgylchiadau presenol, llawer gwell yw gweled y bobl yn ei afael, na'u gweled mor ddirywiedig ag ymfoddloni i aberthu egwyddorion penaf rhyddid a llywodraeth dda, er mwyn tawelwch i fudrelwa yn nheml Mammon, o dan aden lladron dynion.

'The warlike spirit which is in the country is not a thing to be desired, yet under the present circumstances it is much better to see the people possessing it than to see them so debased as to be content with sacrificing the foremost principles of freedom and good government for the sake of earning dirty profits in the temple of Mammon under the thieves of men.'

Having earlier described the actions of the Confederacy's leaders as 'Satanic treason against Freedom', this minister sustains his fire-and-brimstone assault on the Southern enemy, describing the slave market as 'the temple of Mammon'. Typical of the period, he employs that Aramaic word for 'wealth' or 'money' which was borrowed into Greek and Latin and left untranslated in nineteenth-century Welsh Bibles; whereas the 1986 Welsh translation uses the word *Arian*, 'Money' – for example, in Matthew 6:24 ('You cannot serve God and Money') – earlier translations kept the word *Mammon*.[7] This highly-charged biblical language is augmented by that simple phrase which Welsh abolitionists had been using for years to describe slave owners: *lladron dynion*, 'thieves of men'.

As has been seen repeatedly in this study, a number of Welsh America's religious leaders turned their backs on the pacifism which they had embraced at one time in order to support what they saw as a war against slavery. In this essay Dewi Emlyn states plainly that 'nobody is more enthusiastic about carrying on the struggle against the rebels than many of the leaders of the Peace Society' ('nid oes neb yn fwy brwdfrydig dros ddygiad yn mlaen yr ymdrech yn erbyn y gwrthryfelwyr, na llawer o flaenoriaid y Gymdeithas Heddwch').[8] He then presents a theological interpretation of the war, stating that the conflict was the manner in which the prayers of the slaves had been answered.

Y mae Caethiwed wedi dwyn barn a chosb ar bob gwlad a'i harferodd. . . . Bu pobl yr Unol Dalaethau am yspaid hir yn prysur hau y gwynt gyda chaethiwed, ac yn awr maent yn gorfod medi corwynt aruthrol o ddialedd. Caethiwyd, gorweithiwyd a chamdriniwyd y Negroaid am flynyddau hirion. Y mae plant werthid oddiwrth rieni, rhieni amddifaddid o'u plant, gwyr a gwragedd werthid oddiwrth eu gilydd, a merched anmherchid yn greulawn a bwystfilaidd, wedi anfon ocheneidiau, cwynion a thrist-weddiau fyrdd i fyny at Dduw o ddydd i dydd. Atebir hwynt yn awr.[9]

'Slavery has brought judgement and punishment upon every country which has practised it. . . . The people of the United States have for a long time been busily sowing the wind with slavery, and now they must reap a terrible whirlwind of vengeance. The Negroes were enslaved, overworked and mistreated for long years. Children sold away from parents, parents deprived of their children, husbands and wives sold away from each other, and women cruelly and monstrously dishonoured have sent sighs, complaints and a myriad of sorrowful prayers up to God from day to day. They are answered now.'

Dewi Emlyn's reading of the Civil War and its causes carried a corollary which, though implied rather than made explicit, was extremely powerful: if this is God's way of answering the prayers of the oppressed, who can question it?

Like those other Welsh-American ministers and writers discussed in Chapter Three, Dewi Emlyn's interpretation of the war also carried a distinct millennialistic aspect. One of his 'lessons' is given the heading 'Bod Duw cyfiawn yn goruwchlywodraethu amgylchiadau gwledydd y byd', 'That a just God is ultimately governing the circumstances of the countries of the world'.[10] According to this intensely politicized evangelical discourse, the war was cleansing the nation of the sin of slavery and thus ushering in a new era. This leads to his next lesson, one looking to the post-war future of the United States: 'Bod y cyfeiriad gymera pethau yn bresenol yn arwyddo fod gan Dduw fwriadau gwerthfawr a gogoneddus o barthed i dynged America yn y dyfodol'; 'That the direction which things are taking at present means that God has valuable and glorious intentions relating to the fate of America in the future'. This section of his essay makes manifest his millennialistic reading of recent events in no uncertain terms; he writes that, 'after removing slavery' ('yn ol dileu caethiwed') it will take but 'one shower of the Spirit's influences' ('un gawod o ddylanwadau yr Yspryd') 'to usher in the millennium in America' ('i ddarwain i mewn y milflwyddiant yn America').[11]

It will be remembered that other minister-writers of Welsh America accompanied their condemnation of the slave-owning South with accusations aimed at the North's complicity in the national sin. While R. D. Thomas described the war as a 'scourge' (*fflangell*), Erasmus Jones called it 'Jehovah's chastising rod' (*gwialen geryddol Jehofah*), and both wrote that God's punishing whip was being set upon the North as well as the South.[12] This line of reasoning runs through the final section of Dewi Emlyn's essay, asking readers to learn one last lesson, 'that it is a responsibility of countries to conform to God's will in their actions and laws' ('Bod yn ddyledswydd ar wledydd a llywodraethau gydffurfio ag ewllys Duw yn eu gweithrediadau a'u cyfreithiau').[13] This minister from Ohio presents an extremely detailed analysis of what he saw as 'God's will', interpreting the suffering which the war was visiting upon the North as part of the divine plan. Arguing that God's will in relation to slavery was clear from the start, Dewi Emlyn states that Lincoln's government had invited suffering by refusing to yoke the war directly to the struggle against that immoral institution.

> Pan ddywedai Rhagluniaeth ddwyfol mewn modd digamsyniad, 'Rhyddhewch y caethion os mynwch ddarostwng y gwrthryfel', ni thelid nemawr sylw, ond elid yn mlaen i frolio ein hadnoddau mawrion, lluosogrwydd ein byddinoedd, a medrusrwydd ein cadflaenoriaid. . . . Ceisiwyd llethu allan y gwrthryfel a gadael caethiwed yn ddianaf; ond gwgodd Duw ar y cynllun hwnw; daeth aflwydd ar sodlau aflwydd; gwasgwyd y wlad o binacl uchel hunanddigonoldeb i geunant

ddofn gwasgfa a chaledi. Tra daliai y Llywydd a rhai o'i gydgynghoriaid yn ol rhag ymosod ar yr anghenfil oedd yn achos o'r holl gythrwfl, gadawai Duw i'r wlad gael ei tharo yn drymach drymach.[14]

'When divine Providence said in unmistakable terms, "Free the slaves if you desire to put down the rebellion', hardly any notice was given, but rather people continued to boast of our great resources, the size of our armies, and the capability of our generals. . . . An attempt was made to wipe out the rebellion and leave slavery unharmed; but God frowned upon this plan; failure followed failure; the country was pushed from the high peak of self-satisfaction to the deep ravine of distress and hardship. While the President and some of his cabinet members held back from attacking the monster which was the cause of the entire disturbance, God allowed the country to be afflicted ever more severely.'

A host of abolitionists had for years been likening the Southern slave-owners to the Old Testament's Pharaoh, the archetypical autocrat who refused repeatedly to release an enslaved people. This writer also draws heavily upon the story of the biblical Exodus, yet he sees the North as partaking of Pharaoh's fate as well.

O'r diwedd canfu y wlad nad oedd ond Duw allasai ei gwaredu. Dechreuwyd galw o ddifrif arno. Daeth y Llywydd hefyd yn ddigon gostyngedig i wrando ar lais Rhagluniaeth, ac addawodd ryddid i'r caeth y calan nesaf. Yn y cyfamser bydded i blant yr Arglwydd wneud amgylchiadau y wlad yn destyn gweddi daer a beunyddiol at Dduw. Ei fraich estynedig ef yn arwain ei bobl o dy'r caethiwed, sydd i'w chanfod yn amgylchiadau presenol y wlad. Gweddiau aneirif trueiniaid gorthrymedig y De am hirfeithion flynyddau, a atebir yn awr yn nghanol plaau Duw. Costiodd yr oruchwyliaeth waedlyd i'r Gogledd waed llawer o'i meibion . . . Diolch ei bod yn gwawrio ar y caethion yn awr. Daeth Duw allan mor amlwg ag yn yr Aifft o'u plaid.[15]

'At last the country perceived that there was nothing but God that could save it. It started calling seriously upon him. The President also became humble enough to listen to the voice of Providence, and he promised freedom to the slave next New Year. In the meantime let the children of the Lord make the circumstances of the country the subject of earnest daily prayers to God. His extended arm leading his people from the house of slavery is to be perceived in the present circumstances of the country. The innumerable prayers of the South's oppressed sufferers for many a long year have now been answered in the middle of God's plagues. The bloody overseeing has cost the North the blood of many of its sons . . . Thanks be that it is dawning upon the slaves now. God came out in support of them as obviously as [he did] in Egypt.'

The defeats suffered by the Union army during the first year and a half of war are made to resemble the plagues which God visited upon Egypt through the hand of Moses, and the Northern sons killed on Southern battlefields are likened to the first-born of Egypt whose death is described in Exodus 12:29. However, unlike Pharaoh, who changed his mind and pursued the Israelites, the president learned his lesson, becoming 'humble' and thus recognizing 'divine Providence'.

Dewi Emlyn is referring directly to Abraham Lincoln's Emancipation Proclamation; he cites the fact that the president had 'promised freedom to the slave' on 1 January 1863 as proof that Lincoln had accepted God's will. Interestingly enough, the president himself described the Proclamation as the result of a promise made to God. In the words of James McPherson:

> On September 22, five days after the battle of Antietam, Lincoln called his cabinet into session. He had made a covenant with God, said the president, that if the army drove the enemy from Maryland he would issue his Emancipation Proclamation. . . . The cabinet approved[.][16]

Although the document was not to be signed until 1 January 1863, Lincoln's intentions were made public that week in September 1862, roughly a month before this Welsh essay appeared in print.[17] Dewi Emlyn's text can only be fully understood as part of an extremely specific historical context, the three-and-a-half month period which separated the promise of emancipation from the presidential act which would change the legal status of slavery within the United States. This is *y cyfamser*, 'the mean time', to which he refers, a period of intense emotion and anticipation for slave and abolitionist alike.

LAURA GRIFFITHS'S POLITICAL CHRISTMAS CAROL

Dewi Emlyn's essay on 'War's Lessons' was not the only text published in the November 1862 issue of *Y Cenhadwr Americanaidd* which referred directly to the Emancipation Proclamation. Laura Griffiths's poem 'Y Dysgwyliad am Ryddid y Caeth', 'The One Waiting for the Slave's Freedom', also appeared in that issue of the Congregationalists' monthly journal.[18] While the poem itself refers in unmistakable terms to the news that Lincoln was going to sign the Proclamation on the first day of 1863, Laura Griffiths emphasized the relationship between her composition and the political developments in Washington by including a short explanatory note: 'Gwnaethum hyn o benillion pan glywais bod i'r caeth gael d'od yn rhydd'; 'I made these verses when I heard that the enslaved were to become free.'[19]

She was by no means the only woman who was composing and publishing Welsh-language poetry in the United States at the time, and neither was she the only one publishing anti-slavery poetry, yet Laura Griffiths was by all accounts a remarkable individual. Originally from the Llŷn peninsula in North Wales, she emigrated to the United States with her family at a 'very young' age.[20] Laura Griffiths spent most of her life in the town of Prospect, in Oneida County, New York, where she worked as a maid in the household of the Revd Morris Roberts. One of several Welsh ministers in the area who took a leading role in the abolition movement, Roberts had worked with Robert Everett, the *Cenhadwr*'s editor, since the late 1830s. Though Laura Griffiths came from a relatively poor family and worked all her adult life as a servant, she was held in great respect by the community of Welsh-American writers and abolitionists of which she was an active member. Griffiths also published prose, yet she was best known for her verse, and by 1862 a considerable number of her poems had appeared in the *Cenhadwr*.[21]

While the role of the Welsh bard had since the Middle Ages been defined in what were often overtly masculine terms, Laura Griffiths was one of several nineteenth-century Welsh women (and Welsh-American women) who successfully occupied the traditional role of public poet, composing and publishing verse designed to serve the wider community.[22] In addition to writing poetry in response to her community's needs – for example, celebrating a wedding or mourning the dead – Griffiths published her own religious poetry in the pre-war years. One of the best examples appeared in 1860; entitled 'Ychydig Benillion ar Ddyfodiad Crist i'r Byd', 'A Few Verses on the Coming of Christ to the World', this poem combines the traditional Christmas-carol references to the 'stable' (*stabal*) and 'manger' (*preseb*) with an expression of mystical wonder at Jesus' incarnation on earth: 'Mewn dychymyg af i'r anedd / At y Maban bach a'i fam, / Gwel'd ein Crewr, O Mae'n rhyfedd!'; 'In my imagination I travel to the shelter / To the little Boy and his mother, / To see our Creator, Oh it is wondrous!'[23] According to the author of her short biography, Laura Griffiths was a 'woman of detailed observation and astute opinion' ('Dynes ydoedd o sylw manwl a barn graff') who 'possessed an extensive comprehension of various branches of knowledge, especially Theology and Poetry' ('Meddai ddirnadaeth helaeth ar wahanol gangenau gwybodaeth yn neillduol mewn Duwinyddiaeth a Barddoniaeth'). Though praising Griffiths's 'genius, namely her mental ability' ('ei hathrylith, sef ei gallu meddyliol'), her biographer stressed that 'her religion . . . was the glory' which crowned 'all her other superior qualities' ('ei chrefydd . . . ydoedd gogoniant ei holl ragorion eraill').[24]

Laura Griffiths's poem on the Emancipation Proclamation displays all these qualities, bringing an analysis of the current political situation into harmony with a deep faith in God's benevolent guidance. The 'extensive comprehension' of poetry for which she was known is in this case used to produce a piece which combines a clear and easily understood message with an enticing musicality. In a period characterized by religious cliché and conservative conformity, this poem is marked by a strikingly personal voice which speaks to the reader (or listener) in fresh and earnest tones. Despite its freshness, Laura Griffiths's poem is not without precedents; her emphasis on the wonder (*rhyfedd*) of God's presence on earth as well as the cadence of her free-metre song recall the immensely popular hymns of Ann Griffiths (1776–1805).[25] Also like the verse which Ann Griffiths used to express her religious experiences, this poem can be described as a song of praise which injects the vitality of the Welsh folk-song tradition into the genre of the hymn.

While Laura Griffiths was ultimately concerned with praising what she saw as God's actions on behalf of the slaves, she used her first verse to praise Lincoln directly for drafting the Emancipation Proclamation.

O mor hyfryd genyf glywed,
Dewch diolchwn bawb yn llu,
I fod Lincoln ar gyhoeddi
Rhyddid cyflawn i'r dyn du,
Byddai rhyw eiddigedd ynof
Wrth wel'd rhyfel yn ein gwlad,
A dim sôn am dori'r gadwen
Sydd yn dala'r caeth dan draed.[26]

'Oh how lovely it is for me to hear,
Come let all of us give thanks together,
That Lincoln is about to announce
Complete Freedom for the black man.
There was within me a kind of jealousy
At seeing war in our country
Yet with no talk of breaking the chain
Which holds the enslaved under foot.'

Like Dewi Emlyn's discussion of the government's reluctance to recognize 'God's will' during the early phase of the war, Laura Griffiths describes the abolitionist's displeasure at 'seeing' a Civil War not connected directly to an effort to free the slaves. The personal voice which gives this poem so much of its force describes a change in the poet's internal state, a movement from the 'jealousy' described in the opening verse to the wondrous joy which fuels her song.

This transformation is described in terms of a physical omen, a star rising over Washington. The poem's title refers to *disgwyliad*, which can mean 'watcher' or 'one who waits' for a sign in addition to 'expectation'; like the astrologers of Matthew 2.2 who obseve the rising of the star signalling Christ's birth, the poet describes her joy at seeing a long-awaited portent in the sky over the United States capital. The *Ond* – 'but', 'yet', 'however' – which opens her second verse is a conjunction which swings the poem's emotional hinge from the jealousy described above to the state of joyous thanks which is the poems *raison d'être*.

Ond ni welwn draw ryw seren
  Sydd yn blaenu bore wawr,
Draw o Washington mae 'n dyfod,
  Brysia, gwawria'r hyfryd awr.[27]

'But we see yonder a kind of star
  Which heralds the morning dawn,
Yonder from Washington it comes,
  Hurry, let the lovely hour dawn.'

This 'dawn' is then defined as 'the new year, eighteen-hundred and sixty three' ('[y] flwyddyn newydd / Deunaw cant chwe deg a thri'), a 'day' (*diwrnod*) which 'will be long remembered' ('hir y cofir') by those enslaved.[28]

Laura Griffiths opens her third verse by repeating the phrase *hir y cofir*, referring this time to the fame which Lincoln will achieve by signing the Emancipation Proclamation into being: 'Hir y cofir enw Lincoln / Os bydd iddo wneud y gwaith'; 'Long will Lincoln's name be remembered / If he does do the job'. The praise is entirely conditional upon completion of the work at hand. Other Welsh-American writers were describing themselves proudly as 'children of Lincoln', providing a logical war-time extension of the overwhelming support which Welsh-speaking Americans gave Lincoln during the 1860 election. Given the fact that it was difficult to reconcile an unconditional commitment to abolition with the way in which Lincoln's government had dodged the issue of slavery prior to September 1862, many of the country's Welsh abolitionists simply turned a blind eye to their president's failure to act. However, like Dewi Emlyn, Laura Griffiths viewed Lincoln's actions through a critical lens; the president was yet to prove that he could measure up to the moral standard by making good his promise to emancipate the slaves. While the conjunction *Ond*, 'but', provides a hinge swinging the poem from despairing 'jealousy' to joyful hope, the word *Os*, 'if', is used to emphasize the fact that the president's praiseworthy work is not yet complete. Having referred in the poem's opening lines to the 'Freedom' promised to 'the black man', she finishes this verse by foreseeing the manner in which formerly enslaved women will praise Lincoln: 'Fe fydd llawer mam o'r gaeth-glud, / A'i dagrau 'n llifo dros ei grudd, / Yn dysgu i'w baban spelio ei enw'; 'Many a mother out of bondage, / With her tears pouring over her cheek, / Will teach her baby to spell his name.'[29]

The word translated here as 'bondage', [*c*]*aeth-glud*, has had distinctly biblical connotations since it was used (and apparently coined) by William Morgan in his 1588 translation of the Bible.[30] As is seen in Dewi Emlyn's reference to the plagues in Egypt, Welsh authors of anti-slavery literature, like many Anglophone abolitionists, often drew a comparison between the enslavement of the Israelites in Egypt and the enslavement of African Americans in the American South, and the term *caeth-glud* played an important role in this kind of discourse. This poem's main biblical tenor, however, is provided not by reference to the Old Testament Exodus, but rather by an echo of the story of Christ's birth. Laura Griffiths's 'watcher' evokes the astrologers of Matthew 2.2, the star rising over Washington reflects the light of the star of Bethlehem, and the new, free era promised by this omen is meant to recall the deliverance which the coming of Jesus is supposed to have promised to humanity.

This poet knew that her published text would be reaching readers across the United States at various times during November and December 1862, a fact which invites us to read this text in the context of Christmas. Indeed, the focus on the 'wondrous' nature of Christ's incarnation on earth which characterizes Griffiths's pre-war Christmas carol also informs this poem's discussion of Lincoln's Proclamation. Like Dewi Emlyn's essay on 'War's Lessons', this is a text thoroughly embedded in the historical context of which it was a part. The period of time which separated 22 September 1862 from 1 January 1863 also included the celebration of Christmas, a fact exploited by Laura Griffiths in her political Christmas carol; this is a song anticipating the emancipation of the slaves designed to resonate with the ways in which Welsh-Americans were celebrating the birth of Jesus on (and around) 25 December 1862.

The final verse intensifies this aspect of the poem, as Laura Griffiths moves from her conditional praise of Lincoln to unconditional praise for Jesus.

Ond mae rhywun mwy na Lincoln
A'i fysedd heddyw ar y llyw,
Iesu ydyw, dyma ei enw,
Llywydd mawr y bydoedd yw,
O nid rhyfedd iddo ddisgyn,
Iddo glywed cwyn y caeth,
A dod i waered i'w gwaredu
O'u cadwynau tynion wnaeth.[31]

'Yet there is somebody greater than Lincoln
Whose fingers are on the rudder today,
He is Jesus, that's his name,
Great Leader of the universe,[32]
Oh, it is not strange that he has descended,
That he has heard the slave's complaint,
And that he has come down to deliver them
From their constraining chains.'

The noun *llyw*, meaning 'rudder' or 'helm', is the basis for the word *llywydd*, translated here as 'leader'. This word was also used in the nineteenth century to mean 'president' (a term which was supplanted by the modified form *arlywydd* in the twentieth century). The president or *llyw-ydd* is, literally, the 'helmsman', the one with his 'fingers' on the *llyw* or 'rudder'. If the star which Laura Griffiths sees rising over Washington is an American recasting of the star of Bethlehem, it is also a navigational co-ordinate, an astrological sign by which the 'helmsman' of the United States guides the ship of state towards a new, free country. However, this navigational metaphor does not eclipse the star's biblical aspect; while it is hoped that Lincoln will prove to be a good helmsmen, he is ultimately a worldly instrument for Jesus, the 'great helmsman', 'president' or 'leader' responsible for steering the entire 'universe'.

As the first part of the composition resonates with Matthew 2:2, so the final lines of this abolitionist carol ask us to consider the birth of Jesus. Like the star of Bethlehem which signalled Christ's incarnation on earth, the star which Laura Griffiths discerns over Washington is a sign that Jesus is descending to the world. And, as the earthly birth of Jesus is widely interpreted as an act of God designed to deliver humankind, so this poet describes His 'descending' as a way of 'delivering' the slaves. The best known anti-slavery song produced during the Civil War was surely Julia Ward Howe's 'The Battle Hymn of the Republic', a purposeful 'hymn' sung by civilians as well as thousands of marching soldiers. By means of that poem Howe asked Northern soldiers to consider Christ's sacrifice and declare 'As He died to make men holy, let us die to make men free'.[33] A similar relationship between holiness and freedom lies at the heart of this Welsh poem; by means of her literary star Laura Griffiths bathed Washington with the light of Bethlehem, thus suggesting that Jesus, having once come down to earth 'to make men holy', was now descending again in order 'to make them free'.

BREAKING THE CHAINS: THE 22ND WISCONSIN INFANTRY IN KENTUCKY

Abolitionists were in a state of restless anticipation during that period which separated the promise made on 22 September 1862 from the fulfilment which was to come on the first day of 1863, and the conditional nature of Laura Griffiths's praise for Lincoln conveys the mood which gripped abolitionists across the North as they waited for the president to turn his word into law. Judging by the evidence discussed in Chapter Four, a great many Welsh-speaking soldiers were also looking forward to the first day of 1863. Several months before the news of Lincoln's September 1862 decision was made public, Edward Thomas – the soldier-poet known as 'Awenydd' discussed in Chapter Eight – published a poem in *Y Cyfaill o'r Hen Wlad* entitled 'Ar Ddiangfa y Caethwas', 'On the Slave's Escape'.[34] Composed during the period before the star-like news of the pending Proclamation was radiating from Washington, this poet chose to focus on the dramatic way in which individual slaves achieved their own freedom. Thomas's emotional poem presents a heroic slave who rails against the injustice of his situation, asking 'Why . . . am I a slave? / And who made my master a master over me?' ('Pa ham . . . yr ydwyf yn gaethwas? / A phwy wnaeth fy meistr yn feistr arnaf fi?').[35] At the dramatic crescendo of this versified narrative, the slave takes his fate into his own hands, striking out for freedom while uttering a Patrick Henry-like declaration:

'Ai dyn yw efe? Diau dyn ydwyf finau,
A dyn mor ardderchog ac uchel ag yntau:
Ha! Drylliaf ei gadwyn, ffarweliaf â'i rwymau:
Fy rhyddid, fy rhyddid! Neu angeu i mi!'[36]

' "Is he a man? Surely I myself am I man,
And as high and exalted a man as he:
Ha! I will shatter his chain, I will bid farewell to his bonds:
[Give me] my freedom, my freedom! Or [give] me death!" '

This poet was an ardent abolitionist, and his anti-slavery beliefs surely informed his decision to volunteer for the Union army. As it turned out, Edward Thomas's regiment, the 2nd Minnesota Cavalry, was posted to the north-western territories, a development which ensured that he would have few opportunities to encounter real slaves during his military service. Rather than laying his hands on the slaves' chains in a literal fashion, he had to use the poetic inspiration or *awen* which give him his bardic name – Awenydd – to imagine the heroic slave's struggle for his own freedom.

Many other Welsh-American soldiers did encounter slaves while serving in the Union army, and some of them took a direct part in aiding their escape from bondage. The 22nd Wisconsin Infantry, which before the end of the war would earn the title 'the abolitionist regiment', contained a large number of Welsh-speaking volunteers. As was discussed in Chapter Three, they served together in Captain Owen Griffiths's Company F, a unit nick-named 'the Cambrian Guards'. It will be remembered that before these soldiers left for war, their neighbours in Racine, Wisconsin, organized a 'war meeting', and that the resolutions which the community adopted during that gathering included anti-slavery advice aimed at the United States government.[37] Racine's Welsh volunteers joined the civilian members of their home community in asking Lincoln to declare 'all slaves owned by rebel masters . . . hereafter and forever . . . free'.[38] Letters published by some of the 22nd Wisconsin's Welsh soldiers suggest that they welcomed the news of the Emancipation Proclamation with a joy akin to that expressed by Laura Griffiths. Indeed, even before the president signed the Proclamation they were taking direct action in order to pursue that anti-slavery agenda which they had embraced so publicly back in Racine.

The 22nd Wisconsin Infantry had been organized during the last week of August 1862, and on 16 September the new soldiers boarded a train headed for Cincinnati. On 22 September 1862 – the very day on which Lincoln was meeting with his cabinet to finalize the plans for his Emancipation Proclamation – the regiment crossed the Ohio river and entered Kentucky.[39] The Welsh-Americans from Wisconsin were now in a slave state, most likely for the first time in their lives. Kentucky was, of course, one of the border slave states which had not seceded from the Union, and early in the war Lincoln's government had taken care not to do anything which might drive loyal (or 'neutral') slave-owning Kentuckians to support the Confederates. The situation in Kentucky was assessed by one of the 22nd Wisconsin's volunteers, a writer who used the pen-name 'Gomer'. In a letter which he published in *Y Drych*, this soldier implied that his views on the question of slavery in the border state were shared by his fellow Welsh-speaking soldiers.[40]

> Fel y mae yn eglur i bawb sydd wedi . . . sylwi fel y mae pethau yn cael eu cario yn mlaen yn y Llywodraeth, fod gan Kentucky lawer iawn o ddylanwad o'r dechreu hyd yn bresenol. Y gwirionedd yw, fod ein holl flaenoriaid o'r bron trwy y Dalaeth yn ochri caethiwed hyd eithaf eu gallu; a chredaf hefyd pe buasai y Llywydd yn gwrthod gwrandaw cymaint ar y 'Kentucky neutral Politicians' ag a wnaeth o'r dechreu, y buasai y gwrthryfel ofnadwy hwn wedi terfynu yn mhell cyn hyn.[41]

> 'As is clear to everybody who has taken . . . notice of the way things are carried on in the Government, Kentucky has a very great amount of influence . . . The truth is, that nearly all of our leaders throughout the State side with slavery to the utmost of their ability; and I believe in addition that if the President had refused to listen as much to the 'Kentucky neutral Politicians' as he has done from the start, then this horrible rebellion would have ended long before now.'

Gomer's political analysis is used to contextualize the news which constituted his main reason for writing to the newspaper, the praiseworthy actions taken by his regiment's colonel, William Utley: 'Ef allai y bydd ymddygiad Col. Utley, o'r 22ain Wisconsin, yn foddion i agor llygaid rhai mewn swyddi uchel yn y Wladwriaeth'; 'Perhaps the conduct of Col. Utley, of the 22nd Wisconsin, will be a means to open the eyes of those in high offices in the Government.'[42]

This soldier-writer sets the stage for the dramatic episode he is about to relate by noting the significance of his news: 'mae rhai pethau mewn cysylltiad a'r Gatrawd hon sydd o bwys i'r holl wlad'; 'there are some things in relation to this Regiment which are of relevance to the entire country.'[43] He also prepares readers for what is coming by presenting his colonel's anti-slavery credentials: 'mae Col. Utley o Racine, yn ddyngarwr egwyddorol, nid yw ddim gwahaniaeth ganddo pa liw yw y croen, os bydd rhyw arwydd fod yno ddynoliaeth oddi fewn'; 'Col. Utley of Racine is a principled humanitarian, it makes no difference what colour the skin is, if there is some sign that there is humanity within'. All of this prefacing is used to build up to an account of the manner in which the regiment aided fugitive slaves in Kentucky.

> Pan ar ein taith o Cincinnati i'r lle hwn, daeth amryw o honynt i fewn i'r *lines*. Mor fuan ag y daeth y peth i wybodaeth y Cad. Gillmore, dyma orchymyn penodol oddiwrtho at Col. Utley, am iddo eu hanfon ato ef yn uniongyrchol.[44]

> 'While on our journey from Cincinnati to this place [Danville, Kentucky], several of them [escaped slaves] came into our lines. As soon as the knowledge reached Gen. Gillmore, there was a specific order from him to Col. Utley for him to send them directly to him.'

Brigadier General Quincy A. Gillmore was Colonel Utley's commanding officer, yet the 22nd Wisconsin's colonel refused to surrender the fugitive slaves to him, a fact attested by other, more official, sources.[45]

Gomer then provided *Y Drych*'s readers with a complete Welsh translation of what he calls 'yr ohebiaeth a fu rhyngddynt', 'the correspondence which took place between them'. He first gives the General's letter, which contained a curt order: 'Colonel, – Bydd i chwi anfon i fy Headquarters yn uniongyrchol y pedwar Contraband . . . pa rai sydd yn perthyn i ddynion da, ac ufudd i'r Llywodraeth'; 'Colonel, – You will send to my Headquarters directly the four Contrabands . . . who belong to good men, loyal to the Government.'[46] Utley's reply, or at least Gomer's Welsh version of his colonel's reply, combined some elaborate moral and political reasoning with bold defiance.

> Cad. Gillmore – *Syr* – Yr wyf newydd dderbyn eich gorchymyn i roddi i fyny ryw Gontrabands, pa rai y dywedwch sydd yn fy nghatrawd. Goddefwch imi ddweud fy mod yn cydnabod eich awdurdod i'm rheoli yn mhob peth perthynol i'r fyddin a'i symudiadau, ond nid wyf yn edrych ar hyn fel yn perthyn i'r dosbarth hwn. Nid wyf yn cydnabod awdurdod neb ar yr achos o roddi i fyny Contrabands, ond yn unig Llywydd yr Unol Daleithiau. Y mae yn ddiamheu genyf eich bod yn hysbys o'r *Proclamation* dyddiedig Medi 22, 1862 . . . Diweddwyf trwy ddweyd na fu genyf ddim i'w wneyd tu ag at iddynt ddyfod i fewn i'r *lines*, ac ni fydd genyf a wnelwyf at eu gyru allan. Ydwyf eich ufudd wasanaethwr. Wm. L. Utley, Col. 22ain Gat. Wis. Vol.[47]

> 'Gen. Gillmore – *Sir* – I have just received your order to give up some Contrabands, which you say are in my regiment. Allow me to say that I acknowledge your authority to command me in everything relating to the army and its movements, but that I look upon this as relating to a different category. I do not acknowledge the authority of anybody in the matter of giving up Contrabands, except only the President of the United States. I am certain that you know of the Proclamation dated September 22, 1862 . . . I end by saying that I did nothing to make them come into our lines, and I will have nothing to do with sending them out. I am your obedient servant. Wm. L. Utley, Col. 22nd Wis. Vol.'

Many of the Welsh newspaper's readers must have sensed a kind of pointed irony in Utley's closing remarks; the defiant colonel described himself as his commanding general's 'obedient servant' at the end of a letter which stated in unmistakable terms that he was refusing to obey that general's direct order![48] A few years before the start of the war the anti-slavery orator Charles Sumner was elevated to the status of hero by the Welsh-American press, a process which included the publishing of a complete translation of his 'Crime Against Kansas' speech.[49] Similarly, Gomer was working with *Y Drych*'s editor in order to hold Colonel Utley up before all of Welsh America as a 'principled humanitarian' worthy of their praise.

Utley told his commanding general that he 'did nothing to make' the escaped slaves come into his regiment's lines; the fugitives were, like the fictional character described in Awenydd's poem, individuals who took their freedom into their own hands. As several historians have emphasized, fugitive slaves who sought refuge within the ranks of the Northern army were forcing the Union's leaders – both military and civilian – to face the problem of slavery directly.[50] The 22nd Wisconsin's Welsh soldiers facilitated this process, matching their colonel's brave words with direct action taken in defence of the escaped slaves who had asked for their protection. In a second letter to *Y Drych*, Gomer described the way in which slave catchers had shadowed the regiment as it moved through Kentucky: 'mae y gallu caethiwol wedi ein dilyn ni o naill ben y Dalaeth i'r llall, fel bwystfilod rheibus ar ôl eu hysglyfaeth'; 'the slaving powers have followed us from one end of the State to the other, like rapacious beasts tracking their prey'.[51] The conflict between the soldiers from Wisconsin and the slave catchers came to a dramatic conclusion on the streets of Louisville as the regiment marched to the steamboats which were to carry them away from Kentucky.

> Cawsom orchymyn i fyned ar yr agerfadau . . . yr oedd y gweddill o'r adran wedi myned . . . ac yr oedd y *Nigger stealers* wedi llwyddo i fyned a'r caethion druain allan o bob catrawd hyd yn hyny. . . . darfu i'r Mil. Utley orchymyn i ni i fyned trwy'r heolydd gyda'n bidogau ar ein drylliau . . . daethom yn ddigon tawel hyd nes darfu i ni droi i'r heol oedd yn myned i'r *levee;* gyda hyn dyma ddyn yn rhuthro at un o'r *contrabands* ac yn ymaflyd yn ei war mewn eiliad; dyma glic mwrthwl llawddryll o law y Negro, ond yn anffodus ni thaniodd; gyda hyn dyma haner dwsin o fidogau yn erbyn mynwes Mr. 'Dynleidr,' a da oedd ganddo ollwng ei afael er achub ei fywyd. Gwelodd y dinasyddion fod yr 22ain Wis. yn benderfynol o amddiffyn eu hegwyddorion hyd at waed os oedd rhaid, ac mai ofer oedd iddynt dreio yn hwy i fyned a'r Negroes allan o'r *ranks*.[52]

> 'We received an order to go onto the steamboats . . . the rest of the division had gone [already] . . . and the Nigger stealers had succeeded in taking the poor slaves out of every regiment up to that point. . . . Col. Utley commanded us to go through the streets with our bayonets fixed on our rifles. . . . we went quietly enough until we turned into the street which goes to the levee; at this there was a man rushing

> to one of the contrabands and in a second he took hold of the nape of his neck; there was a click of the hammer of a pistol in the Negro's hand, but unfortunately it did not fire; at this there were a half-dozen bayonets against the chest of Mr. 'Humanthief', and he was happy to let go in order to save his life. The citizens saw that the 22nd Wis[consin] were determined to defend their principles to the point of blood if necessary, and that it was useless for them to try any longer to take the Negroes out of our ranks.'

Not surprisingly, Gomer noted with relief 'that the 22nd Wis. has left Kentucky at last, and I think that all of the soldiers are happy that we have left' ('fod yr 22ain Wis. wedi gadael Kentucky o'r diwedd, ac yr wyf yn meddwl fod yn dda gan bawb o'r milwyr ein bod wedi myned').[53] Summarizing his analysis of the situation in the border state, he added with disgust 'that slavery was their "Alpha and Omega", and in truth their everything' ('amlwg mai caethiwed i'w eu "Alpha ac Omega", ac mewn gwirionedd eu cyfan').[54]

While Gomer's letters were published early in 1863, the events which they describe took place during that same period of time which formed the context for Laura Griffiths's poem and Dewi Emlyn's essay, the three and a half months which separated the promise made on 22 September and Lincoln's fulfilment of that promise on the first day of 1863. A number of connected discourses run through Gomer's epistles, all involving different aspects of the struggle against slavery. In addition to revealing (what he saw as) Kentucky's 'Alpha and Omega', this soldier was also providing a public record of his regiment's anti-slavery stance, a record which promoted Colonel William Utley as a praise-worthy abolitionist while also holding up the Welsh soldiers' actions as a model for others to follow. Moreover, Gomer was using his prose to celebrate the bravery of the former slaves, for he described in detail the actions which they themselves took to secure their own freedom.

Gomer's first letter can also be seen as a literary reaction to the Emancipation Proclamation, containing as it does a Welsh translation of Utley's reference to 'the President's declaration'. This epistle was written before the 1 January 1863 signing of the Proclamation and published afterwards, and Gomer's second letter, though not published until March 1863, was presented to readers as a direct sequel to the first text's narrative. Together they provide a memorable example of the way in which political context informed this kind of literary text. The Emancipation Proclamation was itself a text which became political reality – or what we might call historical context – when it was signed by Lincoln. This text-becoming-context constituted an event which many abolitionists viewed as the greatest moral milestone of the Civil War, and this event formed the context in which Gomer enmeshed his own texts. He asked his readers to consider their president's actions, including his past mistakes (in attempting to appease 'the Kentucky neutral politicians') as well as the welcome decision to emancipate the slaves. By stressing the fact that the narrative of his regiment's actions in Kentucky contained 'things . . . which are of relevance to the entire country' Gomer was producing a text which stressed the importance of following words with actions.

THE RISING OF FREEDOM'S SUN: POETRY COMPOSED AFTER 1 JANUARY 1863

Before the sun set on the first day of 1863, telegrams were travelling across America bearing the news that Lincoln had indeed matched his words with action and signed the Emancipation Proclamation. However, the news that the Proclamation had been signed was not enough for many abolitionists; they wanted to know the exact words of the document. In his memorable description of the celebration held that day in Boston's Tremont Temple, Frederick Douglass wrote that 'Judge Thomas Russell went himself to the telegraph office and rushed back into Tremont Temple with the text in hand' and that those words were then read aloud to the assembled crowd.[55] Douglass summarized the reaction succinctly: 'I never saw Joy before'.[56] Welsh-Americans also wanted to familiarize themselves with the exact wording of the Emancipation Proclamation, and to that end *Y Drych* published a complete translation on 17 January 1863.[57] Like other texts stemming from the national struggle against slavery – ranging from Sumner's 'Crime Against Kansas' speech to Colonel Utley's written refusal to surrender fugitive slaves – Lincoln's Proclamation was transformed into a Welsh-language text and, by means of the printing press, presented to Welsh-Americans across the Northern United States.

The news was accompanied by a flood of Welsh poetry. One composition, Iago Ddu's long poem on 'Rhyddid' ('Freedom'), was apparently designed to appear concurrently with the news that the Proclamation had been signed, for it was published in the January 1863 issue of *Y Cyfaill o'r Hen Wlad*. While Laura Griffiths had described the September 1862 promise of emancipation as a hope-bringing star rising over Washington, this poet could by January 1863 see the 'great sun . . . of the slaves' hopes' rising in the American sky ('haul mawr . . . gobaith y caethion').[58] The light of this new celestial body was going to drive slavery from the land once and for all:

> Goleuni dy wyneb sy'n dychryn caethiwed,
> Diflana o'r ddaiar, ymguddia yn abred;
> Cythreuliaid a'th welant, a chrynant gan arswyd,
> Eu llwyddiant a beidia, eu teyrnas sy'n ysgwyd;
> Ehed dy wawl nefol ar edyn yr engyl,
> Ac agor heiyrn ddorau, gwna le i'r efengyl.[59]

> 'The light of your face frightens slavery,
> It disappears from the earth, it hides itself away;

Devils will see you, and quake with fear,
Their success will end, their kingdom is falling;
Your heavenly dawn will fly on the wings of angels,
And opening iron doors, it will make a place for the gospel.'

The *Cyfaill*'s editor followed Iago Ddu's praise for the sun of freedom with another anti-slavery poem, one by a poet using the name Bardd Cwmcelyn. This piece, presented under a title given to many similar compositions, 'Cwyn y Caethwas' ('The Slave's Complaint'), was apparently composed originally during the campaign against the British slave trade which had come to a conclusion decades earlier; it begins 'O Brydain, clyw a gwrando gri, / Hiraethus gŵyn y caethwas du'; 'Oh Britain, hear and listen to the cry, / The longing complaint of the black slave'.[60] By printing – or reprinting – this poem, the journal's editor was helping readers to interpret texts written in response to recent events within a broader historical context, reminding them that Welsh poets had been attacking slavery in verse for some time. Significantly, slavery in Britain and its colonies had been abolished not by war but through legislation, and this poetic reminder of that earlier emancipation might thus have prompted readers to consider the events transpiring in Washington in a new light, reminding them that Lincoln was using law in addition to the sword.

R. H. Evans of Columbus, Ohio, used that same title, 'Cŵyn y Caethwas' ('The Slave's Complaint'), for a poem written in direct response to the Emancipation Proclamation.

Fe fu cri y caeth yn esgyn
Yn y Dê am lawer blwyddyn;
Ond mae'r amser wedi gwawrio,
A Duw y nefoedd wedi gwrando!

Y mae'r fasnach fwyaf aflan
Luniodd uffern ddu ei hunan,
'N cael ei hysgwyd i'w gwaelodion,
Gan Gyhoeddiant Abraham Lincoln![61]

'The slave's cry ascended
In the South for many a year;
But the time has dawned,
And the God of heaven has listened!

'The most despicable trade
Which dark hell itself ever fashioned,
Is being shaken to its foundations
By Abraham Lincoln's Proclamation!'

Like Laura Griffiths and Dewi Emlyn, this poet from Ohio took the president's actions as a sign that God had listened to the cries of the oppressed.

All the poems discussed thus far in this chapter avoid the kind of martial boasting which characterizes so many other war-time compositions. Unlike those Welsh-American writers who saw the war as a way of washing away the stain of slavery with sacrificial blood, these poets completely ignore the language of war, focusing instead on the freedom which Lincoln was promising to the slaves. However, these celebrations of emancipation partake of a store of religious references which also inform those more violent millennialistic compositions; if other writers seem to welcome the violent way in which the nation was being cleansed of its original sin, poets such as R. H. Evans see God moving Lincoln to attack the workings of hell. Like Dewi Emlyn's discussion of Jefferson Davis's 'Satanic treachery against Freedom', and like Iago Ddu's description of slavery as the 'success' of 'devils' whose 'kingdom' is shaken by the Proclamation, Evans sees the president's measure as a blow aimed at 'The most despicable trade / Which dark hell itself ever fashioned.'

These poets described the struggle over slavery as the worldly manifestation of a contest between the supernatural forces good and evil, represented in distinctly Christian terms as the heavenly powers of God and the hellish legions of Satan. On the other hand, Evan ab Owen chose to address a different kind of supernatural force, the *awen* which, according to Welsh tradition, descends upon and inspires the poet. His short verse, 'Rhyddid i'r Caethion' ('Freedom for the Slaves'), also takes as its starting-point the fact that Lincoln had signed the Proclamation. Echoing Laura Griffiths's prefatory reference to the promise made in September, this poet prefaced his poem with a note making clear the connection between his text and the president's actions: '[c]lyfansoddwyd ar ol clywed am gyhoeddiad rhyddid i'r caethion gan A. Lincoln yn nechreu y fl. hon, 1863'; 'composed after hearing about the proclamation of freedom for the slaves made by A. Lincoln at the start of this year, 1863'.[62] According to Evan ab Owen, the president's Proclamation was capable of awakening the *awen* and thus enabling the poet to produce his own versified proclamation:

Awen lesg dihuna'r awrhon,
  Paid a hepian dim yn hwy
Cyfod gwrando cenad Lincoln
  Yn cyhoeddi rhyddid mwy.[63]

'Lifeless *awen*, awake now,
  Do not sleep any longer,
Get up and listen to Lincoln's message
  Announcing [that there will be] freedom henceforth.'

Like those other poetic celebrations of emancipation composed after 1 January 1863 discussed here, Evan ab Owen's verse avoids direct reference to battlefield bloodshed, concentrating instead on the fact that Lincoln's *cenad* or 'message' promised the deliverance of those who had 'received no reward for their work, / except the whip on the back' ('Heb gael gwobr am eu llafur, / Ond y fflangell ar y cefn').[64]

COLUMBIA'S TORTURED BODY

Lincoln's actions on the first day of 1863 did not change the way in which all Welsh-American poets discussed the relationship between the war and slavery, a fact exemplified by a poem which J. W. Nichols of New York published in *Y Cyfaill o'r Hen Wlad* in March 1863, two full months after that fateful day. While welcoming the promise of freedom which had been made, this poet presented a sustained condemnation of the entire United States (which he calls 'Columbia') for maintaining slavery for so long.[65]

Columbia! Columbia! 'r wyt heddyw yn yfed
 Y cwpan dychrynllyd gymysgaist dy hun,
Effeithiau gorthrymder – dylanwad caethiwed –
 Canlyniad dirmygu holl iawnderau dyn;
Bu'th faner yn gysgod i haid o forladron,
 Na welwyd yn oesoedd y ddaiar eu bath,
Yn lloches i feistriaid ffroenuchel a chreulon,
 Yn ddychryn i'r Negro – yn felldith i'r caeth.[66]

'Columbia! Columbia! you are today drinking
 The terrible cup which you yourself have prepared,
The effects of oppression – the influence of slavery –
 The result of scorning all of man's rights;
Your banner has been shelter for a pack of pirates,
 The likes of which had never been seen in the ages of the earth,
A shelter for haughty and cruel masters,
 A terror to the Negro – a curse to the slave.'

Earlier in the war a poet calling himself 'Ab Morydd' had published a poem in *Y Cenhadwr Americanaidd* confessing that 'Our flag was made, by the devil's churlish children, / A disgrace to our country on the borders of Africa's land' ('Ein baner fu cynt, gan filain blant y fall, /Yn warthrudd i'n gwlad ar ororau tir Affric'); like a range of other Welsh-American writers, Ab Morydd interpreted the Civil War as an opportunity to erase the stain of slavery from the American flag.[67] Though writing after Lincoln signed the Emancipation

Proclamation into being, J. W. Nichols chose to present this kind of interpretation of American history, focusing unflinchingly on the fact that Columbia's banner had sheltered slavery.

Bu mamau yn dyoddef dan gysgod dy luman,
A'u cefnau yn gwysi rhedegog o waed,
Dan bwysau y fflangell na chlywai eu gruddfan,
Cyfreithlawn yn unig drwy gyfraith ein gwlad;
Ti blygaist dy liniau i allu caethwasiaeth,
Dirdynaist dy wiw gyfansoddiad dy hun,
Mae swm dy ddeddf-lyfrau yn warth i ddynoliaeth,
Yn her i'r Goruchaf – yn ddirmyg ar ddyn.[68]

'Mothers suffered under the shadow of your flag,
And their backs were furrows flowing with blood
Under the weight of the whip which heard not their cry,
Only legal by the law of our land;
You bent your knee to the slave powers,
You tortured your own worthy body,
The sum of your law books is a shame to humanity,
A challenge to the Almighty – a contempt for man.'

Unlike those other Welsh-American poets discussed in this chapter, Nichols does not refer directly to the Emancipation Proclamation. He does, however, use language which asks readers to consider the relationship between official legislation and slavery; the line 'Dirdynaist dy wiw gyfansoddiad dy hun', translated above as 'You tortured your own worthy body', might also be rendered as 'you tortured your own worthy constitution'. The word *cyfansoddiad*, meaning 'physique' or '(bodily) constitution', was also used to refer to the United States Constitution, 'Cyfansoddiad yr Unol Daleithiau'.[69] Though addressing a personified nation, a 'Columbia' who, within the logic of the poem thus had a 'body', this poet was also describing the way in which the United States had perverted or 'tortured' its own Constitution, using a document which should have promised freedom for all to shelter slavery for nearly a century.

As has been seen already, much of the Welsh-language literature composed in reaction to the Emancipation Proclamation presented various meditations on the relationship between words and actions. In his essay on 'War's Lessons', Dewi Emlyn interpreted the thousands of battlefield deaths inflicted upon the Union forces as God's deliberate work. Likening the war's carnage to the biblical plagues visited upon Egypt, he invited readers to note that both 'plagues' can be seen as divine acts designed to force a powerful man to produce specific words. As Pharaoh, in Exodus 12.31–32, finally utters the words which release the Israelites from Egypt, so Abraham Lincoln finally signed his name to the words which promised emancipation to the Confederacy's slaves. Laura Griffiths praised the process which Lincoln set in motion in September 1862 by declaring that he was 'about to announce . . . Freedom'. She then shifted her praise from this presidential speech act to the divine force which she thought had inspired it, described in terms provided by what is perhaps the most celebrated act in Christian tradition, the 'descent' of Jesus to earth. By the same token, the narratives which 'Gomer' published in *Y Drych* describing the way in which his regiment aided fugitive slaves in Kentucky stressed the importance of backing words with action.

J. W. Nicols also partakes of this discourse. Columbia's physical body elides with the *Cyfansoddiad*, the country's written Constitution, a significant collection of words which have been 'tortured' just as the backs of enslaved mothers have been turned into 'furrows flowing with blood'. While other poets chose to focus on the freeing power of the president's words, this Welsh-American bard forces us to consider the horrible reality which some words call into being. The 'sum' of the country's 'law books' constitutes an oppressive weight, one which 'is a shame to humanity [and a] challenge to the Almighty'.

Despite emphasizing the negative power of words, this poem converges with those other Welsh-American meditations on emancipation at another point; Nichols also finds God's will at work within that web of relations connection words with actions. Before finishing his poem, we learn that God has answered this 'challenge'.

Mae Duw yn ei allu a nerth ei gyfiawnder,
 Yn galw i'r farn drigolion ein gwlad,
Yn talu y pwyth i holl bleidwyr gorthrymder.[70]

'God in his power and the strength of his justice
 Is calling the inhabitants of our country to judgement,
Retaliating against all slavery's supporters.'

However, unlike Dewi Emlyn, Laura Griffiths and R. H. Evans, this poet does not cite Lincoln's Proclamation as the instrument of God's will. Instead, he echoes those other millennialistic poems which Welsh-American poets had been publishing since the fall of Fort Sumter, viewing the war itself as God's answer to the slaves' cry. As the backs of so many mothers had been turned into 'furrows' or 'rows' of blood, so the stripes of the Stars and Stripes were marked with blood.

Mae'th faner yn rhuddgoch gan waed yr anedwydd,
 Dan rwymau haiarnaidd caethwasiaeth yn byw,
Heb ddigon o ddyfroedd yn nyfnder y Werydd
 I olchi ei rhesau, i adfer ei lliw.[71]

'Your banner is red with the blood of the unfortunate ones
Living under the iron bonds of slavery,
There is not enough waters in the depths of the Atlantic
To wash its stripes, to restore its colour.'

It is God who has called the country 'to judgement' on the battlefield, and it is He who is now cleansing the flag of its stain. Rather than washing it clean with the 'waters . . . of the Atlantic', He has chosen to rinse it clean with blood. J. W. Nichols tells us that, as the banner was 'fouled with blood' ('A gwaed [ei] llychwinwyd'), so 'it will be washed [clean] with blood' ('fe'i golchir â gwaed').[72] His final verse emphasizes this interpretation of the relationship between the war and slavery, stating in unmistakable terms that peace and freedom will only thrive after this horrible cleansing.

Gwneir, golchir a gwaed ein baner odidog,
Ei rhesau ddysgleiriant ryw ddiwrnod uwchben,
Pelydra pob seren yn hardd ac ardderchog,
Wrth chwifiaw yn dawel yn awel y nen,
O draethau y Werydd hyd lanau'r Mor Tawel,
O wely'r St. Lawrence hyd Gulfor y Dê,
A phawb dan ei chysgod mor rhydded a'r awel,
A hedd a brawdgarwch yn llanw pob lle.[73]

'It will be done, our glorious banner will be washed with blood,
Its stripes will shine one day overhead,
Every star will radiate beautifully and majestically,
As it waves quietly in the breeze of heaven,
From the beaches of the Atlantic to the shores of the Pacific,
And everybody under its shadow will be as free as the breeze,
And peace and brotherhood will fill every place.'

Abraham Lincoln hoped the war would bring 'a new birth of freedom', and many writers interpreted his Emancipation Proclamation as the herald of that freedom.[74] Others, including this Welsh-American poet from New York, suggested that it would take more than words to erase the stain of slavery from the Stars and Stripes, and that Columbia's tortured body would have to shed still more blood before 'everybody under its shadow' could be 'free as the breeze'.

NOTES

1 *Y Cenhadwr Americanaidd*, November 1862.
2 Ibid.
3 Ibid.
4 Ibid.
5 Ibid. This argument is developed in the following sentences: 'Peth erchyll a cholledus yw rhyfela â'r caethfeistri, ond buasai yn llawer erchyllach, ac yn fil mwy colledus i adael iddynt ddinystrio llywodraeth y bobl dan eu traed' ('War with the slave masters is a horrible and destructive thing, yet it would be much more horrible, and a thousand times more destructive, to allow them to destroy the people's government under their feet').
6 See Chapter Six, pages 250–4.
7 *The New English Bible* (Oxford, 1970), p. 10.
8 *Y Cenhadwr Americanaidd*, November 1862. This was far from being true; the Civil War caused a rift between many of Welsh America's religious leaders and the Welsh leaders of the British Peace Movement. See Robert Huw Griffiths, 'The Welsh and the American Civil War c.1840–1865' (unpublished PhD thesis, Cardiff University, 2004), Chapter 4, 'The Contrasting Experiences of Samuel Roberts and Henry Richard'.
9 *Y Cenhadwr Americanaidd*, November 1862.
10 Ibid.
11 Ibid.
12 See Chapter Three, pages 95–7.
13 *Y Cenhadwr Americanaidd*, November 1862.
14 Ibid.
15 Ibid.
16 James M. McPherson, *Battle Cry of Freedom* [:] *The American Civil War* (Oxford, 1988), p. 557.
17 As early as 23 September 1863, one day after Lincoln met his cabinet, Horace Greely was praising the Emancipation Proclamation on the pages of the *New York Tribune*. See James McPherson, *Crossroads of Freedom* (Oxford, 2002), pp. 139–40.
18 In most contexts the noun *disgwyliad* carries the meaning 'expectation' or 'anticipation', and thus this poem's title can also be rendered as '(The) Anticipation of the Slave's Freedom'. However, the meaning 'watcher' or 'one who watches for' is also attested, and given the use of the definite article, *y*, I have chosen this translation. *Geiriadur Prifysgol Cymru* (Cardiff, 1950–2002), p. 1045.
19 *Y Cenhadwr Americanaidd*, November 1862.
20 The source of this information is a biographical sketch which R. F. Jones published in *Y Cenhadwr Americanaidd* in August 1864.
21 Laura Griffiths published a number of elegies; see, for example: *Y Cenhadwr Americanaidd*, March 1858; March, June, October and December 1859; January, November and December 1860; July, September, and November 1861. Another example of the way in which she put her verse to use in serving the community can be seen in a poem she composed on behalf of her chapel, thanking the Welsh Congregational Chapel of New York City for the gift of 'communion dishes' (*llestri cymundeb*); *Y Cenhadwr Americanaidd*, August 1860.
22 See Jane Aaron, *Pur Fel y Dur* [:] *Y Gymraes yn Llên Menywod y Bedwaredd Ganrif ar Bymtheg* (Cardiff, 1998).

23 *Y Cenhadwr Americanaidd*, May 1860.
24 *Y Cenhadwr Americanaidd*, August 1864.
25 The two women were not related; both Ann and Laura took the name Griffiths from their husbands, and they came from different parts of Wales.
26 *Y Cenhadwr Americanaidd*, November 1862.
27 Ibid.
28 Ibid.
29 Ibid.
30 *Geiriadur Prifysgol Cymru*, p. 385.
31 *Y Cenhadwr Americanaidd*, November 1862.
32 The word *bydoedd*, the plural of the noun *byd*, 'world', 'realm' or 'state', is here translated as 'universe', as it seems to imply a multiplicity of 'worlds' or 'realms', a totality which includes all possible lands, worlds and states.
33 Richard Marius (ed.) and Keith Frome (associate ed.), *The Columbia Book of Civil War Poetry* (New York, 1994), pp. 55–6.
34 *Y Cyfaill o'r Hen Wlad*, March 1862.
35 Ibid.
36 Ibid.
37 See Chapter Three, pages 103–5. On the abolitionist beliefs of the 22nd Wisconsin's' Welsh soldiers, see also Chapter Four, pages 183–4.
38 Eugene Walter Leach, *The Racine County Militant* (Racine, 1915), p. 81.
39 Frank J. Welcher and Larry G. Ligget, *Coburn's Brigade* (Carmel [Indiana], 1999), p. 24.
40 *Y Drych*, 24 January 1863. The letter was written in 'Camp Baird', near Danville, Kentucky, on 22 December 1862. Like many of those soldier-writers discussed in Chapter Five, Gomer's opening sentence suggests that he is corresponding with the paper on behalf of all of the regiment's Welsh soldiers; he describes his own letters as 'ychydig oddiwrth yr 22ain Wisconsin', 'a little [news] from the 22nd Wisconsin'.
41 *Y Drych*, 24 January 1863.
42 Ibid.
43 Ibid.
44 Ibid.
45 Frank J. Welcher and Larry G. Ligget, *Coburn's Brigade*, p. 37.
46 *Y Drych*, 24 January 1863.
47 Ibid.
48 It is clear that many Union officers serving in border states were often either ignorant of the current legislative measures applying to escaped slaves or chose to ignore or misinterpret such measures. According to James McPherson, 'the Republican majority in Congress enacted a new article of war on March 13, 1862, forbidding army officers to return escaped slaves to their masters – even those masters who claimed to be loyal Unionists.' James M. McPherson, *Crossroads of Freedom* [:] *Antietam: The Battle That Changed the Course of the American Civil War* (London, 2003), p. 65.
49 See Chapter Two, pages 49–50.
50 For a summary of this line of interpretation, see Peter Kolchin, *American Slavery* (London, 1993), p. 203.
51 *Y Drych*, 28 March 1863.
52 Ibid.

53 Ibid.

54 Ibid.

55 Quoted in William S. McFeeley, *Frederick Douglass* (New York, 1991), p. 215.

56 Ibid.

57 *Y Drych*, 17 January 1863. The title is given as 'Y Cyhoeddiad Rhyddid'; *rhyddid* means 'freedom', and *cyhoeddiad* can be translated as 'announcement', 'publication', 'declaration', or 'proclamation'.

58 *Y Cyfaill o'r Hen Wlad*, January 1863.

59 Ibid.

60 Ibid.

61 *Y Cyfaill o'r Hen Wlad*, July 1864.

62 *Y Cenhadwr Americanaidd*, August 1863.

63 Ibid.

64 Ibid.

65 Note that this J. W. Nichols of New York is not the J. J. Nicholas who published poetry in *Y Seren Orllewinol*, discussed elsewhere in this study.

66 *Y Cyfaill o'r Hen Wlad*, March 1863. The poem's title is 'Columbia! Columbia!'

67 *Y Cenhadwr Americanaidd*, May 1862.

68 *Y Cyfaill o'r Hen Wlad*, March 1863.

69 *Geiriadur Prifysgol Cymru*, p. 679.

70 *Y Cyfaill o'r Hen Wlad*, March 1863.

71 Ibid.

72 Ibid.

73 Ibid.

74 The words 'a new birth of Freedom' were included in Abraham Lincoln's 'Gettysburg Address'; this speech was delivered on 19 November 1863, ten months after the Emancipation Proclamation. See, for example, Stanley Appelbaum (ed.), *Abraham Lincoln* [:] *Great Speeches* (Mineola [New York], 1991), pp. 103–4.

11

Pulling Down the Pillars: Recording the Service of African-American Soldiers

Since long before the start of the Civil War, the Welsh-American press had been publishing a considerable body of literature which took as its starting-point the belief that emancipation was a moral, religious and political necessity. As soon as the war started bringing freedom to Southern slaves, Welsh abolitionists began publishing discussions of how best to aid those recently freed people. The Revd Franklin Jones, chaplain to the 1st New York Volunteers, was pondering this question in depth during the early months of the war. His regiment, which was occupying the newly-captured area around Newport News, Virginia, was coming into contact with a considerable number of African Americans, many of whom were in that earlier stage of the war suspended in an ambiguous legal state somewhere between slavery and freedom.

> Yr wyf yn gweled, a phan yn gweled nis gallaf lai na theimlo fod y rhyfel hwn wedi bod yn achlysur i agor drws llydan ac effeithiol o ddefnyddioldeb yn mhlith pobl y rhai hyd yn hyn a gauwyd allan oddiwrth fendithion a buddiannau ein cydymdeimlad Cristnogol. Yr wyf yn cyfeirio at y boblogaeth gaeth yn Virginia, ac yn fwyaf neillduol at y rhai a adawyd gan eu meistri, neu a ffoisant oddiwrthynt, ac a ymofynasant am nodded oddiwrth rwymau y gorthrymydd yn ein gwersylloedd.[1]
>
> 'I see, and when seeing I cannot but feel that this war has been an occasion for opening a wide and effective door of usefulness among people who up to now have been shut out of the blessings and benefits of our Christian sympathy. I am referring to the enslaved population in Virginia, and most specifically to those who have been abandoned by their masters, or who have fled from them, and who have sought protection from the bonds of the oppressor in our camps.'

This letter, a copy of which was sent 'at Gymdeithas Gristionogol y Gwyr Ieuainc' – 'to the Young Men's Christian Association' – of New York, was published in *Y Cenhadwr Americanaidd* in October 1861. Jones admired the manner in which the (former) slaves had maintained their own religious culture under the harshest possible conditions, and he was hoping to recruit missionaries to help him 'in providing them with religious education' ('i roddi iddynt addysg crefyddol').[2]

A year later Dewi Emlyn would publish his essay on 'War's Lessons' in the same journal. As was discussed in the last chapter, this minister from Ohio argued that God was punishing the United States in a manner akin to the plagues visited upon Egypt; by the same token, the Revd Franklin Jones employed a reference to Exodus, suggesting that the (former) slaves were akin to the homeless Israelites who, having fled into the wilderness from Egypt, were praying to God for help.

> Yn amddifad a digysur fel y maent, maent yn ymdrechu cadw i fyny gyfarfodydd crefyddol ar y Sabboth; a phrin yr ymddangosodd erioed i lygad y dyngarwr a'r Christion olgyfa fwy toddedig na chynulliad y trueniaid di-dŷ a di-gartref hyn o feibion Affrica, yn estyn eu dwylaw erfyniol yn brysur at Dduw, yn nghanol y ddiffeithfa arswydol bresenol.[3]

> 'Orphaned and without comfort as they are, they try to keep up religious meetings on the Sabbath; and hardly has a more heart-melting scene appeared to the eyes of the humanitarian and the Christian than the congregation of these poor houseless and homeless sons of Africa, busily extending their beseeching hands to God, in the middle of the terrible wilderness [in which they find themselves] at present.'

To further stimulate interest in the religious culture of Virginia's African Americans, Jones included a translation of a letter which another missionary had sent him containing detailed observations on their manner of worship. Hymnology was a central part of nineteenth-century Welsh culture, and no poets were revered more than William Williams of Pantycelyn and Ann Griffiths, both remembered primarily for the popular hymns which they had composed. Like Franklin Jones, the *Cenhadwr*'s editor, Robert Everett, must have known that this information would interest his journal's readers.

> Mae rhyw bethau neillduol iddynt yn eu dull o addoli. . . . Eu hymnau ydynt ddefosiynol; ond y mae ganddynt fath o fyrdwn ar ddiwedd yr Emyn a ganant yn aml, yn y geiriau hyn:
> 'Go down to Egypt – tell Pharaoh
> Thus saith my servant Moses, Let my people go.'
> Gan roddi yr aceniad ar y sill ddiweddaf o'r ddwy linell, ac ail ganu y byrdwn drosodd a throsodd – yr hyn, byddaf yn meddwl, a swnia nod o rybudd parhaus yn nghlustiau gormes.[4]

> 'There are some unique things in their manner of worship. . . . Their hymns are devotional; but they have a kind of refrain at the end of the Hymn which they sing frequently, in these words:
> "Go down to Egypt – tell Pharaoh
> Thus saith my servant Moses, Let my people go."
> Placing the stress on the last syllable of the two lines, and singing the refrain over and over again – which, I think, sounds a note of continual warning in the ears of oppression.'

An appeal to readers interested in musicological detail is combined with a powerful example of the way in which people seeking freedom used religious song to interpret their own situation. Franklin Jones painted a literary portrait of 'the homeless sons of Africa' using colours drawn from the story of Exodus, but he was inspired ultimately by the way in which those people made creative use of religious language.[5]

Y Cenhadwr Americanaidd can be translated as 'The American Missionary'; not surprisingly, this journal would continue to publish appeals for missionaries to work with former slaves right up to the end of the war. For example, one writer calling himself 'Ysgallen' published a piece in the *Cenhadwr* in July 1864 describing the 'Gwyl Flynyddol' or 'Yearly Festival' held at Lane Seminary, a theological college in Cincinnati. His main purpose was to describe the dynamic intellectual and cultural life of the institution and to note the fact that 'nifer go fawr o'r Cymry', 'a considerably large number of the Welsh', had graduated there recently.[6] However, he also referred to the end of the war which he thought was near at hand, beseeching members of his 'nation' (*cenedl*) 'to go as Missionaries amongst the four million Negroes, who are about to enjoy their freedom' ('i fyned yn Gennadau i blith y pedair miliwn Negroaid, sydd ar fwynhau eu rhyddid').[7] Ysgallen suggested that the freedom which he discerned on the horizon was a sign that 'the millennium had dawned' ('y mil blynyddoedd wedi gwawrio') and that Christians should rise to meet it by undertaking this missionary work.[8] A number of Welsh-Americans did travel south to work with former slaves as missionaries or teachers, including Cynthia Everett, one of the daughters of Robert Everett, the *Cenhadwr*'s editor.[9]

Of course, by the time these Northern civilians reached the camps, schools and missions constructed for recently freed people, hundreds of Welsh-speaking soldiers had for some time been encountering slaves freed by the course of war. About the same time that the 22nd Wisconsin Infantry's Welsh volunteers were aiding fugitive slaves in Kentucky (as discussed in the last chapter), another soldier, David J. Evans, was encountering 'contrabands' in North Carolina. In a letter which his mother forwarded for publication in the *Cenhadwr*, Evans contemplated the future relationship between freed men and the Union army.

> Llaweroedd o negroaid o bob parth o'r dalaeth ydynt yn ymgasglu o fewn ein llinellau i feddiannu y rhyddid na feddiannasant erioed o'r blaen. Rhyfedd mor gyflym y deuant, ddydd ar ol dydd yn ymdyru o bob parth o'r wlad. Y trueniaid anffodus! llawer o honynt wedi gorfod gadael eu gwragedd a'u rhai bychain ar ol. Maent yn cael eu defnyddio i godi gwrthgloddiau ac amddiffynfeydd, ac arbedir i'r milwyr felly lawer o waith caled. Yn gyfunol â chyhoeddeb ein Llywydd, ffurfir yn fuan gatrodau o'r rhai galluog o honynt.[10]

> 'Many negroes from every part of the state are gathering within our lines in order to take possession of the freedom which they never before possessed. It is wondrous how quickly they come, thronging day after day from every part of the

> country. The unfortunate poor people! Many of them have had to leave their wives and their little ones behind. They are being used to raise earthworks and defences, and the soldiers are thus spared much hard work. In keeping with our President's proclamation, regiments will be formed from those who are capable.'

The Emancipation Proclamation did indeed refer to the president's ability to enlist what were to be called 'coloured troops', yet this was only the latest of a number of measures which had been slowly opening a door which the Union army had previously closed to African-American men.[11]

Some abolitionists had been calling for the enlistment of coloured troops since the fall of Fort Sumter. Frederick Douglass had put the point eloquently back in May 1861: 'Let the slaves and free colored people be called into service, and formed into a liberating army, to march into the South and raise the banner of emancipation among the slaves.'[12] However, racial prejudice had led many Northerners to view the conflict as 'a white man's war'; confined by the restraints of their own bigotry, they assumed that black men would not make good soldiers and that enlisting them would demean the service of the Union's white soldiers.[13]

A few Union generals had taken actions of their own accord in order to recruit former slaves, most notably David Hunter who in March 1862 began enlisting freed slaves in South Carolina, Georgia and Florida.[14] While Hunter's actions were not supported by the president, the government was slowly coming around, and Congress passed the Militia Act on 17 July 1862, authorizing the use of 'persons of African descent . . . for any military or naval service for which they may be found competent.'[15] Though Lincoln was slow to put this Act into action, politicians and generals in Kansas and Louisiana were taking the initiative and using African-American soldiers in combat by the end of 1862. The president himself came to change his mind, and in May 1863 'the War Department established the Bureau for Colored Troops to regularize their recruitment and organization'.[16]

FORGING A NEW KIND OF FAMILY

Unlike the army, the United States navy had allowed African Americans to serve from the start. By the time the Bureau for Colored Troops was being organized, a Welsh-American sailor, John B. Morgan from Newport, Ohio, had been working side by side with black sailors on the U.S.S. *Vermont* for some time. A letter which he had sent to a friend was forwarded for publication in *Y Drych*:

> Gyda golwg ar y llong, y mae yn llestr mawr dychrynllyd, yn un o'r llestri mwyaf sydd yn rhodio brig y don y dyddiau hyn. Y mae mwy na hanner ei theulu (cynwysa wyth cant i gyd) yn fechygn duon; ac y maent o ddefnydd rhyfeddol yma; hebddynt nis gwn beth a wnaethai ein Llywodraeth.[17]

> 'With regard to the ship, it is a terribly big vessel, one of the biggest vessels which travels over the waves these days. More than half of its crew (it contains eight hundred in total) are black lads; and they are of wondrous use here; I do not know what our Government would do without them.'

The word *teulu*, translated here as 'crew', was used in the medieval and early modern periods to mean 'a military retinue', 'war band' or 'host'. However, by the 1860s it was most commonly used to mean 'family'; John Morgan is referring to the 'host' of sailors serving on his ship, yet he is using a word which also describes that crew as a 'family'.

Soldiers have through the ages used familial metaphors in describing 'the band of brothers' of which they were a part, and some Welsh volunteers in the Union army were defining themselves as 'plant eu hen dad, Abraham Lincoln', 'the children of their old father, Abraham Lincoln'.[18] This sailor describes a multi-racial family, one in which white and black men exist in harmony as they fight for the same cause.

> Yr oeddwn yn rhyfedd dros ryddhad y caeth cyn myned o Newport; mewn gwirionedd, dyna oedd fwyaf ar fy meddwl i'm tueddu i godi arfau yn erbyn y *rebels;* ond er cymaint yr oeddwn yn dymuno eu rhyddhad y pryd hwnw, yr ydwyf yn dymuno eu rhyddhad yn fwy heddiw. Y mae y dynion duon erbyn hyn yn fy adnabod agos oll, am y rheswm fy mod yn treulio cymaint o fy amser yn eu plith, yn gwrando arnynt yn adrodd eu helynt, gyda *Massa* ar y . . . *rice plantations* . . . Y mae yn destun syndod fel y maent yn llafurio i ddysgu darllen; a gallaf sicrhau i chwi nad yw yr ysgrifenydd yn ol o wneuthur ei oreu, yn ol ei allu, i'w haddysgu; nid oes ond ychydig o honynt yn medru darllen, ond y maent yn dyfod yn y blaen yn gyflym; medra rhai ohonynt ddarllen yn weddol yn bresenol, ac yn fuan iawn fe fydd llawer ohonynt yn gallu darllen yn weddol; ni welais neb erioed mor awyddus am ddysgu a'r rhai hyn. O fe garent weld y rhyfel erchyll hwn wedi darfod, ond i'r Gogledd fod yn orchfygol.[19]

> 'I was wondrously in favour of freeing the slave before leaving Newport [, Ohio]; in truth, that was what was most on my mind motivating me to take up arms against the rebels; yet however much I desired their freedom at that time, I desire it more today. The black men all know me well by now, because I spend so much of my time amongst them, listening to them relate their tribulations with Massa on the . . . rice plantations . . . The way they labour to learn to read is a cause of wonder; there are naught but a few of them who can read, yet they are making progress quickly; and I can assure you that the writer is not remiss in trying his best, according to his ability, to teach them; some of them can read fairly well at present, and very soon many of them will be able to read fairly well; I never saw anybody so eager for learning as these people. Oh, they would love to see this horrible war finished, as long as the North be victorious.'

While the chaplain Franklin Jones was asking for volunteers to work with freedmen and women, this Welsh-American sailor took it upon himself to aid the former slaves with whom he served, helping them to acquire the knowledge which would help them in their new lives as free people.

Before finishing, John Morgan restates his desire to see all slaves emancipated, adding criticism aimed at the authorities who had refused for so along to allow African Americans to enlist in the Union army.

> Wel, fy nymuniad i ydyw eu gweled oll yn mwynhau y rhyddid y maent yn deilwng o hono, cyn y bydd yn rhaid imi daflu fy arfau i lawr; oblegid nid wyf yn ewyllysio dychwelyd yn ol yna, a gadael y Negro mewn caethiwed; ac yr ydwyf yn foddlon i fyned trwy lawer o galedi er mwyn ei ryddhau o'i gaethiwed. Ond yr wyf am weled y dynion duon hefyd yn cael dyfod i faes y gwaed ag arfau yn eu dwylaw. Carwn weld cant neu ddau o filoedd o honynt yn ymladd dros eu hiawnderau.[20]

> 'Well, my wish is to see them all enjoying the freedom of which they are worthy before I must through down my arms; for I do not desire to return there and leave the Negro in slavery; and I am content to go through much hardship in order to free him from his slavery. However, I also want to see the black men being allowed to take to the field of blood with weapons in their hands. I would love to see one or two hundred thousand of them fighting for their rights.'

Significantly, this letter was written and published during that very period which saw Lincoln's government finally opening the legislative paths which would permit African Americans 'to take to the field of blood with weapons in their hands'. John Morgan's reference to 'one or two hundred thousand of them' was to prove prophetic; before the end of the Civil War more than 180,000 black soldiers would serve in the Union army.[21] However, these new military units were not organized on the same lines as those used by the navy. In addition to serving in separate regiments, coloured troops were to operate in separate brigades and even separate divisions; the army, though finally opening its doors to African Americans, was not to replicate the kind of multiracial 'family' described by the sailor John Morgan.

One of Lincoln's most loyal Welsh-American 'sons' was neither a sailor nor a soldier, but a civilian who worked for the government. Isaac Cheshire left his home in Wisconsin shortly after the start of the war in order to work for the Department of the Interior in Washington; known to other Welsh-Americans for his talents as a singer and as one of the main supporters of Wisconsin's *eisteddfod* culture, it was his talents as a book-keeper which brought him to the attention of Lincoln's administration.[22] During the war he functioned as a kind of political analyst for *Y Drych*, providing readers with detailed discussions of current events. In May 1863 Cheshire published an essay discussing the newly formed Bureau for Colored Troops. Though he had always espoused anti-slavery views, Cheshire's passionate support for Lincoln made him into an apologist for the president, and in this piece he misrepresented Lincoln's original stance on the question of coloured troops, claiming falsely that he had always been in favour of the idea.

> Y mae yr Arlywydd o'r dechreu i'r diwedd . . . wedi rhoddi ei droed i lawr gyda golwg ar gwestiwn y Negro yn ei berthynas a'r rhyfel. Cânt, heblaw rhawiau i balu, a chawgiau i gogino i'r wlad, arfau goreu yr arfdy i ymladd drosti hefyd.[23]
>
> 'The President has since the start . . . put his foot down with respect to the question of the Negro's relationship with the war. They will receive, in addition to shovels to dig with, and pans to cook with for the country, the best arms of the armoury to fight for it as well.'

Placing the blame not on Lincoln but rather on other unnamed 'people', Cheshire offered proof of the president's good judgement in 'putting his foot down' in this manner, referring to the first coloured regiment which was mustered officially into federal service, Thomas Wentworth Higginson's 1st South Carolina Volunteers.

> Wel! gymaint . . . ydoedd dallineb a thywyllwch ofergoelus y bobl fel y bu yn angenrheidiol dinystrio byddinoedd mawrion . . . llanw mynwesau dirif â galar am eu hanwylion, ac i golledigaeth ei hunan ymrithio o flaen eu llygaid cyn y llwyddwyd i gael ganddynt weled y gwirionedd a'i gredu. Y mae amser gwerthfawr wedi ei golli hefyd; os yw yr hanes yn wir am y *1st South Carolina* . . . eu bod yn *marchio* ac yn myned drwy orchwylion y gwersyll yn gampus; ac heblaw hyny, yn talu yn ol i'w hen feistriaid yn eu pwyth eu hunain, sef rhoddi iddynt ergyd am ergyd ar y maes. Os gwir hyn . . . beth fuasai y canlyniad erbyn heddyw o ymgymeryd a'r cynllun o'r dechreuad . . .? Mentraf ddweyd y buasai genym gorfflu o gan' mil o filwyr o'r duon, y buasent yn fwy o ddychryn i Jeff. Davis na hyny o filwyr gwynion a gafwyd yn y *Border States*.[24]
>
> 'Well! So great . . . was the blindness and superstitious ignorance of the people that it was necessary to destroy great armies . . . [and] fill innumerable bosoms with grief for their dear ones, and for defeat itself to appear before their eyes before they were successfully made to see the truth and believe it. And valuable time has been lost as well, if the news is true regarding the 1st South Carolina . . . that they march and go through the duties of camp excellently; and besides that, pay back their old masters in their own coin, that is giving them blow for blow upon the field. If this be true . . . what would the result be by today if the plan had been undertaken from the start . . .? I venture to say that we would have a force of one hundred thousand black soldiers, who would be more frightening to Jeff Davis than those white soldiers who were had in the Border States.'

Ignoring the fact that Lincoln himself had repeatedly stressed the military importance of the border states early in the war, Cheshire's pleasure at reporting on the success of coloured troops was as consistent with the way in which other Welsh-American writers voiced support for the African-American soldiers as it was inconsistent with the facts regarding Lincoln's views on the subject prior to 1863.

A host of other Welsh-American writers noted with pleasure the fact that African-American soldiers were becoming an increasingly common sight. In a letter to *Y Cenhadwr Americanaidd*, the Revd Ben Chidlaw described the freed men he had seen in Union camps on the banks of the Mississippi: 'Gwelais dros 2,000 o honynt wedi enlistio i'r fyddin, ac y maent yn sicr o wneud milwyr gwrol a medrus. Maent yn barod i ymladd dros eu gwlad, ac i farw (os bydd raid) yn ei hachos'; 'I saw more than 2,000 of them enlisted in the army, and they are certain to make capable and brave soldiers. They are ready fight for their country, and to die (if need be) for its sake.'[25] For Chidlaw, this was a sign that the end of the war was near: 'Mae amgylchiadau ein gwlad yn ddyrus, ond yn gwella, a dydd ein llwyddiant yn gwawrio'; 'The circumstances of our country are complex, but improving, and the day of our success is dawning.'[26]

A Wisconsin soldier, John Griffith Jones, wrote home to his family praising the coloured troops who joined his regiment in camp: 'Mau yma [nifer] o gatrodau o filwyr duon yn caul eu drilio. Y maunt yn dysgu yn rhagorol'; 'There are a number of regiments of black soldiers being drilled. They are learning exceptionally well.'[27] In another letter Jones suggested that, in addition to the military aid they were providing for the Union cause, the coloured troops offered a welcome addition to the army's social life.

> Y mau yma amryw o coler[e]d regiments, ac y mae ganddynt hwy bregethwyr 'run lliw. Yn wir, y maunt yn pregethu yn ardderchog; y maunt yn tynu sylw'r milwyr yn fwy na'n pregethwyr ni ein hunain. Y mau ganddynt ddoniau mawr. Y mau cystal genyf welad y milwyr duon a gwelad y rhai gwynion.[28]
>
> 'There are various coloured regiments here, and they have preachers of the same colour. Truly, they preach wonderfully; they attract the attention of the soldiers better than our own preachers. They have great talents. I am just as happy to see the black soldiers as I am to see the white ones.'

'LIKE GOLD PURIFIED BY FIRE'

It is perhaps significant that Jones uses the word *pregethwyr*, 'preachers', and not *gweinidogion*, 'ministers', suggesting that these men were lay preachers rather than professional pastors. Even more significantly, he does not call them *caplaniaid*, 'chaplains'; African Americans were for the most part barred from becoming commissioned officers and, while '[b]lacks had greatest success in obtaining commissions as regimental chaplains', this success extended to only thirteen chaplain posts (out of a total of well over one hundred).[29] One of the white ministers employed in this position was the Revd Erasmus Jones, a

Welsh-American Congregationalist from Oneida County, New York. A committed abolitionist, Erasmus Jones had joined Robert Everett in his anti-slavery campaigning back in the early 1840s. Though nearly fifty years old, he volunteered for service, seeking specifically to serve with coloured troops, and early in 1864 he was commissioned chaplain with the 21st United States Colored Infantry.[30]

Like the famous scholar after whom he was named, Erasmus Jones was something of a renaissance man. While earning his living as a minister, Jones also made a name for himself as a singer, writer and orator, and he employed these talents in the service of abolition. According to one biographer writing years later, in 'the Anti-Slavery debates he was a recognized force, a power real and original, and he was hailed as a genius.'[31] He published in both English and Welsh, producing poetry as well as a body of prose which ranged from short factual essays to long romantic novels.[32] Since long before the start of the war Jones had been competing (and winning) in various Welsh-American literary festivals, and before the end of the century he would leave his mark upon the country's English-language literary culture by publishing in journals such as *The Atlantic Monthly*. As befitted a writer working in two languages, Erasmus Jones also had an interest in translation, and in 1893 he was to win $100 for 'the best translation from Welsh into English of the King Arthur stories' at the huge *eisteddfod* held in connection with Chicago's World Fair.[33] Jones used these literary talents to record his service with the 21st US Colored Infantry; after his regiment reached Morris Island, South Carolina, he sent a lengthy letter to his old abolitionist colleague, Robert Everett, knowing that Everett would publish it in *Y Cenhadwr Americanaidd*.

> Chwi welwch, Mr. Everett, fy mod yn awr yn Carolina Ddeheuol, yn dal perthynas â'r fyddin Undebawl, sydd yn yr ymdrech clodwiw o roddi i lawr y gwrthryfel mwyaf dieflig a gymerodd le er pan gyfododd Satan a'i angylion yn erbyn llywodraeth gyfiawn Brenin y brenhinoedd. Peidied neb a fy nghamgymeryd. Nid yw eich anheilwng was, hyd yma, wedi cymeryd i fyny arfau milwriaeth *gnawdol*. Mae yn y fyddin yn dilyn yr un alwedigaeth a phan oedd gartref, sef pregethu Crist . . . cefais fy awdurdodi i fod yn *Chaplain of the 21 Regt. United States Colored Troops*. Mae y Regiment i ba un yr wyf yn perthyn, oddigerth ei swyddogion, wedi ei chyfansoddi yn hollol o bobl *dduon*. Ac nid hyny yn unig, ond yr oeddynt oll ychydig amser yn ol yn *gaethion*; yn cael eu hystyried gan eu perchnogion (?) yn werth hyn a hyn o ddoleri, ac yn cael eu prynu a'u gwerthu, a'u gwasgaru, yma a thraw, fel creaduriaid direswm.[34]

> 'You see, Mr. Everett, that I am now in South Carolina, holding a position with the Union army, which is [engaged] in the praiseworthy struggle to put down the most devilish rebellion which has ever taken place since Satan and his angels rose up against the just government of the King of kings. Do not misunderstand me. Your unworthy servant, thus far, has not taken up the arms of *bodily* soldiering. He is following the same calling in the army as when at home, namely preaching

> Christ . . . I was authorized as Chaplain of the 21 Regt. United States Colored Troops. The Regiment to which I belong, except its officers, is composed entirely of *black* people. And not only that, but a little time ago they were *slaves*; considered by their owners (?)[35] to be worth so many dollars, being bought and sold and scattered here and there, like senseless creatures.'

Erasmus Jones describes the enemy in Satanic terms which recall the imagery used by some of the poets discussed in the last chapter. Like those other Welsh-American writers, Jones assumed that his readers would accept his views on the justness of the cause which he was serving and that they would welcome this portrayal of the enemy.

Having worked with Robert Everett during the early days of the campaign to radicalize Welsh-Americans and mobilize them against slavery, Jones made it clear in some of his later writings that he regarded Everett as an important moral leader. Indeed, the respect he held for the *Cenhadwr*'s editor is suggested by the way in which he addressed this letter: '*Anwyl Frawd, Dr. Everett*, neu yn hytrach anwyl *dad* yn yr efengyl'; '*Dear Brother, Dr. Everett*, or rather dear *father* in the gospel.'[36] Erasmus Jones would have been aware of the fact that Everett, once a supporter of the peace movement, had been moved by the events of 'bleeding Kansas' and, finally, by the start of the Civil War, to support an armed struggle which he interpreted as a fight against slavery. As has been seen repeatedly in this study, the relationship between abolition and pacifism constituted a dynamic and changing part of the constellation of beliefs which characterized Welsh America's religious culture during the 1850s and early 1860s; it is within this complex context that the first part of the chaplain's letter should be interpreted. Having announced in his opening sentence the fact that he had joined the army, Erasmus Jones takes a playful step backwards, adding that, unlike most soldiers, he is not fighting with what he calls 'the arms of *bodily* soldiering'. However, the very sentence which assures readers that this minister is not 'taking up' weapons also includes the qualifying statement *hyd yma*, 'thus far' or 'up to now'. The Revd Jones is suggesting, however playfully, that a minister could pick up weapons in order to put down the 'devilish rebellion' of the Southern slave owners.

After considering the implications of his own military service, the chaplain provides a much more detailed discussion of the work being accomplished by the former slaves with whom he served. Jones was writing more than a year after the Bureau for Colored Troops was formed, and the racist refrain of those anti-war Democrats or 'copperheads' in the North had long been proven false.

> Erbyn hyn y mae y dyn du wedi rhoddi prawfiadau digonol i'r wlad, ei fod yn feddianol ar wir elfenau milwrol; ac mae yr hen 'dinc' bengoprog hono – 'A Nigger can't fight,' bron wedi destewi. Ychydig amser yn ol fel y mae eich darllenwyr yn gwybod eisoes, gwnaed ymosodiad ar James Island. . . . Dangosodd y milwyr duon . . . fwy o wrolder a phenderfyniad na'r milwyr gwynion; ac unwaith o

leiaf, pan drodd ein milwyr gwynion eu cefnau, rhuthrasant y'mlaen, nes ffoi o'r gelynion oddiar y maes. 'Parch i'r hwn y mae parch yn ddyledus'.[37]

'By now the black man has given sufficient proof to the country that he possesses true military qualities; and that old copperheaded ditty – "A Nigger can't fight," is nearly silenced. A little while ago, as your readers already know, an attack was made on James Island. . . . The black soldiers displayed more heroism and determination . . . than the white soldiers; and at least once, when our white soldiers turned their backs, they rushed forward, so that the enemy fled from the field. "Respect for he to whom respect is due." '

The 21st US Colored Infantry was on James Island as part of the siege of Charleston, and the regiment was to remain in the area until that city finally fell. Throughout this period, the soldiers whom Erasmus Jones served were fighting side by side with a number of other coloured units, including the 54th Massachusetts Infantry.

No regiment of African-American soldiers received more attention at the time than the 54th Massachusetts Infantry. Frederick Douglass himself recruited for it, and his sons Charles and Lewis had been among the first to enlist. Moreover, it was led by Colonel Robert Gould Shaw, son of some of Boston's more prominent abolitionists.[38] The death of many of the regiment's soldiers during a heroic yet futile assault upon Fort Wagner, South Carolina, on 18 July 1863 was taken by many as a turning-point regarding Northern attitudes towards the new coloured regiments. According to the New York *Tribune*, the 54th Massachusetts 'had made Fort Wagner such a name to the colored race as Bunker Hill has been for ninety years to the white Yankees'.[39] Shaw, who died leading his soldiers in the assault on Fort Wagner, was soon immortalized in a range of literary tributes, including poems by Ralph Waldo Emerson and James Russell Lowell.[40]

As if to emphasize the site's symbolic importance in the struggle for the rights of (former) slaves, Erasmus Jones made a pilgrimage to Fort Wagner after the Confederates were finally forced to surrender it. The chaplain described this pilgrimage for the *Cenhadwr*'s readers: 'Gwelais y fan lle y syrthiodd y gwrol Col. Shaw o'r 54 Mass. wrth arwain ei fechgyn *duon* yn erbyn y gelyn; ac yn y gwastadedd ger llaw, y tawel hunant ynghyd'; 'I saw the place where the heroic Col. Shaw of the 54th Mass. fell while leading his *black* lads against the enemy; and in the nearby lowlands, they sleep quietly together.'[41] The fact that Shaw had been buried with his soldiers was widely publicized at the time. In the words of Joseph T. Glatthaar:

The Confederates . . . laid Shaw to rest in a pit with his men, or as a Confederate supposedly explained when the Federals sought his body under a flag of truce, 'We have buried him with his niggers!' Clearly the Confederates had intended to insult the sensibilities of whites; instead, it became a rallying-cry across the North and helped to immortalize Col. Robert Gould Shaw. One month later, when

> Shaw's father learned that Gen. Gillmore was attempting to secure the remains, he requested that his son's body lie with his men[.][42]

The circumstances of Shaw's death and burial were to provide potent material for generations of American writers, ranging from Paul Laurence Dunbar's mournful description of post-war segregation, 'Robert Gould Shaw' ('Since thou and those who with thee died for right / Have died, the Present teaches, in vain!'), to Robert Lowell's modernist meditation, 'On the Union Dead' ('Shaw's father wanted no monument / except the ditch, / where his son's body was thrown / and lost with his "niggers" ').[43] Erasmus Jones provided *Y Cenhadwr Americanaidd*'s readers with an early example of this kind of discourse, emphasizing the fact that the white colonel and black enlisted men were 'sleeping . . . together' (*hun*[o] *ynghyd*). The chaplain was presenting Welsh-Americans with a more sombre version of what John Morgan described as a 'family' (*teulu*).

Also like John Morgan, Erasmus Jones described the manner in which his comrades strove to attain the literacy which slavery had denied them.

> Mae yn dra hysbys i ddarllenwyr y *Cenhadwr* . . . fod y caethion druain yn cael eu dwyn i fyny yn hollol amddifad o addysg. Ie cospir i'r eithaf bawb a geir yn euog o addysgu y caethwas yn ei 'A B C.' Mae yn wir fod rhyw nifer fach o honynt wedi *lladratta* ychydig o addysg, er gwaethaf eu cyfreithiau; ond nid yw y rhai 'n gymaint ag un o gant. . . . O fel y maent yn sychedu am wybodaeth! Ac y mae y cynydd a wnant o dan yr amgylchiadau, yn ganmoladwy dros ben. Pan ddaethant o'r gaethglud, ni wyddent lythyren ar lyfr. Mae nifer mawr o honynt yn awr yn darllen ac yn ysgrifenu hefyd; ac mae nifer mwy [o] honynt yn 'cyrchu at y nod'[.][44]

> 'It is very well known to the *Cenhadwr*'s readers . . . that the poor slaves are brought up completely deprived of education. Truly, anybody found guilty of teaching a slave his ABCs is punished to the utmost. It is true that some small number have *stolen* a little education, despite their laws; but these are not as many as one in a hundred. . . . Oh how they thirst for knowledge! And the progress which they make under the circumstances is extremely praiseworthy. When they came out of slavery, they could not recognize one letter in a book. Now a great number of them read and write as well; and a greater number of them are "moving towards the target"[.]'

Jones was helping hundreds of men in their transition from slavery to free life, and the text which he published in the *Cenhadwr* underscored the importance of that undertaking. Erasmus Jones had been serving as a minister in Oneida County for over fifteen years, and, like a number of Welsh America's more prominent religious leaders, he was able to travel back to Wales in order to conduct a preaching tour in the 1850s. These facts would have been known to the journal's readers, adding dramatic weight to the description of his service with the 21st US Colored Infantry: 'Mae'n lled debyg na fu eto adeg er pan wyf yn y weinidogaeth mwy manteisiol imi fod yn ddefnyddiol i fy nghyd-ddynion na'r adeg bresenol'; 'It is most likely that there has never been a time since I first started in the ministry better suited for me to be useful to my fellow men than the present.'[45]

Lewis Williams, another Welsh-American who helped African-American soldiers attain literacy, described his work in similar terms: 'ni fuom mewn gwaith mwy difyr erioed'; 'we were never engaged in more pleasing work.'[46] The Revd Ben Chidlaw seemed to be everywhere during the war, travelling extensively with the Union army in the service of a number of causes, including the Sunday school movement, temperance and abolition. Chidlaw also worked with the network of freedmen's aid societies, channelling resources provided by the Welsh of his home state, Ohio, to former slaves.[47] This project brought him into contact with the Revd J. W. Campbell, who was serving as chaplain with a coloured regiment operating in the west. A translation of Campbell's letter of thanks was published in *Y Cenhadwr Americanaidd*: 'Cymeraf hyfrydwch mawr mewn cydnabod derbyniad y gist o Lyfrau (*Primers*) a ddanfonwyd genych i'r gatrawd hon'; 'I take great pleasure in acknowledging the receipt of a chest of Books (Primers) which you sent to this regiment.'[48] Like the letter which Erasmus Jones published in the same journal, this text assured the *Cenhadwr*'s readers that former slaves were 'striving to garner the knowledge which others tried to keep from them *by law*' ('yn ymdrechu casglu y wybodaeth a geisiwyd ei chadw oddiwrthynt *trwy gyfraith*') while also noting 'that they were making good soldiers – that fact has been proved enough' ('eu bod yn gwneud milwyr da – mae'r ffaith hono wedi ei phrofi yn ddigonol').[49]

In addition to publishing this letter in *Y Cenhadwr Americanaidd*, Robert Everett included his own note, adding the weight of his editorial authority to the momentum which missionaries like Chidlaw had achieved. He urged other Welsh-American communities to follow the example of the Ohioans:

> *Anwyl Gymry* yn mhob Sefydliad Cymreig yn America, Deffrown i gymeryd rhan yn y gwaith hwn o ddarparu at addysgu y miloedd a ddeuant yn rhydd o'u cadwynau y dyddiau rhyfedd hyn, y rhai y mae yr angen mwyaf arnynt am gael eu haddysgu. Onid ein dyledswydd a'n braint fel cenedl Gristionogol a chrefyddol ydyw hyn?[50]
>
> 'Dear Welsh People in every Welsh Settlement in America, Let us awaken to take part in this work of preparing for the education of the thousands who are being freed from their chains these wondrous days, those who have the greatest need of being educated. Is this not our duty and our privilege as a Christian and religious nation?'

Another Welsh-American minister who had 'awakened' to this work was the Revd Jonathan E. Thomas, who was taking part in an important project in Arkansas by the start of 1864. Like the better publicized 'Port Royal Experiment', entire families of former slaves were organizing a new, free community, and they were guarded from Confederate raiders by regiments of coloured troops. Thomas discussed the venture on the pages of *Y Cenhadwr Americanaidd*.

> Yr amcan yw gwneud treial ar y dynion duon i gynal eu hunain. Yr oedd dadleu mawr gan wahanol swyddwyr yn y fyddin ar y pen hwn. Er mwyn gwneuthur prawf aethum yn feichiai iddynt, er cael y gwahanol arfau i gario ymlaen eu gorchwylion, gwerth $300. Cymerodd hyn le er's tua deufis yn ol; ac yr wyf yn awr gwedi talu pob cent, a chenyf arian dros ben, ac y mae y General wedi ysgrifenu i Washington yr wythnos ddiweddaf fy mod wedi gwneud y prawf ac wedi ei ddwyn i ben yn llwyddiannus. Y mae genyf filwyr o'r bobl dduon yma i'n hamddiffyn . . . Gwragedd a phlant yw llawer o'r rhai sydd dan fy ngofal – mae y rhan fwyaf o'r gwyr yn filwyr . . . Yr ydwyf yn cael llawer o bleser crefyddol gyda hwy. Os byddaf byw ychydig amser yn eu plith yr ydwyf yn bwriadu ffurfio eglwys yma, os yr Arglwydd a'i myn.[51]

> 'The intention is to conduct a trial as to whether the black men can support themselves. There were great arguments amongst the various officers in the army on this subject. In order to conduct a test I went as surety for them, in order to get different tools for carrying on their tasks, worth $300. This took place two months ago; and I have now paid every cent, and I have money left over, and the General has written to Washington last week saying that I have conducted the test and have concluded it successfully. We have black soldiers here to defend us . . . Many of those in my care are women and children – the majority of the men are soldiers . . . I have a great deal of religious pleasure with them. If I [am able to] live a little time among them, I plan to form a church here, if the Lord desires it.'

Thomas added that, with the help of a Quaker schoolteacher from Ohio, they were also helping the former slaves to learn to read.[52]

Like Erasmus Jones, all these writers were creating a printed record of the fact that the coloured troops with whom they were working were individuals 'for whom respect was due' ('parch i'r hwn y mae parch yn ddyledus'). These Welsh-Americans stressed that, in addition to earning respect on the battlefield, former slaves were earning respect by taking hold of their own destiny and acquiring the education which would serve them in their new, free lives after the war. The manner in which they interpreted the unfolding history of African-American soldiers bears a relationship to the way in which Welsh-American writers were interpreting their own participation in the Civil War; it was a way of proving irrefutably that they had earned United States citizenship.

Robert Everett, in urging Welsh-Americans to aid those chaplains and missionaries working with former slaves, asked his readers to meet the challenge of what he called 'y dyddiau rhyfedd hyn', 'these wondrous days'. Ysgallen, writing from Cincinnati's Lane Seminary, described that charged period as the 'dawning' of 'y mil blynyddoedd', 'the millennium'. Erasmus Jones, who was witnessing with his own eyes the feats achieved by former slaves on the battlefield, also described the period of history in which he was living in millennialistic terms. His fiery description of 'Jehovah's chastising rod', quoted earlier in this study, is, in fact, contained in the epistle which Jones published in the *Cenhadwr* describing his service with the 21st US Colored Infantry. It is worth quoting it again here:

> Mae Duw mewn modd rhyfeddol wedi bod yn goruwch lywodraethu yn y rhyfel hwn. Nid wyf yn meddwl fod yr Arglwydd wedi bod yn cynhyrfu caethfeistri y De i gyfodi yn erbyn y llywodraeth. O'r 'pwll diwaelod' y daeth hyn. Ond mae y Brenhin mawr wedi arfaethu goruwchlywodraethu eu cynddaredd er ei ogoniant, yn *rhyddhad y caethion* yn ogystal a chospi eu gorthrymwyr. Mae yr Unol Daleithau yn awr, y Gogledd fel y De, o dan wialen geryddol Jehofa. Mae gwaedd wylofus pedair miliwn o eneidiau 'dros ba rai y bu Crist farw' wedi cryhaedd clustiau Arglwydd y lluoedd ac wedi llwyddo yn y llys fry. Lled gyndyn ydym wedi bod, mae'n wir, i gydnabod llais Jehofa uwch ein penau yn gwaeddi 'torrwch bob iau a gollwngwch y gorthrymedig yn rhydd!' Bu gorfod i Dduw lindagu y llywodraeth cyn iddi addaw gwneud cyfiawnder â'r negro. Diolch iddo, hyd yn oed am *geryddon*! Credaf fod ein 'hymwared yn agoshau.' Caiff ein gwlad ei 'hadgenedlu drachefn i obaith bywiol'. O'r bedydd gwaed, cawn 'gyfodi i newydd-deb buchedd.' Ar ol y gwyntyllio ofnadwy ceir ni yn wenith mwy pur, a deuwn allan o'r 'ffwrn danllyd boeth' fel aur wedi ei buro trwy dân.[53]

> 'God has in a wondrous fashion been supremely directing [things] in this war. I do not mean that the Lord has been motivating the South's slave-masters to rise up against the government. It is from 'the bottomless pit' that this came. But the great King has arranged supremely to direct their rage for his glory, [turning it into] *freedom for the slaves* as well as punishing their oppressors. The United States now, the North and South alike, are under Jehovah's chastising rod. The doleful cry of four million souls "for whom Christ died" has reached the ears of the Lord of hosts and has been heard in the court on high. We have been fairly reluctant, it's true, to recognize Jehovah's voice above us crying "sever every yoke and set the oppressed free!" God had to strangle the government before it would promise to do justice to the negro. Thank Him, even for *chastisements*! I believe that our "deliverance is growing near". Our land will be "born again to living hope". From this baptism of blood we will be able "to awaken to the newness of life". After this horrible winnowing we will be found to be purer wheat, and we will come out of the "hot fiery furnace" like gold purified by fire.'

Like those other abolitionists who employed the resources of evangelical Protestantism in producing a millennialistic interpretation of the war, Erasmus Jones viewed the bloodshed as a tortuous fire ignited by God in order to cleanse the country of the sin of slavery. He describes this process as working towards a moral purity, likening an idealized post-war nation to the 'purer wheat' which is had after the chaff is removed and to 'gold purified by fire'. During the war – and for a long time afterwards – racist Americans in the North as well as the South were equating steps taken to promote the rights of African Americans with what they saw as a loss of national 'purity'. The Revd

Jones is suggesting the exact opposite; he writes that 'freedom for the slaves' and the kind of equality suggested by Shaw's interment with his soldiers was part of God's way of moving the United States towards purity.

To this end, Erasmus Jones connected the service rendered by coloured regiments in South Carolina to the broader military context, what he called 'the glorious news which is heard from the Union armies' ('y newyddion gogoneddus y clywir oddiwrth fyddinoedd yr Undeb').[54] Like the recent victories achieved by Northern forces in other parts of the country, the work being accomplished by the 21st U. S. Colored Infantry in South Carolina was proof that the end was near:

> Fel hyn mae colofnau *Rebeldom* y naill ar ol y llall yn cwympo ac yn fuan daw yr hen adeilad pwdr i lawr bendramwnwgl y'nghanol banllefau gorfoleddus miliwnau o feibion Affrica, 'A'u holl gadwynau'n chwilfriw mân.'[55]
>
> 'It is like this that the pillars of Rebeldom are falling, the one after the other, and soon the old rotten building will come down in a heap amidst the joyous cries of millions of Africa's sons, "With all of their chains in tiny fragments." '

Three years before Erasmus Jones published this piece in *Y Cenhadwr Americanaidd*, another Welsh-speaking Union chaplain, Franklin Jones, had written to the same journal in order to ask for missionaries to work with the South's recently freed slaves. As was discussed at the start of this chapter, Reverend Jones reproduced for the *Cenhadwr*'s readers a detailed essay which praised the religious culture which slaves had managed to create and maintain while in bondage.[56] In addition to describing the manner in which the 'sons of Africa' ('[m]eibion Affrica') regularly 'extended their beseeching hands . . . to God' ('estyn eu dwylaw erfyniol . . . at Dduw'), that piece discussed their enslaved condition using language which evoked the 'the terrible wilderness' ('y ddiffeithfa arswydol') in which the Israelites of Exodus had found themselves.[57]

In describing the 'devotional hymns' sung by those (former) slaves, that essay quoted a popular phrase which also indexed the biblical enslavement of God's people in Egypt: 'Go down to Egypt – tell Pharaoh / Thus saith my servant Moses, Let my people go.'[58] The readers of the Welsh-American journal were thus asked to consider the liberating power of poetry, the manner in which emotionally charged words like these could 'sound a note of continual warning in the ears of oppression' ('swni[o] nod o rybudd parhaus yn nghlustiau gormes').[59] Three years later, *Y Cenhadwr Americanaidd* was offering its readers Erasmus Jones's observations on men whom he also called 'sons of Africa', men who had replaced the chains of slavery with the free soldier's weapons. This chaplain referred to the hymns of freedom as well, prophesying that the end of the war would be accompanied by 'banllefau gorfoleddus miliwnau o feibion Affrica', 'the joyous cries of millions of Africa's sons'. And for Erasmus Jones, the arming of this African Exodus was a central part of the process which was pulling down the 'pillars' of the slave-holding Pharaoh's 'rotten' temples.

NOTES

1 *Y Cenhadwr Americanaidd*, October 1861. The letter was sent from 'Camp Butler', Newport News, Virginia. Significantly, the Union General Benjamin Butler after whom this camp was named was at this time developing the practice which would label these former slaves as 'contraband of war', thus allowing them to retain their freedom. See, for example, James M. McPherson, *Crossroads of Freedom* [:] *Antietam: The Battle That Changed the Course of the American Civil War* (London, 2003), p. 63.

2 Compare Joseph T. Glatthaar, *Forged in Battle* [:] *The Civil War Alliance of Black Soldiers and White Officers* (Baton Rouge, 1990), pp. 224–5.

3 *Y Cenhadwr Americanaidd*, October 1861.

4 Ibid. The original was composed by the Revd L. C. Lockwood. The lengthy letter was translated and published, apparently in its entirety, in this number of the *Cenhadwr*. Jones notes that Lockwood sent it to him on 4 September 1861.

5 Lewys Glyn Dyfi published similar observations in *Yr Eurgrawn Wesleyaidd*, March 1863. As Welsh America's Wesleyans did not have their own journal, writers like Lewys Glyn Dyfi at times used their denomination's journal in Wales, sometimes publishing in a special column for American news.

6 *Y Cenhadwr Americanaidd*, July 1864.

7 Ibid.

8 Ibid.

9 Papers in the collection of Michael Everett.

10 *Y Cenhadwr Americanaidd*, May 1863.

11 See, for example, Dudley Taylor Cornish, *The Sable Arm* [:] *Black Troops in the Union Army, 1861–1865* (Lawrence [Kansas], 1987), pp. 95–6.

12 *Douglass' Monthly*, May 1861.

13 Joseph T. Glatthaar, *Forged in Battle*, pp. 11–33.

14 Ibid., pp. 6–7

15 Quoted in Joseph T. Glatthaar, *Forged in Battle*, p. 7.

16 Dudley Taylor Cornish, *The Sable Arm*, p.xiv.

17 *Y Drych*, 11 April 1863. The letter itself was written on 12 March.

18 The phrase 'band of brothers', or at least its application to a group of soldiers serving together, seems to have originated with the Saint Crispian's Day speech in Shakespeare's *The Life of Henry the Fifth*, IV.iii; G. Blakemore Evans *et al* (eds), *The Riverside Shakespeare* (Boston, 1974), p. 960.

19 *Y Drych*, 11 April 1863.

20 Ibid.

21 See, for example, Noah Andre Trudeau, *Like Men of War* [:] *Black Troops in the Civil War 1862–1865* (Boston, 1998), p. xvi.

22 E. Hughes *et al* (eds), *Hanes Cymry Minnesota* (Mankato, 1895), pp. 162–3.

23 *Y Drych*, 9 May 1863.

24 Ibid.
25 *Y Cenhadwr Americanaidd*, July 1863.
26 Ibid.
27 The letters of John Griffith Jones, National Library of Wales Manuscript 22421D.
28 Ibid.
29 Joseph T. Glatthaar, *Forged in Battle*, p. 180.
30 Erasmus Jones might have ended up with this specific regiment because of a pre-war acquaintance; Augustus Bennett, the 21st US Colored Infantry's lieutenant colonel was, like Jones, from Oneida County, New York. See Donald M. Wisnoski, *The Opportunity is at Hand* [:] *Oneida County, New York Colored Soldiers in the Civil War* (Lynchburg, 2003), p. 66.
31 *Black River and Northern New York Conference Memorial*, vol. III (May, 1923), p. 362.
32 Ibid, pp. 362–3.
33 Ibid. pp. 363–4.
34 *Y Cenhadwr Americanaidd*, November 1864.
35 The parenthetical question mark, (?), was included by Jones (or by his editor, Robert Everett) in the original, obviously a way of expressing dissatisfaction with the very idea that one person could be considered to 'own' another.
36 *Y Cenhadwr Americanaidd*, November 1864.
37 Ibid.
38 Noah Andre Trudeau, *Like Men of War*, p. 72.
39 New York *Tribune*, 18 September 1865, quoted in James M. McPherson, *The Negro's Civil War* (New York, 2003), p. 195.
40 James Russell Lowell, 'Memoriae Positum R. G. Shaw', in H. E. Scudder (ed.), *The Complete Poetical Works of James Rusell Lowell*; Ralph Waldo Emerson, 'Voluntaries', *The Atlantic Monthly* (September, 1863).
41 *Y Cenhadwr Americanaidd*, November 1864.
42 Joseph T. Glatthaar, *Forged in Battle*, p. 140. See also the letters which James Henry Gooding, one of the 54th's soldiers, was publishing at the time in the New Bedford (Massachusetts) *Mercury*; Virginia M. Adams (ed.), *On the Altar of Freedom* [:] *A Black Soldier's Civil War Letters from the Front* (Amherst, 1991).
43 Robert Lowell's 'On the Union Dead' war first published in *The Atlantic Monthly*, November 1960. Paul Lawrence Dunbar's 'Robert Gould Shaw' quoted from Richard Marius (ed.) and Keith Frome (associate ed.), *The Columbia Book of Civil War Poetry* (New York, 1994), p. 312.
44 *Y Cenhadwr Americanaidd*, November 1864.
45 Ibid.
46 *Y Cenhadwr Americanaidd*, June 1864. Williams was a college student living in New Haven, Connecticut; according to the piece which he published in the *Cenhadwr*, he and his fellow-students (of both Yale College and the 'Seminary') helped educate the soldiers of the 19th Connecticut Volunteers (Colored).
47 Before the end of the war a number of charities were formed in the North to aid former slaves, including the National Freedmen's Relief Association, the Western Freedmen's Aid Commission, and the New England Freedmen's Aid Society. See James M. McPherson, *Battle Cry of Freedom* [:] *The American Civil War* (Oxford, 1988), pp. 709–70.
48 *Y Cenhadwr Americanaidd*, August 1863.
49 Ibid.
50 Ibid.

[51] *Y Cenhadwr Americanaidd*, March 1864.
[52] Ibid.
[53] *Y Cenhadwr Americanaidd*, November 1864.
[54] *Y Cenhadwr Americanaidd*, November 1864.
[55] Ibid.
[56] *Y Cenhadwr Americanaidd*, October 1861.
[57] Ibid.
[58] Ibid.
[59] Ibid.

12

'Heroic Descendants of the Ancient Britons . . . Remember the Eighth of November!': The Election of 1864

Erasmus Jones's letter describing the war as a divine 'fire' designed to 'purify' the nation's metal appeared in *Y Cenhadwr Americanaidd* on 1 November 1864, exactly one week before the presidential election. The vast majority of Welsh-Americans had voted Republican in 1856 and 1860, and the Revd Jones was doing his bit to ensure that 1864 would be no different.

> Unwaith eto, yr ydym yn ymyl etholiad llywyddol, a barnwyf mai dyma yr un mwyaf pwysig o un etholiad a fu yn ein gwlad erioed. Mae ein hiachawdwriaeth, neu ynte ein darostyniad oesol, *fel gwlad*, yn crogi wrth ddydd yr etholiad – yr 8fed o Dachwedd nesaf. Mae y mwyafrif o flaenoriaid y blaid a enwasant G. B. McClellan fel ymgeisydd, yn *fradwyr trwyadl* yn eu calonau. 'Wrth eu ffrwythau yr adnabyddwch hwynt.' Mae pob buddugoliaeth o eiddo byddinoedd yr Undeb yn dristwch i'w heneidiau, tra y dirgel *orfoleddant* pan glywant rywbeth yn ffafriol o fyddin *Jeff Davis*.[1]

> 'Once again, we are nearing a presidential election, and I judge that this is the most important election which has ever been in our country. Our salvation, or else our eternal subjugation *as a country* hangs upon election day – the 8th of November. The majority of the party which has named G. B. McClellan as a candidate are *thorough traitors* in their hearts. "You shall know them by their fruits." Each of the Union armies' victories is a sadness to their souls, while they secretly *rejoice* when they hear something favourable concerning the army of *Jeff Davis*.'

In addition to nominating George B. McClellan as their presidential candidate, the Democratic Party had offered him to voters on a platform which called for an immediate end to the war. In the words of James McPherson, the Democrats were making 'peace the first priority and Union a distant second'.[2] Their election platform also contained a 'pledge to preserve "the rights of the States unimpaired"' which, McPherson adds, was 'a code phrase for slavery'.[3]

During the 1862 mid-term elections, a small group of Welsh Democrats had produced *Yr Amserau*, an abortive paper which sank immediately without trace.[4] Just as the failure of *Y Gwron Democrataidd* ('The Democratic Hero') in 1856 helped ensure that the Republicans would have a free run on the pages of the Welsh-American press in 1860, so the failure of the Democrats' 1862 venture was followed by silence in 1864. Whatever the number of Welsh-speaking Democrats by November 1864, the surviving print record contains little evidence of their activities. Had there been Democrats willing to answer Erasmus Jones in print, they surely would have refused the label of 'traitor', arguing that – as an opposition party contesting an election in a democracy – they had the right to offer a different vision for the country's future. It is equally certain that Erasmus Jones would have ignored any such arguments. Jones had been committed to abolition for more than twenty years, and when he wrote his exhortation he was serving with a regiment of former slaves fighting to set other slaves free. Whatever the political reality in 1864, abolitionists like Erasmus Jones were working to realize their vision of an ideal nation, and it was this nation which was being threatened by the Democrats' election platform.

As was seen in the last chapter, the chaplain's letter described a number of allied forces which were pulling down what he called the 'pillars of Rebeldom', including recent Union victories and the fact that former slaves were now being allowed to fight for their own freedom. Continuing his architectural metaphor, Jones suggested that a Republican victory in the 1864 election would knock down the last remaining pillar supporting the crumbling Confederate edifice.

> Bydded i 'old Abe' cael ei ail ethol, a dyma ergyd angeuawl i annibyniaeth y De. Mae y *Confederacy* eisoes bron a syrthio. Mae yn crynu drwyddo draw, a phan welir Lincoln wedi ei ail sefydlu am bedair blynedd yn ychwanegol yn y gadair lywyddol bydd yr Undeb Americanaidd yn *sicr*. Llethir ein gelynion gan *anobaith*, a bydd y gwrthryfel ar ben. O Gymry America! Hiliogaeth wrol yr Hen Frutaniaid, – gelynion cyneddfol caethwasiaeth, cofiwch – cofiwch yr *wythfed o Dachwedd!*[5]

> 'Let "old Abe" be re-elected, and this will be a death blow to the South's independence. The Confederacy is already nearly falling down. It is shaking through and through, and when Lincoln is seen re-established for four more years in the presidential chair the American Union will be *secure*. Our enemies will be overpowered with *despair*, and the rebellion will be at an end. Oh Welsh people of America! Heroic descendants of the Ancient Britons, – instinctive enemies of slavery, remember – remember *the eighth of November!*'

Erasmus Jones was by no means the only writer claiming that Welsh people were naturally or 'instinctively' inclined to be 'enemies of slavery'. Nor was he the only one to describe Welsh-Americans as 'the heroic descendants of the Old Britons'; as has been seen elsewhere in this study, the heroic traditions of medieval Wales were employed by a number of writers and poets as part of the process of creating literary constructions of Welsh-American identity.

The words *Brutaniaid* and *Hen Frutaniaid* are usually rendered as 'Britons' and 'Ancient Britons'. However, they held a powerful range of associated meanings for nineteenth-century Welsh speakers, and the semantic force is not adequately represented in English by referring simply to 'Britons' or 'people of Britain'. Since at least the Middle Ages, Welsh writers had maintained that the *Brutaniaid* derived their name from Brutus, legendary founder of Britain. Given memorable shape in a twelfth-century Latin narrative composed by Geoffrey of Monmouth and presented to medieval and early modern readers in a dizzying number of Welsh versions, 'Brut y Brenhinedd' – the *Brut* or 'History of the Kings' – claimed that Brutus was the first king to rule over the island which was subsequently given his name: Brut-ain or Britain.[6] In addition to reminding Welsh people that they were the original inhabitants of Britain before the coming of the Romans, English and Normans, this tradition presented a conquered people with an imagined heroic past; the legendary descendants of Brutus included a host of gallant figures, most notably King Arthur himself. Erasmus Jones was addressing some of the youngest Welsh-speaking communities on earth – those spread out across the United States – using a term drawn from traditions surrounding what was considered to be the oldest Welsh community, the original inhabitants of the Island of Britain.

Whatever the politics of the 'heroic' warriors of 'the Ancient Britons', the Union's Welsh-speaking soldiers were standing behind 'their old father, Abraham Lincoln'.[7] John Griffith Jones, serving with the 23rd Wisconsin Infantry in Louisiana, described his comrades' view on the election in a letter to his family:

> Y mau y milwyr bron i gyd yn mynd am Lincoln, Abraham. Y mau y bobl yn lled benderfynol mai fo geith ei electo. Os y fo fydd yn enill y dydd gallaf sicrhau iti na fydd fawr o ymladd y tymor nesaf ond amball i guirela o achos mi welant na fydd dim dichon ymladd. Mi fyn yr hen Abe ei ffordd gan [ei] fod wedi dechra.[8]

> 'The soldiers are almost all for Lincoln, Abraham. The people are most determined that he will be elected. If he wins the day I can assure you that there will not be much fighting next season except for an occasional guerrilla, because they will see that nothing will come of fighting. Old Abe will have his way because he has started it.'

This young soldier wrote these sentences on 20 September 1864, about six weeks before the election. He was killed in combat on 5 October, and thus never had a chance to vote. About the same time as news of his death was reaching his family in Wisconsin, the October 1864 issue of *Y Cenhadwr Americanaidd* was reaching readers across the United States and offering them a long letter by the Revd J. D. Jones, chaplain with the 117th New York Infantry. Jones concluded his epistle by referring to the coming election: 'Unig obaith y gelyn yn awr yw llwyddiant y Penau-Copr yn y Gogledd; os etholir *Undebwr* yn Llywydd, pwy bynag fyddo, gwyddant fod eu hachos ar ben'; 'The enemy's only hope now is the success of the copperheads in the North; if a *Unionist* is elected President, whoever he may be, they know that their cause is lost.'[9]

While soldiers such as John Griffith Jones and Erasmus Jones continued to invoke Lincoln by name, proudly declaring him to be their chosen leader or 'father', the fact that this chaplain avoided the president's name, resorting instead to the qualifying statement 'whoever [the elected Unionist] may be', might have been related to recent tensions experienced within the ranks of Northern abolitionists. Many anti-slavery campaigners still felt that Lincoln was not doing enough for the (former) slaves, and 'these radicals met in Cleveland on May 31, 1864 to nominate John C. Frémont for the presidency on a platform of equal rights for the Negroes of the South'.[10] This third party option soon disappeared, however, when Frémont withdrew from the race in order to clear the way for Lincoln to defeat McClellan. Frederick Douglass himself had given public support to Fremont, yet by the middle of September he too had returned to Lincoln's camp.[11]

Perhaps significantly, Welsh America's abolitionists had for the most part remained silent regarding Fremont's challenge to Lincoln. As was seen in the last chapter's discussion of Isaac Cheshire's political commentaries, many Welsh-American writers turned a blind eye to the fact that Lincoln did not actually support the kind of abolition which they espoused. It is true that some voiced criticism prior to 1863; as was seen in Chapter Ten, Dewi Emlyn suggested that the pre-Emancipation Proclamation Lincoln was similar to the Pharaoh of Exodus, while Laura Griffiths expressed the 'jealousy' of the abolitionist who was forced to witness a Civil War not linked directly to the anti-slavery cause.[12] However, the majority followed Isaac Cheshire and either attributed the government's cold feet on the issue of emancipation to people other than Lincoln, or simply ignored the political reality. Rather than treating the realities of Lincoln's policies and actions in all of their complexities, these writers opted for an idealized portrait of the president. The Lincoln described by most Welsh-American writers was an icon which they themselves had fashioned, a construct designed to reflect their own interpretation of the war as a struggle which was against slavery as much as it was for Union.

Thus it was only in October 1864 that *Y Seren Orllewinol*'s editor revealed his true feelings; Frémont had withdrawn from the race by that time, and breaking the conspiracy of silence no longer presented a danger to Lincoln's bid for re-election.

> Yr ydym hyd yma wedi ymatal rhag dywedyd nemawr am yr etholiad dyfodol, am y teimlem yn ffafriol i'r Cad. Fremont a'i egwyddorion, ond o'r dechreu yn barnu fod ei etholiad ef ar hyn o bryd yn anghyrhaeddadwy. Ond yn awr gan ei fod ef ei hun wedi amlygu ei ddymuniad i ymneillduo o'r gystadleuaeth, o herwydd ei fod yn rhagweld na fyddai iddo trwy aros ar y maes ond cryfhau y blaid a ystyria yn gefnogol i'r gwrthryfelwyr, nis [sic] oes genym bellach ond dewis rhwng y tocynau Gwerinaidd a Democrataidd, neu rhwng Lincoln . . . a McCleallan . . . Tra yr ydym o'n calon yn pleidio heddwch, nid ydym yn barnu mai ein dyledswydd yw gwneud hyny ar draul sathru egwyddorion cyfiawnder a

> rhyddid. Nid yw gair Duw nac esiampl Iesu Grist yn ein dysgu i wneud hyn: ond barnwn y byddai etholaid McClellan ar yr adeg bresennol yn galondid nid bychan i'r gwrthryfelwyr.[13]
>
> 'We have up until now refrained from saying just about anything regarding the future election, because we felt favourably towards Gen. Fremont and his principles, yet from the start judged that his election was at this time unattainable. But now that he himself has made known his desire to withdraw from the competition, because he foresees that he would by remaining on the field only strengthen the hand of the party he considers as supporting the rebels, we no longer have any choice but to choose between the Republican and Democratic tickets or between Lincoln . . . and McClellan . . . While we support peace from the heart, we do not judge that it is our duty to do that [peace] at the expense of trampling on the principles of justice and freedom. Neither the word of God nor the example of Jesus teaches us to do this: rather we judge that the election of McClellan at the present time would be no small reassurance to the rebels.'

Eight years earlier, when Frémont was standing as the Republican Party's first presidential candidate, the October 1856 issue of the *Y Seren Orllewinol* had been entirely devoted to supporting his campaign. The journal's editor, Richard Edwards, had apparently always remained inclined to support 'Frémont and his principles', yet, despite Lincoln's more moderate stance on slavery, Edwards (like many other abolitionists) had leant his support to Lincoln when the principles of political expediency dictated that he do so.

If the support which the *Seren*'s editor gave the president in 1864 was lukewarm, other sections of Welsh-American society were marshalling energetically in order to help secure Lincoln's re-election. When Pennsylvania's Welsh Congregationalists held their annual assembly in mid-October 1864, they had no qualms about mixing politics with religion.[14] A considerable amount of the denomination's resources were diverted directly into Lincoln's campaign.

> Neillduwyd pwyllgor i sylwi ar sefyllfa'r wlad, a mabwysiadwyd y penderfyniadau canlynol: . . . Ein bod yn ddiolchgar i'r Arglwydd am ei nawdd i Lywydd ein gwlad . . . yn benaf am ei wisgo â chymaint o ddoethineb a phwyll . . . Ein bod yn llawenychu yn ddirfawr yn y goleuni tanbaid a lewyrcha allan yn Nghynllun (*Platform*) Cynadledd Baltimore gyda golwg ar helaethiad rhyddid a llwyr ddilead caethiwed. . . . Yr ymegniwn i sicrhau ailetholiad Abraham Lincoln i lywyddiaeth ein gwlad fel cynrychiolydd yr egwyddorion mawrion o ryddid a chyfartalwch dynoliaeth.[15]
>
> 'A committee was detailed to discuss the situation of the country, and the following resolutions were adopted: . . . That we are thankful to the Lord for his support of our country's President . . . especially for investing him with so much wisdom and intelligence . . . That we take great joy in the fiery light which shines from the Platform of the Baltimore Convention [i.e. the Republican Party

> Convention held earlier that year] with a view to expanding freedom and completely removing slavery. That we shall strive to ensure the re-election of Abraham Lincoln to the presidency of our country as the representative of the great principles of freedom and the equality of humanity.'

Ignoring Fremont altogether (and perhaps ignoring the realties of Lincoln's actions prior to the Emancipation Proclamation), Pennsylvania's Welsh Congregationalists committed themselves to the president, describing Lincoln as the very embodiment of 'freedom' and 'equality'.

When election day came, Welsh America acted in accordance with these writers' wishes. One Wisconsin soldier, Cadwaladr Pugh, recorded a tally of the votes cast in his regiment: '*Tach. 8fed, yn y prydhawn.* – Mae yr etholiad wedi pasio yn ein Catrawd. Rhif y pleidleisiau a roddwyd i mewn oedd 381 – sef 371 i Lincoln a 10 i McClellan'; '*Nov. 8th, in the afternoon.* – The election has passed in our Regiment. The number which was turned in was 381 – namely 371 for Lincoln and 10 for McClellan'.[16] In his discussion of the 1864 election, James McPherson provides a detailed analysis of the soldier vote:

> Twelve of the states allowing absentee voting provided for the separate tabulation of soldier ballots. Lincoln received 119,754 of them to McClellan's 34,291, a majority of 78 per cent for the president compared with 53 per cent of the civilian vote in those states. The absentee soldier-vote majority for Republicans in the other seven states was probably at least as great.[17]

Cadwaladr Pugh served with Company F of the 22nd Wisconsin Infantry, one of the army's Welsh companies. If his comrades can be considered representative of Welsh-speaking soldiers, then it is safe to assume that Welsh-Americans in the army voted for Lincoln at a rate even higher than the 78 per cent majority described by McPherson.

Following the pattern established in 1856 and confirmed in 1860, Welsh-American civilians also voted Republican. At times this support extended beyond simply casting a vote; according to *Y Seren Orllewinol*, Columbia, Pennsylvania, was the scene of rioting the night before the election, as Welsh supporters of Lincoln clashed with Irish Democrats. The violence was resumed on election day itself as a 'man from the Emerald Isle' ('gwr o'r Ynys Werdd') assaulted a Welshman with a bowie knife. According to the *Seren*, the knife-wielding Democrat was 'paid back immediately' and forced 'to go home with his wounds' ('cafodd . . . ei dalu yn ol yn ddioed ac aeth adref dan ei glwyfau').[18]

When Lincoln's victory was announced, there was a considerable amount of celebrating throughout Welsh America. The editor of *Y Cyfaill o'r Hen Wlad* joyously proclaimed that 'the people's verdict' had come down in favour of continuing the Union's war effort.

> Felly mae y Weinyddiaeth bresenol wedi cael ei chefnogi gan lais y wlad yn y modd mwyaf penderfynol; a dedfryd y bobl yw fod y rhyfel presenol i gael ei gario yn mlaen yn egniol yn erbyn y gwrthryfelwyr hyd nes byddant yn barod i ymostwng i'r llywdroaeth haelionus, yn erbyn yr hon y codasant i fyny eu harfau.[19]
>
> 'Thus the present Administration has been supported by the country's voice in the most decisive manner; and the people's verdict is that the present war is to be carried on energetically against the rebels until they are ready to submit to the generous government, against which they took up their weapons.'

The *Cyfaill* also marked the occasion by publishing a celebratory hymn.[20] Like some of those poetic meditations on the Emancipation Proclamation discussed earlier in this study, this hymn eschewed praising Lincoln directly, concentrating instead on the divine 'Leader'.

> Duw, cadw ein gwladwriaeth,
> A'n cyfiawn annibyniaeth,
> Rho wenau dy Ragluniaeth
> Fendithiol ar y wlad;
> Bydd i ni yn Arweinydd,
> Yn Noddwr a Chynnalydd,
> Yn Dduw a thirion Arglwydd,
> Anfeidrol Nefol Dad.[21]
>
> 'God, keep our country,
> And our just independence,
> Let your beneficent Providence
> Smile upon the land;
> Be for us Leader,
> Protector and Supporter,
> God and gentle Lord,
> Eternal Heavenly Father.'

This song, described explicitly as an 'Emyn Cenedlaethol' or 'National Hymn', was apparently meant to be performed publicly following the election; it was published along with suggestions as to the tune to which these words were to be sung.[22]

Like the Calvinistic Methodist who edited *Y Cyfaill o'r Hen Wlad*, the Congregationalist Robert Everett interpreted the election's significance for the readers of his denomination's journal, *Y Cenhadwr Americanaidd*. Amongst other things, he asked Welsh-Americans to consider Lincoln's victory within an international context.

> Llawer o bobl yr Hen Wledydd a dybiant nad oes grym mewn Gweriniaeth, ond mai gyda y Pencoronog y mae grym, ac o herwydd hyny mai dyna y ffurflywodraeth oreu. Ond galwn sylw gwyr yr Hen Wledydd at ein hetholiad Llywyddol yn 1864, er eu hargyhoeddi o'u camgymeriad yn hyn.[23]
>
> 'Many people of the Old Countries think that there is no strength in a Republic, but that it is with the Crowned Head that power lies, and because of this that [a monarchy] is the best form of government. But we call the attention of the men of the Old Countries to our Presidential election in 1864 in order to convince them as to their mistake in this.'

Robert Everett was by no means the only American who desired to call the attention of 'the Old Countries' to Lincoln's success. According to Dean B. Mahin, the president made similar comments himself: 'Lincoln told a crowd at the White House that the election demonstrated to the world the viability of popular republican government.'[24]

Despite the unspecified nature of Everett's reference to the monarchies of 'the Old Countries', it is safe to assume that his readers would have been thinking first and foremost of Queen Victoria's 'Crowned Head'. Britain had been less than supportive of Lincoln during the war, and Welsh immigrants who revelled in what they saw as an escape from an oppressive life in the 'Old Country' were aware of the fact that many British conservatives were looking forward to celebrating the death of the American Republic.

The ways in which writers like Robert Everett discussed the election were conditioned by a mode of discourse which had been established well before November 1864. One recurring theme in the discussion of Welsh-American identity involved equating the Southern slave-owners with the 'aristocrats' who had oppressed the Welsh in Britain. More than twenty years before Everett published his post-election comments, similar ideas had been fielded on the pages of *Y Dyngarwr*, that short-lived journal which he had devoted solely to the causes of temperance and abolition. As was seen in Chapter Two, one writer published an essay in 1843 asking readers to view the struggle against American slavery in the same historical context as 'The Slavery of Wales' ('Caethiwed Cymru'), a condition which, he claimed, had existed ever since the Anglo-Norman conquest of Wales in 1282.[25] In addition to these kinds of extended essays, certain turns of phrase which suggested a conceptual link between the Southern slave-owners and the British aristocracy pervaded Welsh-American writing of the period. Perhaps the best example is a label which Robert Everett often applied to Southern leaders: 'Aristocratiaid y De' – 'the Aristocrats of the South'. Having adopted this expression before the war, he continued to employ it right up to the end of the conflict, constantly asking his readers to view the powers behind the Southern Confederacy in terms which recalled the old social hierarchy of Britain.[26]

English-speaking Americans also referred to the 'Southern Aristocrats', and some of the country's most influential abolitionists incorporated the concept into their own extended meditations on slavery's injustice. For example, in 1861 Wendell Phillips provided a memorable articulation of the view that Southern society was preserving an oppressive medieval system:

> This nation is made up of different ages . . . Not homogeneous, but a mixed class of different centuries. The North *thinks* . . . [it] is the nineteenth century . . . The South dreams, it is the thirteenth and fourteenth century – baron and serf, noble and slave.[27]

America's Welsh writers were by no means the only Northerners who characterized Southern slave-owners as 'aristocrats', yet their articulation of the concept was often coloured with specific, comparative references to Welsh and British history.

Isaac Cheshire presented this kind of argument to *Y Drych*'s readers as part of a comparative, class-based analysis of French, British and American history. The Southern 'aristocracy' maintained its status by oppressing others, and thus Cheshire argued that the ultimate cause of the Civil War was merely an American version of the kind of injustice which had for centuries conveyed wealth and privilege to the aristocrats of Britain and Europe.

> [Y] drwg ydyw na chafodd Gweriniaeth erioed chwareu teg. Y mae ei gelynion mor gyfrwys, maent yn cymeryd eu safle ar yr ochr ddall i ddynoliaeth, a thrwy dwyll geiriau teg, trais a gormes, gyrant y werin i'r ffosydd a baratowyd iddynt yn Ffrainc a Lloegr. Yma yn America, ni fynai caethfeistriaid *Ddemocracy* yr Undeb i deyrnasu arnynt . . . Meddyliwyf hefyd fod yn hen bryd i'r werin – y canolradd a'r iselradd (ein gwir frodyr) yn Lloegr ddechreu gwastadhau pethau yno, yn enwedig pan y gwelir fod yr *aristocracy* yn ceisio gyru cyfranwyr y dorth a'r derbynwyr i benau eu gilydd.[28]

> 'The problem is that Republicanism has never had fair play. Its enemies are so clever, they take their position on the blind side of humanity, and by means of the deceit of fair words, violence and oppression, they drive the common people into the ditches which have been prepared for them in France and England. Here in America, the slave-masters do not want the Union's Democracy to rule them . . . I also think that it is about time for the common people – the middle class and the lower class (our true brothers) in England to begin levelling things there, especially when one sees the aristocracy trying to set the producers of the bread and those who receive it against each other.'

Two words central to his discussion require some explanation. First of all, the term *Gweriniaeth* was used by nineteenth-century writers to mean 'Democracy' as well as 'Republicanism'. Secondly, it is formed from the noun *gwerin*, which also appears in this passage, and which is translated here as 'common people'. This word has an extremely complex history, being used to refer to what

English writers might call the 'folk', the 'masses' or the 'working class'. During the middle of the nineteenth century this term was accruing layers of heightened meaning, and by the century's end it was soundly entrenched in the centre of a field of discourse used to portray the *gwerin* as the heroic farmers and workers of Wales who, despite being poor economically, were the privileged bearers of a wealthy cultural tradition.[29]

The writer calling himself Undebwr – or 'Unionist' – employed the same comparison, using it as part of a sustained attack upon one of the Old Country's papers, *Baner Cymru*, 'The Banner of Wales'. The press in Wales was anti-slavery on the whole, as was stressed in Chapter Six. Moreover, most of the Old Country's newspapers and journals either supported the Union directly or condemned the Confederates for maintaining a war to preserve slavery. There were, however, publications in Wales which broke these ideological ranks, and *Baner Cymru* was one of them; this paper translated and published a number of anti-Union pieces which had appeared in the *London Times*. Thus Undebwr directed his fire across the sea, bombarding the Welsh newspaper with words meant to dismiss it as an 'organ' of the British aristocracy.

> Nid yw yn rhyfeddod fod y *London Times, Herald, Advertizer, etc.*, yn amddiffyn y De, canys *organs* y dosbarthiadau llywodraethol ac aristocrataidd ydynt hwy . . . Ond y mae gweled . . . *Banner Cymru* . . . yn cymeryd ochr y De, yn rhywbeth nad allaf mo'i esponio.[30]

> 'It is no wonder that the *London Times, Herald, Advertizer, etc.*, are defending the South, because they are the organs of the governing classes and the aristocrats . . . But seeing . . . *Baner Cymru* . . . take the side of the South is something which I can not explain.'

Undebwr added that Welsh journalists who followed the line of the English aristocratic press 'were no better than moral and mental slaves to the *London Times* and its brothers!' ('yn ddim amgen na caethion moesol, a meddyliol i'r *London Times* a'i frodyr!').[31] This writer was in many ways ahead of his time; it would be half a century and more before this kind of description of British-English culture's hegemonic pressure upon the public life of Wales would become central to Welsh nationalistic discourse. However, the rhetorical strategies which Undebwr employed were similar to those being adopted by other Welsh-American writers during the Civil War; in addition to attacking the 'aristocracy', he was, by calling the Welsh paper a 'slave' to the *London Times*, enforcing the connection between the Southern slave-owners and the British upper classes.

These writers were providing a markedly *Welsh* articulation of their anti-slavery beliefs. By forging a conceptual link between British aristocrats and 'the aristocracy of the South' they were also creating a meaningful connection between enslaved African Americans and the Welsh people. This highly charged comparison was part of an analytical framework which allowed Welsh-

Americans to hold their interpretation of the Civil War and its causes in productive association with discussions of their own national and culture identity (or identities). Indeed, in addition to providing Welsh-Americans with a way of relating their opposition to slavery to the expression of their own identity, references to the historical oppression of the Welsh people were bound up with another subject central to the allied processes of constructing, analysing and articulating that identity: the reasons which had led immigrants to leave Wales in the first place.

The Civil War years in fact witnessed a flurry of activity centring on the concept of a *glwadychfa Gymreig* or 'Welsh colony'. This was instigated to a large extent by Michael D. Jones, a prominent minister and radical thinker who had travelled to the United States in 1848 because he was 'very eager to understand the advantages and disadvantages which existed for the Welsh in America' ('yn awyddus iawn am ddeall y manteision a'r anfanteision oedd i'r Cymry yn America').[32] After two years in Cincinnati, Michael D. Jones returned to Wales, where he began generating plans for establishing a new Welsh settlement. Rather than throwing his intellectual weight behind one of the Welsh communities already existing in the United States, Jones decided to start a new *gwladychfa* in Patagonia, South America. In addition to spreading the idea back in Wales, Jones published a string of essays in the Welsh-American press designed to garner support for his Patagonian settlement, and he was answered by a number of enraged American writers who argued that, in addition to insulting those people who had been maintaining Welsh-language culture in the United States, he was endangering the future existence of Welsh America.[33]

In April 1863 David James of Minersville, Pennsylvania, entered into the discussion by publishing an essay in *Y Drych* on 'Y Wladychfa Gymreig' ('The Welsh Colony'). Rather than taking any particular side in the struggle between the North American and South American factions, he simply voiced support for the general concept of establishing a homeland for the Welsh away from the oppression which had plagued them in Britain.

> Mae sefyllfa y Cymry yn bresenol yn galw am yr anturiaeth. Gwyddys fod eu cyflwr yn yr hen wlad wedi myned yn anfeddyginiaethol heb i ryw sefydliad Cymreig gael ei wneuthur mewn rhyw barth o'r ddaiar. Yr ydym fel cenedl wedi colli ein gwlad, a chael ein hymlid i'r mynyddoedd a'r creigiau fel geifr gwylltion gan y Saesoniaid, y rhai ydynt wedi meddianu y rhan oreu o'r wlad, ac ydynt wedi ymgyfoethogi ac wedi chwyddo mewn balchder a meddianu bron yr holl ddyffrynoedd a orweddant rhwng y mynyddoedd hyny. . . . Ac nid yn unig y mae epil fradwrus Hengist a Horsa wedi meddianu y dyffrynoedd, ond ymlusgant fel locustiaid dros y bryniau hefyd. Gellir mewn gwirionedd alw miloedd o amaethwyr Cymry yn gaethion i'w meistriaid tir. Rhoddant eu llafur trwy y flwyddyn i gyfoethogi Saeson, pengrymant i foesgyfarch Saeson, talant drethi trymion i gadw Saeson diog a digywilydd, ac nid oes gan Gymry lais teg a phriodol yn ngosodiad y cyfreithiau y rhaid iddynt ymostwng iddynt, gan mai

> Saeson yn y cyffredin sydd yn eu cynrychioli yn y Senedd. Gan mai hwynt ydynt y tirfeddianwyr, rhaid i'r amaethwyr anfon eu meistradoedd i'w cynrychioli . . . er na fydd eu meistriaid hyny yn deall iaith y rhai y cymerant arnynt eu cynrhychioli, nac yn teimlo mwy drostynt nag ydyw y Deheuwyr dros eu caethion crwyndduon[.][34]

> 'The situation of the Welsh at present calls out for the venture. It is known that their condition in the old country has become untreatable, except that some Welsh settlement be created in some part of the earth. We as a nation have lost our country, and we have been driven to the mountains and the cliffs like wild goats by the English, who have taken possession of the best part of the country, and who are growing rich and swelling with pride and taking possession almost entirely of the valleys which lie between those mountains. . . . And not only have the treacherous offspring of Hengist and Horsa taken possession of the valleys, but they slither like locusts over the hills as well. It is possible in truth to call thousands of Welsh farmers slaves of their landlords. They give their labour throughout the year to make the English wealthy, they bow their heads to salute the English, they pay heavy taxes in order to support the lazy and shameless English, and the Welsh do not have a fair and appropriate voice in the creation of the laws to which they must submit, since it is generally English people who represent them in the Parliament. Since they are the landowners, the farmers have to send their masters to represent them . . . even though those masters do not understand the language of those whom they take it upon themselves to represent, nor do they feel any more for them than do the Southerners for their black slaves.'

Like Robert Everett, Isaac Cheshire and Undebwr, David James forged an emotionally charged link connecting the 'English masters' of the Welsh to the Southern slave-masters. In detailing the historical basis for his comparison, this Welsh Pennsylvanian described the English as 'the treacherous offspring of Hengist and Horsa'; he was employing an old tradition which held that these two Anglo-Saxon leaders were responsible for bringing the ancestors of the English to Britain, where they would take the lands of the *Hen Frutaniaid* or 'Ancient Britons'.[35]

As has been seen at a number of junctures in this study, the ways in which Welsh-American writers reacted to the Civil War were at times fuelled by themes and images draw from (what was originally) medieval Welsh history and legend. One young soldier, Thomas D. Thomas, invoked the memory of a thirteenth-century Welsh prince who had fought the invading Anglo-Norman armies; he asked other Welsh-Americans to support the Union cause, suggesting that by fighting the Confederates they could prove their 'relation to the most famous Prince Llywelyn' ('perthyn i'r gorenwog Dywysog Llywelyn').[36] Vermont's most famous Welsh bard, Ionoron Glan Dwyryd, delved even deeper into the past, fashioning a versified call to arms which described Welsh-American volunteers as the sons of 'Arthur, our father' ('Arthur, ein tad'). Ionoron implied that, by 'fighting with the rebellious supporters of Slavery' ('ymladd â phleidwyr gwrthnysig Caethiwed'), they could display the same spirit which had characterized Arthur's fight for the freedom of his people.[37]

Arthur's people were, of course, the 'Ancient Britons' to whom Erasmus Jones referred in his exhortation on the eve of the 1864 election. While twentieth-century historians have suggested that the historical Arthur was more of a battle-leader than a ruler, he has always been known to the people of Wales as 'y Brenin Arthur', 'King Arthur'; moreover, the lineage to which he belonged was conceived of explicitly as a line of kings. Geoffrey of Monmouth's twelfth-century Latin text was called *Historia Regum Britanniae*, 'The History of the Kings of Britain', and the Welsh version which was copied into so many medieval and early modern manuscripts was called *Brut y Brenhinedd*, 'The *Brut*' – or 'History' – 'of the Kings'. It will be remembered that the very word for this kind of text, *Brut* (plural *Brutiau*), was derived from the name Brutus, the first in that legendary line of kings. This fanciful pseudo-history was followed by a kind of historical sequel, 'Brut y Tywysogion', 'The History of the Princes', a chronicle which ends with the death of Llywelyn in 1282 and the Anglo-Norman conquest of Wales. As Dafydd Glyn Jones has stressed, this historiographical tradition focuses to a great extent upon loss; just as the historical sequel ends with the death of the last prince of Wales, so the earlier narrative ends when Cadwaladr, the last of the Ancient Britons' kings, is forced to relinquish his people's hold on the Island of Britain.

> Dyma lle mae Brut y Brenhinedd yn cloi, gydag ymadawiad Cadwaladr . . . yr olaf (fe honnir) o frenhinoedd y Brytaniaid i ddal meddiant yr Ynys . . . Dyma hefyd . . . lle mae Brut y Tywysogion yn dechrau. Nid yw'r gwir hanes yn gwadu'r ffug-hanes. I'r gwrthwyneb, y mae'n ei gymryd yn fan cychwyn ac yn ei asio'i hun wrtho. Fe gawsom gan Sieffre hanes y brenhinoedd, o'r cyntaf hyd yr olaf; bydd y Brut arall yn rhoi inni hanes y tywysogion, hyd yr olaf eto . . . hyd 1282.[38]
>
> 'This is where The Brut of the Kings ends, with the departure of Cadwaladr . . . the last (it is claimed) of the kings of the Britons to hold possession of the Island . . . This also . . . is where the Brut of the Princes begins. The real history does not deny the pseudo-history. To the contrary, it takes it as its starting place and grafts itself onto it. From Geoffrey we had the history of the kings, from the first to the last; the other Brut will give us the history of the princes, from the first to the last again . . . up to 1282.'

The substantial body of (pseudo-)history contained in these two closely associated texts was recycled throughout the early modern period, providing the basis for a series of extremely popular books, including Theophilus Evans's *Drych y Prif Oesoedd* (1716 and 1740).[39] Despite being laced with fantastical embellishments and romantic exaggerations, this historiographical tradition preserved a truth which was extremely meaningful to successive generations of Welsh readers; it reminded them that their ancestors were the original inhabitants of both Britain and Wales, and that they had been displaced and dispossessed by a series of invasions and occupations. This loss, or series of losses, was almost always remembered in terms of losing kingship. As Dafydd Glyn Jones summarizes by highlighting a phrase central to the *Brutiau*: ' "Colli coron teyrnas," dyna sy'n brifo o hyd'; ' "The loss of a realm's crown", that is what always hurts.'[40]

All the writers mentioned in this chapter – and all the Welsh-American writers discussed in this book – would've been aware of this historiographical tradition. Indeed, many of them would have read (and perhaps owned) books such as *Drych y Prif Oesoedd*. This version of their people's past provided nineteenth-century writers with robust models for constructing or re-constructing Welsh identity, and Welsh-speaking Americans such as Thomas D. Thomas, Ionoron Glan Dwyryd and Erasmus Jones utilized the cultural resources provided by this tradition while interpreting what the Civil War meant in terms of Welsh-American identity. Recycling elements of this regal history provided these writers with a means of articulating their interpretations of the relationship between the war and Welsh America; however, while invoking King Arthur and Prince Llywelyn, they were supporting anything but the concept of monarchical rule. On the contrary, as is exemplified by several texts discussed in this chapter, the ideological constellation constructed and maintained by Welsh America's war-time writers also included a pronounced commitment to republicanism, a belief that electing a president democratically was better than deferring to what Robert Everett called a *Pencoronog* or 'Crowned Head'. The 'Ancient Britons' may have been ruled by a line of kings, but when Erasmus Jones asked their 'heroic descendants' to turn out for Lincoln he was addressing a people who were committed to the principle of republicanism.

NOTES

1 *Y Cenhadwr Americanaidd*, November 1864.
2 James M. McPherson, *Battle Cry of Freedom* [:] *The American Civil War* (Oxford, 1988), p. 772.
3 Ibid., p. 772.
4 See Chapter Six, pages 237–8.
5 *Y Cenhadwr Americanaidd*, November 1864.
6 See, for example, Brynley F. Roberts, *Brut y Brenhinedd* (Dublin, 1971), pp. ix–xxxi.
7 See the Prologue, pages vi–viii.
8 The letters of John Griffith Jones, National Library of Wales Manuscript 22421D.
9 *Y Cenhadwr Americanaidd*, October 1864.
10 James M. McPherson, *The Negro's Civil War* (New York, 2003), p. 307.
11 James M. McPherson, *The Negro's Civil War* (New York, 2003), p. 310; see also William S. McFeely, *Frederick Douglass* (New York, 1991), pp. 231–5.
12 See Chapter Ten, pages 388–95.
13 *Y Seren Orllewinol*, October 1864.
14 *Y Cenhadwr Americanaidd*, December 1864.

15 Ibid.
16 *Y Cenhadwr Americanaidd*, September 1865.
17 James M. McPherson, *Battle Cry of Freedom*, p. 804.
18 *Y Seren Orllewinol*, November 1864.
19 *Y Cyfaill o'r Hen Wlad*, December 1864.
20 *Y Cyfaill o'r Hen Wlad*, November 1864. 'Berwyn' was the poet's bardic name; his or her real identity is not known.
21 Ibid.
22 Ibid. 'Mae Alaw ar y mesur hwn gan J. Ambrose Lloyd wedi ei gyhoeddi yn Rhif. I. "Greal y Corau." '
23 *Y Cenhadwr Americanaidd*, December 1864.
24 Dean B. Mahin, *One War at a Time* [:] *The International Dimensions of the American Civil War* (Washington, 1999), p. 245.
25 See Chapter Two, page 66.
26 See, for example, *Y Cenhadwr Americanaidd*, January 1865.
27 Quoted by Melinda Lawson, *Patriot Fires* [:] *Forging a New American Nationalism in the Civil War North* (Lawrence [Kansas], 2002), pp. 136–7.
28 Y Drych, 9 May 1863
29 *Geiriadur Prifysgol Cymru* (Cardiff, 1950–2002), p. 1643.
30 *Y Drych*, 10 January 1863.
31 Ibid.
32 E. Pan Jones, *Oes a Gwaith M. D. Jones, Bala* (Bala, 1903), p. 31.
33 See, for example, 'Iwan' in *Y Drych*, 4 April 1864. For a discussion of this passage within the broader context of Welsh-American identity, see Jerry Hunter, 'Y Traddodiad Llenyddol Coll', *Taliesin* (Spring, 2003).
34 *Y Drych*, 25 April 1863.
35 A range of medieval and early modern texts name Horsa and Hengist as the leaders of the Saxon invasion. For example, one of the 'Triads of the Island of Britain' describes the 'Three Oppressions that came to this Island, and not one of them went back', citing 'the Saxons, with Horsa and Hengist as their leaders' as the 'third Oppression'. See Rachel Bromwich (ed. and trans.), *Trioedd Ynys Prydein* (Cardiff, 1978), pp. 84, 159 and 406–7. According to *Geiriadur Prifysgol Cymru*, by the middle of the nineteenth century several Welsh words formed from the name Hengist were being used to denote Englishness; *Hengistaidd*, 'English' or 'Anglicized' (first attested in 1837), and *Hengistiaith*, 'the English language' (*c.* 1820). *Geiriadur Prifysgol Cymru* (Cardiff, 1950–2002), p. 1852.
36 See Chapter Three, page 142.
37 See Chapter Three, pages 137–41.
38 Dafydd Glyn Jones, *Agoriad yr Oes* [:] *erthyglau ar lên, hanes a gwleidyddiaeth Cymru* (Talybont, 2001), p. 72.
39 The title of Theophilus Evans's *Drych y Prif Oesoedd* translates as 'A Mirror of the Primary Ages'. See Gwyn Thomas, 'Two Prose Writers: Ellis Wynne and Theophilus Evans', in Branwen Jarvis (ed.), *A guide to Welsh literature c. 1700–1800* (Cardiff, 2000), pp. 55–62; Dafydd Glyn Jones, *Agoriad yr Oes*, pp. 10–43.
40 Dafydd Glyn Jones, *Agoriad yr Oes*, p. 73.

13

'The Ashes of Nations': Endings and Beginnings

Erasmus Jones wrote his exhortation to 'the heroic descendants of the Ancient Britons' while encamped on Morris Island, South Carolina. The regiment which he served as chaplain, the 21st US Colored Infantry, was taking part in the siege of Charleston. This city was a potent symbol of everything which they were fighting against; Charleston's cannons had fired the opening shots in the Civil War, handing the Confederacy its first military victory with the surrender of Fort Sumter. It also had one of the South's largest concentrations of businesses trading in slaves; in fact, a number of the soldiers serving with Erasmus Jones were 'formerly slaves in the city of Charleston'.[1] Like the rest of his regiment, the Welsh-American chaplain was eagerly anticipating the city's fall.

> Oddeutu pedair neu bum' milldir i'r deorllewin gwelwn *Charleston*. Dyma'r fan lle y ganwyd ac y magwyd y gwrthryfel presenol; ac nid anghyson y gelwir hi 'The cradle of Rebellion'. Erbyn heddyw mae ei gorwychder wedi ei ddarostwng, a'i uncheldrem wedi ei ddwyn i'r llwch. . . . gobeithiaf yn lled hyderus, y caf y pleser *anraethol* o ysgrifenu ychydig o lythyrau i'm teulu o ddinas Charleston.[2]

> 'About four or five miles to the south-west we can see *Charleston*. This is the place where the present rebellion was born and raised; and it is not inconsistent that it is called "The cradle of Rebellion". By today its splendour has been subdued, and its ambition has been turned to ashes. . . . I hope fairly confidently that I will have the *indescribable* pleasure of writing a few letters to my family from the city of Charleston.'

In addition to having that 'indescribable pleasure', the former slaves with whom Erasmus Jones served were to be the first Union soldiers to march through the streets of Charleston after the Confederates yielded the city in February 1865. A reporter for the *Boston Evening Journal*, Charles Coffin, was there to describe the event:

> With the old flag above them, its fadeless stars and crimson folds waving in the . . . breeze, keeping step to freedom's drumbeat, up the grass grown streets, past the slave marts where their wives and children, their brothers and fathers, where they themselves had been sold in the public stables, laying aside their arms, working the fire engines to extinguish the flames, and in the spirit of the redeemer of men, saving that which was lost.[3]

It is not known whether Erasmus Jones described the scene in writing himself; no such text has been uncovered by present research. However, when readers of *Y Cenhadwr Americanaidd* received news of Charleston's fall, they could turn to that letter which the chaplain had published three months earlier and say, with his words, that the Confederacy's 'old rotten building' was at last 'coming down in a heap' ('daw yr hen adeilad pwdr i lawr bendramwnwgl').[4]

William Tecumseh Sherman was the Union general in charge of the war in the Carolinas, and he was praised extensively on the pages of the Welsh-American press. One poet, Daniel Thomas, published 'Verses which were composed while the General W. T. Sherman was taking the Rebellion out of Charleston, South Carolina' ('Pennillion a gyfansoddwyd pan ydoedd y Cad. W. T. Sherman yn dwyn y Gwrthryfel allan o Charleston, S. C.').[5] As was seen in Chapter Three, Ionoron Glan Dwyryd published a recruiting song early in the war which asked American 'sons of Arthur' to turn South Carolina 'into a river of blood' ('yn afon o waed').[6] The poem which Daniel Thomas published in *Y Seren Orllewinol* in effect describes the realization of that violent vision. After first declaring that 'Our banner is waving [again] over the remains of Fort Sumter' ('Ein baner sy'n chwifio ar weddill Caer Sumpter'), he turns to address a personified South Carolina whose impending 'burial' has been announced by Charleston's fall.

Carolina, Carolina, dy dynged a seliwyd,
 Dy orchest orchfygwyd, ymlidiwyd dy lu;
Hen nythle bythgofus y sarff felldigedig,
'Nawr yno'r anadlir hoff ryddid mwyn cu; . . .
Mae dydd i dy gladdu yn awr yn dynesu,
 Mae Charleston a'r gaerfa yn awr gennym ni.[7]

'Carolina, Carolina, your fate has been sealed,
 Your feat is defeated, your host has been routed;
Always remembered as the old nesting place of the accursed serpent,
 It is now there that dear, tender freedom is being breathed; . . .
The day of your burial is now growing closer,
 We now posses Charleston and the fort.'

Erasmus Jones had anticipated the fall of 'the cradle of Rebellion', using a phrase popular with the Northern press; Daniel Thomas employed the same image in drawing attention to the special significance of the city's capture: 'Ei bedd i'r sarff dorchog yw'r lle bu ei chryd'; 'The coiled serpent's grave is the place where its cradle was.'[8]

Also like Erasmus Jones, who wrote that the city's capture would reduce Charleston's 'ambition to ashes', this poet described the ruins of Fort Sumter as a funeral pyre on which the Confederacy's leaders would be reduced to 'ashes'.

Wel llosger ar Sumpter gynnllwynwyr enciliad,
A'u llwch i Gaergwdion dyrchafed y gwynt;
Na foed iddo ddisgyn ar lanerch o'n daear,
A brigwyn y tonau na chaffont eu hynt;
Pur awyr gwladgarwch wasgaro eu drewdod,
Eu llwybrau fo'n darfod o olwg y byd;
Hurrah for the heros, mae'r amser yn agos
Y derfydd gobeithion y bradwyr i gyd.[9]

'Well, let the plotters of secession be burnt upon Sumter,
And may the wind lift their ashes to the Milky Way;
Do not let it settle upon any clearing of our earth,
And may the white crest of the waves not know their course;
May the pure air of patriotism scatter their stench,
May their traces disappear from the sight of the world;
Hurrah for the heroes, the time is close
When all of the traitors' hopes will be at an end.'

It is perhaps no coincidence that this poet chose to praise Sherman's soldiers in the same stanza which also describes the cremation of the Confederacy; the 'heroes' to whom he paid tribute did indeed 'burn' their way through South Carolina. While his devastating march through Georgia has been better remembered in American popular culture, William Tecumseh Sherman ensured that South Carolina was, in the words of one historian, 'more intensely pillaged and burned'.[10]

Although Charleston itself escaped this fate, many of South Carolina's villages – as well as half the city of Columbia – were reduced to ashes. The deliberate destruction was in part planned by Sherman in order to break the crumbling Confederacy's morale, and it was amplified substantially by thousands of unchecked Northern soldiers who took their own revenge upon 'the cradle of the rebellion'.[11] The praise which this poet fashioned for Sherman and his army suggests a great deal about the way in which some sectors of Welsh-American society had come to accept – and even embrace – the harsh realities of warfare. The main stream of America's Welsh-language writing had long since flowed away from the pacifism which some of its writers had once embraced, a fact which had been signalled four years previously when bards such as Ionoron Glan Dwyryd began publishing their blood-thirsty recruiting songs. Now Daniel Thomas was celebrating what can only be described as one of the crueller aspects of the conflict, a nineteenth-century version of total war.

This poem also suggests something about the way in which traditional Welsh cultural resources were reworked and applied to the circumstances of the American Civil War. In asking the wind to take the secessionists' ashes to the 'Milky Way', Daniel Thomas uses the word *Caergwdion*, a version of the expression *Caer Gwydion*, meaning 'Gwydion's Fort'.[12] A nineteenth-century Welsh speaker who wanted to describe the luminous pathway visible in the night sky had several expressions from which to choose; in addition to *Caer Gwydion*, the phrases *Y Llwybr Llaethog* (literally, 'the Milky Path'), *Y Ffordd Laethog* ('The Milky Way'), *Y Ffordd Wen* ('The White Way'), *Y Ffordd Laethwen* ('The Milk-white Way') and *Llwybr y Gwynt* ('The Path of the Wind') were all available.[13] Daniel Thomas, however, chose to describe the Milky Way as 'Gwydion's Fort'. Besides being one of many expressions applied to the same celestial phenomenon, the word *Caergwdion* plays no part in this poem's rhyme-scheme; both of these facts compel us to ask why Thomas employed this exact word.

The magician Gwydion is one of the main characters in the Fourth Branch of the Mabinogi, a text considered to be one of medieval Welsh literature's crowning jewels. It is of course possible that, by the nineteenth century, the words *Caer Gwydion* and *Caergwdion* had become linguistic fossils to an extent, and that for many Welsh people they carried no associations other than referring to the Milky Way. However, in addition to the possibility that oral traditions concerning Gwydion were handed down, a number of publications which appeared during the first half of the nineteenth century ensured that the medieval narrative of his exploits was reintroduced to literary-minded Welsh people.[14] Whatever Thomas's understanding of the figure of Gwydion, he refers to his 'Fort' as a kind of otherworld, a place totally removed from 'our earth' (*ein daear*). Daniel Thomas is not only willing the total destruction of the Secessionists, he is also voicing a kind of curse, wishing that every trace of the enemy 'disappear from the sight of the world' for ever. However, rather than damning them to a 'hell' described in Christian terms, he scatters their ashes to the otherworld of *Caer Gwydion*. This place is defined in opposition to the known world, and it is included as a way of signalling the end of the Confederates' 'hopes' on earth. Perhaps significantly, the popular book which Ellis Wynne published early in the eighteenth century, *Gweledigaetheu y Bardd Cwsc* ('The Visions of the Sleeping Bard'), mentions *Caer Gwydion* as one of the features which the narrator passes on his journey to visit Hell.[15] While it is impossible to know exactly what meaning or meanings Daniel Thomas hoped to convey by including the reference in his poem, it is certain that the word *Caergwdion* had the ability to index a range of possible meanings, images and associations.

It is also worth stressing that, while most Welsh expressions for the Milky Way are based on one of two words, *ffordd* ('way') and *llwybr* ('path'), this phrase calls it a *caer* or 'fort'. Since the start of the Civil War – and, indeed, since the prewar tensions concerning the federal soldiers garrisoned there – this word had been used in the Welsh-American press to describe Fort Sumter.[16] This poem, it will be remembered, in fact begins by referring to *Caer Sumpter*: 'Ein baner sy'n chwifio ar weddill Caer Sumpter, / A'n harwydd brithresol yn chwiban y gwynt'; 'Our banner is waving over the remains of Fort Sumter, / Our spangled flag in the whipping of the wind'. The wind which brings animation to the Union banner in the opening couplet is the same wind which will take the ashes of the Union's enemies to Caer Gwydion. By the same token, that supernatural fortress to which they are exiled for ever is a reminder of the fort in Charleston which those same enemies had captured in their first military victory.

This is in many ways a strange poem. In addition to celebrating the violent subjugation of the rebellion's 'cradle', it also presents a wish for peace which is similar to a number of other Welsh poems published during the final months of the war:[17] 'Mor anwyl i'n calon yw gweled argoelion / O gadw'r mangelau, a gweinio y cledd'; 'So dear to our heart is seeing signs / Of putting away the cannons, and sheathing the sword.'[18] This stanza, with its invocation of peace, is the penultimate verse of the poem; the final verse is in fact the one quoted above, that stanza which imagines Fort Sumter as a funeral pyre from which the wind will carry the rebels' ashes to Caer Gwydion. The plea for peace, then, is followed by the darkest of wishes, a desire to see the enemies killed, their ashes scattered, and all 'traces' of their being wiped off of the face of the world for ever.

While some of Welsh America's poets and writers meditated on the fires which were reducing the last bastions of the Confederacy to ashes, others turned their attention to a legislative battle which was being waged in Washington. In order to outlaw slavery permanently throughout the United States, Lincoln had introduced the Thirteenth Amendment to the Constitution. Although the Senate had passed it on 8 April 1864, the House contained a number of Democrats who were not inclined to support the plans of the Republican administration, and thus Lincoln pursued an intense lobbying campaign that winter.[19] He managed to secure enough votes, and the amendment was passed by the House on 31 January 1865.[20] As had been the case two years previously when the Emancipation Proclamation forged an official link between the government's war aims and the abolition of slavery, the Thirteenth Amendment inspired a number of Welsh America's poets and writers.

Robert Everett, editor of *Y Cenhadwr Americanaidd*, told his readers that, while they were 'bound' to thank God for the Union's recent military victories, they were even more obliged to thank Him for the new era of freedom which was dawning: 'A mwy eto yw ein rhwymau i gydnabod rhagluniaeth ddaionus yr Arglwydd am . . . beri mai rhyddid trwy yr holl wlad . . . fydd canlyniad y gyflafan fawr hon'; 'And greater still are we bound to acknowledge the Lord's beneficent providence for . . . ensuring that freedom throughout the entire country . . . will be the result of this great massacre.'[21] An abolitionist seasoned by more than twenty-five years of anti-slavery work, Everett now rejoiced in the fact that 'all America was going to be a free country . . . with men of every colour and means enjoying their rights' ('bydd America . . . yn wlad rydd trwyddi oll . . . a dynion o bob lliw ac amgylchiadau yn cael mwynhau eu hianwderau').[22]

Y Seren Orllewinol published a poem on 'Rhyddhad y Caethion yn America,' 'The Freeing of the Slaves in America,' by a bard calling himself 'Crwydryn' (or 'Wanderer').[23] As if playing upon the persona suggested by his pen-name, this Wanderer's opening lines suggest that the news had travelled across some distance in order to reach the poet who, though far from the centres of government and power, was nonetheless attuned to events of national significance.

Ust! Ust! pa beth yw'r adsain glywaf draw?
Mae anian deg ei hun fel pe mewn braw!
Gwefreiddiodd natur lon. A ddaeth y dydd
I ollwng caethwas du yn berffaith rhydd?[24]

'Hush! Hush! what is the echo I hear yonder?
It is as if fair life itself is startled!
It has animated glad nature. Has the day come
To set the black slave perfectly free?'

Having established the monumental nature of the news, Crwydryn then offers a prayer of gratitude, asking his readers to join him in 'giving thanks to Heaven for such a gift' ('i'r Nef diolchwn am fath rodd').[25] This 'gift' is defined explicitly as 'freeing' (*rhyddhau*) the slaves, who are in turn described as the Welsh-Americans' 'brothers' (*brodyr*): 'a chalon pwy na thodd / Pan welwn frodyr ini o'r un cnawd, / Rhai gynt fu'n gorfod goddef y fath wawd'; 'and whose heart would not melt / When we see brothers of ours from the same flesh, / Those who formerly had to suffer such contempt.'[26]

One American *eisteddfod* even made the Thirteenth Amendment the subject of a poetry contest; competing bards were instructed to compose 'Chwech Penill Ar Welliant Cyfansoddiad y Talaethau Unedig o barth Rhyddid y Caethion' – 'Six Stanzas On the Improvement of the United States Constitution regarding Freedom of the Slaves.'[27] This kind of competition was an extremely public manifestation of Welsh-American literary culture; the organizers were thus announcing to the wider community that they deemed the Thirteenth Amendment to be, quite literally, the stuff of poetry. The victorious poet, J. B. Jones of Providence, Pennsylvania, eventually published his 'six stanzas' in *Y Cenhadwr Americanaidd*. In both imagery and ideology, this poem is typical of the kinds of texts being composed and published by other Welsh-Americans; Jones, for example, announces that 'the slaves who have surely been taken from their chains / Will glorify the delights of their rights' ('Y caethion yn ddiau a gaed o'u cadwynau / Mawrygant fwynderau eu breiniau o'r bron').[28] The poem's conclusion, however, is more curious:

Trefnidaeth fasnachol mewn cig a gwaed dynol,
Ddarfyddodd yn hollol weithredol ar hyn.
Ni fydd i feib Affric elynion mileinig
I'w dwyn i'r Amerig mewn sarug ddull syn.[29]

'The commercial enterprise in human flesh and blood
Was totally and actively ended with this.
The sons of Africa will no longer have cruel enemies
Bringing them to America in a shocked, dejected state.'

The first line in this concluding stanza presents an apt description of the kind of 'enterprise' being 'ended' as Union troops occupied Charleston and closed down the businesses which had been so central to the country's domestic slave trade. However, it is clear that the final lines of this poem refer to the trans-Atlantic slave trade; J. B. Jones was describing an institution which had been outlawed by the United States government more than half a century before the start of the Civil War.[30] This reference to 'sons of Africa' being carried to America may be read simply as historical inaccuracy, as an anachronistic slip which mars a poem otherwise devoted to recent events.

Examined from another angle, this aspect of the poem can be read as part of a strategy designed to help readers locate the significance of the Thirteenth Amendment within a broader historical context. Since the eighteenth-century campaigns to abolish Britain's slave trade, Welsh-language poetry had been used to attack what J. B. Jones calls 'the commercial enterprise in human flesh and blood'.[31] As was seen in Chapter Two, one of the first Welsh bards to place his poetry at the service of abolition, Iolo Morganwg, was later held up by the Welsh-American press as a moral exemplar.[32] In harking back to the days of the trans-Atlantic slave trade, J. B. Jones was suggesting that the amendment was finally ending what had been a long, nasty business. While the connection which this poet made between the Thirteenth Amendment and the international slave trade was relatively unique, an attempt to interpret recent events in terms of large-scale historical processes characterized much of the literature which was produced during the final phase of the Civil War.

'THE ALTAR OF THEIR CRUELTY': THE LITERATURE OF ANDERSONVILLE

One of the more interesting Welsh poems published in the wake of the Thirteenth Amendment was composed by a poet from Summit Hill, Pennsylvania, who used the name 'Alwyn'.[33] Appearing in *Y Seren Orllewinol* in June 1865, the piece is entitled 'Meibion Rhyddid yn y De', 'The Sons of Freedom in the South'. This poem in fact presents two different kinds of 'freedom's sons', linking them thematically by means of a protracted narrative. The nineteenth century witnessed a number of Welsh experiments with narrative verse, as critics and *eisteddfod* organizers in Wales worked to foster a climate which might help produce an *arwrgerdd* or 'epic' of Miltonic proportions.[34] While not approaching the most ambitious narrative poems being composed in the Old Country (some of which were thousands of lines in length), the ninety-two lines of this poem provided Alwyn with enough room to create an impressive historical panorama. He begins with the causes of the Civil War, describing in his opening stanza the 'horrible treachery' ('erchyll fradwriaeth') which Southerners planned in order to 'injure Freedom, and bring down her throne' ('Rhyddid i'w chlwyfo, a'i gorsedd i gwympo'). The Rebels' march to war is imagined as a move to seal the doom of the slaves:

Mae calon miliwnau o blant y cadwynau,
  Bron ysgar yn ddarnau gan arswyd a braw
Rhag ellyll bradwriaeth gael llwyr oruchafiaeth,
  A chladdu eu gobaith[.][35]

'The hearts of millions of the children of the chains
  Are nearly shattered in pieces by terror and fear
Lest treachery's fiends gain complete supremacy,
  And bury their hope.'

This memorable description of the slaves as 'children of the chains' is central to the poem's ideational structure, for they are soon to be redefined as 'freedom's sons'. This versified narrative's thematic focus on different kinds of 'children' or 'sons' is expanded to include the Confederates as well; while presented as 'treachery's fiends' in the first verse, the Southern soldiers are subsequently characterized as 'the children of rebellion' ('[p]lant y gwrthryfel').

Alwyn then turns to consider the Union's march to war, depicting a brotherhood of 'soldiers who join together at the trumpet's beckoning' ('Ar awgrym yr udgorn y milwyr a unant') and fight to wrest 'freedom . . . from the middle of the fire' ('rhyddid . . . o ganol y tan').[36] Other Welsh-American poets were applying phrases such as 'children of Lincoln' and 'sons of Arthur' to Northern volunteers; this poet, however, calls them 'Sons of Freedom', using the same epithet which he gives to the slaves these soldiers were fighting to free. After a stylized description of the two armies clashing in battle, Alwyn provides a poetic version of the most horribly prosaic kind of text produced during the war – the official casualty list. Just as the military authorities categorized losses as 'killed', 'wounded' and 'missing,' so he states that 'A multitude is dead, a host is injured' ('Mae torf wedi marw, mae llu wedi eu clwyfo'), before proceeding to detail at length the condition of 'the sons of the mighty who were placed in prison' ('A meibion y cedyrn mewn carchar a gaed').[37]

Mae eto laweroedd o'n bechgyn gorhoewon,
Eu calon yn isel, a'u cyflwr yn gaeth,
Heb frwydro dros ryddid ac Undeb Columbia,
Ond araf ymfarw, heb ymborth na maeth[.][38]

'There are still many [more] of our lively boys
Whose hearts are low, and whose condition is enslaved,
Not able to fight for freedom and Columbia's Union,
But slowly wasting to death, without food or nourishment.'

Thus the full meaning of the second part of the title becomes clear; just as the words *yn y De* – 'in the South' – serve to locate the slaves described in the first part of the poem, so this same phrase also refers to the Southern prisons holding these Northern 'sons of freedom'.

Having taken the field in order to fight for the slaves' freedom, the imprisoned soldiers are now made to share those slaves' fate. In addition to using the adjective *caeth*, 'enslaved', Alwyn calls the Northerners *caethion*, 'slaves', similarly describing their situation as [*g*]*orthrwm caethiwed*, 'slavery's oppression'. While many of his contemporaries were using the word *carcharorion* in discussing 'prisoners' of war, this poet avoids that term in order to employ the exact language which Welsh-American writers normally applied to Southern slaves. Beneath the surface of this poem's dramatic narrative and patriotic blustering lies a studied consideration of abstracted ideals. While suggesting that different groups of Americans can claim to be the 'sons of freedom', this work also proposes that the opposite condition, slavery, is a great equalizer; Alwyn suggests that bondage, like freedom, can focus attention on the common quality of humanity. This point is made clear by the narrative's main character, an imprisoned Union officer who addresses his comrades as '"Fy mrodyr anwylaf, fy nghydradd mewn dirmyg" ' – ' "My dearest brothers, my equal in contempt" ' – while interpreting the meaning of their suffering for them, describing it as 'aberth prydweddol', a 'fitting sacrifice'.

For all his heroic rhetoric, this poet tries to approach the painful reality of the prisoner's life. The unnamed officer continues his soliloquy, describing their harsh treatment as deliberate cruelty, enforcing the portrait which the poet has already drawn of imprisoned soldiers 'slowly wasting to death, without food or nourishment'.

'Syrthiasom, syrthiasom i ddwylaw y gelyn,
Diderfyn yn ddiau yw'r ingoedd a gawn;
Mae'n trethu adnoddau ei greulawn feddyliau
Er llenwi'i ffiolau a dagrau yn llawn.'[39]

'We have fallen, we have fallen into the enemy's hands,
It is sure that the pains we will have will be unending;
He will tax the resources of his cruel thoughts
In order to fill his cups to the top with tears.'

While also a meditation on the connection between the war and slavery, it becomes increasingly clear that this poem is one of many texts written in direct response to the horror stories which travelled north from Southern prisons.

Alwyn was by no means the first Welsh-American poet to examine the prisoner's fate. More than a year before he published his meditation on the two kinds of 'Freedom's Sons' being 'enslaved' in the South, *Y Seren Orllewinol* presented its readers with 'Cwyn y Milwr yn Ngharchar Richmond' – 'The Complaint of the Soldier in Prison in Richmond'. The poet called himself 'Ciw Gwydd' or 'Gosling'; while he might have been a veteran who was captured early in the war and paroled before the system of prisoner exchange deteriorated, it is more likely that Ciw Gwydd was, like Alwyn, a civilian who filtered the stories about Southern prisons through his bardic imagination.[40] Like Alwyn's long composition, this is a narrative poem, yet the two are pitched in entirely different literary registers. While 'The Sons of Freedom in the South' looks towards the more ambitious experiments being produced for Welsh *eisteddfodau*, the prisoner's 'Complaint' is a ballad akin to hundreds of texts which were printed as broadside or pamphlet and sold for popular consumption in Welsh fairs and markets during the eighteenth and nineteenth centuries.

Ciw Gwydd places his narrative in the mouth of the eponymous 'Soldier', and he begins by addressing his imagined audience in a manner which recalls the style adopted by many other Welsh balladeers.[41]

Holl ie'ngctyd gwlad Columbia,
Gwych emau, bloda'r byd,
Gwrandewch ar air o ganu,
Mae'n alar, bron i gyd[.][42]

'All youth of Columbia's country,
Splendid gems, flowers of the world,
Listen to a word of song,
It is grief, almost entirely.'

This narrator then presents the reader (or listener) with the history of his military career, moving through a summary of his service under 'Maclelan' to a climactic battle. This is described in three melodramatic stanzas: the regiment is surrounded, the soldiers run out of ammunition, and they are ordered to attack with the bayonet. At this point in the narrative the focus narrows, shifting attention from the fate of the entire regiment to the circumstances of the individual soldier:

Yn awr dangoswyd calon,
Gan gewri'n catrawd ni;
Yn gweithio'u ffordd trwy'r gelyn,
Ond O, fe'm clwyfwyd i!
Tan glwyfau 'nawr fe'm cludwyd
I'r carchar, dyma'r gwir;
A'm gwaed yn llanw'm 'sgidiau
Nis gallaf ddweyd fy nghur![43]

'Now bravery was displayed
By the heroes of our regiment
Working their way through the enemy,
But Oh, I was wounded!
Now I was taken with my wounds
To the prison, that's the truth;
With my blood filling my shoes
I cannot voice my pain!'

With the 'soldier' imprisoned, the ballad draws to a close, finishing with three stanzas which constitute the 'the soldier's complaint in prison', narrowly defined. He tells us that the pain caused by longing for his mother, father and home is compounded by neglect:

Ond ofer i mi gwyno,
Na cheisio dweyd fy lo's,
Heb feddyg yn ymweled
A'm clwyfau ddydd na nos[.][44]

'Yet it is useless for me to complain,
Or attempt to voice my worries,
Without a doctor to attend
My wounds day and night.'

The final stanza shifts the focus again, expanding outwards this time in order to move from the narrator's own 'worries' to a consideration of all Union prisoners of war:

Mae'n galed arnaf yma,
'Rwy'n dweyd y gwir yn siwr;
I filwyr Abram Lincoln

'Does dim ond bara' dwr;
A'r dwr yn llwyd fel llaca,
A'r bara'n brin a drwg,
A ninau wrth ei dderbyn
Nis beiddiwn dangos gwg.[45]

'It's hard on me here,
I am surely telling the truth;
For Abraham Lincoln's soldiers
There is naught but bread and water;
And the water is brown like mud,
And the bread little and bad,
And while receiving it we
Dare not show a frown.'

Like the portrait which Alwyn presented of prisoners 'slowly wasting to death, / without food or nourishment', Ciw Gwydd ends by drawing attention to the lack of food in Southern prisons. Similarly, both poets present this as a manifestation of the Confederates' intentional cruelty.

Historians today still dispute the intentional nature of that cruelty, with some placing the blame squarely on the Confederate authorities and others arguing that the climate of deprivation and hardship which the war brought to the South was the real culprit.[46] Whatever the ultimate cause or causes of the suffering, the fact that great numbers of Union prisoners were dying in horrendous conditions in Southern prisons was widely known in the North well before the end of the war.[47] Thus, while a number of texts published during the final phase of the conflict focussed on the *llwch* – the 'ashes' or 'dust' – of the ruined Confederacy, other Welsh-American writers were drawing attention to the ruined bodies of prisoners of war. (Significantly, none of these poets and writers refer to the condition of Confederates being held in Northern prisons.)[48]

As with Northerners in general, Welsh-speaking Americans came to use Andersonville as a byword for Southern cruelty. An open-air camp surrounded by a stockade, the compound in Andersonville, Georgia, was designed originally to hold 10,000 men. However, as James McPherson explains, it was soon over-crowded:

> 33,000 men were packed [in the camp] by August 1864 . . . without shade in a Deep South summer and with no shelter except what they could rig from sticks, tent flies, blankets, and odd bits of cloth. . . . During some weeks in the summer of 1864 more than a hundred prisoners died every day in Andersonville. Altogether 13,000 of the 45,000 men imprisoned there died of disease, exposure, or malnutrition.[49]

The long rows of tightly packed graves in Andersonville's cemetery would become one of the lasting images of the war's horrors. Even before the Confederates' final surrender was announced, many Welsh-Americans had come to learn of the special significance which these graves held for them. Of the twenty-one Welsh-speaking soldiers who had enlisted in the 9th Minnesota Infantry, seven were captured and sent to Andersonville. One of them, Edward S. Evans, managed to escape; after finding his way to the Union lines, he would be one of those survivors who provided Northerners with a first-hand account of life in the Southern prison.[50] Of the six who remained, only one, John Jenkins, was to survive. In April 1865 *Y Cenhadwr Americanaidd* recorded the deaths of the others: John G. Roberts, David Breese, William Rees, Evan J. Davies, and Lewis Lewis.[51] This last soldier had enlisted at the age of fourteen; though only seventeen when he died, Lewis Lewis had served in the Union army for nearly three years.[52]

The same issue of *Y Cenhadwr Americanaidd* also recorded the deaths of two friends from Granville, Ohio. Both had been imprisoned in Andersonville, and one of them was buried there.

> At y rhestr hirfaith o enwau y rhai a newynwyd yn nwylaw gelynion ein gwlad, y mae genym y gorchwyl poenus o gofnodi enwau a marwolaeth dau wr ieuanc o ardal Granville, Ohio, y rhai a syrthiasant yn aberth i gynddaredd y gelynion . . . Joshua Hughes. Bu farw yn ngharachar Andersonville, Georgia, Medi 4, 1864, yn 21 mlwydd oed. . . . Bu farw John S. Davies yn nhŷ ei rieni, Granville, Ohio, . . . o fewn ychydig ddyddiau i 19 mlwydd oed. Bu yn garcharor yn nwylaw y gelyn am chwe mis, yn Llofrudd-dai Andersonville a Florida. Dioddefodd ddirfawr galedi, trwy anwyd, noethni a newyn. Dirwasgwyd ef yn ysgerbwd dignawd, fel miloedd eraill, cyn ei ollwng yn rhydd. Cyrhaeddodd dŷ ei dad, a'i gnawd wedi duo gan newyn, dri diwrnod cyn ei farwolaeth. Cafodd adrodd ychydig o hanes ei ddioddefiadau mawrion yn y carcharau.[53]

> 'To the long list of names of those who were starved to death in the hands of our country's enemies, we have the painful task of recording the names and deaths of two young men from the district of Granville, Ohio, who fell as a sacrifice to the rage of the enemies . . . Joshua Hughes died in the prison at Andersonville, Georgia, 4 September 1864, 21 years of age. . . . John S. Davies died in the house of his parents, Granville, Ohio . . . within a few days of [turning] 19 years of age. He had been a prisoner in the hands of the enemy for six months, in the slaughter-houses of Andersonville and Florida. He suffered enormous hardship, from cold, nakedness and starvation. He was turned into a fleshless skeleton, like thousands of others, before being set free. He reached the house of his father, with his flesh having blackened from starvation, three days before his death. He was able to relate a little of the history of his great sufferings in the prisons.'

As is also seen in the history of Edward Edwards's escape from Andersonville, it was not only second-hand news which Welsh America received from Southern prisons. The *Cenhadwr* emphasized this point, making it clear that John Davies was returned to his parents as a living 'skeleton'; this young soldier, suspended between life and death, was able to tell family and friends who gathered in his home in Ohio 'a little of the history of his great sufferings' before dying.

These kinds of stories were incorporated into the constellation of causes which the Union's pro-war writers used as justification for the continued use of violence. Just as the *New York Times* cited Andersonville as proof that the slave masters were 'born to tyranny and reared to cruelty', so *Y Cenhadwr Americanaidd* accompanied the obituaries of these two soldiers from Ohio with a protracted discussion of the significance of their deaths.[54]

> O'r holl drueni cysylltiedig â'r gwrthryfel . . . nid oes dim i'w gydmaru mewn creulondeb, i ymddygiad dideimlad y gwrthryfelwyr tuag at ein milwyr ffyddlawn y rhai a fu mor anffodus a syrthio yn garcharorion i'w dywlaw haiarnaidd ac annynol. Y mae miloedd o'n gwyr ieuainc cryfion a phrydferth wedi cael eu haberthu ar allor eu creulondeb a'u cynddaredd.[55]

> 'Of all of the wretchedness connected with the rebellion . . . there is nothing comparable in cruelty to the unfeeling behaviour of the rebels towards those of our faithful soldiers who were so unfortunate as to fall as prisoners into their iron-like and inhuman hands. Thousands of our strong and comely young men have been sacrificed on the altar of their cruelty and their rage.'

The writer who produced this piece for the *Cenhadwr* was David Price; he was well known to Welsh-American readers, having published a considerable amount of prose and poetry over the years (sometimes using the bardic name Dewi Dinorwig). Price was also a Congregational minister, and during the war he served the Welsh communities of Granville and Newark in Ohio. The Revd Price had in fact been in the ministry for more than thirty-five years, and he had written several works of religious instruction. He knew his Bible, and he was well aware of the implications carried by the words *aberthu* ('to sacrifice') and *allor* ('altar').[56]

As was seen in Chapter Four, some Welsh-speaking volunteers described their commitment to the Union cause in terms of making a 'sacrifice' upon the nation's 'altar', thus re-inscribing familiar biblical terms with a new patriotic meaning. Steven E. Woodworth, in discussing the adaptation of these concepts by Civil War soldiers, stressed the special significance of the way in which the words 'sacrifice' and 'altar' were combined:

> Things sacrificed on an altar were offered directly to the deity whose altar that was, for the purpose of propitiating that god or atoning for wrongdoing. The Old Testament Scriptures spoke of sacrificing animals to the God of Israel as a token of the final sacrifice that God would provide Himself. . . . The ultimate sacrifice in the Bible has been Christ[.][57]

In interpreting the treatment meted out to the Union's soldiers by their Confederate captors, Price describes an entirely different kind of altar. By purposefully adapting biblical rhetoric, he deprives the rebels of human reason just as he deprives them of any moral faculty; they use their 'inhuman hands' to 'sacrifice' their prisoners 'on the altar of their cruelty and their rage'.

Like that poet from Summit Hill who used the name Alwyn, this minister from Ohio saw Andersonville's cruelty as the direct result of a deliberate Confederate policy: 'mae ganddynt eu cynlluniau bwriadol i newynu i farwolaeth y sawl a ddelir yn gaeth ganddynt'; 'they have their plans intended to starve to death whoever is held as prisoner by them.' Also like Alwyn, David Price thought that the treatment of prisoners of war reflected the way in which Southerners treated their slaves; he claimed that the same 'bloody dogs' ('cŵn gwaedlyd') used to track down escaped slaves were used in places like Andersonville, adding that men who were once slave-catchers were now prison guards. These men, Price continued, were themselves no better than 'human bloodhounds, not fit . . . to untie the shoelaces' of those whom they oppressed ('[g]waedgwn o ddynion, nid ydynt deilwng . . . i ddatod carai eu hesgidiau').[58] Employing a range of rhetorical skills which he had honed in the pulpit as well as in numerous *eisteddfodau*, David Price examined the moral implications of the Confederates' actions from a number of angles. These included the vantage-point provided by a protracted historical analysis:

> Y mae barbareidd-dra caethfeddianwyr y De yn taflyd creulonderau yr oesau tywyllaf i'r cysgod. Darllenasom am wasgeuon carcharorion y Bastile yn Ffrainc, ond nid oeroedd ein gwaed i'r fath raddau ag wrth ddarllen am gythreuligrwydd swyddogion carcharau Millen a Castle Thunder. Buom yn rhyfeddu at galongaledwch ceidwaid mileing daeargelloedd y chwilys pabaidd yn Spaen, ond yr oeddynt yn drugarogion mewn cydmariaeth i lywodraethwyr carcharau Andersonville a Florida y wlad hon.[59]

> 'The barbarity of the South's slave-holders overshadows the cruelties of the darkest ages. We have read about the afflictions of the Bastille's prisoners in France, yet our blood did not grow cold to the extent as when reading about the devilishness of the prison officers in Millen and Castle Thunder. We were amazed at the hard-heartedness of the savage guards of the papist inquisition's underground cells in Spain, yet they were merciful in comparison with the governors of the prisons of Andersonville and Florida in this country.'

This essay can be read as an attempt to traverse the emotional distance which separates the second-hand knowledge gained by 'reading' about these kinds of stories from the first-hand testimony provided by former prisoners such as John S. Davies. After referring to the 'cruelties' which the young Ohioans had to endure in Andersonville, Price adds that 'there is no language which is able to set out their wretchedness' ('Nid oes iaith a ddicohon osod allan eu trueni').

However, while claiming that his prose, like that produced by any writer, was inadequate in the face of such suffering, David Price was doing so in a context which also authorized his own knowledge of that suffering. He knew John Davies and his parents personally; if he was not one of those who gathered beside the dying soldier's bed, then he certainly heard 'the history of his great sufferings' from the young man's family, for they asked him to perform John's funeral sermon. The Revd Price in fact read a funeral sermon for both of these young soldiers, delivering it in Granville as well as the nearby community of Newark. He provided the *Cenhadwr*'s readers with a synopsis, noting that he marked 'the occasion of the death of these promising young men' ('ar achlysur marwolaeth y gwyr ieuainc gobeithiol uchod') by preaching on the text of Job 3.18: 'Y rhai a garcharwyd a gant yno lonydd y'nghyd, ni chlywant lais y gorthrymydd'; 'those imprisoned will receive peace there, they will not hear the oppressor's voice.'[60] This concludes an essay which, among other things, focuses attention on the relationship between the harshest kinds of experience and the ways in which people try to express that suffering. Price asks his readers to consider the nature of the eye-witness testimony which John Davies provided before dying, setting it against the inadequate 'language' (*iaith*) used by writers such as himself. Similarly, he draws attention to 'the oppressor's voice', suggesting that those responsible for the suffering implicate language itself in their crimes.[61]

Another Welsh-American who meditated on that suffering was Humphrey Griffiths of Iowa City. His teenage son, Joseph, had been captured while serving in Georgia with the 5th Iowa Cavalry.[62] He was sent to Andersonville, and some time early in 1865 the family received news that Joseph had died in prison. The father composed an elegy, eventually publishing it in *Y Cenhadwr Americanaidd*.[63] The title of the published poem presents the subject in raw prose: 'Llinellau yn goffadwriaeth am Joseph Griffiths, sef fy anwyl fab, yr hwn a gafodd ei newynu yn y carchar yn Georgia'; 'Lines in memory of Joseph Griffiths, namely my dear son, who was starved to death in the prison in Georgia'.[64]

After first describing the way in which his family received the news, Humphrey Griffiths turns to consider those whom he held responsible for his son's death. While David Price described the Southern 'barbarity' (*barbareidd-dra*), this dead soldier's father stated that 'barbarians' (*barbariaid*) in the remotest corners of the world 'would be completely terrified' ('arswydent i gyd') should they hear about the manner in which his son had died. Placing blame at the door of the Confederacy's leaders, he adds that, because of Andersonville's atrocities, even 'barbarians' would avoid 'going near to Davis and Lee' ('Rhag myned yn agos i Davis na Lee').[65]

Like its metrical structure, the diction of this elegy is simple and unpretentious. Echoing the message conveyed by the title, Humphrey Griffiths signed his elegy 'ei dad mewn galar', 'his father in mourning'; even though this poem was eventually published, it belongs first and foremost to the personal realm of the family's grief. Humphrey Griffiths himself referred to the tension between this private sphere and the public context of print culture in a note explaining why the elegy was not published until August 1865.

> Yr wyf wedi meddwl eu hanfon er's amryw fisoedd, ond ryw fodd teimlwyf fy hun yn wan, trwy na arferais anfon erioed o'r blaen, yn nghyd ag ofn y beirdd, ond fy nheimlad yw, yn fy ngalar, ac nid canu. Felly dymunwyf iddynt oll basio heibio imi am eu cyhoeddi.[66]

> 'I have thought to send [these lines] for several months, but somehow I feel myself to be inadequate, seeing as I have never sent [poetry to be published] before, in addition to fear of the bards; yet this is my feeling, in my mourning, and not poetry. Thus I desire for all of them to pass me by for publishing them.'

In asking America's Welsh poets to excuse him, Humphrey Griffiths says that his elegy is not *canu*, a word translated above as 'poetry'. A verbal-noun which can mean 'to sing' as well as 'song', this word is used in literary contexts to refer to the public body of a poet's work. It is also employed by critics to describe those qualities which, literally, make a poem 'sing'. What is interesting in terms of the history of Welsh literary criticism is the fact that Humphrey Griffiths contrasts the *canu* which 'the bards' (*y beirdd*) might expect with the pure 'feeling' (*teimlad*) which possesses him in his 'mourning' (*galar*).

Nineteenth-century Welsh poetry was conditioned to a great extent by a kind of Romanticism (which was either 'new', 'late' or 'neo-', depending on how it is defined and whether or not it is discussed in reference to the earlier Romantic movements which swept through other European literatures).[67] Both the producers and the consumers of verse set the expression of emotion at the centre of the poet's vocation, and, as many scholars have noted, a fetish was made out of 'feeling' (*teimlad*).[68] John Ceiriog Hughes, surely the most popular poet of Victorian Wales, argued for the pre-eminence of one emotion, 'love' (*cariad*), proclaiming famously that 'a second-rate poem on this subject . . . is certain to receive a better reception than a better poem on other subjects' ('mae cân ailraddol ar y testyn yma . . . yn sicr o gael gwell derbyniad na chân well ar destynau eraill').[69] A great deal of verse was also being devoted to *hiraeth*, the feeling of intense longing for an absent something or someone.[70] The cult of this feeling would gather so much prestige that, by the early twentieth century, one leading Welsh critic could write that 'longing is the subject of all poetry' ('hiraeth yw testun pob prydyddiaeth').[71] While engaged in the process of writing obituaries for soldiers killed by the suffering of Andersonville, David Price was moved to contemplate the inadequacy of language in the face of such a subject. By the same token, Humphrey Griffiths refused the label of 'poetry' or 'song' (*canu*), claiming instead that his simple 'lines' were an expression of his authentic 'feeling' (*teimlad*). Like those soldiers discussed in Chapter Nine who examined the difference between reading about battle and experiencing it first-hand, this soldier's father was making a distinction between the reality of experience and the artifice of literature. As a result, he exploded – perhaps unwittingly – one of Welsh criticism's favourite aesthetic principles.

The 'feeling' which engulfed this grieving father was expressed as hatred for the Confederate leaders, as was seen above. However, the elegy's final two stanzas use an entirely different lens to bring his emotion into focus, thus moving away from these political recriminations in order to concentrate on the private realm of the grief-stricken family.

Wel ffarwel, fab anwyl, ti est i dy fedd,
O gyrraedd y fagnel, y bicell a'r cledd,
Ti gefaist y carchar i ddyoddef dy ran,
A thithau yn ieuanc ac hefyd yn wan.

Mae'r teimlad sydd ynom ni heddiw yn dear
I'th gladdu yn barchus yn ymyl dy chwaer,
Ond anodd yw hynny mae gormod o drwch
O'th ffyddlon gydfilwyr yn gymysg â'th lwch.[72]

'Well, farewell, dear son, you have gone to your grave,
Out of reach of the cannon, the bayonet and the sword.
You for your part suffered in prison,
And you being young and also delicate.

The feeling which is within us today is strong
To bury you respectably beside your sister,
But that is not easy: too great is the bulk
Of your faithful fellow-soldiers mixed with your dust.'

Although this poet distanced his elegy from the label of *canu*, the rhyming words which anchor his final couplet work in powerful harmony to create an arresting description of the Andersonville cemetery. Translated here as 'bulk', the noun *trwch* can also be rendered as 'density', 'thickness', 'mass', 'depth', or as 'a deep layer'.[73] While *llwch* can be used to mean 'ashes' (as in the meditations on Charleston's fall discussed above), it in this case refers to the 'dust' to which decomposing bodies are reduced. Shortly after the war, Dorence Atwater, a former prisoner who had kept a list of Andersonville's dead, returned to the site with Clara Barton in order to catalogue and mark the graves, and their reports were eventually published.[74] Whether or not Humphrey Griffiths learned that – out of more than 13,000 burials – his son's grave was given the number 12,560, he was nonetheless aware of the staggering number of 'fellow-soldiers' forming the *trwch* or 'deep layer' of which Joseph's 'dust' was a small part.

The discussion of Andersonville's 'inhuman' cruelties continued for some time after the end of the war, for the Welsh-American press, like the American press in general, gave considerable attention to the trial and execution of Henry Wirz, the Confederate officer who had been in charge of the prison camp.[75] The prisoners' suffering became an emotional benchmark, a point of reference to be used in future discussions of the war's horrors. Thus, when Evan Griffiths sat down to write a letter of commiseration shortly after the end of the war, his thoughts turned to Andersonville. His friends, the Revd and Mrs William D. Williams, had lost two sons in the war, and Evan Griffiths asked them to take consolation in the fact that their children did not die in the Southern prison: 'Tybiaf y clwyfasid y teimlad yn fwy, pe buasent wedi eu newynu fel miloedd yn Andersonville'; 'I suppose that your feelings would be wounded more, had they been starved to death like thousands in Andersonville.'[76]

THE ANGEL OF PEACE

Like the recipients of so many letters composed during the war, the Revd and Mrs Williams thought that the contents of Evan Griffiths's post-war epistle would benefit the wider reading community; it was forwarded to Robert Everett, and he transformed the private letter into a public text by publishing it. These words of consultation appeared in *Y Cenhadwr Americanaidd* in August 1865, three months after the journal's readers were presented with a description of the war's close:

> Y Cadf. Grant a ddanfonodd genadwri ysgrifenedig at Lee . . . yn galw arno i roi ei arfau i lawr a therfynu y brwydrau. Ac ar ol rhai llythyrau yn ol a blaen mewn canlyniad i hyn, ar ddydd Sabboth, Ebrill y 9fed, y Cadf. Robert E. Lee a'i fyddin a roddasant eu harfau i lawr.[77]
>
> 'Gen. Grant sent a written message to Lee . . . calling upon him to put down his arms and bring the battles to an end. And after some letters back and forth as a result of this, on Sunday, April the 9th, Gen. Robert E. Lee and his army put down their arms.'

Considering the magnitude of the event being described, the *Cenhadwr*'s description of Lee's surrender at Appomattox Court House is fairly subdued. This is perhaps explained by the fact that the news was already three weeks old by the time this issue of the journal was produced at the start of May 1865.

William Rowlands, editor of *Y Cyfaill o'r Hen Wlad*, marked the end of the conflict with more boisterous tones, proclaiming 'thanks to Almighty God for this last crowning victory of a lawful government over an unjust and unjustifiable rebellion' ('diolch i Dduw Hollalluog am y fuddugoliaeth goronawl ddiweddaf hon o lywodraeth gyfreithlon ar wrthryfel diachos ac anghyfiawnadwy').[78] Rowlands was able to produce an issue of his journal midway through April, and he was thus able to provide his readers with the record of an experience which was still fresh:

> GORFOLEDD!
> 'Yr Arglwydd a wnaeth i ni bethau mawrion; am hyny yr ydym yn llawen!' Nid heb ei ddymuno, eithr heb ei ddysgwyl mor fuan, o leiaf, yn tynu at ganolnos nos Sabboth, y 9fed, deffrowyd ni gan sŵn clychau a chyflegrau, yn rhoi ar ddeall fod rhyw newydd da o bwys wedi cyrhaedd ar adenydd y fellten, a'u bod yn methu ei gadw dan y boreu. Gwyddem nad oedd un Petersburgh na Richmond arall idd-eu cymeryd – ond wedi codi ac ymholi, y newydd gorfoleddus oedd bod y Cadf. Lee wedi rhoddi i fyny ei hun a'i fyddin i'r Cadraglaw Grant. Teimlem yn ddigon boddlawn gael ein deffroi erbyn hyny, ac i gyduno yn y teimladau gorfoleddus. Heddwch bellach, ni a hyderwn. . . . Amlyga ein Llywydd galluog bob parodrwydd i faddeu, anghofio a derbyn yn ol; ond saif fel y graig dros fod yn rhaid i bob trefniad o hyn allan fod yn darostyngedig i'r *Proclamasiwn*, yn cynnwys dilead bythol CAETHWASIAETH yn y Talaethau Unedig. Y mae gallu cyhoeddi y newyddion gorfoleddus hyn, bythefnos yn gynt nag yn ol yr hen drefn misol, yn llawenydd i'r Golygdd.[79]
>
> 'REJOICING!
> ' "The Lord has done great things for us; for that we are joyful!" Not without wishing it, but rather without expecting it so soon, at least, drawing towards midnight on the night of Sunday, the 9th, we were awakened by the sound of bells and cannons providing the understanding that some good news of import had arrived upon the wings of the lightning-bolt, and that they could not keep it until the morning. We knew that there was not one more Petersburg nor Richmond to be taken – but, after getting up and inquiring, the joyous news was that Gen. Lee had surrendered himself and his army to Lieutenant General Grant. We felt content enough to be awakened at this, and to partake of the joyous feelings. Today and henceforth, we shall take heart. . . . Our capable President will display every readiness to forgive, forget and receive back; but he will stand like a rock on the point that every measure from now on must be in keeping with the Proclamation, including the eternal abolition of SLAVERY in the United States. The ability to publish this joyous news, a fortnight earlier than the old monthly arrangement, gives joy to the Editor.'

Despite the many sombre tones which inflected the way in which the press discussed the war's end, Welsh America's print culture was not completely devoid of humour at this time. In June 1865 *Y Seren Orllewinol* published an illustration depicting the former Confederate president dressed in woman's clothing, attempting to flee while his bonnet flies behind him and his spurred boots emerge conspicuously from beneath his petticoats. Under the caption

'Dal Jeff Davis a'i Gyfeillion', 'Catching Jeff Davis and his Friends', a short explanatory paragraph was included:

> Daliwyd yr Arch-fradwr, Jeff. Davis, yn nghyd a'i deulu ac amryw o'i gynghorwyr, gan y Mil. Prichard, y 4ydd Gwyr Meirch Michigan, gyda chant a hanner o'i wyr, ar foreu y 10fed o Fai, yn Irwinville, Ga. Amcanodd Jeff. ddiangc yn nillad ei wraig, ond sylwodd y milwyr ar ei fotasau.[80]
>
> 'The Arch-traitor, Jeff Davis, along with his family and several of his advisers, were caught by Col. Prichard of the 4th Michigan Cavalry, with a hundred and fifty of his men, on the morning of the 10th of May, in Irwinville, Georgia. Jeff intended to escape in his wife's clothing, but the soldiers noticed his boots.'

Like most of the country's Welsh publications, *Y Seren Orllewinol* made little use of illustrations; the acquisition and reproduction of visual images was a luxury which was beyond the normal means of the journal's editor.[81] While this picture was a simple cartoon, unsophisticated in its execution, it nonetheless testifies to the fact that the *Seren*'s editor thought that his readers should be treated with a portrait of the cross-dressing Jefferson Davis.

More characteristic of the period were the solemn meditations which Welsh America's poets continued to provide for some time after the war's conclusion. One of the more memorable compositions is an *englyn* which Rowland Walter published in the November 1865 issue of *Y Cenhadwr Americanaidd*. This quarryman from Vermont, it will be remembered, had achieved literary fame before the war under the bardic name Ionoron Glan Dwyryd, and throughout the war years he employed his verse to interpret and memorialize different aspects of the conflict. In addition to examining the tragedy of war from a fictional vantage point in poems such as 'Bedd y Milwr Cymreig yn America' ('The Welsh Soldier's Grave in America'), he published elegies for young soldiers from Vermont killed in battle. Moreover, Ionoron had also placed his verse at the service of the Union cause in a more propagandistic fashion, composing patriotic recruiting songs such as 'Baner yr Undeb' ('The Union Banner'), which appeared in print late in 1861.[82] This is the piece which addresses the sons of 'our father Arthur' ('Arthur ein tad'), asking them to turn 'South Carolina into a river of blood' ('A South Carolina yn afon o waed'). The central device of this poem, it will also be remembered, is the Union's 'Guardian Angel' ('Angel Gwarcheidiol'), a martial figure whose violent passions mirror the cataclysmic energies which were engulfing the land after the fall of Fort Sumter:

> A'i drem yn melltenu eiddigedd ei fron;
> A chan ei ddigofaint, mae cefnfor ymchwyddol
> Dros wyneb Columbia yn gwthio ei don[.][83]

'And his gaze flashed the lightning of his heart's jealous passion;
And because of his wrath, a swelling sea
Is throwing its waves across the face of Columbia[.]'

The strict-metre stanza which Ionoron published in November 1865 also takes an angel as its governing image; this poem focuses on a 'cherub' to whom the bard directs his meditation on 'Heddwch' ('Peace'). While both images draw upon the popular iconography of nineteenth-century Christianity, the heavenly messenger of the *englyn* is worlds away from the vengeful angel of the earlier poem.

Heddwch
Esgyll cerub yw'th wisgoedd, – angyles
Yn ngolwg y nefoedd;
Llawer gwaith, yn llu ar g'oedd,
Anadlaist lwch cenedloedd.[84]

'Peace
A cherub's wings are your raiments, – an angel
In heaven's view;
Many a time, marshalled publicly,
You have breathed the ashes of nations.'

As was stressed in Chapter Three's discussion of Ionoron's recruiting song, Welsh distinguishes between the masculine noun *angel* 'angel' and the corresponding feminine noun *angyles*. The figure of the wrathful Guardian constructed by Ionoron in his 1861 poem is, like the angels of scripture, explicitly male; on the other hand, this 'cherub' is made to be explicitly female; she is an *angyles*, literally 'a female angel'. For this poet, the supernatural herald of war was masculine and the corresponding messenger of peace was feminine.

Although the opposite of the Angel of Peace is not invoked by name, this compact stanza invites a meditation on the relationship between peace and war. This is presented by means of an extremely arresting image: 'Peace' is depicted as an angel who travels after war, breathing in the 'dust' or 'ashes' (*llwch*) which are left in its wake. At this time the Northern press was celebrating the restoration of the Union and many abolitionists were publishing pieces welcoming the new era of freedom which was dawning. However, while Ionoron Glan Dwyryd had published poetry which was markedly pro-Union and anti-slavery, he commemorated the end of war with this *englyn*, a poem which, other than the title's reference to 'peace', is constructed beyond the borders of that celebratory realm. Rather than singing the praises of a newly-restored nation, Ionoron uses this poem to ponder the ruins of a plurality of 'nations' destroyed by war.

For it is a plurality which is suggested by the final word of this poem; *cenedloedd* – now spelled *cenhedloedd* – is the plural of the noun *cenedl*, meaning 'nation', 'race' or 'people.' As has been seen throughout this study, Welsh-American writers often addressed their readers as their *cyd-genedl*, modifying that charged word *cenedl* with the prefix *cyd-* ('fellow' or 'co-'). This word, it will be remembered, was central to the way in which Welsh America's weekly newspaper, *Y Drych*, described itself: *Newyddiadur Cenedlaethol at Wasanaeth Cenedl y Cymry yn y Talaethau Unedig*; 'A National Newspaper at the Service of the Nation of the Welsh in the United States'.[85] If readers who encountered Ionoron's verse on the pages of *Y Cenhadwr Americanaidd* were wondering what the coming of peace meant for the United States, they were also contemplating the post-war future of that discrete *cenedl* or 'nation' to which they also belonged, Welsh America.

Some writers began discussing this subject even before the Civil War had ended. In addition to the Confederacy's reduction to ashes and the incorporation of the abolition of slavery into the country's constitutional fabric, another historical process was receiving attention during the final months of the war – the expansion of Welsh America. New communities were being established in the lands won 'for freedom' by the Union armies, and the press was used to garner support for these ventures. For example, in December 1864 *Y Cenhadwr Americanaidd* carried a piece by the Revd R. M. Evans boasting about 'the Welsh Settlement in the Northern part of Missouri' ('Y Drefedigaeth Gymreig yn Ngogleddbarth Missouri').[86] Evans directed his comments to readers living in Welsh America's older communities, suggesting that they too could move westwards and avail themselves of Missouri's 'substantial advantages':

> Da genyf weled fod cynifer o hil Gomer wedi prynu yno yn barod . . . Bydded i blant Gomer ddal gafael yn y cyfleustra sydd o'u blaen yn bresenol er sicrhau iddynt eu hunain artref rhad ac am byth mewn gwlad fras a ffrwythlon sydd a'i hinsawdd yn iachus a'i manteision yn helaeth.[87]

> 'I am pleased to see that so many of Gomer's descendents have bought [land] there already . . . May Gomer's children seize the opportunity which is before them at present in order to obtain cheaply an eternal home for themselves in a rich and fertile land with a healthy climate and substantial advantages.'

Many years before the start of the Civil War writers had begun describing immigrants and their children as 'Hil Gomer yn America', 'the Descendants of Gomer in America'.[88] Like other charged phrases which were drawn from medieval Welsh pseudo-history, this expression was used to invoke an ancient lineage thought to stretch beyond the kings of the 'Ancient Britons' to Gomer, grandson of Noah.[89] This tradition's continued popularity with Welsh-speaking Americans is exemplified, among other things, by the fact that a number of writers adopted Gomer as a pen-name, including at least one Union soldier who published extensively during the war.[90] Now, as the war entered its final phase, R. M. Evans was claiming that Gomer's children were finding a new home in northern Missouri.[91]

According to the essay which Evans published in *Y Cenhadwr Americanaidd*, it was the end of slavery which had cleared the way for this new community. He described a Welsh-American utopia, an ideal place where the labours of industrious craftsmen were accompanied by a flourishing of the arts, and he stated explicitly that this free, peaceful community was being built upon land previously sullied by slavery and violence.

> Mae pob peth yn ymddangos yn obeithiol yn bresenol y bydd y sefydliad yn un blodeuog a llafur y Cymro gweithgar i lwyddo, ac y bydd i swn morthwyl y gôf i'w glywed ar yr eingion a bwyll y saer ar yr adeiladaeth a phob cangen mewn celfyddyd yn llwyddo, yn lle swn y fflangell ar gefn y dyn du a'i ocheneidiau a'i ruddfanau yn hollti yr awyr uwch ben, y bydd trais caethiwed, gormes a gwrthryfel wedi darfod o'r tir a heddwch a rhyddid a chyfiawnder yn ffynu trwy yr holl wlad.[92]

> 'Everything suggests hopefully at present that the settlement will be a flourishing one and that the labours of the industrious Welshman will thrive, and that the sound of the blacksmith's hammer upon the anvil and the axe of the carpenter upon the building will be heard and every branch of art will thrive, instead of the sound of the whip on the back of the black man with his sighs and cries rending the sky over head, and that the violence of slavery, oppression and rebellion will have disappeared from the land as peace and freedom and justice prosper throughout the entire country.'

Although several months of bloodshed were yet to come when these sentences appeared in print, the hopes expressed by R. M. Evans were already being voiced in a variety of ways by different sectors of Northern society. The most memorable articulation of this kind of optimistic vision had been provided a year earlier by Abraham Lincoln himself, when he said in his Gettysburg Address that 'this nation . . . shall have a new birth of freedom'.[93] Evans was describing the role which Welsh-Americans could play in that process, building a new home for themselves while also contributing to the greater project of constructing a new, freer nation.

One of the first Welsh immigrants to settle in northern Missouri was William B. Jones, a poet, writer and entrepreneur.[94] Jones had been a co-owner of *Y Drych* in the 1850s and would continue to write for the paper up to his death in 1887.[95] In November 1865 the newspaper published a poem which Jones had composed the previous April, a few days before the end of the war.[96] Entitled 'Dymuniad y Bardd', 'The Poet's Wish', it is a simple, single-stanza composition (using a free metre, rather than the strict *englyn* form employed by Ionoron

Glan Dwyryd in his meditation on 'Peace'). Employing the oft-quoted biblical reference to beating swords into ploughshares, this 'wish' unites praise for peace with a celebration of slavery's end.

Mae'r amser hyfryd bron wrth law,
Daw terfyn ar y rhyfel maith;
A'r milwr gyda'i gaib a'i raw
Yn lle y cledd fydd wrth ei waith:
A'r Negro saif yn ngoleu dydd,
Heb gadwyn ar ei ddwylaw mwy
Yn DDYN, yn 'ddeiliad,' ac yn RHYDD,
Trwy haeddiant Crist a'i Farwol Glwy.[97]

'The beautiful time is nearly at hand,
This long war will come to an end;
And the soldier with his ploughshare and shovel
Instead of the sword will go to work:
And the Negro will stand in the light of day,
No longer with chain upon his hands,
A MAN, a "citizen", and FREE,
By the right of Christ and his Mortal Wound.'

The weapons of the past are discarded, and instead of concentrating on the wounds left by war Jones refers only to the grace-bringing wound of Christ. This 'Mortal Wound' is cited to establish the unquestionable right which former slaves have to their freedom, their citizenship and their humanity. It also serves to establish divine authorization for the bright future which this poet sees for the industrious former soldier.

Like R. M. Evans, William B. Jones devoted considerable energy to promoting the new community which they were establishing in Missouri.[98] Also like Evans, Jones placed that process in productive association with a meditation on the end of the war and the demise of slavery. If both Welsh-Americans were concerned with the same literal piece of land in northern Missouri, both also used writing to present similar constructions of the same idealized post-war community. The former soldier imagined in 'The Poet's Wish' employs his 'ploughshare and shovel' in peaceful industry, just as the blacksmith and carpenter of Evans's vision place their tools at the service of a new utopian society. Similarly, just as Evans asks us to hear the sounds of freedom – the noise created by 'the blacksmith's hammer . . . and the axe of the carpenter' displacing the slave's 'sighs and cries' – so Jones invites us to see the former slave standing, a free man, 'in the light of day'. While Ionoron Glan Dwyryd was contemplating 'the ashes of nations', writers like these were focusing on the new Welsh-American nation which they hoped to construct out of the ruins of war.

NOTES

1 *Boston Evening Journal*, 2 March 1865, quoted by Noah Andre Trudeau, *Like Men of War* [:] *Black Troops in the Civil War 1862–1865* (Boston, 1998), p. 357. I am grateful to Nicole Green, curator of the Slave Mart Museum, Charleston, for information on the history of the city's slave trade.

1 *Y Cenhadwr Americanaidd*, November 1864.

2 Ibid.

3 *Boston Evening Journal*, 2 March 1865, quoted by Noah Andre Trudeau, *Like Men of War*, p. 357.

4 *Y Cenhadwr Americanaidd*, November 1864.

5 *Y Seren Orllewinol*, December 1865. While the poem was not published until December, and thus several months after the war had ended, the poet states that he composed it while Sherman's army was in the process of conquering South Carolina.

6 See Chapter Three, pages 140–1.

7 *Y Seren Orllewinol*, December 1865.

8 Ibid.

9 Ibid.

10 James M. McPherson, *Battle Cry of Freedom* [:] *The American Civil War* (Oxford, 1988), p. 826.

11 Ibid., pp. 825–30.

12 *Geiriadur Prifysgol Cymru* (Cardiff, 1950–2002), p. 384.

13 All of these are attested in print or writing before the time of the American Civil War; see *Geiriadur Prifysgol Cymru*, pp. 1304, 2084, and 2238.

14 William Owen Pughe published the text of the Fourth Branch, *Math fab Mathonwy*, in the *Cambro-Briton* in 1820–1, and the work of this enterprising scholar was much discussed at the time. These medieval texts achieved their most popular nineteenth-century incarnation, however, with Lady Charlotte Guest's English translation, which first appeared in 1838. See Glenda Carr, 'William Owen Pughe and the London Societies', in Branwen Jarvis (ed.), *A guide to Welsh literature c. 1700–1800* (Cardiff, 2000), pp. 184–5.

15 Ellis Wynne, *Gweledigaetheu y Bardd Cwsc* (London, 1703; reprint: Cardiff, 1960), p. 85.

16 The variant *caerfa* was also used; see, for example, the essay which takes Sumter's fall as its starting point, published in *Y Cenhadwr Americanaidd*, May 1865.

17 See Chapter Seven, pages 291–311.

18 *Y Seren Orllewinol*, December 1865.

19 James McPherson, *Battle Cry of Freedom*, pp. 838–9.

20 The final stage in the process was not achieved until December 1865, when three-quarters of the states ratified the amendment. James McPherson, *Battle Cry of Freedom*, p. 840; Peter Kolchin, *American Slavery* (London, 1993), p. 207.

21 *Y Cenhadwr Americanaidd*, January 1865.

22 Ibid.

23 *Y Seren Orllewinol*, March 1866.

24 Ibid.

25 Ibid.

26 Ibid.

27 *Y Cenhadwr Americanaidd*, August 1867; this poem is described as *buddugol*, 'victorious.' It is not known exactly which *eisteddfod* held this competition.

[28] Ibid.

[29] Ibid.

[30] Hugh Thomas, *The Slave Trade* [:] *The Story of the Atlantic Slave Trade: 1440–1870* (New York, 1997), p. 552: 'a bill in favor of abolition of the slave trade passed the Senate on January 27, 1807, and in the House of Representatives on February 11. President Jefferson signed it on March 2. It stated unequivocally that, from January 1, 1808, it would be illegal to introduce into the United States any "negro, mulatto, or person of colour, as a slave." '

[31] See E. Wyn James, 'Caethwasanaeth a'r Beirdd, 1790–1840,' *Taliesin* (Summer 2003).

[32] See Chapter Two, pages 78–9.

[33] *Y Seren Orllewinol*, June 1865.

[34] See E. G. Millward, *Yr Arwrgerdd Gymraeg: Ei Thwf a'i Thranc* (Cardiff, 1998).

[35] *Y Seren Orllewinol*, June 1865.

[36] Ibid.

[37] Ibid.

[38] Ibid.

[39] Ibid.

[40] *Y Seren Orllewinol*, April 1864. Ciw Gwydd gave 'Danville' as his home; there were many towns of that name in the North, and it is not clear which one was his place of residence.

[41] See, for example, the songs of Abel Jones (Bardd Crwst), one of the best known ballad-mongers in Wales; to cite one parallel, the opening of 'Cân o glod i weision a morwynion Cymru mewn perthynas i aredig': 'Fechgyn ifainc cywrain, Cymru, / Dowch i wrando arna'i i'n traethu / Mae rhyw ganiad fwynaidd felys / Gyda ni . . .'; Ben Bowen Thomas, *Drych y Baledwr* (Llandysul, 1958), p. 70.

[42] *Y Seren Orllewinol*, April 1864.

[43] Ibid.

[44] Ibid.

[45] Ibid.

[46] James M. McPherson, *Battle Cry of Freedom*, pp. 797–8 and 801–2; John L. Ransom, *John Ransom's Andersonville Diary* [:] *Life Inside the Civil War's Most Infamous Prison* (New York, 1986), pp. 259–81.

[47] For example, James M. McPherson, *Battle Cry of Freedom*, p. 797.

[48] Earlier in the war some writings were published by Welsh-speaking soldiers detailed to guard Confederate prisoners; see Jerry Hunter, *Llwch Cenhedloedd* (Llanrwst, 2003), p. 230. See also James M. McPherson, *Battle Cry of Freedom*, pp. 801–2.

[49] James M. McPherson, *Battle Cry of Freedom*, p. 196.

[50] Thomas E. Hughes, David Edwards, Hugh G. Roberts and Thomas Hughes (eds), *Hanes Cymry Minnesota* (Mankato, 1895), pp. 189–90.

[51] *Y Cenhadwr Americanaidd*, April 1865.

[52] *Hanes Cymry Minnesota*, p. 240.

[53] *Y Cenhadwr Americanaidd*, April 1865.

[54] *New York Times*, 22 April 1864; quoted by McPherson, *Battle Cry of Freedom*, p. 797.

[55] *Y Cenhadwr Americanaidd*, April 1865.

[56] Born in 1804, David Price was ordained in Wales in 1829. His religious texts included *Y Catecism Cyntaf* (Oswestry, 1840), *Darlith ar Ryddid Crefyddol* (Llanrwst, 1844) and *Adeiladydd Teuluaidd* (Denbigh, 1844), which translate as 'The First Catechism', 'A Lecture on Religious Freedom', and 'A Family Instructor'. All these

were published in Wales before Price emigrated in 1857; after settling in the United States, he seems to have confined his religious publications to short pieces produced for *Y Cenhadwr Americanaidd*, his denomination's Welsh-language journal.

57 Steven E. Woodworth, *While God is Marching On* [:] *The Religious World of Civil War Soldiers* (Lawrence [Kansas], 2001), p. 106.

58 *Y Cenhadwr Americanaidd*, April 1865.

59 Ibid.

60 Ibid.

61 My discussion of this aspect of David Price's essay is influenced by some of the European writers who, a century after the American Civil War, discussed the relationship between language and the much greater cruelties enacted in the Nazis' concentration camps. See, for example, Theodor Adorno, 'After Auschwitz', Theodor W. Adorno, *Negative Dialectics*, trans. E. B. Ashton (London, 1973). The original German text, *Negative Dialektik*, was published in Frankfurt in 1966. George Steiner, 'Silence and the Poet', *Language and Silence* [:] *Essays 1958–1966* (London, 1967).

62 Papers in the collection of Joan F. Huff.

63 *Y Cenhadwr Americanaidd*, August 1865. It has, according to papers in the collection of Joan F. Huff, also survived in manuscript. It is possible, however, that this manuscript version was copied from the text printed in the journal. No further details are available.

64 Ibid.

65 Ibid.

66 Ibid.

67 See Huw M. Edwards, 'The Lyric Poets,' in Hywel Teifi Edwards (ed.), *A guide to Welsh Literature c. 1800–1900*.

68 See, for example, E. G. Millward, *Cenedl o Bobl Ddewrion* [:] *Agweddau ar Lenyddiaeth Oes Victoria* (Llandysul, 1991), p. 45.

69 Quoted by Hywel Teifi Edwards, *Ceiriog* (Caernarfon, 1987), p. 26.

70 For example, the title 'Hiraeth Cymro am ei Wlad mewn Bro Estronawl' ('A Welshman's longing for his Country in a Foreign Land') was set as the subject for an *eisteddfod* held in Wrexham in 1820. The winning *awdl* (or long strict-metre poem), by Ieuan Glan Geirionydd, enjoyed considerable popularity throughout the century.

71 W. J. Gruffydd, quoted by Alun Llywelyn-Williams, *Y Nos, Y Niwl a'r Ynys* (Cardiff, 1960), p. 165. While his book concentrates on the period 1890–1914, the final chapter of Llywelyn-Williams's study of Welsh Romanticism is devoted to 'Y Gair Hiraeth' ('The Word *Hiraeth*').

72 *Y Cenhadwr Americanaidd*, August 1865.

73 *Geiriadur Prifysgol Cymru*, p. 3625.

74 Dorence Atwater, *A list of the Union soldiers buried at Andersonville: copied from the official record in the surgeon's office at Andersonville* (New York, 1866).

75 To cite but one example, *Y Cyfaill o'r Hen Wlad*, September 1865: 'Prawf Wirz' ('The Trial of Wirz').

76 *Y Cenhadwr Americanaidd*, August 1865. According to the published version of the letter, the original personal epistle was written on 19 June 1865.

77 *Y Cenhadwr Americanaidd*, May 1865.

78 *Y Cyfaill o'r Hen Wlad*, April 1865.

79 *Y Cyfaill o'r Hen Wlad*, April 1865.

80 *Y Seren Orllewinol*, June 1865.

81 *Y Cyfaill o'r Hen Wlad* was able to include illustrations more frequently; moreover, they were also on the whole of higher quality then the one published by the *Seren* in June 1865.

82 See Chapter Three, pages 136–42.

83 *Y Cyfaill o'r Hen Wlad*, December 1861.

84 *Y Cenhadwr Americanaidd*, November 1865.

85 See Chapter One, pages 12–13.

86 *Y Cyfaill o'r Hen Wlad*, December 1864.

87 Ibid.

88 See, for example, *Y Seren Orllewinol*, March 1847.

89 See Chapter One, pages 16–17.

90 See Chapter Ten, pages 397–401.

91 There were only a few isolated Welsh families in Missouri before the war, most of them living in the city of St Louis. The extension of the Hannibal and St. Joseph Rail Road into northern Missouri in the late 1850s helped pave the way for the new Welsh settlement which, by the end of the Civil War, was named New Cambria. See R. D. Thomas, *Hanes Cymry America* (Utica, 1872), pp. 86–9.

92 *Y Cyfaill o'r Hen Wlad*, December 1864.

93 Abraham Lincoln, 'Address Delivered at the Dedication of the Cemetery at Gettysburg, November 19, 1863', in (ed.) Stanley Appelbaum, *Abraham Lincoln* [:] *Great Speeches* (New York, 1991), p. 104.

94 R. D. Thomas, *Hanes Cymry America* (Utica, 1872), p. 88.

95 Aled Jones and Bill Jones, *Welsh Reflections* [:] *Y Drych and America 1851–2001* (Llandysul, 2001), p. 12.

96 While the poet himself gave 10 April 1865 as the date of composition, the poem was not published in *Y Drych* until 9 November 1865.

97 *Y Drych*, 9 November 1865.

98 R. D. Thomas, *Hanes Cymry America* (Utica, 1872), p. 88.

14

'Our Lincoln'

When William Rowlands published that mid-month issue of *Y Cyfaill o'r Hen Wlad* in April 1865 he was able to present his immediate reactions to the end of the war. Looking optimistically to the future, the editor placed his hopes in the nation's 'capable President' ('Llywydd galluog'), for Rowlands was sure that Lincoln would heal the country's wounds, 'forgiving, forgetting and receiving back' while also 'standing like a rock over . . . the eternal abolition of Slavery' ('i faddeu, anghofio a derbyn yn ol'; 'saif fel y graig dros . . . [dd]ilead bythol Caethwasiaeth').[1] However, by the time the *Cyfaill*'s subscribers were reading these words, the editor's optimistic sentences had accrued a sad irony. Abraham Lincoln was shot by John Wilkes Booth on 14 April 1865, and their 'capable President' would never witness the fulfilment of his plans for post-war reconstruction.

Thus when the May issue of *Y Cyfaill o'r Hen Wlad* was published, its main story was presented under the headline 'Newyddion Dychrynllyd – Brad-laddiad y Llywydd Lincoln'; 'Frightening News – The Assassination of President Lincoln'.[2] The journal's news was old by the time it reached its Welsh-American readers; many of them had already taken part in the public displays of grief which were to help enshrine an idealized image of Lincoln in the nation's memory. According to Melinda Lawson, 'No event contributed more to the making of Lincoln as a national symbol than his funeral, an extraordinary event that lasted fourteen days and took place across seven states.'[3] After first lying in state in Washington, on 21 April Lincoln's body was placed on the funeral train which was to bear him slowly westwards to his grave in Springfield, Illinois. Millions of Americans came to view the coffin as it stopped along the way, and millions more lined the tracks to catch a glimpse of the passing train. Those who were not able to witness the funeral procession found a variety of ways of expressing their grief in their own communities. As Lawson summarizes:

> Americans mourned President Lincoln as they had mourned no public figure in their history. Businesses and schools closed; men and women wept openly in the streets. Buildings and homes were decorated with black muslin, rosettes, and flags flown at half-mast. . . . Across the North, in churches and schoolhouses, people held memorial services and town meetings to proclaim their grief.[4]

Several of America's Welsh poets examined the way in which this large-scale mourning engulfed Northern society. Rowland Walter, that quarryman from Vermont known to readers as Ionoron Glan Dwyryd, addressed a personified nation, characterized as a black-clad widow: 'Priodol it', wlad, ydyw gwisgo / Dy ddu i arwylo ar hyn'; 'It is fitting for you, country, to wear / Your black to mourn at this.' The poet imagined that the vestments of mourning were being adopted by everybody and everything:

Priodol iwch, longau yr eigion,
 Yw cario eich duon uwch dw'r,
A throi eich hwylbreni yn dystion
 Fod genych barch-gofion i'r gwr.

Priodol i frenin alaru
 A rhodio mewn du gyda'i arch, –
Heb gadw yn ol o wneyd unpeth,
 A dangos trwy bobpeth ei barch[.][5]

'It is fitting for you, ships of the sea,
 To carry your black clothes above the water,
And turn your masts into witnesses testifying
 That you have respectful memories for the man.

'It is fitting for a king to mourn
 And walk in black with his coffin, –
Without refraining from doing anything
 And displaying with everything his respect.'

Far away from the Welsh communities of the North, one anonymous soldier serving near Mobile, Alabama, reacted to the news of Lincoln's death by sending a single stanza to *Y Cenhadwr Americanaidd*, addressing 'anwyl Abra'm Lincoln' – 'dear Abraham Lincoln' – and stating simply that 'Thousands of patriots / are now in deep mourning, / With their tears flowing freely' ('Mae miloedd o wladgarwyr / Mewn galar dwys yn awr, / A'u dagrau'n llifo'n hidl').[6]

If its poets were moved to describe the climate of grief which had transformed the land, Welsh America at large was taking part in the public mourning. On 23 April, the first Sunday after the funeral train had begun its journey, Welsh-speaking Congregationalists in Johnstown, Pennsylvania, gathered to hear the Revd Thomas Jenkins deliver a *pregeth angladdol* or 'funeral sermon' for the president, while Scranton's Welsh Congregationalists heard the Revd Samuel Williams deliver his 'sermon on the death and burial of the Honorable Abraham Lincoln, late President of the United States' ('Pregeth ar farwolaeth a chladdedigaeth yr Anrhydeddus Abraham Lincoln, diweddar Lywydd yr

Unol Dalaethau').[7] Farther to the north, Calvinistic Methodists in the town of Freedom, New York, held a *cyfarfod gweddi* or 'prayer meeting' to mark the occasion, as did dozens of Welsh-speaking chapels across the United States.[8]

In addition to expressing grief and respect for the murdered president, these public ceremonies helped to articulate participants' views on the relationship between the individual, his or her local community, and the national 'family' which united in mourning its dead 'father'. A range of public services and performances served to elide the distinction between individual and nation, just as the gathering crowds travelling to view Lincoln's coffin sought to transcend the distance separating them from the person they were mourning. As Elizabeth Young has observed, this kind of 'ritual of public display both sanctified the martyred president and elevated his viewing audience, uniting them as members of the Lincolns' national "family" mourning his death'.[9] Print culture facilitated this process, allowing individuals to fashion public testimonies from the grief which linked isolated individuals. Such a link was fashioned by Robert Everett when he published a letter which E. R. Lewis had sent to him.

> *Fy hoff Frawd Dr. Everett*, – Y mae yn ddiamheu genyf eich bod – fel miliynau trwy'r wlad – yn teimlo yn wir drallodus, oblegid mwrddrad y dyn da, y gwladgarwr pur, a'r arweinydd profiadol, doeth a llwyddiannus A. Lincoln, diweddar Lywydd yr Unol Dalaethau. Y mae fy nghalon wedi bod yn friw er ddoe pan glywais y newydd trist, yr wyf yn methu a bwyta na chysgu na chael un tawelwch.[10]
>
> 'My dear Brother Dr. Everett, – I am certain that you – like millions throughout the country – are feeling sincerely afflicted because of the murder of the good man, the pure patriot and the adept, wise and experienced leader, A. Lincoln, late President of the United States. My heart has been injured since yesterday when I heard the sad news; I can neither eat nor sleep nor find any peace.'

The same journal which brought Lewis's letter into the public sphere, *Y Cenhadwr Americanaidd*, also created a public record of some of the funeral sermons mentioned above. An explanatory note prefacing the printed version of the Revd Jenkins's text claimed that the collective community of Johnstown's Welsh Congregationalists was responsible for having it published. After preaching on the night of 23 April 1865, the minister was subjected to the 'desire and determination of the congregation' ('[d]ymuniad a phenderfyniad y gynulleidfa'), and thus forced to send the sermon to the *Cenhadwr* for the 'benefit' (*lles*) of the wider Welsh-American public.[11]

As has been stressed at various junctures in this study, a great number of Welsh America's poets, writers and editors had, since the very beginning, placed Lincoln upon a literary pedestal of their own creation. Rather than analysing the differences between their president's policies and their own anti-slavery beliefs, these *literati* chose instead to construct an idealized president to whom they could then gesture as an icon representing the ideology which they themselves embraced. The moderate Republican who had weathered more than a year of war before drawing up the Emancipation Proclamation was made to reflect the way in which they were interpreting the connection between the war, slavery and the Union.[12] As was discussed in Chapter Ten, a few isolated voices did express criticism of Lincoln's pre-Emancipation Proclamation actions, but these same writers and poets also cited the Proclamation as proof that the president had come to acknowledge what they saw as God's will.[13] If many of Welsh America's writers and poets had turned a blind eye to Lincoln's less than perfect record as an abolitionist, the literature which they produced after their president's death carried that process of idealization to new extremes. This was a Welsh-American version of a phenomenon described by Melinda Lawson:

> Lincoln's eulogists . . . struggled to plumb the meaning of his patriotism. Here they were faced with a fundamental tension, for Lincoln's patriotism contained contradictions that were compounded by his death. . . . Like [the abolitionist Wendell] Phillips, many Northerners questioned the value of a freedom unaccompanied by state protection on some level, and wondered whether Lincoln's policy of charity would not undermine the ideals of liberty to which he was also committed. . . . For many, however, the tensions inherent in Lincoln's patriotism were swept away by the emotional power of his martyrdom.[14]

This is particularly evident in the texts printed by Welsh America's denominational journals. The sermon which John Williams published suggested that Lincoln's efforts had ensured that a better country would sprout from the ashes of war: 'y byddo i'r egwyddorion o gyfiawnder a rhyddid, a blanwyd eisoes gan ein diweddar Lywydd, wreiddio ac ymehangu trwy yr holl dir'; 'may the principles of justice and freedom which have already been planted by our late President take root and spread throughout the entire land.'[15]

Despite this organic metaphor, the governing image of Williams's sermon was not derived from the world of plants. Six months earlier, the Congregational minister Erasmus Jones had told *Y Cenhadwr Americanaidd*'s readers that the Civil War was a divine conflagration designed to cleanse the nation of slavery's sin. The United States, Jones had suggested, would emerge from the furnace of war 'fel aur wedi ei buro trwy dân', 'like gold purified by fire'.[16] The sermon which John Williams presented to the country's Welsh-speaking Methodists by means of *Y Cyfaill o'r Hen Wlad* was written after the fires of that furnace had finished their work. Borrowing his Congregationalist colleague's metallurgic imagery, the Revd Williams suggested that Lincoln's assassination was part of the process which had transformed the nation into 'y mŵn gwerthfawrocaf . . . aur puredig', 'the most precious of minerals . . . purified gold'.[17]

The themes of these eulogistic sermons overlapped to a great extent with the ways in which other Northerners were paying tribute to the murdered president. Like many of their Anglophone compatriots, Welsh-American ministers described Lincoln as an American Moses, having 'laboured for the salvation of his people, liberated a race from bondage, only to perish before he glimpsed the promised land'.[18] Thus the funeral sermon which Samuel Williams delivered in Scranton, Pennsylvania, took as its starting-point Numbers 27.12: 'A dywedodd yr Arglwydd wrth Moses, Dring i'r Mynydd Abarim hwn, a gwel y tir a roddais i feibion Israel'; 'And the Lord said to Moses, Climb this Mt. Abarim, and see the land which I gave to the sons of Israel.'[19] The Revd E. R. Lewis employed the same comparison in his letter to the *Cenhadwr*'s editor:

> Dyna Moses, gwas yr Arglwydd, yr *Aboltionist* mawr hwnw, yr hwn a aberthodd bob mantais dymorol er mwyn y caethion tlawd yn yr Aifft – cymerodd eu hachos yn achos iddo ei hun, daeth yn *Emancipator* iddynt, er fod hyny yn costio pob peth iddo[.][20]

> 'There is Moses, the Lord's servant, that great Abolitionist, he who sacrificed every worldly advantage for the sake of the poor slaves in Egypt – he took their cause as his own cause, he became an Emancipator for them, although that cost him everything.'

Lewis melds biblical past with American present, describing Lincoln as the freer of Egypt's slaves while simultaneously applying the political language of the 1860s – 'Abolitionist' and 'Emancipator' – to Moses.

Moses was not the only biblical figure to whom writers turned for imagery to use in sanctifying Lincoln. As Edmund Wilson noted more than forty years ago, '[a]fter Lincoln's assassination, when the great crusade had been successful, when Mrs. Howe's militant God was no longer needed and Lincoln's martyrdom had made him a saint, he was often assimilated to Jesus.'[21] Some Northerners applied the words which Jesus uttered on the cross to the president's assassination – 'Father forgive them, they know not what they do' – including the poet Edmund Clarence Stedman and James Garfield, a Union general and future president of the United States.[22] The Revd Thomas Jenkins drew a slightly more subtle comparison in his funeral sermon, suggesting that 'the good men of every age' ('dynion da pob oes') have suffered 'the treatment, the scorn and the cruelty which the Son of God received' ('y driniaeth, y gwawd a'r creulondeb a gafodd Mab Duw').[23]

The best-known example of the process by which Lincoln was 'assimilated to Jesus' is perhaps found in Herman Melville's poem 'The Martyr'. Drawing a parallel between one of Christianity's central narratives and the death which some Northerners were already proclaiming to be the central martyrdom of American history, Melville linked Lincoln's April assassination to the annual commemoration of the crucifixion: 'Good Friday was the day / Of the prodigy and crime, / When they killed him in his pity, / When they killed him in his prime.'[24] A number of Welsh America's poets were describing him in similar terms, including Glaswelltyn, a bard from Wisconsin for whom Lincoln was 'ein merthyr mwyn' – 'our dear martyr'.[25] Similarly, David Price – the minister from Ohio who had provided an extended explication of Andersonville's significance – published a poem that August depicting Lincoln as 'a Martyr for his country's life' ('Yn Ferthyr dros fywyd ei wlad').[26]

These poets also spelt out what they saw as the exact reasons for Lincoln's martyrdom. Just as other Welsh-Americans had, five years earlier, made John Brown 'a martyr', so these bards spun elegies which cast the president as a hero who died in order to set others free. Glaswelltyn's poem is in many ways typical of this strain of writing, for his long composition begins by asking – and then answering – this central question:

Ow Lincoln pa'm merthyrwyd di?
Ai am roi rhyddid hoff i lu
Oe'nt gynt yn gaeth gan rwymau cry'
    Ymhell o'u gwlad?
Do toraist un o seiliau'r ddraig,
Er gwaetha'r seirff a'u gwenyn aig,
Rhoist i gaethiwed farwol saig,
    Ein Llywydd mâd.[27]

'Oh Lincoln, why were you martyred?
Was it for giving dear freedom to a multitude
Who were formerly enslaved with strong bonds
    Far from their country?
Yes, you broke one of the dragon's foundations,
Despite the serpents and their poisonous host,
You served slavery a mortal dish,
    Our good President.'

This poem is entitled 'Deigryn Hiraeth am ein parchus Lywydd Abraham Lincoln', 'A Tear of Longing for our respectable President Abraham Lincoln', and one of the forms which the poet's 'longing' takes is an imagined visit to the martyr's tomb. Published at the start of July, two months after Lincoln was buried in Springfield, Glaswelltyn dreams of travelling from Wisconsin to the fresh grave in Illinois:

    Ehedeg wnawn
Dros fryniau cribog dyrys daith
A thros y llynoedd llydain llaith,
Ar lan dy fedd cysegrwn iaith
  O barch yn llawn.[28]

'I would fly
Over the crested mountains on a difficult journey
And over the wide wet lakes,
And at the side of your grave I would consecrate language
Of respect completely.'

This desire, shot through the prism of the poet's imagination, is what produces the elegy itself. These lines present a metapoetical meditation on the genesis of the poem of which they are a part, described here as 'language' which the poet 'consecrates' to the memory of the martyr.

The long journey of Lincoln's funeral train, purposefully drawn out and well publicized, invited poets to employ this kind of imagery in their elegies. Most famously, Walt Whitman meditated on the 'Coffin that passes through lanes and streets, / Through day and night with the great cloud darkening the land'.[29] David Price described 'The great procession' ('Gorymdaith fawreddog') which accompanied the body, noting that the people who constituted it were drawn from 'every degree and every language' ('gan bob gradd a phob iaith').[30] And, while Whitman focuses his reader's attention on the single mourner offering his solitary 'sprig of lilac' to the 'coffin that slowly passes', Price focuses on a mass of dying flowers brought by the throngs of mourners who lined the route from Washington to Springfield:

Y blodau prydferthion eu lliw,
A dduodd, a gwywodd eu gwedd,
Calonau myrddyniau sydd friw,
Mae Abraham Lincoln mewn bedd,
'R holl wlad sy'n wylofain, pob teml a phob tŷ
A wasgwyd â galar a wisgwyd â du.[31]

'The flowers of beautiful colours
Have blackened, and their form has withered,
The hearts of multitudes are bruised,
Abraham Lincoln is in a grave,
The entire country is weeping, every church and every house
Has been afflicted with grief dressed with black.'

Glaswelltyn – whose bardic name suggests an organic, Whitmanesque 'Blade of Grass' – avoided these withering floral tributes, offering instead a living plant. This Wisconsin poet declared that, after journeying to 'consecrate' his 'language of respect' at the side of Lincoln's grave, he would 'plant in splendid fashion a willow of peace, / to weep its tears over your grave' ('Gwych blanu wnawn helygen hedd, / I wylo'i dagrau uwch dy fedd').[32] The weeping willow was a stock image central to the Victorian era's symbology of mourning. This poet, however, puts the familiar image to good use, incorporating it in his meditation on the relationship between grief and the poetry designed to express that grief. Glaswelltyn, it will be remembered, described his composition as 'Deigryn Hiraeth', 'A Tear of Longing' for the martyred president; the weeping willow represents his desire to create a permanent reminder of the ephemeral tears shed over the tomb, just as the poem itself is a lasting record of the flood of public mourning which swept over the country in the spring of 1865.

Glaswelltyn's fantastic journey 'over crested mountains' and 'wide lakes' ends at the grave in Illinois, a site which the poet's imagination locates in a 'pleasant glade'. In that *englyn* which Ionoron Glan Dwyryd addressed to personified 'Peace', he portrayed her as an angel travelling in the wake of war's destruction; in the final verse of his elegy, Glaswelltyn asks for 'angels of peace' to watch over Lincoln's grave and ensure that the enemies who plagued him in life leave him undisturbed.

Dymunwn i anglyion hedd
I wylio'n dyner iawn dy fedd,
Fel na chai gelyn byth mwy sedd
    O'th amgylch di:
Na golwg ar y llanerch clyd,
Sy'n cynwys trysor hoffa'r byd,
A deilad Iawn yr angau drud,
    Ein Lincoln ni.[33]

'I would ask that angels of peace
Watch your grave most tenderly
So that no enemy ever again take a seat
    Beside you
Nor gaze upon the pleasant glade
Which contains the dearest treasure of the world,
And subject of costly death's Atonement,
    Our Lincoln.'

Significantly, the poet capitalizes the word *Iawn*. The common noun *iawn* can mean 'truth', 'justice', or 'redress' (and the word is also frequently used as an adjective). When written *Yr Iawn*, it becomes a theological term, a reference to 'The Expiation' or 'Atonement' for sins.[34] Nineteenth-century Welsh Bibles used the word in 1 John 2.2: 'Ac efe yw yr iawn dros ein pechodau ni: ac nid dros yr eiddom ni yn unig, eithr dros bechodau yr holl fyd'; 'And he is the atonement for our sins: and not ours only, but for the sins of the entire world.'[35] In addition to portraying Lincoln explicitly as a 'martyr', Glaswelltyn interpreted his 'sacrifice' using language and concepts which, in the words of Edmund Wilson, 'assimilated [him] to Jesus'. According to the First Epistle of John, Christ is 'the atonement for our sins' and 'for the sins of the entire world'; this Welsh-American poet describes the martyred Lincoln as 'the dearest treasure of the world' and as one who provided 'Atonement' (*Iawn*) by dying.

While it became commonplace to describe Lincoln as a 'martyr' (*merthyr*) and his death as a 'sacrifice' (*aberth*), not all Welsh America's poets agreed as to the exact articulation of these concepts. When Pittston, Pennsylvania, held its *eisteddfod* that December, competing poets were asked to compose two stanzas in the strict-metre *englyn unodl union* form which could serve as Lincoln's 'Beddargraff' or 'Epitaph'.[36] The judge, Dewi Emlyn, was extremely critical of an image employed by one contestant who described the president's death as 'lludw aberth gwlad-gymod', 'the burnt offering' or 'ashes of sacrifice' of 'national reconciliation'. A great many Northerners were suggesting just this, describing the 'martyrdom' as 'the final realization of the nation'.[37] Poets writing in both Welsh and English contributed to this vision of national reconciliation, including Ionoron Glan Dwyryd who addressed the dead Lincoln, saying 'your wound has dulled the sword; / Peace reigns throughout the country' ('A'th archoll ddifiniodd y cledd; / Mae heddwch trwy'r wlad yn teyrnasu').[38] Dewi Emlyn, however, could not stomach this kind of discourse:

> Y mae'r syniad fod gweddillion marwol Lincoln yn 'Lludw aberth gwlad-gymod' yn rhy erchyll i'w oddef. Ni bu aberthiad Lincoln yn foddion i gymodi y wlad, ac nid oes unrhyw sail i farn ei bod yn fwy cymodol yn awr na phe buasai ef yn fyw.[39]
>
> 'The idea that Lincoln's mortal remains are "the burnt offering of national reconciliation" is too horrible to suffer. Lincoln's sacrifice was not the means of reconciling the country, and there is no basis for the opinion that it is more inclined to be reconciled now then when he was alive.'

It was not the biblical language of altars and sacrifice with which Dewi Emlyn took issue, but rather the political reality which this language was used to express.

The poet who fashioned this phrase, however, was committed to his sacrificial imagery; he signed his composition 'Isaac', thus incorporating an implicit reference to the ultimate sacrifice which God demands of Abraham in the Book of Genesis. The pen-names which competing bards used for Pittston's *eisteddfod* are in themselves suggestive as to the way in which the public mourning of Lincoln was incorporated into Welsh-American literary culture. Poets who took their names from Welsh history and legend – 'Shon Tydur', 'Caswallon', 'Twm Sion Catti' – competed with one calling himself 'Lincolnist'. Another competitor, perhaps hoping to gain sympathy points by revealing his status as a veteran, described himself as 'Y Milwr a'r Gwallt Melyn' ('The Soldier with the Yellow Hair'). The melding of Welsh culture and American geography was suggested by 'Telynor o Santelena', 'The Harpist from St. Helena', while two – 'Galarwr Parhaus' ('Continual Mourner') and 'Gomer Ddu' ('Black Gomer') – adopted names which allowed them to wear the badge of mourning on their sleeves. The bard who devised the moniker 'Gomer Ddu' took a name honoured by generations of Welsh writers and coloured it 'black', a move which readers could interpret as suggesting grief as well as the recently freed slaves.

As is seen in the criticism which he levelled at Isaac's interpretation of the 'sacrifice', Dewi Emlyn's discussion of the strict-metre epitaphs reveals his well-defined views on the way in which poetry was to be used in interpreting and glorifying the deceased president's actions. Thus, while 'Lincolnist' was praised for his command of the *englyn* form, the judge was not entirely satisfied with his poem's content: 'nid yw ef wedi cyfeirio yn ddigon penodol at ryddhad y caethion, yr hyn a gyfansodda brif enwogrwydd Lincoln tra parhao oesau'r ddaiar'; 'he does not refer specifically enough to the freeing of the slaves, which will constitute Lincoln's chief fame as long as the ages of the earth shall continue'. The strict rules governing the *englyn unodl union* dictate that there are thirty syllables in a stanza. Poets competing in the Pittston *eisteddfod* could only compose two stanzas each, and thus were limited to a total of sixty syllables. Despite these demands, Dewi Emlyn expected them to make 'specific' reference to the emancipation of the slaves. The kind of the thing which he had in mind is exemplified by the final line of one of winning stanzas; it declared in no uncertain terms that Lincoln was 'A hero who set the Negro free' ('Gwron roes y Negro'n rhydd').[40]

In Melinda Lawson's analysis, those writers who 'strove to understand and give meaning to Lincoln's death . . . revisited many of the themes about patriotism and the nation that had informed their wartime thinking'.[41] This process is particularly evident in the elegies produced by Welsh-American bards. As the critic Dewi Emlyn emphasized, the literary culture to which these poets belonged expected them to 'refer specifically . . . to the freeing of the slaves'. Just as a great amount of Welsh America's war-time literature consistently misrepresented Lincoln's stance on abolition, constructing an ideal version of the president which reflected the writers' own anti-slavery beliefs, so the country's Welsh-speaking poets did their part to ensure that the dead president would be remembered first and foremost as the Great Emancipator.

Notwithstanding the numerous bardic tributes, one of the more memorable Welsh-language manifestations of this process is found in a piece of prose published by the Revd E. R. Lewis in the May 1865 issue of *Y Cenhadwr Americanaidd*.[42] Attempting to distil an interpretation of recent events which encompassed the end of the war as well as Lincoln's death, Lewis began by thanking God for the news that the war had ended, adding that 'Peace is now hovering with its white wings in the air, ready to descend amongst us and distribute its best blessings' ('mae Heddwch yn awr a'i hadneydd gwyn yn hofran yn yr awyr, yn barod i ddisgyn i'n mysg, i wasgaru eu bendithion goreu').[43] The discussion which follows this flowery description of 'Peace' in effect crystallizes the main interpretive strategies which the Welsh-American press had brought to bear upon the war and its causes from the start. Lewis summarized the result of four bloody years succinctly as 'freedom and justice . . . for every colour and class' ('rhyddid ac iawnder . . . i bob lliw a gradd').[44] He also revisited the more complex ways in which some of Welsh America's religious writers had interpreted the war, viewing the bloodshed in millennialistic terms as divine retribution for 'slavery, that dirty black spot which was upon the bright face of our adopted country [and which] had to be wiped away . . . with blood' ('caethwasiaeth, yr ysmotyn du brwnt hwnw, oedd ar wyneb llachar ein gwlad fabwysiedig, i gael ei sychu ymaith . . . â gwaed').

Like other Welsh writers before him, the Revd Lewis echoed John Brown's gallows-day prophecy that 'the crimes of this guilty land' could not 'be purged away but with blood'. Significantly, the Revd Lewis enshrined Brown alongside Lincoln in a gallery of patriotic heroes:

> Fe godir Abraham Lincoln, y dyn gwir dda hwn, awdwr yr Emancipation Proclamation, i ochr yr anfarwol Washington, a bydd ei enw yn berarogl am oes America. Bydd enw John Brown, y merthyr, – Ioan Fedyddiwr goruwchwyliaeth rhyddid – yn fwy parchus. Bydd enwau Wm. Lloyd Garrison, Wendell Phillips, &c, &c, yn fwy swynol i glustiau Americanaidd yn y dyfodol nag y buont yn yr amser a aeth heibio.[45]
>
> 'Abraham Lincoln, this truly good man, author of the Emancipation Proclamation, will be raised up to the side of the immortal Washington, and his name will be treasured as long as America lives. The name of John Brown the martyr – John the Baptist of freedom's stewardship – will be more respectable. The names of William Lloyd Garrison, Wendell Phillips, &c, &c will be more charming to American ears in the future than they have been in the time which has passed.'

While the flood of elegies which followed the president's death cast Lincoln as the great national 'martyr', this writer applies the word specifically to John Brown. Lewis was rejuvenating that discourse which had been presented on the pages of the Welsh-American press following Brown's execution, the radical interpretation of his violent anti-slavery actions which, in the words of Eos Glan Twrch, made Brown 'A martyr . . . at freedom's gate' ('Merthyr . . . yn mhorth rhyddyd').[46]

Lewis was equating abolition with patriotism. A more objective historian could point to a serious imperfection in the rhetorical fabric of his essay by noting that George Washington had himself owned slaves. Whether or not Lewis was aware of this fact, Washington, the archetypical founding father, is included in order to establish the patriotic nature of the realm to which he is consigning these heroes. Like so many other Welsh-American writers, and like so many Americans in general, this writer ignored Lincoln's record prior to the

Emancipation Proclamation, choosing instead to present an idealized construction of the Great Emancipator. In reality an ideological chasm divided Lincoln's actions from those of the abolitionist leaders whom Lewis names:

> William Lloyd Garrison believed that 'the Republican party means to do nothing, can do nothing, for the abolition of slavery in the slave states.' Wendell Phillips even went so far as to call Lincoln 'the Slave Hound of Illinois' because he refused to advocate repeal of the fugitive slave law.[47]

A similar gulf separated the Great Emancipator from the man whom Lewis calls 'the martyr'; while noting that Brown 'agreed with us in thinking slavery wrong', Lincoln had condemned his actions thoroughly, declaring emphatically that 'John Brown was no Republican'.[48] Such historical details have no place in Lewis's prose. He is concerned instead with interpreting the actions of the 'truly good man, author of the Emancipation Proclamation' as part of the process which has created 'the future', a new moral climate in which the names of Garrison and Phillips 'will be more charming to American ears' and 'the name of John Brown . . . will be more respectable'. Although not describing Lincoln explicitly in terms of the crucified Christ, this minister's characterization of Brown as 'John the Baptist' is an implicit invitation for readers to consider a bold (re)interpretation of the relationship between these men within the broader history of emancipation. Made explicit, this radical reading casts Brown as the herald of Lincoln's anti-slavery epiphany; like John the Baptist, he is the prophet in the wilderness whose words, actions and death serve to prefigure the sacrifice of the messiah whose coming he had announced.

The millennialistic cleansing of national sin and the 'martyrdom' of John Brown were not the only themes revisited by E. R. Lewis in this piece of prose. Lewis also partakes of the discourse which a number of Welsh-American writers had employed throughout the war in order to portray the Confederate leaders as 'aristocrats' and place the war within the international context of the struggle between republicanism and the 'oppressors of the common people'.[49]

> Bydd yma waith i ddarfelydd y bardd, beirniadaeth yr hanesydd, a ffynonell dihysbydd i'r ffug-chwedleuydd. Y mae gormeswyr a phendefigion pob gwlad wedi bod yn edrych gyda phryder arnom. Bydd darllen hanes ein buddugoliaethau yn creu ofn ynddynt. Y mae cyfeillion rhyddid a miliynau tlodion gorthrymedig y byd wedi bod yn edrych a gwrando yn bryderus. Bydd hanes ein llwyddiant yn dderbyniol ganddynt, cyffroa eu gobeithion a nertha eu calonau. Bydd yn arddangosfa i'r holl fyd, y gall y *Bobl* fyw yn annibynol ar y bendefigaeth, y gallant ddal i fyny eu llywodraeth a'u sefydliadau yn anrhydeddus. Saif yn ddychryn i ormeswyr y werin.[50]

> 'Here there will be work for the poet's fancy, the historian's criticism, as well as an inexhaustible source for the writer of fiction. The oppressors and noblemen of every country have been looking with worry upon us. Reading the history of our

> victories will instil fear in them. The friends of freedom and millions of the world's oppressed poor have been looking and watching anxiously. Our success will be acceptable to them, it will excite their hopes and strengthen their hearts. It will be a demonstration to the entire world that the *People* can live independent of the nobility, that they can maintain their government and their institutions honourably. It will stand as a terror to the oppressors of the common people.'

It is literature which is to ensure that the American Civil War remains for ever as a warning to 'oppressors' everywhere. The act of 'reading' will be the means of 'instilling fear' in the aristocratic enemies of *y werin* – the 'folk' or 'common people' – and the victories achieved by Lincoln and his Union soldiers are to be sustained in the future by the 'poet', the 'historian' and 'the writer of fiction'. This writer's prose was, of course, part of the very process which he sought to describe. Using the themes and images which had characterized a great deal of Welsh-American war writing, E. R. Lewis created what he called an *arddangosfa* – a public 'display' or 'demonstration' – designed to give heart to the 'friends of freedom' and the 'oppressed poor'. A central part of Lewis's literary 'display' was his construction of an idealized Lincoln, the same abolitionist hero being praised in so many Welsh elegies. In effect, all these writers and poets were creating their own Welsh Lincoln.

The desire to claim the martyred president for Welsh America at times exceeded the bounds of literary artifice. Some writers attempted to construct a Welsh pedigree for the dead president, while others focused their attention on his widow. Rumours that Mary Todd Lincoln was Welsh circulated during the months following her husband's funeral, and in June 1865 the story found its way to the pages of *Y Cyfaill o'r Hen Wlad*.

> Dywedir mai Cymraes yw Mrs. Lincoln, gweddw-wraig ein diweddar Lywydd hybarch, a'i bod yn enedigol o'r Cas-Newydd, Sir Fynwy, nid yn mhell o hen gartref Golygydd Y CYFAILL. Os bydd hi yn aros, fel y dywedir y bydd, am dymhor, ger llaw Chicago, dysgwyliwn i un o'r ddau Frawd Parchedig Dafydd neu Moses Williams, o'r ddinas hono, bysbysu y genedl yn nghylch hyny.[51]

> 'It is said that Mrs. Lincoln, wife of our greatly respected late President, is a Welsh woman, and that she is a native of Newport, Monmouthshire, not far from the old home of Y CYFAILL's editor. If she stays, as it is said she will, for a while near Chicago, then we expect that one of the Reverend Brothers, Dafydd or Moses Williams, of that city will inform the nation in that respect.'

The journal's editor, William Rowlands, hoped that Mrs Lincoln would prove to be a living link between his 'old home' in Wales and the inner circle of the president's family. As this question was of great concern to the entire 'nation' (*cenedl*) of Welsh America, Rowlands was counting on some of Chicago's most prominent Welshmen to keep his readers informed.

As it turned out, the president's family was not claimed for Welsh America in this literal fashion, and the 'nation' would have to content itself with the Lincoln being constructed by its poets and writers. After all, since the start of the war the Welsh-American press had been telling its readers that they were part of Lincoln's metaphorical family. Like that Union soldier who had described himself and his comrades as 'plant eu hen dad, Abraham Lincoln' – 'the children of their old father, Abraham Lincoln' – the poet David Price could address the dead president as 'ein tad', 'our father'.[52] If not always described as 'our father', he was almost always described as 'ours'. In the course of his imagined journey to the president's tomb, Glaswelltyn employs the phrase 'Ein merthyr mwyn', 'Our dear martyr'. By the same token, Glaswelltyn's closing lines describe him as 'the dearest treasure of the world, / And subject of costly death's Atonement, / Our Lincoln' ('trysor hoffa'r byd, / A deilad Iawn yr angau drud, / Ein Lincoln ni').[53] In all these texts the possessive pronoun *ein* – 'our' – is meaningfully ambiguous. These writers and poets were staking a claim in the greater national family which included all Americans who mourned for Lincoln, yet they were also addressing the specific community of Welsh-Americans for whom they wrote. Welsh-speaking Americans could not, in the end, join William Rowlands in addressing Mary Todd Lincoln as a *Cymraes* or 'Welsh woman'. They could, however, describe their martyred president with the closing line of Glaswelltyn's elegy, using the words of their native language to call him, simply, *Ein Lincoln ni*: 'Our Lincoln'.

NOTES

1 *Y Cyfaill o'r Hen Wlad*, April 1865.

2 *Y Cyfaill o'r Hen Wlad*, May 1865.

3 Melinda Lawson, *Patriot Fires* [:] *Forging a New American Nationalism in the Civil War North* (Lawrence, KS, 2002), p. 175.

4 Melinda Lawson, *Patriot Fires*, p. 172.

5 Rowland Walters, 'Marwnad Abraham Lincoln' ('An Elegy for Abraham Lincoln'), in *Caniadau Ionoron* (Utica, 1872), p. 300. This long poem was originally published in *Y Cenhadwr Americanaidd*.

6 *Y Cenhadwr Americanaidd*, July 1865.

7 Ibid.

8 *Y Cyfaill o'r Hen Wlad*, July 1865.

9 Elizabeth Young, *Disarming the Nation* [:] *Women's Writing and the American Civil War* (Chicago, 1999), p. 131.

10 *Y Cenhadwr Americanaidd*, May 1865.

11 *Y Cenhadwr Americanaidd*, July 1865.

12 For a concise discussion of Lincoln's (changing) stance on slavery, see Peter Kolchin, *American Slavery* (New York, 1993), pp. 201–2: 'Lincoln had promised that the new Republican Administration, though opposed to the *expansion* of slavery, would pose no threat to slavery in the states where it already existed . . . Lincoln's

caution stemmed not from moral equivocation – he consistently reiterated his belief that slavery was wrong and ought to be abolished – but from potent practical considerations.'

13 See Chapter Ten, pages 388–95.
14 Melinda Lawson, *Patriot Fires*, pp. 174–5.
15 *Y Cyfaill o'r Hen Wlad*, July 1865.
16 *Y Cenhadwr Americanaidd*, November 1864.
17 *Y Cyfaill o'r Hen Wlad*, July 1865.
18 Melinda Lawson, *Patriot Fires*, p. 173.
19 *Y Cenhadwr Americanaidd*, July 1865.
20 *Y Cenhadwr Americanaidd*, May 1865.
21 Edmund Wilson, *Patriotic Gore* [:] *Studies in the Literature of the American Civil War* (New York, 1962), p. 97.
22 Melinda Lawson, *Patriot Fires*, p. 173; Edmund Wilson, *Patriotic Gore*, p. 97.
23 *Y Cenhadwr Americanaidd*, July 1865.
24 Richard Marius and Keith Frome (eds), *The Columbia Book of Civil War Poetry* (New York, 1994), p. 333.
25 *Y Cenhadwr Americanaidd*, July 1865.
26 *Y Cenhadwr Americanaidd*, August 1865.
27 *Y Cenhadwr Americanaidd*, July 1865.
28 Ibid.
29 Walt Whitman, 'When Lilacs Last in the Dooryard Bloom'd' (first published 1865), quoted from Ronald Gottesman, Francis Murphy, Laurence B. Holland, Hershel Parker, David Kalstone and William H. Pritchard (eds), *The Norton Anthology of American Literature*, vol. 1 (New York, 1979), p. 1951.
30 *Y Cenhadwr Americanaidd*, August 1865.
31 Ibid.
32 *Y Cenhadwr Americanaidd*, July 1865.
33 Ibid, July 1865.
34 *Geiriadur Prifysgol Cymru* (Cardiff, 1950–2002), pp. 2002–3.
35 William Morgan's 1588 translation is the basis for this (with minor orthographic variations, for example, *tros* instead of *dros*). The 1988 Welsh Bible has changed the translation of this verse substantially: 'ac ef sy'n foddion ein puredigaeth oddi wrth ein pechodau, ac nid puredigaeth ein pechodau ni yn unig, ond hefyd bechodau'r holl fyd'; *Y Beibl Cymraeg Newydd* (Aberystwyth, 1988), Testament Newydd, p. 24. This 1988 Welsh version is aptly translated by the words of the *New English Bible* (Oxford, 1970): 'He is himself the remedy for the defilement of our sins, not our sins only but the sins of all the world.'
36 *Y Drych*, 25 January 1866.
37 Melinda Lawson, *Patriot Fires*, p. 173: 'The idea that Lincoln's death proclaimed the final realization of the nation was expressed in both religious and secular terms.'
38 Rowland Walter, *Caniadau Ionoron*, p. 301.
39 *Y Drych*, 25 January 1866.
40 Ibid.
41 Melinda Lawson, *Patriot Fires*, p. 72.
42 *Y Cenhadwr Americanaidd*, May 1865. Note that, while this essay appears in the same issue as the letter by Lewis quoted earlier in this chapter, they are two separate texts.
43 Ibid.

44 Ibid.

45 Ibid.

46 Eos Glan Twrch's poem was published in a number of places, including *Y Cenhadwr Americanaidd*, June 1862.

47 James M. McPherson, *Battle Cry of Freedom* [:] *The American Civil War* (Oxford, 1988), p. 227.

48 Stephen B. Oates, *To Purge This Land With Blood* [:] *A Biography of John Brown* (Amherst [Mass.], 1970), pp. 310–11.

49 See especially the writings of Isaac Cheshire, 'Undebwr', Robert Everett and Erasmus Jones, discussed in Chapter Twelve, pages 436–40.

50 *Y Cenhadwr Americanaidd*, May 1865.

51 *Y Cyfaill o'r Hen Wlad*, June 1865.

52 *Y Drych*, 31 January 1863; *Y Cenhadwr Americanaidd*, August 1865.

53 *Y Cenhadwr Americanaidd*, July 1865.

Index